Lecture Notes in Computer Science 5160

Commenced Publication in 1973
Founding and Former Series Editors:
Gerhard Goos, Juris Hartmanis, and Jan van Leeuwen

Editorial Board

John S. Fitzgerald   Anne E. Haxthausen
Husnu Yenigun (Eds.)

Theoreticl Aspects of Computing - ICTAC 2008

5th International Colloquium
Istanbul, Turkey, September 1-3, 2008
Proceedings

 Springer

Volume Editors

John S. Fitzgerald
Newcastle University, School of Computing Science
Newcastle NE1 7RU, UK
E-mail: John.Fitzgerald@ncl.ac.uk

Anne E. Haxthausen
Technical University of Denmark
Informatics and Mathematical Modelling
2800 Lyngby, Denmark
E-mail: ah@imm.dtu.dk

Husnu Yenigun
Sabanci University, Faculty of Engineering and Natural Sciences 2094
Orhanli, Tuzla 34956, Istanbul, Turkey
E-mail: yenigun@sabanciuniv.edu

Library of Congress Control Number: 2008933379

CR Subject Classification (1998): F.1, F.3, F.4, F.2, D.2

LNCS Sublibrary: SL 1 – Theoretical Computer Science and General Issues

ISSN   0302-9743
ISBN-10   3-540-85761-3 Springer Berlin Heidelberg New York
ISBN-13   978-3-540-85761-7 Springer Berlin Heidelberg New York

Springer is a part of Springer Science+Business Media

springer.com

© Springer-Verlag Berlin Heidelberg 2008
Printed in Germany

Typesetting: Camera-ready by author, data conversion by Scientific Publishing Services, Chennai, India
Printed on acid-free paper   SPIN: 12458417   06/3180   5 4 3 2 1 0

Preface

Research on theoretical aspects of computing has a direct impact on the practice of computer systems development. Over many decades, fundamental theories have emerged to describe functionality, temporal behavior and resource consumption. Theories of application domains are beginning to be exploited for modelling and analyzing intended computing systems before the expensive commitment is made to real programs and hardware. Recent years have seen major improvements in the cost-effectiveness of tools supporting the exploitation of theories through proof, model-checking and testing. Against this encouraging background, we are pleased to present papers that show something of the liveliness and diversity of research in theoretical aspects of computing today.

ICTAC 2008, the 5th International Colloquium on Theoretical Aspects of Computing, was held on 1-3 September 2008 in Istanbul, Turkey, hosted by Sabancı University. The ICTAC series was founded by the International Institute for Software Technology of the United Nations University (UNU-IIST). It brings together practitioners and researchers from academia, industry and government to present results and to exchange ideas and experience addressing challenges in both theoretical aspects of computing and in the exploitation of theory through methods and tools for system development. The series also promotes cooperation in research and education between participants and their institutions, from developing and industrial countries, in accordance with the mandate of the United Nations University. The previous ICTAC colloquia were held in Guiyang, China (2004, LNCS 3407), Hanoi, Vietnam (2005, LNCS 3722), Tunis, Tunisia (2006, LNCS 4281) and Macau SAR, China (2007, LNCS 4711).

This year, over 70 submissions were received and each paper had three reviews. We thank the members of the Program Committee and the other specialist referees for the effort and skill that they invested in the review and selection process, which was managed using easychair. Some 27 papers were accepted to accompany keynote talks from three invited speakers: Jean-Raymond Abrial, Jan Peleska and Bill Roscoe. Each invited speaker also offered a tutorial on their work, and these were held at Sabancı University on 31 August. Co-located workshops included the International Workshop on Quality Aspects of Coordination (QAC 2008), chaired by Sun Meng and Farhad Arbab; the 2nd International Workshop on Harnessing Theories for Tool Support in Software, chaired by Jianhua Zhao and Volker Stolz; and the International Workshop on Foundations of Computer Science as Logic-Related, chaired by Walter Carnielli.

Events such as ICTAC are community efforts and can not succeed without the generosity of sponsors. ICTAC 2008 was kindly supported by UNU-IIST, Sabancı University and the Scientific and the Technological Research Council of Turkey (TUBITAK). Prof. Peleska's lecture was made possible by financial support from Formal Methods Europe.

We are grateful to our publisher, especially to Alfred Hofmann and Nicole Sator at Springer's Computer Science Editorial, for their help in creating this volume. Finally, we would like to thank our fellow organizers of ICTAC 2008: our colleagues in Istanbul, our Publicity Chair Jeremy Bryans and, at UNU-IIST, Kitty Chan and Clark Chan. We have been greatly helped by the advice, experience and enthusiasm of Zhiming Liu, Mike Reed (Director of UNU-IIST), and the ICTAC Steering and Advisory Committees.

June 2008

J. S. Fitzgerald
A. Haxthausen
H. Yenigun

Organization

ICTAC 2008 was organized by Sabancı University in cooperation with the United Nations University International Institute for Software Technology.

Conference Committee

General Chair	George Michael Reed (UNU-IIST, Macau)
Program Chairs	John S. Fitzgerald (Newcastle University, UK)
	Anne Haxthausen (Technical University of Denmark)
Organization Chair	Husnu Yenigun (Sabancı University, Turkey)
Publicity	Jeremy Bryans (Newcastle University, UK)

ICTAC Steering Committee

John S. Fitzgerald (Newcastle University, UK)
Martin Leucker (Technische Universität München, Germany)
Zhiming Liu (Chair) (UNU-IIST, Macao)
Tobias Nipkow (Technische Universität München, Germany)
Augusto Sampaio (Universidade Federal de Pernambuco, Brazil)
Natarajan Shankar (SRI, USA)
Jim Woodcock (University of York, UK)

Program Committee

Keijiro Araki	Lindsay Groves	Wolfgang Reisig
Jonathan Bowen	Michael R. Hansen	Augusto Sampaio
Michael Butler	Ian Hayes	Bernhard Schaetz
Ana Cavalcanti	Dang Van Hung	Natarajan Shankar
Patrice Chalin	Tomasz Janowski	Serdar Tasiran
Christine Choppy	He Jifeng	Helen Treharne
Jim Davies	Joe Kiniry	Ji Wang
Jin Song Dong	Maciej Koutny	Alan Wassyng
George Eleftherakis	Kung-Kiu Lau	Jim Woodcock
Esra Erdem	Martin Leucker	Husnu Yenigun
Wan Fokkink	Peter Mosses	Naijun Zhan
Marcelo Frias	Ernst-Rdiger Olderog	
Kokichi Futatsugi	Paritosh K Pandya	
Chris George	Anders Ravn	

External Reviewers

Marco Aiello
Yuji Arichika
Rilwan Basanya
Anirban Bhattacharyya
Jens Calamé
Sagar Chaki
Yuki Chiba
Robert Colvin
Phan Cong-Vinh
Marcio Cornelio
Charles Crichton
Kriangsak Damchoom
Zhe Dang
Brijesh Dongol
Elsa Estevez
Radu Grigore
Alexander Gruler
Tingting Han
Benjamin Hummel
Ryszard Janicki
Mikolas Janota
Christian Damsgaard Jensen
Christophe Joubert
Weiqiang Kong
Kemal Kilic
Daniel Klink
Alexander Knapp
Istvan Knoll
Stephan Korsholm
Shigeru Kusakabe
Edmund Lam
Wanwei Liu
Xiaodong Ma
Nicolas Markey
Manuel Mazzara
Michael Meier
Roland Meyer

Hiroshi Mochio
Sotiris Moschoyiannis
Alexandre Mota
Mohammad Reza Mousavi
Masaki Nakamura
Viet Ha Nguyen
Ioannis Ntalamagkas
Kazuhiro Ogata
Adegboyega Ojo
Joseph Okika
Yoichi Omori
Elisabeth Pelz
Franck Pommereau
Rodrigo Ramos
Tauseef Rana
Wolfgang Reisig
Markus Roggenbach
David Rydeheard
Lily Safie
Mar Yah Said
Cesar Sanchez
Jeff Sanders
Cem Say
Jun Sun
Cuong Minh Tran
Anh Hoang Truong
Robert Walters
Zhaofei Wang
Michael Weber
James Welch
Kirsten Winter
Stephen Wright
Berrin Yanikoglu
Naijun Zhan
Wenhui Zhang
Xian Zhang

Table of Contents

Using Design Patterns in Formal Methods: An Event-B Approach

(Extended Abstract)

J.-R. Abrial and Thai Son Hoang

ETH Zurich
{jabrial,htson}@inf.ethz.ch

Motivation. Formal Methods users are given sophisticated languages and tools for constructing models of complex systems. But quite often they lack some systematic methodological approaches which could help them. The goal of introducing *design patterns* within formal methods is precisely to bridge this gap.

A design pattern is a general reusable solution to a commonly occurring problem in (software) design ... It is a description or template for how to solve a problem that can be used in many different situations (Wikipedia on "Design Pattern").

The usage of design patterns in Object Oriented technology results (in its simplest form) in *adapting* and *incorporating* some pre-defined pieces of codes in a software project.

The usage of design patterns in Formal Methods technology will follow a similar strategy, namely to *adapt* and *incorporate* a pre-defined proved and refined mini-model into a larger one. Such an incorporation would not only save re-inventing something that already exist but also save re-doing the corresponding refinements and proofs of correctness.

Typical examples of design patterns are the notions of actions and reactions (and chains thereof) in reactive systems, or the notions of message transmission, acquisition, and response in synchronous as well as asynchronous protocols. In such systems, there are many instances of such patterns. Of course, modelling and proving such systems without design patterns is possible (this has been done for many years) but the usage of such patterns results in very systematic constructions, which can also be explained in a far easier way than without them.

In this presentation, we propose to explain how to introduce this technology within Event-B, which is the name of a mathematical (set-theoretic) approach used to develop *complex discrete systems*, be they computerized or not. This will be done within the framework of the Rodin Platform.

The Rodin platform is an open tool set devoted to supporting the development of such systems. It contains a modeling database surrounded by various plug-ins: static checker, proof obligation generator, provers, model-checkers, animators, UML transformers, requirement document handler, etc. The database

J.S. Fitzgerald, A.E. Haxthausen, and H. Yenigun (Eds.): ICTAC 2008, LNCS 5160, pp. 1–2, 2008.

itself contains the various modeling elements needed to construct discrete transition system models: essentially variables, invariants, and transitions (events).

Formal development. With the help of this palette, users can develop mathematical models and refine them. In doing so, they are able to reason, modify, and decompose their models before starting the effective implementation of the corresponding systems. Such an approach is well known and widely used in many mature engineering disciplines where reasoning on a abstract representation of the future system is routine. Just think of the usage of blueprints made by architects within a building construction process.

An Event-B formal development is made of a sequence of models, where each model is a refinement of the previous one (if any) in the sequence. A refinement corresponds to an enrichment of the more abstract model. Each refined model is subjected to proofs showing that it is not contradictory with its abstraction. This is precisely in such a refinement process that one can incorporate some predefined patterns.

An Event-B design pattern is a small model (with constants, variables, invariants, and events) devoted to formalise a typical well known sub-problem. The idea is to have a library of such design patterns which could be either quite general or domain dependent. Each design pattern will be stored with the corresponding refinements and proofs.

The adaptation of an Event-B design pattern essentially consists in instantiating (repainting) its constants, variables and events in order to have them corresponding to some elements of the problem at hand.

The incorporation of an Event-B design pattern within a larger model whose construction is in progress consists in *composing* the design pattern events within some existing events of the model so that the resulting effect is a refinement of the large model. This is to be done in a completely syntactic way so that no refinement proofs are necessary.

Tool. As the Rodin Platform is implemented on top of Eclipse, it is intended to construct on Eclipse a design pattern repository (the library) as well as a design pattern plug-in to facilitate the systematic adaptation and incorporation of Event-B design patterns. This work is presently in progress.

Result. Two case studies have been developed which are very encouraging: a reactive system and a business system. They will be incorporated in this presentation.

A Unified Approach to Abstract Interpretation, Formal Verification and Testing of C/C++ Modules

Jan Peleska

Department of Mathematics and Computer Science
University of Bremen
Germany
jp@tzi.de

Abstract. In this paper, a unified approach to abstract interpretation, formal verification and testing is described. The approach is applicable for verifying and testing C/C++ functions and methods and complies with the requirements of today's applicable standards for the development of safety-critical systems in the avionics and railway domains. We give an overview over the techniques required and motivate why an integrated approach is not only desirable from the verification specialists' perspective, but also from the tool builders' point of view. Tool support for our approach is available, and it is currently applied in industrial verification projects for railway control systems. All techniques can be adapted to model-based testing in a straightforward way. The objective of this article is to describe the interplay between the methods, techniques and tool components involved; we give references to more comprehensive descriptions of the underlying technical details.

1 Introduction

1.1 Overview

Starting from the perspective of safety-critical systems development in avionics, railways and the automotive domain, we advocate an integrated verification approach for C/C++ modules[1] combining abstract interpretation, formal verification by model checking and conventional testing. It is illustrated how testing and formal verification can benefit from abstract interpretation results and, vice versa, how test automation techniques may help to reduce the well known problem of false alarms frequently encountered in abstract interpretations. As a consequence, verification tools integrating these different methodologies can provide a wider variety of useful results to their users and facilitate the bug localisation processes involved. From the practitioners' point of view, our approach is driven by the applicable standards for safety-critical systems development in the railway and avionic domains: The methods and techniques described should help

---

[1] We use the term *module* to denote both C functions and C++ methods.

J.S. Fitzgerald, A.E. Haxthausen, and H. Yenigun (Eds.): ICTAC 2008, LNCS 5160, pp. 3–22, 2008.

to (1) fulfil the software-quality related requirements of these standards more efficiently and (2) facilitate the formal justification that these requirements have been completely fulfilled.

We present an overview of the methods required to achieve these goals for C/C++ code verification. The tasks involved can be roughly structured into six major building blocks (see Figure 1): (1) A parser front-end is required to transform the code into an intermediate model representation which is used for the analyses to follow. The intermediate model representation contains a suitably abstracted memory model which helps us to cope with the problems of aliasing, type casts and mixed arithmetic and bit operations typically present in C/C++ code. (2) Verification tasks have to be decomposed into sub-tasks investigating sub-models. A sub-model selector serves for this purpose. (3) Concrete, symbolic and abstract interpreters are required to support the process of constraint generation, the abstract interpreter serving the dual purpose of runtime error checking and of constraint simplification. (4) A constraint generator prepares the logical conditions accumulated by the interpreters for the (5) constraint solver which is needed to calculate concrete solution vectors as well as over and under approximations of the constraint solution sets. (6) For automated test case generation, test data is constructed as solutions to the constraints associated with a specific reachability goal. The test data has to be integrated in test procedures automatically invoking the tested modules, feeding the input data to their interfaces and checking the modules' behaviour against expected results specifications. Test procedures are internally represented as abstract syntax trees, so that different syntax requirements of test execution environments can be conveniently met.

Our presentation focuses on the interplay between these building blocks and provides references to more detailed elaborations of the technical problems involved.

In section 2 the requirements of standards related to safety-critical systems development are sketched. Section 3 contains the main part of this paper. It describes the work flow between the tool components listed above which conforms

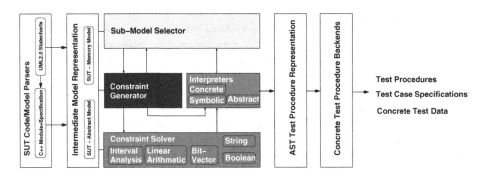

Fig. 1. Building blocks of test automation, static analysis and property verification tool platform

to these standards. Moreover, the methods used to implement the component functionality are sketched. Section 4 presents a conclusion.

1.2 Related Work

The work presented here summarises and illustrates results previously published by the author and his research team in cooperation with Verified Systems International GmbH [3,17,19,16,15].

Many authors point out that the syntactic richness and the semantic ambiguities of C/C++ present considerable stumbling blocks when developing analysis tools for software written in these languages. Our approach is similar to that of [11] in that we consider a simplified syntactic variant – the GIMPLE code – with the same expressive power but far more restrictive syntax than the original language: GIMPLE [10] is a control flow graph representation using 3-address code in assignments and guard conditions. Since the gcc compiler transforms every C/C++ function or method into a GIMPLE representation, this seems to be an appropriate choice: If tools can handle the full range of GIMPLE code, they can implicitly handle all C/C++ programs accepted by gcc. Therefore we extract type information and GIMPLE code from the gcc compiler; this technique has been described in [14]. In contrast to [11], where a more abstract memory model is used, our approach can handle type casts.

The full consideration of C/C++ aliasing situations with pointers, casts and unions is achieved at the price of lesser performance. In [6,5], for example, it is pointed out how more restrictive programming styles, in particular, the avoidance of pointer arithmetics, can result in highly effective static analyses with very low rates of false alarms. Conversely it is pointed out in [25] that efficient checks of pointer arithmetics can be realised if only some aspects of correctness (absence of out-of-bounds array access) are investigated. As another alternative, efficient static analysis results for large general C-programs can be achieved if a higher number of false alarms (or alternatively, a suppression of potential failures) is acceptable [8], so that paths leading to potential failures can be identified more often on a syntactic basis without having to fall back on constraint solving methods.

On the level of binary program code verification impressive results have been achieved for certain real-world controller platforms, using explicit representation models [22]. These are, however, not transferable to the framework underlying our work, since the necessity to handle floating point and wide integer types (64 or 128 bit) forbids the explicit enumeration of potential input values and program variable states.

All techniques described in this paper are implemented in the RT-Tester tool developed by the author and his research group at the University of Bremen in cooperation with Verified Systems International GmbH [26]. The approach pursued with the RT-Tester tool differs from the strategies of other authors [6,5,25]: We advocate an approach where verification activities focus on small program units (a few functions or methods) and should be guided by the expertise of the development or verification specialists. Therefore the RT-Tester tool provides mechanisms for specifying preconditions about the expected or admissible input data for the unit under inspection as well as for semi-automated stub ("mock-object") generation showing user-defined behaviour whenever invoked by the unit to be analysed. As a consequence, programmed units can be verified immediately – this may be appealing to developers in favour of the *test-driven development* paradigm [4] – and interactive support for bug-localisation and further investigation of potential failures is provided: A debugger supports various abstract interpretation modes (in particular, interval analysis) and the test case generator can be invoked for generating explicit input data for reaching certain code locations indicating the failure of assertions.

With the recent progress made in the field of Satisfiability Modulo Theory [20] powerful constraint solvers are available which can handle different data types, including floating point values and associated non-linear constraints involving transcendent functions. The solver implemented in the tool relies on ideas developed in [9] as far as Boolean and floating point constraints are involved, but uses additional techniques and underlying theories for handling linear inequations, bit vectors, strings and algebraic reasoning, see, e. g. [23]. Most methods for solving constraints on interval lattices used in our tool are based on the interval analysis techniques described in [12].

2   Background and Motivation: Industrial Safety-Critical Systems Development and the Deployment of Formal Methods

According to the standards [21,7,1] the generation of 100% correct software code is not a primary objective in the development of safety-critical systems. This attitude is not unjustified, since code correctness will certainly not automatically imply system safety. Indeed, safety is an *emergent* property [13, p. 138], resulting from a suitable combination of (potentially failing) hardware and software layers. As a consequence, the standards require that

– the contribution of software components to system safety (or, conversely, the hazards that may be caused by faulty software) shall be clearly identified, and
– the software shall be developed and verified with state-of-the art techniques and with an effort proportional to the component's criticality.

Based on the criticality, the standards define clearly which techniques are considered as appropriate and which effort is sufficient. The effort to be spent on verification is defined most precisely with respect to testing techniques: Tests should (1) exercise each functional requirement at least once, (2) cover the code completely, the applicable coverage criteria (statement, branch, modified condition/decision coverage) again depending on the criticality, (3) show the proper integration of software on target hardware. Task (3) is of particular importance, since analyses and formal verifications on source code level cannot prove that the module will execute correctly on a specific hardware component.

These considerations motivate the main objectives for the tool support we wish to provide:

1. Application of the tool and the results it provides have to be associated clearly with the development phases and artifacts to be produced by each activity specified in the applicable standards.
2. Application of the tool should help to produce the required results – tests, analysis and formal verifications – faster and at least with the same quality as could be achieved in a manual way.

Requirement 1 is obviously fulfilled, since the tool functionality described here has been explicitly designed for the module verification phase, as defined by the standards mentioned above. Requirement 2 motivates our *bug finder* approach with respect to formal verification and static analysis: These techniques should help to find errors more quickly than would be possible with manual inspections and tests alone – finding *all* errors of a certain class is not an issue. As a consequence the tool can be designed in such a way that state explosions, long computation times, false alarms and other aspects of conventional model checkers and static analysis tools, usually leading to user frustration and rejection of an otherwise promising method, simply do not happen: Instead, partial verification results are delivered, and these – in combination with the obligatory tests – are usually much better than what a manual verification could produce within affordable time.

3   Abstract Interpretation, Formal Verification and Testing – An Integrated Approach

3.1   Specification of Analysis, Verification and Test Objectives

In our approach functional requirements of C/C++ modules are specified by means of pre- and post-conditions (Fig. 2). Optionally, additional assertions can be inserted into an "inspection copy" of the module code. The *Unit Under Test (UUT)*[2] is registered by means of its prototype specification preceded by the @uut keyword and extended by a {@pre: ... @post}; block. Pre- and post-conditions are specified as Boolean expressions or C/C++ functions, so that – apart from a few macros like @pre, @post, @assert and the utilisation of the method name as place holder for return values – no additional assertion language syntax is required. The pre-condition in Fig. 2, for example, states that the specified module behaviour is only granted if input i is in range $0 \leq i \leq 9$ and inputs x, y satisfy $\exp(y) < x$. The post-condition specifies assertions whose applicability may depend on the input data: The first assertion globx == globx@pre states that the global variable globx should always remain unchanged by an execution of f(). The second assertion (line 9) only applies if the input data satisfies $-10.0 < y \wedge \exp(y) < x$. Alternatively (line 12), the return value of f() shall be negative.

---

[2] We use this term in general for any module to be analysed, verified and/or tested.

```
1        double globx;
2
3        @uut double f(double x, double y, int i) {
4          @pre:
5              0 <= i and i <= 9 and exp(y) < x;
6          @post:
7              @assert( globx == globx@pre );
8              if ( -10.0 < y and exp(y) < x ) {
9                  @assert( f == 1.0/(x - exp(y)) );
10             }
11             else {
12                 @assert( f < 0 );
13             }
14       };
15
```

Fig. 2. Example: Module specification by pre- and post-conditions

It is well-known that pre-/post-condition specifications are considerably facilitated by the optional utilisation of *auxiliary variables* [2, p. 192]: These variables are characterised by the fact that they are never read in control conditions or assignments to non-auxiliary variables. As a consequence, the existence of auxiliary variables and their associated assignments does not change the (untimed) behaviour of the UUT. Assignments can either be directly inserted into the UUT code (so-called *code instrumentation*) or into the UUT specification by way of pre- and post-processing statements.

Since module behaviour is not only defined by its input-output relation but also by the sequence of sub-function and method invocations, it is necessary to specify

- the expected number and sequence of sub-function invocations,
- the expected input data to be passed by the UUT to its sub-functions,
- constraints about the sub-function behaviour, depending on the input data it receives.

Sub-functions are specified in the same way as the UUT itself. Using auxiliary variables and associated assignments recording the calls and their parameters, the assertions related to sequencing of sub-function calls can be expressed by means of predicates referring to these auxiliary variables. For test purposes, our system automatically generates *test stubs* (also called *mock objects* in object-oriented settings): These are functions replacing the original sub-functions invoked by the UUT, and showing the specified sub-function behaviour. The utilisation of stubs has the advantage, that exceptional behaviour which rarely occurs in the original sub-function (e. g. report of an arithmetic exception or a hardware error) can easily be simulated in the stub, so that execution of the associated code sections in the UUT can be triggered in a simple way.

Complementary to functional testing, it is required to perform *structural testing*. The goal of structural testing consists in covering the UUT control structures, statements, calls to sub-functions and interfaces, while still checking that the functional requirements are met. Currently, we support the coverage criteria required in the standards [21,7]:

- Statement coverage (C0): Every statement is executed at least once.
- Decision coverage (C1): C0 coverage plus the requirement that every decision is evaluated at least once with result `true` and at least once with result `false`. This is required, for example, for testing avionic software of criticality level B (A = highest criticality level).
- Multiple condition/decision coverage (MC/DC): C1 coverage plus the requirement that every condition in a decision in the module has taken all possible outcomes at least once, and each condition in a decision has been shown to independently affect that decision's outcome. A condition is shown independently to affect a decision's outcome by varying just that condition while holding fixed all other possible conditions. This is required, for example, for testing avionic software of criticality level A.

The specification of pre-/post-conditions and internal assertions, in combination with the optional utilisation of auxiliary variables, allows to specify safety conditions about the module behaviour. As a consequence, the verification goals are represented by reachability problems which are very similar to the structural coverage test goals: If we consider augmented module versions where each safety condition ψ is represented by an auxiliary code branch `if (`$\neg\psi$`) then { raiseError(); }` located at the appropriate place in the code, a test reaching the `raiseError()`-statement would uncover the violation of ψ and at the same time provide a counter example. Conversely, if this statement can be proven to be "dead code", this proves validity of ψ.

Furthermore, the objective to achieve *functional* test coverage can also be reduced to the problem of achieving *structural* test coverage, that is, it can also be transformed into a set of reachability problems. To illustrate this we consider a typical post-condition pattern

$$Q \equiv \bigwedge_i (C_i(\boldsymbol{v}, \boldsymbol{v}') \Rightarrow Q_i(\boldsymbol{v}, \boldsymbol{v}'))$$

Given variable vector pre-states $\boldsymbol{v}$ and post-states $\boldsymbol{v}'$, this post-conditions states a number of conditions $C_i(\boldsymbol{v}, \boldsymbol{v}')$ about the situations to be distinguished. Depending on the applicable situation $C_i(\boldsymbol{v}, \boldsymbol{v}')$, additional assertions $Q_i(\boldsymbol{v}, \boldsymbol{v}')$ shall also hold. Functional test coverage would now require to create each of the situations $C_i(\boldsymbol{v}, \boldsymbol{v}')$, so that the expected outcome $Q_i(\boldsymbol{v}, \boldsymbol{v}')$ can be checked. Instead of UUT `f()`, we now consider the augmented function `f`$_{\text{aug}}$`()` shown in Fig. 3. Obviously, statement coverage of `f`$_{\text{aug}}$`()` implies functional coverage of `f()` in the sense exemplified above.

```
1        void f_aug(t1 x1, ..., tn xn) {
2          t r;
3          if ( P(v) ) {
4            // This branch is entered when input data
5            // satisfied pre-condition P(v)
6
7            v0 = v;                  // Create copy of pre-states
8            r = f(x1, ...,xn); // Call the UUT
9
10           // Post-state has changed variable vector v,
11           // pre-state is saved in auxiliary variable v0.
12
13           if ( C_1(v0,v) ) {
14              assert( Q_1(v0,v) );
15           }
16           ...
17           if ( C_k(v0,v) ) {
18              assert( Q_k(v0,v) );
19           }
20         }
21       }
22
```

Fig. 3. Branch coverage of f_aug() implies functional test coverage of f()

For the abstract interpretation objective *"absence of run-time errors"* no user-defined specifications are required, since the analysis obligations can be directly extracted from the code. It is possible, however, to choose between *bug finder mode* and *proof mode*: The former mode only uncovers run-time errors along the module paths which have been investigated in order to reach the specified test coverage and verification goals. Each uncovered run-time error is associated with a test case uncovering the erroneous module state; potential runtime errors for which no test cases could be constructed are not reported. The proof mode tries to prove the absence of *any* runtime error within the module, provided that the specified pre-conditions are met.

3.2   Transformation into an Intermediate Model Representation

To facilitate the re-use of algorithms for testing and verifying programs written in other programming languages and to support model-based testing and verification approaches, all algorithms operate on an *intermediate model representation IMR*. Conceptually, IMRs consist of collections of transition systems $T = (S, S_0, \longrightarrow)$ which may be connected by a decomposition relation (e. g. transition system state $s \in S$ is decomposed into one or more sub-ordinate transition systems $T_1, \ldots, T_n$) and a parallelism relation (transition system T_1 is executed in parallel to T_2).

Since we do not impose any restrictions on the size of the data types involved, explicit transition system state space representations of C/C++ modules in the IMR would be impossible. Instead, the IMR encodes the transition relation, using a combined explicit and symbolic technique: The full transition system state space S is structured into *locations Loc* and variable valuations $V \not\rightarrow D$, i. e., $S = Loc \times (V \not\rightarrow D)$, where V denotes the set of symbols and D a suitable domain capturing all symbol types involved. Note that the valuation mappings are partial, because at different states different symbols may be present in the state-dependent scope. Moreover, V may be infinite to allow for symbols specified by de-referenced pointer expressions (such as `*(p->next->...->next->x)`) or array elements with arbitrary index expressions (like `a[i`$_0$` + ... + i`$_n$`]`).

A directed *location graph* $L = (Loc, \longrightarrow_L \subseteq Loc \times Label \times Loc)$ with labelled edges explicitly represents an abstraction of the transition system. The abstraction hides all concrete symbol valuations. The Edges $e = l_0 \longrightarrow_L l_1$ of L may be labelled by *guard conditions* $g(e)$, that is, predicates with symbols from V as free variables. The guard conditions specify the constraints on variables valuations to be fulfilled for having an associated transition in the concrete transition system $T = (Loc \times (V \not\rightarrow D), S_0, \longrightarrow)$. Furthermore, edges e can be annotated with symbolic transition relations specifying *actions* $\epsilon(e)$, that is, changes $\sigma_1 = \epsilon(e)(\sigma_0)$ on symbol valuations accompanying a $(l_0, \sigma_0) \longrightarrow_L (l_1, \sigma_1)$-transition in the concrete transition system T. Similarly, nodes l_1 of the location graph can be annotated by *entry actions* $\alpha(l_1)$, specifying changes on symbol valuations occurring when entering location l_1. Furthermore, they can be labelled with *invariants* $inv(l)$ and *do-actions* $\delta(l)$ to encode models specified in timed, potentially hybrid, formalisms and supporting urgent and non-urgent transitions.

A pre-requisite for a concrete transition $(l_0, \sigma_0) \longrightarrow (l_1, \sigma_1)$ to take place in T is that there exists an edge $l_0 \xrightarrow{[g]/a}_L l_1$ in the location graph such that $\sigma_0 \models g$, that is, $g(\sigma_0(x_0)/x_0, \ldots, \sigma_0(x_n)/x_n)$ evaluates to `true`. This is obviously independent on the concrete formalism encoded in the IMR. The more specific rules for deriving possible T-transitions depend on the underlying formalism. As a consequence, we instantiate specific interpreters implementing the concrete transition rules with each supported formalism. This necessity suggests an object-oriented approach for the IMR.

For C/C++ module testing, each module $f()$ corresponds to one transition system $T(f)$ and transition system states correspond to computation states of the module. A call from $f()$ to a sub-module $h()$ corresponds to a state s representing the call which is related to a sub-ordinate transition system $T(h)$. The IMR uses GIMPLE control flow graphs (CFG) as location graphs for C/C++ modules (see [10]). These graphs have one dedicated *entry node* **BLOCK 0** and one *exit node* **EXIT**. Each location is associated with an entry action, and these are the only actions defined for CFGs; do-actions, invariants and actions associated with edges are not needed. Actions are defined in imperative programming language style according to the GIMPLE syntax and in 3-address code[3]. Each CFG node l has at most two outgoing edges $l \xrightarrow{[g_0]}_L l', l \xrightarrow{[g_1]}_L l''$ corresponding to if-else-conditions, so $g_1 = \neg g_0$. The symbol set V consists of the variable symbols occurring in $f()$ plus additional atomic variables introduced to support the 3-address code representation. Each concrete transition of T can be derived from the rule

$$\frac{l_0 \xrightarrow{[g]}_L l_1, \ \sigma_0 \models g}{(l_0, \sigma_0) \longrightarrow (l_1, \alpha(l_1)(\sigma_0))}$$

A *run* of a C/C++ module is a finite computation, that is, a sequence

$$r = \langle (l_0, \sigma_0), \ldots, (l_n, \sigma_n) \rangle$$

such that $(l_0, \sigma_0) \in S_0$ and

$$\forall \, i \in \{0, \ldots, n-1\} : \exists \, l_i \xrightarrow{[g_i]}_L l_{i+1} : \sigma_i \models g_i \wedge \sigma_{i+1} = \alpha(l_{i+1})(\sigma_i)$$

A path $l_0 \longrightarrow l_1 \longrightarrow, \ldots, \longrightarrow l_n$ through the location graph $L(T)$ is called *feasible* if an associated run in T can be constructed, otherwise the path is *infeasible*.

If the entry action of the target node consists of a function call then the following rule for the calculation of $\alpha(l_1)(\sigma_0)$ is applied:

$$\frac{\alpha(l_1) = \{\mathbf{x_0} = \mathbf{h}(\mathbf{x_1}, \ldots, \mathbf{x_n});\}, \ (BLOCK \ 0, \sigma_0|_h) \longrightarrow_h^* (EXIT, \sigma_1)}{\alpha(l_1)(\sigma_0) = (\sigma_1|_f)[x_0 \mapsto \sigma_1(h_{return})]}$$

This rule is interpreted as follows: If $T(f)$ may perform a transition into location l_1 which has a function call as entry action, then the effect of this action is defined by $T(h)$. If $T(h)$ transforms entry valuation $\sigma_0|_h$ into exit valuation σ_1 then the symbols still visible at the level of $f()$ (that is, everything but the formal parameters and stack variables of $h()$) carry the new valuation σ_1, and the return value of $h()$ is assigned to the target variable x_0 of the assignment. The symbol $|$ in $\sigma_0|_h$ denotes (1) the extension of dom σ_0 to the scope of $h()$: dom σ_0 is now extended by the formal parameters and stack variables of $h()$. (2) The assignment of actual parameter values used in the call to h to formal parameter valuations visible inside h. Observe that for reference parameters the formal parameter gets an address assignment from the associated actual parameter. Conversely, $\sigma_1|_f$ denotes (1) the domain restriction of valuation function σ_1; formal parameters and local variables of $h()$ are no longer visible, and (2) the assignment of the return value of $h()$ to an intermediate variable h_{return} visible at the level of $f()$.

Due to the aliasing effects possible in C/C++, the sub-function $h()$ may indirectly change local variables of $f()$ via assignments to de-referenced pointers. As a consequence, the effect of the $h()$-execution on symbol valuations "apparently" outside the scope of $h()$ can be quite complex. The memory model and the associated valuation rules described below have been designed to cope with these problems. For the moment it suffices to observe that an assignment to a

---

[3] Exceptions are calls to modules with more than 3 parameters $\mathbf{y} = \mathbf{f}(\mathbf{x_1}, \ldots, \mathbf{x_n})$ and access to multi-dimensional array $\mathbf{y} = \mathbf{a}[\mathbf{x_1}] \ldots [\mathbf{x_n}], n > 2$.

symbol inside the scope of $h()$ may implicitly change the valuation of (due to recursive data structures and pointer de-referencing) possibly infinitely many other symbols which may even be outside the scope of $h()$.

3.3   The Sub-model Generator

The reason for using a mixed explicit (location graph) and symbolic (specification of transition effects on valuations) intermediate model representation lies in the fact that this allows us to distribute the elaboration of reachability strategies onto two tool components – the solver and the sub-model generator – instead of only one (the solver). It has been pointed out in [3] that the reachability goals associated with structural test coverage and with the verification of safety properties can always be expressed as a goal to cover specific edges in a location graph; for C/C++ this is the GIMPLE CFG or a semantically equivalent transformation thereof. The task of the sub-model generator is therefore to restrict the complete transition system collection representing the UUT into a collection of restricted sub-systems by eliminating as many original transitions that will never be visited by any path leading to the destination edges as possible. Since this should be performed in an efficient manner *before* a constraint solver is involved, the sub-model generator performs a conservative approximation based on the location graph alone, that is, without calculating symbol valuations. Furthermore, the sub-model generator receives feed-back from the constraint solver about infeasible paths through the location graph and applies learning strategies for avoiding to pass infeasible sub-models to the solver. Finally, this tool component keeps track of the location graph coverage achieved.

The simplest sub-models are paths through the location graph, more complex ones are

- trees leaving a higher degree of freedom for the solver in order to construct runs to the destination edges, and
- sub-graphs representing if-else branches both leading back to the same path to the destination edge.

Example 1. Consider a C/C++-UUT whose transition relation is encoded by the CFG depicted in Fig. 4. For structural testing it is useful to know all paths up to a certain depth leading to any given edge. For this purpose, the sub-model generator maintains a tree of depth k as depicted in Fig. 5, associated with a function ϕ_k mapping edges e of the location graph to lists of nodes n in the tree, such that a path in the tree from root to n corresponds to a path trough the transition graph reaching e. For the configuration described by Fig. 4 and 5 we have, for example, $\phi_6(f) = \langle (l_5, 3), (l_5, 5), (l_5, 4), (l_5, 7) \rangle$. If one path, say, the one specified by $(l_5, 3)$, to the destination edge is identified by the solver to be infeasible, the tree is pruned at the target node of the destination edge. In our example, edges in the sub-tree starting at $(l_5, 3)$ would never be suggested again by the sub-model generator. If all paths specified by $\phi_k(f)$ turned out to be infeasible, the tree can be expanded if possible, but only at leaves which do not reside in sub-trees already pruned.

For structural testing it will be too costly to expand the tree of Fig. 5 further, if most of the edges have already been covered. The sub-model generator now constructs another tree structure capturing all (still potentially feasible) paths to an edge still uncovered.

More details about the algorithms for generating sub-models can be found in [3].   □

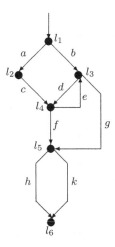

Fig. 4. Location graph example

3.4   Interpreters

Symbolic Interpretation. Given the IMR of a spcification or C/C++ module, the symbolic interpreter performs symbolic computation of runs through a sub-model of the location graph. This interpreter is the core component for generating the constraints to be solved for the inputs of a module, in order to reach a given edge.

As a consequence of the aliasing problems of C/C++ it may be quite complex to determine the valuation of a variable in a given module state: the memory location associated with the variable may have been changed not only by direct assignments referring to the variable name, but also indirectly by assignments to de-referenced pointers and memory copies to areas containing the variable. Therefore we introduce a memory model that allows us to identify the presence of such aliasing effects with acceptable effort. Computations are defined as sequences of memory configurations, and the memory areas affected by assignments or function/method executions are specified by means of base addresses, offsets and physical length of the affected area. Moreover, the values written to these memory areas are only specified *symbolically* by recording the value-defining expression (e. g. right-hand side of an assignment or output parameter

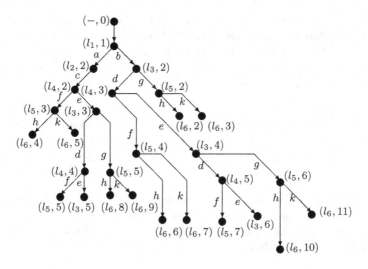

Fig. 5. Tree sub-model with paths to *all* edges in the location graph

of a procedure call) without resolving them to concrete or abstract valuations. This motivates the term *symbolic interpretation*. Global, static and stack variables x induce base addresses &x in the data and stack segment, respectively. Dynamic memory allocation (malloc(), new ...) creates new base addresses on the heap. A memory configuration *mem* consists of a collection of *memory items*, each item *m* specified by base address, offset, length and and value expression (Fig. 6). Since some statements will only conditionally affect a memory area, it is necessary to associate memory items with constraints specifying the conditions for the item's existence.

$$m.v_0 \mid m.v_1 \mid m.a \mid m.t \mid m.o \mid m.l \mid m.val \mid m.c$$

$m.v_0$ First computation step number where m is valid
$m.v_1$ Last computation step number where m is valid or ∞ for items valid beyond the actual computation step
$m.a$ Symbolic base address
$m.t$ Type of specified value $m.val$
$m.o$ Start offset from base address in bits, where value is stored
$m.l$ Offset from base address to first bit following the stored value, so $m.l - m.o$ specifies the bit-length of the memory location represented by the item
$m.val$ Value specification
$m.c$ Validity constraint

Fig. 6. Structure of a memory item m

Symbolic computations – that is, sequences of memory configurations related by transition relations – are recorded as *histories*, in order to reduce the required storage space: Memory items are associated with a validity interval $[m.v_0, m.v_1]$ whose boundaries specify the first and last computation step where the item was a member of the configuration.

Example 2. Suppose that variables $\mathtt{float}$ $\mathtt{x}, \mathtt{y}, \mathtt{z}$; are defined in the stack frame of the UUT on a 32-bit architecture, and the current computation step n performs an assignment $\mathtt{x} = \mathtt{y} + \mathtt{z}$. This leads to the creation of a new memory item

$$m =_{\mathrm{def}} \boxed{n \mid \infty \mid \&x \mid \mathtt{float} \mid 0 \mid 32 \mid y_n + z_n \mid \mathtt{true}}$$

Item m is first valid from step n on, and has not yet been invalidated by other writes affecting the memory area from start address $\&x$ to $\&x + 31$. The value depends on the valuation of y and z, taken in step n. This is denoted by the version index n in the value expression $y_n + z_n$. □

For the representation of large memory areas carrying identical or inter-dependent values it is useful to admit additional bound parameters in the offset, value and constraint specifications:

$$m_{p_0,\ldots,p_k} =$$

$$\boxed{v_0 \mid v_1 \mid a \mid t \mid o(p_0,\ldots,p_k) \mid l(p_0,\ldots,p_k) \mid val(p_0,\ldots,p_k) \mid c(p_0,\ldots,p_k)}$$

defines a *family of memory items* by means of the definition

$$
\begin{aligned}
m_{p_0,\ldots,p_k} =_{\mathrm{def}} \{m' \mid\ & m'.v_0 = v_0 \wedge m'.v_1 = v_1 \wedge m'.a = a \wedge m'.t = t\ \wedge \\
& (\exists p_0',\ldots,p_k' : m'.o = o[p_0'/p_0,\ldots,p_k'/p_k]\ \wedge \\
& m'.l = l[p_0'/p_0,\ldots,p_k'/p_k]\ \wedge \\
& m'.val = val[p_0'/p_0,\ldots,p_k'/p_k]\ \wedge \\
& m'.c = c[p_0'/p_0,\ldots,p_k'/p_k])\}
\end{aligned}
$$

Example 3. Suppose that array $\mathtt{float}$ $\mathtt{a}[10]$; is defined in the stack frame of the UUT on a 32-bit architecture, and is currently represented by a family of memory items

$$m_p =_{\mathrm{def}}$$

$$\boxed{n \mid \infty \mid \&a[0] \mid \mathtt{float} \mid 32 \cdot p \mid 32 \cdot p + 32 \mid \mathtt{sinf}((float)p) \mid 0 \leq p \wedge p < 10}$$

Family m specifies one memory item for each $p \in \{0,\ldots,9\}$, each item located at a p-dependent offset from the base address $\&a[0]$ and carrying a p-dependent value. □

Symbolic interpretation (denoted below by transition relation $\longrightarrow_G$, "G" standing for "GIMPLE operational semantics") is performed according to rules of the pattern

$$\frac{n_1 \overset{g}{\longrightarrow}_{CFG} n_2}{(n_1, n, mem) \longrightarrow_G (n_2, n+1, mem')},$$

so a transition can be performed on symbolic level whenever a corresponding edge exists in the control flow graph ($\xrightarrow{g}_{CFG}$ denotes the edge-relation in the module's CFG, with guard condition g as label). It may turn out, however, on abstract or concrete interpretation level, that such a transition is infeasible because no valuation of inputs exists where the constraints of all memory items involved evaluate to true. Informally speaking, a statement changing the memory configuration is processed according to the following steps: (1) For every base address and offset possibly affected by the statement, create a new memory item m', to be added to the resulting configuration. (2) For each new item m' check which existing items m may be invalidated: Invalidation occurs, if m' refers to the same base address as m and the data area of m' has a non-empty intersection with that of m. (3) For each invalidated item m create new ones m'' specifying what may still remain visible of m: m'' equals to m if m' does not exist at all (i. e., constraint $m'.c$ evaluates to false), or m' and m do not overlap. Moreover, m'' specifies the resulting value representation of m in memory for the situation where m' and m only partially overlap.

In [16,15], formal transition rules have been specified for $\longrightarrow_G$, as well as the algorithms required for rule application. Here we will only present an example, in order to illustrate the effect of these rules on the symbolic memory state.

Example 4. A stack declaration int a[10]; followed by assignments a[i] = m + n; a[j] = 0; is represented in GIMPLE as

```
1       int a[10];
2       i_0 = i;
3       D_4151 = m + n;
4       a[i_0] = D_4151;
5       j_1 = j;
6       a[j_1] = 0;
```

After having processed lines 1 — 6, the associated computation results in the following history of memory items:

$$m_p^1 = (1, 3, \&a[0], 32 \cdot p, 32 \cdot p + 32, \text{int}, \text{Undef}, 0 \le p \wedge p < 10)$$

$$m^2 = (2, \infty, \&i\_0, 0, 32, \text{int}, i_1, \text{true})$$

$$m^3 = (3, \infty, \&D\_4151, 0, 32, \text{int}, m_2 + n_2 \text{true})$$

$$m_p^4 = (4, 5, \&a[0], 32 \cdot p, 32 \cdot p + 32, \text{int}, \text{Undef}, 0 \le p \wedge p < 10 \wedge p \ne i\_0_2)$$

$$m^5 = (4, 5, \&a[0], 32 \cdot i\_0_2, 32 \cdot i\_0_2 + 32, \text{int}, D\_4151_3, 0 \le i\_0_2 \wedge i\_0_2 < 10)$$

$$m^6 = (5, \infty, \&j\_1, 0, 32, \text{int}, j_4, \text{true})$$

$$m_p^7 = (6, \infty, \&a[0], 32 \cdot p, 32 \cdot p + 32, \text{int}, \text{Undef}, 0 \le p \wedge p < 10 \wedge p \ne i\_0_2 \wedge p \ne j\_1_5)$$

$$m^8 = (6, \infty, \&a[0], 32 \cdot i\_0_2, 32 \cdot i\_0_2 + 32, \text{int}, D\_4151_3,$$

$$0 \le i\_0_2 \wedge i\_0_2 < 10 \wedge i\_0_2 \ne j\_1_5)$$

$$m^9 = (6, \infty, \&a[0], 32 \cdot j\_1_5, 32 \cdot j\_1_5 + 32, \text{int}, 0, 0 \le j\_1_5 \wedge j\_1_5 < 10)$$

Initially, the declared array a is undefined because it resides in the stack segment where no variable initialisation takes place (memory item m_p^1). The assignment to a[i_0] in line 4 invalidates the original item m_p^1 representing the symbolic valuation of a, so $m_p^1.v_1 = 3$. This leads to the creation of two new items: m^5 specifies the effect of the assignment in line 4, and m_p^4 specifies the array elements which are still undefined. A further invalidation of m_p^4, m^5 is caused by the assignment in line 6 and generates the new items m_p^7, m^8, m^9. Item m^8, for example, specifies the situation where the original value written to a[i_0] in line 4 is still visible after the new assignment in line 6.   □

Abstract Interpretation. The *abstract interpreters* evaluate one or more abstractions of the memory model. Starting with (lattice) abstractions of the module's input data, they operate on abstractions of the symbolic memory model. The purpose of this activity is threefold:

- Identification of runtime errors.
- Using over-approximation, an abstract interpreter can find sufficient conditions to prove that a computation "suggested" by path generator and symbolic interpreter is infeasible. Since abstract interpretation can be performed at comparably low cost this is more effective than waiting for the constraint solver to find out that a path cannot be covered.
- Using under-approximation, the abstract interpreters speed up the solution process for non-linear constraints involving floating point variables and transcendent functions.

Concrete Interpretation. The concrete interpreter applies concrete GIMPLE semantics [16] in order to find out the paths through the IMR that are covered with concrete sets of input data. It is applied

- in verification to present counter examples,
- in structural testing to determine the location graph edges following a reachable destination edge which are also covered before the exit point of a module execution is reached.

3.5   Constraint Generation

As we have seen in the previous section, the guard conditions to be fulfilled in order to cover a specific path or a sub-graph of a module's CFG are already encoded in the memory items associated with the symbolic memory configurations involved. The most important task for the constraint generator is now to resolve the value components of the memory items involved, so that the resulting expressions are free of pointer and array expressions, and are represented in an appropriate format for the solver.

Example 5. Let us extend Example 4 by two additional statements

```
7 D_4160 = a[i_0];
8 if ( D_4160 < 0 ) { ...(*)... }
```

and suppose we wish to reach the branch marked by (*). The constraint generator now proceeds as follows: (1) Initialise constraint Φ as $\Phi := \mathtt{D\_4160} < 0$.

(2) Resolve $\mathtt{D\_4160}$ to $\mathtt{a[i\_0]}$, as induced by the memory item resulting from the assignment in line 7. Since $\mathtt{a[i\_0]}$ is an array expression, we have to resolve it further, before adding the resolution results to Φ.

(3) $\mathtt{a_7[i\_0_7]}$ matches with items m_p^7, m^8, m^9 for $\mathtt{a}$ and m^2 for $\mathtt{i\_0}$ in Example 4, since the other items with base address $\&\mathtt{a[0]}$ are already outdated at computation step 7; this leads to resolutions

$$
\begin{aligned}
\Phi = {} & \mathtt{D\_4160} < 0 \wedge ((\mathtt{D\_4160} = \mathtt{Undef} \wedge \mathtt{i\_0_7} = \mathtt{p} \wedge 0 \le \mathtt{p} \wedge \mathtt{p} < 10 \wedge \mathtt{p} \neq \mathtt{i\_0_2} \wedge \mathtt{p} \neq \mathtt{j\_1_5}) \vee \\
& (\mathtt{D\_4160} = \mathtt{D\_4151_3} \wedge \mathtt{i\_0_7} = \mathtt{i\_0_2} \wedge 0 \le \mathtt{i\_0_2} \wedge \mathtt{i\_0_2} < 10 \wedge \mathtt{i\_0_2} \neq \mathtt{j\_1_5}) \vee \\
& (\mathtt{D\_4160} = 0 \wedge \mathtt{i\_0_7} = \mathtt{j\_1_5} \wedge 0 \le \mathtt{j\_1_5} \wedge \mathtt{j\_1_5} < 10)) \wedge \\
& \mathtt{i\_0_7} = \mathtt{i\_0_2} \wedge \mathtt{i\_0_2} = \mathtt{i_1} \wedge \mathtt{j\_0_5} = \mathtt{j_4} \wedge \mathtt{j_4} = \mathtt{j_1}
\end{aligned}
$$

Observe that at this stage Φ has been completely resolved to atomic data types: The references to array variable $\mathtt{a}$ have been transformed into offset restrictions (expressions over $\mathtt{i\_0_7}, \mathtt{i\_0_2}, \mathtt{j\_1_5}, \ldots$), and the array elements involved (in this example $\mathtt{a[i\_0]}$) have been replaced by atomic variables representing their values ($\mathtt{D\_4160}$). References to C-structures would be eliminated in an analogous way, by introducing address offsets for each structure component and using atomic variables denoting the component values.

Further observe that we have already eliminated the factors 32 in Φ, initially occurring in expressions like $32 \cdot \mathtt{i\_0_7} = 32 \cdot \mathtt{j\_1_5}$. These factors are only relevant for bit-related operations; for example, if an integer variable is embedded into a C-union containing a bit-field as another variant, and a memory item corresponding to the integer value is invalidated by a bit operation.

(4) Simplify by means of abstract interpretation: Using interval analysis for symbols of numeric type, some atoms of the constraint can be quickly verified or falsified, in order to simplify the constraint finally passed to the solver. Suppose, for example, that $\mathtt{i}$, $\mathtt{j}$ were inputs to the module and fulfilled the pre-conditions $0 \le \mathtt{i} < 2$, $2 \le \mathtt{j} < 10$ The interval analysis would yield $\mathtt{true}$ for condition $\mathtt{i\_0_2} \neq \mathtt{j\_1_5}$ for all elements i, j satisfying the pre-condition, so conjunct $\mathtt{i\_0_2} \neq \mathtt{j\_1_5}$ could be deleted in Φ.

(5) Prepare the constraint for the solver: Following the restrictions for admissible constraints described in [9], our solver requires some pre-processing of Φ: (a) Inequalities like $\mathtt{i\_0_2} \neq \mathtt{j\_1_5}$ are replaced by disjunctions involving $<, >$, e. g. $\mathtt{i\_0_2} < \mathtt{j\_1_5} \vee \mathtt{i\_0_2} > \mathtt{j\_1_5}$. (b) Inequalities $a < b$ are only admissible if a or b is a constant. Therefore atoms like $\mathtt{i\_0_2} < \mathtt{j\_1_5}$ are transformed with the aid of *slack variables* s, so that non-constant symbols are always related by equality. For example, the above atom is transformed into $\mathtt{i\_0_2} + \mathtt{s} = \mathtt{j\_1_5} \wedge 0 < \mathtt{s}$. (c) Three-address-code is enforced, so that – with the exception of function calls $\mathtt{y} = \mathtt{f}(\mathtt{x_0}, \ldots, \mathtt{x_n})$ and array expressions $\mathtt{y} = \mathtt{a[x_1]} \ldots [\mathtt{x_n}]$ – each atom refers to at most 3 variables. Since the introduction of slack variables may lead to four variables in an expression originally expressed with three symbols only, auxiliary variables are needed to reinstate the desired three-address representation. For example, $x + y < z$ leads to $x + y = z + s \wedge s < 0$ which is subsequently

transformed into $aux = z + s \wedge x + y = aux \wedge s < 0$. (d) The constraint is transformed into conjunctive normal form CNF. Constraint Φ in this example already indicates a typical problem to be frequently expected when applying the standard CNF algorithm: Some portions of Φ resemble a disjunctive normal form. This is caused by the necessity to consider alternatives – that is, $\vee$-combinations – of memory items, where the validity of each item is typically specified by a conjunction. As a consequence, the standard CNF algorithm may result in a considerably larger formula. Therefore we have implemented both the standard CNF algorithm and the Tseitin algorithm [24] as an alternative, together with a simple decision procedure indicating which algorithm will lead to better results.

3.6 Constraint Solver

The solver handling the conditions prepared by the constraint generator has been developed according to the *Satisfiability Modulo Theory (SMT)* paradigm [20]. It uses a combination of techniques for solving partial problems of specific type (e. g., constraints involving bit vector arithmetic, strings, or floating point calculations). For the solution of constraints involving floating point expressions and transcendent functions the solver applies *interval analysis* [12] and learning strategies designed by [9], see also [3] for more details of solver application in the context of test automation.

4 Conclusion

We have described an integrated approach for automated testing, static analysis by abstract interpretation and formal verification by model checking (reachability analysis for safety properties). The main focus of the presentation was on the verification of C/C++ modules. It has been indicated, however, how more abstract specification models can be encoded in the same intermediate model representation IMR used for code verification. As a consequence, the algorithms operating on the IMR can be directly applied to model-based testing and model verification. The techniques described in this paper, together with the tool support provided by the test automation system RT-Tester [26] are applied in industrial projects in the fields of railway control systems and avionics, the model-based approach is currently applied in the railway and automotive domains. More details about model-based testing can be found in [18].

References

1. IEC 61508 Functional safety of electric/electronic/programmable electronic safety-related systems. International Electrotechnical Commission (2006)
2. Apt, K.R., Olderog, E.R.: Verification of Sequential and Concurrent Programs. Springer, Heidelberg (1991)
3. Badban, B., Fränzle, M., Peleska, J., Teige, T.: Test automation for hybrid systems. In: Proceedings of the Third International Workshop on SOFTWARE QUALITY ASSURANCE (SOQUA 2006), Portland Oregon, November 2006, USA (2006)

4. Beck, K.: Test-Driven Development. Addison-Wesley, Reading (2003)
5. Cousot, P., Cousot, R., Feret, J., Mauborgne, L., Miné, A., Monniaux, D., Rival, X.: Combination of abstractions in the ASTRÉE static analyzer. In: Okada, M., Satoh, I. (eds.) ASIAN 2006. LNCS, vol. 4435, pp. 1–24. Springer, Heidelberg (2008)
6. Blanchet., B., et al.: Design and implementation of a special-purpose static program analyzer for safety-critical real-time embedded software. In: Mogensen, T.A., et al. (eds.) The Essence of Computation. LNCS, vol. 2566, pp. 85–108. Springer, Heidelberg (2002)
7. European Committee for Electrotechnical Standardization. EN 50128 – Railway applications – Communications, signalling and processing systems – Software for railway control and protection systems. CENELEC, Brussels (2001)
8. Fehnker, A., Huuck, R., Jayet, P., Lussenburg, M., Rauch, F.: Goanna - a static model checker. In: Proceedings of 11th International Workshop on Formal Methods for Industrial Critical Systems (FMICS), Bonn, Germany (2006)
9. Fränzle, M., Herde, C., Teige, T., Ratschan, S., Schubert, T.: Efficient solving of large non-linear arithmetic constraint systems with complex boolean structure. Journal on Satisfiability, Boolean Modeling and Computation (2007)
10. GCC, the GNU Compiler Collection. The GIMPLE family of intermediate representations, http://gcc.gnu.org/wiki/GIMPLE
11. Goubault-Larrecq, J., Parrennes, F.: Cryptographic protocol analysis on real C code. In: Cousot, R. (ed.) VMCAI 2005. LNCS, vol. 3385, pp. 363–379. Springer, Heidelberg (2005)
12. Jaulin, L., Kieffer, M., Didrit, O., Walter, É.: Applied Interval Analysis. Springer, London (2001)
13. Leveson, N.G.: Safeware. Addison-Wesley, Reading (1995)
14. Löding, H.: Behandlung komplexer Datentypen in der automatischen Testdatengenerierung. Master's thesis, University of Bremen (May 2007)
15. Peleska, J.: Integrated and automated abstract interpretation, verification and testing of C/C++ modules. In: Dams, D.R., Hannemann, U., Steffen, M. (eds.) Correctness, Concurrency and Compositionality – Festschrift for Willem-Paul de Roever. LNCS Festschrift series. Springer, Heidelberg (2008)
16. Peleska, J., Löding, H.: Symbolic and abstract interpretation for c/c++ programs. In: Proceedings of the 3rd intl Workshop on Systems Software Verification (SSV 2008), February 2008. Electronic Notes in Theoretical Computer Science, Elsevier, Amsterdam (2008)
17. Peleska, J., Löding, H., Kotas, T.: Test automation meets static analysis. In: Koschke, R., Rödiger, K.-H., Herzog, O., Ronthaler, M. (eds.) Proceedings of the INFORMATIK 2007, Band 2, Bremen, Germany, September 24-27, pp. 280–286 (2007)
18. Peleska, J., Möller, O., Löding, H.: Model-based testing for model-driven development with uml/dsl. In: Proceedings of the Software & Systems Quality Conference (SQC 2008) (to appear, 2008), http://www.informatik.uni-bremen.de/agbs/agbs/jp/jp_papers_e.html
19. Peleska, J., Zahlten, C.: Integrated automated test case generation and static analysis. In: Proceedings of the QA+Test 2007 International Conference on QA+Testing Embedded Systems, Bilbao (Spain), October17 - 19 (2007)
20. Ranise, S., Tinelli, C.: Satisfiability modulo theories. TRENDS and CONTROVERSIES–IEEE Magazine on Intelligent Systems 21(6), 71–81 (2006)
21. SC-167. Software Considerations in Airborne Systems and Equipment Certification. RTCA (1992)

22. Schlich, B., Salewski, F., Kowalewski, S.: Applying model checking to an automotive microcontroller application. In: Proc. IEEE 2nd Int'l Symp. Industrial Embedded Systems (SIES 2007), IEEE, Los Alamitos (2007)

23. Strichman, O.: On solving presburger and linear arithmetic with sat. In: Aagaard, M.D., O'Leary, J.W. (eds.) FMCAD 2002. LNCS, vol. 2517, pp. 160–170. Springer, Heidelberg (2002)

24. Tseitin, G.S.: On the complexity of derivation in propositional calculus. In: Slisenko, A.O. (ed.) Studies in Constructive Mathematics and Mathematical Logic, Part 2, Consultants Bureau, New York, p. 115 (1962)

25. Venet, A., Brat, G.: Precise and efficient static array bound checking for large embedded c programs. In: Proceedings of the PLDI 2004, Washington, DC, June 9-11, 2004, ACM Press, USA (2004)

26. Verified Systems International GmbH, Bremen. RT-Tester 6.2 – User Manual (2007)

The Three Platonic Models of Divergence-Strict CSP

A.W. Roscoe

Oxford University Computing Laboratory
Bill.Roscoe@comlab.ox.ac.uk

Abstract. In an earlier paper [13], the author proved that there were three models of CSP that play a special role amongst the ones based on finite observations: the traces ($\mathcal{T}$), stable failures ($\mathcal{F}$) and stable revivals ($\mathcal{R}$) models are successively more refined, but all further models refine $\mathcal{R}$. In the present paper we prove the corresponding result for the divergence-strict models: ones that treat any process that can diverge immediately as the least in the refinement order. We define what it is to be a divergence-strict model, both for general and finitely nondeterministic CSP, and find that in order to get our result we need to add a new but natural operator into the language.

1 Introduction

The process algebra CSP [5,10] is traditionally studied via behavioural models, namely combinations of sets of linear observations that might be made of them. The reference point for making these observations is CSP's standard LTS-based operational semantics as set out in Chapter 7 of [10] (perhaps with definitions for operators not considered there). In order to be a *model*, a representation has to be a congruence (it must be possible to deduce the observations of the result of applying any CSP operator from the observations of its arguments) and there must be a way of working out the operationally correct value of any recursive term from the function the recursion represents over the model.

One can divide the models of CSP into three categories:

- The models such as finite traces $\mathcal{T}$ and stable failures $\mathcal{F}$ (representing a process as its sets of finite traces, and stable failures (s, X) where the process can, after trace s, reach a state in which neither an internal τ action nor a member of X is possible). All the observations made of processes in this class of models are *finite*: they can be completed in a finite time.
- The divergence-strict models such as failures/divergences $\mathcal{N}$ in which, in addition to some finite observations, we are allowed to record some behaviours that take infinitely long. At any time when we are recording an observation, we will record the process diverging if it does, and furthermore we choose not to care about what our process might do on any observation that extends such a divergence. (A process diverges when it performs an infinite unbroken sequence of τ actions.)

J.S. Fitzgerald, A.E. Haxthausen, and H. Yenigun (Eds.): ICTAC 2008, LNCS 5160, pp. 23–49, 2008.

This class is particularly important since $\mathcal{N}$ and its extension to include infinite traces are the simplest that allow (respectively for finitely nondeterministic and general processes) one to specify that a process, offered a set X of events, *must* accept one of them. They also give the expressive power to define the concept of *determinism* [10].

Divergence strictness is useful for two reasons: firstly it permits (as we shall see later) the modelling of finitely branching processes without a separate representation of infinite traces, and secondly because it enormously simplifies the semantics of recursion. If one always regards divergence as an error, there is no need for models that distinguish beyond it.

– Models that record infinite behaviour but are not subject to divergence strictness. The first examples of these that are not just Cartesian products of the other two types were demonstrated in [12].

In [13], the author introduced a new family of models based on observing slightly more than in *failures*-based models and less than in either *ready-set* (sometimes termed *acceptance-set*) models or *refusal testing* models. In this family, we choose to observe not only failures (s, X) (where our process can perform the trace s and then stably refuse X) but also, when X is not the set of all visible events, single actions a that the state witnessing the refusal of X can perform. Thus processes include in their representations their *deadlock* traces (representing the traces on which the process can refuse anything) and their *revivals* (s, X, a). This family of models was inspired by the conformance equivalence of Fournet *et al* [1].

We discovered there that the stable failures model plays a special role in the van Glabbeek hierarchy [2,3], since it was shown to complete a fundamental initial sequence. Specifically, we showed that, with respect to the CSP language used in that paper, any non-trivial finite observation model that is not one of the increasingly refined sequence $\mathcal{T}$, $\mathcal{N}$ and $\mathcal{R}$ must refine $\mathcal{R}$. Furthermore there is no model $\mathcal{R} \prec \mathcal{M}$ such that every CSP model strictly refining $\mathcal{R}$ must refine $\mathcal{M}$. (For one congruence $\mathcal{B}$ to refine another $\mathcal{A}$ means that any pair of processes identified by $\mathcal{B}$ are identified by $\mathcal{A}$. We will sometimes write this $\mathcal{A} \preceq \mathcal{B}$.) These three initial models are seemingly forced on us and can be compared (perhaps fancifully) to the Platonic solids of geometry.

In that paper the author conjectured that essentially the same result would hold in the class of divergence-strict models. The purpose of the present paper is to resolve that conjecture: in fact it is true, but not quite in the terms that the author envisaged, since the language needs to be extended in a subtle way. The main structural result of this paper is the following theorem.

Theorem 1. *For a suitably extended (see Section 5) language CSP+, the three congruences* $\mathcal{T}^{\Downarrow\omega}$, $\mathcal{F}^{\Downarrow\omega}$ *and* $\mathcal{R}^{\Downarrow\omega}$ *(i.e. the finite observation models extended by strict divergence traces and infinite traces) are more abstract than every other nontrivial model of this language.*

The first thing we need to do, even to fully understand this statement, is decide what qualifies as a divergence-strict CSP model. We establish this via the creation of the most refined such model of them all. We also establish relationships between models for the full CSP language and ones for finitely nondeterministic CSP – which we abbreviate fCSP and whose standard models are denoted $\mathcal{T}^{\Downarrow}$ etc – that allow us to restrict our attention for the rest of the paper to the latter. This is a considerable bonus since we only have to consider behaviours over which we can use induction, and find we can restrict attention to finite restrictions of processes.

Having done this we are able to prove the first stage of the main result, namely that the divergence-strict traces model $\mathcal{T}^{\Downarrow}$ is refined by *every* nontrivial such CSP congruence, with respect to the same language used in [13].

It came as a surprise to the author that, with this same dialect of CSP, there is a curious congruence that is not quite as refined as the failures-divergences model $\mathcal{N}$. The discovery of this congruence (previously noted in [9]) leads to the observation that no CSP operator treats processes in a specific way that seems operationally natural, namely for some action of a given process P leading directly to the operator turning P off. We therefore add such an operator to the language, obtaining a language we term CSP+. We show that there is a surprisingly stark contrast between the relative roles of our new operator – $P \ominus_a Q$ that allows P to throw control to Q by communicating a – and the more usual interrupt operator $P \triangle Q$.

With this enhanced language we are able to complete the proof of the main result in two steps, one to prove that $\mathcal{N}$ is the weakest proper refinement of $\mathcal{T}^{\Downarrow}$, and the second to prove that the divergence-revivals model $\mathcal{R}^{\Downarrow}$ is the weakest proper refinement of this.

There is an appendix of notation. We do not give detailed descriptions in this paper of well-established CSP models or the semantics of CSP over them. The interested reader can easily find these in [10] or [13].

2   Background

In this paper, as in [13], we restrict ourselves to the study of models where the overall alphabet Σ is finite. However we only consider potential models that make sense for any size of Σ and have the property that a pair of processes defined over Σ_1 are equivalent over a model defined over Σ_1 if and only if they are equivalent over the same model defined over every larger Σ_2, because the model over Σ_1 is a natural restriction of the larger one. This means, for example, that we can establish properties of an equivalence between processes defined over Σ_1 by introducing a finite number of extra events and studying the equivalence over the resulting larger Σ_2. We might also note the following:

- The CSP renaming operator – with its ability to apply an arbitrary permutation to a process's alphabet – implies that any congruence for CSP must be essentially symmetric in events.
- Combinations of prefixing, renaming, parallel and hiding allow CSP to bring differences between processes forward or to postpone them. This suggests that CSP congruences must discriminate behaviours happening at any point in a process's execution uniformly.

Certainly all established models obey these two principles.

2.1 The CSP Language

Our starting point for CSP in this paper is the same language as in [13], but without the two (*SKIP* and ;) related to successful termination. This latter omission is just to make our arguments simpler[1] – the results of this paper are still valid with them added. The constant processes are thus

- *STOP* which does nothing – a representation of deadlock.
- **div** which performs (only) an infinite sequence of internal τ actions – a representation of divergence or live-lock.
- *CHAOS* which can do anything except diverge.
- *RUN(A)* which always offers the actions A.

and the operators

- $a \rightarrow P$ communicates the event $a \in \Sigma$ before behaving like P. This is *prefixing*.
- $?x : A \rightarrow P(x)$ communicates any event from $A \subseteq \Sigma$ and then behaves like the appropriate $P(x)$. This is *prefix choice*.
- $P \sqcap Q$ lets the process decide to behave like P or like Q: this is *nondeterministic* or *internal* choice. It can be used as a binary operator like this or over nonempty sets of processes $\sqcap S$. The only difference between CSP and fCSP is that in the latter we may not use $\sqcap$ over infinite sets.
- $P \square Q$ offers the environment the choice between the initial Σ-events of P and Q. If the one selected is unambiguous then it continues to behave like the one chosen; if it is an initial event of both then the subsequent behaviour is nondeterministic. The occurrence of τ in one of P and Q does *not* resolve the choice (unlike CCS +), and if one of P and Q can terminate then so can $P \square Q$. This is *external* choice.
- $P \rhd Q$ may choose to offer the visible actions of P but, unless one of these is followed, *must* offer the initial choices of Q. This is *asymmetric* or *sliding* choice and can be said to give an abstract (and untimed) representation of P timing out, if none of its initial actions are accepted, and becoming Q. This is considered primitive for reasons set out in [13].
- $P \parallel_X Q$ runs P and Q in parallel, allowing each of them to perform any action in $\Sigma - X$ independently, whereas actions in X must be synchronised between the two. It terminates when both P and Q have, a rule which is equivalent to stating that $\checkmark$ is synchronised like members of X. All other CSP parallel operators can be defined in terms of this one.
- $P \setminus X$, for $X \subseteq \Sigma$, *hides* X by turning all P's X-actions into τs.
- $P[\![R]\!]$ applies the *renaming* relation $R \subseteq \Sigma \times \Sigma$ to P: if $(a, b) \in R$ and P can perform a, then $P[\![R]\!]$ can perform b.

---

[1] The chief benefit is that we do not have to allow for processes terminating in the many contexts we create for them in this paper. The reader can see this effect in [13].

– $P \triangle Q$ runs like P but if at any time the environment communicates an initial visible action of Q, then (nondeterministically if that event is also currently offered by P) P shuts down and the process continues like Q. This is the *interrupt* operator.

We will discover some interesting things about $\triangle$ in Section 5.

The final CSP construct is recursion: this can be single or mutual (including mutual recursions over infinite parameter spaces), can be defined by systems of equations or (in the case of single recursion) in line via the notation $\mu \, p.P$, for a term P that may include the free process identifier p.

2.2   The Hierarchy of CSP Models

CSP models traditionally represent processes by sets of observations which can be made of a process. These observations are always ones that it is reasonable for someone interacting with the process to see in some finite or infinite linear interaction with it (in other words things are seen in some definite succession, with no branching). We work here under the same postulates as in [13], namely that the things that our observer can see are:

(a) Visible actions from Σ.
(b) The fact that a process is stable (is unable to perform any further actions without the co-operation of its environment), *and then*
   (i) whether it refuses a set of actions $X \subseteq \Sigma$ it is offered and
   (ii) the actual set of actions from Σ it is offering.

We note here that the ability to observe refusal sets is implied by the ability to observe acceptance (sometimes called *ready set*) information.

We specifically exclude the possibility that our observer might see that some action happens when the process is *unstable*. It is hard to justify that one could observe that some τ action was possible without actually following it, and such observations would imply some highly undesirable inequalities between processes.

This means that the most refined model for CSP based on finite observations is $\mathcal{FL}$, in which behaviours of the form

$$\langle A_0, a_0, A_1, a_2, \ldots, A_{n-1}, a_{n-1}, A_n \rangle$$

are recorded, with the a_i visible events and the A_i *generalised acceptances*, being either $\bullet$, meaning that stability was not observed at this point, or the acceptance set of the stable state that occurred at the relevant point. In this second case we expect $a_i \in A_i$. The set of all such sequences will be termed FLO (finite linear observations). We will denote them by Greek letters $\beta, \gamma, \ldots$, which will also sometimes denote the same sort of alternating sequence beginning or ending in an event rather than a generalised acceptance, and even infinite sequences of these forms.

The healthiness conditions are that (the representation of) a process P must satisfy

FL0 P is nonempty: specifically $\langle \bullet \rangle \in P$

FL1 P is prefix closed: if $\beta^\frown \gamma \in P$ and β ends in a generalised acceptance, then $\beta \in P$.

FL2 P is closed under observing less stability: if $\beta^\frown \langle A \rangle^\frown \gamma \in P$, then so is $\beta^\frown \langle \bullet \rangle^\frown \gamma$.

FL3 All proper acceptances can be realised: if $\beta^\frown \langle A \rangle \in P$ and $A \neq \bullet$, then $\beta^\frown \langle A, a, \bullet \rangle \in P$ for all $a \in A$.

It is straightforward to construct semantic clauses for all operators in our language over this model.

In [13], the author defined a finite-observation CSP model to be any model that represents a process as a finite tuple of relational images of its image in $\mathcal{FL}$. The number of such relations needs to be independent of the size of the alphabet Σ, and the equivalences induced over processes over Σ must be independent of which $\Sigma' \supseteq \Sigma$ is used to construct the model. We can also expect, thanks to the observations at the start of Section 2, that all the relations will be symmetric under permutations of Σ. All the standard models fit comfortably into this definition. We will find in this paper, however, that we can generalise it a little. The finite observation models other than $\mathcal{FL}$ that were studied in [13] were

$\mathcal{T}$ the finite trace model [4],

$\mathcal{F}$ the stable failures model [10], which records a process's finite traces and stable failures,

$\mathcal{R}$ the stable revivals model, which records a process's finite traces, deadlock traces and stable revivals as described above,

$\mathcal{A}$ the stable acceptances model (based on [7]), which records finite traces and pairs (s, A) in which A is a stable acceptance set at the end of the trace s, and

$\mathcal{RT}$ the stable refusal testing model (based on [8,6]), in which behaviours have the same appearance as for $\mathcal{FL}$, but where (subset closed) refusal sets replace acceptances.

Each of the above models can be extended to a divergence-strict one in two ways: one that handles only fCSP and an extension which handles the whole language. For a given finite-observation model $\mathcal{M}$, these two divergence-strict analogues are written $\mathcal{M}^{\Downarrow}$ and $\mathcal{M}^{\Downarrow\omega}$ respectively. These notations are explained thus:

– A divergence-strict model's role is much more about telling us when a process must stabilise if left alone, rather than when it diverges. After all, the basic assumption of the model is that once a process can diverge we don't care what else it does. In other words, every trace that is not a divergence is one on which the process definitely *converges* or becomes stable. $P \Downarrow$ often means "P is convergent" in the literature.

– A^ω is a common notation for infinite sequences of members of A, and it is necessary to include infinite sequences of actions etc explicitly in models to deal with the combination of divergence and the CSP hiding operator.

$\mathcal{M}^{\Downarrow}$ simply adds a component of "divergences" to $\mathcal{M}$. A *divergence* is generally anything that $\mathcal{M}$ allows us to record during an incomplete behaviour after which the observed process might diverge (perform an infinite unbroken series of τs). Thus, for $\mathcal{T}^{\Downarrow}$, $\mathcal{F}^{\Downarrow}$ ($= \mathcal{N}$), $\mathcal{R}^{\Downarrow}$ and $\mathcal{A}^{\Downarrow}$, a divergence is a trace, for $\mathcal{RT}^{\Downarrow}$ it is a refusal trace ending in $\bullet$ and for $\mathcal{FL}^{\Downarrow}$ it is an acceptance trace ending in $\bullet$. It turns out that the addition of the divergences component to $\mathcal{F}$, $\mathcal{R}$ and $\mathcal{A}$ allows the removal of the finite traces component: after any finite trace a process must either diverge or become stable.

In each case the model is made *divergence strict* by including a healthiness condition that says that if β is any divergence recorded in the model $\mathcal{M}$, then every extension of β (whether a divergence or another type of behaviour) is automatically included in a process P's representation *whether the operational P can actually be observed performing this extension or not.*

A process's representation in $\mathcal{FL}^{\Downarrow}$ therefore takes the form of a pair (B, D) of subsets of FLO, with every member of D ending in $\bullet$: B represents those that can be observed of the process, and D represents the ones on which it can diverge. Both, of course, are extended by extensions of divergences. The healthiness conditions FL0–FL3 still apply, as do:

FLD1 $\beta^\frown\langle\bullet\rangle \in D$ imples $\beta^\frown\gamma \in B$ for all suitably-formed γ.
FLD2 $\beta^\frown\langle\bullet\rangle \in D$ imples $\beta^\frown\gamma'^\frown\langle\bullet\rangle \in D$ for all suitably-formed γ'.
FLD3 $\beta^\frown\langle\bullet\rangle \in B - D$ implies that there is $A \neq \bullet$ such that $\beta^\frown\langle A\rangle \in B$.

The first two of these impose divergence strictness, and the last says that after any observation a process either eventually becomes stable or diverges.

We can represent (B, D) either explicitly like this or as a single set in which the two forms of behaviour are both present, only with the final compulsory $\bullet$ of each divergence replaced by $\Uparrow$. These two are clearly equivalent, and we will move between them as convenient.

The following property of $\mathcal{FL}^{\Downarrow}$ makes the close relationship between it and the CSP language clear, and also clarifies the meaning of some of our later arguments.

Theorem 2. *Every member of $\mathcal{FL}^{\Downarrow}$ is the semantics of a CSP process.*

PROOF.   The author proved a number of similar results for other models in [13]. The construction we use here is similar to that used for other divergence-strict models there.

Before we start we will observe the following: if $(B, D) \in \mathcal{FL}^{\Downarrow}$ and $\beta \in B$, then we can define a process $(B, D)/\beta$ – the behaviour *after* β by the following, where $\beta = \beta'^\frown\langle A\rangle$ for some A.

   div   if $\beta'^\frown\langle\bullet\rangle \in D$,   and otherwise

$$(\{\gamma \mid \beta'^\frown\gamma \in B\}, \{\gamma \mid \beta'^\frown\gamma \in D\}) \qquad\qquad \text{if } A = \bullet$$
$$(\{\langle A'\rangle^\frown\gamma \mid \beta^\frown\gamma \in B \wedge A' \in \{\bullet, A\}\}, \{\langle A'\rangle^\frown\gamma \mid \beta^\frown\gamma \in D \wedge A' \in \{\bullet, A\}\}) \text{if } A \neq \bullet$$

We can now define a process $INT(B, D)$ that represents a formal interpreter for an arbitrary member of $\mathcal{FL}^{\Downarrow}$. If $\langle\bullet\rangle \in D$ (i.e. the process can diverge immediately) then $IND(B, D) = $ **div**. Otherwise, by FLD3 we know that the set

$ACCS = \{A \neq \bullet \mid \langle A \rangle \in B\}$ is nonempty, so we can define $INT(B, D)$ to be as follows, where $B^0 = \{a \mid \langle \bullet, a, \bullet \rangle \in B\}$.

$$?x : B^0 \to INT((B, D)/\langle \bullet, a, \bullet \rangle)$$
$$\rhd \bigsqcap \{?x : A \to INT((B, D)/\langle A, a, \bullet \rangle) \mid A \in ACCS\}$$

Note that this can perform every action that the target (B, D) can initially, unstably. Also for every stable acceptance A that the target has initially, our interpreter can offer A and then carry on in any way that (B, D) can after observatiing $\langle A \rangle$.. This completes the proof of Theorem 2. ∎

As discussed in [10,12], in models that involve strict divergence it works far better (for example in finding the fixed points of recursions) to approximate processes from below in the refinement order, or even the "strong order" described in [11] in which the only way to move up (at least amongst models that do not model infinite behaviours *other* than divergences) is to convert some divergent behaviour into non-divergent.

In a related fashion, all of the known finite-nondeterminism models of CSP are naturally turned into (ultra) metric spaces by considering the *restriction* $P \downarrow n$ of any process to $n \in \mathbb{N}$ to be all behaviours of P up to and including the nth events in its traces, with the $P \downarrow n$ becoming divergent after these nth events. So $P \downarrow 0$ is equivalent to the immediately divergent process **div**. The distance between a pair of processes P and Q is

$$d(P, Q) = \inf\{2^{-n} \mid P \downarrow n = Q \downarrow n\}$$

Noting that a process's image in $\mathcal{FL}^{\Downarrow}$ is *already* a divergence-strict construction, we can expect that it will usually not be necessary to re-inforce this once more. We can therefore specify that a *natural* divergence-strict model $\mathcal{M}$ for fCSP is formed from a finite number of components, the observations of each of which are either a relational image of B or of D, where the process's value in $\mathcal{FL}^{\Downarrow}$ is (B, D). We can describe these two collections of images as NB and ND. These must satisfy:

(i) The induced equivalence is a congruence, with $\sqsubseteq$ (i.e. reverse containment) giving a congruent least-fixed-point semantics for recursion.
(ii) The images of of B and D are separate components of the image.
(iii) If $P \neq_{\mathcal{M}} Q$ then there exists $n \in \mathbb{N}$ such that $P \downarrow n \neq_{\mathcal{M}} Q \downarrow n$

We view (ii) as a clarity assumption: since $D \subset B$ it avoids ambiguity over how to create members of NB. (iii) holds automatically provided (as in all known models) the behaviours of $\mathcal{M}$ partition into lengths that correspond (even to within a constant factor) to the lengths of their pre-images in $\mathcal{FL}^{\Downarrow}$.

The above definition can be generalised in the following way that, as we will find later, allows the concept of divergence strictness to be interpreted more liberally. In other words it will allow a model to be *more* divergence strict than a simple image of $\mathcal{FL}^{\Downarrow}$ would allow.

A *general* divergence-strict model identifies each process P with $f(B, D)$, where (B, D) is its image in $\mathcal{FL}^{\Downarrow}$ and f is a $\sqsubseteq$-continuous function from $\mathcal{FL}^{\Downarrow}$ to a partial order $\mathcal{O}$. Here, by $\sqsubseteq$-*continuous*, we mean that if C is any linearly ordered set of processes over $\mathcal{FL}^{\Downarrow}$, then $f(\bigsqcup C) = \bigsqcap(\{f(P) \mid P \in C\})$, where this greatest lower bound exists in the range of f. The choice of $\bigsqcap$ rather than $\bigsqcup$ here is a convention – it says that we associate the direction of the order on $\mathcal{O}$ with the refinement order on processes, and indeed will think of it as refinement.

This last continuity property is always true of the relational image definition by construction, and it implies that f is monotone. The resulting model $\mathcal{M}$ (a subset of $\mathcal{O}$) is $\{f(P) \mid P \in \mathcal{FL}^{\Downarrow}\}$: it must be a congruence for fCSP with $\sqsubseteq$-least fixed points giving the congruent denotation for recursions, and satisfy $P \neq_M Q \Rightarrow \exists n.f(P \downarrow n) \neq f(Q \downarrow n)$.

Note that, as a result of Theorem 2 and our definition above, every member of every general divergence-strict model is expressible in CSP.

We can similarly generalise the definition of finite observation models, again using the $\sqsubseteq$-continuity property. The proofs in [13] still work, with little alteration. The author has yet to find a good reason for *wanting* this generalisation from plain relational images over finite-observation models, however. If we are to model a process as one or more classes of individual finitely and linearly observable things, it is hard to see why these should need to be inferred from sets of members of FLO as opposed to individual ones.

3   Finitary Versus General Models of CSP

The metric described above works because all the behaviours in $\mathcal{FL}^{\Downarrow}$ have a finite length: the best definition for this is the number of visible actions in the corresponding trace if it ends in divergence, and this number plus one otherwise. The range of behaviours we allow our notional observer to see in constructing $\mathcal{FL}^{\Downarrow}$ do not cover all possibilities, since they do not include the records of interactions that take infinitely long and include an infinite number of visible actions rather than ending in permanent stable refusal or divergence. To create a full record in the spirit of $\mathcal{FL}^{\Downarrow}$ we could also record ones taking the form of sequences $\langle A_0, a_0, A_1, a_1, A_2, \ldots \rangle$ that have the same structure as the $\mathcal{FL}$ behaviours FLO except that they go on for ever.

There is an important reason for this omission: all fCSP processes, like the finitely branching LTS's that are their operational semantics, have a natural closure property. Their infinite behaviour can be deduced from the behaviours we record in models like $\mathcal{T}^{\Downarrow}$ and $\mathcal{FL}^{\Downarrow}$ that only explicitly record finite traces and similar; a summary proof of this follows below (for $FL^{\Downarrow}$).

Suppose γ is an infinite behaviour of the above form, all of whose prefixes belong to some node P of a finitely branching LTS. Consider the tree formed by unrolling the behaviour of P, with all parts not reachable in a prefix of γ pruned away. By assumption, since γ has arbitrarily long prefixes, this tree is infinite; it is also finitely branching by assumption. König's Lemma tells us there is an infinite path through it. We consider two possibilities: either the actions of that path contain an infinite sequence of consecutive τs or they do not. If they do then there is a prefix of γ that is divergent in P. γ is then a member of P's $\mathcal{FL}^{\Downarrow\omega}$ by closure under divergence strictness. If they do not then the nodes in this sequence are easily seen to be witnesses of the full behaviour γ. This completes our proof.

This is not true if we extend our interest to general CSP, and we therefore take the obvious step of adding such infinite behaviours into the representation of a process in the extended model $\mathcal{FL}^{\Downarrow\omega}$. Each process becomes a triple (B, D, I) with I consisting of these infinite behaviours.

The next natural question to ask is when such a triple is the representation of a reasonable process – or, in other words, how to formulate natural *healthiness conditions*. Fortunately we have a well-established way of determining this via the principle that

(*) every CSP process is equivalent to the nondeterministic choice of all its finitely nondeterministic refinements, or equivalently its set of *closed refinements*.

Here, a process (B, D, I) is *closed* if and only if I consists precisely of those infinite behaviours all of whose finite prefixes belong to B. Refinement, as ever, is defined by superset.

To understand this condition, note first that any process of the form of such a nondeterministic composition is, by Theorem 2 and one use of nondeterministic choice, expressible in CSP. To prove that every process's representation can be expressed thus, consider any behaviour γ of the node P of an arbitrary LTS. As above, we can unroll P's behaviour into a tree T (where no node is reachable in more than one way, or from itself through a non-empty path). Identify an infinite path through the tree that either witnesses γ or some divergent prefix. Now systematically prune the tree subject to two constraints:

- In the resulting tree T' no node has more than one outward action with any particular label from $\Sigma \cup \{\tau\}$, but always has exactly the same set of initial actions as the corresponding node in T.
- All nodes of T no longer reachable from its root are discarded.
- Every node and action on the path identified above is preserved.

The behaviour of the root state of T' is a process that (a) has the behaviour γ, (b) refines the original process P, and (c) is finitely branching and therefore has a closed image in our model. This means that every behaviour of P is one of a closed refinement of P, justifying our assertion that every process is just the sum of the behaviours of its closed refinements.

Infinite behaviours make no contribution to the calculation of the restrictions $P \downarrow n$ over $\mathcal{FL}^{\Downarrow\omega}$, although these processes do have infinite behaviours thanks to divergence strictness. Closed processes are precisely those such that $P = \bigsqcup\{P \downarrow n \mid n \in \mathbb{N}\}$.

We can now define a divergence-strict natural model of full CSP to be a finite tuple of relational images of a process's image in $\mathcal{FL}^{\Downarrow\omega}$ satisfying the following:

(i) It provides a congruence.

(ii) The images of the three components (B, D, I) are disjoint, and the images of the components (B, D) provide a natural divergence-strict model for fCSP that gives the same congruence as $\mathcal{M}$ itself over these processes and which satisfies our definition of such models above

The rationale behind (ii) is much the same as in the earlier definition: it ensures that the infinite behaviours of $\mathcal{FL}^{\Downarrow\omega}$ are not used to reveal details that could equally have been deduced from the finite behaviour components.

The properties of relational imaging guarantee that every such model $\mathcal{M}$ satisfies property (*), so that with respect to the particular infinite details that have been recorded, the congruence on finitely nondeterministic CSP determines that on the full language.

Given that every model of full CSP is a model of fCSP, and the strong results we will prove later showing that there are no interesting general, as opposed to natural, models for an extended fCSP that interfere with our structural result, we choose not to attempt a generalisation of the concept of a "general model" involving infinite behaviours.

It is highly relevant to the subject matter of this paper to ask whether any any finitary model $\mathcal{F}$ can have more than one extension to the full language, through the use of different sets of infinite behaviours. By this, of course, we mean sets of infinite behaviours that give rise to different equivalences over CSP. The main determining factor in this is the semantics of hiding.

We can show that every divergence-strict model of full CSP must distinguish processes based on their infinite traces:

Lemma 1. *Suppose that $\mathcal{M}$ is a divergence-strict congruence for full CSP. Then two processes that have different infinite traces as judged in $T^{\Downarrow\omega}$ must be mapped to different processes in $\mathcal{M}$. Furthermore, each such natural model for full CSP has a distinct relational image or images for each infinite trace u.*

PROOF. Suppose P and Q are processes with different sets of infinite traces but are identified by $\mathcal{M}$. We can assume that P has an infinite trace u that Q lacks. (And for any given u we could easily create a specific P and Q for this u.) We can create a special process XI_u that has every possible behaviour that does not imply the presence of u:

$$XI_u = \bigsqcap \{ V \mid V \text{ is a closed process without the trace } u \}$$

We can also create a process that performs u but only in unstable states US_u:

$$US_{\langle a \rangle^\frown u} = (a \rightarrow US_u) \rhd STOP$$

Let $PT = (P \parallel_{\Sigma} US_u) \sqcap XI_u$ and $QT = (Q \parallel_{\Sigma} US_u) \sqcap XI_u$. These two processes are equivalent in all their finitely observable and deadlock behaviour, and cannot perform the infinite trace u except that PT can do so from unstable states all the way along the trace if it cannot diverge on a prefix of u.

Let T_u be the process that simply steps in turn through the events of u (each offered stably). Consider the context $C[X] = (X \parallel_{\Sigma} T_u) \setminus \Sigma$. Operationally, it is clear that $C[PT]$ can diverge immediately, but $C[QT]$ cannot: in fact the latter process is equivalent to $STOP$.

Since $R \,\square\, \mathbf{div} = \mathbf{div}$ and $R \,\square\, STOP = R$ for all CSP processes R in all CSP models, it follows that our model $\mathcal{M}$ must distinguish $\mathbf{div}$ and $STOP$. Therefore (from the action of $C[\cdot]$ and the fact that $\mathcal{M}$ is a congruence), it must also distinguish PT and QT; and P and Q in turn. However the only recordable behaviour on which PT and QT differ is the everywhere unstable infinite trace u. It follows that the relations that create $\mathcal{M}$ from $\mathcal{FL}^{\Downarrow\omega}$ must map this behaviour to an image that is distinct from those of all other behaviours other than ones that also contain the same infinite trace.

We can therefore conclude that $\mathcal{M}$ must contain enough information to deduce what all the infinite traces of a process are. This concludes the proof of Lemma 1.∎

Now suppose that γ_0 is the infinite $\mathcal{FL}^{\Downarrow\omega}$ behaviour representing the observation of the whole of u performed unstably (i.e. the events of the trace u with •s between), and that γ_1 is any other behaviour in which u is performed: necessarily γ_1 has some first observation of stability (via a particular acceptance set) in it. We can write γ_1 as $\langle \bullet, a_1, \bullet, \ldots, a_{r-1}, A_r, a_r \rangle^\smallfrown \xi$.

There are processes that contain γ_0 in their $\mathcal{FL}^{\Downarrow\omega}$ representation but not γ_1: an example is the process US_u as defined above.

The following technical lemma is what will allow us to achieve the main result of this section, namely proving that, as far as the main structural result of this paper is concerned, we can restrict our attention to models of fCSP.

Lemma 2. *Suppose that γ_0 and γ_1 are as specified above. Then we can find a pair of finitely nondeterministic, closed and divergence-free processes P and Q that are equivalent up to the acceptance set model $\mathcal{A}^{\Downarrow\omega}$, where P has the behaviour γ_1, and Q has γ_0 but not γ_1.*

PROOF. We can straightforwardly define a process that has any infinite $\mathcal{FL}^{\Downarrow\omega}$ behaviour η as follows:

$$II(\langle \bullet, a \rangle^\smallfrown \eta) = a \rightarrow II(\eta) \rhd STOP$$
$$II(\langle A, a \rangle^\smallfrown \eta) = STOP \sqcap (a \rightarrow II(\eta) \,\square\, ?x : A - \{a\} \rightarrow STOP)$$

In the second case necessarily $a \in A$. These behaviours have been designed so that when $\eta_1 \leq \eta_2$ (i.e. η_1 is obtained from η_2 by replacing some A_i with •), we have $II(\eta_2) \sqsubseteq II(\eta_1)$.

The following process does not have η unless all the "acceptances" are •, but it does have the associated infinite trace and all the trace/acceptance pairs (s, A) that the presence of η implies.

$$FSI(\langle \bullet, a \rangle^\smallfrown \eta) = a \rightarrow FSI(\eta) \rhd STOP$$
$$FSI(\langle A, a \rangle^\smallfrown \eta) = a \rightarrow FSI(\eta) \rhd (STOP \sqcap (?x : A \rightarrow STOP))$$

$FSI(\eta)$ is equivalent, in the finite acceptances model $\mathcal{A}$, to $II(\eta)$:

- Clearly they have the same finite traces: the finite prefixes of η's trace extended by any event a that belongs to an acceptance of η in the appropriate place.
- They have the same infinite traces, namely $\{u\}$.
- Both can deadlock after any trace.
- Both can offer any proper acceptance offered by η at the appropriate point in the trace.

Since these processes are both divergence free and finitely nondeterministic, this equivalence extends to $\mathcal{A}^{\Downarrow\omega}$.

The lemma is therefore established by setting $P = II(\gamma_1)$ and $Q = FSI(\gamma_1)$.∎

We are now in a position to prove a strong result about the infinite extensions of a class of models that includes all those that are central to our main structural result.

Theorem 3. *Each of the models $\mathcal{T}^{\Downarrow}$, $\mathcal{F}^{\Downarrow} = \mathcal{N}$, $\mathcal{R}^{\Downarrow}$ and $\mathcal{A}^{\Downarrow}$ has, judging by the equivalence represented on processes and transition systems, a unique extension to become a natural infinitary model.*

PROOF. We know [13] that each of them can be so extended by the addition of the component of infinite traces. By Lemma 1 we know that any such extension contains a distinct relational image for each infinite trace. If any infinite behaviour γ_1 had a relational image distinct from the corresponding infinite trace, then the finitary processes P and Q created by Lemma 2 would be distinguished by our hypothetical extension, even though they are equivalent in $\mathcal{A}^{\Downarrow}$ and hence in each of $\mathcal{T}^{\Downarrow}$, $\mathcal{F}^{\Downarrow}$ and $\mathcal{R}^{\Downarrow}$. This would contradict the fact that an extension must yield the same equivalence on finitary terms as the model being extended.   ∎

It follows from this, and Lemma 1, that if our main structural result holds for finitary models, then it also holds for general models: any non-trivial model of full CSP must refine $\mathcal{T}^{\Downarrow\omega}$, and so on.

We note in passing that Theorem 3 does not extend to models of finitary CSP that are richer than those listed. Specifically it does not seem to hold for models where an arbitrarily long series of refusals and/or acceptances are recorded. It turns out, for example, that $\mathcal{FL}^{\Downarrow}$ has at least three different extensions: we can choose to record

- As many as infinitely many acceptance sets in a trace, as in $\mathcal{FL}^{\Downarrow\omega}$.
- An arbitrarily large finite number of acceptance sets in a trace, so that any infinite behaviour has an infinite tail of •s.
- An arbitrarily long finite string of acceptance sets or •, followed by an infinite string of refusal sets or •.

4   Stage 1: Every Model Refines $\mathcal{T}^{\Downarrow}$

What we now seek to prove is that every nontrivial general model of fCSP satisfies one of the following:

- It represents the same equivalence as $\mathcal{T}^{\Downarrow}$.
- It represents the same equivalence as $\mathcal{F}^{\Downarrow} = \mathcal{N}$.
- It refines $\mathcal{R}^{\Downarrow}$.

We break our analysis of this into three stages:

1. Showing that every such model refines $\mathcal{T}^{\Downarrow}$.
2. Showing that every such model that is not $\mathcal{T}^{\Downarrow}$ refines $\mathcal{F}^{\Downarrow}$.
3. Showing that every such model that is not $\mathcal{T}^{\Downarrow}$ or $\mathcal{F}^{\Downarrow}$ refines $\mathcal{R}^{\Downarrow}$.

In [13], the author used two different patterns of proof for the corresponding results. In each case he was proving that every congruence $\mathcal{M}$ for CSP that strictly refines some congruence $\mathcal{A}$, must also refine some second congruence $\mathcal{B}$. (Stage 1 has this form if we allow $\mathcal{A}$ to be the trivial congruence that identifies all processes.) In both styles of proof we can start out by assuming that there are a pair of processes P and Q such that $P \neq_M Q$ but $P =_A Q$. From this it is easily deduced, by considering $P \sqcap Q$ (which cannot be $\mathcal{M}$-equivalent to both P and Q), that without loss of generality we can assume $P \sqsubseteq_M Q$.

In the first pattern of proof we assume we have a pair of processes such that $V \not\sqsubseteq_B U$ and $U =_A V$, and construct a context such that $C[U] = P$ and $C[V] = Q$ (equality holding in all models of the class being considered, so certainly $\mathcal{M}$). Since P and Q are being mapped to those processes that are distinct in $\mathcal{M}$, it follows that P and Q are themselves distinct in $\mathcal{M}$, which is what we wanted to prove.

The second pattern, which we will see in Sections 6 and 7, operates on similar principles but depends on showing by technical analysis that we can choose very special P and Q that make a more difficult construction of $C[\cdot]$ possible.

In [13], the first style of proof was used for the first two steps of the overall result, namely proving that $\mathcal{T}$ is the unique minimally refined finite-observation model and that $\mathcal{F}$ is uniquely minimal amongst the rest of this class of models.

In the case of divergence-strict models, the author has only found a way of doing this for the first stage, though this is remarkably straightforward. Indeed it follows from an argument essentially the same as our proof of Lemma 1 above.

Theorem 4. *If $\mathcal{M}$ is a non-trivial divergence-strict model for CSP, then $\mathcal{T}^{\Downarrow} \preceq \mathcal{M}$.*

PROOF. We will follow the first pattern above. However the fact that $\mathcal{M}$ is divergence strict allows us to be specific about P: we can clearly set it equal to **div** and choose Q to be any process that is not $\mathcal{M}$-equivalent to **div**.

If U and V are processes that are distinguished by $\mathcal{T}^{\Downarrow}$, then without loss of generality we can assume that $V \not\sqsubseteq_{TD} U$. In other words *either* U has a divergence trace s not in V, or the divergence sets are equal and U has a trace t not in V.

In the first case let $D[X] = (T(s) \parallel X) \setminus \Sigma$ where $T(\langle \rangle) = STOP$ and $T(\langle a \rangle^\frown s) = a \rightarrow T(s)$. It is easy to see that in general $D[X] = STOP$ unless X

has s as a divergent trace, in which case $D[X] = \mathbf{div}$, this equality holding in $\mathcal{FL}^{\Downarrow}$ and hence in all divergence-strict models.

In the second let $D[X] = (T^{\Uparrow}(t) \parallel_{\Sigma} X) \setminus \Sigma$ where $T^{\Uparrow}(\langle\rangle) = \mathbf{div}$ and $T^{\Uparrow}(\langle a\rangle^{\frown}t) = a \to T^{\Uparrow}(t)$. Again, it is easy to see that $D[X] = STOP$ if X does not have the trace t, and $D[X] = \mathbf{div}$ if it does.

In either case let $C[X] = D[X] \;\square\; Q$. $C[U]$ can diverge immediately because $D[U]$ can. As all immediately divergent processes are equivalent to $\mathbf{div}$ in divergence-strict models, this tells us that $C[U] = \mathbf{div}$ in all of them. On the other hand $C[V] = STOP \;\square\; Q$, and since $STOP \;\square\; Q = Q$ in all known CSP models including $\mathcal{FL}^{\Downarrow}$, we have $C[V] = Q$.

Thus the CSP context $C[\cdot]$ maps U and V to two processes that are distinct in $\mathcal{M}$. We can deduce from the fact that $\mathcal{M}$ is a congruence that U and V must themselves be distinct in $\mathcal{M}$. This completes the proof of Theorem 4.   ∎

5   An Unexpected Congruence and How to Avoid It

After establishing Theorem 4, the author moved on to try to prove that every model for fCSP that properly refines $\mathcal{T}^{\Downarrow}$ in turn refines $\mathcal{F}^{\Downarrow} = \mathcal{N}$. These efforts failed, and he was disappointed to discover that there is a model that lies strictly between these two models.

The language as defined in Section 2.1 has a modified – and slightly more abstract – version of $\mathcal{N}$ as a model. This has all the usual healthiness conditions plus one more:

$$(s, X) \in F \wedge s^{\frown}\langle a\rangle \in D \Rightarrow (s, X \cup \{a\}) \in F$$

The interpretation of this is that we choose not to care about whether events that lead immediately to divergence are refused or not. The resulting extended refusals are included in the model rather than excluded so as to make the theory of refinement as set containment work: this decision is analogous to the one to include rather than exclude all post-divergence behaviours.

For example this model identifies $a \to \mathbf{div}$ with $STOP \sqcap a \to \mathbf{div}$, which are distinct in $\mathcal{N}$.

It is not a *natural model* in the sense described earlier for two reasons. Firstly, the extra refusals each depend on an arbitrary number of divergences. Secondly there is more cross play between the divergence and non-divergence behaviours than is allowed in the definition of a natural model. What it creates is a strangely amplified notion of divergence strictness: to create this we need to use the machinery set out in the definition of a general model.

The immediate question that comes to mind when seeing this model, which we will call $\mathcal{N}^-$, is "How can this be a congruence?" To answer this we need to look to the operational semantics of CSP (viewable online at [10], Chapter 7). All of the operators in the usual language, and hence the whole language, satisfy the following principle:

– Suppose the context $C[P]$ can perform the initial action a and become the process Q, and P itself performs some action $P \xrightarrow{b} P'$ that is part of a (i.e. the operational rules that generate a depend on P performing b). Then the term Q always involves P' and is divergence strict in it – in other words, if P' can perform an infinite sequence of τs then so can Q.

Putting it another way, no CSP operator ever allows an argument to perform an action and then immediately disposes of that argument. (A number of operators including $\square$ dispose of *other* arguments when one performs a visible action.)

What this means is that if the argument P of $C[P]$ performing b leads immediately to divergence, then so does the derived action a of $C[P]$. Clearly we would expect the issue of whether P can refuse b or not to affect whether $C[P]$ can refuse a – but what we have discovered is that:

– The refusal by P of an action that leads immediately to divergence can only affect the refusal by $C[P]$ of actions that lead immediately to divergence.

Another way of reading this is that discarding the information about whether P can refuse b or not can only mean that we are unable to discover information about whether $C[P]$ can refuse other actions that lead directly to divergence. It should therefore not come as too much of a surprise to discover that throwing away all such information from all processes (which is what $\mathcal{N}^-$ does) yields a congruence for fCSP.

This congruence had previously been identified for a sub-language in [9], but the author was not aware of it until the failure of the proof of the natural step 2 of the structural theorem forced him to rediscover it.

There seems no good reason at all why there is no operator in CSP that throws away a process as soon as it has performed an action. (Actually, in a sense, the sequential composition operator ; does, but the assumptions and restrictions conventionally placed on the termination signal $\checkmark$ mean that this exception is not decisive.) Implementing such an operator would not cause any particular problem. Evidently there is just no such concept in concurrency that Hoare thought was necessary to include in CSP. In fact, given the importance of operating system ideas in Hoare's initial work (see, for example [5], Chapters 5–7) including exception handling (Chapter 5), the author expected to find that Hoare had discussed an operator that allowed a process to throw an exception and pass on control to a second process or some external context. In fact there is no such operator, since all the exceptions that Hoare's operators handle are triggered by external events rather than internally generated ones. Correspondence between the author and Hoare ensued, during which we were unable to discover any such operator in previous work but agreed that it would be perfectly natural to add one.

In particular the following *exception throwing* operator seems very natural: $P \,\Theta_a\, Q$ behaves like P until P communicates a, at which point it starts Q:

$$\frac{P \xrightarrow{x} P'}{P \,\Theta_a\, Q \xrightarrow{x} P' \,\Theta_a\, Q}(x \neq a) \qquad \frac{P \xrightarrow{a} P'}{P \,\Theta_a\, Q \xrightarrow{a} Q}$$

We will add it to the language: we will call the result CSP+.

$\mathcal{N}^-$ is not a model for CSP+ because it is not a congruence: recall that $a \rightarrow \textbf{div}$ and $STOP \sqcap a \rightarrow \textbf{div}$ are identified by $\mathcal{N}^-$. On the other hand $(a \rightarrow \textbf{div}) \Theta_a STOP = a \rightarrow STOP$ and $(STOP \sqcap a \rightarrow \textbf{div}) \Theta_a STOP = STOP \sqcap a \rightarrow STOP$, and these two processes are *not* equivalent over $\mathcal{N}^-$, which they would have to be if it was a congruence.

In a subsequent paper, the author will demonstrate that in an important sense Θ_a can be said to *complete* the CSP language, since it means that every operator which is expressible in a natural class of operational semantics can be expressed in CSP+. For the time being, however, we will examine its relationship with the CSP language described in [13].

In fact, it has a very interesting relationship with $\triangle$. Recall that it was necessary to include $\triangle$ in the CSP language in [13] to obtain the structural result for finite-observation models. This very fact means that $\triangle$ cannot be expressed in terms of the rest of the language in a general finite-observation model. It therefore comes as something of a surprise to discover the following result.

Lemma 3. *In $\mathcal{FL}^{\Downarrow\omega}$, and therefore in every divergence-strict model, $\triangle$ can be expressed using the other operators of CSP.*

PROOF. The easiest way to prove this lemma is to give the equivalent expression: extend the alphabet from Σ_0 to $\Sigma = \Sigma_0 \cup \Sigma_1$ where $\Sigma_1 = \{a' \mid a \in \Sigma_0\}$ (the map from a to $'$ being injective and $\Sigma_0 \cap \Sigma_1 = \emptyset$). The relations *Prime* and *Unprime* respectively map every member a of Σ_0 to a', and every $a' \in \Sigma_1$ to a, leaving other events unchanged.

$$P \triangle' Q = (P \ ||| \ Q[\![Prime]\!]) \underset{\Sigma}{||} Reg)[\![Unprime]\!], \quad \text{where}$$

$$Reg = (?x : \Sigma_0 \rightarrow Reg) \ \square \ (?x : \Sigma_1 \rightarrow RUN(\Sigma_1))$$

What this construct does is to allow P to proceed until Q communicates an event, at which point P is blocked (by *Reg*) from performing any further actions. This is, of course, very nearly the desired effect of the interrupt operator $\triangle$. The only difference is that after Q has performed a visible action, P can still perform internal actions in the above construct whereas in $P \triangle Q$ it is actually turned off. This can make the difference between a process being stable or unstable: $\textbf{div} \triangle' Q$ can never be stable – and therefore have stable acceptances – and $\textbf{div} \triangle Q$ can. These two versions are different in any finite observation model that is richer than traces. The difference with divergence-strict models, however, is that for the two versions to be semantically different in finite observation models, P has to be in a state where it can diverge at the point where it is interrupted. It follows that the interruption must be of a potentially divergent state of $P \triangle Q$ also. Thus the differences only appear beyond the point where $P \triangle Q$ can diverge, and so they are eliminated by divergence strictness, which obliterates such distinctions.

So in fact, over divergence-strict models, $\triangle$ and $\triangle'$ are equivalent. This completes the proof of Lemma 3.   ∎

$P \Theta_a Q$ can be defined correctly over all standard CSP models. For example, over $\mathcal{FL}^{\Downarrow}$ we can define:

$$P \Theta_a Q = \{\beta \in P \mid trace(\beta) \in (\Sigma - \{a\})^*\}$$
$$\cup \{\beta^\frown\gamma \mid \beta^\frown\langle\bullet\rangle \in P, \gamma \in Q, trace(\beta) \in (\Sigma - \{a\})^*\{a\}\}$$
$$\cup \{\beta^\frown\gamma \mid \beta^\frown\langle\Uparrow\rangle \in P, trace(\beta) \in (\Sigma - \{a\})^*\}$$

Here, we are using the representation of processes as single sets containing both ordinary and divergent behaviours, and $trace(\beta)$ is the sequence of visible events in β. The third line is needed to achieve divergence strictness.

It is possible, in general, to define $\triangle$ in terms of Θ_a. Define

$$P \triangle'' Q = (((P \mathbin{|\!|\!|} a' \to STOP) \Theta_{a'} STOP)[\![R]\!]) \mathbin{\underset{\Sigma_1}{\|}} Q[\![Prime]\!])[\![Unprime]\!]$$

where a' is an arbitrary member of Σ_1 and $R = \{(a', x) \mid x \in \Sigma_1\}$.

The $\mathcal{N}^-$ model shows that one cannot in general express Θ_a in terms of the other operators, but interestingly one can over finite observation models:

Lemma 4. *The following operator is equivalent to Θ_a over $\mathcal{FL}$, and hence over every finite observation model.*

$$P \Theta_a' Q = ((P \triangle (c \to Q[\![Prime]\!])) \mathbin{\underset{\Sigma_0}{\|}} Reg_\theta)[\![Unprime]\!] \setminus \{c\}$$
$$Reg_\theta = ?s : (\Sigma_0 - \{a\} \to Reg_\theta) \mathbin{\square} (a \to c \to STOP)$$

where c is an event not in either Σ_0 or Σ_1.

PROOF. This construction allows P to proceed normally until it has performed an a, whereupon (i) Reg_θ blocks P from further visible actions, (ii) the event c is allowed which permits the interrupt to occur and (iii) after this event Q runs. Since the c is the only event available when it happens, and it is hidden, its effects from the outside are invisible. This behaviour is exactly like that of $P \Theta_a Q$ except that the argument P is discarded at the point when the hidden-c τ occurs, just after the a when it is discarded in $P \Theta_a Q$. Since that τ can certainly happen, $P \Theta_a' Q$ has all the real, externally-visible behaviours of $P \Theta_a Q$ in any of our models. The only thing that $P \Theta_a' Q$ can do extra is have P perform τs between the a and the hidden c. This creates a real difference in models where divergence is recorded, since these τs might create divergence. No extra finitely observable behaviour is created however, since $P \Theta_a' Q$ cannot become stable or perform any visible action after the a until the hidden c has occurred. ∎

This last result is reassuring, since it shows us that adding Θ_a gives no extra expressibility over finite-observation models, the domain where [13] succeeded without it.

From now on in this paper we will be considering the language CSP+, and can be safe in the knowledge that adding an extra operator (with respect to which $\mathcal{T}^\Downarrow$ is a congruence) cannot invalidate Theorem 4: that result remains true with fCSP replaced by fCSP+.

6   Stage 2: $\mathcal{N}$ Is the Weakest Proper Refinement of $\mathcal{T}^{\Downarrow}$

For this step of the proof it is clear (thanks to the existence of $\mathcal{N}^-$) that Θ_a will need to play a role. As stated earlier, we will use a more technical style of proof since the author has failed to find a way of following the first proof outline here.

We begin with a lemma that has much in common with the ideas used to prove full abstraction results.

In this section and the next, when we write "$P = Q$" or "$P \sqsubseteq Q$" between two fCSP terms or finitely branching transition system nodes, we will mean equality or refinement as judged over $\mathcal{FL}^{\Downarrow}$: the most refined relevant model. We will write other forms as $P =_{FD} Q$ or similar (this meaning failures-divergences, in other words equivalence over $\mathcal{N}$). So, in particular, the "=" in the conclusion of the following lemma means equivalence over $\mathcal{FL}^{\Downarrow}$.

Lemma 5

If $U =_{TD} V$ but $U \not\sqsupseteq_{FD} V$, then there is a context $C[\cdot]$ such that $C[U] = STOP \sqcap (a \to STOP)$ and $C[V] = a \to STOP$.

PROOF. Under these assumptions we know that U and V have the same divergence-strict sets of traces and divergences, but that there is some failure (s, X) (necessarily with s not in the common divergence set and with $X \neq \emptyset$) such that (s, X) is a failure of U but not V. We can assume that the event a can never be communicated by either U or V other than through divergence strictness, since if not we can apply a renaming (perhaps extending the alphabet) to obtain U' and V' satisfying this. Let $\Sigma_0 = \Sigma - \{a\}$.

Let $IdDp = \{(x, b), (x, c) \mid x \in \Sigma_0\}$ be the renaming that maps every member of Σ_0 to a fixed pair of further additional events b and c. Define

$$FT(\emptyset, Y) = ?x : \Sigma_0 - Y \to STOP$$

$$FT(\langle x \rangle^\frown t, Y) = (x \to FT(t, Y)) \rhd a \to STOP$$

$$CF0(t, Y)[P] = (FT(s, Y) \parallel_{\Sigma_0} P)[\![IdDp]\!]$$

$$Reg_{FT}(0) = c \to STOP \quad \text{and} \quad Reg_{FT}(n+1) = b \to Reg_{FT}(n)$$

$$CF1(t, Y)[P] = (((CF0(t, Y)[P] \parallel_{\{b,c\}} Reg_{FT}(\#t)) \setminus \{b\}) \Theta_c STOP)[\![a/c]\!]$$

$$CF2(t, Y)[P] = CF1(t, Y)[P] \sqcap a \to STOP$$

$CF2(s, X)$ can serve as the context required by the lemma, as we now demonstrate.

Consider first $CF0(s, X)[V]$. This process cannot diverge until perhaps after it has performed one more event than $\#s$, because we know that V cannot on any prefix of s. Imagine the progress of the process V within this context. If it has completed the trace s then, since it cannot then refuse X, it cannot deadlock with $FT(s, X)$ when offered $\Sigma_0 - X$. So in this state there is certainly an action in Σ_0 available at the level of the parallel operator, meaning that some event(s) are offered stably. Thus, after $\#s$ copies of b or c, $CF0(s, X)[V]$ definitely offers $\{b, c\}$.

The effect of $CF1(s, X)[V]$ is to hide the first $\#s$ of these, and only allow the next one to be c, and then turn this into a through renaming. The effect of the Θ_c operator is to cut off this behaviour immediately after this renamed c, in particular ensuring that any divergence of V at that point does not map to a divergence of the context. Any a's arising from the choice in $\rhd$ not to pursue a proper prefix of s remain available: whatever route of internal progress this process follows, a will eventually be offered stably and the process will then $STOP$. Thus $CF1(s, X)[V] = a \to STOP$ and so $CF2(s, X)[V] = a \to STOP$ also.

On the other hand $CF0(s, X)[U]$ evidently can deadlock after the trace s inside the renaming, so $CF1(s, X)[U]$ can deadlock on the empty trace thanks to the hiding. Depending on whether $s = \langle\rangle$ and what other refusals U has after s, $CF1(s, X)[U]$ may or may not be able to offer and perform an a. But $CF2(s, X)[U]$ certainly can, meaning that $CF2(s, X)[U] = STOP \sqcap a \to STOP$ as required. This completes the proof of Lemma 5.   ∎

Without the Θ_c, we could have proved an analogous lemma mapping the two processes to $a \to \mathbf{div}$ and $STOP \sqcap a \to \mathbf{div}$ but this would not have been strong enough to use in our later proof. Note in particular that this pair of processes are equivalent in $\mathcal{N}^-$.

We are now in a position to prove the main result of this section.

Theorem 5. *Any divergence-strict model* $\mathcal{M}$ *of* fCSP+ *that is not* $\mathcal{T}^{\Downarrow}$ *is a refinement of* $\mathcal{N}$*: in other words if* $\mathcal{N}$ *distinguishes a pair of processes then so does* $\mathcal{M}$.

PROOF. We may, following the outline proofs set out in Section 4, assume that P and Q are a pair of processes that are identified by $\mathcal{T}^{\Downarrow}$, distinguished by $\mathcal{M}$ and such that $P \sqsubseteq Q$. By our assumptions about the nature of divergence-strict models $\mathcal{M}$, we can assume that $P = P \downarrow N$ and $Q = Q \downarrow N$ for some $N \in \mathbb{N}$. This means that every behaviour of P and Q that is longer than N is implied by one of length N through divergence strictness.

There is a countable infinity of possible members of the two components of a member of $\mathcal{FL}^{\Downarrow}$ thanks to our assumption that the overall alphabet is finite, and the fact that only finite traces are involved. Only finitely many of them have length N or less.

We can therefore list the ones of length N or less that belong to P and not Q as $\beta_1, \beta_2 \beta_3 \dots \beta_K$. To enable these behaviours to appear in a single list, we assume the representation of processes as single sets with divergences ending in $\Uparrow$.

By our assumption that P and Q are equivalent in $\mathcal{T}^{\Downarrow}$, it is certain that every β_i contains at least one non-• acceptance. Denote the first position of one in β_i by $fa(i)$ (i.e. if $\beta_i = \langle A_1, a_1, \dots A_{r-1}, a_{r-1}, A_r \rangle$ then $A_{fa(i)}$ is a proper acceptance and $A_j = \bullet$ for all $j < fa(i)$.

We make a further assumption about this series: if $fa(i) > fa(j)$ then $j < i$. In other words we arrange this finite list so the ones with the most delayed first acceptance come early. This means that if we take β_i and replace the $A_{fa(i)}$ by •, then either the resulting behaviour is in Q or it comes earlier in the list.

We will construct a series of processes $Q_i \sqsupseteq P$ where $Q_0 = Q$ and $Q_{n+1} \sqsubseteq Q_n$ has the behaviour β_{n+1}. We need to show how to build Q_{n+1} in general.

If Q_{n+1} already contains β_{n+1} then we need do nothing. Otherwise consider the behaviours Ψ_{n+1} of P that agree with β_{n+1} up to and including the acceptance at $fa(n+1)$.

We know by our choice of enumeration of the β_i, the observation above and elementary consequences of divergence strictness that Q_n contains each $\gamma \in \Psi_{n+1}$ with the acceptance at $fa(n+1)$ replaced by $\bullet$.

Let $Q_{n+1} = Q_n \cup \Psi_{n+1}$. This belongs to $\mathcal{FL}^{\Downarrow}$ and contains β_{n+1}. Theorem 2 means that we do not need to worry about giving a CSP construction for this process, as there is one automatically. This completes our construction of the Q_i. Clearly $Q_K = P$.

Over $\mathcal{M}$, the Q_n cannot all be equivalent, by our assumption that $P \neq_M Q$. So choose n so that Q_{n+1} is the first to be $\mathcal{M}$-inequivalent to Q. It follows that adding Ψ_{n+1} to Q_n creates a process that is different in $\mathcal{M}$ from it.

What we therefore have, in Q_{n+1} and Q_n, are a pair of processes that are differentiated by $\mathcal{M}$, and identified by $\mathcal{T}^{\Downarrow}$, but where the relationship between them is much more constrained than in a general pair such that $P \sqsubseteq_M Q$ and $P =_{TD} Q$. Now that we have constructed them we will essentially run through the same structure of proof as Theorem 4, with Q_{n+1} and Q_n playing the roles that **div** and Q did there.

We know that Q_n has the behaviour γ which consists of all the actions before $fa(n+1)$ (with all acceptances $\bullet$).

Now add an extra element a to the alphabet of our processes, and let Q^* be the process as Q_{n+1} except that after γ, when offering $A_{fa(n+1)}$, it can additionally perform a (as an addition to acceptance sets), and this a leads to the behaviour Q_n/γ.) Q^* can be defined in terms of CSP operators, Q_{n+1} and Q_n in a similar fashion to our earlier constructions. This extra behaviour is not available if any of the members of γ have been performed from *stable* states.

The crucial properties of Q^* are (i) $Q^* \underset{\{a\}}{\|} STOP = Q_{n+1}$ because all the extra behaviour is blocked, and (ii) $Q^* \setminus \{a\} = Q_n$ because this process cannot become stable after γ until after the hidden a.

Let Σ_0 be all visible events other than a.

If $U \neq_{FD} V$ but $U =_{TD} V$ then, by Lemma 5 we can assume without loss of generality that there is $C1[\cdot]$ such that

$$C1[U] = STOP \sqcap a \rightarrow STOP$$

$$C1[V] = a \rightarrow STOP$$

Suppose X is either $a \rightarrow STOP$ or $STOP \sqcap a \rightarrow STOP$ in

$$C2[X] = ((Q^* \underset{\{a\}}{\|} X) \setminus \{a\})$$

As Q^* cannot perform a more than once, it is clear that $Q^* \underset{\{a\}}{\|} a \rightarrow STOP = Q^*$. It follows by our earlier remarks about $Q^* \setminus \{a\}$ and $Q^* \underset{\{a\}}{\|} STOP$ that

$$- \quad C2[a \rightarrow STOP] = Q^* \setminus \{a\} = Q_n$$

$- \ C2[STOP \sqcap a \to STOP] = (Q^* \ \underset{\{a\}}{\|} \ STOP) \sqcap Q^* \setminus \{a\} = Q_{n+1} \sqcap Q_n =$
Q_{n+1}

Let $C[X] = C2[C1[X]]$. Then, by what we have already shown, $C[U] = Q_{n+1}$ and $C[V] = Q_n$. So $C[U] \neq_M C[V]$. This completes the proof of Theorem 5. ∎

7 Stage 3: Every Proper Refinement of $\mathcal{N}$ Refines $\mathcal{R}^{\Downarrow}$

The final stage in our proof follows along very similar lines to the second, only just a little bit more intricate. First we establish a lemma very similar to Lemma 5.

Lemma 6
If $U =_{FD} V$ but $U \not\sqsupseteq_{RD} V$, then there is a context $C[\cdot]$ such that

$$C[U] = STOP \sqcap (a \to \ STOP) \ and \ C[V] = (a \to STOP) \rhd STOP$$

PROOF   Note that, as one would expect, the two result processes here are failures but not revivals equivalent, just as the two used in Lemma 5 are traces but not failures equivalent. These two processes are identical in $\mathcal{FL}^{\Downarrow}$ except that $STOP \sqcap a \to STOP$ has the observations $\langle \{a\}, a, \bullet \rangle$ and $\langle \{a\}, a, \emptyset \rangle$ unlike $(a \to STOP) \rhd STOP$, where a can only happen after $\bullet$.

Since U and V are equivalent in $\mathcal{N}$, it follows that they have the same sets of traces, deadlock traces and divergence traces. We know, therefore, that there is some revival (s, X, b) of U but not V. (This means U can perform the trace s, refuse the set X in a stable state, and then perform the visible action $b \notin X$.) On the other hand (s, X) is certainly a failure of V.

The following context forces a process W down the trace s (which is hidden from the outside), then offers both X and b. This may very well deadlock *before* reaching the possibility of X and b.

$$CR1[W] = ((FT(s, \Sigma - (X \cup \{b\})) \ \underset{\Sigma}{\|} \ W)[\![D]\!] \ \underset{\Sigma}{\|} \ Reg_R(\#s)) \setminus \Sigma_0, \quad \text{where}$$

$$\Sigma_1 = \{x' \mid x \in \Sigma_0\} \quad \Sigma = \Sigma_0 \cup \Sigma_1$$

$$D = \{(x, x'), (x, x) \mid x \in \Sigma_0\}$$

$$Reg_R(0) = ?x : \Sigma_0 \to STOP \quad Reg_R(n+1) = ?x : \Sigma_1 \to Reg_R(n)$$

If $W \in \{U, V\}$ then this process definitely has the trace $\langle b \rangle$, and does not diverge on $\langle \rangle$. If $W = V$ then it can definitely deadlock on the empty trace (because, after s, V can refuse X but not offer b). In this case it might also be able to offer some sets that include b', but definitely not $\{b'\}$ since V cannot offer b without some member of X. If $W = U$ then $CR1[W]$ can definitely offer $\{b'\}$ on $\langle \rangle$, because W can refuse X and then perform b.

$CR1[U]$ and $CR1[V]$ might well diverge after a single event, because U or V can diverge after a trace of the form $s\hat{\ }\{x\}$ for $x \in X \cup \{b\}$. We can eliminate this possibility using the Θ_a operator, as we had to in Section 6:

$$CR2[W] = (CR1[W][\![R]\!] \,\Theta_c\, STOP) \,\Theta_a\, STOP, \quad \text{where}$$

$$R = \{(x', c) \mid x \in X\} \cup \{(b', a)\}$$

This can now perform the event a from the statement of the lemma when W performs its special b, and an arbitrary fixed event c when W accepts a member of X. Observe that $W[U]$ can offer just $\{a\}$, while if $W[V]$ offers a stably its acceptance set is $\{a, c\}$. Now let

$$CR3[W] = ((a \to STOP) \rhd STOP) \sqcap CR2[W] \setminus \{c\}$$

Every behaviour of $CR2[V] \setminus \{c\}$ is one of $(a \to STOP) \rhd STOP$, but since

$$a \to STOP \sqsupseteq CR3[U] \sqsubseteq STOP \sqcap a \to STOP$$

and $((a \to STOP) \rhd STOP) \sqcap a \to STOP = STOP \sqcap a \to STOP$ we know that $CR3[U] = STOP \sqcap a \to STOP$. Thus $CR3[\cdot]$ is the context required by the statement of our lemma.   ∎

Theorem 6. *Every divergence-strict model $\mathcal{M}$ of fCSP+ that is a proper refinement of $\mathcal{N}$ is in turn a refinement of $\mathcal{R}^{\Downarrow}$.*

PROOF. This time we will have a pair of processes such that $P =_{FD} Q$, $P \sqsubseteq Q$ and $Q \neq_M P$. Again we can assume that $P = P \downarrow N$ and $Q = Q \downarrow N$ for some N, so that the difference between the behaviour sets of P and Q is finite apart from ones implied by divergence strictness. Once again we choose an enumeration $\beta_1, \beta_2, \ldots, \beta_K$ of this difference so that $fa(i) > fa(j) \Rightarrow i < j$.

Notice that, for each i, β_i is a witness for P having the failure $(s, \Sigma - A_{fa(i)})$, where s are the events in β_i preceding the first proper acceptance $A_{fa(i)}$. Since P and Q are failures equivalent, it follows that Q must have a behaviour in which the events of s are followed by a proper acceptance $B_i \subseteq A_{fa(i)}$.

We use exactly the same construction as in the proof of Theorem 5 to create the series of processes Q_i where $Q_0 = Q$, $Q_{n+1} \sqsubseteq Q_n$ contains β_{n+1} and $Q_K = P$. Once again we can therefore concentrate on the first pair Q_n and $Q_{n+1} = Q_n \cup \Psi_{n+1}$ of processes distinguished by $\mathcal{M}$.

Let s be the trace represented by β_{n+1} up to the first non-• acceptance $A (= A_{fa(n+1)})$. Let γ be β_{n+1} up to and including this first acceptance A. We know that all the differences between Q_{n+1} and Q_n are extensions of γ, and in particular all the behaviours obtained by changing the first A in a member of Ψ_{n+1} to • are already in Q_n by the structure of our enumeration of the β_i.

As we have done a number of times before, we will extend our alphabet to $\Sigma_0 \cup \Sigma_1$ where $\Sigma_1 = \{x' \mid x \in \Sigma_0\}$ and Σ_0 contains all the events used by our processes. We extend the priming notation x' to sets, behaviours etc, simply meaning it is applied to all their members.

Let ρ be the behaviour that consists of all the events of s preceded by •, with the acceptance B at the end, namely the witness in Q of the failure $(s, \Sigma_0 - A)$. And let σ be the same except that the final acceptance is $A' \cup B$. Now define

$$R = Q_n \cup \{\sigma^\frown \nu^\dagger \mid \gamma^\frown \nu \in Q_{n+1}\} \cup \{\sigma^\frown \nu \mid \rho^\frown \nu \in Q\}$$

where $\nu^\dagger$ is the same as ν except that the first event only is primed.

In other words, R behaves like Q_{n+1} except (i) that events picked from the special acceptance A after s are primed and (ii) that it only has the option to behave outside the range allowed by Q_n when it has offered $A' \cup B$ after ρ, and selecting a member of B leads it to behave like Q would in analogous circumstances.

Consider, then

$$C4[X] = (R \underset{\Sigma_1}{\parallel} X[\![AP]\!])[\![Unprime]\!]$$

where $AP = \{(a, x') \mid x \in B\}$ maps the event a from the statement of Lemma 6 to every member of A'. Note that the parallel composition allows R to run completely freely except that any member of A' is affected by how X offers a if at all.

If $X = (a \to STOP) \rhd STOP$ then we need to consider two cases of what happens when R has completed s and is offering $A' \cup B$.

- X might deadlock, meaning that R is blocked from performing events from A'. In this case the context just offers B and continues like Q would in the same circumstances.
- X might perform a unstably, meaning that the offer of $A' \cup B$ becomes $\bullet$ in the combination. The continuing behaviour is one of Q if a member of B is chosen, or one of Q_n with one event primed if a member of A' is chosen, the latter because of our choice of enumeration.

It follows easily from this that $C4[(a \to STOP) \rhd STOP] = Q_n$.

On the other hand, if $X = (a \to STOP) \sqcap STOP$, then X has the option of offering a stably. This means that R's complete offer of $A' \cup B$ goes forward, which becomes A after the $Unprime$ renaming. Since this offer of A can be followed by every behaviour Q_{n+1} can exhibit after γ, it follows that $C4[(a \to STOP) \sqcap STOP] \sqsubseteq Q_{n+1}$

It would be nice if this were an equality, but it may not be since Q may have behaviours after ρ than Q_{n+1}, and indeed P, need not have after γ. This does not matter in the big picture of our proof, however, since

$$(P_1 \sqsubseteq P_2 \sqsubseteq P_3 \wedge P_2 \neq_M P_3) \Rightarrow P_1 \neq_M P3$$

by the monotonicity of the assumed abstraction map from $\mathcal{FL}^{\Downarrow}$ to $\mathcal{M}$.

It follows that if $U \neq_{RD} V$ then without loss of generality we can, using $C4[C3[\cdot]]$, map U to $C4[(a \to STOP) \sqcap STOP]$ and Q_n respectively, two processes known to be distinct in $\mathcal{M}$. Hence $U \neq_M V$, so $\mathcal{M}$ refines $\mathcal{R}^{\Downarrow}$. This completes the proof of Theorem 6. ∎

8   Conclusions

In this paper we have given details of the most refined divergence-strict models for both finitary fCSP and the language that allows infinite nondeterminism, as well as proposing definitions for what a divergence-strict model looks like in general. We found a rather counter-intuitive congruence that in essence is created because CSP has no operator of a sort that seems, with the benefit of hindsight, to be natural. We therefore added an extra operator Θ_a from this extra class, creating CSP+. Interestingly, this new operator adds no semantic expressive power over the class of *finite observation* models that the earlier paper [13] considered.

We studied the relationship between finitary models such as $\mathcal{T}^{\Downarrow}$ and $\mathcal{R}^{\Downarrow}$ and their infinitary extensions, in particular proving the uniqueness of this extension for some of more abstract models including all those that play a key role in our structural theorem. We are therefore able to restrict attention, in the proof of that theorem, to the finitary models.

This structural result was completed using three separate Theorems, each a qualified uniqueness theorem for one of the three models we identify as "Platonic". As one would expect, these arguments are sometimes delicate and require many intricate CSP+ contexts to be created.

In [13], the author proved a further result, namely that the stable revivals model $\mathcal{R}$ is the greatest lower bound (as a congruence) of the stable acceptances model $\mathcal{A}$ and the stable refusal testing model $\mathcal{RT}$. A corollary of this result is that the initial linear sequence of models does not continue beyond $\mathcal{R}$. The proof of that result carries forward easily to the class of divergence-strict models, from which we can deduce that the initial sequence is again limited to length 3.

In [13], the author conjectured that the classification problem for CSP models would become significantly more complex once one moves beyond the initial three models, and if one ventures outside the relatively controlled and homogeneous worlds of finite-observation, and divergence-strict models. His suspicion has only grown stronger during the investigations underlying the present paper, both because of something we have written about and something we have not mentioned yet. The first of these was the observation that beyond the realm of Theorem 3 we can expect multiple infinitary extensions of a given fCSP model. The second is that we may similarly have freedom to vary how much information we record about divergences: for example, it seems likely that the variant of $\mathcal{FL}^{\Downarrow}$ in which only trace divergences, as opposed to ones with acceptances too, would be a congruence.

Since the results of the present paper and the corresponding ones from [13] were largely unanticipated by the author, he does not exclude the possibility that there may be nice classification results in the reaches beyond revivals. However, he doubts there are!

There is no space in the present paper to report on a fascinating by-product of our work here. That is the idea that our extended language CSP+ can be shown to be a universal language for a wide class of languages of concurrency, namely ones with *CSP-like* operational semantics. Thus, for any such language, all the usual models of CSP together with their refinement properties, and susceptibility to FDR and CSP compression functions, will apply just as much as they do for CSP. The author expects to report on this further work soon.

Acknowledgements

This is one of a series of papers that was inspired by the work of Jakob Rehof, Sriram Rajamani and others in deriving *conformance*, a revivals-like congruence for a CCS-like language. My work on this paper benefited greatly from conversations with Jakob, Antti Valmari and Tony Hoare.

References

1. Fournet, C., Hoare, C.A.R., Rajamani, S.K., Rehof, J.: Stuck-free conformance. In: Alur, R., Peled, D.A. (eds.) CAV 2004. LNCS, vol. 3114. Springer, Heidelberg (2004)
2. van Glabbeek, R.J.: The linear time - Branching time spectrum I. In: The handbook of process algebra. Elsevier, Amsterdam (2001)
3. van Glabbeek, R.J.: The linear time - Branching time spectrum I. In: Best, E. (ed.) CONCUR 1993. LNCS, vol. 715. Springer, Heidelberg (1993)
4. Hoare, C.A.R.: A model for communicating sequential processes. In: On the construction of programs, Cambridge University Press, Cambridge (1980)
5. Hoare, C.A.R.: Communicating sequential processes. Prentice-Hall, Englewood Cliffs (1985)
6. Mukkaram, A.: A refusal testing model for CSP. D.Phil thesis. Oxford University, Oxford (1993)
7. Olderog, E.R., Hoare, C.A.R.: Specification-oriented semantics for communicating processes. Acta Informatica 23, 9–66 (1986)
8. Phillips, I.: Refusal testing. Theoretical Computer Science 50, 241–284 (1987)
9. Puhakka, A.: Weakest congruence results concerning "any-lock". In: Kobayashi, N., Pierce, B.C. (eds.) TACS 2001. LNCS, vol. 2215. Springer, Heidelberg (2001)
10. Roscoe, A.W.: The theory and practice of concurrency. Prentice-Hall International, Englewood Cliffs (1998), http://web.comlab.ox.ac.uk/oucl/work/bill.roscoe/publications/68b.pdf
11. Roscoe, A.W.: An alternative order for the failures model, in 'Two papers on CSP', technical monograph PRG-67; also appeared in Journal of Logic and Computation 2(5), 557–577 (1988)
12. Roscoe, A.W.: Seeing beyond divergence. In: Abdallah, A.E., Jones, C.B., Sanders, J.W. (eds.) Communicating Sequential Processes. LNCS, vol. 3525. Springer, Heidelberg (2005)
13. Roscoe, A.W.: Revivals, stuckness and the hierarchy of CSP models (submitted), http://www.comlab.ox.ac.uk/people/bill.roscoe/publications/105.pdf

Appendix: Notation

This paper follows the notation of [10], from which most of the following is taken.

Σ	(Sigma): alphabet of all communications
τ	(tau): the invisible action
Σ^τ	$\Sigma \cup \{\tau\}$
A^*	set of all finite sequences over A
$\langle\rangle$	the empty sequence
$\langle a_1, \ldots, a_n \rangle$	the sequence containing $a_1, \ldots, a_n$ in that order
$s\hat{\ }t$	concatenation of two sequences
$s \leq t$	($\equiv \exists u.s\hat{\ }u = t$) prefix order
$\bullet$	non-observation of stability
FLO	the alternating sequences of acceptances/$\bullet$ and members of Σ.

Processes:

$\mu\,p.P$	recursion
$a \to P$	prefixing
$?x : A \to P$	prefix choice
$P \square Q$	external choice
$P \sqcap Q, \quad \sqcap S$	nondeterministic choice
$P \parallel_X Q$	generalised parallel
$P \setminus X$	hiding
$P[\![R]\!]$	renaming (relational)
$P[\![a \mapsto A]\!]$	renaming in which a maps to every $b \in A$
$P[\![A \mapsto a]\!]$	renaming in which every member of A maps to a
$P \triangleright Q$	"time-out" operator (sliding choice)
$P \triangle Q$	interrupt
$P \Theta_a Q$	exception throwing
$P[x/y]$	substitution (for a free identifier x)
$P \xrightarrow{a} Q$	($a \in \Sigma \cup \{\tau\}$) single action transition in an LTS

Models:

$\mathcal{T}$	traces model
$\mathcal{N}$	failures/divergences model (divergence strict)
$\mathcal{F}$	stable failures model
$\mathcal{R}$	stable revivals model
$\mathcal{A}$	stable ready sets, or acceptances, model
$\mathcal{RT}$	stable refusal testing model
$\mathcal{FL}$	the finite linear observation model
$\mathcal{M}^{\Downarrow}$	the model $\mathcal{M}$ extended by strict divergence information
$\mathcal{M}^{\Downarrow,\omega}$	$\mathcal{M}$ extended by strict divergences and infinite traces or similar
$\mathcal{M}^{\#}$	$\mathcal{M}$ extended by non-strict divergences and infinite traces or similar
$\mathcal{X} \preceq \mathcal{Y}$	$\mathcal{X}$ identifies all processes identified by $\mathcal{Y}$
$\sqsubseteq$	refinement (over $\mathcal{FL}^{\Downarrow\omega}$ by default)

Monotonic Abstraction in Action
(Automatic Verification of Distributed Mutex Algorithms)

Parosh Aziz Abdulla[1], Giorgio Delzanno[2], and Ahmed Rezine[1]

[1] Uppsala University, Sweden
{parosh, Rezine.Ahmed}@it.uu.se
[2] Università di Genova, Italy
giorgio@disi.unige.it

Abstract. We consider verification of safety properties for *parameterized distributed protocols*. Such a protocol consists of an arbitrary number of (infinite-state) processes that communicate asynchronously over FIFO channels. The aim is to perform *parameterized verification*, i.e., showing correctness regardless of the number of processes inside the system. We consider two non-trivial case studies: the distributed Lamport and Ricart-Agrawala mutual exclusion protocols. We adapt the method of *monotonic abstraction* that considers an over-approximation of the system, in which the behavior is monotonic with respect to a given pre-order on the set of configurations. We report on an implementation which is able to fully automatically verify mutual exclusion for both protocols.

1   Introduction

In this paper, we consider automatic verification of safety properties for *parameterized distributed protocols*. Such a protocol consists of an arbitrary number of concurrent processes communicating asynchronously. The aim is to prove correctness of the protocol regardless of the number of processes.

Several aspects of the behavior of distributed protocols make them extremely difficult to analyze. First, the processes communicate asynchronously through channels and shared variables. Each process may operate on *heterogeneous* data types such as Boolean, integers, counters, logical clocks, time stamps, tickets, etc. Furthermore, such protocols often involve *quantified* conditions. For instance, a process may need to receive acknowledgments from *all* the other processes inside the system, before it is allowed to perform a transition. Finally, these protocols are often *parameterized* meaning we have to verify correctness of an infinite family of systems each of which is an infinite-state system. Here, we refine the method of [3,2] based on *monotonic abstractions* to perform fully automatic verification of two difficult examples; namely the distributed mutual exclusion algorithm by Lamport [17]; and its modification by Ricart and Agrawala [21].

We model a parametrized distributed system (or a distributed system for short) as consisting of an arbitrary number of processes. Each process is an extended finite-state automaton which operates on a number of Boolean and numerical (natural number) variables. Each pair of processes is connected through

J.S. Fitzgerald, A.E. Haxthausen, and H. Yenigun (Eds.): ICTAC 2008, LNCS 5160, pp. 50–65, 2008.

a number of bounded FIFO-channels which the processes use to interchange messages. A transition inside a process may be conditioned by the local variables and the messages fetched from the heads of the channels accessible to the process. The conditions on the numerical variables are stated as *gap-order constraints*. Gap-order constraints [19] are a logical formalism in which we can express simple relations on variables such as lower and upper bounds on the values of individual variables; and equality, and gaps (minimal differences) between values of pairs of variables. Also, as mentioned above, one important aspect in the behavior of distributed protocols is the existence of *quantified* conditions. This feature is present for instance in the Lamport and Ricart-Agrawala protocols. Here, the process which is about to perform a transition needs to know (or receive) information (e.g., acknowledgments) from the other processes inside the system. Since a process cannot communicate directly with the other processes, it keeps instead information locally about them. This local information is stored through a number of variables which we call *record variables*. A process has a copy of each record variable corresponding to each other process inside the system. As an example, consider a system with n processes. Suppose that, in the protocol, a process needs to receive acknowledgments from all the other processes. The protocol then uses a Boolean variable *ack* to record information about received acknowledgments. Then, a process (say process i) will have $n - 1$ copies of the variable *ack*, where each copy corresponds to another process (the copy corresponding to process j records whether process i has received an acknowledgment from process j). When process i receives an acknowledgment from process j through the relevant channel, it assigns *true* to its copy of *ack* corresponding to process j. Process i performs the transition by *universally* quantifying over all its copies of *ack*, i.e., checking that all of them are set to true. We can also have existential quantification in which case the process checks that *some* local copy has a certain value (rather than *all* local copies).

In this paper, we report on two case studies where we use our model of distributed systems to describe parameterized versions of the distributed Lamport and Ricart-Agrawala protocols. We have verified fully automatically the protocols, using a tool which adapts the method of *monotonic abstractions* reported in [3,2]. The idea of monotonic abstraction is to make use of the theory of *monotonic programs*. In fact, one of the widely adopted frameworks for infinite-state verification is based on the concept of transition systems which are monotonic with respect to a given pre-order on the set of configurations. This framework provides a scheme for symbolic backward reachability analysis, and it has been used for the design of verification algorithms for various models including Petri nets, lossy channel systems, timed Petri nets, broadcast protocols, etc. (see, e.g., [5,12,13,1]). The main advantage of the method is that it allows to work on (infinite) sets of configurations which are upward closed with respect to the pre-order. These sets have often very efficient symbolic representations (each upward closed set can be uniquely characterized by its minimal elements) which makes them attractive to use in reachability analysis. Unfortunately, many systems do not fit into this framework, in the sense that there is no nontrivial (useful) ordering for which these systems are monotonic.

The idea of *monotonic abstractions* [3,2] is to compute an over-approximation of the transition relation. Given a preorder $\preceq$, we define an abstract semantics of the considered systems which ensures their monotonicity. Basically, the idea is to consider that a transition is possible from a configuration c_1 to c_2 if it is possible from c_1 to a larger configuration $c_3 \succeq c_2$. The whole verification process is fully automatic since both the approximation and the reachability analysis are carried out without user intervention. Observe that if the approximate transition system satisfies a safety property then we can safely conclude that the original system satisfies the property, too. Based on the method, we have implemented a prototype and applied it for *fully automatic* verification of the distributed Lamport and Ricart-Agrawala protocols. Termination of the approximated backward reachability analysis is not guaranteed in general.

Related Work. This paper gives detailed descriptions of two non-trivial case studies, where we adapt monotonic abstraction [2,3,4] to the case of distributed protocols. Compared to the methods of [3] and [2,4] which operate on simple Boolean and integer variables respectively, our formalism allows the modeling of heterogeneous data types such as FIFO queues, logical clocks, etc, which are very common in the deigns of distributed protocols.

In [24], the authors consider distributed protocols with a bounded number of processes, and also build for heterogeneous systems (e.g., with Booleans and integers) on top of the Omega-based solver. Here, we have a tool for heterogeneous data types built on top of our verification method [2,3,4] which allows to deal with unbounded numbers of components. There have been several works on verification of parameterized systems of *finite-state processes*, e.g., regular model checking [15,6,8] and counter abstraction methods [11,14,12,13]. In our case, the processes are infinite-state, and therefore our examples cannot be analyzed with these methods unless they are combined with additional abstractions. Furthermore all existing automatic parameterized verification methods (e.g., [15,6,8,10,11,3,2]) are defined for systems under the (practically unreasonable) assumption that quantified conditions are performed atomically (globally). In other words, the process is assumed to be able to check the states of all the other processes in one atomic step. On the other hand, in our quantified conditions, the process can only check variables which are local to the process. Non-atomic versions of parameterized mutual exclusion protocols such as the Bakery algorithm have been studied with heuristics to discover invariants, ad-hoc abstractions, or semi-automated methods in [7,16,18,9,10]. In contrast to these methods, our verification procedure is fully automated and is based on a more realistic model.

A parameterized formulation of the Ricart-Agrawala algorithm has been verified semi-automatically in [22], where the STeP prover is used to discharge some of the verification conditions needed in the proof. We are not aware of other attempts of fully automatic verification of parameterized versions of the Ricart-Agrawala algorithm or of the distributed version of Lamport's distributed algorithm.

Outline. In the next section, we give preliminaries, and in Section 3 we describe our model for distributed systems (protocols). In Section 4, we give the operational semantics by describing the (infinite-state) transition system induced by a distributed system. In Section 5, we introduce an ordering on the set of configurations of the system, and explain how to specify safety properties (such as mutual exclusion) as reachability of a set which is upward closed with respect to the ordering. In Section 6 and 7 we give the modeling of the distributed Lamport and the Ricart-Agrawala protocols respectively. In Section 8, we give an overview of the method of monotonic abstractions used to perform reachability analysis. Section 9 reports the result of applying our prototype on the two case studies. Finally, we give some conclusions and directions for future research.

2   Preliminaries

We use $\mathcal{B}$ to denote the set $\{true, false\}$ of Boolean values; and use $\mathcal{N}$ to denote the set of natural numbers. We assume an element $\bot \notin \mathcal{B} \cup \mathcal{N}$ and use $\mathcal{B}_\bot$ and $\mathcal{N}_\bot$ to denote $\mathcal{B} \cup \{\bot\}$ and $\mathcal{N} \cup \{\bot\}$ respectively. For a natural number n, let $\overline{n}$ denote the set $\{1, \ldots, n\}$. We will work with sets of variables. Such a set A is often partitioned into two subsets: *Boolean* variables $A_\mathcal{B}$ which range over $\mathcal{B}$, and *numerical* variables $A_\mathcal{N}$ which range over $\mathcal{N}$. We denote by $\mathbb{B}(A_\mathcal{B})$ the set of Boolean formulas over $A_\mathcal{B}$. We will also use a simple set of formulas, called *gap formulas*, to constrain the numerical variables. More precisely, we let $\mathbb{G}(A_\mathcal{N})$ be the set of formulas which are either of the form $x = y$ or of the form $x \sim_k y$ where $\sim \in \{<, \leq\}$, $x, y \in A_\mathcal{N}$, and $k \in \mathcal{N}$. Here $x <_k y$ stands for $x + k < y$. We use $\mathbb{F}(A)$ to denote the set of formulas which has members of $\mathbb{B}(A_\mathcal{B})$ and of $\mathbb{G}(A_\mathcal{N})$ as atomic formulas, and which is closed under the Boolean connectives $\wedge, \vee$. For instance, if $A_\mathcal{B} = \{a, b\}$ and $A_\mathcal{N} = \{x, y\}$ then $\theta = (a \supset b) \wedge (x + 3 < y)$ is in $\mathbb{F}(A)$. Sometimes, we write a formula as $\theta(y_1, \ldots, y_k)$ where $y_1, \ldots, y_k$ are the variables which may occur in θ; so we can write the above formula as $\theta(x, y, a, b)$.

A *substitution* is a set $\{x_1 \leftarrow e_1, \ldots, x_n \leftarrow e_n\}$ of pairs where x_i are variables, and e_i are all constants or all variables. For each $i : 1 \leq i \leq n$, e_i is of the same type as x_i. Here, we assume that all the variables are distinct, i.e., $x_i \neq x_j$ if $i \neq j$. For a formula θ and a substitution S, we use $\theta[S]$ to denote the formula we get from θ by simultaneously replacing all occurrences of the variables $x_1, \ldots, x_n$ by $e_1, \ldots, e_n$ respectively. Observe that, if $e_1, \ldots, e_n$ are constants, then all variables appearing in θ will be replaced. In such a case, the formula $\theta[S]$ evaluates either to *true* or to *false*. Sometimes, we may write $\theta[S_1][S_2] \cdots [S_m]$ instead of $\theta[S_1 \cup S_2 \cup \cdots \cup S_m]$. As an example, if $\theta = (x_1 < x_2) \wedge (x_3 <_2 x_4)$ then $\theta[x_1 \leftarrow y_2, x_4 \leftarrow x_3][x_2 \leftarrow x_3] = (y_2 < x_3) \wedge (x_3 <_2 x_3)$.

3   Parameterized Distributed Systems

In this section, we introduce a basic model for parameterized distributed systems with heterogeneous data types.

A *parameterized distributed system* (or *distributed system* for short) consists of an arbitrary (but finite) number n of identical processes. Each process has a number of *local* variables and communicates asynchronously with the other processes through a set of bounded *FIFO channels*. To simplify, we assume, in this and in the next section, that each channel is of size one. It is straightforward to extend the results to the case of channels of any (finite) size. Furthermore, a process maintains a number of *record* variables which are used to store information about the local states and values of local variables of the other processes. All the variables and channels are assigned either Boolean or integer variables. A process is modeled as an extended finite-state automaton where the transitions check and update the values of the variables and channels accessible to the process. A transition is of one of three types. A *local* transition involves only the local variables of the process. In a *quantified* transition, the process may also check and update the values of the record variables. Such a transition is called *quantified* since (as we shall see below) it may involve an arbitrary number of variables. Finally, in a *communication* transition, also the contents of the channels can be checked and updated. A distributed system, described in this manner, induces an infinite family of (infinite-state) systems, namely one for each size n. The aim is to verify correctness of the systems for the whole family.

To simplify, we assume that each process is indexed by a natural number $i : 1 \leq i \leq n$. The index of the process does not appear in the transition rules, and hence has no relevance for the behavior of the process. Sometimes, we simply write "process i" to refer to the process with index i. In the sequel, we assume the sets L, R, and Ch of *local*, *record*, and *channel* variables, respectively. The set L is partitioned into $L_\mathcal{B}$ (which range over $\mathcal{B}$) and $L_\mathcal{N}$ (which range over $\mathcal{N}$). A variable in L assumes values in $\mathcal{B}$ or $\mathcal{N}$ depending on its type. Also, the other sets R and Ch are partitioned in a similar manner. In case of a channel variable, the variable will take values from $\mathcal{B}_\perp$ and $\mathcal{N}_\perp$ where the value $\perp$ indicates that the channel is empty. Each process i has one copy of the set L. Also, for each record variable $x \in R$ and pairs of processes i and j, process i has a local copy of x corresponding to j. Process i then uses that particular copy of x to record information about the state of process j. Finally, for each channel variable $x \in Ch$ and pairs of processes i and j, there is one copy of x which i can write to and j can read from; and (symmetrically) another copy which j can write to and i can read from. Notice that, for an instance of n processes, there will be n copies of L and $n(n-1)$ copies of R and Ch.

To describe the transitions of the system, we introduce the set $L^{next} = \{x^{next} \mid x \in L\}$ which contains the *next-value* versions of the variables in L. A variable $x^{next} \in L^{next}$ represents the next value of x when performing a transition. The sets R^{next} and Ch^{next} are defined in a similar manner. Formally, a *distributed system* $\mathcal{D}$ is a pair (Q, T), where Q is a finite set of *local states*, and T is a finite set of *transition rules*. A transition is of the form

$$t : \left[q \rightarrow q' \, \rhd \, \theta \right] \tag{1}$$

where $q, q' \in Q$ and θ is either a *local*, a *quantified*, or a *communication condition*. Intuitively, the process which makes the transition changes its local state from q to q'. In the meantime, the values of the variables and channels accessible to the process are checked and updated according to θ. Below, we describe how we define local, quantified, and communication conditions.

A *local condition* is a formula in $\mathbb{F}(L \cup L^{next})$. The formula specifies how the local variables of the process are updated with respect to their current values. A *quantified condition* θ is either of the form $\forall \cdot \theta_1$ (i.e., it is universal), or of the form $\exists \cdot \theta_1$ (i.e., it is existential), where $\theta_1 \in \mathbb{F}(L \cup L^{next} \cup R \cup R^{next})$. The universal condition checks the local variables of the process (say with index i) which is about to make the transition (through L), and the copies of the record variables inside i corresponding to *all* the other processes (through R). It also specifies how these variables are updated (through L^{next} and R^{next}). The existential case can be explained analogously, with the difference that the record variables corresponding so *some* other (unspecified) process (rather than all other processes) will be checked and updated. A *communication condition* θ is of the form $Com \cdot \theta_1$ where θ_1 belongs to $\mathbb{F}(L \cup L^{next} \cup R \cup R^{next} \cup Ch \cup Ch^{next})$. Intuitively, the process (say with index i) chooses some other process (say with index j). Process i performs the transition checking and updating its local variables and its copies of the record variables corresponding to process j (in a similar manner to above). Furthermore, process i can read the values of the channels to which j can write and i can read (through Ch); and update the channels to which i can write and j can read (through Ch^{next}). Here, we assume that the transition is enabled only if it does not try to read the value of an empty channel, or to write to a channel which is full (occupied). Notice that the transition is implicitly existentially quantified, in the sense that process i checks and updates record variables and channel contents corresponding only to one other process.

Remark 1 (Finite Variables). The case where the variables range over finite domains can be handled in a straightforward manner.

Example. Assume local states q_1, q_2 and q_3, a local numerical variable *clock*, a Boolean record variable *checked* and a numerical channel variable c. In the rest of the paper, we introduce some syntactic sugar to improve readability. We assume that non-mentioned *next-value* forms of local and record variables equal their current value. Follow examples of local, universally quantified and communication transitions.

Local. The process changes local state from q_1 to q_2. It assigns a new value to the local (numerical) variable *clock* which is larger than its current value.

$$q_1 \rightarrow q_2 \triangleright (clock < clock^{next})$$

Universally quantified. The process changes local state from q_2 to q_3. It also changes the value of *clock* as above, and checks whether the values of all copies of the record variable *checked* are equal to *true*. Furthermore, the process resets all these values to *false*.

$$q_2 \rightarrow q_3 \triangleright \forall (clock < clock^{next} \wedge checked \wedge \neg(checked^{next}))$$

Communication. A process (say with index i) at local state q_2 changes the value of *clock* as above, and chooses some other process (say with index j). Process i checks whether its copy of *checked* corresponding to process j is *false*. In such a case, it sets *checked* to *true*, and sends the value of its updated logical clock to process j along the relevant copy of channel c (the copy to which process i writes to and process j reads from).

$$q_2 \rightarrow q_2 \triangleright Com \cdot \left(\begin{array}{c} clock < clock^{next} \\ \wedge \neg checked \wedge checked^{next} \wedge c^{next} = clock^{next} \end{array} \right)$$

4   Operational Semantics

In this section, we define the transition system associated with a distributed system. In general, a *transition system* $\mathcal{T}$ is a pair $(D, \Longrightarrow)$, where D is an (infinite) set of *configurations* and $\Longrightarrow$ is a binary relation on D. A distributed system $\mathcal{D} = (Q, T)$ induces a transition system $\mathcal{T}(\mathcal{D}) = (C, \longrightarrow)$ as follows. A configuration is defined by the local states and the values of the local variables in the processes, the values of the record variables, and the contents of the channels. Formally, a *configuration* c (of *size* n) is a tuple (n, s, u, v, w) where

- s is a mapping $\overline{n} \rightarrow Q$. For each process (with index i) the value of $s(i)$ defines the local state of the process.
- u is a mapping $\overline{n} \rightarrow L \rightarrow (\mathcal{B} \cup \mathcal{N})$. For each process (with index i) and local variable x, the value of $u(i)(x)$ defines the value of the copy of x in process i. The value may be in $\mathcal{B}$ or $\mathcal{N}$ depending on the type of x.
- v is a mapping $\overline{n} \rightarrow \overline{n} \rightarrow R \rightarrow (\mathcal{B} \cup \mathcal{N})$. For processes (with indices i and j), and record variable x, $v(i)(j)(x)$ defines the value of the copy of x in process i corresponding to process j.
- w is a mapping $\overline{n} \rightarrow \overline{n} \rightarrow Ch \rightarrow (\mathcal{B}_\perp \cup \mathcal{N}_\perp)$. For processes (with indices i and j), and channel variable x, the value of $w(i)(j)(x)$ defines the content of the copy of channel x to which i can write and j can read. If $w(i)(j)(x) = \perp$ then the channel is empty.

Now, we are ready to define the transition relation $\longrightarrow$. Consider two configurations $c_1 = (n, s_1, u_1, v_1, w_1)$ and $c_2 = (n, s_2, u_2, v_2, w_2)$ of the same size n. Consider a transition t rule of the form of (1) and a natural number $1 \leq i \leq n$. Intuitively, we will describe the effect of process i performing transition t. We write $c_1 \xrightarrow{t, i} c_2$ to denote that the following conditions are satisfied:

- $s_2(j) = s_1(j)$, $u_2(j) = u_1(j)$, $v_2(j) = v_1(j)$ for each $j : 1 \leq j \neq i \leq n$. Furthermore, $w_2(j)(k) = w_1(j)(k)$, if $1 \leq j \neq i \leq n$ and $1 \leq k \neq i \leq n$, and $j \neq k$. The other processes do not change their local states, local variables, or their record variables. The channels which cannot be read from or written to by process i are not changed either.
- $s_1(i) = q$ and $s_2(i) = q'$. The current and new local states of process i should be consistent with those given in the transition rule.
- One of the following conditions holds:
  - θ is a local condition and the formula $\theta [\rho_1] [\rho_2]$ holds, where the substitutions are defined by $\rho_1 = \{x \leftarrow u_1(i)(x) | \ x \in L\}$, and by $\rho_2 = \{x^{next} \leftarrow u_2(i)(x) | \ x \in L\}$. Furthermore, $v_2 = v_1$ and $w_2 = w_1$. The current and new values of the local variables of i are consistent with θ.

- $\theta = \forall \cdot \theta_1$ is a universal quantified condition and $\theta_1 [\rho_1] [\rho_2] \left[\rho_3^j\right] \left[\rho_4^j\right]$ holds for each $j : 1 \leq j \neq i \leq n$. The substitutions ρ_1 and ρ_2 are defined as in the previous case, while $\rho_3^j = \{x \leftarrow v_1(i)(j)(x)| \ x \in R\}$, and $\rho_4^j = \{x^{next} \leftarrow v_2(i)(j)(x)| \ x \in R\}$. Furthermore $w_2 = w_1$. In addition to the local variables, process i may check and update the values of its record variables. The manner in which the variables are changed should be consistent with the condition for each other process j.

- $\theta = \exists \cdot \theta_1$ is an existential quantified condition and $\theta_1 [\rho_1] [\rho_2] \left[\rho_3^j\right] \left[\rho_4^j\right]$ holds for some $j : 1 \leq j \neq i \leq n$. Furthermore $w_2 = w_1$. All the substitutions are defined as in the previous case. The difference is that the variable changes should be consistent with the condition of the transition for *some* other process j (rather than all other processes).

- $\theta = Com \cdot \theta_1$ is a communication condition. In this case, the formula $\theta_1 [\rho_1] [\rho_2] \left[\rho_3^j\right] \left[\rho_4^j\right] \left[\rho_5^j\right] \left[\rho_6^j\right]$ holds for some $j : 1 \leq j \neq i \leq n$. The substitutions ρ_1, ρ_2, ρ_3^j, and ρ_4^j are defined as above, while ρ_5^j is defined by $\{x \leftarrow w_1(j)(i)(x)| \ x \in Ch\}$ and ρ_6^j by $\{x^{next} \leftarrow w_2(i)(j)(x)| \ x \in Ch\}$. Furthermore the following conditions are satisfied for each $x \in Ch$:
  * either x does not occur in θ_1 or both $w_1(j)(i)(x) \neq \bot$ and $w_2(j)(i) = \bot$. The channel can be read only if it is not empty. After the reading operation, the channel becomes empty.
  * either x^{next} does not occur in θ_1 or $w_1(i)(j)(x) = \bot$. A channel can be written to only if it is empty.

We write $c_1 \longrightarrow c_2$ to denote that $c_1 \xrightarrow{t,\, i} c_2$ for some t and i.

5   Safety Properties

Following the methodology of [3,2], we introduce an ordering on configurations, which we use to define the safety problem. Assume a distributed system $\mathcal{D} = (Q, T)$. We assume that, the system starts executing from an *initial* configuration, where each process starts running from an (identical) *initial* local state, with predefined initial values in the local and record variables, and with empty channels. In the induced transition system $\mathcal{T}(\mathcal{D}) = (C, \longrightarrow)$, we use *Init* to denote the set of initial configurations. Notice that this set is infinite, since there is a different initial configuration for each instance (size) of the system.

We define an ordering on configurations. To do that, we first introduce a notation. Consider a configuration $c = (n, s, u, v, w)$, a variable $x \in L \cup R \cup Ch$, and i, j where $1 \leq i \neq j \leq n$. Abusing notation, we define $c(x)(i)(j)$ to be $u(i)(x)$ if $x \in L$, $v(i)(j)(x)$ if $x \in R$, and $w(i)(j)(x)$ if $x \in Ch$. Consider two configurations $c_1 = (n_1, s_1, u_1, v_1, w_1)$ and $c_2 = (n_2, s_2, u_2, v_2, w_2)$. We write $c_1 \preceq c_2$ to denote that there is an injection $h : \overline{n_1} \to \overline{n_2}$ such that the following conditions are satisfied for each $i, j, l, m : 1 \leq i, j, l, m \leq n_1$:

1. $s_1(i) = s_2(h(i))$.
2. $c_1(i)(j)(x) = \bot$ iff $c_2(h(i))(h(j))(x) = \bot$ for all $x \in Ch$.

3. $c_1(i)(j)(x) = true$ iff $c_2(h(i))(h(j))(x) = true$ for all $x \in L_\mathcal{B} \cup R_\mathcal{B} \cup Ch_\mathcal{B}$.
4. $c_1(i)(j)(x) = c_1(l)(m)(y)$ iff $c_2(h(i))(h(j))(x) = c_2(h(l))(h(m))(y)$ for all $x, y \in L_\mathcal{N} \cup R_\mathcal{N} \cup Ch_\mathcal{N}$.
5. $c_1(i)(j)(x) <_{k_1} c_1(l)(m)(y)$[1] implies that there is a $k_2 \geq k_1$ such that $c_2(h(i))(h(j))(x) <_{k_2} c_2(h(l))(h(m))(y)$ for all $x, y \in L_\mathcal{N} \cup R_\mathcal{N} \cup Ch_\mathcal{N}$.

A set of configurations $D \subseteq C$ is *upward closed* (with respect to the ordering $\preceq$) if $c \in D$ and $c \preceq c'$ implies $c' \in D$. For sets of configurations $D, D' \subseteq C$ we use $D \longrightarrow D'$ to denote that there are $c \in D$ and $c' \in D'$ with $c \longrightarrow c'$.

The *coverability problem* for parameterized systems is defined as follows:

PAR-COV

Instance

- A distributed system $\mathcal{D} = (Q, T)$.
- Two sets of configurations *Init* and C_F, with C_F upward closed.

Question *Init* $\xrightarrow{*} C_F$?

It can be shown, using standard techniques (see e.g. [23]), that checking many classes of safety properties, e.g. mutual exclusion, can be translated into instances of the coverability problem. Therefore, checking safety properties amounts to solving PAR-COV (i.e., to the reachability of upward closed sets).

6   Distributed Mutex by Lamport

We describe the distributed mutual exclusion algorithm by Lamport [17] in our model. In this algorithm, a number of processes compete for a shared resource and communicate by message passing. The protocol guarantees mutual exclusion by allowing only the process with the *earliest* request to access its critical section. Here, *earliest* is defined by means of *logical clocks* [17], one per process. A logical clock is a local numerical variable that is strictly increased each time a process performs a transition. The value of the local logical clock is appended to each sent message. Each time a process receives a time-stamped message, it updates its logical clock to a value that is strictly larger than the maximum of the time stamp in the message, and of the previous value of the clock. Ties are broken by giving priority to the process to the left. Here we model the relative positions of the processes by introducing a Boolean local variable *right* that is unmodified once initialized. This gives a total ordering that uniquely defines the process with the earliest request.

In our model (table 1) of the algorithm, each process is in one of five local states, namely *idle, ask, wait, use* and *free*. The logical clock of a process is represented by a numerical local variable *clock*. The process has a local variable *last* which it uses to record the value of its logical clock at the time when it last started sending requests to other processes. The process has also a Boolean record variable *checked* which it uses to keep track of other processes to (from) which it has already sent (received) messages such as requests, acknowledgments,

---

[1] Recall $x <_{k_1} y$ iff $x + k_1 < y$.

etc. Another record variable, namely *Queue*, is used to store the time stamps associated with the requests received from other processes. Finally, the system has two channel variable c and ts. A process uses its copies of the channels to send timed-stamped messages. For instance, when a process wants to send a time-stamped request to another process, then it puts the message req to the relevant copy of c (the one writable by the current process and readable by the other process) and the time stamp to the relevant copy of ts.

Each time a process takes a transition, its logical clock is increased using the formula $clock < clock^{next}$. Initially, all processes are in their initial local state *idle*. When a process wants to enter the critical section, it first sends requests to all other processes. This is done in three steps (transitions t_1, t_2, and t_3). In t_1, the process moves from local state *idle* to local state *ask*. In doing this, it also records the new value of its logical clock in the local variable *last*. Notice that t_1 is a local transition. In *ask*, the process loops sending requests to the other processes, one at a time. This is done through t_2 which is a communication transition. In each execution of t_2, the process chooses another process , and checks whether it has already sent a request to that process (using the record variable *checked*). If this is not the case then it sets *checked* to true, and sends a time-stamped request to the other process on channels c and ts. More precisely, it sends the request message req through c and the new value of its logical clock through ts. In t_3, the process checks whether it has sent a request to all the other processes, by testing that all its copies of the record variable *checked* are equal to *true*. Observe that t_3 is a universally quantified transition.

A process can at any time receive a request from another process. This is done by transition t_9 which is a communication transition. The process receives a request from another process through channel c, and the associated time stamp through channel ts. It assigns to its logical clock a new value which is strictly larger than both the old value of the logical clock (the formula $clock < clock^{next}$) and the received time stamp (the formula $ts < clock^{next}$). It assigns the time stamp to the copy of the record variable *Queue* corresponding to the other process; then it sends back an acknowledgment to the other process together with a time stamp which is equal to the new value of its logical clock.

After sending the requests, a process starts collecting acknowledgments (in state *wait*). This is done by the communication transition t_4. The process receives an acknowledgment from the copy of channel c corresponding to another process together with the corresponding time stamp from channel ts. It updates its logical clock, and marks it has received an acknowledgment from the other process in a similar manner to above (see e.g., the explanation of t_2).

The process enters the critical section (transition t_5) only if it has received acknowledgments from all other processes, and if its request is the earliest among the received requests. The process request is the earliest if for each other process j in the system, one of the three following conditions holds; either (i) no request was received from process j (checked with $Queue = zero$); or the time stamp associated with the received request (stored in *Queue*) is (ii) strictly larger than *last*; or (ii) equal to *last* but process j is to the right of the current process ($right \wedge last = Queue$).

Finally a process releases the resource by sending a release message to all the other processes in the system. This is done in three steps (transitions t_6, t_7 and t_8).These steps are similar to the three steps of sending requests to the other processes (transitions t_1, t_2 and t_3). A process that receives a release message (transition t_{10}), updates its local clock, and removes from its local queue the corresponding request.

Table 1. Lamport Distributed Mutex

States:	$Q = \{idle, ask, wait, use, free\}, any \in Q$

Local:	$clock, last$ are *naturals originally zero*
Record:	*checked* is a *Boolean originally false*
	Queue is a *natural originally zero*
Channel:	c is in $\{req, ack\}_\perp$ *originally* $\perp$
	ts is in $\mathcal{N}_\perp$ *originally* $\perp$

$$t_1 : idle \rightarrow ask \triangleright \left(clock < clock^{next}\right) \wedge \left(last^{next} = clock^{next}\right)$$

$$t_2 : ask \rightarrow ask \triangleright Com \cdot \left(\begin{array}{l} \left(clock < clock^{next}\right) \\ \wedge \left(c^{next} = req\right) \wedge \left(ts^{next} = clock^{next}\right) \\ \wedge \left(\neg checked \wedge checked^{next}\right) \end{array}\right)$$

$$t_3 : ask \rightarrow wait \triangleright \forall \left(\begin{array}{l} \left(clock < clock^{next}\right) \\ \wedge \left(checked \wedge \neg(checked^{next})\right) \end{array}\right)$$

$$t_4 : wait \rightarrow wait \triangleright Com \cdot \left(\begin{array}{l} \left(clock < clock^{next}\right) \\ \wedge (c = ack) \wedge \left(ts < clock^{next}\right) \\ \wedge \left(\neg checked \wedge checked^{next}\right) \end{array}\right)$$

$$t_5 : wait \rightarrow use \triangleright \forall \left(\begin{array}{l} \left(clock < clock^{next}\right) \\ \wedge \left(checked \wedge \neg(checked^{next})\right) \\ \wedge \left(\begin{array}{l} (Queue = zero) \vee (last < Queue) \\ \vee (right \wedge (last = Queue)) \end{array}\right) \end{array}\right)$$

$$t_6 : use \rightarrow free \triangleright \left(clock < clock^{next}\right)$$

$$t_7 : free \rightarrow free \triangleright Com \cdot \left(\begin{array}{l} \left(clock < clock^{next}\right) \\ \wedge \left(c^{next} = rel\right) \wedge \left(ts^{next} = clock^{next}\right) \\ \wedge \left(\neg checked \wedge checked^{next}\right) \end{array}\right)$$

$$t_8 : free \rightarrow idle \triangleright \forall \left(\begin{array}{l} \left(clock < clock^{next}\right) \\ \wedge \left(checked \wedge \neg(checked^{next})\right) \end{array}\right)$$

$$t_9 : any \rightarrow any \triangleright Com \cdot \left(\begin{array}{l} \left(clock < clock^{next}\right) \\ \wedge (c = req) \wedge \left(ts < clock^{next}\right) \\ \wedge \left(Queue^{next} = ts\right) \\ \wedge \left(c^{next} = ack\right) \wedge \left(ts^{next} = clock^{next}\right) \end{array}\right)$$

$$t_{10} : any \rightarrow any \triangleright Com \cdot \left(\begin{array}{l} \left(clock < clock^{next}\right) \\ \wedge (c = rel) \wedge \left(ts < clock^{next}\right) \\ \wedge \left(Queue^{next} = zero\right) \end{array}\right)$$

The set of configurations violating mutual exclusion is the set where at least two processes are in state *use*.

7   Distributed Mutex by Ricart-Agrawala

The Ricart-Agrawala algorithm [21] is a modification of Lamport's distributed mutex. The modification aims at diminishing the number of exchanged messages

Table 2. Ricart-Agrawala Distributed Mutex

States:	$Q = \{idle, ask, wait, use, free\}$,
	$grant \in \{idle, free\}, hold \in \{ask, wait, use\}$

Local:	$clock, last$ are *naturals originally zero*
Record:	$checked, deferred$ are *Booleans originally false*
Channel:	c is in $\{req, ack\}_\perp$ *originally* $\perp$
	ts is in $\mathcal{N}_\perp$ *originally* $\perp$

$t_1: idle \rightarrow ask \triangleright \left(clock < clock^{next}\right) \wedge \left(last^{next} = clock^{next}\right)$

$t_2: ask \rightarrow ask \triangleright Com \cdot \begin{pmatrix} \left(clock < clock^{next}\right) \\ \wedge \left(c^{next} = req\right) \wedge \left(ts^{next} = clock^{next}\right) \\ \wedge \left(\neg checked \wedge checked^{next}\right) \end{pmatrix}$

$t_3: ask \rightarrow wait \triangleright \forall \begin{pmatrix} \left(clock < clock^{next}\right) \\ \wedge checked \wedge \neg(checked^{next}) \end{pmatrix}$

$t_4: wait \rightarrow wait \triangleright Com \cdot \begin{pmatrix} \left(clock < clock^{next}\right) \\ \wedge (c = ack) \wedge \left(ts < clock^{next}\right) \\ \wedge \left(\neg checked \wedge checked^{next}\right) \end{pmatrix}$

$t_5: wait \rightarrow use \triangleright \forall \left(\left(clock < clock^{next}\right) \wedge checked \wedge \neg(checked^{next})\right)$

$t_6: use \rightarrow free \triangleright \left(clock < clock^{next}\right)$

$t_7: free \rightarrow free \triangleright Com \cdot \begin{pmatrix} \left(clock < clock^{next}\right) \\ \wedge \left(c^{next} = ack\right) \wedge \left(ts^{next} = clock^{next}\right) \\ \wedge \left(deferred \wedge \neg(deferred)^{next}\right) \end{pmatrix}$

$t_8: free \rightarrow idle \triangleright \forall \left(\left(clock < clock^{next}\right) \wedge (\neg deferred)\right)$

$t_9: grant \rightarrow grant \triangleright Com \cdot \begin{pmatrix} \left(clock < clock^{next}\right) \\ \wedge (c = req) \wedge \left(ts < clock^{next}\right) \\ \wedge \left(c^{next} = ack\right) \wedge \left(ts^{next} = clock^{next}\right) \end{pmatrix}$

$t_{10}: hold \rightarrow hold \triangleright Com \cdot \begin{pmatrix} \left(clock < clock^{next}\right) \\ \wedge (c = req) \wedge \left(ch1_{ts} < clock^{next}\right) \\ \wedge \left((ts < last) \vee (ts = last \wedge \neg right)\right) \\ \wedge \left(c^{next} = ack\right) \wedge \left(ts^{next} = clock^{next}\right) \end{pmatrix}$

$t_{11}: hold \rightarrow hold \triangleright Com \cdot \begin{pmatrix} \left(clock < clock^{next}\right) \\ \wedge (c = req) \wedge \left(ts < clock^{next}\right) \\ \wedge \left((last < ts) \vee (ts = last \wedge right)\right) \\ \wedge \left(\neg deferred \wedge deferred^{next}\right) \end{pmatrix}$

per entry to the critical section. This is achieved by not sending release messages, and modifying the conditions for sending acknowledgment messages. In a similar manner to our model of Lamport's algorithm, each process can have one of the five states: *idle, ask, wait, use* and *free*. We use two local numerical variables *clock* and *last*, three Boolean record variables *checked, right* and *deferred*, and two channel variables c and ts. Except for *deferred*, all variables play the same roles as in Lamport's algorithm. This variable is used to remember the processes to which an acknowledgment should be sent when releasing the critical section.

Like in Section 6, a process sends requests by means of three transitions (t_1, t_2 and t_3). A process that receives a request while in state *idle* or *free*, updates its logical clock and sends back an acknowledgment (transition t_9). If a process receives the request when in states *ask, wait* or *use*, then it may take one of two actions. If the time stamp received with the request is (i) strictly smaller than the value of the local variable *last*, or is (ii) equal to *last* and the sender of the request is to the left of the receiver, then the receiver sends back an acknowledgment (transition t_{10}). Otherwise, this is deferred (transition t_{11}).

After sending the requests, a process collects acknowledgments (transition t_4). A process that did receive acknowledgments from all other processes can access its critical section (transition t_5). Finally a process releases the resource by sending an acknowledgment message to each other process with a deferred request (transitions t_6, t_7 and t_8).

The set of configurations violating mutual exclusion is the set where at least two processes are in state *use*.

8   Approximation and Scheme Overview

In this section, we use a methodology introduced in [3,2] for solving PAR-COV. The methodology consists in over-approximating the transition relation $\longrightarrow$ of Section 4 by a new monotonic transition relation $\rightsquigarrow \ = \longrightarrow \cup \rightsquigarrow_1$. Intuitively, the relation $\rightsquigarrow_1$ corresponds to the deletion of all processes (together with the corresponding record and channel variables) violating a condition θ_1 when taking a quantified universal transition $t = \forall \cdot \theta_1$. Observe that a negative answer to *Init* $\overset{*}{\rightsquigarrow} C_F$ implies a negative answer to PAR-COV. We check *Init* $\overset{*}{\rightsquigarrow} C_F$ using a scheme based on backward reachability analysis. The scheme symbolically represents sets of configurations by constraints. We write $[\![\phi]\!]$ to refer to the (infinite) upward closed set of configurations represented by a constraint ϕ. For a (finite) set of constraints Φ, we define $[\![\Phi]\!] = \bigcup_{\phi \in \Phi} [\![\phi]\!]$. We also write $Pre(\phi)$ to mean a set of constraints, such that $[\![Pre(\phi)]\!] = \{c | \exists c' \in [\![\phi]\!] . c \rightsquigarrow c'\}$. The set $[\![Pre(\phi)]\!]$ needs to be upward closed in order to be represented by a set of constraints. The monotonicity of $\rightsquigarrow$ ensures upward closedness.

Scheme. Given a finite set Φ_F of constraints representing the set C_F, we check whether *Init* $\overset{*}{\rightsquigarrow} [\![\Phi_F]\!]$. We perform backward reachability analysis, generating a sequence $[\![\Phi_0]\!] \subseteq [\![\Phi_1]\!] \subseteq [\![\Phi_2]\!] \subseteq \cdots$, of finite sets of constraints such that $\Phi_0 = \Phi_F$, and $\Phi_{j+1} = \Phi_j \cup Pre(\Phi_j)$. The procedure terminates when we reach a point j where $[\![\Phi_j]\!] \supseteq [\![\Phi_{j+1}]\!]$. Notice that the termination condition implies that Φ_j characterizes the set of all predecessors of $[\![\phi_F]\!]$. This means that $Init \overset{*}{\leadsto} [\![\Phi_F]\!]$ iff $(Init \cap [\![\Phi_j]\!]) \neq \emptyset$. Observe that, in order to implement the scheme (i.e., transform it into an algorithm), we need to be able (for any constraints ϕ, ϕ') to (i) check that $(Init \cap [\![\phi]\!]) = \emptyset$, (ii) compute the set $Pre(\phi)$; (iii) check that $[\![\phi]\!] \subseteq [\![\phi']\!]$. The definitions of constraints and the operations on them are similar to [20] and are introduced in the appendix.

9   Experimental Results

The method has been implemented in a prototype. The tool starts from specifications of bad states (at least two processes in state *use*). We report on the obtained results, using a 1.6 Ghz laptop with 1G of memory.

Mutual exclusion of both distributed algorithms has been checked fully automatically. We give the number of iterations and constraints (in the final set resulting from the fixpoint analysis), together with the required time in seconds and memory in megabytes.

Table 3. Obtained results

	# iterations	# constraints	time(sec)	memory(MB)
Distr. Lamport	30	4676	85	18
Distr. Ricart-Agrawala	32	1205	13	< 5

10   Conclusions and Future Research

We have shown how to instantiate the monotonic abstraction scheme [3,2] for automatic verification of parameterized distributed protocols. We have described how the method works on two non-trivial case studies, namely the distributed Lamport and the Ricart-Agrawala mutex protocols. Both protocols are verified automatically in our prototype without the need for manual intervention.

An interesting direction for future work is to extend the method to systems whose configurations can be modeled by graphs such as cache coherence protocols and dynamically allocated data structures. There are also several other interesting classes on problems for which monotonic abstraction seems to be relevant. For instance, we are currently working on applying monotonic abstraction to perform *shape analysis* on memory heaps. The idea is to find suitable pre-orders which allow to perform an abstract (over-approximate) reachability analysis using upward-closed sets of heap graphs.

References

1. Abdulla, P.A., Čerāns, K., Jonsson, B., Tsay, Y.-K.: Algorithmic analysis of programs with wqo domains. Information and Computation 160, 109–127 (2000)
2. Abdulla, P.A., Delzanno, G., Rezine, A.: Parameterized verification of infinite-state processes with global conditions. In: Damm, W., Hermanns, H. (eds.) CAV 2007. LNCS, vol. 4590, pp. 145–157. Springer, Heidelberg (2007)
3. Abdulla, P.A., Henda, N.B., Delzanno, G., Rezine, A.: Regular model checking without transducers. In: Grumberg, O., Huth, M. (eds.) TACAS 2007. LNCS, vol. 4424, pp. 721–736. Springer, Heidelberg (2007)
4. Abdulla, P.A., Henda, N.B., Delzanno, G., Rezine, A.: Handling parameterized systems with non-atomic global conditions. In: Logozzo, F., Peled, D.A., Zuck, L.D. (eds.) VMCAI 2008. LNCS, vol. 4905. Springer, Heidelberg (2008)
5. Abdulla, P.A., Jonsson, B.: Verifying programs with unreliable channels. Information and Computation 127(2), 91–101 (1996)
6. Abdulla, P.A., Jonsson, B., Nilsson, M., d'Orso, J.: Regular model checking made simple and efficient. In: Brim, L., Jančar, P., Křetínský, M., Kucera, A. (eds.) CONCUR 2002. LNCS, vol. 2421, pp. 116–130. Springer, Heidelberg (2002)
7. Arons, T., Pnueli, A., Ruah, S., Xu, J., Zuck, L.: Parameterized Verification with Automatically Computed Inductive Assertions. In: Berry, G., Comon, H., Finkel, A. (eds.) CAV 2001. LNCS, vol. 2102, pp. 221–234. Springer, Heidelberg (2001)
8. Boigelot, B., Legay, A., Wolper, P.: Iterating Transducers in the Large. In: Hunt, J.W.A., Somenzi, F. (eds.) CAV 2003. LNCS, vol. 2725, pp. 223–235. Springer, Heidelberg (2003)
9. Chkliaev, D., Hooman, J., van der Stok, P.: Mechanical verification of transaction processing systems. In: ICFEM 2000 (2000)
10. Clarke, E., Talupur, M., Veith, H.: Proving ptolemy right: Environment abstraction principle for model checking concurrent system. In: Ramakrishnan, C.R., Rehof, J. (eds.) TACAS 2008. LNCS, vol. 4963. Springer, Heidelberg (2008)
11. Delzanno, G.: Automatic verification of cache coherence protocols. In: Emerson, E.A., Sistla, A.P. (eds.) CAV 2000. LNCS, vol. 1855, pp. 53–68. Springer, Heidelberg (2000)
12. Emerson, E., Namjoshi, K.: On model checking for non-deterministic infinite-state systems. In: Proc. LICS, pp. 70–80 (1998)
13. Esparza, J., Finkel, A., Mayr, R.: On the verification of broadcast protocols. In: Proc. LICS 1999 (1999)
14. German, S.M., Sistla, A.P.: Reasoning about systems with many processes. Journal of the ACM 39(3), 675–735 (1992)
15. Kesten, Y., Maler, O., Marcus, M., Pnueli, A., Shahar, E.: Symbolic model checking with rich assertional languages. TCS 256, 93–112 (2001)
16. Lahiri, S.K., Bryant, R.E.: Indexed predicate discovery for unbounded system verification. In: Alur, R., Peled, D.A. (eds.) CAV 2004. LNCS, vol. 3114, pp. 135–147. Springer, Heidelberg (2004)
17. Lamport, L.: Time, clocks and the ordering of events in a distributed system. Communications of the ACM 21(7), 558–565 (1978)
18. Manna, Z., Anuchitanukul, A., Bjørner, N., Browne, A., Chang, E., Colón, M., de Alfaro, L., Devarajan, H., Sipma, H., Uribe, T.: STEP: the Stanford Temporal Prover. Draft Manuscript (June 1994)
19. Revesz, P.: A closed form evaluation for datalog queries with integer (gap)-order constraints. Theoretical Computer Science 116(1), 117–149 (1993)

20. Rezine, A.: Parameterized Systems: Generalizing and Simplifying Automatic Verification. PhD thesis, Uppsala University (2008)
21. Ricart, G., Agrawal, A.K.: An optimal algorithm for mutual exclusion in computer networks. Communications of the ACM 24(1), 9–17 (1981)
22. Sedletsky, E., Pnueli, A., Ben-Ari, M.: Formal verification of the ricart-agrawala algorithm. In: Proc. CFSTTCS 2000 (2000)
23. Vardi, M.Y., Wolper, P.: An automata-theoretic approach to automatic program verification. In: Proc. LICS, pp. 332–344 (June 1986)
24. Yavuz-Kahveci, T., Bultan, T.: A symbolic manipulator for automated verification of reactive systems with heterogeneous data types. STTT 5(1) (2003)

Non-interleaving Semantics with Causality for Nondeterministic Dataflow

Oana Agrigoroaiei[1] and Gabriel Ciobanu[1,2]

[1] Romanian Academy, Institute of Computer Science
Blvd. Carol I no.8, 700505 Iaşi, Romania
oanaag@iit.tuiasi.ro
[2] "A.I.Cuza" University of Iaşi, Faculty of Computer Science
Blvd. Carol I no.11, 700506 Iaşi, Romania
gabriel@info.uaic.ro

Abstract. We present a denotational model of nondeterministic dataflow in which an explicit notion of causality is introduced. We define a set of labelled flows over a set of fixed channels and two orders which induce cpo structures. Labelled flows are based on a conflict relation which allows to express several behaviours (configurations) at once. A netflow is a continuous function over configurations used to represent a dataflow network. We use a form of Galois connection in which such a function is the upper adjoint to correlate the possible outputs with their causes. The feedback operation is defined using a fixed point construction. Russell's example is used to show how this formal approach solves causal anomalies of nondeterministic dataflow.

1 Introduction

Dataflow is a sound, simple, and powerful model of parallel computation. The dataflow model describes computation in terms of locally controlled events; each event corresponds to the "firing" of an action. Such an action can be a single instruction, or a sequence of instructions, and an action fires when all the inputs it requires are available. In a dataflow execution, many actions may be ready to be executed simultaneously (locally controlled by their operand availability), and thus these actions represent asynchronous concurrent computation events.

As a model of computation, dataflow has a long history. A history of the evolution of the dataflow computation models and related architecture models are presented in [9]. The Kahn process networks were defined in early 1970s, and Kahn dataflow was used to model concurrency. In [8], Kahn has given a fixed point denotational semantics; the central idea is that each Kahn dataflow network can be described as a continuous function transforming a string of input values into a string of output values. The relational generalisation of this model to the nondeterministic case was shown not to be compositional by Brock and Ackerman [3]. The example they use, simplified as in [7], is the following: consider the dataflow networks N_i, $i \in \{1, 2\}$ and F, as pictured in Figure 1. The intuitive description of the networks is: $5\,5-merge$ takes the first data item from α, merges

J.S. Fitzgerald, A.E. Haxthausen, and H. Yenigun (Eds.): ICTAC 2008, LNCS 5160, pp. 66–80, 2008.
© Springer-Verlag Berlin Heidelberg 2008

it with the sequence 5 5 and outputs the resulting sequence on β; buf_1 takes a data item from β and outputs it on δ, repeats this behaviour once and then stops; buf_2 takes two data items from β and outputs them on δ, then stops; $fork$ takes a data item from δ and sends it on both δ_1 and δ_2; $+1$ adds 1 to each data item from δ_1, outputting it to α.

The input-output correspondence is $a_1 a_2 \ldots a_n \ldots \mapsto \{5\,5, 5\,a_1, a_1\,5\}$ for both N_1 and N_2. However, when N_1 and N_2 are placed in the context formed by $+1$ linked with $fork$, forming networks M_1 and M_2, the input-output correspondence is no longer the same. Note that since the input channel α of N_i is connected to the output channel of $+1$, there is no input channel for M_i, so in this case the correspondence is output related only. For M_1 the output is 5 5 or 5 6 while for M_2 the only possible output is 5 5. This discrepancy is caused by the fact that the input-output relation does not take causality into consideration.

Fig. 1. The dataflow networks N_i and M_i, $i \in \{1, 2\}$

In this paper we present a model of dataflow networks which is based on labelled flows, which are a particular type of labelled event structures. We introduce labelled flows to express the possible behaviours in a single mathematical structure. Each element of a labelled flow represents a communication event on a specific channel of the dataflow network, and it is labelled with a data value which passes through that channel. An order relation and a conflict relation are defined over the elements. The order relation represents temporal precedence of data on a channel. The conflict relation expresses the fact that two communication events cannot both be a part of the same behaviour. We formalise a behaviour by the notion of configuration (finite conflict-free labelled flow).

We represent graphically a labelled flow by a set of trees where the elements are tree nodes, and the edges give the order relation over the elements: $x < y$ in a labelled flow if y is up on a branch starting from x.

We also define two orders $\sqsubseteq$ and $\leq$ over the labelled flows. Considering two labelled flows f and g, by $f \sqsubseteq g$ we understand that the number of possible behaviours expressed by f is smaller that the number of possible behaviours expressed by g, and each behaviour expressed by f is a part of a behaviour expressed by g. This is equivalent to the fact that the elements of f are also elements of g and f has more conflicts than g. By $f \leq g$ we understand that the elements of f are also elements of g and f has the same conflicts as g. The set of labelled flows on a fixed set of channels is a bounded complete cpo with respect to $\sqsubseteq$ and a cpo with respect to $\leq$. To model a dataflow network we use a monotone function which takes configurations into labelled flows, which respects a name invariance condition and behaves as the upper adjoint of a Galois connection. The lower adjoint of the Galois connection is the causality map. The causality map applied to a configuration D from the output provides the configuration C from the input which is the least input configuration for which D is part of the output. In other words, the data carried by the elements of C represents the data sequence which has to be read by the dataflow network before the data sequence carried by D appears.

Name invariance is imposed to ensure that the function does not depend on the names of the elements: when two labelled flows have the same structure, so do their images by the function. The second condition provides a clear definition of causality in terms of configurations. This function has an extension to labelled flows which is continuous with respect to both $\leq$ and $\sqsubseteq$.

We provide a non-interleaving compositional semantics for nondeterministic dataflow whose strength resides in the approach of causality. Usually in event structures the order relation is considered to provide causality: if $x < y$ then x causes y. To obtain this non-interleaving semantics we use a different vision of causal correlation of input and output given by a Galois connection which is based on more than simply temporal precedence.

The structure of the rest of the paper is as follows. In section 2 we define labelled flows, present our motivation in using them to model nondeterminism, and state some properties of the set of labelled flows over a set of channels. In section 3 we introduce the dataflow model consisting of netflows, and we present sequential and parallel composition together with feedback. We also prove that in the deterministic case the model is in concordance with Kahn's semantics. Section 4 contains conclusions and directions for further research.

2   Labelled Flows

We begin by reviewing some notions from domain theory.

A subset S of a poset (partially ordered set) P is called a *lower subset* if whenever $x \leq y$ in P and $y \in S$, then $x \in S$, where $\leq$ is the order relation on P. $S \subseteq P$ is called *directed* if any finite subset of S has a upper bound in S.

A poset P is called *directed complete* if any directed subset S has a supremum in P and *bounded complete* if any bounded subset S has a supremum $\sup S \in P$. A directed complete poset with a least element is called a *cpo* (complete partial order). An element c of a cpo P is called *compact* if whenever $S \subseteq P$ is directed and $c \leq \sup S$, then there exists $s \in S$ such that $c \leq s$. If P and Q are cpos, a function $f : P \to Q$ is called *(Scott-)continuous* if $f(\sup S) = \sup f(S)$ for every directed $S \subseteq P$. More information on these notions is available in [2].

We consider that all dataflow networks accept as input elements of a fixed set V.

Definition 1. *Given a finite set A, a labelled flow f on A is defined by:*

1. *a carrier set $|f| \subseteq A \times S$, for some at most countable set S;*
2. *a labelling function $l_f : |f| \to V$;*
3. *an order relation $\leq_f$ such that*
    (a) $y \leq_f x, z \leq_f x \Rightarrow z \leq_f y$ or $y \leq_f z$;

(b) $\{y \mid y \leq_f x\}$ is finite for all $x \in |f|$;

(c) $(\alpha, s) \leq_f (\alpha', s') \Rightarrow \alpha = \alpha'$;

4. a conflict relation $\#_f$, namely a symmetric irreflexive relation on $|f|$, such that

(a) if $a = (\alpha, s), a' = (\alpha, s')$ then either $a \leq_f a'$, $a' \leq_f a$ or $a \#_f a'$;

(b) if $a \leq_f b$ and $a \#_f c$ then $b \#_f c$ (conflict inheritance).

We denote by $Lflow(A)$ the class of all labelled flows on A. We use the notation $[f]$ for the labelled poset structure $(|f|, \leq_f, l_f)$ of f. We denote by $f(\alpha)$ the subset $\{a \mid a = (\alpha, s)\}$ of $|f|$, and by ε_A the empty labelled flow on A ($|\varepsilon_A| = \emptyset$).

The fact that $|f| \subseteq A \times S$ says that each element $x \in |f|$ has a tag with the channel on which the communication event represented by x takes place. The labelling function l_f gives the data $l_f(x)$ transmitted in the communication event x. The order relation represents temporal precedence of communication events. Condition 3a gives the graphical representation as a set of trees for a labelled flow. We consider that elements with different channel tags are not ordered (Definition 1, 3c) because we give a non-interleaving semantics. Note that a labelled flow is also an event structure [10].

Why introduce a conflict relation? We use it to express the output of a non-deterministic dataflow network as a set of possible outputs which may conflict, in the sense that these outputs may not occur both. An example of such an output is presented in Figure 2, where $|f| = \{(\alpha, x), (\alpha, y), (\beta, u), (\beta, v), (\beta, w)\}$, with $(\alpha, x) \leq_f (\alpha, y)$, $(\beta, u) \leq_f (\beta, v)$, $(\beta, u) \leq_f (\beta, w)$, $(\beta, v) \#_f (\beta, w)$ (by definition), $(\alpha, x) \#(\beta, v)$ and $l(\alpha, x) = l(\beta, u) = 1, l(\alpha, y) = l(\alpha, v) = 2, l(\beta, w) = 3$. The meaning is that the output on channel β is 1 followed by 2 or 3; if 2 follows 1 then there is no output on channel α; if 3 follows 1 then the output on channel α is 1 followed by 2.

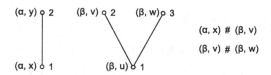

Fig. 2. The labelled flow f on $A = \{\alpha, \beta\}$

If f and g are labelled flows on A, we say that $q : f \to g$ is an isomorphism if $q : |f| \to |g|$ is a bijection such that $x \leq_f y$ iff $q(x) \leq_g q(y)$ and $x \#_f y$ iff $q(x) \#_g q(y)$ and $l_f = l_g \circ q$. For $B \subseteq A$ we denote by $f|_B \in Lflow(B)$ the restriction of f to B, i.e. $|f|_B| = \cup_{\beta \in B} f(\beta)$ with the order and conflict relations induced by the inclusion $|f|_B| \subseteq |f|$.

An element f of $Lflow(A)$ is called a *configuration* if it is finite and conflict free: $\#_f = \emptyset$. We denote by $\mathcal{C}(A)$ the class of all configurations in $Lflow(A)$ and we use $C, D, E \ldots$ to denote configurations. A configuration C is called *prime* if there exist $x, y \in C$, not necessarily distinct, such that for all $z \in C$, $z \leq x$ or $z \leq y$. In other words, a prime configuration in $Lflow(A)$ is one which has values on at most two channels $\alpha, \beta \in A$. The definition of a prime configuration is due to the fact that we work with the binary relation #; a configuration with values on more than three channels is entirely determined by the prime configurations which it contains. We use configurations to represent inputs for dataflow networks.

Definition 2. *Let f, g be two labelled flows on A. We say that*

- *$[f] \prec [g]$ if:*
  - *$|f| \subseteq |g|$;*
  - *for each $x \in |f|$, $l_f(x) = l_g(x)$;*
  - *if $x, y \in |f|$ then $x \leq_f y$ if and only if $x \leq_g y$;*
  - *$|f|$ is a lower subset of $|g|$: if $x \leq_g y$ and $y \in |f|$ then $x \in |f|$.*
- *$f \sqsubseteq g$ if $[f] \prec [g]$ and $\#_f \supseteq \#_g|_{|f| \times |f|}$ (in other words, g has less conflicts than f on $|f|$, which means more possible combinations of received or sent values);*
- *$f \leq g$ if $f \sqsubseteq g$ and $\#_f = \#_g|_{|f| \times |f|}$ (g can have more elements than f, but has exactly the same conflicts as f on $|f|$).*

Note that if C is a configuration (and so C is conflict free) and f a labelled flow, then $C \sqsubseteq f$ iff $C \leq f$. In such a situation we use the latter notation, in order to underline that f has no conflicts on its subset $|C|$.

Proposition 3.

- *$(\text{Lflow}(A), \sqsubseteq)$ is a bounded complete cpo, $(\mathcal{C}(A), \leq)$ is bounded complete, and $(\text{Lflow}(A), \leq)$ is a cpo which is not bounded complete.*
- *If $\{f_i\}_{i \in I}$ is a directed family in $(\text{Lflow}(A), \leq)$ then the supremum of the family in $(\text{Lflow}(A), \leq)$ is equal to its supremum in $(\text{Lflow}(A), \sqsubseteq)$.*

Proof (Sketch). Let $\{f_i\}_{i \in I}$ be a directed or bounded family in $(Lflow(A), \sqsubseteq)$. Then $\sup_i f_i = f$ where:

1. $|f| := \cup_i |f_i|$; $l_f(x) = l_{f_i}(x)$ if $x \in |f_i|$;
2. $x \leq_f y$ iff $\exists i \in I$ such that $x \leq_{f_i} y$;
3. $x \#_f y$ iff $x \#_{f_i} y$, for all $i \in I$ such that $x, y \in |f_i|$.

Let $\{g_i\}_{i \in I}$ be a directed family in $(Lflow(A), \leq)$. Then the supremum of $\{g_i\}_{i \in I}$ in $(Lflow(A), \leq)$ is g where:

1. $|gf| := \cup_i |g_i|$; $l_g(x) = l_{g_i}(x)$ if $x \in |g_i|$;
2. $x \leq_g y$ iff $\exists i \in I$ such that $x \leq_{g_i} y$;
3. $x \#_f y$ iff $\exists i \in I$ such that $x \#_{g_i} y$

To prove that $g = sup_i g_i$ (i.e. g is also the supremum of $\{g_i\}$ in $(Lflow(A), \sqsubseteq)$) it is enough to see that because $g_i \leq g$, if $x, y \in |g_i|$ such that $(x, y) \in \#)g_i$ then for any $j \in J$ such that $x, y \in |g_j|$ we also have $(x, y) \in \#)g_j$.

Let $\{C_i\}_{i \in I}$ be a bounded family in $(\mathcal{C}(A), \leq)$. Then $\sup_i C_i = C$ where:

1. $|C| := \cup_i |C_i|$; $l_C(x) = l_{C_i}(x)$ if $x \in |C_i|$;
2. $x \leq_C y$ iff $\exists i \in I$ such that $x \leq_{C_i} y$;
3. $\#_C = \emptyset$. $\square$

Corollary 4. *Restriction to a subset of channels preserves suprema of bounded or directed families in* $(\text{Lflow}(A), \sqsubseteq)$, *of bounded families in* $(\mathcal{C}(A), \leq)$ *and of directed families in* $(\text{Lflow}(A), \leq)$.

We denote by $\text{Sup}_i C_i$ and $\text{Inf}_i C_i$ the supremum and infimum, respectively of a family $\{C_i\}_{i \in I}$ of configurations in $(\mathcal{C}(A), \leq)$, to differentiate them from $\sup_i f_i$ and $\inf_i f_i$, which we use for the supremum and infimum of a family $\{f_i\}_{i \in I}$ of labelled flows in $(Lflow(A), \sqsubseteq)$.

Proposition 5. *Configurations are compact elements in* $(\text{Lflow}(A), \sqsubseteq)$*: if* C *is a configuration in* $\text{Lflow}(A)$ *such that* $C \leq h = \sup_i h_i$ *and* $\{h_i\}_{i \in I}$ *is a directed family then* $\exists k \in I$ *such that* $C \leq h_k$. *The same result holds if* $\{h_i\}_{i \in I}$ *is just bounded, case in which* C *should be prime.*

Proposition 6. *If* f *is a labelled flow in* $\text{Lflow}(A)$ *then*

$$f = \sup \{C \mid C \leq f, C \text{ prime configuration }\}$$

3 Denotational Model of Dataflow Networks

In order to describe a dataflow network with input channels A and output channels B we consider a map which sends configurations on A into labelled flows on B. Besides monotonicity, which is a natural requirement, we require a notion of causality as a part of the map's definition.

Definition 7. *We call* netflow *a map* $\varphi : \mathcal{C}(A) \rightarrow \text{Lflow}(B)$ *for which the following hold:*

- φ *is monotone with respect to* $\leq$: *if* $C \leq D$ *then* $\varphi(C) \leq \varphi(D)$;
- *If* $\{C_i\}_{i \in I}$ *is a family of configurations, bounded in* $(\text{Lflow}(A), \sqsubseteq)$, *then the family* $\{\varphi(C_i)\}_{i \in I}$ *is also bounded in* $(\text{Lflow}(A), \sqsubseteq)$;
- *there exists a map* $\text{cause}_\varphi : \mathcal{C}(B)_\varphi \rightarrow \mathcal{C}(A)$ *such that* $\forall E \in \mathcal{C}(A)$

$$C \leq \varphi(E) \Leftrightarrow \text{cause}_\varphi(C) \leq E$$

where $\mathcal{C}(B)_\varphi = \{C \in \mathcal{C}(B) \mid \exists D \in \mathcal{C}(A) : C \leq \varphi(D)\}$;

We also require a name invariance *property: if there exists an isomorphism* $r : C \rightarrow D$ *then there exists an isomorphism* $q : \varphi(C) \rightarrow \varphi(D)$ *such that if* $C' \leq C$ *then* $\varphi(r(C')) = q(\varphi(C'))$.

Remark 8. We impose the name invariance condition to ensure that the behaviour of a netflow φ depends only on the sequence of labels of the input configuration. Moreover, the condition is strong enough to prove that isomorphic configurations have isomorphic causes:

$$\text{if } E \leq \varphi(C) \text{ then } r(\text{cause}_\varphi(E)) = \text{cause}_\varphi(q(E))$$

Remark 9. Note the similarity between the definition of cause_φ and the notion of Galois connection [4]. Just like the lower adjoint of a Galois connection, cause_φ preserves suprema: if $\{C_i\}_{i \in I}$ is a family of configurations in $\mathcal{C}(B)_\varphi$ such that $\exists \text{Sup}_i C_i = C$ and C is in $\mathcal{C}(B)_\varphi$ then $\exists \text{Sup}_i \text{cause}_\varphi(C_i) = \text{cause}_\varphi(C)$.

Remark 10. If $\varphi : \mathcal{C}(A) \to Lflow(B)$ is a netflow and $B' \subseteq B$ then $\varphi|_{B'}$ defined by $\varphi|_{B'}(f) = \varphi(f)|_{B'}$ is a netflow.

The importance of the causality notion as part of the definition of a netflow can be seen by looking at the Brock - Ackerman example presented in the introduction. Recall that the only difference between the dataflow networks N_1 and N_2 was given by the two processes buf_1 and buf_2. When presented with an input sequence of length greater than 1, they both output the first two elements of that sequence. The difference between them is given by causality, and we see this in their netflow representations B_1 and B_2. The input sequence $a_1 \ldots a_n \ldots$ of length greater than 1 is represented by a configuration C on α with elements $x_1 < \ldots < x_n < \ldots$, $l_C(x_k) = a_k, \forall k$. Let the configuration D on β denote $B_i(C)$. Then D is a configuration with two elements, $y_1 < y_2$, $l_D(y_1) = l_D(y_2)$. The action of the netflows B_1 and B_2 on the configuration C can be seen in Figure 3. Let $D_1 \leq D$ be the configuration with only one element: y_1. Consider the configurations $C_1, C_2 \leq C$ such that C_1 has only the element x_1, and C_2 has the elements $x_1 < x_2$. Then $cause_{B_1}(D_1) = C_1$ because $B_1(C_1) = D_1$ and $B_1(\varepsilon_{\{\beta\}}) = \varepsilon_{\{\delta\}}$. However, $cause_{B_2}(D_1) = C_2$ because $B_2(C_2) = D_1$ and $B_2(C_1) = \varepsilon_{\{\delta\}}$. In other words, the first data item a_1 produced as output by B_2 is caused by the input sequence $a_1 a_2$, not just by a_1.

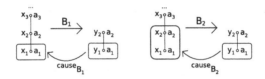

Fig. 3. The netflows B_1 and B_2

Let $\mathcal{N}(A, B)$ denote the class of netflows from $\mathcal{C}(A)$ to $Lflow(B)$. The map φ is also continuous with respect to $\leq$ because if $C = \text{Sup}_i C_i$ for a directed family of configurations $\{C_i\}$, then (similarly to Proposition 5) it follows that $C = C_{i_0}$ and so $\varphi(C)$ is indeed the supremum of $\{\varphi(C_i)\}_{i \in I}$ in $(Lflow(B), \leq)$.

The following result will be used to extend φ to a map which takes labelled flows into labelled flows.

Lemma 11. *If C is a configuration and f is a labelled flow in* Lflow(A) *such that $C \leq \sup\{\varphi(D) \mid D \leq f\}$, then there exists a configuration $E \leq f$ such that $C \leq \varphi(E)$.*

Proof. If $A = \{\alpha_1, \ldots, \alpha_n\}$ and for $i \in \{1, \ldots, n\}$ let x_i be the maximal element in $[C(\alpha_i)]$. Let $C_i = \{y \mid y \leq_C x_i\}$ and $C_{ij} = \{y \mid y \leq_C x_i \text{ or } y \leq_C x_j\}$ (such that $C_i, C_{ij} \leq C$). Since C_i, C_{ij} are prime configurations and $C \leq \sup\{\varphi(D) \mid D \leq f\}$, from Proposition 5 it follows that $C_{ij}, C_i \in \mathcal{C}(B)_\varphi$ and so there exist $E_i = cause_\varphi(C_i)$ and $E_{ij} = cause_\varphi(C_{ij})$. Since $C_{ij} = \text{Sup}\{C_i, C_j\}$ we have $E_{ij} = \text{Sup}\{E_i, E_j\}$ (according to Remark 9). We prove now that there exists $\text{Sup}_i E_i$. Consider E given by $E(\alpha_k) = \cup_i E_i(\alpha_k)$, with $x \leq_E y$ iff there exists i such that $x \leq_{E_i} y$, and $\#_E = \emptyset$. Then E is well defined (because there exists $\text{Sup}\{E_i, E_j\}$), and it is the supremum of E_i in $\mathcal{C}(A)$. We prove that $C \leq \varphi(E)$. Since $C_{ij} \leq \varphi(E)$ it follows that $|C| \prec |\varphi(E)|$. If $x, y \in |C|$ such that $(x, y) \in \#_{\varphi(E)}$ then $x \in C(\alpha_{i_1}), y \in C(\alpha_{i_2})$ therefore $x, y \in |C_{i_1 i_2}|$, so $(x, y) \in \#_{C_{i_1 i_2}}$. We have obtained that $\varphi(E)$ has no conflicts in $|C|$, and thus we reach the conclusion. $\square$

We build an extension of φ to $Lflow(A)$ by

$$\bar{\varphi} : Lflow(A) \rightarrow Lflow(B), \bar{\varphi}(f) = \sup\{\varphi(D) \mid D \leq f\}$$

Lemma 11 can be rephrased as: if $C \leq \bar{\varphi}(f)$ then $\exists\ cause_\varphi(C) \leq f$.

Proposition 12. $\bar{\varphi}$ is continuous with respect to both $\leq$ and $\sqsubseteq$.

Proof. First, we prove that $\bar{\varphi}$ is monotone with respect to $\leq$. Consider two labelled flows $f \leq g$ in $Lflow(A)$. By the definition of $\bar{\varphi}$ it follows that $\bar{\varphi}(f) \sqsubseteq \bar{\varphi}(g)$. We prove that $\#_{\bar{\varphi}(g)}|_{|\bar{\varphi}(f)| \times |\bar{\varphi}(f)|} \supseteq \#_{\bar{\varphi}(f)}$.

Consider $x, y \in |\bar{\varphi}(f)|$ such that $(x, y) \notin \#_{\bar{\varphi}(g)}$. Let C be the labelled flow $C \leq \bar{\varphi}(g)$ with x, y the only maximal elements; C is a configuration because $(x, y) \notin \#_{\bar{\varphi}(g)}$. Let C_x be the labelled flow $C_x \leq \bar{\varphi}(f)$ with x the only maximal element and we define C_y similarly; C_x and C_y are also configurations. By Lemma 11 there exist $E = cause_\varphi(C)$, $E_x = cause_\varphi(C_x)$ and $E_y = cause_\varphi(C_y)$. Since $\bar{\varphi}(f) \sqsubseteq \bar{\varphi}(g)$ it follows that $C = \text{Sup}\{C_x, C_y\}$; then $E = \text{Sup}\{E_x, E_y\}$ by Remark 9. Since $f \leq g$ and $E \leq g$ it follows that $\inf\{E, f\}$ is a configuration which we denote by D. It follows that $E_x, E_y \leq D$, so $E \leq D$; therefore $E \leq f$. We have obtained that $C \leq \bar{\varphi}(f)$, so $(x, y) \notin \#_{\bar{\varphi}(f)}$.

Secondly, we prove that if $\{f_i\}_{i \in I}$ is a directed family in $(Lflow(A), \sqsubseteq)$ then $\bar{\varphi}(\sup_i f_i) = \sup_i \bar{\varphi}(f_i)$. Clearly, $\bar{\varphi}$ is monotone with respect to $\sqsubseteq$, so $\bar{\varphi}(\sup_i f_i) \sqsupseteq \sup_i \bar{\varphi}(f_i)$. Let C be a configuration such that $C \leq \bar{\varphi}(\sup_i f_i)$. Then there exists $D \leq \sup_i f_i$ such that $C \leq \varphi(D)$. Since $\{f_i\}$ is directed, by Proposition 5 it follows that there exists $i_0 \in I$ such that $D \leq f_{i_0}$. We have obtained that $C \leq \sup_i \bar{\varphi}(f_i)$, hence the conclusion.

Thirdly, if $\{f_i\}$ is a directed family with supremum f in $(Lflow(A), \leq)$ then $\{f_i\}$ is also a directed family with supremum f in $(Lflow(()A), \sqsubseteq)$. Moreover, $\{\bar{\varphi}(f_i)\}_{i \in I}$ is directed in $(Lflow(A), \leq)$ and so it has a supremum g. Since g is also the supremum of $\{\bar{\varphi}(f_i)\}$ in $(Lflow(()A), \sqsubseteq)$ it follows by the continuity of $\bar{\varphi}$ with respect to $\sqsubseteq$ that $g = \bar{\varphi}(f)$. $\square$

The reason for introducing an extension is provided by the definition of sequential composition. If $\varphi \in \mathcal{N}(A, A')$ and $\psi \in \mathcal{N}(A', A'')$ we define their sequential composition $\psi * \varphi : \mathcal{C}(A) \rightarrow Lflow(A'')$ by $\psi * \varphi = \bar{\psi} \circ \varphi$.

Proposition 13. *The sequential composition of two netflows is a netflow. Moreover, the sequential composition $*$ is associative.*

To prove name invariance for sequential composition we use the following result:

Lemma 14. *Consider $\varphi \in \mathcal{N}(A, B)$ and $f, g \in$ Lflow(A). If $r : f \to g$ is an isomorphism, then there exists an isomorphism $q : \bar{\varphi}(f) \to \bar{\varphi}(g)$ such that $f' \leq f$ implies $q(\varphi(f')) = \varphi(r(f))$.*

To introduce parallel composition of netflows we first define the parallel composition of two labelled flows.

Definition 15. *Let A_1, A_2 be two disjoint finite sets. If $g_1 \in$ Lflow(A_1) and $g_2 \in$ Lflow(A_2) we denote by $g_1 || g_2$ the labelled flow $\in$ Lflow$(A_1 \cup A_2)$ defined by*

- $|g_1 || g_2| = |g_1| \cup |g_2|$;
- $x \leq y$ in $[g_1 || g_2]$ iff $\exists i$ such that $x, y \in |g_i|$ and $x \leq_{g_i} y$;
- $x \# y$ in $g_1 || g_2$ iff $\exists i$ such that $x, y \in |g_i|$ and $x \#_{g_i} y$, for $i \in \{1, 2\}$.

Note that because A_1 and A_2 are disjoint the tags of elements from $|g_1|$ are distinct from tags of elements from $|g_2|$ so $|g_1| \cap |g_2| = \emptyset$.

Definition 16. *Let A_1, A_2, B_1, B_2 be finite sets such that $A_1 \cap A_2 = B_1 \cap B_2 = \emptyset$. The parallel composition of two netflows $\varphi_i \in \mathcal{N}(A_i, B_i)$, $i \in \{1, 2\}$ is*

$$\varphi_1 || \varphi_2 : \text{Lflow}(A_1 \cup A_2) \to \text{Lflow}(B_1 \cup B_2), \varphi_1 || \varphi_2(C) = \varphi_1(C_1) || \varphi_2(C_2)$$

where C_i is the restriction $C|_{A_i}$ of the configuration C to the set of channels A_i.

Proposition 17. *$\varphi_1 || \varphi_2$ is a netflow. Moreover, parallel composition of netflows is associative.*

3.1 Feedback

Another operation on netflows is feedback, through which we infer the behaviour of a dataflow network obtained by connecting some output channels to some (corresponding) input channels starting from the behaviour of that dataflow network. Let A, B, O be three sets such that $O \cap A = O \cap B = \emptyset$. For $\varphi \in \mathcal{N}(O + A, O + B)$ we look for a netflow $\uparrow^O \varphi$ which behaves as φ with every output channel $\omega \in O$ connected to the input channel with the same name. We start from the deterministic case. A netflow is called deterministic if it takes configurations into configurations. Since every netflow is name invariant, a deterministic netflow is equivalent to a continuous function between sets of strings. *Kahn's principle* states that deterministic dataflow networks are modelled by continuous functions between sets of strings over V and that feedback is obtained by setting $\uparrow^O f(t) = f|_B(s_t, t)$, where f is such a continuous function taking sets of strings indexed by $O \cup A$ to sets of strings indexed by $O \cap B$ and s_t is the least fixed point of the function $s \mapsto f|_O(s, t)$ (see Figure 4).

This procedure cannot be applied directly to the nondeterministic case; suppose we consider g_D the fixed point of the function $g \mapsto \bar{\varphi}|_\omega(g || D)$ and take $\uparrow^O \varphi(D) = \bar{\varphi}|_B(g_D || D)$. Then among the configurations of g_D will be some which contain elements which have appeared before the elements which cause them to appear (in a previous iteration).

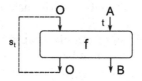

Fig. 4. Feedback in deterministic dataflow

Example 18. We consider a dataflow network which whenever receives two numbers (on channel ω or α) it outputs their sum on channel ω and their product on channel β. Let $\varphi \in \mathcal{N}(\{\omega, \alpha\}, \{\omega, \beta\})$ be a netflow which models it. We look for g_D when the input D is the sequence 1-3-5-7, i.e. for example the configuration $D = \{(\alpha, x) < (\alpha, y) < (\alpha, z) < (\alpha, t)\}$ with $l(\alpha, x) = 1, l(\alpha, y) = 3, l(\alpha, z) = 5$ and $l(\alpha, t) = 7$ (recall that *name invariance* assures us it does not matter what are the names of the elements of D). Then $g_D = \sup\{h_n| \ h_n = \bar{\varphi}|_O(h_{n-1}||D)\}$, $h_0 = \varepsilon_O$. We have $h_1 = \{(\omega, a) < (\omega, b)| \ l(\omega, a) = 4, l(\omega, b) = 12$ therefore in $h_2 = \bar{\varphi}|_O(h_1||D)$ the value $4+1$ can appear as label for one of the elements. Since $h_2 \leq g_D$ it follows that 5 can also appear as label in g_0 which clearly should not happen, since 4 is caused by 1 (see Figure 5).

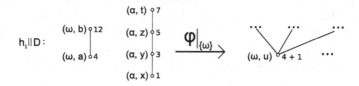

Fig. 5. $h_2 = \bar{\varphi}|_O(h_1||D)$

To "prune" such configurations from the tree structure of g_D we define $\uparrow^O\varphi$ as follows:

Definition 19. *Let $\varphi : \mathcal{C}(O \cup A) \rightarrow$ Lflow$(O \cup B)$ be a netflow. Let $F\bar{\varphi} :$ Lflow$(O \cup A) \rightarrow$ Lflow$(O \cup B)$ be given by*

$$F\bar{\varphi}(f) = \sup\{C| \ C \leq \bar{\varphi}(f), C \text{ valid configuration }\}$$

where a configuration C is valid *if (cause$_\varphi C$)$|_O \leq C|_O$.*

For any configuration D in Lflow(A) *let g_D be the least fixed point of the function $g \mapsto F\bar{\varphi}|_O(g||D)$ and we define*

$$\uparrow^O\varphi : \mathcal{C}(A) \rightarrow \text{Lflow}(B), \uparrow^O\varphi(D) = F\bar{\varphi}|_B(g_D||D)$$

This definition ensures that all elements which appear in g_D are preceded by their cause. It also ensures that all elements which appear in $\uparrow^O\varphi(D)$ are obtained by processing the input in the correct order - we select from $\bar{\varphi}|_B(g_D||D)$ only those configurations which are not in conflict with their own cause from $Lflow(O)$, cause which we already know is valid.

Let us look again at the previous example, that of the dataflow network which adds and multiplies whichever two numbers it receives. First, we find the fixed point g_D. We have $g_D = \sup\{g_D^1, \ldots, g_D^n, \ldots\}$ where $g_D^n = F\bar{\varphi}|_O(g_D^{n-1}||D)$ and $g_D^0 = \varepsilon_\omega$. Then $g_D^1 = \{(\omega, a) < (\omega, b)| \ l(\omega, a) = 4, l(\omega, b) = 12\}$. We have $g_D^2 \leq \varphi|_\omega(g_D^1||D)$. The reasoning by which we find g_D^2 can be followed by looking at Figure 6 (the elements in bold font are those which remain after discarding non-valid configurations).

Let C be one of the configurations in $\varphi|_\omega(g_D^1||D)$ that has $4+1$ as label for the first element x_0. If C is valid then $cause_\varphi(C_{x_0}||\varepsilon_B)|_\omega \leq C_{x_0} = \{x_0| \ l(x_0) = 5\}$. But $cause_\varphi(C_{x_0}||\varepsilon_B)|_\omega = \{(\omega, a)| \ l(\omega, a) = 4\}$, which leads to a contradiction. Similarly, any configuration on ω with label $4 + 12$ for its first element can be discarded. Therefore the only valid configurations can be found among those with label $1+3$ for the first element on the channel ω. The options for the label of the second element are $4+12$, $4+5$ or $5+7$. If a valid configuration has label $4+12$ for its second element let C' be the simple finite configuration formed of the first and second element. But $(cause_\varphi C'||\varepsilon_B)|_\omega = g_D^1$ and clearly $g_D^1 \not\leq C'$. Therefore the label of the second element can only be $4 + 5$ or $4 + 7$. In the first case, the only possibility for the label of a third element is $12 + 7$ and that produces a non-valid configuration. In the second case, the only possibility for the label of a third element is $4 + 12$ and that produces a valid configuration. There are no more possibilities left, so g_D^2 is given by $g_D^2(\omega) = \{(\omega, a), (\omega, b), (\omega, c), (\omega, d)\}$ where $l(\omega, a) = 4$, $l(\omega, b) = 12$, $l(\omega, c) = 16$, $l(\omega, d) = 9$ and $(\omega, a) < (\omega, b) < (\omega, c)$, $(\omega, a) < (\omega, d)$, $(\omega, b)\#(\omega, d)$. By repeating this reasoning we find that $g_D = g_D^3$, where g_D^3 is given by $g_D^3(\omega) = \{(\omega, a), (\omega, b), (\omega, c), (\omega, d), (\omega, e)\}$ such that $g_D^2 \leq g_D^3$ and $l(\omega, e) = 16$, $(\omega, d) < (\omega, e)$.

Fig. 6. Finding g_D^2

Let us look now at the output on channel β. The expected output is a labelled flow with only two configurations, one with the string of labels $1 \cdot 3$ - $4 \cdot 5$ - $9 \cdot 7$ and the other with the string of labels $1 \cdot 3$ - $5 \cdot 7$ - $4 \cdot 12$, which have the first element in common. Let $C_1 = \{(\omega, a) < (\omega, b) < (\omega, c)\}$ and $C_2 = \{(\omega, a) < (\omega, d) < (\omega, e)\}$ be the two maximal configurations of g_D. The reasoning involved in finding all valid configurations in $\varphi(g_D||D)$ can be followed by looking at Figure 7.

Let E be a valid configuration in $\varphi(g_D||D)$. Suppose the label of the first element y_1 of $E|_B$ is $4 \cdot 1$; then the label of the first element u_1 of $cause_\varphi(C_{y_1})|_\omega$ is 4, which is obtained by adding 1 with 3 and is therefore in conflict with the

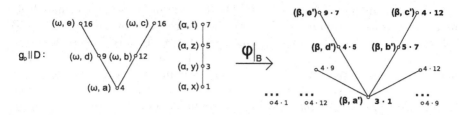

Fig. 7. Finding $\uparrow^O \varphi(D)$

first element of $E|_B$. Similarly we find out that the label of y_1 cannot be $4 \cdot 9$ or $4 \cdot 12$, i.e. $y_1 = (\beta, a')$. If $E|_B$ has a second element y_2 its label can be $4 \cdot 9$, $4 \cdot 12$, $4 \cdot 5$ or $5 \cdot 7$. Suppose that label is $4 \cdot 12$. Then $cause_\varphi(C_{y_2})|_\omega$ has a second element u_2 with label 12; u_2 has been produced by adding 5 to 7 so it is in conflict with y_2. Similarly we prove that the label of y_2 cannot be $4 \cdot 12$. If it is $4 \cdot 5$ or $5 \cdot 7$ then $\{y_1 < y_2\}$ is a valid configuration. Suppose the label of y_2 is $4 \cdot 5$, i.e. $y_2 = (\beta, d')$. If E has a third element y_3 then its label can be $9 \cdot 7$ or $12 \cdot 7$. If it is $12 \cdot 7$ then we should have $cause_\varphi(C_{y_3})|_\omega = (\{(\omega, a) < (\omega, d)\} < E|_\omega$ but (ω, d) is in conflict with (β, d'), the second element of E. Thus $y_3 = (\beta, e')$. Following a similar reasoning for the case $y_2 = (\beta, b')$ we find that the output is the expected one.

In these examples we have identified elements by their labels even if the labels are not used in defining feedback in order to avoid complicating the explanation by using a large number of names for the elements.

To prove the correctness of Definition 19 we need two lemmas.

Lemma 20. *If C is a configuration such that $C \leq F\bar\varphi(f)$ and there exists $g \leq f$ such that $C \leq \bar\varphi(g)$ and $g|_O \leq \bar\varphi|_O(g)$ then $C \leq F\bar\varphi(g)$.*

Lemma 21. *If $f \leq g$ and $f|_O \leq \bar\varphi|_O(f)$ then $F\bar\varphi(f) \leq F\bar\varphi(g)$. Moreover, $F\bar\varphi$ preserves suprema for directed families $\{f_i\}$ with respect to $\leq$ and $\sqsubseteq$ if every f_i has the property $f_i|_O \leq \bar\varphi|_O(f_i)$.*

Theorem 22. *$\uparrow^O \varphi : \mathcal{C}(A) \to \mathrm{Lflow}(B)$ is correctly defined and is a netflow.*

Proof. First, consider $g_D = \sup_n g_D^n$, where $g_D^{n+1} = F\bar\varphi|_O(g_D^n||D)$ and $g_D^0 = \varepsilon_O$. We see that $g_D^n \leq g_D^{n+1}$ inductively because of Lemma 21 and because $g_D^n||D$ verifies the condition. Therefore g_D is the least fixed point of $g \mapsto F\bar\varphi|_O(g||D)$, also from Lemma 21. Moreover, $\uparrow^O \varphi$ is monotone with respect to $\leq$ because $D \leq E$ implies $g_D \leq g_E$, by induction.

Secondly, we prove the existence of $cause_{\uparrow^O\varphi}$. Consider C such that $C \leq F\bar\varphi|_B(g_D||D)$. Then $\varepsilon_O||C \leq \bar\varphi(g_D||D)$ so, by Lemma 11, $\exists F_0 = cause_\varphi(\varepsilon_O||C) \leq g_D||D$. Because $g_D \leq \bar\varphi|_O(g_D||D)$ we can define inductively a sequence of configurations F_n such that $F_{n+1} = cause_\varphi(F_n|_O||\varepsilon_B)$ and $F_{n+1}|_O \leq g_D, F_{n+1}|_A \leq D$. Then there exists $G = Sup_n F_n|_A \leq D$ and we set $cause_{\uparrow^O\varphi}(C) = G$. Note that G does not depend on D. We now prove that

$C \leq \uparrow^O \varphi(E)$ if and only if $cause_{\uparrow^O \varphi} \leq E$. The direct implication is immediate from the mode of construction of G. To prove the reverse we show that $C \leq \uparrow^O \varphi(G)$ and we use the monotonicity of $\uparrow^O \varphi$ with respect to $\leq$. To this purpose note that $F_0|_O \leq g_D = \sup g_D^n$ and $\{g_D^n\}_n$ is a directed family in $(Lflow(O), \leq)$. Therefore there exists m such that $F_0|_O \leq g_D^m$; we obtain inductively that $F_n|_O \leq g_D^{m-n}$, for $n \leq m$. This means that $F_m|_O = \varepsilon_B$ and so $F_m \leq g_G||G$. Therefore $F_{m-1}|_O||\varepsilon_B \leq \varphi(F_m) \leq \bar\varphi(g_G||G)$. Using Lemma 20 and the fact that $g_G \leq g_D$ and $(g_G||G)|_O = g_G \leq \bar\varphi(g_G||G)$ we obtain that $F_{m-1}|_O||\varepsilon_B \leq F\bar\varphi(g_G||G)$ i.e. $F_{m-1}|_O \leq g_G$. In the end we obtain $\varepsilon_O||C \leq \varphi(F_0) \leq \bar\varphi(g_G||G)$. The conclusion follows from Lemma 20 and the fact that $\varepsilon_O||C \leq F\bar\varphi(g_D||D)$.

Thirdly, we prove name invariance. Let $h_0 : D \to E$ be an isomorphism. We construct inductively a sequence $h_{n+1} : F\bar\varphi(g_D^n||D) \to F\bar\varphi(g_E^n||E)$ of isomorphisms such that $h_{n+1}(g_D^n) = g_E^n$, $\forall n \geq 1$, as follows. There exists $\bar h_1 : \bar\varphi(\varepsilon_O||D) \to \bar\varphi(\varepsilon_O||E)$, by name invariance and since $F\bar\varphi(\varepsilon_O||D) = \bar\varphi(\varepsilon_O||D)$, there exists the isomorphism h_1. Since $h_1|_{g_D^1} : g_D^1 \to g_E^1$ is an isomorphism there exists $\bar h_2 : \bar\varphi(g_D^1||D) \to \bar\varphi(g_E^1||E)$ isomorphism. We show that $\bar h_2(F\bar\varphi(g_D^1||D)) = F\bar\varphi(g_E^1||E)$ and we set h_2 to be the restriction of $\bar h_2$ to $F\bar\varphi(g_D^1||D)$. We have $\bar h_2(g_D^1) = \bar\varphi|_O(h_1(g_D^0||D)) = g_E^1$. Consider $C \leq \bar\varphi(g_D^1||D)$. Then C is valid if and only if $\bar h_2(C)$ is valid because $cause_\varphi(C)|_O \leq g_D^1$, therefore $cause_\varphi(C)|_O \leq C|_O$ if and only if $h_1(cause_\varphi(C)|_O) = \bar h_2(cause_\varphi(C)|_O) \leq \bar h_2(C|_O)$ iff $cause_\varphi(\bar h_2(C))|_O \leq \bar h_2(C)|_O$. We have proved the existence of h_2; the inductive construction is continued in the same manner. We now define an isomorphism $h : F\bar\varphi(g_D||D) \to F\bar\varphi(g_E||E)$ by setting $h(x) = h_{n+1}(x)$, where $x \in |F\bar\varphi(g_D||D)|$. Then h is well defined because $h_{n+1}(g_D^n) = h_n(g_D^n)$; by the construction of suprema of directed labelled flows we see that h is a order and conflict preserving bijection.   □

We now return to the deterministic case. It is clear that the sequential or parallel composition of deterministic netflows produce deterministic netflows. The following proposition states that the fixpoint construction we have presented coincides, in the deterministic case, with Kahn's fixpoint construction.

Proposition 23. *If φ is deterministic then $\uparrow^O \varphi(D) = \varphi|_B(C_D||D)$, where C_D is the least fixed point of the function $g \mapsto \varphi|_O(g||D)$.*

Proof. Let $C_D^{n+1} = \varphi|_O(C_n||D)$, $C_0 = \varepsilon_O$ and $g_D^{n+1} = F\bar\varphi|_O(g_D^n||D)$, $g_D^0 = \varepsilon_O$. Then $C_D = \sup_n C_D^n$ and $g_D = \sup_n g_D^n$. We prove by induction on n that $g_D^n = C_D^n$ for all $n \geq 0$. We know that $g_D^0 = C_0$. If for some n we have $g_D^n = C_n$, then we prove that $g_D^{n+1} = C_D^{n+1}$. Let $E := \varphi(C_D^n||D)$; then E is valid because $cause_\varphi(E)|_O =\leq C_D^n \leq C_D^{n+1} = \varphi|_O(C_D^n||D) = E|_O$. Therefore $C_D^{n+1} = F\bar\varphi(g_D^n||D) = g_D^{n+1}$. Therefore $C_D = g_D$. Then $\varphi(C_D||D)$ is valid and so $F\bar\varphi(g_D||D) = \varphi(C_D||D)$, thus $\uparrow \varphi(D) = \varphi|_B(C_D||D)$.   □

The explicit notion of causality that we introduced is strong enough to ensure that the well-known causal anomalies (like the one presented by Brock and Ackerman [3]) are avoided. Here we treat the example provided by Russell [11], following the variant described in [12].

Consider a dataflow network P_1 which either outputs a token before receiving any input token and stops, or outputs a token and when it receives an input token outputs another token and stops. Consider also a dataflow network P_2 which outputs a token before receiving any input token and stops, or when it receives an input token, outputs two tokens and stops. Note that P_1 and P_2 have the same input-output relation: $\{(\varepsilon, t), (t, t), (t, tt)\}$, where t represents a token. However, there exists a context which distinguishes between P_1 and P_2. Let F be the *fork* network, which copies every input it receives on its two output channels. If Q_i is the network obtained by composing F with P_i and connecting one of the output channels of F to the input channel of P_i, then Q_1 outputs one or two tokens while Q_2 outputs only one token. This example shows that a denotational semantics for nondeterministic dataflow must have a notion of causality more descriptive than that given by the input/output relation.

We model each P_i by $\xi_i : \mathcal{C}(\{\omega\}) \to Lflow(\{\beta\})$ and F by $\phi : \mathcal{C}(\{\beta\}) \to Lflow(\{\omega, \omega'\})$. Then ϕ is given by $\phi(D) = D_1 || D_2$ where $D_1 = D$ and D_2 is in $\mathcal{C}(\{\omega'\})$ such that if (ω, u) is an element of D the corresponding element of D_2 is (ω', u). Let $C \in \mathcal{C}(\{\omega\})$ and $h_i, k_i \in Lflow(\{\beta\})$ be as follows: $|C| = C(\omega) = \{x\}$; $|h_1| = h_1(\omega) = \{a, b\}$ with $a\#b$; $|k_1| = k_1(\omega) = \{a, b, x'\}$ with $a\#b$, $b < x'$; $|h_2| = h_2(\omega) = \{a\}$; $k_2 = \{a, x_1, x_2\}$ with $a\#x_1$, $x_1 < x_2$. Then ξ_i are given by $\xi(\varepsilon_w) = h_i$ and $\xi_i(f) = k_i$ for $i \in \{1, 2\}$; also, if D is a configuration with first element x_0 then $\xi_i(D) = \xi_i(C_{x_0})$ which is isomorphic to $\xi_i(C)$. The description of ξ_i is also given graphically in Figure 8 (we omit the labels of the elements since they are all t). Clearly, $\xi_1 \neq \xi_2$. Moreover, by using definition 19 we obtain the expected output: $\uparrow_w \phi * \xi_1$ has two configurations, one with one element and the other with two elements, while $\uparrow_w \phi * \xi_2$ has only one configuration, that being h_2.

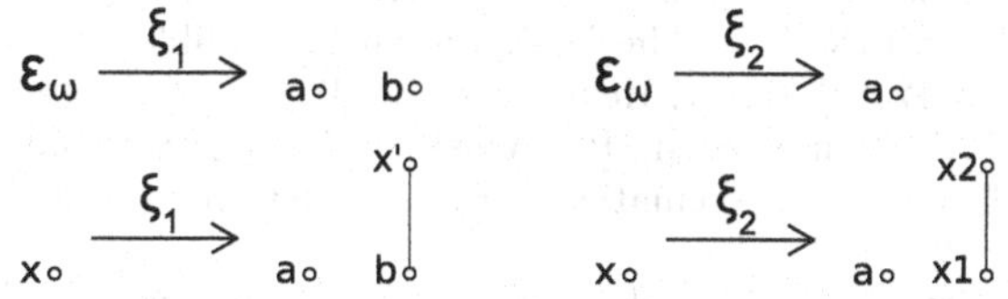

Fig. 8. ξ_1 and ξ_2

4   Conclusion

Labelled flows provide an intuitive way of expressing nondeterminism for dataflow networks. The order relations defined on sets $Lflow(A)$ yield a rich mathematical structure for the model we present in this paper, which integrates causality in a functional setting. To our knowledge such a representation of causality is novel. The problem of expressing causality is not a trivial one; the greatest difficulties appear when describing feedback. As can be seen in the proof of Theorem 22, it is not easy to define the cause of a configuration which appears in the output of $\uparrow^O \varphi$ in terms of its cause with respect to φ.

There are several models describing the nondeterministic case, of which we mention a few. Jonsson has presented a fully abstract interleaving semantics based on traces (i.e., sequences of communication events) [7]. Gaifman and Pratt have presented a semantics based on partially ordered multisets (pomsets) [6]. Abramsky has generalised Kahn's principle to a family of models which include both the trace and the pomset model [1]. Hildebrandt, Panangaden and Winskel present the trace model as an instance of a traced monoidal category, using profunctors as generalisation of relations [5]. Saunders-Evans and Winskel describe a model based on spans of event structures which are representations of certain profunctors [12].

Several of these papers present interleaving semantics. The difference from these papers is that we present a non-interleaving semantics. With respect to the papers presenting non-interleaving semantics, the difference resides in the explicit treatment of causality. In this way we solve the well-known causal anomalies (e.g., Brock and Ackerman anomaly). We use the example provided by Russell to show how our formal approach solves causal anomalies of nondeterministic dataflow.

References

1. Abramsky, S.: A Generalized Kahn Principle for Abstract Asynchronous Networks. In: Schmidt, D.A., Main, M.G., Melton, A.C., Mislove, M.W. (eds.) MFPS 1989. LNCS, vol. 442, pp. 1–21. Springer, Heidelberg (1990)
2. Abramsky, S., Jung, A.: Domain Theory. In: Handbook of Logic in Computer Science, vol. III, pp. 1–168. Clarendon Press (1994)
3. Brock, J., Ackerman, W.: Formalization of Programming Concepts. LNCS, vol. 107, pp. 252–259. Springer, Heidelberg (1981)
4. Erné, M., Koslowski, J., Melton, A., Strecker, G.E.: A Primer on Galois Connections. In: Paulisch, F.N. (ed.) The Design of an Extendible Graph Editor. LNCS, vol. 704, pp. 103–125. Springer, Heidelberg (1993)
5. Hildebrandt, T.T., Panangaden, P., Winskel, G.: A Relational Model of Non-Deterministic Dataflow. Mathematical Structures in Computer Science 14, 613–649 (2004)
6. Gaifman, H., Pratt, V.R.: Partial Order Models of Concurrency and the Computation of Functions. Logic in Computer Science, 72–85 (1987)
7. Jonsson, B.: A Fully Abstract Trace Model for Dataflow Networks. Principles of Programming Languages, 155–165 (1989)
8. Kahn, G.: The Semantics of a Simple Language for Parallel Programming. In: IFIP Congress, pp. 471–475 (1974)
9. Najjar, W.A., Lee, E.A., Gao, G.R.: Advances in the Dataflow Computational Model. Parallel Computing 25, 1907–1929 (1999)
10. Nielson, M., Plotkin, G.D., Winskel, G.: Petri Nets, Event Structures and Domains. Rechnerstrukturen und Betriebsprogrammierung 13, 85–108 (1981)
11. Russell, J.R.: Full Abstraction for Nondeterministic Dataflow Networks. Foundations of Computer Science, 170–175 (1989)
12. Saunders-Evans, L., Winskel, G.: Event Structure Spans for Nondeterministic Dataflow. Electronic Notes of Theoretical Computer Science 175, 109–129 (2007)

Symbolic Reachability for Process Algebras with Recursive Data Types

Stefan Blom and Jaco van de Pol[*]

Formal Methods and Tools, Department of Computer Science, University of Twente,
P.O. Box 217, 7500AE Enschede, The Netherlands
{sccblom,vdpol}@cs.utwente.nl

Abstract. In this paper, we present a symbolic reachability algorithm for process algebras with recursive data types. Like the various saturation based algorithms of Ciardo et al, the algorithm is based on partitioning of the transition relation into events whose influence is local. As new features, our algorithm supports recursive data types and allows unbounded non-determinism, which is needed to support open systems with data. The algorithm does not use any specific features of process algebras. That is, it will work for any system that consists of a fixed number of communicating processes, where in each atomic step only a subset of the processes participate. As proof of concept we have implemented the algorithm in the context of the μCRL toolset. We also compared the performance of this prototype with the performance of the existing explicit tools on a set of typical case studies.

1   Introduction

High level formalisms, such as Petri Nets and Process Algebras are powerful languages for specifying systems. When combined with recursive data types, they become even more powerful. However, we have to pay a price for this expressiveness. Analyzing these specifications with symbolic techniques is difficult, because it is not easy to translate them to a formalism where the state is a vector of booleans. Thus, toolsets for process algebras with data, such as CADP [1,2], FDR [3] and μCRL [4] rely on explicit state techniques. The former two exploit compositional techniques to extend the size of the state space that can be dealt with. For the latter, we present a symbolic technique based on decision diagrams in this paper.

Computing the set of reachable states is a good way to perform model checking tasks such as the verification of safety properties. But it can be an expensive computation. Therefore much work has gone into avoiding doing so. The entire fields of bounded model checking and on-the-fly model checking are devoted to developing methods that can give useful results without having to perform a complete reachability analysis. However, any exhaustive technique will need to perform a reachability analysis somehow, so we use this as a first step towards building a complete symbolic tool chain.

* This work has been partially funded by the EU under grant number FP6-NEST STREP 043235 (EC-MOAN).

J.S. Fitzgerald, A.E. Haxthausen, and H. Yenigun (Eds.): ICTAC 2008, LNCS 5160, pp. 81–95, 2008.

Contribution and related work. In the area of quantitative evaluation, symbolic techniques already exist. The Petri Net based tool SMART [5] implements a powerful technique called saturation [6]. Also, symbolic techniques have been developed for a stochastic process algebra and implemented in the tool CASPA [7,8]. The most general algorithm is the one used in SMART. But, it does not have support for two features that are fundamental for the process algebra μCRL and an optional extension for Petri Nets: infinite data types and non-deterministic events.

Infinite data types are due to the fact that in μCRL one can define recursive data types. Non-deterministic events arise if one needs to model a random input while modeling an open system. For example, in μCRL, we can write a 1-place buffer as follows:

$$X = \sum_{x \in \mathbb{N}} read(x).write(x).X \text{ where } \mathbb{N} ::= 0 \mid \mathsf{succ}(\mathbb{N}) \ .$$

If a *read*-event happens then the argument must be chosen from an infinite set. In practice, choices like this will be from a finite set, which is not known a priori. Thus, we do not know a priori a limit on the branching degree. In a classical Petri Net, events are deterministic: once an event is chosen the result is fixed because no matter which tokens are selected the result will be identical. In a colored Petri Net, events can also be non-deterministic. If an event is chosen then selecting tokens with different colors can still lead to different results. If a finite superset of the used colors is known in advance a colored Petri Net can be encoded as a monochrome Petri Net. The algorithms, which are implemented in SMART rely on deterministic events. In our tool we extend the algorithms to deal with non-deterministic events. As the underlying data structure, we do not use MDDs with in-place updates, as in [9]. We use a decision diagram formalism which mixes features from MDDs and ZDDs instead. Moreover, we use a classical BDD style next state computation rather than in-place updates.

Overview. The remainder of this paper is organized as follows. In the next section, we discuss some of the basics of explicit state space generation and symbolic reachability analysis. In Sect. 3 we discuss the principle of event locality and how that notion leads to a partitioning of the symbolic transition relation and a refactoring of the next state code for explicit tools. This is followed by a presentation of our grey box reachability algorithm. The next section contains some remarks on how this algorithm was implemented for the μCRL toolset. Section 6 presents the results of a few experiments performed with that prototype and we conclude with a discussion of the results so far and future work.

2   Preliminaries

The semantics of modeling formalisms used in model checking are always some form of transition system. The basic structure of a transition system is defined below.

Definition 1. *A transition system (TS) is a tuple $\langle S, R, s^0 \rangle$, where S is a set of states, $R \subseteq S \times S$ is the transition relation and $s^0 \in S$ is the initial state*

For practical purposes, one needs to attach labels to either states (e.g. atomic propositions) or the transitions (e.g. actions) or both. These labels are not essential to the presentation in this paper, so we omit them. What is essential is that states have a vector structure. In this paper, we assume that a state is a fixed length vector. From now on N will stand for the length of the vector and D_i for $i = 1 \cdots N$ will be the domain of the ith element. Thus the set of states S is given as

$$S = D_1 \times \cdots \times D_N .$$

When the set of states is defined as a tuple like this, it is inevitable that not all states are reachable. In fact, for μCRL many sets D_i are the semantics of a recursive data type and hence infinite. In the remainder, we assume a *single initial state* and a *finite set of reachable states*.

Definition 2. *Given a transition system $\mathcal{L} \equiv \langle S, R, s^0 \rangle$. The set of reachable states is*

$$V = \{s \in S \mid s^0 \ R^* \ s\} .$$

A state $s \in S$ is reachable if $s \in V$.

Usually, we build the set of reachable states using a breadth first strategy. Thus, we define level i (denoted L_i) as the set of states whose distance to the initial state is i. The set of states at distance less than or equal to i is denoted V_i. The union of all V_i is V:

Proposition 1. *Given a transition system $\mathcal{L} \equiv \langle S, R, s^0 \rangle$. Let*

$$
\begin{aligned}
L_0 &= \{s^0\} & V_0 &= \{s^0\} \\
L_{i+1} &= \{s' \in S \mid \exists s \in L_i : \ s \ R \ s' \wedge s' \notin V_i\} & V_{i+1} &= V_i \cup L_{i+1}
\end{aligned}
$$

then

$$V = \bigcup_{i=0}^{\infty} V_i .$$

A simple algorithm that computes the set of reachable states is given in Table 1. How this algorithm is implemented depends on how the transition system is given. Next, we shortly review explicit state space generation from an on-the-fly interface and symbolic reachability.

For explicit state model checking, the fundamental way of implementing a transition system is by implementing the two functions in Table 2. The first function simply returns the initial state and the second returns the set of successors $\{s' \mid s \ R \ s'\}$ of a given state s as a list. The data structure used to implement sets is typically a hash table. Using this representation, the implementation of line 5 of Table 1 boils down to a simple loop that calls GetNext many times. Because this interface does not give away any details about the internal structure, we call it a black box interface.

Table 1. Basic reachability algorithm

```
1   proc reach ()
2       V := {s⁰}
3       L := V
4       while L ≠ ∅ do
5           L := {y | ∃x ∈ L : x R y}
6           L := L \ V
7           V := V ∪ L
8       end
9       return V
10  end
```

Table 2. Black Box on-the-fly API

```
state          GetInitial ();
state list     GetNext(state s);
```

For symbolic reachability, the data structures for both sets and the transition relation are some form of decision diagram. That is, a set $S' \subseteq S$ is represented by a boolean expression $\mathcal{S}'(\boldsymbol{x})$ such that

$$\boldsymbol{x} \in S' \Leftrightarrow \mathcal{S}'(\boldsymbol{x})$$

where the expression is stored as a decision diagram and $\boldsymbol{x}$ stands for the vector $x_1, \cdots x_n$. Similarly the transition relation is stored as a boolean expression $\mathcal{R}(\boldsymbol{x}, \boldsymbol{x}')$, such that

$$\boldsymbol{x} \: R \: \boldsymbol{x}' \Leftrightarrow \mathcal{R}(\boldsymbol{x}, \boldsymbol{x}')$$

Given a level as a formula $\mathcal{L}(\boldsymbol{x})$, we can compute the next level using the expression:

$$(\exists \boldsymbol{x}.(\mathcal{L}(\boldsymbol{x}) \wedge \mathcal{R}(\boldsymbol{x}, \boldsymbol{x}')))[\boldsymbol{x}' := \boldsymbol{x}]$$

Which provides us with the symbolic implementation of line 5.

The major advantage of symbolic techniques is that the representation of a set of states can be very compact. For example, the set of bit vectors with even parity can be represented by a decision diagram with a number of nodes that is linear in the length of the vector. The same holds for transition relations. Of course not every relation is represented easily. For example, multiplication of two n-bit numbers will produce a diagram that is exponential in n. (See [10].)

Although it is easy to apply explicit techniques to a symbolic model, it is not so easy to apply symbolic techniques to a given explicit model. The problem is that to compute a symbolic version of the transition relation, we must basically enumerate all possible transitions and collect them in a symbolic structure. In the next section, we explain how to modify the explicit interface in such a way that symbolic techniques can be applied efficiently.

3   Locality

The key to applying symbolic techniques to on-the-fly models is *event locality*. The notion of event locality refers to the fact that even though in a state several events could be enabled, each event separately affects just a small part of the state vector. For example, if one has a system which is composed of several processes running in parallel then in many models there are just two kinds of events: events in which one of the processes performs a step and events in which two of the processes synchronize to perform a step. In these cases, the enabledness and result of steps is decided by looking at the global variables (if any) and the local variables of the processes involved.

As an example, let us consider two ways of solving the 8-queens problem. The efficient way of solving the problem with a non-deterministic program is

```
for  i = 1 to 8 do
    put queen i in any row in column i
    if  for some 0 < j < i queen i on the same row or diagonal as queen j  then
        fail
    end
end
success
```

A solution to the problem is a path that ends in success. Putting the first queen is a very local event: we just put the queen somewhere in the first column. This affect the counter i and the position of the first queen only. The 8th step however is completely non-local: we need to check the counter i, test the positions of queens $1, \cdots, 7$ and write the position of queen 8.

To get event locality, we may rewrite the problem as follows:

```
for  i = 1 to 8 do put queen i on row 1 of column i end
while true
    if  ∃0 < i, j ≤ 8: queen i on the same row or diagonal as queen j  then
        move queen i to any row in column i
    end
end
```

A solution to the problem is a path to deadlock: if no two queens are in the same row, the same diagonal or the same column then no move is possible. However, every step is local: every move requires testing the positions of two queens and if enabled writing one of them.

To exploit event locality, one can partition the set of possible transitions into groups of transitions, such that each group affects part of the state only.

For the algorithm we present in the next section, we need to extend the black box interface to support group information. Because the extension exposes more structure than the black box interface, we have called it the grey box interface. The grey box interface is presented in Table 3 and uses five functions. The first function returns the length of the state vector (N). The second returns the number of groups, which from now on we will refer to as K. The third function

Table 3. Grey Box State Space API

```
int               GetStateLength ();
int               GetGroupCount ();
int list          GetGroupInfluenced(int group);
data list         GetInitialState ();
data list list    GetNext(data list src ,int group);
```

returns (a list representation of) the set of indices that is influenced (either read or written) while computing the enabledness and next states of the given group. This set of indices will be referred to as I_g, for any group g. The fourth function returns the initial state as a list of length N. The fifth function returns a list of projected next states, given a projected state and a group. That is, the length of src and each of the next states is the size of I_g if the group is g.

In terms of symbolic algorithms, event locality means that we can partition the transition relation into a disjunction (over the separate groups) of conjunctions (collections of local transitions) as follows:

$$\mathcal{R}(\boldsymbol{x}, \boldsymbol{x}') = \bigvee_{g=1}^{K} \mathcal{D}_g(\boldsymbol{x}, \boldsymbol{x}') = \bigvee_{g=1}^{K} \left(\mathcal{R}_g(\pi_g(\boldsymbol{x}), \pi_g(\boldsymbol{x}')) \wedge \bigwedge_{i \notin I_g} [x_i = x_i'] \right),$$

where we define the projection to a group as $\pi_g(\boldsymbol{x}) = (x_j)_{j \in I_g}$.

4   Grey Box Reachability Algorithm

In this section, we describe our symbolic reachability algorithm for grey box models. The variables and constant used are listed in Table 4. The set operations are listed in Table 5 and the algorithm itself is presented as Table 6.

The algorithm performs a breadth first analysis. That is, the visited set and the current level are set to singleton initial state and the visited part of each group is set to empty. Next, we repeat the main loop in which we replace the current level by the new states reachable from that level until the current level is empty.

In each iteration of the main loop we first extend the local symbolic transition relations of the groups to include all necessary transitions. (See lines 9-15.) That is, for every group we project the current level to the sub-vector used by the group and for all of the new sub-vectors we explore the next states and insert any transition found into the local transition relation. The second half of the main loop is building the new level by computing the next states of the level set according to each of the group relations. (See lines 16-21.) This involves a symbolic next state computation for each group that changes the members of the sub-vector and leaves all other variables unchanged. From this the next level is then computed.

Table 4. Reachability Variables and Constants

K	Number of groups	constant number
I_i	Indices in the state vector, which are Influenced by group i	explicit list
V	Visited states	symbolic
L	current Level	symbolic
L^p	projection of current level to influenced variables of current group	symbolic
V_i^p	projected states Visited for group i	symbolic
R_i^p	projected transition Relation for group i	symbolic
N	Next level	symbolic
s^p	projected state	explicit vector

Table 5. Operations on sets

$\cdot \setminus \cdot$	set minus	symbolic
$\cdot \cup \cdot$	set union	symbolic
$\text{project}(\cdot,\cdot)$	projection to a sub-vector	symbolic
$\text{step}(\cdot,\cdot,\cdot)$	result of one step in a relation applied to a sub-vector	symbolic
$\text{next}_i^p(\cdot)$	next state function of the ith group	explicit
$\{\cdot \mid \cdot\}$	building a set by inserting elements one element at a time	mixed

The set operations project and step can be written as symbolic set operations as follows:

$$\text{project}(\mathcal{S}(\boldsymbol{x}), I) = \exists (x_i)_{i \notin I}.\mathcal{S}(\boldsymbol{x})$$
$$\text{step}(\mathcal{S}(\boldsymbol{x}), \mathcal{R}((x_i)_{i \in I}, (x_i')_{i \in I}), I) =$$
$$(\exists (x_i)_{i \in I}(\mathcal{S}(\boldsymbol{x}) \wedge \mathcal{R}((x_i)_{i \in I}, (x_i')_{i \in I})))[x_i' := x_i \mid i \in I]$$

The function call $\text{next}_i^p(s)$ is shorthand for the call GetNext(s,i).

5 Implementation

We have implemented a prototype of the algorithm presented in the previous section on top of the μCRL tool set ([4],[11]). The concept of this toolset is to take a specification and compile it into a linear process equation (LPE). An LPE is a process given as an initial state and a recursive equation:

$$X(\boldsymbol{x}) = \sum_{i=1}^{K} \underbrace{\sum_{e_i \in E_i} C_i \Rightarrow a(t_{i,0}).X(t_{i,1}, \cdots, t_{i,n})}_{\text{summand } i}$$

where C_i and $t_{i,j}$ are expressions over $e_i, x_1, \cdots, x_n$. The intended meaning of this equation is that to perform a step, one has to first non-deterministically select $1 \leq i \leq K$ (determining a summand), then non-deterministically select some $e \in E_i$, evaluate the condition C_i to see if the step is enabled and if it is enabled then the label of the step is the result of the expression $a(t_{i,0})$ and the next state is $t_{i,1}, \cdots, t_{i,n}$.

Table 6. Symbolic reachability algorithm for grey box models

```
1   proc mixed_reach ()
2       V := {s^0}
3       L := V
4       for i = 1 to K do
5           V_i^p := ∅
6           R_i^p := ∅
7       end
8       while L ≠ ∅ do
9           for i = 1 to K do
10              L^p := project ( L , I_i )
11              for s^p in L^p \ V_i^p do
12                  R_i^p := R_i^p ∪ {(s^p, d^p) | d^p ∈ next_i^p(s^p)}
13              end
14              V_i^p := V_i^p ∪ L^p
15          end
16          N := ∅
17          for i = 1 to K do
18              N := N ∪ step ( L , R_i^p , I_i )
19          end
20          L := N \ V
21          V := V ∪ N
22      end
23      return V
24  end
```

Hence, an LPE has a natural partitioning into groups by treating each summand as a group. Selecting this partitioning, the influenced variables of each summand are as follows:

$$I_i^X = \{x_j \mid t_{j,k} \neq x_j \lor \exists k \neq j : x_j \text{ occurs in } C_j \text{ or } t_{j,k}\}$$

We implemented this natural partitioning and we used it for the tests presented in this paper.

The μCRL toolset uses the ATerm library ([12]). To make interfacing with the decision diagrams easy we used a simple decision diagram library for manipulating sets, which we implemented on top of the ATerm library. The ATerm library was developed for the manipulation of large terms. It uses maximal sub-term sharing to keep its memory footprint minimal, which is the equivalent of a global unique table. It also provides garbage collection, but it does not provide advanced caching strategies. The resulting data structure for sets of vectors is a form of multi-way decision diagram (MDD). We call it List Decision Diagram (LDD), because instead of having one node with many edges we have a linked list.

By using the ATerm library, we automatically get maximal sharing (a global unique table), so there are no duplicate nodes. We can further classify our structure as a quasi-reduced version [13] rather than the fully-reduced version [14]. This choice was made because the set of possible values at each level is dynamic.

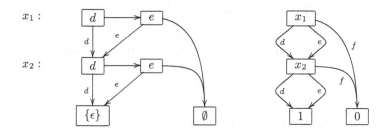

Fig. 1. The set {dd,de,ed,ee} as LDD and MDD

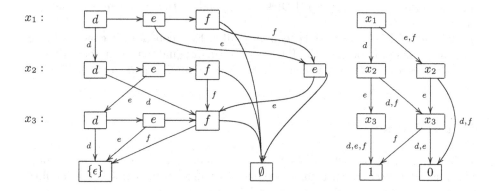

Fig. 2. The set {def,eef,fef,ddf,dff,ded,dee} as LDD and MDD

In a fully-reduced setting every extension of the set of values requires an update of every diagram, in the quasi-reduced setting this operation has no impact at all. For the same reason we do not use nodes with multiple successors, but just nodes with 2 successors that form a sorted list.

An LDD is a DAG. In this dag we have three types of nodes. The node types $\{\epsilon\}$ (or true) and $\emptyset$ (or false) do not have successors. That is, they are constants. The third type of node has a label (a) and two successors (n_1, n_2) and is written as $\text{node}(a, n_1, n_2)$. The semantics $[\![S]\!]$ of an LDD S is as follows:

$$
\begin{aligned}
[\![\{\epsilon\}]\!] &= \{\epsilon\} \\
[\![\emptyset]\!] &= \emptyset \\
[\![\text{node}(a, n_1, n_2)]\!] &= \{a\,w \mid w \in [\![n_1]\!]\} \cup [\![n_2]\!]
\end{aligned}
$$

To illustrate the relation between MDDs and our own LDDs, we have drawn the set $\{dd, de, ed, ee\}$ ($\{d, e\} \times \{d, e\}$) and the set $\{def, eef, fef, ddf, dff, ded, dee\}$ (Hamming distance to def no more than 1) in both formats in Fig. 1 and 2 respectively. The MDD's are over the domain $D = \{d, e, f\}$. To make these four diagrams easier to read, we have added edge labels that allow us to check for membership of a vector by checking if there is a path from the root to $\{\epsilon\}$ or 1 such that the string of edge labels along the path is the vector. To save clutter

Table 7. Reachability for Distributed Lift

legs	states	mem	time	mem/state	states/sec
2	391	30,668	1.08	80,317.22	362.04
3	7,369	56,236	4.32	7,814.58	1,705.79
4	129,849	79,820	29.48	629.47	4,404.65
5	2,165,446	181,592	250.10	85.87	8,658.32
6	33,949,609	661,724	2,344.03	19.96	14,483.44
7	501,505,138	2,246,788	17,995.72	4.59	27,868.02

an edge labeled d, e means two edges, one labeled d and one labeled e. Note that the edges without label in the LDDs correspond to the linked lists "building" the MDD nodes.

The sizes of LDDs and MDDs can only differ by a constant: it can be proven that the number of nodes in an MDD is less than or equal to the number of nodes in the corresponding LDD, which is in turn less than or equal to the number of edges in the MDD.

6   Experiments

In this section, we describe two sets of experiments that have been carried out. The first set of experiments measures the performance of our symbolic reachability analysis on two parametrized problems. The second set of experiments compares the performance of state space generation for a set of five problems and three tools.

To test the performance of our symbolic reachability analysis, we used two series of problems:

- A distributed lift system [15]. This model describes a system that can lift large vehicles by using one leg for each wheel of the vehicle. These legs are connected in a ring topology. The number of legs is a parameter.
- A version of the sliding window protocol [16]. This model is parametrized by both the number of data elements in the alphabet and the windows size. (The buffer is a fixed 1 place lossy buffer.)

To test the performance for these models, we used a dual Intel Xeon E5335 (2.0GHz) machine with Intel 5000P chipset and 8GB memory. We ran one experiment at a time. The results for the lift problem are in Table 7. Those for the sliding window protocol are in Table 8. Both tables contain the number of states in each of the models and the time and memory usage. Time is measured in time elapsed and in number of states processed per second. Memory is measured in maximum resident set (RSS) in kB and in number of bytes per state. The first table contains both forms, the second table has just the second form of the time and memory numbers.

The explicit state space generator of the μCRL has a lower bound of 16 bytes per state, excluding hash tables and other overhead. Since a hash table easily accounts for another 8 bytes per state, anything below 24 is good. The reason for these high numbers is that we have used the ATerm library in 64-bit

Table 8. Reachability for Sliding Window Protocol

states / mem/state (B) / states/sec		→ windows size							
		1	2	3	4	5	6	7	8
	1	156	1,860	10,608	43,320	146,740	442,524	1,235,528	3,269,680
		36,785.23	6,355.41	1,749.53	499.90	149.17	50.05	20.62	12.32
		111.43	1,273.97	6,548.15	20,826.92	48,589.40	83,652.93	110,020.30	109,171.29
	2	390	10,156	126,138	1,132,248	8,487,750	56,793,060	351,503,922	
		28,262.40	1,821.34	174.08	24.31	7.28	4.79	9.79	
		267.12	6,269.14	46,545.39	114,600.00	140,688.71	96,365.59	34,239.62	
	3	708	32,124	719,460	12,075,000	174,187,380			
		15,955.89	657.04	34.54	5.55	5.19			
		468.87	18,149.15	125,779.72	189,560.44	89,441.99			
↓ elements	4	1,110	78,156	2,829,570	79,474,200				
		9,819.33	280.12	10.87	3.31				
		760.27	37,575.00	201,536.32	189,694.00				
	5	1,596	161,812	8,746,248	375,691,704				
		7,114.11	135.50	5.88	6.91				
		1,093.15	67,421.67	269,945.93	113,410.54				
	6	2,166	299,820	22,789,098					
		5,137.96	73.29	4.28					
		1,483.56	103,030.93	301,802.38					
	7	2,820	512,076	52,280,988					
		3,683.50	43.42	3.45					
		1,931.51	139,530.25	314,094.25					
	8	3,558	821,644	108,715,890					
		3,143.95	30.87	2.52					
		2,356.29	179,398.25	294,822.75					

mode which uses about twice as much memory as in 32-bit mode. A carefully designed symbolic set library should work with half the memory or less. The rate of state exploration in the purely explicit instantiator is typically around a few thousand states per second. Values of over 100,000 obtained for some sliding window protocol instances are therefore a big improvement.

Our second experiment used the same set of 5 problems that we used in an earlier paper where we studied the performance of distributed state space generators [17]. We list the number of levels (iterations needed), the size of the state space and a brief description of each problem:

lift5. This model has 103 levels, 2,165,446 states and 8,723,465 transitions. It describes an elevator system with 5 legs in order to lift large vehicles [15].

SWP. This model has 61 levels, 19,466,100 states and 93,478,264 transitions. It is a version of the sliding window protocol [16]. This instance has 3 data elements, window size 2 and 3-place lossy buffers for communication.

1394fin. This model has 170 levels, 88,221,818 states and 152,948,696 transitions. It describes the physical layer service of the 1394 or firewire protocol and also the link layer protocol entities. [18,19] We use an instance with 3 links and 1 data element.

franklin53. This model has 82 levels, 84,381,157 states and 401,681,445 transitions. It describes a leader election protocol for anonymous processes along a bidirectional ring of asynchronous channels, which terminates with probability one [20,21]. We chose an instance with 5 nodes and 3 identities.

Table 9. Comparison of state space generation tools

problem/order		symbolic		mixed		explicit	
		time(s)	mem(kB)	time(s)	mem(kB)	time(s)	mem(kB)
lift5	G	861	378	535	195	408	230
lift5	R	217	181	398	101	319	226
swp	G	30,322	345	2,073	111	1,426	1,308
swp	R	29,232	342	1,850	107	1,264	1,308
1394fin	G	768	214	46,787	2,356	41,560	5,592
franklin53	G	out of memory		97,005	23,875	6,745	7,844
franklin53	R1	4,970	2,187	17,649	653	6,557	5,533
franklin53	R2	12,712	6,989	15,448	662	6,565	5,529
ccp33	G	out of memory		out of memory		44,855	7,741
ccp33	R	146,127	44,214	82,379	2,895	46,092	6,419

CCP33. This model has 297 levels, 97,451,014 states and 1,061,619,779 transitions. It describes and instance of the cache coherence protocol *Jackal* for Java programs with 3 processes and 3 threads [22].

The main goal of this test was to compare the performance of our symbolic prototype and the sequential state space generator of the μCRL toolset. However, we also wanted to have an indication of the memory cost of the operations on decision diagrams. Thus, we implemented a mixed state space generator. This mixed tool is a direct implementation of reachability in which we enumerate the successors of each state explicitly, but which uses the symbolic set structure instead of a hashtable for the set of visited states and the level sets.

All three tools were using version 2.18.0 of the μCRL toolset. To run these tests, we used a server with dual Intel Xeon X5365 (3.00GHz) processor and an Intel 5000P chipset with 64GB memory. We ran one experiment at a time.

The problems as they were formulated for the testing of the distributed tools, could only be dealt with by the symbolic tool in 3 out of 5 cases. The remaining cases ran out of memory. To fix this, we reordered the variables using the heuristic that the distance between variables that interact should be low.

The data collected in this test is summarized in Table 9. For each of the tools, we have two columns: time (in seconds) and maximum memory (in kB). The first column of the table indicates the problem, the second column contains the variable order, where G means given and R means reordered.

The given variable ordering of the franklin problem was first all processes then all channels. We changed this to process variables and channel variables interleaved, either starting with a process (R1) or starting with a channel (R2). While the reordering didn't affect the mixed tools very much, it did have a large influence on the symbolic tool. It is left as future work to find out if a reason for this difference can be found.

To compare the performance of the various tools, we compare the best runs for each tool within each of the groups for lift5, swp, 1394fin, franklin and ccp33. For memory the score (symbolic vs mixed vs explicit) is 1-4-0. For time the score is 3-0-2.

What can we learn from these experiments? Looking at the data of the first test, it seems that the bigger the model the better the performance in both states/sec and mem/state of the symbolic tools. This is a clear improvement over the explicit tools where performance usually decreases slightly as the models grow. It should be noted however, that this trend is broken for the three largest instances of SWP. We think that this is due to performance issues in our symbolic set implementation, but that is a conjecture only.

From the second test, we get some data to compare approaches. If we compare the memory usage of the symbolic tool with the mixed tool then we see that with one exception, the mixed tool uses less memory. This is to be expected because the mixed tool uses the symbolic sets for storage only, whereas the symbolic tool computes with these sets, which requires additional memory for the operation cache and intermediate results. If we compare the mixed tool and the explicit tool on time then the mixed tool looses. This is not surprising because insert/lookup is much more expensive for the symbolic set than for the hash table set. Comparing the symbolic tool with the explicit tool, then we get a mixed result. In two cases (lift5,franklin) the results do not differ substantially. In the other three cases the symbolic tool is substantially better in memory and time (1394fin), substantially worse in time but better in memory (swp) and substantially worse in both time and memory (ccp33). The conclusion is that the symbolic tool even in its current form is a very useful addition, but not capable of replacing the explicit tool. Replacing the explicit tool will not be an option for some time anyway, as there are a number of issues left open, which will be discussed in the next section.

7   Conclusion

In this section, we discuss some of the open issues that need to be solved to make the symbolic tool more useful and summarize the results.

On the implementation side, the most important task is to replace the current ATerm based symbolic set implementation with a much higher performance decision diagram package. This is needed not only for performance, but also to allow our back-end to interface with other modeling formalisms. For example, we plan on writing an interface to NIPS (see [23]) which is a virtual machine which is compatible with SPIN (see [24]). To do this, we also need to extend the implementation from fixed vector length to variable vector length.

Independently, we will investigate the effects of the search order on the size of the intermediate structures. So far, we have used a breadth first search (BFS) strategy. One of the strategies we need to look at is saturation. Ciardo et al. have shown that this strategy is much better for Petri Nets. As explanation they state that it reduces the difference between the size (in numbers of nodes) of the reachable state space and the peak size of the set of visited states considerably. If we look at the peak/final differences for our typical models then we find they are small. Thus, it is not a priori clear if saturation will work well.

By implementing a symbolic tool for a modeling language that has until now had support for explicit exploration only, we are in a situation where we can compare the performance of explicit and symbolic tools. One of the things that we need to do is see how far we can get with applying the symbolic tool to existing models. We have started this in the second test by looking at five models, but all five of the problems were message passing systems. Such systems have a high degree of locality. This is not always the case. In timed systems one usually has global synchronisation steps which involve nearly the entire state. We will study examples with global steps in order to find common features that allow an efficient embedding into our tool.

Another issue is that so far, we have written models in a way that is optimized for explicit enumeration. For example consider the 8-queens problem. Finding all solutions using the first algorithm (directed search) requires looking at 2,058 states. If we use the second algorithm (random moves) we get 16,777,216 states. Using explicit tools we would never consider the second approach for practical purposes. However, the worst size of the diagram representing the set of states for the first approach is 2,655 nodes and the worst size for the second approach is 166. And there are many other modeling techniques that are good for explicit exploration but bad for symbolic techniques, such as path reduction by making sequences of steps atomic.

We have shown that a generalized version of the conjunctive/disjunctive partitioning scheme implemented in SMART for Petri nets can be successfully extended to allow non-deterministic transitions and implemented for the process algebra μCRL. The initial results with the prototype show that symbolic exploration should be a part of the future of process algebra's, but also that retiring the explicit tools is not an option yet.

References

1. Garavel, H., Mateescu, R., Lang, F., Serwe, W.: CADP 2006: A Toolbox for the Construction and Analysis of Distributed Processes. In: Damm, W., Hermanns, H. (eds.) CAV 2007. LNCS, vol. 4590, pp. 158–163. Springer, Heidelberg (2007)
2. Fernandez, J.C., Garavel, H., Kerbrat, A., Mounier, L., Mateescu, R., Sighireanu, M.: CADP - A Protocol Validation and Verification Toolbox. In: Alur, R., Henzinger, T.A. (eds.) CAV 1996. LNCS, vol. 1102, pp. 437–440. Springer, Heidelberg (1996)
3. Roscoe, B.: The theory and practice of concurrency. Prentice-Hall, Englewood Cliffs (amended, 1998) (2005)
4. Blom, S., Fokkink, W., Groote, J.F., van Langevelde, I., Lisser, B., van de Pol, J.: μCRL: A Toolset for Analysing Algebraic Specifications. In: Berry, G., Comon, H., Finkel, A. (eds.) CAV 2001. LNCS, vol. 2102, pp. 250–254. Springer, Heidelberg (2001)
5. Ciardo, G., Miner, A.S.: SMART: The Stochastic Model checking Analyzer for Reliability and Timing. In: QEST, pp. 338–339. IEEE Computer Society, Los Alamitos (2004)
6. Ciardo, G., Yu, A.J.: Saturation-Based Symbolic Reachability Analysis Using Conjunctive and Disjunctive Partitioning. In: Borrione, D., Paul, W. (eds.) CHARME 2005. LNCS, vol. 3725, pp. 146–161. Springer, Heidelberg (2005)

7. Kuntz, M., Siegle, M.: Deriving Symbolic Representations from Stochastic Process Algebras. In: Hermanns, H., Segala, R. (eds.) PROBMIV 2002, PAPM-PROBMIV 2002, and PAPM 2002. LNCS, vol. 2399, pp. 188–206. Springer, Heidelberg (2002)
8. Kuntz, M., Siegle, M., Werner, E.: Symbolic Performance and Dependability Evaluation with the Tool CASPA. In: Núñez, M., Maamar, Z., Pelayo, F.L., Pousttchi, K., Rubio, F. (eds.) FORTE 2004. LNCS, vol. 3236, pp. 293–307. Springer, Heidelberg (2004)
9. Ciardo, G., Marmorstein, R.M., Siminiceanu, R.: The saturation algorithm for symbolic state-space exploration. STTT 8, 4–25 (2006)
10. Bryant, R.E.: On the Complexity of VLSI Implementations and Graph Representations of Boolean Functions with Application to Integer Multiplication. IEEE Trans. Computers 40, 205–213 (1991)
11. Blom, S., Groote, J.F., van Langevelde, I., Lisser, B., van de Pol, J.: New developments around the μCRL tool set. In: Arts, T., Fokkink, W. (eds.) Eighth International Workshop on Formal Methods for Industrial Critical Systems (FMICS 2003). ENTCS, vol. 80 (2003)
12. Brand, M.G.J.v.d., Jong, H.A.d., Klint, P., Olivier, P.A.: Efficient Annotated Terms. Software – Practice & Experience 30, 259–291 (2000)
13. Kimura, S., Clarke, E.: A parallel algorithm for constructing binary decision diagrams. Computer Design: VLSI in Computers and Processors. Proceedings. ICCD 1990, 220–223 (1990)
14. Bryant, R.E.: Graph-Based Algorithms for Boolean Function Manipulation. IEEE Trans. Computers 35, 677–691 (1986)
15. Groote, J.F., Pang, J., Wouters, A.G.: A Balancing Act: Analyzing a Distributed Lift System. In: Gnesi, S., Ultes-Nitsche, U. (eds.) Proc. 6th Workshop on Formal Methods for Industrial Critical Systems, pp. 1–12 (2001)
16. Badban, B., Fokkink, W., Groote, J.F., Pang, J., van de Pol, J.: Verification of a sliding window protocol in μCRL and PVS. Formal Aspects of Computing 17, 342–388 (2005)
17. Blom, S., Lisser, B., van de Pol, J., Weber, M.: A database approach to distributed state space generation. In: Haverkort, B., Černa, I. (eds.) Proceedings of the 6th International Workshop on Parallel and Distributed Methods in verification, vol. 198 (2007)
18. Luttik, S.: Description and formal specification of the link layer of P1394. In: Technical Report SEN-R9706, Amsterdam, The Netherlands (1997)
19. Sighireanu, M., Mateescu, R.: Verification of the Link Layer Protocol of the IEEE-1394 Serial Bus (FireWire). An Experiment with E-LOTOS. STTT 2, 68–88 (1998)
20. Bakhshi, R., Fokkink, W., Pang, J., van de Pol, J.: Leader Election in Anonymous Rings: Franklin Goes Probabilistic. In: Accepted for 5th IFIP International Conference on Theoretical Computer Science (2008)
21. Franklin, W.R.: On an Improved Algorithm for Decentralized Extrema Finding in Circular Configurations of Processors. Commun. ACM 25, 336–337 (1982)
22. Pang, J., Fokkink, W.J., Hofman, R.F., Veldema, R.: Model checking a cache coherence protocol of a Java DSM implementation. JLAP 71, 1–43 (2007)
23. Weber, M.: An Embeddable Virtual Machine for State Space Generation. In: Bosnacki, D., Edelkamp, S. (eds.) SPIN 2007. LNCS, vol. 4595, pp. 168–186. Springer, Heidelberg (2007)
24. Holzmann, G.J.: The SPIN Model Checker: Primer and Reference Manual. Addison-Wesley, Reading (2003)

Inclusion Test Algorithms for One-Unambiguous Regular Expressions*

Haiming Chen and Lei Chen

State Key Laboratory of Computer Science, Institute of Software,
Chinese Academy of Sciences
Beijing 100080, China
{chm,chl}@ios.ac.cn

Abstract. One-unambiguous regular expressions are used in DTD. It is known that inclusion for one-unambiguous regular expressions is in PTIME. However, there has been no study on algorithms for the inclusion. In this paper we present algorithms for checking inclusion of one-unambiguous regular expressions. A classical way is based on automata, following which one algorithm is provided and improvements are given. The other algorithm is based on derivatives, utilizing a property introduced here that the number of derivatives of a one-unambiguous regular expression is finite. We conducted preliminary experiments by implementing typechecking of XML using the algorithms. The results show that typechecking using the new algorithms is more efficient than the typechecking used for XDuce.

Keywords: One-unambiguous regular expression, inclusion, algorithm.

1 Introduction

Extensible Markup Language (XML) is a simple, very flexible text format for structured data, which becomes popular for the Web and other applications. Usually in applications XML data are provided with schemas that the XML data must conform to. These schemas are very helpful for XML processing. In many tasks it is required to check inclusion of schemas, for example, in query processing, schema update, typechecking, and so on. Since in many cases the inclusion problem of XML schemas is closely related to the inclusion problem of regular expressions [16], it is useful to study the inclusion problem of regular expressions used in XML schemas.

Many results for the complexity of the inclusion problem for regular expressions exist. For general regular expression, inclusion is PSPACE-complete [20]. Martins, Neven, and Schwentick [16] give complexity of decision problems for several subclasses of regular expressions called simple regular expressions occurring in practice in XML schemas. Their results show that inclusion is already

---

* Work supported by the National Natural Science Foundation of China under Grants Nos. 60573013, 60721061.

J.S.Fitzgerald,A.E.Haxthausen,andH.Yenigun(Eds.):ICTAC2008,LNCS5160, pp. 96–110, 2008.

CONP-complete for very innocent expressions such as expressions with factors of the form a or a^*. Several authors give complexity for regular expressions with interleaving and/or numerical occurrence indicators [17,15,11]. Inclusion for these expressions is in EXPSPACE. In order to get tractable inclusion checking, Suzuki [21] proposes a polynomial-time algorithm for solving a subproblem of the inclusion problem defined by edit operations.

The most commonly used XML schema languages are Document Type Definition (DTD) and XML Schema which are recommended by W3C [5,19]. *One-unambiguous regular expressions* [7] are used in DTD. In particular, the complexity of inclusion problem for DTDs reduces to the complexity of inclusion problem of the corresponding regular expressions. For XML Schema, investigation reveals that most definitions in XML Schema in practice are actually DTDs according to [4]. Therefore algorithms for one-unambiguous regular expressions are useful in practice. There are also some suggestions on using some other regular expressions instead of one-unambiguous ones in DTDs mainly because the latter is not a syntactic concept. However the complexity of inclusion problem will probably become higher as well by this, and here we mainly focus on one-unambiguous regular expressions. One-unambiguous regular expressions reflect the requirement that a symbol in the input word be matched uniquely to a position in a regular expression without looking ahead in the word. Since one-unambiguous regular expressions can be transformed to deterministic finite automata (DFA) in polynomial time, inclusion for one-unambiguous regular expressions is in PTIME. However, there has been no study on algorithms for the inclusion for this kind of regular expressions in the literature.

In this paper we first present two algorithms for checking inclusion of one-unambiguous regular expressions. A classical way to this problem is based on automata. The Glushkov automaton for a one-unambiguous regular expression is deterministic [7]. We have shown in [9] that for a one-unambiguous regular expression in star normal form, the equation automaton [1] is deterministic, and the Brzozowski's deterministic automaton [8] can be easily computed. Hence any one of the above DFA can be used in the algorithm. However here we just use Glushkov DFA as example. It is easy to use other types of the above DFA. One easy algorithm in this approach is provided. Improvements on the basic algorithm are then given, which may reduce time and space requirements in practice. Another algorithm is based on derivatives [8]. For one-unambiguous regular expressions, we give an equivalent calculation of derivatives, and show that the number of derivatives is finite, while this may be infinite for regular expressions. Then an algorithm for inclusion is given, which repeatedly calculates the derivatives of the expressions and will give an answer in this process.

Then we introduce experiments with the algorithms. We conducted some preliminary experiments by implementing typechecking of XML using the algorithms. The examples for running typechecking are from XDuce [23], an XML processing language which supports regular tree languages as schemas. The results show that typechecking using both algorithms are faster than the type-checking of XDuce.

Section 2 introduces notations and notions required in the paper. Section 3 presents the automata-based algorithm. Section 4 gives the derivative-based algorithm. Section 5 describes the experiments. Section 6 contains related work. Section 7 gives concluding remarks.

2   Notations and Notions

We assume the reader to be familiar with basic regular language and automata theory, e.g., from [22], so that we introduce here only some notations and notions used later in the paper.

2.1   Regular Expressions

Let Σ be an alphabet of symbols. $|\Sigma|$ denotes the size of Σ, ε denotes the empty word. Σ^* is the set of all words over Σ. A regular expression over Σ is $\emptyset, \varepsilon$ or $a \in \Sigma$, or is obtained from these by applying the following rules finitely many times: for two regular expressions E_1 and E_2, the union $E_1 + E_2$, the concatenation $E_1 E_2$, and the star E_1^* are regular expressions. For a regular expression E, the language specified by E is denoted by $L(E)$. The size of E is denoted by $|E|$ and is the length of E when written in postfix (parentheses are not counted). $\|E\|$ denotes the number of symbol occurrences in E, or the alphabetic width of E. Σ_E denotes the symbols that occur in E, which is the smallest alphabet of E.

2.2   One-Unambiguous Regular Expressions

One-unambiguous regular expressions are also called deterministic regular expressions, the name came from Brüggemann-Klein and Wood [7].

For a regular expression we can mark symbols with subscripts so that in the marked expression each marked symbol occurs only once. For example $(a_1 + b_1)^* a_2 b_2 (a_3 + b_3)$ is a marking of the expression $(a + b)^* ab(a + b)$. A marking of an expression E is denoted by E'. The reverse of marking is the dropping of subscripts from the marked symbols, denoted by $\natural$.

One-unambiguous expressions are defined as follows:

An expression E is one-unambiguous if and only if, for all words $uxv, uyw \in L(E')$ where $|x| = |y| = 1$, if $x \neq y$ then $x^\natural \neq y^\natural$. A regular language is one-unambiguous if it is denoted by some one-unambiguous expression.

As shown by Brüggemann-Klein [6], we have the following result.

Proposition 1. *It can be decided in linear time whether a regular expression is one-unambiguous.*

2.3   Glushkov Automaton and Star Normal Form

The Glushkov automaton (or position automaton) is introduced independently by Glushkov [13] and McNaughton and Yamada [18].

For a regular expression E over Σ, we define the following functions:

$$first(E) = \{a \mid aw \in L(E), a \in \Sigma, w \in \Sigma^*\}$$
$$last(E) = \{a \mid wa \in L(E), w \in \Sigma^*, a \in \Sigma\}$$
$$follow(E,a) = \{b \mid uabv \in L(E), u,v \in \Sigma^*, b \in \Sigma\}, \text{for } a \in \Sigma$$

The Glushkov automaton for E is defined as follows:

$$M_E = (Q_E, \Sigma, \delta_E, q_E, F_E)$$

1. $Q_E = \Sigma_{E'} \cup \{q_E\}$
2. $\delta_E(q_E, a) = \{x \mid x \in first(E'), x^\natural = a\}$, for $a \in \Sigma$
3. $\delta_E(x, a) = \{y \mid y \in follow(E', x), y^\natural = a\}$, for $x \in \Sigma_{E'}$ and $a \in \Sigma$
4. $F_E = \begin{cases} last(E') \cup \{q_E\}, & \text{if } \varepsilon \in L(E), \\ last(E'), & \text{otherwise} \end{cases}$

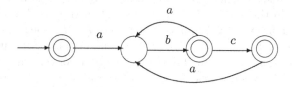

Fig. 1. The Glushkov automaton corresponding to $(ab(c + \varepsilon))^*$

Example 1. The Glushkov automaton M_{E_1} of the regular expression $E_1 = (ab(c + \varepsilon))^*$ is in Figure 1.

Let $L(M)$ denote the language accepted by the automaton M. As shown by Glushkov [13], McNaughton and Yamada [18] and Brüggemann-Klein and Wood [7], we have the following properties.

Proposition 2. $L(M_E) = L(E)$.

Proposition 3. *A regular expression E is one-unambiguous if and only if M_E is deterministic.*

A naive algorithm to compute Glushkov automata takes time cubic in the size of the expression. A quadratic time algorithm is given by Brüggemann-Klein [6], which has linear running time for one-unambiguous regular expressions. The algorithm uses the star normal form.

For a regular expression E over Σ, define

$$followlast(E) = \{b \mid vbw \in L(E), v \in L(E), v \neq \varepsilon, b \in \Sigma_E\}$$

Star normal form of regular expressions is defined as follows [6]:

A regular expression E is in star normal form if, for each starred subexpression H^* of E, $followlast(\overline{H}) \cap first(\overline{H}) = \emptyset$ and $\varepsilon \notin L(H)$.

Brüggemann-Klein and Wood [7] prove each regular expression can be transformed into star normal form.

3   Automata Based Method

3.1   The Algorithm

A classical way to check inclusion of regular expressions is to convert the regular expressions to automata and compare the automata. Since one-unambiguous regular expressions can be directly converted to DFA, inclusion test in this way is quite easy. We have shown in [9] that the equation automaton [1] for a one-unambiguous regular expression in star normal form is deterministic, and the Brzozowski's deterministic automaton [8] can be easily computed for a one-unambiguous regular expression in star normal form. Hence any one of the Glushkov, Brzozowski's, or equation DFA can be used in the algorithm. However here we just use Glushkov DFA as example. It is easy to use other types of the above DFA. In this section we give a basic algorithm used in this approach. Given two one-unambiguous regular expressions E_1, E_2, our aim is to determine whether the relation $L(E_1) \subseteq L(E_2)$ is true or false. An automata based method for this is as follows. In the method we first convert the expressions to Glushkov automata, then check inclusion of the automata. Since $\Sigma_{E_1} \not\subseteq \Sigma_{E_2}$ implies $L(E_1) \not\subseteq L(E_2)$, we assume $\Sigma_{E_1} \subseteq \Sigma_{E_2}$ in the following.

(1) Construct the corresponding automata from the expressions. The Glushkov DFA can be computed by the algorithm in [6]. $M_{E_1} = (Q_{E_1}, \Sigma_{E_1}, \delta_{E_1}, q_{E_1}, F_{E_1})$ *with* $\|E_1\| + 1$ *states,* $M_{E_2} = (Q_{E_2}, \Sigma_{E_2}, \delta_{E_2}, q_{E_2}, F_{E_2})$ *with* $\|E_2\| + 1$ *states.*

(2) Compute the automaton for the complement of $L(M_{E_2})$*.*

We need first make M_{E_2} *complete if it is not. Suppose the complete one is* $M'_{E_2} = (Q'_{E_2}, \Sigma_{E_2}, \delta'_{E_2}, q_{E_2}, F_{E_2})$*, then* $M' = (Q'_{E_2}, \Sigma_{E_2}, \delta'_{E_2}, q_{E_2}, Q'_{E_2} - F_{E_2})$*, such that* $L(M') = \overline{L(M'_{E_2})} = \overline{L(M_{E_2})}$*.*

(3) Construct an automaton B*, such that* $L(B) = L(M_{E_1}) \cap L(M')$*.*

The automaton is constructed by the product construction. $B = (Q_{E_1} \times Q'_{E_2}, \Sigma, \delta, (q_{E_1}, q_{E_2}), F_{E_1} \times (Q'_{E_2} - F_{E_2})), \Sigma = \Sigma_{E_1} \cup \Sigma_{E_2}, \delta((p, q), a) = (\delta_{E_1}(p, a), \delta'_{E_2}(q, a))$*.*

(4) Check if $L(B) = \emptyset$*?*

This can be solved by a search on the graph $G = (Q, E)$*, where* $Q = Q_{E_1} \times Q'_{E_2}$*,* E *is the set of transitions, or edges. If there is a path from the start state to an accepting state then* $L(B)$ *is not empty.*

Then $L(E_1) \subseteq L(E_2) \iff L(B) = \emptyset$*.*

Correctness of the algorithm: The overall process implements checking $L(E_1) \cap \overline{L(E_2)} = \emptyset$*.*

In step (1), the computation of M_{E_1} and M_{E_2} can be done in $O(|E_1|)$ and $O(|E_2|)$ time respectively [6]. This is due to the use of star normal form. In step (2), the computation of M'_{E_2} can be done in $O(|Q_{E_2}||\Sigma_{E_2}|) = O((\|E_2\|+1)|\Sigma_{E_2}|)$ time. The construction of M' is in linear time. In step (3), the construction of B can be computed in $O((\|E_1\|+1)(\|E_2\|+2)(|\Sigma_{E_1} \cup \Sigma_{E_2}|)) = O(\|E_1\| \cdot \|E_2\| \cdot |\Sigma_{E_1} \cup \Sigma_{E_2}|)$ time. In step (4), for a DFA B, $|E| \leq |Q| \cdot |\Sigma_{E_1} \cup \Sigma_{E_2}|$. It is known that a search on G can be done in $O(|Q|+|E|)$ time ([10, p. 534]). Therefore the time complexity is $O(|Q|+|E|) = O(\|E_1\| \cdot \|E_2\| \cdot |\Sigma_{E_1} \cup \Sigma_{E_2}|)$. The running time of the overall computation is $O(\|E_1\| \cdot \|E_2\| \cdot |\Sigma_{E_1} \cup \Sigma_{E_2}|)$. By the assumption of $\Sigma_{E_1} \subseteq \Sigma_{E_2}$, $O(\|E_1\| \cdot \|E_2\| \cdot |\Sigma_{E_1} \cup \Sigma_{E_2}|) = O(\|E_1\| \cdot \|E_2\| \cdot |\Sigma_{E_2}|)$. The space required by the algorithm is $O(\|E_1\| \cdot \|E_2\| \cdot |\Sigma_{E_2}|)$.

3.2   Improvements

By using properties of the above automata, we can have a simpler construction of B. Let us define a path in an automaton as a sequence $x_1 y_1 x_2 y_2 \ldots x_n y_n x_{n+1}$ where x_i are states and y_i are symbols, and there are transitions from x_i to x_{i+1} on input y_i. Since M' is complete and deterministic and, by assumption, $\Sigma_{E_1} \subseteq \Sigma_{E_2}$, we have

Property 1. Let $P_1 = \{h \mid h$ is a path starting from (q_{E_1}, q_{E_2}) in $B\}$, $P_2 = \{k \mid k$ is a path starting from q_{E_1} in $M_{E_1}\}$, then $P_1[(p,q)\backslash p] = P_2$, and $|P_1| = |P_2|$.

$P_1[(p,q)\backslash p]$ denotes the set in which for any path $h \in P_1$ every state (p,q) in h is replaced by the left component p.

Proof. Given $h \in P_1$, by the definition of B, $h[(p,q)\backslash p] \in P_2$. Given $k \in P_2$, since M' is complete and $\Sigma_{E_1} \subseteq \Sigma_{E_2}$, there exists a path $h \in P_1$ such that $h[(p,q)\backslash p] = k$. So $P_1[(p,q)\backslash p] = P_2$. Since M' is deterministic, the number of paths in B could not be more than the number of paths in M_{E_1}. On the other hand, since M' is complete and $\Sigma_{E_1} \subseteq \Sigma_{E_2}$, the number of paths in B could not be less than the number of paths in M_{E_1}. □

Property 2. Let $P_1 = \{h \mid h$ is a path starting from (q_{E_1}, q_{E_2}) and ending with an accepting state in $B\}$, $P_2 = \{k \mid k$ is a path starting from q_{E_1} and ending with an accepting state in $M_{E_1}\}$, then $P_1[(p,q)\backslash p] \subseteq P_2$, and $|P_1| \leq |P_2|$.

Proof. It follows from Property 1 and the fact of $F_{E_1} \times (Q'_{E_2} - F_{E_2}) \subseteq F_{E_1} \times Q'_{E_2}$. □

An automaton is called a trim automaton if it only contains states reachable from the start state. From the above, the transition function of the trim version of B can be calculated from M_{E_1} as follows.

$Q = \{(q_{E_1}, q_{E_2})\}$,
For $(p,q) \in Q$ and (p,q) is unmarked and $\delta_{E_1}(p,a)$ is defined
    $\delta((p,q),a) = (\delta_{E_1}(p,a), \delta'_{E_2}(q,a))$,
    $Q = Q \cup \{(\delta_{E_1}(p,a), \delta'_{E_2}(q,a))\}$,
    mark (p,q) in Q

This is more efficient than the previous construction of B. Denote the resulting automaton as B_c. It is clear $L(B) = L(B_c)$.

Then checking $L(B) = \emptyset$ can be done simply by checking if B_c contains an accepting state. If B_c dose not contains accepting state, then $L(B) = \emptyset$, otherwise $L(B) \neq \emptyset$.

Since what we need is to check if there is no accepting state in B, we can have further improvement of steps (3) to (4) by a M_{E_1}-directed search on M_{E_1} and M', without building the automaton for the intersection.

$Q = \{(q_{E_1}, q_{E_2})\}$,
For $(p, q) \in Q$ and (p, q) is unmarked and $\delta_{E_1}(p, a)$ is defined
    If both $\delta_{E_1}(p, a)$ and $\delta'_{E_2}(q, a))$ are accepting states then return FALSE,
    else
        $Q = Q \cup \{(\delta_{E_1}(p, a), \delta'_{E_2}(q, a))\}$,
        mark (p, q) in Q
return TRUE

In the search, if there is an accepting state, then it immediately returns FALSE and stops. Only if there is no accepting state, a complete search will be done, which equals to the construction of B_c. Therefore, it has the same time complexity as the one using B_c if $L(B) = \emptyset$, and is more efficient otherwise. It is more efficient in space since B_c is not constructed.

Example 2. Let E_1 be the one from Example 1, $E_2 = (abc^*)^*$, then the constructed Glushkov automaton M_{E_1} is shown in Figure 1, and Figure 2 shows the computation by the algorithm.

In step (3), the construction of B_c can be computed in $O((\|E_1\| + 1)(\|E_2\| + 2)|\Sigma_{E_1}|) = O(\|E_1\| \cdot \|E_2\| \cdot |\Sigma_{E_1}|)$ time. In step (4), checking an accepting state is in linear time. Indeed, the accepting states have been marked in the construction of automata. If in step (3) we use a variable to keep this information, then whether there is an accepting state is already known and the checking is done in constant time. The running time of the overall computation is $O(\|E_1\| \cdot \|E_2\| \cdot |\Sigma_{E_1}|)$. The space complexity is $O(\|E_1\| \cdot \|E_2\| \cdot |\Sigma_{E_1}|)$.

For the M_{E_1}-directed search algorithm, the time complexity is $O(\|E_1\| \cdot \|E_2\| \cdot |\Sigma_{E_1}|)$, but the space complexity is $O(\|E_1\| \cdot |\Sigma_{E_1}| + \|E_2\| \cdot |\Sigma_{E_2}|)$.

4   Derivative Based Method

In this section an algorithm to determine the inclusion of two one-unambiguous regular expressions, based on the derivatives of regular expressions, is presented. This is inspired by the algorithm to determine inequalities of regular expressions based on partial derivatives [2].

Derivatives of regular expressions were introduced by Brzozowski [8].

Given a regular expression E and a symbol a, the derivative $d_a(E)$ of E with respect to a is defined inductively as follows:

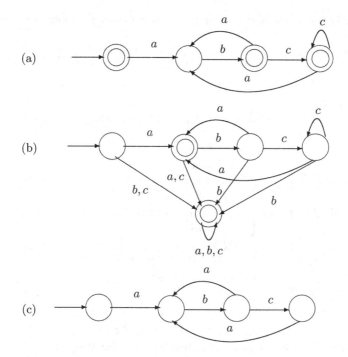

Fig. 2. (a) The Glushkov automaton corresponding to $(abc^*)^*$; (b) The automaton M'; (c) The automaton B_c

$$da(\emptyset) = d_a(\varepsilon) = \emptyset$$
$$d_a(b) = \begin{cases} \varepsilon, \text{ if } b = a \\ \emptyset, \text{ otherwise} \end{cases}$$
$$d_a(F + G) = d_a(F) + d_a(G)$$
$$d_a(FG) = \begin{cases} d_a(F)G + d_a(G), \text{ if } \varepsilon \in L(F) \\ d_a(F)G, \qquad\qquad \text{ otherwise} \end{cases}$$
$$d_a(F^*) = d_a(F)F^*$$

Derivatives with respective to a word is $d_\varepsilon(E) = E$, $d_{wa}(E) = d_a(d_w(E))$.

As shown by Brüggemann-Klein and Wood [7], the derivatives of a one-unambiguous regular expression in star normal form are also one-unambiguous regular expressions in star normal form.

Proposition 4. ([7]) Let E be in star normal form.
$E = \emptyset, E = \varepsilon$, or $E = a \in \Sigma$: E is one-unambiguous.
$E = F + G$: E is one-unambiguous iff F and G are one-unambiguous and $first(F) \cap first(G) = \emptyset$.
$E = FG$: If $L(E) = \emptyset$, then E is one-unambiguous. If $L(E) \neq \emptyset$ and $\varepsilon \in L(F)$, then E is one-unambiguous iff F and G are one-unambiguous, $first(F) \cap first(G) = \emptyset$, and $followlast(F) \cap first(G) = \emptyset$. If $L(E) \neq \emptyset$ and $\varepsilon \notin L(F)$, then E is one-unambiguous iff F and G are one-unambiguous and $followlast(F) \cap first(G) = \emptyset$.

$E = F^*$: E is one-unambiguous iff F is one-unambiguous and $followlast(F) \cap first(F) = \emptyset$.

When one-unambiguous expressions are concerned, we also have the following construction of derivatives.

Proposition 5. *For a one-unambiguous regular expression E in star normal form, the derivative of E by a symbol a can be computed as follows:*

$$d_a(\emptyset) = d_a(\varepsilon) = \emptyset$$

$$d_a(b) = \begin{cases} \varepsilon, \text{ if } b = a \\ \emptyset, \text{ otherwise} \end{cases}$$

$$d_a(F + G) = \begin{cases} d_a(F), \text{ if } a \in first(F) \\ d_a(G), \text{ if } a \in first(G) \\ \emptyset, \quad \text{ otherwise} \end{cases}$$

$$d_a(FG) = \begin{cases} d_a(F)G, \text{ if } a \in first(F) \\ d_a(G), \quad \text{ if } a \in first(G) \text{ and } \varepsilon \in L(F) \\ \emptyset, \quad \text{ otherwise} \end{cases}$$

$$d_a(F^*) = d_a(F)F^*$$

Proof. We need to prove only for $E = F + G$ or FG.

If $E = F + G$, then $first(F) \cap first(G) = \emptyset$ by Proposition 4. So if $a \in first(F)$ then $a \notin first(G)$, then $d_a(G) = \emptyset$, $d_a(E) = d_a(F)$. The same is for $a \in first(G)$. If both $a \notin first(F)$ and $a \notin first(G)$, then $d_a(E) = \emptyset$.

If $E = FG$, by definition $d_a(E) = d_a(F)G + d_a(G)$ if $\varepsilon \in L(F)$, or $d_a(F)G$ otherwise. First we show $first(F) \cap first(G) = \emptyset$. If $L(E) = \emptyset$, obviously $first(F) \cap first(G) = \emptyset$, otherwise $L(F), L(G) \neq \emptyset$ which means $L(E) \neq \emptyset$. If $L(E) \neq \emptyset$, then from Proposition 4 $first(F) \cap first(G) = \emptyset$. Then, the remaining proof is similar to that of the above for $E = F + G$.

Checking if $\varepsilon \in L(E)$ for a regular expression E is simple.

For two one-unambiguous regular expressions E_1, E_2, to determine if $L(E_1) \subseteq L(E_2)$, first transform E_1, E_2 into star normal forms respectively, then use the following algorithm. In the algorithm A contains expression pairs and is set initially to empty.

```
include(E₁, E₂, A)
(1) if ε ∈ L(E₁) and ε ∉ L(E₂) then return False
(2) if first(E₁) ⊄ first(E₂) then return False
(3) A = A ∪ {E₁, E₂}
(4) for all a ∈ first(E₁) do
(5)    t₁ = dₐ(E₁), t₂ = dₐ(E₂),
(6)    if (t₁, t₂) ∉ A then
(7)        if include(t₁, t₂, A)=False then return False
(8) return True
```

$include(E_1, E_2, A)$ returns True if $L(E_1) \subseteq L(E_2)$ and False otherwise.

Example 3. Let E_1, E_2 be the ones from Example 1, 2 respectively. We will determine if $L(E_1) \subseteq L(E_2)$. Since E_1, E_2 are in star normal form, we directly go to the algorithm.

$E_1 = (ab(c + \varepsilon))^*$,
$E_2 = (abc^*)^*$,
$first(E_1) = first(E_2) = \{a\}$,
$A = \{(E_1, E_2)\}$,
$d_a(E_1) = b(c + \varepsilon)(ab(c + \varepsilon))^*$ r_{11},
$d_a(E_2) = bc^*(abc^*)^*$ r_{21},
$first(r_{11}) = first(r_{21}) = \{b\}$,
$A = \{(E_1, E_2), (r_{11}, r_{21})\}$,
$d_b(r_{11}) = (c + \varepsilon)(ab(c + \varepsilon))^*$ r_{12},
$d_b(r_{21}) = c^*(abc^*)^*$ r_{22},
$first(r_{12}) = first(r_{22}) = \{a, c\}$,
$A = \{(E_1, E_2), (r_{11}, r_{21}), (r_{12}, r_{22})\}$,
$d_a(r_{12}) = r_{11}$,
$d_a(r_{22}) = r_{21}$,
$(d_a(r_{12}), d_a(r_{22})) \in A$,
$d_c(r_{12}) = E_1$,
$d_c(r_{22}) = r_{22}$,
$first(E_1) = \{a\}, first(r_{22}) = \{a, c\}$,
$A = \{(E_1, E_2), (r_{11}, r_{21}), (r_{12}, r_{22}), (E_1, r_{22})\}$,
$d_a(E_1) = r_{11}$,
$d_a(r_{22}) = r_{21}$,
$(d_a(E_1), d_a(r_{22})) \in A$.

Therefore `include` returns True, so $L(E_1) \subseteq L(E_2)$.

In general, the derivatives of a regular expression may constitute a infinite set without some reduction by similarity. But in the case of one-unambiguous regular expressions, the number of derivatives is finite, as shown below.

Theorem 1. *For a one-unambiguous regular expression E in star normal form, the cardinality of the set $D(E)$ of derivatives is less than or equal to $\|E\| + 1$.*

Proof. Since $d_\varepsilon(E) = E$, we only need to prove that the number of derivatives of E with respect to non-empty words, denoted $nd(E)$, is less than or equal to $\|E\|$. We prove this by induction.

Base. If $E = \emptyset, \varepsilon$, or a, $a \in \Sigma$, the above is obvious.

Induction. 1. $E = F + G$. It is easily verified from definitions in Proposition 5 that, for a non-empty word $w \in \Sigma^+$, (conditions of rhs are omitted in the sequel of the proof)

$$dw(F + G) = \begin{cases} d_w(F) \\ d_w(G) \\ \emptyset \end{cases}$$

Hence $nd(F + G) \leq nd(F) + nd(G) \leq \|F\| + \|G\| = \|E\|$.

2. $E = FG$. Using the definitions in Proposition 5, we have

$$d_w(FG) = \begin{cases} d_w(F)G \\ d_v(G) & \text{forall } v \in \Sigma^+ \text{ such that } w = uv, u \in \Sigma^* \\ \emptyset \end{cases}$$

So $nd(FG) \le nd(F) + nd(G) \le \|F\| + \|G\| = \|E\|$.

3. $E = F^*$. Similarly, we have

$$d_w(F^*) = \begin{cases} d_v(F)F^* & \text{forall } v \in \Sigma^+ \text{ such that } w = uv, u \in \Sigma^* \end{cases}$$

Therefore $nd(F*) \le nd(F) \le \|F\| = \|E\|$. This concludes the inductive step.

The bound is worst case optimal, one example is the expression abc.

Therefore the number of pairs of expressions to be checked for inclusion in `include` is bounded to $\|E_1\| \cdot \|E_2\|$; This ensures termination of the algorithm.

Although the algorithm is rather simple, the worst case complexity is higher than the automata-based algorithm. Recall from [1], any partial derivative of E is either ε or a subexpression of E or a concatenation of subexpressions where the number of subexpressions is no greater than the number of occurrences of concatenation and Kleene star appearing in E. Therefore, in the worst case, a partial derivative of E may have a size up to $|E|^2$. According to [9], derivatives of a one-unambiguous regular expression has the same form as the partial derivatives of the expression. In the above algorithm, consider the comparison in (6), the worst-case time complexity is $O((|E_1|^2 + |E_2|^2)\|E_1\|^2\|E_2\|^2)$. Also the worst-case space complexity is $O(|E_1|^2\|E_1\| + |E_2|^2\|E_2\|)$. However, in practice, computation rarely reaches the upper bounds. For example, in Example 3, there could be up to $4 \times 4 = 16$ pairs of derivatives, but there are only 5 pairs in A and 5 comparisons done. In fact, as we will see in the next section, in the experiments the derivative-based algorithm is faster than the automata-based one.

Virtually the search strategy of the algorithm is similar to the M_{E_1}-directed search introduced in the previous section. However, here it is not needed to compute all the derivatives in advance.

5   Experiments

The algorithms for the inclusion of one-unambiguous regular expressions can be used in many tasks as mentioned in Section 1. We have conducted some preliminary experiments where the algorithms introduced in previous sections are applied to one of the tasks, i. e., typechecking. As a first step to this application we have just implemented checking one-unambiguous regular expressions, and some other work such as exhaustiveness checking was not integrated. In the experiments the algorithms can be compared with each other, and our type-checking implementations can be compared with other typechecking algorithm.

The examples for running typechecking are from XDuce [23], an XML processing language which supports regular tree languages as schemas. Our typechecking implementations are restricted to one-unambiguous regular expressions. The original examples may first be modified so that expressions that are not one-unambiguous are filtered out.

The examples are as follows.

ex1: addrbook. The common example used in XDuce papers. Constructs a new file which contains the name and the tel number by extracting from the XML file which contains the address information.

ex2: bookmarks. Takes a Netscape bookmarks file as input file which is a subset of type HTML and extracts a file including contents, body and links between them, which is the full HTML type.

ex3: html2latex. Imports an external DTD named xhtml1-transitional.dtd and takes as input an HTML file(of type HTML) and converts it into LaTeX (a value of type string).

ex4: ns2xbel. Imports an external DTD named xbel-1.0.dtd and takes as input a bookmark file which is in the Netscape format and converts it into the XBEL format.

In ex1 there is 1 regular expression which is not one-unambiguous and the corresponding equation which contains this expression is removed from the example. In ex2 there are 2 regular expressions which are not one-unambiguous and the corresponding equations are removed. In ex3 and ex4 there is no such regular expression and the examples need no modification.

ex1, ex4 : millisecond

ex2, ex3 : 100 milliseconds

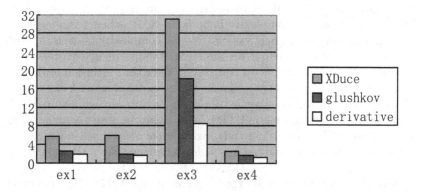

Fig. 3. Results of the experiments

Figure 3 shows the concrete results from the experiments. The examples are taken from XDuce [23], therefore the typechecking algorithm of XDuce is also used in the experiments. Some examples are small in size, and some are not.

XDuce [14] is a typed XML processing language which supports regular expression types. Its typechecking algorithm is based on tree automata.

The time in the figure indicates the time of the process to, given two expressions, check the inclusion of the expressions. In the experiments the time used for other operations such as checking exhaustiveness of pattern matching by the type checker of XDuce was not counted. The environment of the experiments is as follows: Intel Pentium 4 CPU 3.0GHz, 512MB RAM, Ubuntu 7.04-alternate-i386, XDuce 0.5.0, OCaml 3.10.0.

The results of the experiments show that our typechecking implementations both are more efficient than XDuce, and that the derivative-based algorithm is more efficient than the automata-based one. Of course the experiments we did are still very preliminary; more examples would be very useful, and the implementations of the two inclusion algorithms can still be improved.

Of course, the algorithms are targeted to applications which use DTDs. As mentioned before, most XML schemas used in practice are DTDs. Furthermore, when more general schemas are supported, it is possible to use our algorithms for checking inclusion of DTDs and more general algorithms for other schemas.

6   Related Work

A schema S_2 includes a schema S_1 if for any document d that is valid against S_1, d is valid against S_2. For DTD, the inclusion problem reduces to the inclusion problem of the corresponding regular expressions. Martins, Neven, and Schwentick [16] study the relations between complexity for decision problems for DTD and XML Schema (single-type SDTD) and complexity for decision problems for the corresponding regular expressions, and show that for inclusion the complexity bounds for the regular expressions carry over to DTD and XML Schema, so it suffices to restrict attention to the complexity of regular expressions to derive complexity bounds for XML schema languages.

Martins, Neven, and Schwentick [16] give complexity of decision problems for several subclasses of regular expressions called simple regular expressions occurring in practice in XML schemas. Their results show that inclusion is already CONP-complete for very innocent expressions such as expressions with factors of the form a or a^*. If the number of occurrences of the same symbol in expressions is bounded by some k ($RE^{\leq k}$), inclusion is in PTIME. Several authors give complexity for regular expressions with interleaving and/or numerical occurrence indicators [17,15,11]. These expressions are allowed in schema languages like XML Schema and Relax NG. Inclusion for these expressions is in EXPSPACE.

One-unambiguous regular expressions are used in DTD. Since one-unambiguous regular expressions can be transformed to DFA in linear time, inclusion for this kind of expressions is in PTIME. However, there has been no algorithm for the inclusion.

For DTD inclusion, Suzuki [21] proposes a polynomial-time algorithm for solving a subproblem of the inclusion problem for regular expressions defined by edit operations. However, the algorithm does not cover the inclusion problem for one-unambiguous regular expressions.

Ghelli, Colazzo, and Sartiani [12] propose a restricted class of regular expressions with interleaving and counting, for which inclusion is in PTIME. The class also dose not cover one-unambiguous regular expressions.

Typechecking algorithms are proposed in languages like XDuce, CDuce [3], and so on. These algorithms solve the inclusion problem for regular tree languages. Inclusion is EXPTIME-complete in general, and there is no complexity results for the algorithms in the case of DTD or XML Schema.

A rewriting method to determine inequalities of regular expressions, based on partial derivatives, has been proposed [2]. It rewrites an inequality to a set of subinequalities. The derivative-based algorithm is inspired by and similar in spirit to it. We can use derivatives here, and hence make a simpler algorithm, because the number of derivatives of a one-unambiguous expression is finite.

7 Concluding Remarks

We presented two algorithms for checking inclusion of one-unambiguous regular expressions. One algorithm is based on automata. The other one is based on derivatives. We also conducted some experiments by applying the algorithms to typechecking of XML. The results show that both the algorithms are quite efficient. Of course the algorithms are targeted to applications which use DTDs. As discussed in Section 5, when more general schemas are supported, it is possible to integrate our algorithms with more general algorithms. In the experiments the automata-based algorithm is slower than the derivative-based one. This may partly be because in practice usually the number of pairs of derivatives to be checked is very small. In addition, derivatives often are subexpressions of a regular expression, since actual DTDs usually contain very simple regular expressions. Thus derivatives often are smaller in size than the regular expression. Also, it is not needed to compute all of the derivatives in advance, whereas the whole automata have to be built in advance. Of course, the experiments are preliminary, more experiments are very useful.

Future work includes: experiments with more examples; a complete type checker for regular tree languages, which uses the above algorithms. Comparison with other typed XML processing languages like CDuce [3] are useful. The algorithms can also be used to other tasks of XML processing that require checking inclusion of schemas.

Acknowledgement. We thank Zheng Lixiao for her careful reading and helpful comments on the writing of the paper.

References

1. Antimirov, V.: Partial derivatives of regular expressions and finite automaton constructions. Theoretical Computer Science 155, 291–319 (1996)
2. Antimirov, V.: Rewriting regular inequalities. In: FCT 1995. LNCS, vol. 965, pp. 116–125. Springer, Heidelberg (1995)

3. Benzaken, V., Castagna, G., Frisch, A.: CDuce: An XML centric general-purpose language. In: ACM SIGPLAN International Conference on Functional Programming (ICFP), Uppsala, Sweden, pp. 51–63 (2003)
4. Bex, G.J., Neven, F., Bussche, J.V.: DTDs versus XML schema: a practical study. In: WebDB 2004, pp. 79–84 (2004)
5. Bray, T., et al.: XML 1.1, W3C Recommendation, 2nd edn. (2006)
6. Bruggemann-Klein, A.: Regular expressions into finite automata. Theoretical Computer Science 120, 197–213 (1993)
7. Bruggemann-Klein, A., Wood, D.: One-unambiguous regular languages. Information and Computation 142(2), 182–206 (1998)
8. Brzozowski, J.A.: Derivatives of regular expressions. J. ACM 11(4), 481–494 (1964)
9. Chen, H.: Derivatives and automata of one-unambiguous regular expressions (submitted, 2008)
10. Cormen, T.H., Leiserson, C.E., Rivest, R.L., Stein, C.: Introduction to Algorithms. MIT Press, Cambridge (2001)
11. Gelade, W., Martens, W., Neven, F.: Optimizing schema languages for xml: numerical constraints and interleaving. In: Schwentick, T., Suciu, D. (eds.) ICDT 2007. LNCS, vol. 4353. Springer, Heidelberg (2006)
12. Ghelli, G., Colazzo, D., Sartiani, C.: Efficient inclusion for a class of XML types with interleaving and counting. In: Arenas, M., Schwartzbach, M.I. (eds.) DBPL 2007. LNCS, vol. 4797, pp. 231–245. Springer, Heidelberg (2007)
13. Glushkov, V.M.: The abstract theory of automata. Russian Math. Surveys 16, 1–53 (1961)
14. Hosoya, H., Pierce, B.: XDuce: a statically typed XML processing language. ACM Transactions on Internet Technology 3(2), 117–148 (2003)
15. Kilpelainen, P., Tuhkanen, R.: Regular expressions with numerical occurrence indicators - preliminary results. In: SPLST 2003, pp. 163–173 (2003)
16. Martens, W., Neven, F., Schwentick, T.: Complexity of decision problems for simple regular expressions. In: Fiala, J., Koubek, V., Kratochvíl, J. (eds.) MFCS 2004. LNCS, vol. 3153, pp. 889–900. Springer, Berlin (2004)
17. Mayer, A.J., Stockmeyer, L.J.: Word problems - this time with interleaving. Information and Computation 115(2), 293–311 (1994)
18. McNaughton, R., Yamada, H.: Regular expressions and state graphs for automata. IEEE Trans. on Electronic Computers 9(1), 39–47 (1960)
19. Sperberg-McQueen, C.M., Thompson, H.: XML Schema, http://www.w3.org/XML/Schema
20. Stockmeyer, L.J., Meyer, A.R.: Word problems requiring exponential time: Preliminary report. In: STOC 1973, pp. 1–9. ACM Press, New York (1973)
21. Suzuki, N.: An edit operation-based approach to the inclusion problem for DTDs. In: Adams, C., Miri, A., Wiener, M. (eds.) SAC 2007. LNCS, vol. 4876, pp. 482–488. Springer, Heidelberg (2007)
22. Yu, S.: Regular Languages. In: Rozenberg, G., Salomaa, A. (eds.) Handbook of Formal Languages, vol. I, pp. 41–110. Springer, Berlin (1997)
23. XDuce Webpage, http://xduce.sourceforge.net/

Refinement of Kripke Models for Dynamics

Francien Dechesne[1], Simona Orzan[1], and Yanjing Wang[2]

[1] Department of Computer Science, Eindhoven University of Technology,
P.O. Box 513, NL-5600MB, Eindhoven, The Netherlands
[2] Centrum voor Wiskunde en Informatica,
P.O. Box 94079, NL-1090 GB Amsterdam, The Netherlands

Abstract. We propose a property-preserving refinement/abstraction theory for Kripke Modal Labelled Transition Systems incorporating not only state mapping but also label and proposition lumping, in order to have a compact but informative abstraction. We develop a 3-valued version of Public Announcement Logic (PAL) which has a dynamic operator that changes the model in the spirit of public broadcasting. We prove that the refinement relation on *static* models assures us to safely reason about any *dynamic* properties in terms of PAL-formulas on the abstraction of a model. The theory is in particular interesting and applicable for an epistemic setting as the example of the Muddy Children puzzle shows, especially in the view of the growing interest for epistemic modelling and (automatic) verification of communication protocols.

1 Introduction

Epistemic logics are modal logics for reasoning about knowledge, traditionally used to describe the distribution of information among parties. Recently, these logics have become interesting also from a more practical perspective, i.e. for modelling knowledge development during communication protocols, by the addition of dynamics: mathematical constructions that enable to reason about knowledge and information *change* [8,1,2]. Methods based on epistemic logics have been developed for the analysis of complex communication protocols: e.g. BAN logic [4], the theory of function views [13] and interpreted systems [8,10,19]. These approaches are also more and more tool-supported, and interesting protocol properties are assessed or discarded by (automatic) model checking [11,19,22].

The structures on which epistemic formulas can be evaluated are Kripke models as in usual modal logic, with multiply labelled transitions representing different agents' uncertainties. Inevitably, when epistemic modelling is applied to complex situations, very large epistemic models can be expected. One way to deal with this, is to import the refinement and abstraction techniques developed for labelled transition systems (LTS), e.g. [16,15,20]. The refinement method intuitively relates a detailed model (refined model) with a coarser one (abstract model) in which some information may be lost, but the information kept is faithful to the detailed model. In the Kripke models of the epistemic setting, there are often transitions with different labels that might be similar to each other — for instance if they express

J.S. Fitzgerald, A.E. Haxthausen, and H. Yenigun (Eds.): ICTAC 2008, LNCS 5160, pp. 111–125, 2008.

uncertainties of agents playing similar roles in a multi-agent system. Another specific characteristic of epistemic Kripke models is that in modelling practical situations, numerous different basic propositions might be used. We may expect to lump some of those transitions with different labels or combine states with different propositional valuations to obtain a more compact abstraction. However, the traditional LTS abstraction techniques do not perform this type of reductions, so an adaptation is needed. Moreover, when we include the dynamic modalities, which essentially change the model, into the language (e.g announcements or actions, cf. [8,1,12,7]), it is a challenge to adapt the LTS abstraction theory such that a suitable abstraction relation will preserve the truth values of the dynamic formulas on the abstract model.

In this paper, we extend the refinement theory for *Kripke Modal Labelled Transition Systems* (KMLTSs), incorporating not only state mapping but also label- and proposition lumping, in order to obtain compact but informative abstractions. We develop a 3-valued Public Announcement Logic (PAL) and prove that the refinement relation on *static* models *can* assure us to safely verify any *dynamic* properties in terms of PAL-formulas on the abstractions of a KMLTS. Thus the theory can be used to abstract Kripke models, since Kripke models can be regarded as special case of KMLTSs. This theory is in particular applicable for an epistemic setting as the example of the Muddy Children shows.

In the flourishing field of abstraction techniques, to the best of our knowledge, no work on the abstraction of Kripke models exists yet reducing both the number of labels and of basic propositions. The literature related most closely to the current paper is the work on abstraction of LTSs [20] in which the labels could be grouped. Since both temporal and knowledge properties can be expressed using box- and diamond modalities of modal languages, model checkers on LTSs are sometimes employed to verify epistemic properties [11,19,22]. However, LTS abstractions were never used in this context. A complementary technique for escaping the epistemic explosion problem is symbolic model checking discussed in [17].

Section 2 introduces Kripke Modal Labelled Transition Systems, together with a 3-valued interpretation of PAL. In Section 3, the notions of refinement and abstraction are introduced and the preservation results are proven. Section 4 contains two examples of applying abstraction to some real epistemic models. We conclude in Section 5.

2   Preliminaries

In this section we introduce the 3-valued Public Announcement Logic (PAL) interpreted on 3-valued Kripke Modal Labelled Transition Systems.

2.1   Kripke Modal Labelled Transition System

A standard Kripke model consists of a set of states S, the labelled relations R among them and a 2-valued valuation V which assigns a truth value to each

basic proposition in each state[1]. In order to define abstractions of Kripke models
the standard definition is extended in the following sense:

- To incorporate the approximation of propositional information in the abstract model, we use 3-valued valuations instead of 2-valued ones. Besides
  true and *false*, atomic propositions can now have a third truth value $\perp$ which
  is intended to mean *unknown*.
- To incorporate the approximation of relations, two types of relations *must*
  and *may* are introduced as in *Modal Transition Systems* [16], where *must*
  transitions are under-approximations (the relations are necessarily there in
  the concrete model) and *may* for over-approximations (there are possibly
  such relations). Since necessarily existent relations should be at least possible, we require that the *must* relations are included in the *may* relations.

Formally, similar to the definition of Kripke Modal Transition Systems in [14,9],
we have:

Definition 1 (Kripke Modal Labelled Transition System). *A Kripke
Modal Labelled Transition System (KMLTS) is a tuple* $\mathcal{M} = (I, P; S, \rightarrow_\diamond, \rightarrow_\square, V)$
where:

- *I is a non-empty set of labels;*
- *P is a set of basic propositions;*
- *S is a non-empty set of states;*
- $\rightarrow_\diamond$ *is a set of transitions of the form* $s \xrightarrow{i}_\diamond s'$ *where* $i \in I$;
- $\rightarrow_\square$ *is a set of transitions of the form* $s \xrightarrow{i}_\square s'$ *where* $i \in I$;
- *V is a valuation function:* $V : S \rightarrow \{true, false, \perp\}^P$.

We require that $\rightarrow_\square \subseteq \rightarrow_\diamond$. *We call* (I, P) *the signature of* $\mathcal{M}$. *A pointed KMLTS*
$(\mathcal{M}, s)$ *is a pair of a KMLTS* $\mathcal{M}$ *and a distinguished state* s *in it.*

We include the signature (I, P) in the specification of the models as, in general,
the signatures of a model and its abstraction will be different.

A standard Kripke model can be regarded as a special kind of KMLTS, where
must and *may* coincide and the valuation is essentially 2-valued:

Definition 2 (Concrete model). *A KMLTS* $\mathcal{M} = (I, P; S, \rightarrow_\diamond, \rightarrow_\square, V)$ *is a
concrete model if:*

- $\rightarrow_\diamond = \rightarrow_\square$;
- *for all* $s \in S$, *all* $p \in P : V(s)(p) \neq \perp$.

---

[1] In an epistemic setting, the states (also called "possible worlds") are interpreted as
states of affairs that may be considered possible by agents: an *i*-relation from one
state to another means that at the first state agent *i* considers the second possible.

2.2   Public Announcement Logic

Public Announcement Logic (PAL) initiated in [18] is a convenient language to describe announcements and their informational consequences for (a group of) agents. Based on the standard language of epistemic logic (logic of knowledge), a new modality $[\phi]$ is introduced into the language, with $[\phi]\psi$ intended to express "*if ϕ is true then after the announcement of ϕ, ψ is true.*". Various case studies showed this logic to be powerful in helping to understand complicated higher order reasoning about knowledge and announcements such as in the cases of Muddy Children, Sum and Product and the protocol of Dining Cryptographers (we refer interested readers to [21] for detailed explanations).

Formally, given a signature (I, P), the formulas of the *Public Announcement Logic* $\mathcal{L}_{I,P}$ are defined by

$$\phi, \psi ::= p \mid \phi \wedge \psi \mid \neg\phi \mid \Box_i\phi \mid [\phi]\psi$$

where $p \in P$, $i \in I$. As usual, we define $\phi \vee \psi$, $\phi \rightarrow \psi$ and $\Diamond_i\phi$ as abbreviations of $\neg(\neg\phi \wedge \neg\psi)$, $\neg\phi \vee \psi$ and $\neg\Box_i\neg\phi$ respectively.

As we will see in the next section, our overall approach is not constrained to be used only in epistemic settings, as it does not require the model to be $S5$.[2] Not constrained within $S5$ models, we will have more freedom to find suitable abstractions, as we will see in the Muddy Children example.

2.3   Semantics

The semantics for 2-valued public announcement logic is the extension of standard modal logic with relativization operators $[\phi]$: $\mathcal{M}, s \vDash [\phi]\psi \iff [\mathcal{M}, s \vDash \phi$ implies $\mathcal{M}|_\phi, s \vDash \psi]$, where the relativized model $\mathcal{M}|_\phi$ is the restriction of $\mathcal{M}$ to the states where ϕ holds. We extend such relativization, which we call "update" in the context of PAL, to the 3-valued case and take the usual semantics for $\Box$ as in the logics on Modal Transition Systems:

Definition 3 (3-valued Semantics). *The truth value of a $\mathcal{L}_{I,P}$ formula ϕ in a state s of a KMLTS $\mathcal{M} = (I, P; S \rightarrow_\Diamond, \rightarrow_\Box, V)$, written $[\![\phi]\!]^{\mathcal{M},s}$, is defined by:*

$$
\begin{aligned}
[\![p]\!]^{\mathcal{M},s} &= V(s)(p) \\
[\![\neg\phi]\!]^{\mathcal{M},s} &= \neg_3[\![\phi]\!]^{\mathcal{M},s} \\
[\![\phi \wedge \psi]\!]^{\mathcal{M},s} &= [\![\phi]\!]^{\mathcal{M},s} \wedge_3 [\![\psi]\!]^{\mathcal{M},s} \\
[\![\Box_i\phi]\!]^{\mathcal{M},s} &= \begin{cases} true & if \ \forall s' : s \xrightarrow{i}_\Diamond s' \implies [\![\phi]\!]^{\mathcal{M},s'} = true \\ false & if \ \exists s' : s \xrightarrow{i}_\Box s' \ and \ [\![\phi]\!]^{\mathcal{M},s'} = false \\ \bot & otherwise \end{cases} \\
[\![[\phi]\psi]\!]^{\mathcal{M},s} &= \begin{cases} true & if \ [\![\phi]\!]^{\mathcal{M},s} = false \ or \ [\![\psi]\!]^{\mathcal{M}|_\phi,s} = true \\ false & if \ [\![\phi]\!]^{\mathcal{M},s} = true \ and \ [\![\psi]\!]^{\mathcal{M}|_\phi,s} = false \\ \bot & otherwise \end{cases}
\end{aligned}
$$

---

[2] $S5$ is a set of formulas axiomatizing the reading of $\Box$ as knowledge. $S5$ characterizes models in which the relations are equivalence relations.

where:

- $\neg_3(true) = false, \neg_3(false) = true$ *and* $\neg_3(\bot) = \bot$, *and for any* $x, y \in \{true, false, \bot\}$: $x \wedge_3 y = min(x, y)$ *w.r.t.* $\leq_v$: $false \leq_v \bot \leq_v true$.
- $\mathcal{M}|_\phi = (I, P; S' \to'_\diamond, \to'_\Box, V')$ *is defined as follows:*
  - $S' = \{s \in S \mid [\![\phi]\!]^{\mathcal{M}, s} \neq false\}$;
  - $\to'_\diamond = \to_\diamond |_{S' \times S'}$;
  - $\to'_\Box = \to_\Box \cap (S' \times \{s \in S' \mid [\![\phi]\!]^{\mathcal{M}, s} = true\})$;
  - $V'(s) = V(s)$ *for* $s \in S'$.

The intuitive idea behind the semantics of $\Box$ is that $\Box\phi$ is true if all the possible (*may*) relations lead to ϕ-true states, and is false if there exists a necessary (*must*) relation leading to a ϕ-false state.

The updated model $\mathcal{M}|_\phi$ keeps all ϕ-*not-false* states and all the relations among them, except for the *must* relations directed at a ϕ-unknown state.[3] Note that $\mathcal{M}|_\phi$ is still a KMLTS since $\to'_\Box \subseteq \to'_\diamond$ by definition. It is not hard to check that this three valued semantics "coincides" with the standard 2-valued semantics on concrete models. Formally, for any $\mathcal{L}_{I,P}$ formula ϕ, any concrete model $\mathcal{M}$:

$$[\![\phi]\!]^{\mathcal{M}, s} = true \iff \mathcal{M}', s \vDash \phi \qquad [\![\phi]\!]^{\mathcal{M}, s} = false \iff \mathcal{M}', s \nvDash \phi$$

where $\mathcal{M}'$ is the standard Kripke model converted from $\mathcal{M}$ by lumping *may* and *must* relations together. For 2-valued Public Announcement Logic the following reduction axioms hold:

(At)	$[\phi]p$	$\leftrightarrow$	$\phi \to p$
(PF)	$[\phi]\neg\psi$	$\leftrightarrow$	$\phi \to \neg[\phi]\psi$
(Dist)	$[\phi](\psi_1 \wedge \psi_2)$	$\leftrightarrow$	$[\phi]\psi_1 \wedge [\phi]\psi_2$
(Seq)	$[\phi][\psi]\chi$	$\leftrightarrow$	$[\phi \wedge [\phi]\psi]\chi$
(KA)	$[\phi]\Box_i\psi$	$\leftrightarrow$	$\phi \to \Box_i[\phi]\psi$

In the 3-valued case, there are a few cases where the left hand side of $\leftrightarrow$ gives *false* while the right hand side gives $\bot$, all involving the valuation of ϕ to be $\bot$. So if we only consider concrete models then the evaluation of ϕ is either *true* or *false* and the above equivalences hold.

Although our concern in this paper is primarily to develop the theory of epistemic abstrcations, the ultimate goal is to enable automatic verification of large epistemic models. Designing efficient algorithms for checking the satisfaction of 3-valued PAL formulae on KLMTSs, based on the definition above, is an interesting topic in itself and we leave it as further work. We now only note that, looking at similar results in the literature [3], it is to expect that such a model checking algorithm will not be more complex than the ones for checking (2-valued) PAL on KMs or LTSs.

---

[3] The *must*-relations signify *necessary* relations. However, a ϕ-unknown state s is not necessarily there in the updated model, as *unknown* leaves the possibility open that ϕ could 'actually' be *false*, in which case s would not be in the updated model. A relation directed at a possibly but not necessarily existent state, cannot be a necessary relation, so *must*-relations to ϕ-unknown states are removed.

3   Refinement and Logical Characterization

In this section we extend the classic definition of refinement with label and proposition mapping in order to reduce the number of labels and possibly achieve smaller abstraction models. We show that we can reason about properties of the more refined model by model checking the more abstract model.

3.1   Refinement and Abstraction

As observed in [20], to do model checking on infinitely-labelled systems, one needs abstraction to obtain a model with a reduced number of labels. We aim for an abstraction method to reduce the labels also in the finite case, by lumping similar transitions with different labels together into a unified one. This is often applicable in the epistemic case, as several agents may play a similar role and therefore have similar uncertainties. On the other hand, different propositions may also have a similar role on different states, in which case abstractions may combine propositions together as well. In the following, we use two mappings from one signature to the other to capture the above intuitions of lumping labels and propositions. It is important to note that these abstractions produce models with a different signature.

Notation For a function h and x in its range, we use $h^{-1}[x]$ to denote the preimage of x.

Definition 4 (Refinement and Abstraction). *Given two KMLTSs* $\mathcal{M} = (I, P; S, \to_\diamond, \to_\square, V)$ *and* $\mathcal{N} = (I', P'; T, \to'_\diamond, \to'_\square, V')$ *and two surjective functions* $f : I' \to I$ *and* $g : P' \to P$, *a binary relation* $R \subseteq T \times S$ *is called an* f, g-refinement relation between $\mathcal{N}$ and $\mathcal{M}$, *if for all* $t \in T, s \in S$ *with* $(t, s) \in R$ *the following hold:*

- *for any* $p \in P$: $V(s)(p) \neq \bot$ *implies for all* $p' \in g^{-1}[p]$: $V'(t)(p') = V(s)(p)$;
- $t \xrightarrow{i'}_\diamond t'$ *implies* $\exists s' \in S$: $s \xrightarrow{f(i')}_\diamond s'$ *and* $R(t', s')$;
- $s \xrightarrow{i}_\square s'$ *implies* $\forall i' \in f^{-1}[i]$: $\exists t' \in T$ *such that* $t \xrightarrow{i'}_\square t'$ *and* $R(t', s')$.

We say $\mathcal{N}$ *is a* f, g-refinement of $\mathcal{M}$ *(notation:* $\mathcal{N} \Subset_{f,g} \mathcal{M}$*) if there exists an* f, g-refinement relation R between $\mathcal{N}$ and $\mathcal{M}$. *We say* $(\mathcal{N}, t)$ *is an* f, g-refinement of $(\mathcal{M}, s)$ *(notation:* $(\mathcal{N}, t) \Subset_{f,g} (\mathcal{M}, s)$*) if there exists an* f, g-refinement relation R between $\mathcal{N}$ and $\mathcal{M}$ *such that* $(t, s) \in R$.

Correspondingly, $(\mathcal{M}, s)$ *is called an* f, g−abstraction of $(\mathcal{N}, t)$ *iff* $(\mathcal{N}, t)$ *is an* f, g-refinement of $(\mathcal{M}, s)$.

The first condition says that the valuation in the more abstract model can be less informative by making some propositions *unknown* ($\bot$), but never unfaithful. The intuition behind the requirement of *must* is that an i-*must* relation in the more abstract model is like an intersection of corresponding i'-*must* for $i' \in f^{-1}[i]$. For *may*, an $f(i')$-*may* relation in the more abstract model is like a union of those i''-*may* relations in the more refined model for which $f(i'') = f(i')$.

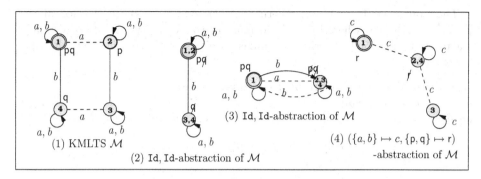

Fig. 1. A pointed KMLTS and three possible abstractions of it. Dot lines are for *may* relations and solid lines for *must*. *May* relations that coincide with corresponding *must* ones are omitted. If there is no arrow on a relation then it is bidirectional. $\overline{p}$ is to mean the value of p is *unknown* ($\bot$) at the current state. For clarity, the states of $\mathcal{M}$ are numbered and the numbers on the states of the abstracted models indicate which original states they represent. In (2), the mappings are the identity functions, and the valuation of proposition q is mapped to $\bot$ for all worlds. In (3), the abstraction is given by the identity functions as well, but collapsing different worlds. In (4), there's an abstraction obtained by lumping both agents and both propositions.

Note that for two 2-valued Kripke models with the same signature (I, P), $\mathcal{N}$ is a refinement of $\mathcal{M}$ in the classical sense of [15] iff $\mathcal{N}$ is an (Id_I, Id_P)−refinement of $\mathcal{M}$ where Id_X is identity function on the domain X.

Fig. 1 shows an example of a KMLTS $\mathcal{M}$ and some abstractions of it.

Since $\to_\square \subseteq \to_\diamond$, we can make a concrete refinement of any KMLTS by dropping *may* relations that do not have a *must* counterpart (i.e. $\to'_\diamond, \to'_\square := \to_\square$) and by adapting the valuation to become two-valued (e.g. by defining $V'(s)(p) = false$ whenever $V(s)(p) = \bot$ and $V'(s)(p) = V(s)(p)$ otherwise). Therefore:

Proposition 1. *A KMLTS $\mathcal{M}$ always has a concrete refinement.*

3.2 Logical Characterization

We will prove a preservation result of satisfaction of formulas between a pointed model $(\mathcal{N}, t)$ and its abstraction $(\mathcal{M}, s)$. Intuitively we want a formula to be true/false at $\mathcal{N}$ if it is true/false at $\mathcal{M}$ respectively, such that we can safely model check the more abstract model to get the information of the more refined one. However, as these models may have different signatures due to the f, g mappings attached to the refinement relation, we need to check different formulas on these two models. Given two pointed models $(\mathcal{M}, s), (\mathcal{N}, t)$, and two formulas ϕ, ψ, we say $[\![\psi]\!]^{\mathcal{M},s} \leq [\![\phi]\!]^{\mathcal{N},t}$ if the following hold:

1. $[\![\psi]\!]^{\mathcal{M},s} = true \implies [\![\phi]\!]^{\mathcal{N},t} = true$;
2. $[\![\psi]\!]^{\mathcal{M},s} = false \implies [\![\phi]\!]^{\mathcal{N},t} = false$.

Then our goal is to check whether $(\mathcal{N}, t) \Subset_{f,g} (\mathcal{M}, s)$ implies for all ϕ: $\llbracket \ulcorner \phi \urcorner \rrbracket^{\mathcal{M},s} \leq \llbracket \phi \rrbracket^{\mathcal{N},t}$ where $\ulcorner \phi \urcorner$ is a formula in the signature of $\mathcal{M}$ corresponding to ϕ. To pinpoint the right formulas to check, we introduce the following translation:

Definition 5 (Translation of formulas). *Given signatures $(I', P'), (I, P)$, and surjective functions $f : I' \to I, g : P' \to P$, we define the translation of an $\mathcal{L}_{I',P'}$-formula ϕ into an $\mathcal{L}_{I,P}$-formula $\ulcorner \phi \urcorner_{f,g}$ inductively as follows:*

$$
\begin{aligned}
\ulcorner p' \urcorner_{f,g} &= g(p') \\
\ulcorner \neg \psi \urcorner_{f,g} &= \neg \ulcorner \psi \urcorner_{f,g} \\
\ulcorner \psi_1 \wedge \psi_2 \urcorner_{f,g} &= \ulcorner \psi_1 \urcorner_{f,g} \wedge \ulcorner \psi_2 \urcorner_{f,g} \\
\ulcorner \Box_{i'} \psi \urcorner_{f,g} &= \Box_{f(i')} \ulcorner \psi \urcorner_{f,g} \\
\ulcorner [\chi] \psi \urcorner_{f,g} &= [\ulcorner \chi \urcorner_{f,g}] \ulcorner \psi \urcorner_{f,g}
\end{aligned}
$$

Before proving the main result of this paper, we first prove a result establishing the refinement relation between the updated models $(\mathcal{N}|_{\chi}, t)$ and $(\mathcal{M}|_{\ulcorner \chi \urcorner_{f,g}}, s)$ for some $\mathcal{L}_{I,P}$-formula χ, given that $(\mathcal{N}, t) \Subset_{f,g} (\mathcal{M}, s)$

Lemma 1. *Suppose $(\mathcal{N}, t), (\mathcal{M}, s)$ are pointed KMLTSs with signatures (I', P') and (I, P) and set of states T and S respectively, such that $(\mathcal{N}, t) \Subset_{f,g} (\mathcal{M}, s)$. Then for any $\mathcal{L}_{I',P'}$ formula χ such that $t \in \mathcal{N}|_{\chi}$ and $s \in \mathcal{M}|_{\ulcorner \chi \urcorner_{f,g}}$, we have $(\mathcal{N}|_{\chi}, t) \Subset_{f,g} (\mathcal{M}|_{\ulcorner \chi \urcorner_{f,g}}, s)$ if for each $t' \in T, s' \in S$ the following condition holds:*

$$(\mathcal{N}, t') \Subset_{f,g} (\mathcal{M}, s') \implies \llbracket \ulcorner \chi \urcorner_{f,g} \rrbracket^{\mathcal{M},s'} \leq \llbracket \chi \rrbracket^{\mathcal{N},t'} \qquad (\star)$$

Proof. Suppose $(\mathcal{N}, t) \Subset_{f,g} (\mathcal{M}, s)$ then there is a relation R which constitutes an f, g-refinement between $\mathcal{N}$ and $\mathcal{M}$ with $(t, s) \in R$. We claim that $R' = R \cap (\mathcal{N}|_{\chi} \times \mathcal{M}|_{\ulcorner \chi \urcorner_{f,g}})$ is an f, g-refinement relation between $\mathcal{N}|_{\chi}$ and $\mathcal{M}|_{\ulcorner \chi \urcorner_{f,g}}$. Note that $(t, s) \in R'$ since $t \in \mathcal{N}|_{\chi}$ and $s \in \mathcal{M}|_{\ulcorner \chi \urcorner_{f,g}}$. Now we check the three conditions of the refinement relation:

- for the condition on p: follows from this property of R and the fact that the valuation of an updated model is just the restriction of the original valuation to the remaining states.
- Suppose $t \xrightarrow{i'}_{\Diamond} t'$ in $\mathcal{N}|_{\chi}$, then $t \xrightarrow{i'}_{\Diamond} t'$ in $\mathcal{N}$ according to the definition of the update. Since $(\mathcal{N}, t) \Subset_{f,g} (\mathcal{M}, s)$, there exists $s' \in \mathcal{M}$: $s \xrightarrow{f(i')}_{\Diamond} s'$ and $(t', s') \in R$. Remains to show that $s' \in \mathcal{M}|_{\ulcorner \chi \urcorner_{f,g}}$. Suppose not, then $\llbracket \ulcorner \chi \urcorner_{f,g} \rrbracket^{\mathcal{M},s'} = false$. Because $(t', s') \in R$ ensures $(\mathcal{N}, t') \Subset_{f,g} (\mathcal{M}, s')$, it then follows from condition $(\star)$ that $\llbracket \chi \rrbracket^{\mathcal{N},t'} = false$. But then $t' \notin \mathcal{N}|_{\chi}$, contradiction.
- Suppose $s \xrightarrow{i}_{\Box} s'$ in $\mathcal{M}|_{\ulcorner \chi \urcorner_{f,g}}$, then $\llbracket \ulcorner \chi \urcorner_{f,g} \rrbracket^{\mathcal{M},s'} = true$ and $s \xrightarrow{i}_{\Box} s'$ in $\mathcal{M}$. Because R is an f, g-refinement between $(\mathcal{N}, t)$ and $(\mathcal{M}, s)$, for any $i' \in f^{-1}[i]$ there exists $t' \in \mathcal{N}$ such that $t \xrightarrow{i'}_{\Box} t'$ and $(t', s') \in R$. To show that $(t', s') \in R'$ for such t', it remains to show that $t' \in \mathcal{N}|_{\chi}$. Since $\llbracket \ulcorner \chi \urcorner_{f,g} \rrbracket^{\mathcal{M},s'} = true$ and $(t', s') \in R$, it then follows from condition $(\star)$ that $\llbracket \chi \rrbracket^{\mathcal{N},t'} = true$. Hence, $t' \in \mathcal{N}|_{\chi}$.

Theorem 1. *Suppose* $\mathcal{N}, \mathcal{M}$ *are KMLTSs w.r.t.* I', P' *and* I, P *respectively.* s *and* t *are two worlds in* $\mathcal{M}$ *and* $\mathcal{N}$ *respectively. Then* $(\mathcal{N}, t) \Subset_{f,g} (\mathcal{M}, s)$ *implies for all* $\phi \in \mathcal{L}_{I', P'}$: $\llbracket \ulcorner \phi \urcorner_{f,g} \rrbracket^{\mathcal{M}, s} \leq \llbracket \phi \rrbracket^{\mathcal{N}, t}$.

Proof. We prove the theorem by induction on the structure of ϕ :

- $\phi = p'$: trivial, follows from the first condition of the definition of refinement.
- $\phi = \neg \psi$: suppose $\llbracket \ulcorner \phi \urcorner_{f,g} \rrbracket^{\mathcal{M}, s} = true$ then according to the semantics $\llbracket \ulcorner \psi \urcorner_{f,g} \rrbracket^{\mathcal{M}, s} = false$. Thus by induction hypothesis $\llbracket \psi \rrbracket^{\mathcal{N}, t} = false$. Therefore $\llbracket \phi \rrbracket^{\mathcal{N}, t} = true$. For the case $\llbracket \ulcorner \phi \urcorner_{f,g} \rrbracket^{\mathcal{M}, s} = false$, similar.
- $\phi = \psi_1 \wedge \psi_2$:
  - suppose $\llbracket \ulcorner \phi \urcorner_{f,g} \rrbracket^{\mathcal{M}, s} = true$ then by the semantics: $\llbracket \ulcorner \psi_1 \urcorner_{f,g} \rrbracket^{\mathcal{M}, s} = true$ and $\llbracket \ulcorner \psi_2 \urcorner_{f,g} \rrbracket^{\mathcal{M}, s} = true$. Thus by induction hypothesis $\llbracket \psi_1 \rrbracket^{\mathcal{N}, t} = true$ and $\llbracket \psi_2 \rrbracket^{\mathcal{N}, t} = true$. Therefore $\llbracket \phi \rrbracket^{\mathcal{N}, t} = true$.
  - suppose $\llbracket \ulcorner \phi \urcorner_{f,g} \rrbracket^{\mathcal{M}, s} = false$ then by the semantics either $\llbracket \ulcorner \psi_1 \urcorner_{f,g} \rrbracket^{\mathcal{M}, s} = false$ or $\llbracket \ulcorner \psi_2 \urcorner_{f,g} \rrbracket^{\mathcal{M}, s} = false$. Without loss of generality, suppose the latter. Thus by induction hypothesis $\llbracket \psi_2 \rrbracket^{\mathcal{N}, t} = false$. Therefore $\llbracket \phi \rrbracket^{\mathcal{N}, t} = false$.
- $\phi = \Box_{i'} \psi$: then $\ulcorner \phi \urcorner_{f,g} = \Box_{f(i')} \ulcorner \psi \urcorner_{f,g}$.
  - suppose $\llbracket \ulcorner \phi \urcorner_{f,g} \rrbracket^{\mathcal{M}, s} = true$ then according to the semantics for all s' with $s \xrightarrow{f(i')}_{\Diamond} s'$ we have $\llbracket \ulcorner \psi \urcorner_{f,g} \rrbracket^{\mathcal{M}, s'} = true$. Suppose in $\mathcal{N}$ there is a world t' such that $t \xrightarrow{i'}_{\Diamond} t'$ then according to the definition of refinement, there is a $s'' \in \mathcal{M}$ such that $s \xrightarrow{f(i')}_{\Diamond} s''$ and $(\mathcal{N}, t') \Subset_{f,g} (\mathcal{M}, s'')$. Thus $\llbracket \ulcorner \psi \urcorner_{f,g} \rrbracket^{\mathcal{M}, s''} = true$. By induction hypothesis, $\llbracket \psi \rrbracket^{\mathcal{N}, t'} = true$. Therefore $\llbracket \Box_{i'} \psi \rrbracket^{\mathcal{N}, t} = true$.
  - suppose $\llbracket \ulcorner \phi \urcorner_{f,g} \rrbracket^{\mathcal{M}, s} = false$ then according to the semantics, there is s' with $s \xrightarrow{f(i')}_{\Box} s'$ such that $\llbracket \ulcorner \psi \urcorner_{f,g} \rrbracket^{\mathcal{M}, s} = false$. By definition of refinement, for any $i'' \in f^{-1}[f(i')]$ there is a $t' \in \mathcal{N}$ such that $t \xrightarrow{i''}_{\Box} t'$ and $(\mathcal{N}, t') \Subset_{f,g} (\mathcal{M}, s')$. By induction hypothesis, for all such t' : $\llbracket \psi \rrbracket^{\mathcal{N}, t'} = false$. Thus for all $i'' \in f^{-1}[f(i')]$: $\llbracket \Box_{i''} \psi \rrbracket^{\mathcal{N}, t} = false$. In particular: $\llbracket \Box_{i'} \psi \rrbracket^{\mathcal{N}, t} = false$.
- $\phi = [\chi] \psi$
  - if $\llbracket \ulcorner \phi \urcorner_{f,g} \rrbracket^{\mathcal{M}, s} = true$ then $\llbracket \ulcorner \chi \urcorner_{f,g} \rrbracket^{\mathcal{M}, s} = false$ or $\llbracket \ulcorner \psi \urcorner_{f,g} \rrbracket^{\mathcal{M}|\ulcorner \chi \urcorner_{f,g}, s} = true$. If $\llbracket \ulcorner \chi \urcorner_{f,g} \rrbracket^{\mathcal{M}, s} = false$ then $\llbracket \chi \rrbracket^{\mathcal{N}, t} = false$ by induction hypothesis, hence $\llbracket \phi \rrbracket^{\mathcal{N}, t} = true$. Otherwise, $\llbracket \ulcorner \psi \urcorner_{f,g} \rrbracket^{\mathcal{M}|\ulcorner \chi \urcorner_{f,g}, s} = true$ and $\llbracket \ulcorner \chi \urcorner_{f,g} \rrbracket^{\mathcal{M}, s} \neq false$, so $s \in \mathcal{M}|\ulcorner \chi \urcorner_{f,g}$. Now suppose $\llbracket \chi \rrbracket^{\mathcal{N}, t} \neq false$, so: $t \in \mathcal{N}|_{\chi}$. We need to show that $\llbracket \psi \rrbracket^{\mathcal{N}|_\chi, t} = true$. By induction hypothesis $(\mathcal{N}, t') \Subset_{f,g} (\mathcal{M}, s') \implies \llbracket \ulcorner \chi \urcorner_{f,g} \rrbracket^{\mathcal{M}, s'} \leq \llbracket \chi \rrbracket^{\mathcal{N}, t'}$ for each $s' \in S, t' \in T$. Therefore from Lemma 1 we have $(\mathcal{N}|_\chi, t) \Subset_{f,g} (\mathcal{M}|_{\ulcorner \chi \urcorner_{f,g}}, s)$. By induction hypothesis, $\llbracket \psi \rrbracket^{\mathcal{N}|_\chi, t} = true$. Thus $\llbracket \phi \rrbracket^{\mathcal{N}, t} = true$.
  - if $\llbracket \ulcorner \phi \urcorner_{f,g} \rrbracket^{\mathcal{M}, s} = false$ then $\llbracket \ulcorner \chi \urcorner_{f,g} \rrbracket^{\mathcal{M}, s} = true$ and $\llbracket \ulcorner \psi \urcorner_{f,g} \rrbracket^{\mathcal{M}|\ulcorner \chi \urcorner_{f,g}, s} = false$. Since $\llbracket \ulcorner \chi \urcorner_{f,g} \rrbracket^{\mathcal{M}, s} = true$ then $\llbracket \chi \rrbracket^{\mathcal{N}, t} = true$ by induction hypothesis. We only need to show $\llbracket \psi \rrbracket^{\mathcal{N}|_\chi, s} = false$. It is clear that $t \in \mathcal{N}|_\chi$ and $s \in \mathcal{M}|_{\ulcorner \chi \urcorner_{f,g}}$, then by the induction hypothesis the condition of Lemma 1 holds, and it follows that $(\mathcal{N}|_\chi, t) \Subset_{f,g} (\mathcal{M}|_{\ulcorner \chi \urcorner_{f,g}}, s)$. Thus by the induction hypothesis we have $\llbracket \psi \rrbracket^{N|_\chi, t} = false$. Therefore: $\llbracket \phi \rrbracket^{\mathcal{N}, t} = false$.

Corollary 1. *Suppose $(\mathcal{N}, t), (\mathcal{M}, s)$ are two pointed KMLTSs w.r.t. (I', P') and (I, P) respectively. If $(\mathcal{N}, t) \Subset_{f,g} (\mathcal{M}, s)$ and $\mathcal{N}$ is a Kripke model converted from a concrete KMLTS then for any formula $\phi \in \mathcal{L}_{I', P'}$:*

- $[\![\ulcorner\phi\urcorner_{f,g}]\!]^{\mathcal{M},s} = true \implies \mathcal{N}, t \vDash \phi$
- $[\![\ulcorner\phi\urcorner_{f,g}]\!]^{\mathcal{M},s} = false \implies \mathcal{N}, t \vDash \neg\phi$

By the above corollary, to know whether ϕ is satisified at a pointed Kripke model, we can instead model check $\ulcorner\phi\urcorner_{f,g}$ on its f, g−abstraction.

To justify the logical characterization, we prove the converse of Theorem 1.

Theorem 2. *Suppose $(\mathcal{N}, t)$ and $(\mathcal{M}, s)$ are pointed KMLTS models with signatures (I', P') and (I, P), and suppose they enjoy image finiteness (i.e. every transition relation has most finitely many successors at any state). If for every formula $\phi \in \mathcal{L}_{I', P'}$: $[\![\ulcorner\phi\urcorner_{f,g}]\!]^{\mathcal{M},s} \leq [\![\phi]\!]^{\mathcal{N},t}$ then $(\mathcal{N}, t) \Subset_{f,g} (\mathcal{M}, s)$.*

Proof. Assume: for every formula $\phi \in \mathcal{L}_{I', P'}$: $[\![\ulcorner\phi\urcorner_{f,g}]\!]^{\mathcal{M},s} \leq [\![\phi]\!]^{\mathcal{N},t}$, and let $R = \{(t', s') \mid \text{for every } \phi : [\![\ulcorner\phi\urcorner_{f,g}]\!]^{\mathcal{M},s'} \leq [\![\phi]\!]^{\mathcal{N},t'}\}$. Then $(t, s) \in R$, and we check the three conditions of definition 4 for R. Suppose $(t', s') \in R$, then:

- The first condition follows from $[\![\ulcorner p'\urcorner_{f,g}]\!]^{\mathcal{M},s'} \leq [\![p']\!]^{\mathcal{N},t'}$ for $p' \in P'$.

- Suppose towards contradiction that $\exists t'' : t' \xrightarrow{i'}_{\Diamond} t''$ in $\mathcal{N}$ but for any $s'' \in S$: $s' \xrightarrow{f(i')}_{\Diamond} s''$ implies $(t'', s'') \notin R$. According to image finiteness, we have only finitely many such s''; call them $s''_0 \dots s''_n$. For each s''_k, since $(t'', s''_k) \notin R$, there must be a formula $\psi_{s''_k}$ such that $[\![\ulcorner\psi_{s''_k}\urcorner_{f,g}]\!]^{\mathcal{M},s''_k} = true$ but $[\![\psi_{s''_k}]\!]^{\mathcal{N},t'} \neq true$.[4] Now $\Box_{f(i')}(\bigvee_{k=0}^{n} \ulcorner\psi_{s''_k}\urcorner_{f,g})$ is *true* at s' but $\Box_{i'}(\bigvee_{k=0}^{n} \psi_{s''_k})$ is not *true* at t', contradicting the assumption that $(t', s') \in R$.

- Suppose towards contradiction that $s' \xrightarrow{f(i')}_{\Box} s''$ in $\mathcal{M}$, but there exists $i'' \in f^{-1}[f(i')]$ such that $\forall t'' \in T: t' \xrightarrow{i''}_{\Box} t''$ implies $(t', s'') \notin R$. According to image finiteness, there are only finitely many such t''; call them $t''_0 \dots t''_n$. For each t''_k, since $(t''_k, s'') \notin R$, there must be a formula $\psi_{t''_k}$ such that $[\![\ulcorner\psi_{t''_k}\urcorner_{f,g}]\!]^{\mathcal{M},s''} = false$ but $[\![\psi_{t''_i}]\!]^{\mathcal{N},t''_i} \neq false$. Note that $\Box_{f(i')}(\bigvee_{k=0}^{n} \ulcorner\psi_{t''_i}\urcorner_{f,g})$ is *false* at s' but $\Box_{i''}(\bigvee_{k=0}^{n} \psi_{t'_i})$ is not *false* at t', contradicting the assumption that $(t', s') \in R$.

4   Examples

4.1   The Muddy Children

A standard example demonstrating the effect of updates on the knowledge within a group of agents, is the epistemic modelling of the Muddy Children Puzzle (cf. the seminal work on reasoning about knowledge [8]). The setting is as follows: out of n children, $k > 1$ got mud on their foreheads while playing. They can see

---

[4] If $[\![\ulcorner\psi_{s''_k}\urcorner_{f,g}]\!]^{\mathcal{M},s''} = false$ but $[\![\psi_{s''_k}]\!]^{\mathcal{N},t''} \neq false$ then $[\![\ulcorner\neg\psi_{s''_k}\urcorner_{f,g}]\!]^{\mathcal{M},s''} = true$ but $[\![\neg\psi_{s''_k}]\!]^{\mathcal{N},t''} \neq true$.

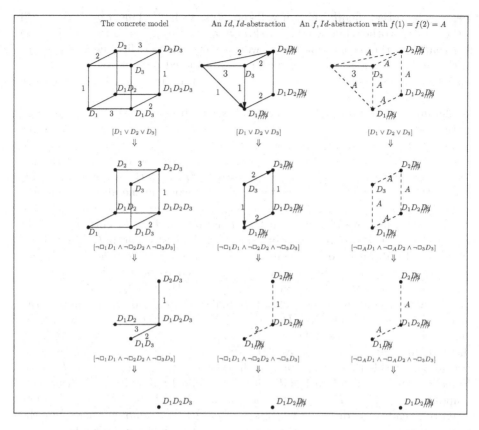

Fig. 2. Abstractions of the Muddy Children for $n = 3$ children. Each world has reflexive *may*-relations for each $i \in I$, some have reflexive *must*-relations, but for simplicity of presentation, all reflexive relations are omitted; $\cancel{D_3}$ means proposition D_3 has valuation $\bot$ in the current state.

whether other kids are dirty, but there is no mirror for them to discover whether they are dirty themselves. Then father walks in and states: "At least one of you is dirty!" Then he requests "If you know you are dirty, step forward now." If nobody steps forward, he repeats his request: "If you now know you are dirty, step forward now." After exactly k requests to step forward, the k dirty children suddenly do so (assuming they are honest and perfect reasoners).

The left column of Fig. 2 shows the standard epistemic model for this setting with three children. Proposition D_i signifies "child i is dirty". After the first update formula ("At least one of you is dirty"), all updates are of the form "nobody knows (yet) he is dirty" (by showing no move). One can check that if only one child is dirty, it will know after the first update. In that case a world satisfying only one D_i is the actual world; from this world in the updated model, child i considers no other worlds possible anymore. If nobody steps forward after the first request (implying nobody knows yet whether he is dirty), and a child sees only one other muddy child, it will know that he himself must be dirty as well (otherwise this other child would have known previously). This is modelled by the fact that after the second update the worlds with only one dirty child disappear in the updated model (they are no longer considered possible by anybody). If then nothing happens (third update), it must be the case that all three are dirty (and everybody knows this).

The middle and right columns of Fig. 2 show abstracted versions of the concrete model on the left. The refinement relation underlying both abstractions relates three pairs of worlds in the concrete model to three single worlds in the abstraction, while the world with all propositions *false* and the world with only D_3 *true* are kept (for example, the world with D_2 *true* and the world with D_2, D_3 *true* in the concrete model are related to the one world in the abstracted model where D_2 is *true* and D_3 *unknown*). In the middle column, the parameters f, g for the refinement are identities, in the right column f maps both 1 and 2 to abstract label A. Let D be the abbreviation of the first update $(D_1 \vee D_2 \vee D_3)$ and K be the abbreviation of the next ones $(\neg\square_1 D_1 \wedge \neg\square_2 D_2 \wedge \neg\square_3 D_3)$. Notice the following significant properties can be verified to be *true* in the two abstractions: (1) In both abstractions, $\ulcorner[D][K][K](\square_1 D_1 \wedge \square_2 D_2)\urcorner_{f,g}$ is *true* at the worlds that correspond to the world which makes D_1, D_2 and D_3 *true* in the original model. Thus $[D][K][K](\square_1 D_1 \wedge \square_2 D_2)$ is *true* in that world in the original model. Namely, in the case all three children are dirty, children 1 and 2 will know they are dirty after three updates. (2) In both abstractions, $\ulcorner[D][K]\square_1 D_1\urcorner_{f,g}$ is *true* at the worlds that correspond to the world which makes D_1 and D_3 *true*. Namely in the case children 1 and 3 are dirty, child 1 will know he is dirty after 2 updates. (3) $\ulcorner[D]\square_3 D_3\urcorner_{f,g}$ is *true* at the worlds with only D_3 *true*. Namely when only child 3 is dirty, he will know after the first announcement. For the generalization to the n children case, similar abstractions can be made.

Note that whereas all relations in the concrete model are equivalence relations ($S5$), this is no longer the case for the abstractions: in the middle abstraction, the *must* relations can be seen to be non-symmetric, and in the right abstraction, the relation labelled A is no longer transitive (in general the union of two equivalence relations is not necessarily transitive). In terms of the axiom set $S5$: some of the axioms are *unknown* rather than *true* in the non-$S5$ abstractions of this example.

4.2   Encoded Broadcast

Consider the following simple situation: a television sender wants to broadcast its programs (i.e., streams of bits) only to paying viewers. Therefore, it encodes the stream with a boolean function, let us consider negation. The encoding function has been shared to the registered clients, indexed $1 \ldots n$, while some other unregistered parties, indexed $n+1 \ldots n+m$, do not know it and it should be the case that they do not get access to the programs. A model of this situation can be seen in Figure 3 (up). $b_1 \ldots b_{n+m}$ are the bits located at the sites of the $n+m$ viewers, currently waiting to be set to the value of the next bit in the stream. The broadcast, to both registered and unregistered users, will consist of one bit c, which is the encoding of the actual next bit. In the actual world

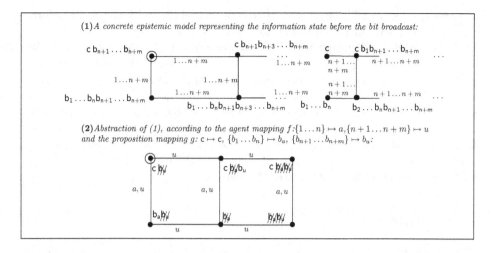

Fig. 3. Epistemic modelling of encoded broadcasting. To keep a clear overview, not all arrows were drawn; the transitive and reflexive closure of the arrow relation forms the intended equivalence. **(up)**: on each row, the first dots stand for a continuation of the sequence of indistinguishable worlds where the valuations range through all the subsets of $\{b_{n+1} \ldots b_{n+m}\}$. The second dots stand for sequences of worlds where the valuations range through all the subsets of $\{b_1 \ldots b_{n+m}\}$ with at least one positive (on top) or negative (on bottom) b_i, with $i \in \{1 \ldots n\}$. In the possible worlds on the top row, $c = true$ and on the bottom row, $c = false$. The registerd users know that the encoding algorithm ensures $\bigwedge_{i \in \{1 \ldots n\}} c \leftrightarrow \neg b_i$, therefore their indistinguishability relations do not reach worlds where this formula is false. The unregisterd users are not able to distinguish between any two possible valuations. **(down)**: b_a and b_u can be seen as the receiving bits of a symbolic registered user a and a symbolic unregistered user u, respectively. The abstraction in (2) is obtained by mapping all concrete states where c is true and $b_1 \ldots b_n$ are false to the abstract state $c\cancel{b_a}\cancel{b_u}$, all other concrete states where c is true and $b_{n+1} \ldots b_{n+m}$ are true to $c\cancel{b_a}b_u$, and the rest of the concrete states where c is *true* to the abstract state $c\cancel{b_a}\cancel{b_u}$ (a similar mapping for states with c is false).

(marked with a circle), let us assume that the next bit in the stream is *false* and hence its encoding is $c = true$. We are interested in checking that, after a bit has been broadcasted, (only) the authorized users have received it correctly.

The size of the epistemic model varies obviously with m and n and can be huge, but it is also very regular. The uncertainty relation for every unauthorized agent $i \in \{n+1 \ldots n+m\}$ is the complete graph. Intuitively, this is because such an agent does not hold any information on the encoding function or on any of the waiting bits $b_1 \ldots b_{n+m}$, so it considers all valuations as possible. An abstraction of this concrete model can be seen in Figure 3 (down). Broadcasting the encoded bit c can be simply modelled by the public announcement of c. The abstract version of this announcement $\ulcorner c \urcorner_{f,g}$ is still c.

The correct receive property by authorized viewers might be formalized as: $\bigwedge_{i \in \{1 \ldots n\}} [c] \Box_i \neg b_i$ (since the transmitted bit was *false*). Its translation to the abstract context is $[c]\square_a \neg b_a$, which is true on model (2) in Figure 3. Therefore, according to Theorem 1, all original formulas are *true*.

The other desired property is that unauthorized users will not receive the intended bit, that is $\bigwedge_{i \in \{n+1...n+m\}} [c] \neg \square_i (\neg b_i)$. The translation of this formula, $[c] \neg \square_u \neg b_u$ can also be evaluated to true on model (2), meaning, again via Theorem 1, that the value of b doesn't leak to the unauthorized agents. Note that *must* relations are needed in order to establish satisfiability of such negative knowledge properties. An interesting observation is that, due to the enormous density of arrows in an epistemic model, *must* relations will occur often enough in abstracted models. This is quite different than the case of LTSs, where most relations in abstracted models are of the *may* type.

5   Conclusion

We proposed a refinement/abstraction framework for KMLTSs, which allows reasoning on small coarse abstract models and transfer the results on refined detailed models. In particular, if the concrete Kripke models are epistemic models, interesting knowledge properties are preserved by refinements and abstractions as shown by two examples.

The theoretical novelty of this work is the extension of traditional abstraction techniques to both the label and proposition mapping, and to a logic containing a dynamic *public announcement* modality. Both features are of fundamental importance in (epistemic) modelling and verification, which is the main motivation of our work. In order to incorporate the full power of dynamic epistemic modelling, more research is needed on integrating general update constructions as formalized by action models [1]. The abstraction of action models is also practically interesting, as it is shown in [6] that they can be of huge size when modelling protocols. Another goal is to adapt this framework to Interpreted Systems [8,19], which combines both epistemic and temporal characteristics.

On a practical side, our framework opens the way to automatic epistemic verification of large or even infinite models. Future research should be dedicated to practical problems like generating abstract models directly from textual or formal, but compact, protocol specifications. A possible starting point is the process algebra language of [5].

Acknowledgement. We thank the anonymous referees for their detailed comments. The authors are supported by Dutch NWO project VEMPS (612.000.528).

References

1. Baltag, A., Moss, L.S.: Logics for epistemic programs. Synthese 139(2), 165–224 (2004)
2. van Benthem, J., van Eijck, J., Kooi, B.: Logics of communication and change. Information and Computation (2006)

3. Bruns, G., Godefroid, P.: Model checking with multi-valued logics. In: Díaz, J., Karhumäki, J., Lepistö, A., Sannella, D. (eds.) ICALP 2004. LNCS, vol. 3142. Springer, Heidelberg (2004)

4. Burrows, M., Abadi, M., Needham, R.: A logic of authentication. In: Practical Cryptography for Data Internetworks. IEEE Computer Society Press, Los Alamitos (1996)

5. Dechesne, F., Mousavi, M., Orzan, S.M.: Operational and epistemic approaches to protocol analysis: Bridging the gap. In: Dershowitz, N., Voronkov, A. (eds.) LPAR 2007. LNCS (LNAI), vol. 4790. Springer, Heidelberg (2007)

6. Dechesne, F., Wang, Y.: Dynamic epistemic verification of security protocols: framework and case study. In: A Meeting of the minds: Proceedings LORI workshop. Texts in Computer Science, pp. 129–144 (2007)

7. van Eijck, J.: DEMO program and documentation (2005),
   http://www.cwi.nl/~jve/demo/

8. Fagin, R., Halpern, J.Y., Moses, Y., Vardi, M.Y.: Reasoning About Knowledge. MIT Press, Cambridge (1995)

9. Godefroid, P., Jagadeesan, R.: Automatic abstraction using generalized model checking. In: Brinksma, E., Larsen, K.G. (eds.) CAV 2002. LNCS, vol. 2404, pp. 137–150. Springer, Heidelberg (2002)

10. Halpern, J.Y., O'Neill, K.R.: Anonymity and information hiding in multiagent systems. Journal of Computer Security, 483–514 (2005)

11. van der Hoek, W., Wooldridge, M.: Model checking knowledge and time. In: Bošnacki, D., Leue, S. (eds.) SPIN 2002. LNCS, vol. 2318, pp. 95–111. Springer, Heidelberg (2002)

12. Hommersom, A., Meyer, J.-J., de Vink, E.P.: Update semantics of security protocols. Synthese 142, 229–267 (2004); Knowledge, Rationality and Action subseries

13. Hughes, D., Shmatikov, V.: Information hiding, anonymity and privacy: A modular approach. Journal of Computer Security 12(1), 3–36 (2004)

14. Huth, M., Jagadeesan, R., Schmidt, D.: Modal transition systems: A foundation for three-valued program analysis. In: Sands, D. (ed.) ESOP 2001. LNCS, vol. 2028. Springer, Heidelberg (2001)

15. Larsen, K.G.: Modal specifications. In: Automatic Verification Methods for Finite State Systems, pp. 232–246 (1989)

16. Larsen, K.G., Thomsen, B.: A modal process logic. In: Proceedings LICS, pp. 203–210 (1988)

17. van der Meyden, R., Su, K.: Symbolic model checking the knowledge of the dining cryptographers. In: Proc. CSFW 2004, pp. 280–291. IEEE, Los Alamitos (2004)

18. Plaza, J.A.: Logics of public communications. In: Proceedings ISMIS 1989, pp. 201–216 (1989)

19. Raimondi, F., Lomuscio, A.: Automatic verification of deontic interpreted systems by model checking via OBDD's. Journal of Applied Logic (2006)

20. van de Pol, J.C., Valero Espada, M.: Modal abstractions in μCRL*. In: AMAST, pp. 409–425 (2004)

21. van Ditmarsch, H., van der Hoek, W., Kooi, B.: Dynamnic Epistemic Logic. Synthese Library, vol. 337. Springer, Heidelberg (2008)

22. van Eijck, J., Orzan, S.M.: Epistemic verification of anonymity. ENTCS, 168 (2007)

Tomorrow and All our Yesterdays: MTL Satisfiability over the Integers[*]

Carlo A. Furia[1] and Paola Spoletini[2]

[1] DEI, Politecnico di Milano, Milano, Italy
[2] DSCPI, Università degli Studi dell'Insubria, Como, Italy

Abstract. We investigate the satisfiability problem for metric temporal logic (MTL) with both past and future operators over linear discrete bi-infinite time models isomorphic to the integer numbers, where time is unbounded both in the future and in the past. We provide a technique to reduce satisfiability over the integers to satisfiability over the well-known mono-infinite time model of natural numbers, and we show how to implement the technique through an automata-theoretic approach. We also prove that MTL satisfiability over the integers is EXPSPACE-complete, hence the given algorithm is optimal in the worst case.

1 Introduction

Temporal logic has become a very widespread notation for the formal specification of systems, temporal properties, and requirements. Its popularity is significantly due to the fact that it provides highly effective conceptual tools to model, specify, and reason about systems [7], and it is amenable to fully automated verification techniques, the most notable being model-checking [4].

In temporal logic frameworks it is customary to model time as infinite in the future and finite in the past, i.e., with an origin; in other words, time is mono-infinite. On the contrary, models where time is infinite both in the future and in the past — i.e., it is *bi-infinite* [12] — have been routinely neglected. The reasons for this strong preference are mainly historical, as it has been pointed out by various authors [7,13]. Namely, temporal logic has been originally introduced for the purpose of reasoning about the behavior of "ongoing concurrent programs" [7], hence a model of time with an origin is appropriate since "computation begins at an initial state" [7]. However, there are various motivations in favor of the adoption of bi-infinite time models [13] as well, and they go beyond the obvious theoretical interest.

The first of such reasons has to do with the usage of temporal logics with operators that reference to the past of the current instant. If past is bounded, we may have to deal with past operators referring to instants that are before the origin of time: this gives rise to so-called *border effects* [5]. For instance, consider *yesterday* operator Y of LTL[1]: Yp evaluates to true at some instant t

---

[*] Work partially supported by the MIUR FIRB ArtDeco project.

[1] Throughout the paper we assume temporal logics with past operators.

J.S. Fitzgerald, A.E. Haxthausen, and H. Yenigun (Eds.): ICTAC 2008, LNCS 5160, pp. 126–140, 2008.
© Springer-Verlag Berlin Heidelberg 2008

if and only if its argument p holds at the previous instant $t - 1$. Then, consider formula Yalarm which models an alarm being raised at the previous instant. If we evaluate the formula at the origin, the reference to the "previous" instant of time is moot as there is no such instant, and whether the evaluation should default to true or to false depends on the role the formula plays in the whole specification. A possible solution to these problems is to introduce two variants of every past operator, one defaulting to true and the other to false [5]; however, this is often complicated and cumbersome, especially in practical applications. On the contrary, the adoption of bi-infinite time gets rid of such border effects single-handedly, in a very uniform and natural manner, because there are simply no "inaccessible" instants of time.

The second main motivation for considering bi-infinite time models is derived from a reason for adopting mono-infinite time models: the fact that ongoing non-terminating processes are considered. Similarly, when modeling processes that are "time invariant" (whose behavior does not depend on *absolute* time values) and where initialization can be abstracted away, a time model which is infinite both in the past and in the future is the most natural and terse assumption.

This paper investigates temporal logic over bi-infinite discrete-time models. More precisely, we consider a linear-time model which is isomorphic to the integer numbers. Correspondingly, Metric Temporal Logic (MTL) [1] is taken as temporal logic notation. It will be clear that, over the adopted discrete-time model, MTL boils down to LTL with a succinct encoding of constants in formulas. Hence, our results will be easily stateable in terms of LTL as well. The main contributions are as follows. First, we present a general technique to reduce the satisfiability problem for MTL over the integers to the same problem over the more familiar mono-infinite time model isomorphic to the natural numbers. Second, we show how the technique can be practically implemented with an automata-theoretic approach — derived from previous work of ours [15] — which can work on top of the Spin model-checker [10]. Third, the complexity of the MTL satisfiability problem over the integer is assessed, and it is shown that, unsurprisingly, it matches the well-known upper and lower bounds for the same problem over mono-infinite discrete time domain [1]. To the best of our knowledge, this is the first work which analyzes the complexity of MTL (and LTL) satisfiability over bi-infinite time and provides a practical algorithm for it.

For the sake of space limits, we omit some proofs and inessential details, while providing some intuitive examples. Missing details can be found in [8].

2   Definitions and Preliminaries

The symbols $\mathbb{Z}$ and $\mathbb{N}$ denote respectively the set of integer numbers and the set of nonnegative integers. For greater clarity, connectives and quantifiers of the meta-language are typeset in a bold underlined font.

2.1   Metric Temporal Logic

We define Metric Temporal Logic (MTL) [1] over mono-infinite and bi-infinite linear discrete time. We always consider the variant with both past and future operators (called MTL^P by some authors [1]).

Syntax. Let $\Pi = \{p, q, \ldots\}$ be a finite set of propositions. MTL formulas are given by $\phi ::= p \mid \neg\phi \mid \phi_1 \wedge \phi_2 \mid \phi_1 \, \mathsf{U}_I \, \phi_2 \mid \phi_1 \, \mathsf{S}_I \, \phi_2$, where $p \in \Pi$, I is an interval of the naturals (possibly unbounded to the right), and the symbols U_I, S_I denote the bounded *until* and *since* operator, respectively.

Standard abbreviations are assumed such as $\top, \bot, \vee, \Rightarrow, \Leftrightarrow$. In addition, we introduce some useful derived temporal operators: *eventually* $\mathsf{F}_I\phi = \top \, \mathsf{U}_I \, \phi$; *always* $\mathsf{G}_I\phi = \neg\mathsf{F}_I\neg\phi$; *next* $\mathsf{X}\phi = \bot \, \mathsf{U} \, \phi$; *release* $\phi_1 \, \mathsf{R}_I \, \phi_2 = \neg(\neg\phi_1 \, \mathsf{U}_I \, \neg\phi_2)$. Each of these operators has its past counterpart; that is, respectively: eventually in the *past* $\mathsf{P}_I\phi = \top \, \mathsf{S}_I \, \phi$; *historically* $\mathsf{H}_I\phi = \neg\mathsf{P}_I\neg\phi$; *previous* or *yesterday* $\mathsf{Y}_k\phi = \mathsf{P}_{[k,k]}\phi$; *trigger* $\phi_1 \, \mathsf{T}_I \, \phi_2 = \neg(\neg\phi_1 \, \mathsf{S}_I \, \neg\phi_2)$. Note that, whenever no interval is specified, $I = (0, \infty)$ is assumed for all operators; also, the singleton interval $[k, k]$ is abbreviated by $= k$.

Precedence of operators is defined as follows: $\neg$ has the highest binding power, then we have the temporal modalities U_I, S_I and derived ones, then $\wedge$ and $\vee$, $\Rightarrow$, and finally $\Leftrightarrow$. $\widetilde{\phi}$ denotes the formula obtained from ϕ by switching every future operator with its past counterpart, and *vice versa*.

The size $|\phi|$ of a formula ϕ is given by the product of its number of connectives $|\phi|_\#$ times the size $|\phi|_M$ of the largest constant used in its formulas, succinctly encoded in binary. A *future* formula ϕ is a formula which does not use any past operator; conversely, a *past* formula π is a formula which does not use any future operator. A formula ψ is *flat* if it does not nest temporal operators.[2] A flat formula is *propositional* if it does not use temporal operators at all.

Words and operations on them. For a finite alphabet Σ, we introduce the sets of right-infinite words (called ω-words), of left-infinite words (called $\widetilde{\omega}$-words), and of bi-infinite words (called $\mathbb{Z}$-words) over Σ, and we denote them as Σ^ω, $^\omega\Sigma$, and $\Sigma^\mathbb{Z}$, respectively. Correspondingly, an ω-language (resp. $\widetilde{\omega}$-language, $\mathbb{Z}$-language) is a subset of Σ^ω (resp. $^\omega\Sigma$, $\Sigma^\mathbb{Z}$).

Given an ω-word $w = w_0 w_1 w_2 \cdots$, $\widetilde{w}$ denotes the $\widetilde{\omega}$-word $\cdots w_{-2} w_{-1} w_0$ defined by the bijection $w_{-k} = w_k$ for $k \in \mathbb{N}$. The same notation is used for the inverse mapping from $\widetilde{\omega}$-words to ω-words. The mapping is also extended to languages as obvious, with the same notation. Given a $\mathbb{Z}$-word $x = \cdots x_{-2} x_{-1} x_0 x_1 x_2 \cdots$ and $k \in \mathbb{Z}$, x^k denotes the ω-word obtained by truncating x at x_k on the left, i.e., $x^k = x_k x_{k+1} x_{k+2} \cdots$; similarly, $^k x$ denotes the $\widetilde{\omega}$-word obtained by truncating x at x_k on the right, i.e., $^k x = \cdots x_{k-2} x_{k-1} x_k$.

The operations of intersection ($\cap$), union ($\cup$), and concatenation (.) for words and languages are defined as usual. Let w and $\overline{w}$ be an ω- and an $\widetilde{\omega}$-word, respectively. The $\mathbb{Z}$-word $\overline{w} \triangleright w$ (*right join*) is defined as $^{-1}\overline{w}.w$, and the $\mathbb{Z}$-word $\overline{w} \triangleleft w$ (*left join*) is defined as $\overline{w}.w^1$. The join operations are extended to

---

[2] In the literature, there exist also different definitions of flatness, e.g., [3].

languages as obvious, with the same notation. Also, $\downarrow^\Sigma$ denotes the projection homomorphism over Σ.

Semantics. We define the semantics of MTL formulas for infinite words over 2^Π, where Π is a finite set of atomic propositions. As it is standard, every letter $y_k \in 2^\Pi$ in such words represents the set of atomic propositions that are true at integer time instant k (also called *position*). We introduce the predicate $\mathbf{valid}(y, i)$ which holds iff i is a valid position in the infinite word y, i.e., iff y is a $\mathbb{Z}$-word and $i \in \mathbb{Z}$, or y is an ω-word and $i \in \mathbb{N}$, or y is an $\widetilde{\omega}$-word and $-i \in \mathbb{N}$.

Let ϕ be an MTL formula, y a generic infinite word over 2^Π, and i an integer such that $\mathbf{valid}(y, i)$. The satisfaction relation $\models$ is defined inductively as:

$$y, i \models p \quad\Leftrightarrow\quad p \in y_i$$
$$y, i \models \neg\phi \quad\Leftrightarrow\quad y, i \not\models \phi$$
$$y, i \models \phi_1 \wedge \phi_2 \quad\Leftrightarrow\quad y, i \models \phi_1 \;\wedge\; y, i \models \phi_2$$
$$y, i \models \phi_1 \, \mathsf{U}_I \, \phi_2 \quad\Leftrightarrow\quad \exists d \in I: (\mathbf{valid}(y, i+d) \;\wedge$$
$$y, i+d \models \psi_2 \wedge \forall 0 < u < d : y, i+u \models \psi_1)$$
$$y, i \models \phi_1 \, \mathsf{S}_I \, \phi_2 \quad\Leftrightarrow\quad \exists d \in I: (\mathbf{valid}(y, i-d) \;\wedge$$
$$y, i-d \models \psi_2 \wedge \forall 0 < u < d : y, i-u \models \psi_1)$$
$$y \models \phi \quad\Leftrightarrow\quad \forall i \in \mathbb{Z} : (\mathbf{valid}(y, i) \Rightarrow y, i \models \phi)$$

Note that we defined $y \models \phi$ to denote "global satisfiability", i.e., the fact that ϕ holds at all valid positions of y. This definition is especially natural over bi-infinite words, where there is no initial instant at which to evaluate formulas. On the contrary, "initial satisfiability" is more common over mono-infinite words where an origin is unambiguously fixed. However, the global satisfiability problem is easily reducible to the initial satisfiability problem, as $\forall i : y, i \models \phi$ iff $y, 0 \models \text{Alw}(\phi)$, where $\text{Alw}(\phi) \equiv \mathsf{G}\phi \wedge \phi \wedge \mathsf{H}\phi$ denotes that ϕ holds always.

For instance, consider formula $\nu = \mathsf{H}_{[0,3]}p$ and its interpretation over ω-word w^+ in Figure 1. According to the semantics defined above, ν is true at 1 because p holds for all *valid* positions between 1 and $1 - 3 = -2$. However, there may be justifications in favor of evaluating ν false at 1: there is no complete interval of size 4 where p holds continuously. This is an example of so-called *border effect*: what is a "reasonable" evaluation of formulas near the origin is influenced by the role the formulas play in a specification.

There is an interesting relation between the reverse $\widetilde{\phi}$ of a formula ϕ and the reverse $\widetilde{w}$ of ω-words w that are models of ϕ, as the following example shows. Consider formula $\theta = \mathsf{H}_{[0,3]}p \Rightarrow \mathsf{F}q$ and its reverse $\widetilde{\theta} = \mathsf{G}_{[0,3]}p \Rightarrow \mathsf{P}q$. θ asserts that whenever p held continuously for 4 time units, q must hold somewhere in the future (excluding the current instant), hence θ is true at position 4 and false at position 11 over ω-word w^+ in Figure 1. If we consider $\widetilde{\omega}$-word w^- obtained by reversing w^+ (also in Figure 1), we see that $\widetilde{\theta}$ is true at position -4 and false at position -11 over w^-.

By generalizing the example, we have the following proposition.

Proposition 1. *Let $w^+ \in \left(2^\Sigma\right)^\omega$ be an ω-word, ϕ be an MTL formula, and $i \in \mathbb{N}$. Then $w^+, i \models \phi$ iff $\widetilde{w^+}, -i \models \widetilde{\phi}$.*

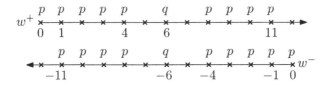

Fig. 1. ω-word w^+ (above) and its reverse $\widetilde{\omega}$-word w^- (below)

Satisfiability and language of a formula. Satisfiability is the following problem: "given a formula ϕ is there some word y such that $y \models \phi$?". It is the verification problem we consider in this paper. For an MTL formula ϕ, let $\mathcal{L}_0^\omega(\phi)$ denote the set of ω-words w such that $w, 0 \models \phi$, let $\mathcal{L}^\omega(\phi)$ denote the set of ω-words w such that $w \models \phi$, and let $\mathcal{L}^{\mathbb{Z}}(\phi)$ denote the set of $\mathbb{Z}$-words x such that $x \models \phi$. Then, the satisfiability problem for a formula ϕ is equivalent to the emptiness problem for the corresponding language.

LTL and expressiveness. LTL is a well-known linear temporal logic based on the unique modality U. We will consider the past-enhanced variant of the logic, and call it simply LTL. For the time models we consider in this paper, MTL is simply LTL with an exponentially succinct encoding (see [8] for a translation): every MTL formula μ can be translated into an LTL formula λ_μ such that $|\lambda_\mu| = |\lambda_\mu|_\# = \exp \mathrm{O}(|\mu|_\# |\mu|_\mathrm{M})$.

2.2 Automata over Infinite Words

Languages definable in MTL can also be described as languages accepted by finite state automata such as Büchi automata (BA) [16]. The size $|\mathcal{A}|$ of a BA $\mathcal{A}$ is defined as the number of its finite states.

Alternating automata (AA, [17]) are an equally expressive but possibly more concise version of BA. AA have two kinds of transitions: nondeterministic transitions (also called existential, corresponding to $\vee$) just like vanilla BA, and parallel transitions (also called universal, corresponding to $\wedge$). Alternation can represent concisely the structure of an LTL formula [17], avoiding the exponential blow-up. In [15] we introduced Alternating Modulo Counting Automata (AMCA), an enriched variant of AA which makes use of (bounded) counters; this new feature can represent succinctly MTL formulas as well, i.e., it can encode succinctly constants used in MTL modalities.

Definition 1 (Alternating Modulo Counting Automaton (AMCA) [15]). *An Alternating Modulo Counting Automaton is a tuple $\langle \Sigma, Q, \mu, q_0, \delta, F \rangle$ where:*

- *Σ is a finite alphabet,*
- *Q is a set of states,*
- *$\mu \in \mathbb{N}_{\geq 1}$ such that $C = [0..\mu]$ denotes a modular finite counter,*

- $q_0 \in Q$ is the initial state,
- $\delta : Q \times C \times \Sigma \rightarrow \mathbb{B}^+(Q \times C)$ is the transition relation,[3]
- $F \subseteq Q$ is a set of accepting states.

For the sake of readability when indicating the elements in $\mathbb{B}^+(Q \times C)$ we will use the symbol / to separate the component in Q from the component in C.
    A run of an AMCA is defined as follows.

Definition 2 (Run of an AMCA). A run (T, ρ) of an AMCA $\mathcal{A}$ on the ω-word $w = w_0 w_1 \cdots \in \Sigma^\omega$ is a $(Q \times C \times \mathbb{N})$-labeled tree, where ρ is the labeling function defined as: $\rho(\epsilon) = (q_0/0, 0)$; for all $x \in T$, $\rho(x) = (q/k, n)$; and the set $\{(q'/h, 1) \mid c \in \mathbb{N}, x.c \in T, h \in C, \rho(x.c) = (q'/h, n+1)\}$ satisfies the formula $\delta(q/k, w_n)$.
    The acceptance condition for AMCA is defined similarly as for regular BA: a path is accepting iff it passes infinitely many times on at least one state in F. Formally, for a sequence $P \in \mathbb{N}^\omega$ and a labeling function ρ, let $\inf(\rho, P) = \{s \mid \rho(n) \in \{s\} \times \mathbb{N} \text{ for infinitely many } n \in P\}$. A run (T, ρ) of an AMCA is accepting iff for all paths P of T it is $\inf(\rho, P)|_Q \cap F \neq \emptyset$.

The size $|\mathcal{A}|$ of an AMCA $\mathcal{A}$ can be defined as the product of $|Q|$ times the size of the counter, succinctly encoded in binary: $|\mathcal{A}| = O(|Q| \log \mu)$. With the usual notation, $\mathcal{L}^\omega(\mathcal{A})$ denotes the set of all ω-words accepted by an automaton $\mathcal{A}$.

3   Automata-Based MTL Satisfiability over the Naturals

A widespread approach to testing the satisfiability of an MTL (or LTL) formula over mono-infinite time models isomorphic to the natural numbers relies on the well-known tight relationship between LTL and finite state automata. In order to test the satisfiability of an MTL formula μ, one translates it into an LTL formula λ_μ, and then builds a nondeterministic BA $\mathcal{A}_{\lambda_\mu}$ that accepts precisely the models of λ_μ, hence of μ. Correspondingly, an emptiness test on $\mathcal{A}_{\lambda_\mu}$ is equivalent to a satisfiability check of μ. This procedure, very informally presented, relies on the following two well-known results.

Proposition 2 ([17]). (1) The emptiness problem for (nondeterministic) BA of size n is decidable in time $O(n)$ and space $O(\log^2 n)$. (2) Given an LTL formula ϕ, one can build a (nondeterministic) BA $\mathcal{A}_\phi$ with $|\mathcal{A}_\phi| = \exp O(|\phi|)$ such that $\mathcal{L}^\omega(\mathcal{A}_\phi) = \mathcal{L}^\omega(\phi)$ and $\mathcal{L}_0^\omega(\mathcal{A}_\phi) = \mathcal{L}_0^\omega(\phi)$.

In practice, however, this unoptimized approach is inconvenient, because the BA representing an MTL formula is in general doubly-exponential in the size of the formula, hence algorithmically very inefficient. On the contrary, we would like to exploit more concise classes of automata (such as AMCA) to represent MTL formulas more efficiently in practice. With this aim, in [15] we proposed a novel approach to model-checking and satisfiability checking over discrete mono-infinite time domains for a propositional subset of the TRIO metric temporal

---

[3] $\mathbb{B}^+(S)$ denotes the set of all *positive* Boolean combinations of elements in S.

logic. It is clear that the subset of TRIO considered in [15] corresponds to MTL as we defined it in this paper. Hence, let us recall from [15] the following result about the translation of MTL formulas in BA and AMCA over the naturals.

Proposition 3 ([15]). *Given a past MTL formula π, one can build two deterministic BA $\mathcal{A}_{\pi^\omega}$ and $\mathcal{A}_{\pi^0}$ such that $\mathcal{L}^\omega(\mathcal{A}_{\pi^0}) = \mathcal{L}_0^\omega(\pi)$, $\mathcal{L}^\omega(\mathcal{A}_{\pi^\omega}) = \mathcal{L}^\omega(\pi)$, and the size of both $\mathcal{A}_{\pi^0}$ and $\mathcal{A}_{\pi^\omega}$ is $\exp O(|\pi|)$. Given a future MTL formula φ, one can build two AMCA $\mathcal{A}_{\varphi^\omega}$ and $\mathcal{A}_{\varphi^0}$ such that $\mathcal{L}^\omega(\mathcal{A}_{\varphi^0}) = \mathcal{L}_0^\omega(\varphi)$, $\mathcal{L}^\omega(\mathcal{A}_{\varphi^\omega}) = \mathcal{L}^\omega(\varphi)$, and the size of both $\mathcal{A}_{\varphi^0}$ and $\mathcal{A}_{\varphi^\omega}$ is $O(|\varphi|)$.*

More precisely, future formulas are translated into AMCA according to the following schema: the AMCA for a future formula φ over alphabet Π is $\mathcal{A}_\varphi = \langle \Sigma, Q, \mu, q_0, \delta, F \rangle$ where:

- $\Sigma = 2^\Pi$,
- $Q = \{\nu \mid \nu$ is a subformula of $\varphi\} \cup \{\neg\nu \mid \nu$ is a subformula of $\varphi\}$,
- $\mu = |\varphi|_M$,
- $q_0 = \varphi$,
- the transition relation δ is defined as follows:
  - $\delta(\chi/0, p) = \top/0$ for $\chi \in \Pi$ and $\chi = p$,
  - $\delta(\chi/0, p) = \bot/0$ for $\chi \in \Pi$ and $\chi \neq p$,
  - $\delta(\psi \wedge \upsilon/0, p) = \delta(\psi/0, p) \wedge \delta(\upsilon/0, p)$,
  - $\delta(\neg\psi/0, p) = \mathsf{dual}(\delta(\psi/0, p))$, where $\mathsf{dual}(\phi)$ is a formula obtained from ϕ by switching $\top$ and $\bot$, $\wedge$ and $\vee$, and by complementing all subformulas of ϕ,
  - $\delta(\psi \, \mathsf{U}_{[a,b]} \, \upsilon/k, p) =$
    $$\begin{cases} \psi \, \mathsf{U}_{[a,b]} \, \upsilon/k + 1 & k = 0 \\ \delta(\psi/0, p) \wedge \left(\psi \, \mathsf{U}_{[a,b]} \, \upsilon/k + 1\right) & 0 < k < a \\ \delta(\upsilon/0, p) \vee \left(\delta(\psi/0, p) \wedge \left(\psi \, \mathsf{U}_{[a,b]} \, \upsilon/k + 1\right)\right) & a \leq k \leq b \\ \bot & k > b \end{cases}$$
    for $a \leq b < \infty$,
  - $\delta(\psi \, \mathsf{U} \, \upsilon/k, p) = \delta(\upsilon/0, p) \vee (\delta(\psi/0, p) \wedge (\psi \, \mathsf{U} \, \upsilon/0))$,
- $F = \{\xi \mid \xi \in Q$ and ξ has the form $\neg(\psi \, \mathsf{U} \, \upsilon)\}$

In the remainder we will show how to exploit such satisfiability checking procedures over the naturals to perform satisfiability checking over the integers.

4   Automata-Based MTL Satisfiability over the Integers

This section presents the main contribution of the paper: a technique to reduce the satisfiability problem for MTL formulas over the integers to the same problem over the naturals, and an automata-based implementation thereof.

Flat normal form. We introduce a suitable normal form where each application of temporal operators can be analyzed in isolation, and we show that any MTL formula can be rendered into this normal form by introducing auxiliary atomic proposition but without changing the asymptotic size of the formula.

An MTL formula ϕ is in *flat normal form* when it is written as:[4] $\phi' = \beta \wedge \bigwedge_{k=1}^{n} \mathrm{Alw}(p_k \Leftrightarrow \psi_k)$, where $\beta \in \mathbb{B}(\Pi)$ and ψ_k is a flat formula, for all $k = 1, \ldots, n$. In addition, if every ψ_k is a pure past formula or a pure future formula, ϕ' is named flat *separated* normal form (FSNF).

Theorem 1. *Let ϕ be an MTL formula over Π; a ϕ' in FSNF can be built efficiently such that $\mathcal{L}^{\mathbb{Z}}(\phi) =\downarrow^{\Pi} \mathcal{L}^{\mathbb{Z}}(\phi')$, $|\phi'|_M = |\phi|_M$, and $|\phi'|_\# = O(|\phi|_\#)$.*

For example, considering formula $\theta = \mathrm{H}_{[0,3]}p \Rightarrow \mathrm{F}q$, we can build θ' by replacing $\mathrm{H}_{[0,3]}p$ and $\mathrm{F}q$ with two new Boolean literals p' and q' respectively. Hence, $\theta' = (p' \Rightarrow q') \wedge \mathrm{Alw}\left(p' \Leftrightarrow \mathrm{H}_{[0,3]}p\right) \wedge \mathrm{Alw}(q' \Leftrightarrow \mathrm{F}q)$.

4.1   Splitting the Evaluation about the Origin

Let ϕ' be an MTL formula in FSNF. The satisfiability of ϕ' can be analyzed by considering each of the $n + 1$ subformulas $\beta, p_k \Leftrightarrow \psi_k|_{1 \leq k \leq n}$ separately. In fact, $x \models \phi'$ iff $x \models \beta$ and $\underline{\forall} k = 1, \ldots, n : x \models p_k \Leftrightarrow \psi_k$. Hence, without loss of generality, we focus on studying the satisfiability of formulas in the form β, $p \Leftrightarrow \psi^+$, and $p \Leftrightarrow \psi^-$, where ψ^+ and ψ^- are flat *until* and *since* formulas, respectively.

More precisely, let us start with the future formula: $\psi = f \Leftrightarrow p \, \mathrm{U}_I \, q \equiv (\neg f \vee p \, \mathrm{U}_I \, q) \wedge (f \vee \neg p \, \mathrm{R}_I \, \neg q)$ In turn, $x \models \psi$ iff $x \models \neg f \vee p \, \mathrm{U}_I \, q$ and $x \models f \vee \neg p \, \mathrm{R}_I \, \neg q$. Correspondingly, we now focus on studying the satisfiability of the simple formula $\neg f \vee p \, \mathrm{U}_I \, q$ over the integers. Then it will be straightforward to extend it to handle the other formula $f \vee \neg p \, \mathrm{R}_I \, \neg q$, as well as the corresponding past formula $f \Leftrightarrow p \, \mathrm{S}_I \, q$.

Behavior about the origin. Let us consider a $\mathbb{Z}$-word x such that $x \models p \, \mathrm{U}_{[l,u]} \, q$ for some $0 \leq l \leq u < \infty$. We aim at splitting the evaluation of $x \models p \, \mathrm{U}_{[l,u]} \, q$ into the evaluation of other related formulas over mono-infinite words x^0 and $^0 x$.

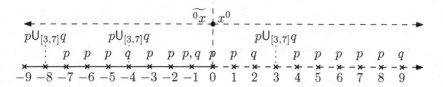

Fig. 2. Splitting the evaluation of $p \, \mathrm{U}_{[3,7]} \, q$ about the origin

---

[4] $\mathbb{B}(\Pi)$ denotes the set of all Boolean combinations of elements in Π.

Before introducing the formal results, let us provide some intuition about our technique, and let $l = 3, u = 7$. First of all, $x \models p \, U_{[3,7]} \, q$ requires in particular that $x^0 \models p \, U_{[3,7]} \, q$: *until* is a future operator, thus its evaluation over x^0 is independent of all instant before the origin, hence $x^0 \models p \, U_{[3,7]} \, q$ iff $\forall k \geq 0$: $x, k \models p \, U_{[3,7]} \, q$. For instance this is the case of instant 3 in Figure 2. Similarly, let us consider any position k of x such that the interval $(k, k + 7] \subset (-\infty, 0]$ is contained completely to the left of the origin, such as position -8 in Figure 2. The evaluation of $p \, U_{[3,7]} \, q$ at k is independent of all instants after the origin, hence $x, k \models p \, U_{[3,7]} \, q$ iff $^0x, k \models p \, U_{[3,7]} \, q$, for all $k + 7 \leq 0$, i.e., $k \leq -7$. Finally, let us consider what happens to the evaluation of $p \, U_{[3,7]} \, q$ at instants k such that the interval $(k, k + 7] \ni 0$ contains the origin; for instance let $k = -4$ and consider again Figure 2. Hence, there exists a $h \in [-1, 3]$ such that $x, h \models q$ and for all $-4 < j < h$ it is $x, j \models p$. Here, we have to distinguish two cases and handle them differently. If $h \leq 0$ such as for $h = -1$ in Figure 2, the evaluation of $p \, U_{[3,7]} \, q$ at -4 is still independent of instants after the origin, hence $x, k \models p \, U_{[3,7]} \, q$ iff $^0x, k \models p \, U_{[3,7]} \, q$. Otherwise, if $h > 0$ such as for $h = 2$ in Figure 2, we consider separately the adjacent intervals $(k, 0]$ and $(0, k+7]$. The fact that p holds throughout $(k, 0]$ is independent of instants after the origin, so $x, k \models G_{(0, -k]} p$ iff $^0x, k \models Gp$. Moreover, $p \, U_I \, q$ holds at the origin for the "residual" interval $(0, 3]$, thus $x, 0 \models p \, U_{[1,3]} \, q$ iff $x^0, 0 \models p \, U_{[1,3]} \, q$.

By generalizing the above informal reasoning, we get the following.

Lemma 1. *For $x \in (2^\Pi)^\mathbb{Z}$, $0 \leq l \leq u < \infty$ such that $u \neq 0$,[5] $1 - u \leq i \leq -1$:*

$$
x, i \models p \, U_{[l,u]} \, q \quad \Leftrightarrow \quad
\begin{array}{c}
x, i \models p \, U_{[l,-i]} \, q \\
\underline{\vee} \\
\left(x, i \models G_{[1,-i]} p \, \underline{\wedge} \, x, 0 \models p \, U_{[\max(1,i+l),i+u]} \, q \right)
\end{array}
\tag{1}
$$

Proof. Let us start with the $\Rightarrow$ direction: assume $x, i \models p \, U_{[l,u]} \, q$. Hence, there exists a $d \in [l, u]$ such that $x, i + d \models q$ and for all $i < j < i + d$ it is $x, j \models p$. If $i + d \leq 0$ then $0 \leq d \leq -i$, hence $x, i \models p \, U_{[l,-i]} \, q$ holds. Otherwise, $i + d > 0$; in this case, p holds throughout $(i, 0]$ and thus $x, i \models G_{[1,-i]} p$ holds. In addition, let $d' = i + d$; note that $1 \leq d' \leq i + u$ and also $i + l \leq d'$, so $x, 0 \models p \, U_{[\max(1,i+l),i+u]} \, q$ holds.

Let us now consider the $\Leftarrow$ direction. If $x, i \models p \, U_{[l,-i]} \, q$, from $1 - u \leq i \leq -1$ we get $1 \leq -i \leq u - 1$, thus $[l, -i] \subseteq [l, u]$ which entails $x, i \models p U_{[l,u]} \, q$. Otherwise, let $x, i \models G_{[1,-i]} p$ and $x, 0 \models p \, U_{[\max(1,i+l),i+u]} \, q$. That is, p holds throughout $(i, 0]$, and there exists a $k \in [\max(1, i + l), i + u]$ such that $x, k \models q$ and p holds throughout $(0, k)$. Let $d = -i + k$; from $k \in [\max(1, i + l), i + u]$ we get $d \in [l, u]$, which establishes $x, i \models p \, U_{[l,u]} \, q$. □

Lemma 1 shows how to "split" the evaluation of an *until* formula into the evaluation of two derived formulas, one to be evaluated to the left of the origin, and

---

[5] This restriction is clearly without loss of generality, as $\phi_1 \, U_{[0,0]} \, \phi_2 \equiv \phi_2$.

one to its right. Next, we use that result to express the satisfiability of a formula of the form $\neg f \vee p\, \mathsf{U}_{[l,u]}\, q$ over a bi-infinite word x as the satisfiability of several different formulas, each evaluated separately either on the whole mono-infinite word x^0 or on the whole mono-infinite word ^0x.[6]

Lemma 2. *Let $x \in (2^{\Pi})^{\mathbb{Z}}$ and $0 \leq l \leq u < \infty$ such that $u \neq 0$; then:*

$$x \models \neg f \vee p\, \mathsf{U}_{[l,u]}\, q \quad \Leftrightarrow \quad \begin{array}{c} x^0 \models \neg f \vee p\, \mathsf{U}_{[l,u]}\, q \;\triangle\; {}^0x \models \neg f \vee p\, \mathsf{S}_{[l,u]}\, q \vee (\mathsf{H}p \wedge \mathsf{H}_{=u}\bot) \\[4pt] \underset{\forall 1 \leq i \leq u-1 \,:}{\wedge} \left(\begin{array}{c} {}^0x \models \mathsf{P}_{=i}\top \wedge \mathsf{H}_{=i+1}\bot \Rightarrow \neg f \vee p\, \mathsf{S}_{[l,u]}\, q \\ \vee \\ x^0,0 \models p\, \mathsf{U}_{[\max(1,-i+l),-i+u]}\, q \end{array} \right) \end{array} \quad (2)$$

Let Φ_{L} and Φ_{R} be the sets of all MTL formulas appearing in left- and right-hand side of Formula (2), respectively (for all values of $1 \leq i \leq u-1$). Note that $u = \exp O(|\Phi_{\mathrm{L}}|_{\mathrm{M}})$, due to the succinct encoding of constants assumption. Then, $|\Phi_{\mathrm{R}}|_{\mathrm{M}} = O(|\Phi_{\mathrm{L}}|_{\mathrm{M}})$ and $|\Phi_{\mathrm{R}}|_{\#} = O(u \cdot |\Phi_{\mathrm{L}}|_{\#}) = |\Phi_{\mathrm{L}}|_{\#} \exp O(|\Phi_{\mathrm{L}}|_{\mathrm{M}})$.

It is not difficult to show that the equivalence of Formula (2) can be exploited to derive an equivalent formulation of the bi-infinite language $\mathcal{L}^{\mathbb{Z}}\!\left(\neg f \vee p\, \mathsf{U}_{[l,u]}\, q\right)$ in terms of mono-infinite ω-languages and composition operations on them.

Theorem 2. *Let $0 \leq l \leq u < \infty$ and $u \neq 0$; then:*

$$\mathcal{L}^{\mathbb{Z}}\!\left(\neg f \vee p\, \mathsf{U}_{[l,u]}\, q\right) = \bigcap_{i=1}^{u-1} \begin{array}{c} \widetilde{\mathcal{L}^{\omega}}\!\left(\neg f \vee p\, \mathsf{S}_{[l,u]}\, q \vee (\mathsf{H}p \wedge \mathsf{H}_{=u}\bot)\right) \triangleright \mathcal{L}^{\omega}\!\left(\neg f \vee p\, \mathsf{U}_{[l,u]}\, q\right) \\[4pt] \cap \\[4pt] \left(\begin{array}{c} \widetilde{\mathcal{L}^{\omega}}\!\left(\mathsf{P}_{=i}\top \wedge \mathsf{H}_{=i+1}\bot \Rightarrow \neg f \vee p\, \mathsf{S}_{[l,u]}\, q\right) \triangleright \left(2^{\Pi}\right)^{\omega} \\ \cup \\ {}^{\omega}\!\left(2^{\Pi}\right) \triangleright \mathcal{L}_0^{\omega}\!\left(p\, \mathsf{U}_{[\max(1,-i+l),-i+u]}\, q\right) \end{array} \right) \end{array} \quad (3)$$

Other operators. So far, we have provided a characterization of flat formulas only in the form $\neg f \vee p\, \mathsf{U}_{[l,u]}\, q$, for finite $l \leq u$. In order to handle every possible subformula in FSNF, we have to present similar characterizations for the subformulas: (1) $\neg f \vee p\, \mathsf{U}_{[l,\infty)}\, q$; (2) $f \vee p\, \mathsf{R}_I\, q$, for any interval I; (3) $f \Leftrightarrow p\, \mathsf{S}_I\, q \equiv (\neg f \vee p\, \mathsf{S}_I\, q) \wedge (f \vee \neg p\, \mathsf{T}_I\, \neg q)$, for any interval I; (4) $\beta \in \mathbb{B}(\Pi')$. Such characterizations are derivable similarly as for the bounded *until*. Hence, in the following we just collect the final results for (1) and (2), while the easily derivable results for past operators are provided only in [8].

$$\mathcal{L}^{\mathbb{Z}}(\neg f \vee p\, \mathsf{U}\, q) = \begin{array}{c} \widetilde{\mathcal{L}^{\omega}}(\neg f \vee p\, \mathsf{S}\, q \vee \mathsf{H}p) \triangleright \mathcal{L}^{\omega}(\neg f \vee p\, \mathsf{U}\, q) \\[4pt] \cap \\[4pt] \left(\widetilde{\mathcal{L}^{\omega}}(\neg f \vee p\, \mathsf{S}\, q) \triangleleft \left(2^{\Pi}\right)^{\omega} \;\cup\; {}^{\omega}\!\left(2^{\Pi}\right) \triangleright \mathcal{L}_0^{\omega}(p\, \mathsf{U}\, q) \right) \end{array} \quad (4)$$

$$\mathcal{L}^{\mathbb{Z}}\!\left(f \vee p\, \mathsf{R}_{[l,u]}\, q\right) = \bigcap_{i=1}^{u-1} \begin{array}{c} \widetilde{\mathcal{L}^{\omega}}\!\left(f \vee p\, \mathsf{T}_{[l,u]}\, q\right) \triangleright \mathcal{L}^{\omega}\!\left(f \vee p\, \mathsf{R}_{[l,u]}\, q\right) \\[4pt] \cap \\[4pt] \left(\begin{array}{c} \widetilde{\mathcal{L}^{\omega}}(\mathsf{P}_{=i}\top \wedge \mathsf{H}_{=i+1}\bot \Rightarrow \mathsf{P}p) \triangleright \left(2^{\Pi}\right)^{\omega} \\ \cup \\ {}^{\omega}\!\left(2^{\Pi}\right) \triangleright \mathcal{L}_0^{\omega}\!\left(p\, \mathsf{R}_{[\max(1,-i+l),-i+u]}\, q\right) \end{array} \right) \end{array} \quad (5)$$

---

[6] Note that $\mathsf{H}_{=k}\bot$ holds exactly at all positions $j < k$ of any ω-word.

$$\mathcal{L}^{\mathbb{Z}}(f \vee p \, \mathsf{R} \, q) \quad = \quad \begin{array}{c} \widetilde{\mathcal{L}^{\omega}}(f \vee (p \, \mathsf{T} \, q \wedge \mathsf{P} p)) \rhd \mathcal{L}^{\omega}(f \vee p \, \mathsf{R} \, q) \\ \cup \\ \widetilde{\mathcal{L}^{\omega}}(f \vee p \, \mathsf{T} \, q) \rhd (\mathcal{L}_0^{\omega}(p \, \mathsf{R} \, q) \cap \mathcal{L}^{\omega}(f \vee p \, \mathsf{R} \, q)) \end{array} \tag{6}$$

In fact, to give some intuition about the formulas for the past operators, consider the example of formula $\theta = \mathsf{H}_{[0,3]} p \Rightarrow \mathsf{F} q$. θ in separated normal form becomes $\theta' = (p' \Rightarrow q') \wedge (p' \Leftrightarrow \mathsf{H}_{[0,3]} p) \wedge (q' \Leftrightarrow \mathsf{F} q)$. Then, subformula $\lambda = p' \vee \neg \mathsf{H}_{[0,3]} p = p' \vee \mathsf{P}_{[0,3]} \neg p = p' \vee \top \, \mathsf{S}_{[0,3]} \, \neg p$ can be directly decomposed into:

$$x \models p' \vee \mathsf{P}_{[0,3]} \neg p \quad \underset{\forall 1 \leq i \leq 2:}{\Leftrightarrow} \quad \left(\begin{array}{c} \widetilde{x^0} \models p' \vee \mathsf{F}_{[0,3]} \neg p \,\underset{\wedge}{\wedge}\, x^0 \models p' \vee \mathsf{P}_{[0,3]} \neg p \vee \mathsf{H}_{=u} \bot \\ \left(x^0 \models \mathsf{P}_{=i} \top \wedge \mathsf{H}_{=i+1} \bot \Rightarrow p' \vee \mathsf{P}_{[0,3]} \neg p \right) \\ \underset{\vee}{\vee} \\ \widetilde{0x}, 0 \models \mathsf{F}_{[1, -i+3]} \neg p \end{array} \right) \tag{7}$$

4.2   From Languages to Automata (to ProMeLa)

In Section 3 we recalled that one can build an automaton that accepts any given MTL ω-language. On the other hand, in the previous section we showed how to reduce MTL satisfiability over $\mathbb{Z}$-languages to MTL satisfiability over ω-languages composed through the operations of $\rhd$, $\lhd$, $\cup$, $\cap$, and $\downarrow^\Pi$.

Indeed, the reduction can be fully implemented. In fact, in [8] we substantiate the claim that both BA and AMCA are closed under intersection and union, in such a way that if $\mathcal{A}_1$ and $\mathcal{A}_2$ are two automata (either BA or AMCA), then $|\mathcal{A}_1 \cup \mathcal{A}_2| = O(|\mathcal{A}_1| + |\mathcal{A}_2|)$ and $|\mathcal{A}_1 \cap \mathcal{A}_2| = O(|\mathcal{A}_1| \cdot |\mathcal{A}_2|)$.

Moreover, consider $\rhd$ and let L be a $\mathbb{Z}$-language defined as $\widetilde{L_1} \rhd L_2$. Then a $\mathbb{Z}$-word x is in L iff $\widetilde{^{-1}x} \in L_1$ and $x^0 \in L_2$. Hence, if we have two automata $\mathcal{A}_1, \mathcal{A}_2$ such that $\mathcal{L}^\omega(\mathcal{A}_1) = L_1$ and $\mathcal{L}^\omega(\mathcal{A}_2) = L_2$ the emptiness of L can be checked noting that $L = \emptyset$ iff $\mathcal{L}^\omega(\mathcal{A}_1) = \emptyset$ or $\mathcal{L}^\omega(\mathcal{A}_2) = \emptyset$. A very similar reasoning holds for $\lhd$. Finally consider the projection: for any MTL formula ϕ over Π let ϕ' be an equi-satisfiable MTL formula over $\Pi' \supseteq \Pi$. Then, $\downarrow^\Pi \mathcal{L}^{\mathbb{Z}}(\phi') = \mathcal{L}^{\mathbb{Z}}(\phi)$, and $\mathcal{L}^{\mathbb{Z}}(\phi) = \emptyset$ iff $\mathcal{L}^{\mathbb{Z}}(\phi') = \emptyset$. Correspondingly, the technique to check the satisfiability over the extended alphabet suffices to complete the satisfiability check on the original formula.

Implementing automata. In [2] we presented TRIO2ProMeLa, a tool that translates TRIO formulas (or, equivalently, MTL formulas) into a ProMeLa representation of the automata presented in Section 3. ProMeLa is the input language to the Spin model-checker [10], hence the tool allows one to check the satisfiability of an MTL formula on top of Spin. This approach is very efficient in practice, since it translates directly compositions (through union and intersection) of BA and AMCA to ProMeLa, obtaining a code of the same size as the original automata composition description. In a nutshell, every state of an AMCA is implemented with a ProMeLa process, existential transitions are implemented as nondeterministic choices, and universal transitions as the parallel run of concurrent processes. The tool also introduces some useful optimizations, such as merging processes when possible. When Spin is run on the automata described in ProMeLa, it unfolds them on-the-fly. This unfolding may lead to a blow-up in the dimension of the automata but it is performed by the model-checker only when needed. This approach is convenient, since in many practical cases, when the original formulas are large, the direct translation to BA and then to ProMeLa is simply unfeasible. We refer the reader to [2,15] for a detailed description of the translation from AMCA and BA to ProMeLa code.

TRIO2ProMeLa can be reused to provide an implementation of our satisfiability checking procedure over the integers. Once a formula is decomposed as explained in the previous sections, each component is translated into the ProMeLa process that represents the equivalent automaton. All the obtained processes are then suitably composed and coordinated by starting them together at time 0. The results of the various emptiness checks are then combined to have a response about the satisfiability of the original formula.

4.3   Summary and Complexity

Let us briefly summarize the satisfiability checking technique we presented in this section and let us analyze its worst-case asymptotic complexity.

Summary of the satisfiability checking algorithm. Given an MTL formula ϕ over Π, the satisfiability over $\mathbb{Z}$-words is checked according to the following steps.

1. From ϕ, build a formula ϕ' in FSNF such that $\mathcal{L}^{\mathbb{Z}}(\phi) = \downarrow^{\Pi} \mathcal{L}^{\mathbb{Z}}(\phi')$ (Theorem 1).
2. For each subformula ϕ'_i of ϕ', build a set of formulas $\{\phi'_{i,j}\}_j$, whose combined satisfiability over ω-words is equivalent to the satisfiability of ϕ'_i over $\mathbb{Z}$-words (e.g., according to (3) for the bounded *until*). Let $\phi''_i = \bigcup_j \{\phi'_{i,j}\}$.
3. Translate each subformula $\phi'_{i,j}$ into an automaton $\mathcal{A}_{i,j}$ according to what is described in Section 3.
4. For each i, compose the various automata $\mathcal{A}_{i,j}$ according to the structure of the corresponding language equivalences (e.g., according to (3) for the bounded *until*). In practice, for every i we can assume to have two automata $\mathcal{A}_i^+, \mathcal{A}_i^-$ such that $\widetilde{\mathcal{L}^\omega}(\mathcal{A}_i^-) \sim \mathcal{L}^\omega(\mathcal{A}_i^+) = \mathcal{L}^{\mathbb{Z}}(\phi'_i)$, where $\sim$ is $\triangleright$ or $\triangleleft$.
5. Let $\mathcal{A}^+, \mathcal{A}^-$ be the automata resulting from the intersection of the various $\mathcal{A}_i^\pm$'s according to the structure of $\mathcal{L}^{\mathbb{Z}}(\phi')$.
6. Since the equivalence $\downarrow^{\Pi} \mathcal{L}^{\mathbb{Z}}(\phi') = \mathcal{L}^{\mathbb{Z}}(\phi)$ holds by construction, the emptiness test on $\mathcal{L}^\omega(\mathcal{A}^+)$ and on $\mathcal{L}^\omega(\mathcal{A}^-)$ is equivalent to the satisfiability check of ϕ over $\mathbb{Z}$-words.

Let us go back to our previous example of $\theta = \mathsf{H}_{[0,3]}p \Rightarrow \mathsf{F}q$, and let θ' be θ in FSNF. One of the subformulas in θ' is $\lambda = p' \vee \mathsf{P}_{[0,3]}p$, which can be decomposed according to the left-hand side of 2. Correspondingly, we would build the following automata: $\mathcal{A}_1$ for $p' \vee \mathsf{P}_{[0,3]}\neg p$; $\mathcal{A}_2$ for $p' \vee \mathsf{P}_{[0,3]}\neg p \vee \mathsf{H}_{=u}\bot$; $\mathcal{A}_3^j$ for $\mathsf{P}_{=j}\top \wedge \mathsf{H}_{=j+1}\bot \Rightarrow p' \vee \mathsf{P}_{[0,3]}\neg p$, $j = 1,2$; $\mathcal{A}_4^j$ for $\mathsf{F}_{[1,-j+3]}\neg p$, $j = 1,2$. The automata would then be composed into: $\mathcal{A}_\lambda^- = \mathcal{A}_1$; $\mathcal{A}_\lambda^+ = \mathcal{A}_2 \cap \bigcap_{j=1}^2 \left(\mathcal{A}_3^j \cup \mathcal{A}_4^j \right)$.

Overall, we build two such automata $\mathcal{A}_i^-$ and $\mathcal{A}_i^+$ for each of the 5 subformulas θ' can be decomposed into. Let $\mathcal{A}^+ = \bigcap_{i=1}^5 \mathcal{A}_i^+$ and $\mathcal{A}^- = \bigcap_{i=1}^5 \mathcal{A}_i^-$. We conclude that θ is satisfiable iff $\mathcal{L}^\omega(\mathcal{A}^+)$ is non-empty and $\mathcal{L}^\omega(\mathcal{A}^-)$ is non-empty.

Complexity of satisfiability checking over the integers. Let us now evaluate an upper bound on the complexity of the above procedure. The worst-case occurs when overall automata $\mathcal{A}^\pm$ are expanded entirely into nondeterministic BA, thus losing entirely the conciseness of AMCA and the implicit representation of intersections.

First of all, let us estimate the size of every $\mathcal{A}_{i,j}$ with respect to the size of ϕ_i'. In Proposition 2 we recalled that the size $|\mathcal{B}|$ of a Büchi automaton $\mathcal{B}$ encoding an LTL formula θ of size $|\theta|$ is $\exp \mathrm{O}(|\theta|)$. Also, every MTL formula η can be translated into an equivalent LTL formula of size $\exp \mathrm{O}(|\eta|_\# |\eta|_\mathrm{M})$. In our case, every formula $\phi_{i,j}'$ is translated into an automaton of size:

$$|\mathcal{A}_{i,j}| = \exp\exp \mathrm{O}\left(\left|\phi_{i,j}'\right|_\# \left|\phi_{i,j}'\right|_\mathrm{M}\right) = \exp\exp \mathrm{O}\left(\left|\phi_{i,j}'\right|_\mathrm{M}\right)$$

because every subformula $\phi_{i,j}'$ has a constant (i.e., independent of $|\phi|$) number of connectives. Also, we noted that $\left|\phi_{i,j}'\right|_\mathrm{M} = |\phi_i'|_\mathrm{M}$, so:

$$|\mathcal{A}_{i,j}| = \exp\exp \mathrm{O}\left(|\phi_i'|_\mathrm{M}\right)$$

Next, let us estimate the size of $\mathcal{A}_i^\pm$. Roughly, $\mathcal{A}_i^\pm$ is the intersection $\bigcap_j \mathcal{A}_{i,j}$, hence its size is upper-bounded by the product of the sizes $|\mathcal{A}_{i,j}|$:

$$|\mathcal{A}_i^\pm| = \prod_j |\mathcal{A}_{i,j}| \le \left(\max_j |\mathcal{A}_{i,j}|\right)^{|\phi_i''|} = (\exp\exp \mathrm{O}(|\phi_i'|_\mathrm{M}))^{\exp \mathrm{O}(|\phi_i'|_\mathrm{M})}$$

where the equivalence between $|\phi_i''|$ and $\exp \mathrm{O}(|\phi_i'|_\mathrm{M})$ was highlighted in Section 4.1. After some manipulation, we get:

$$|\mathcal{A}_i^\pm| = \exp\left((\exp \mathrm{O}(|\phi_i'|_\mathrm{M}))(\exp \mathrm{O}(|\phi_i'|_\mathrm{M}))\right) = \exp\exp \mathrm{O}\left(|\phi_i'|_\mathrm{M}\right)$$

Then, the overall size of $\mathcal{A}^+$ and $\mathcal{A}^-$ can be computed as:

$$|\mathcal{A}^+| + |\mathcal{A}^-| = \mathrm{O}(|\mathcal{A}^\pm|) = \prod_i |\mathcal{A}_i^\pm| \le \left(\max_i |\mathcal{A}_i|\right)^{|\phi'|_\#} = \exp\left(|\phi'|_\# \exp \mathrm{O}(|\phi'|_\mathrm{M})\right)$$

thanks to the equivalence between $|\phi_i'|_\mathrm{M}$ and $\mathrm{O}(|\phi'|_\mathrm{M})$ stated in Remark 4.1.

Finally, Theorem 1 relates the size of ϕ' to that of the original formula ϕ, so we have:

$$|\mathcal{A}^+| + |\mathcal{A}^-| = \exp\left(|\phi|_\# \exp \mathrm{O}(|\phi|_\mathrm{M})\right)$$

From the well-known result that emptiness check of a Büchi automaton takes time polynomial (actually, linear) in the size of the automaton (see Proposition 2), we have established the following.

Theorem 3 (Upper-bound complexity). *The verification algorithm of this paper can check the satisfiability of an MTL formula ϕ over $\mathbb{Z}$-words in time doubly-exponential in the size $|\phi|$ of ϕ.*

The doubly-exponential time performance is worst-case optimal, because the satisfiability problem for MTL over the integers is an EXPSPACE-complete problem, as it is over the naturals [1].

Theorem 4 (Complexity of MTL over the integers). *The satisfiability problem for MTL over the integers is* EXPSPACE-*complete.*

Proof (sketch). From the upper-bound analysis and Proposition 2 it follows also that the problem is is decidable in nondeterministic (singly) exponential space, hence it is in EXPSPACE. For the EXPSPACE-hardness proof, one reduces from the satisfiability of future-MTL over integer-timed ω-words, which is also EX-PSPACE-complete [1]. See [8] for details.   □

5   Discussion

As we discussed in the Introduction, bi-infinite time models for temporal logic have been studied very rarely. Let us briefly consider a few noticeable exceptions.

On the more practical side, Pradella et al. [13] recently developed a tool-supported technique for bounded model-checking of temporal logic specifications over the integers. Bounded model-checking is a verification technique based on reduction to the propositional satisfiability (SAT) problem, for which very efficient off-the-shelf tools exist. The technique is however incomplete, as it only looks for words of length up to a given bound k, where k is a parameter of the verification problem instance. [13] describes a direct encoding of MTL bounded satisfiability as a SAT instance and reports on some interesting experimental results with an implementation. [13] also discusses the appeal of bi-infinite time from a system modeling perspective; some of its considerations are also discussed in the Introduction of the present paper.

In the area of automata theory and formal languages, there exist a few works considering bi-infinite time models. For instance Perrin and Pin [12] introduce bi-infinite words and automata on them, and extend some classical results for mono-infinite words to these new models. In the same vein, Muller et al. [11] establish the decidability of LTL over the integers. However, to the best of our knowledge the complexity of temporal logic over bi-infinite time has never been investigated in previous work.

On the contrary, temporal logic over mono-infinite time models has been extensively studied, and it has been the object of an impressive amount of both practical and theoretical research (e.g., [7,9,17,1,6]). Satisfiability of both LTL [14] and MTL [1] — also with past operators — over mono-infinite discrete time models has been thoroughly investigated. Sistla and Clarke [14] proved that LTL satisfiability over the naturals is PSPACE-complete, with a (singly) exponential time algorithm. Correspondingly, Alur and Henzinger [1] proved that MTL satisfiability over mono-infinite integer timed words is EXPSPACE-complete, and provided a doubly-exponential time algorithm. The same holds for bi-infinite discrete time, as we showed in this paper.

In the future, we plan to work on the implementation of an automated translator from integer-time MTL specifications to Spin models, and to experiment with it to assess the practical feasibility of the approach, also in comparison with similar tools for mono-infinite time models. Also, the related MTL model-checking problem over integer time will be investigated.

References

1. Alur, R., Henzinger, T.A.: Real-time logics: Complexity and expressiveness. Information and Computation 104(1), 35–77 (1993)
2. Bianculli, D., Morzenti, A., Pradella, M., San Pietro, P., Spoletini, P.: Trio2Promela: A model checker for temporal metric specifications. In: ICSE Companion, pp. 61–62 (2007)
3. Bouyer, P., Markey, N., Ouaknine, J., Worrell, J.: The cost of punctuality. In: Proceedings of LICS 2007, pp. 109–120. IEEE Computer Society Press, Los Alamitos (2007)
4. Clarke, E.M., Grumberg, O., Peled, D.A.: Model Checking. MIT Press, Cambridge (2000)
5. Coen-Porisini, A., Pradella, M., San Pietro, P.: A finite-domain semantics for testing temporal logic specifications. In: Ravn, A.P., Rischel, H. (eds.) FTRTFT 1998. LNCS, vol. 1486, pp. 41–54. Springer, Heidelberg (1998)
6. Demri, S., Schnoebelen, P.: The complexity of propositional linear temporal logics in simple cases. Information and Computation 174(1), 84–103 (2002)
7. Emerson, E.A.: Temporal and modal logic. In: van Leeuwen, J. (ed.) Handbook of Theoretical Computer Science, vol. B, pp. 996–1072. Elsevier Science, Amsterdam (1990)
8. Furia, C.A., Spoletini, P.: MTL satisfiability over the integers. Technical Report 2008.2, DEI, Politecnico di Milano (2008)
9. Gabbay, D.M., Hodkinson, I., Reynolds, M.: Temporal Logic: mathematical foundations and computational aspects, vol. 1. Oxford University Press, Oxford (1994)
10. Holzmann, G.J.: The SPIN Model Checker: Primer and Reference Manual (2003)
11. Muller, D.E., Schupp, P.E., Saoudi, A.: On the decidability of the linear Z-temporal logic and the monadic second order theory. In: Proc. of ICCI 1992, pp. 2–5 (1992)
12. Perrin, D., Pin, J.-É.: Infinite Words. Pure and Applied Mathematics, vol. 141. Elsevier, Amsterdam (2004)
13. Pradella, M., Morzenti, A., San Pietro, P.: The symmetry of the past and of the future. In: Proceedings of ESEC/FSE 2007, pp. 312–320 (2007)
14. Sistla, A.P., Clarke, E.M.: The complexity of propositional linear temporal logics. Journal of the ACM 32(3), 733–749 (1985)
15. Spoletini, P.: Verification of Temporal Logic Specification via Model Checking. PhD thesis, DEI, Politecnico di Milano (May 2005)
16. Thomas, W.: Automata on infinite objects. In: van Leeuwen, J. (ed.) Handbook of Theoretical Computer Science, vol. B, pp. 133–164. Elsevier Science, Amsterdam (1990)
17. Vardi, M.Y.: Handbook of Modal Logic. In: Automata-Theoretic Techniques for Temporal Reasoning, pp. 971–990 (2006)

A Theory of Pointers for the UTP

Will Harwood[1], Ana Cavalcanti[2], and Jim Woodcock[2]

[1] Citrix Systems (R & D) Ltd, Venture House, Cambourne Business Park
Cambourne, Cambs, UK
[2] University of York, Department of Computer Science
York, UK

Abstract. Hoare and He's unifying theories of programming (UTP) provide a collection of relational models that can be used to study and compare several programming paradigms. In this paper, we add to the UTP a theory of pointers and records that provides a model for objects and sharing in languages like Java and C++. Our work is based on the hierarchical addressing scheme used to refer to record fields (or object attributes) in conventional languages, rather than explicit notions of location. More importantly, we support reasoning about the structure and sharing of data, as well as their, possibly infinite, values. We also provide a general account of UTP theories characterised by conjunctive healthiness conditions, of which our theory is an example.

Keywords: semantics, refinement, relations, object models.

1 Introduction

Interest in reasoning about pointers is not recent [4], and has been renewed by the importance of sharing in object-oriented languages [1,16]. The classic model of pointers [17] uses two functions: one associates memory addresses to values, and the other associates names to memory addresses. Similarly, most models use indexes to represent memory locations or embed a heap [13,24]. Modern object-oriented languages, however, do not directly support manipulation of addresses.

The unifying theories of programming (UTP) [11] provide a modelling framework for several programming paradigms. It is distinctive in that its uniform underlying alphabetised relational model allows the combination of constructs from different theories, and supports comparison and combination of notations and techniques. Currently, there are UTP theories for imperative languages, functional languages, CSP, timed notations, and so on.

In this paper, we present a UTP theory for pointers based on the hierarchical addressing created by data types defined by recursive records. For example, for a variable l, we have the address l itself, and possibly addresses like $l.label$ and $l.next.item$, if the object value of l contains attributes $label$ and $next$, and the value of $l.next$ is another object with an attribute $item$.

We have three components in our model: a set of (hierarchical) addresses, a function that associates the addresses of attributes that are not object valued to their primitive values, and a sharing relation. Our addresses are particular

J.S. Fitzgerald, A.E. Haxthausen, and H. Yenigun (Eds.): ICTAC 2008, LNCS 5160, pp. 141–155, 2008.

to each variable, and we abstract from the notion of specific locations. This simplifies our theory, as compared, for example, to our own previous work [5].

We assume that all values have a location, including primitive values. Variables are names of locations, as are attribute access expressions like $l.next$, which define composed names of locations. These names, however, also have a value. A distinguishing feature of our model is that it represents sharing in a program as an updatable automaton that also associates (some) addresses to values. This allows us to define a simple de-referencing operator to tie the values in the automaton to those of the programming variables and of attribute accesses. In this way, we can, to a large degree, separate specifications into pure logical expressions on values, and update expressions involving pointers.

We do not assume strong typing, and so can cater for the use of pointers in languages like Lisp and, to some extent, C, although we do not cover pointer arithmetic. Infinite values are constructible by loops in pointer references; they are explicitly definable by fixed points and are generally represented by partial functions. In our model, de-referencing a pointer yields a partial function that can represent an infinite value. Finally, we do not model unreachable locations: we have automatic garbage collection. The only way of naming a location is by a path (composed name) that leads (refers) to it; if there is no path to a location, it does not exist. This does mean that we cannot reason about issues like memory leakage, but have a simpler model to reason about the functionality of a program.

In this paper, we also define a few constructs related to creation and assignment of records. We give their predicate model, and establish the adequacy of the definitions by proving that the predicates are healthy. The reasoning technique encouraged by the UTP is based on algebraic laws of refinement; our theory, however, can also be used to justify the soundness of techniques based on Hoare triples, for example. An account of Hoare logic in the UTP is available in [11].

Our long-term goal is to provide a pointer semantics for an object-oriented language for refinement that supports the development of state-rich, concurrent programs. In particular, we are interested in *OhCircus* [6]; it combines Z and CSP, with object-oriented constructs in the style of Java, and, as such, it has in the UTP an appropriate choice of semantic model. Following the UTP style, we are considering individual aspects of the *OhCircus* semantics separately. The theory presented here will be integrated with the copy semantics of *OhCircus*.

The UTP relational models are defined in a predicative style similar to that adopted in Z or VDM, for example. They comprise a collection of theories that model specifications, designs, and programs; a theory is characterised by a set of alphabetised predicates that satisfy some healthiness conditions.

There is a subtle difficulty in defining a pointer theory that can be easily combined with the existing UTP theories: the UTP is a logical language where variables range over values. To illustrate the issue, we consider a variable l that holds a value of a type $List ::= (label : \mathbb{Z}; \ next : List)$ of recursive records with fields *label* and *next*. After the assignments $l.label := 1$ and $l.next := l$, the value of l is an infinite list, but it is constructed as a pointer structure. Pointers are used for two distinct purposes: to construct infinite values by self-reference, and to share storage. We need a model that records the sharing, but allows appropriate reasoning about values, to simplify specification.

A simple solution is to model storage as a graph and to use fixed points to handle self-references when constructing the denotation of a value. In this case, however, the update operations explicitly use fixed points (for the values) and reasoning is cumbersome. Instead, we create a model where updates act directly on the values associated with the graph as well as on its structure.

A large number of healthiness conditions used to characterise UTP theories are defined by a conjunction. In this case, a function $\mathbf{H}$ from predicates to predicates is defined as $\mathbf{H}(P) = P \wedge \psi$, for some predicate ψ; the healthy predicates are the fixed points of $\mathbf{H}$: those for which $\mathbf{H}(P) = P$. A number of properties are satisfied by these predicates, independently of the particular definition of ψ. We present and prove some of these results; they simplify proof in our theory.

In [5], we also present a theory of pointers and records for the UTP. It is based on the model of entity groups in [21] to formalise rules of a refinement calculus for Eiffel [15]. In that work, the complications of an explicit model of the memory are also avoided; each entity (variable) is associated with the set of variables that share its location (entity group). Here, we use a binary relation to model sharing, and record the set of valid names and values explicitly to simplify definitions and proof. This is in addition to the simplification that arises from the separate treatment of healthiness conditions defined by conjunction.

In the next section, we describe the UTP. Section 3 describes our model informally. In Section 4, we present general results about theories characterised by healthiness conditions defined by conjunctions, before we formalise our theory in Section 5. A model for usual programming constructs is presented in Section 6. Finally, in Section 7 we consider some related and future work.

2   Unifying Theories of Programming

In the unifying theories of programming, relations are defined by predicates over an alphabet (set) of observational variables that record information about the behaviour of a program. In the simplest theory of general relations, these include the programming variables v, and their dashed counterparts v', with v used to refer to an initial observation of the value of v, and v' to a later observation. In the sequel, we use v to stand for the list of all programming variables, and v' to the corresponding list of dashed variables. The set of undecorated (unprimed) variables in the alphabet αP of a predicate P is called its input alphabet $in\alpha P$, and the set of dashed variables is its output alphabet $out\alpha P$. A condition is a predicate whose alphabet includes only input variables.

Theories are characterised by an alphabet and by healthiness conditions defined by monotonic idempotent functions from predicates to predicates. The predicates of a theory with an alphabet A are all the predicates on A which are fixed points of the healthiness conditions. As an example, we consider designs.

The general theory of relations does not distinguish between terminating and non-terminating programs. This distinction is made in the UTP in a theory of designs, which includes two extra boolean observational variables to record the start and the termination of a program: ok and ok'. All designs can be split into precondition/postcondition pairs, making them similar to specification statements of a refinement calculus. The monotonic idempotents used to define the healthiness conditions for designs can be defined as follows, where P is a relation (predicate) with alphabet $\{ok, ok', v, v'\}$.

$$\textbf{H1}(P) \mathrel{\widehat{=}} ok \Rightarrow P \qquad \textbf{H2}(P) \mathrel{\widehat{=}} P \mathbin{;} J, \textbf{ where } J \mathrel{\widehat{=}} (ok \Rightarrow ok') \wedge v' = v$$

If P is **H1**-healthy, then it makes no restrictions on the final value of variables before it starts. If P is **H2**-healthy, then termination must be a possible outcome from every initial state. The functional composition of **H1** and **H2** is named **H**. Our definition of **H2** is different from that in [11], but it is equivalent [7]; it uses the sequence operator that we define below.

Typically, a theory defines a number of programming operators of interest. Common operators like assignment, sequence, and conditional, are defined for general relations. Sequence is relational composition.

$$P \mathbin{;} Q \mathrel{\widehat{=}} \exists\, w_0 \bullet P[w_0/w'] \wedge Q[w_0/w], \textbf{ where } out\alpha(Q) = in\alpha(Q)' = w'$$

The relation $P \mathbin{;} Q$ is defined by a quantification that relates the intermediate values of the variables. It is required that $out\alpha(P)$ is equal to $in\alpha(Q)'$, which is named w'. The sets w, w', and w_0 are used as lists that enumerate the variables of w and the corresponding decorated variables in the same order.

A conditional is written as $P \triangleleft b \triangleright Q$; its behaviour is (described by) P if the condition b holds, else it is defined by Q.

$$P \triangleleft b \triangleright Q \mathrel{\widehat{=}} (b \wedge P) \vee (\neg b \wedge Q), \textbf{ where } \alpha(b) \subseteq \alpha(P) = \alpha(Q).$$

A central concern of the UTP is refinement. A program P is refined by a program Q, which is written $P \sqsubseteq Q$, if, and only if, $P \Leftarrow Q$, for all possible values of the variables of the alphabet. The set of alphabetised predicates form a complete lattice with this ordering. Recursion is modelled by weakest fixed points $\mu X \bullet F(X)$, where F is a monotonic function from predicates to predicates.

The programming operators of a theory need to be closed: they need to take healthy predicates to healthy predicates. In Section 4, we provide some general results for healthiness conditions defined by conjunctions.

3   A Model for Pointers

In this section we introduce a straightforward and intuitive model of a storage graph that we call a pointer machine. Afterwards, in Section 3.2 we introduce an alternative representation for a pointer machine that is easier to model in the UTP. The new UTP theory itself is presented in Section 5.

3.1   The Pointer Machine

A simple model for storage is a labelled graph, in which the labels are names of attributes, and terminal nodes hold values. It is useful to think of this graph as a particular kind of automaton, a *pointer machine* that accepts addresses (attribute by attribute) and produces values when you reach a terminal node.

Intuitively, arcs represent pointers, internal nodes represent storage locations for pointers, and terminal nodes, storage locations for values. A mapping assigns attribute names to arcs for selecting pointers and values, and another gives the values stored at a terminal node. For example, Figure 1 gives a pointer machine for the variable l defined in Section 1. There is only one internal node X, the initial node, and one terminal node, Y. The arcs are $\{\, X \mapsto X, X \mapsto Y\,\}$; we write $a \mapsto b$ to describe the pair (a, b). The set of labels is $\{l, label, next\}$, and the labelling functions are $\{\,(X \mapsto X) \mapsto next, (X \mapsto Y) \mapsto label\,\}$ for the arcs, and just $\{\, Y \mapsto 1\,\}$ for the terminal node.

Fig. 1. A labelled graph representation for a pointer machine

In fact, a pointer machine naturally represents a structure in which there is a single entry point. Conceptually, we regard the start node as a fictional root of all memory, whose arcs correspond to simple variable names.

3.2   A Simpler Model

We represent pointer machines by a triple $\langle A, V, S \rangle$, where A is the set of addresses that the machine accepts, V is a partial function mapping addresses to primitive values, and S is an equivalence relation on addresses, recording that two addresses lead to the same node. The addressing map V defines which addresses yield values: the difference between A and dom V is the set of addresses that are accepted by the machine, but do not yield a primitive value. The set A defines the valid addresses. The storage map S records the sharing. For the pointer machine in Figure 1, A contains l, all the addresses formed only by accesses to *next* ($l.next$, $l.next.next$, and so on), and those that end with an access to *label*, possibly after (repeated) accesses to *next* ($l.label$, $l.next.label$, $l.next.next.label$, and so on). The V function maps all accesses to *label* to 1. Finally, S relates l to all (repeated) accesses to *next*, all these addresses to each other, and all accesses to *label* to each other as well.

The set of finite addresses $FAd \;\widehat{=}\; (\text{seq } Label) \setminus \{\,\langle\,\rangle\,\}$ contains the non-empty sequences of labels. An infinite address is an element of $seq_\infty \;\widehat{=}\; \mathbb{N}_1 \to Label$, that is, a total function from the positive natural numbers to $Label$. Finally, an address in $Ad \;\widehat{=}\; FAd \cup seq_\infty$ can be finite or infinite.

Equality. Two equalities are definable: *value equality*, written $=_v$, and *pointer equality*, which is written $=_p$. The former holds for pointers that have the same value. It establishes that, if you follow the pointers, and use the nodes you arrive at as the start nodes of two pointer machines, say $\langle A_1, V_1, S_1 \rangle$ and $\langle A_2, V_2, S_2 \rangle$, then $A_1 = A_2$ and $V_1 = V_2$, that is, the domains of definition and the addressing map of the machines are the same. This means that two pointers are equal if further addressing off these pointers leads to the same values (and the same failures). Pointer equality holds for pointers that point to exactly the same location.

For a finite p, we define the p-projection $\langle A.p, V.p \rangle$ of the machine with $A.p \mathrel{\hat=} \{ q : Ad \mid p.q \in A \}$ and $V.p \mathrel{\hat=} \{ q : Ad \mid p.q \in \mathrm{dom}\ V \bullet q \mapsto V(p.q) \}$. We use the dot operator to combine addresses, as well as to append an attribute name to the end of an address. The value associated with the object pointed by p is the tree coded by $\langle A.p, V.p \rangle$. Value equality is defined by equality of pointer projections, and pointer equality is defined by the storage map.

$$p =_v q \mathrel{\hat=} (A.p = A.q \wedge V.p = V.q) \qquad p =_p q \mathrel{\hat=} (p, q) \in S$$

For our simple example, we have that $l.next$ is both value and pointer equal to l. The l-projection of the machine described above is formed by stripping off the leading l in all addresses in A and dom V.

4   Conjunctive Healthiness Conditions

We refer to a healthiness condition that is, or can be, defined in terms of conjunction as a conjunctive healthiness condition. In this section, we consider an arbitrary conjunctive healthiness condition $\mathbf{CH}(P) = P \wedge \psi$, for some predicate ψ. All the healthiness conditions of our theory are conjunctive.

Conjunction, disjunction, and conditional are closed with respect to **CH**.

Theorem 1. *If P and Q are **CH**-healthy predicates, then $P \wedge Q$, $P \vee Q$, and $P \lhd c \rhd Q$ are **CH**-healthy.*

The proof of this and every other result in this paper can be found in [10].

To establish closedness for sequence, we consider a specific kind of conjunctive healthiness condition: those in which ψ is itself the conjunction of conditions ψ_i and ψ_i' over the input and output alphabets, respectively. In this case, **CH** imposes similar restrictions on the input and output alphabets. (As expected, the predicate P' is that obtained by dashing all occurrences of the observational variables in P.) With these results, we can prove closedness of sequence.

Theorem 2. *If P and Q are **CH**-healthy, where $\mathbf{CH}(P) = P \wedge \psi \wedge \psi'$, for some condition ψ on input variables, then P; Q is **CH**-healthy as well.*

The set of **CH**-healthy predicates is a complete lattice, since it is the image of a monotonic idempotent healthiness condition [11]. So, recursion can still be defined using weakest fixed points; closedness is established by the next theorem.

Theorem 3. *If F is a monotonic function from* **CH**-*healthy predicates to* **CH**-*healthy predicates, then* $\mu_{ch} X \bullet F(X) = \textbf{CH}(\mu X \bullet F(X))$, *where* $\mu_{ch} X \bullet F(X)$ *is the least fixed point of F in the lattice of* **CH**-*healthy predicates.*

This states that a recursion is a **CH**-healthy predicate, if, for instance, its body is built out of **CH**-healthy predicates itself using closed constructors.

Designs. In general, a theory of **CH**-healthy predicates is disjoint from the theory of designs: on abortion, a design provides no guarantees, but a **CH**-healthy predicate requires ψ to hold. Of course, if ψ is *true*, in which case CH is the identity, we do not have a problem, but for interesting **CH**, there is a difficulty. We follow the UTP approach used to combine the theory of reactive processes and designs to combine the theory of designs with a theory of **CH**-healthy predicates. We take **CH** as a link that maps a design to a **CH**-healthy predicate.

What we have is an approximate relationship between the two theories: for a **CH**-healthy relation P, **CH** $\circ$ **H1**$(P) \sqsubseteq P$. This is a property of a Galois connection that translates between the theories. The healthiness condition **H2** is not a problem: it commutes with **CH**, provided ψ does not refer to ok'.

Theorem 4. CH $\circ$ **H2** $=$ **H2** $\circ$ **CH**, *provided ok' is not free in ψ.*

Galois connection. Our proof of the existence of a Galois connection between the theories of **CH**-healthy predicates and designs relies on two simple lemmas about **H1**, **CH**, and refinement. In fact, instead of considering **H1** in particular, we consider an arbitrary implicational healthiness condition **IH**$(P) = \phi \Rightarrow P$.

Lemma 1 (IH-refinement). **IH**$(P) \sqsubseteq$ **IH**(Q) *if, and only if,*   **IH**$(P) \sqsubseteq Q$.

This lemma lets us cancel an application of **IH** on the right-hand side of the refinement. This works because **IH**(P) is a disjunction, and the cancellation strengthens the implementation. Something similar can be done with **CH**, but since **CH** is a conjunction, the cancellation takes place on the specification side.

Lemma 2 (CH-refinement). $P \sqsubseteq$ **CH**(Q) *if, and only if,*   **CH**$(P) \sqsubseteq$ **CH**(Q).

Applications of the above lemmas justify the main result for a combination of the theories of **IH**-healthy and **CH**-healthy predicates.

Theorem 5. *There is a Galois connection between* **IH**-*healthy and* **CH**-*healthy predicates, where* **CH** *is the right adjoint and* **IH** *is the left one.*

$P \sqsubseteq$ **IH**(Q) *if, and only if,*   **CH**$(P) \sqsubseteq Q$.

Here, P is **IH**-*healthy, and Q is* **CH**-*healthy.*

For designs, more specifically, we have the result below.

Theorem 6. CH *and* **H** *form a Galois connection between designs and* **CH**-*healthy predicates.*

$D \sqsubseteq$ **H**(P) *if, and only if,*   **CH**$(D) \sqsubseteq P$.

Here, D is a design, and P is **CH**-*healthy.*

Proof of closedness of the operators in the combined theories is simple.

5   Pointers and Records in the UTP

The alphabet of our theory includes three new observational variables A, V, and S that record separately the components of the pointer machine.

The first healthiness condition, named **HP1**, guarantees that A is prefix closed. We write $x < y$ when x is a (finite) strict prefix of the address y.

HP1 $P = P \wedge \forall a_1 : A;\ a_2 : FAd \mid a_2 < a_1 \bullet a_2 \in A$

This means that if $x.y.z$, for instance, is a valid address, then $x.y$ and x must be as well. As already said, the healthiness conditions are characterised by functions, so in accordance with the UTP style, we use the name of the healthiness condition as the name of the corresponding function. In the case of **HP1**, for example, we have a function $\textbf{HP1}(P) \cong P \wedge \forall a_1 : A;\ a_2 : FAd \mid a_2 < a_1 \bullet a_2 \in A$.

To formalise **HP2**, we define the subset $term(A)$ of addresses of terminal nodes. In general, $term(X) \cong \{ x : X \cap FAd \mid \neg \ \exists y : X \bullet x < y\}$, that is, a terminal address is finite and has no valid extensions. In **HP2**, we connect $\text{dom } V$ and A by requiring each terminal in A to have a value defined by V.

HP2 $P = P \wedge \text{dom } V = \text{term}(A)$

The third healthiness condition **HP3** connects the programming variables in the alphabet to pointers in the pointer machine. For every variable x, we use $'x$ to refer to its name. We require in **HP3** that $'x$ is a variable in the pointer machine, and that the value of x is consistent with that assigned by V. The variables of the pointer machine are the first elements of the addresses: for a set of addresses X, the variables are $vars(X) \cong \{x : X \bullet x(1)\}$. If $'x$ is a terminal, then x must have value $V('x)$. If $'x$ is not a terminal, then the value of x is a partial function that maps addresses to values defined by the projection of V at $'x$, that is, $V.('x)$. For every x in $in\alpha(P) \setminus \{A, V, S\}$, we define the de-referencing operator $!x$ as follows: $!x \cong \textbf{if } x \in \text{term}(A) \textbf{ then } V(x) \textbf{ else } V.x$. For a dashed variable, the definition is $!(x') \cong \textbf{if } x \in \text{term}(A') \textbf{ then } V'(x) \textbf{ else } V'.x$. In **HP3** we use this operator to constrain the values of the input variables.

HP3 $P = P \wedge\ v_1 = \ !'v_1 \wedge \ldots \wedge v_n = \ !'v_n \wedge \{'v_1, \ldots, 'v_n\} = vars(A)$
         where $\{'v_1, \ldots, 'v_n\} = in\alpha(P) \setminus \{A, V, S\}$

The remaining healthiness conditions are related to S. It should involve only addresses in A and should be an equivalence relation. We use R^* to describe the reflexive, symmetric, and transitive closure of R.

HP4 $P = P \wedge S \in (A \leftrightarrow A) \wedge S = S^*$

Also, if two addresses are equivalent under S, then any extension by the same address should be equivalent. We define an equivalence relation E between addresses to be *forward closed* with respect to a set of addresses A to mean that once two addresses are equivalent, then their common extensions are equivalent, that is $\mathrm{fclos}_A\, E \cong \forall\, x, y, a : Ad \mid (x, y) \in E \wedge (x.a \in A \vee y.a \in A) \bullet (x.a, y.a) \in E.$

HP5 $P = P \wedge \mathrm{fclos}_A\, S$

Finally, if two terminals share a location, then they have the same value.

HP6 $P = P \wedge \forall\, a, b : Ad \mid (a, b) \in S \wedge a \in \mathrm{dom}\, V \bullet b \in \mathrm{dom}\, V \wedge V(a) = V(b)$

We also have extra healthiness conditions **HP7-HP12** that impose the same restrictions on the dashed variables. Our theory is characterised by the healthiness condition **HP**, the functional composition of all these healthiness conditions.

All our healthiness conditions are conjunctive; consequently, **HP** is conjunctive, and moreover, it imposes the same restrictions on S, V, and A, and on S', V' and A', as studied in Section 4. So, we can conclude, based on Theorems 1, 2, and 3, that the usual specification and programming constructs are closed with respect to **HP**. In addition, **HP** and **H** are adjuncts of a Galois connection that defines a theory of pointers for terminating programs. We only need to be careful with the definition of **HP2**. In the theory of pointer designs, ok and ok' are not programming variables, and just like A, V, and S, they are not to have space allocated in the pointer machine. So, ok is not to be included in the vector v of variables considered in **HP2**, and ok' is not to be included in v' in **HP8**.

In the sequel, we define some programming constructs; for that, it is useful to define **HPI** $\cong$ **HP1** $\circ$ **HP2** $\circ$ **HP3** $\circ$ **HP4** $\circ$ **HP5** $\circ$ **HP6**. It imposes restrictions only on the input variables. These definitions illustrate the use of the healthiness conditions also to simplify definitions; in particular **HP9** is very useful, as it relates changes in the machine to changes in values of variables. Most of the healthiness conditions are restrictions that characterise the automata that model pointer machines. In the case of **HP3**, and the corresponding **HP9**, however, we have healthiness conditions that unify the structural and logical views of variables. They are the basis for a reasoning technique that copes in a natural way with (infinite) values whose storage structure is also of interest.

6   Programming Constructs

We can update the pointer machine using a value assignment, which we write $x := e$ for a finite address x in A, or a pointer assignment $x :\!- y$, where both x and y are finite addresses in A. Both types of assignment may change an internal or a terminal node, and consequently alter A, V, and S.

6.1   Value Assignment

We define, for an address x, the set $\mathrm{share}(x) \cong S(\!\mid \{x\} \mid\!)$ of addresses that share its location; $S(\!\mid \{x\} \mid\!)$ is the relational image of $\{x\}$ through S: all elements related to x in S. A value assignment to a terminal address is defined as follows.

$$x := e \cong \mathbf{HPI} \circ \mathbf{HP9}(A' = A \wedge V' = V \oplus \{a : \mathrm{share}_S(x) \bullet a \mapsto e\}) \wedge S' = S)$$

provided $x \in \mathrm{dom}\, V$

The symbol $\oplus$ is used for the functional overriding operator. In the new value of V, x and all the addresses that share its location are associated with the value e. The application of the healthiness condition **HPI** ensures that the input variables are healthy; **HP9** ensures that the values of the programming variables are updated in accordance with the changes to V.

For an internal address, the definition of assignment is a generalisation of that above. Before we present it, we define the set $\text{ext}(x) \mathbin{\widehat{=}} \text{share}_S(x)^\uparrow$ of all addresses that extend x or any of the other addresses that share the location of x. The set $X^\uparrow \mathbin{\widehat{=}} \bigcup\{x : X \cap FAd \bullet x\infty\}$ contains all addresses that extend those in a set X, and $x\infty \mathbin{\widehat{=}} \{\, a : Ad \bullet x.a \,\}$ contains all the extensions of the finite address x. All the addresses in $\text{ext}(x)$ become invalid if x is assigned a value; they are removed from A, from the domain of V, and from the domain and range of S. The operators for domain and range subtraction are $\lhd$ and $\rhd$.

$$x := e \mathbin{\widehat{=}}$$

$$\mathbf{HPI} \circ \mathbf{HP9} \left(\begin{array}{l} A' = A \setminus \text{ext}_S(x) \land \\ V' = (\text{ext}_S(x) \lhd V) \cup \{a : (\text{share}_S(x) \setminus \text{ext}_S(x)) \bullet a \mapsto e\} \land \\ S' = \text{ext}_S(x) \lhd S \rhd \text{ext}_S(x) \end{array} \right)$$

$$\textbf{provided } x \in A \text{ and } x \notin \text{dom } V.$$

For a terminal address x, the set $x\infty \cap A$ is empty, and so is $\text{ext}_S(x) \cap A$. So, in the definition of assignment to a terminal address, we do not change A and S. In V, we include the addresses that share a location with x according to the new storage map S', that is, $\text{share}_S(x) \setminus \text{ext}_S(x)$.

As an example, we consider again the variable l in Figure 1; after the assignment $l.next := 3$, all extensions of $l.next$ become invalid. The set $\text{share}_S(l.next)$ contains l and all accesses to $next$; so, $\text{ext}(l.next)$ contains all addresses in A, except l. So, after $l.next := 3$, A contains only l, S only associates l to itself, and finally, the domain of V is wiped out, and l is added: it is mapped to 3.

The proofs of **HP**-healthiness [10] provide validation for our definitions.

6.2   Pointer Assignment

We present here just the definition of pointer assignment to an internal address. As a motivating example, we consider the variables l, m, and n depicted in Figure 2(a). After the assignment $l :- m.link$, the value and sharing properties of l and its extensions are completely changed, but no other variable is affected: l now points to the same location as $m.link$, but n, for example, does not change. The address l is still valid, but its extensions, like $l.next$, $l.label$, and so on, cease to exist. Instead, all addresses formed by concatenating a suffix of $m.link$ to l are now valid. For example, $l.value$, $l.link$, $l.link.link$ and so on become valid.

Accordingly, in the definition of $x :- y$, we remove $x\infty$ from A, and add the set $\{\, a : A.y \bullet x.a \,\}$ of new addresses. In the case of V, we remove $x\infty$ from its domain, and give x and its new extensions the values defined by y, if any. In our example, after the assignment $l :- m.value$, since $m.value$ is a terminal, with value 3, then l also becomes a terminal with the same value. On the other hand,

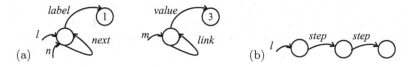

Fig. 2. Two pointer machines

after $l :-\ m.link$, the new terminal locations correspond to those of $m.link$. Namely, we have new terminals $l.value$, $l.link.value$ and so on, all with value 3.

If x and y share the same location, the pointer assignment $x :-\ y$ has no effect and, in particular, S does not change. If, however, they point to different locations, the sharing information for x and all elements of $x\infty$ change. To simplify the definition of S', we define the set $\mathrm{bsh}(x) \mathrel{\widehat{=}} \{x\} \cup x\infty$ of addresses whose sharing is broken. The existing sharing information about these addresses is eliminated, and their new sharing with y and its extensions is recorded.

Conditional expressions are used below: the value of $e_1 \lhd b \rhd e_2$ is e_1 if the condition b holds, otherwise its value is e_2.

$$x :-\ y \mathrel{\widehat{=}}$$

$$\mathbf{HPI} \circ \mathbf{HP9}\left(\begin{array}{l} A' = A \setminus x\infty \cup \{a : A.y \bullet x.a\}\ \wedge \\ V' = \begin{pmatrix} (x\infty \lhd V) \cup \\ (\{x \mapsto V(y)\} \lhd y \in \mathrm{dom}\,V \rhd \emptyset) \cup \\ \{a : \mathrm{dom}\,V.y \bullet x.a \mapsto V(y.a)\} \end{pmatrix}\ \wedge \\ S' = \begin{pmatrix} S \lhd (x,y) \in S \rhd \\ \begin{pmatrix} (\mathrm{bsh}(x) \lhd S \rhd \mathrm{bsh}(x)) \cup \\ (\{x\} \times ((S(\!|\,\{y\}\,|\!) \setminus x\infty) \cup \{x\})) \cup \\ \bigcup\{a : A.y \bullet \{x.a\} \times ((S(\!|\,\{y.a\}\,|\!) \setminus \mathrm{bsh}(x)) \cup \{x.a\})\} \end{pmatrix} \end{pmatrix}^* \end{array}\right)$$

provided $x \notin \mathrm{dom}\,V$ and x is a simple name.

The address x now shares its location with y and all the addresses that already share a location with y: those in $S(\!|\,\{y\}\,|\!)$. It may be the case, however, that y shares a location with an extension of x, and in this case that address does not exist anymore, and needs to be eliminated. In our example, after $l :-\ n.label$, l should be associated with $n.label$, $n.next.label$, $n.next.next.label$ and so on; however $S(\!|\,\{n.label\}\,|\!)$ also includes $l.label$, $l.next.label$, and all other accesses to $label$ via l; these need to be excluded. The same comment applies to the sharing information related to the new extensions $l.a$ of x; they should be related to $S(\!|\,\{y.a\}\,|\!)$, but the extensions of x should be eliminated. If present, x should also be eliminated, as information about it in S is no longer valid. In the case of $S(\!|\,\{y\}\,|\!)$, we know that x does not belong to this set, since $(x,y) \notin S$.

Finally, we need to consider the cases in which $S(\!|\,\{y\}\,|\!)$ is contained in $x\infty$, so that $S(\!|\,\{y\}\,|\!) \setminus x\infty$ is empty, or $S(\!|\,\{y.a\}\,|\!)$ is contained in $\mathrm{bsh}(x)$, so that $S(\!|\,\{y.a\}\,|\!) \setminus \mathrm{bsh}(x)$ is empty. The machine in Figure 2(b) gives us an example: after $l :-\ l.step$, the valid addresses are l and $l.step$, and S' should be the identity. When we eliminate l and all its extensions from S, however, we get the empty relation; furthermore, $S(\!|\,\{l.step\}\,|\!)$ contains only $l.step$, and similarly, $S(\!\mid\{l.step.step\}\mid\!)$ is $\{l.step.step\}$. To guarantee that S' includes all valid addresses, we explicitly associate x and each new $x.a$ to themselves.

A value assignment $x := y$ affects the value of all addresses that share the location of x. In the case of a pointer assignment, however, not all of them are affected. For example, as we discussed above, even if the variables x and z share a location, $x :- y$ does not affect z. On the other hand, $x.a :- y$ affects both $x.a$ and $z.a$, since $x.a$ is an attribute of both x and z. The definition of $x.a :- y$ is similar to that of $x :- y$, but it takes into account the fact that other addresses, and not only $x.a$ and $x.a\infty$ are affected. Details are in [10].

6.3   Object Creation

New structures are created in programming languages by allocating storage. The effect in the pointer machine is to make new addresses available.

In our untyped theory, we define that the attributes of newly created objects have an unspecified value. We introduce a construct $x : new(a)$, which allocates new storage for an object that becomes accessible from x; here a is a list of the attribute names. We use the notation $\{x.a_i\}$ to refer to the set of addresses formed by appending an attribute a_i in a to x. Similarly, we write $\{x.a_i \mapsto v_i\}$ to denote the set of pairs that associate each $x.a_i$ to the corresponding element of a list v of values; similarly $\{x.a_i \mapsto x.a_i\}$ associates each address $x.a_i$ to itself. The definition of $x : new(a)$ is much like that of a pointer assignment to x, and we consider below the case in which x is a simple name.

$$x : new(a) \;\widehat{=}\; \textbf{HPI} \circ \textbf{HP9} \begin{pmatrix} A' = (A \setminus x\infty) \cup \{x.a_i\} \;\wedge \\ \exists v \bullet V' = ((x\infty \cup \{x\}) \triangleleft V) \cup \{x.a_i \mapsto v_i\} \;\wedge \\ S' = \begin{pmatrix} ((x\infty \cup \{x\}) \triangleleft S \triangleright (x\infty \cup \{x\})) \cup \\ \{x \mapsto x\} \cup \{x.a_i \mapsto x.a_i\} \end{pmatrix} \end{pmatrix}$$

$$\textbf{provided } x \in A \text{ and } x \text{ is a simple name.}$$

Its proof of healthiness is similar to that for assignment.

6.4   Variable Declaration and Undeclaration

Pointer variables can be introduced by the operator $begin(x)$ and removed by $end(x)$.

$$begin(x) \;\widehat{=}\; \textbf{HPI} \circ \textbf{HP9} \begin{pmatrix} A' = A \cup \{x\} \;\wedge \\ \exists v \bullet V' = V \oplus \{x \mapsto v\} \;\wedge \\ S' = S \cup \{x \mapsto x\} \end{pmatrix} \quad \textbf{provided } x \notin A$$

In this case **HP9** guarantees that the output alphabet includes x', corresponding to the new variable x, which is now in A.

$$end(x) \;\widehat{=}\; \textbf{HPI} \circ \textbf{HP9} \begin{pmatrix} A' = A \setminus (x\infty \cup \{x\}) \;\wedge \\ V' = (x\infty \cup \{x\}) \triangleleft V) \;\wedge \\ S' = (x\infty \cup \{x\}) \triangleleft S \triangleright (x\infty \cup \{x\}) \end{pmatrix}$$

These constructs correspond to the (**var** x) and (**end** x) operators of the UTP; they do not create a variable block.

7   Conclusions

We have presented a UTP theory of programs with variables whose object values and their attributes may share locations. We capture an abstract memory model of a modern object-oriented language based on (mutually) recursive records.

These have also been considered by Naumann in the context of higher-order imperative programs and a weakest precondition semantics [19]. In that work, many of the concerns are related to record types, and the possibility of their extension, as achieved by class inheritance in object-oriented languages. Here, we are only concerned with record values. We propose to handle the issue of inheritance separately, in a theory of classes with a copy semantics [25].

The idea of avoiding the use of explicit locations was first considered in [3] for an Algol-like language. The motivation was the definition of a fully abstract semantics, which does not distinguish programs that allocate variables to different positions in memory. In that work, sharing is recorded by a function that maps each variable to the set of variables that share its location; a healthiness condition ensures that variables in the same location have the same value. A stack of functions is used to handle nested variable blocks and redeclaration. We do not consider redeclarations, but we handle the presence of record variables, and sharing between record components, not only variables.

Hoare & He present in [12] a theory of pointers and objects using an analogy with process algebras. They draw attention to the similarities between pointer structures, automata and processes, and use of trace semantics and bisimulation in discussing pointers. They use a graph model based on a trace semantics: a set of sets of traces, each set of traces describing the paths that may be used to access a particular object. This work, however, stops short of providing a specification or refinement framework for pointer programs. We take the view that pointer structures are not just like automata, they are automata; this leads naturally to the view that updatable pointer structures are updatable automata. We handle the correspondence between the values of object variables and attribute accesses, and the sharing structure of these variables and their components in the unified context of a programming theory. To manage complexity, we use healthiness conditions to factor out basic properties from definitions.

Work on separation logic [23] and local reasoning [20] also provided inspiration for our work. These approaches establish a system of proof rules to address the frame problem. When a change is made to a data structure, variables not affected by the change maintain their values; standard approaches to reasoning require explicit invariants for every variable that does not change its value, with a large overhead in specification and reasoning. Any effective theory must address this problem in some way. Our work builds a semantic view of pointers which we believe supports derived rules of inference that mirror those used in local reasoning. At the moment, we are concerned with local reasoning, rather than separation logic, because we want to work with classical logic to simplify connection with other UTP theories.

Chen and Sanders' work [8] lifts and extends combinators of separation logic to handle modularisation and abstraction at the levels of specification and design.

This work is based on the model in [12], and as such it also does not consider the relationship between the pointer structure and the values of programming variables and attribute accesses. On the other hand, they present a number of operators and laws to support reasoning about the graph structures.

Möller [18] uses relations to represent pointer graphs; the extension of this work to Kleene algebra [9] provides a natural formalism to capture self-referential structures. Since we adopt the automaton view of pointers, there is inevitably a correspondence with Kleene algebras: all our constructions could be expressed in terms of an updatable Kleene algebra. The difference is one of perspective: if we were concerned with data structures, our work would provide results similar to Möller's, although expressed in terms of automata. We aim, however, at a theory for specification and refinement, so our model is directly linked to the UTP framework via the healthiness conditions that connect the updatable automaton to the program variables.

Bakewell, Plump, and Runciman [2] suggest the explicit use of a graph model to reason about pointers. With this perspective, it is natural to talk about invariants of the graph and about pointer structure manipulations in terms of invariant preservation. This is at the heart of the work in [2], in which a set of invariants are defined for pointer graphs and program safety is defined in terms of preservation of suitable sets of these invariants. The technique would be directly applicable to automaton models, including ours.

The refinement calculus for object systems (rCOS) [14] and TCOZ [22], an object-oriented language that combines Object-Z [26], CSP, and timing constructs, have been given a UTP semantics. In both works, objects have identities which are abstract records of their location in memory. Object identities refer explicitly to storage and, as already discussed, prevent full abstraction.

In the short term, we plan to investigate refinement laws of our theory, and explore its power to reason about pointer programs in general, and data structures and algorithms typically used in object-oriented languages in particular. After that, we want to go a step further in our combination of theories and consider a theory of reactive designs with pointers.

References

1. Back, R.J., Fan, X., Preoteasa, V.: Reasoning about Pointers in Refinement Calculus. In: APSEC 2003, p. 425. IEEE Computer Society Press, Los Alamitos (2003)
2. Bakewell, A., Plump, D., Runciman, C.: Specifying Pointer Structures by Graph Reduction. In: Pfaltz, J.L., Nagl, M., Böhlen, B. (eds.) AGTIVE 2003. LNCS, vol. 3062, pp. 30–44. Springer, Heidelberg (2004)
3. Brookes, S.D.: A Fully Abstract Semantics and a Proof System for an Algol-like Language with Sharing. In: Melton, A. (ed.) MFPS 1985. LNCS, vol. 239, pp. 59–100. Springer, Heidelberg (1986)
4. Burstall, R.M.: Some techniques for proving correctness of programs which alter data structures. Machine Intelligence 7, 23–50 (1972)
5. Cavalcanti, A.L.C., Harwood, W., Woodcock, J.C.P.: Pointers and Records in the Unifying Theories of Programming. In: Dunne, S., Stoddart, B. (eds.) UTP 2006. LNCS, vol. 4010, pp. 200–216. Springer, Heidelberg (2006)

6. Cavalcanti, A.L.C., Sampaio, A.C.A., Woodcock, J.C.P.: Unifying Classes and Processes. SoSyM 4(3), 277–296 (2005)
7. Cavalcanti, A.L.C., Woodcock, J.C.P.: A Tutorial Introduction to CSP in Unifying Theories of Programming. In: Cavalcanti, A., Sampaio, A., Woodcock, J. (eds.) PSSE 2004. LNCS, vol. 3167, pp. 220–268. Springer, Heidelberg (2006)
8. Chen, Y., Sanders, J.: Compositional Reasoning for Pointer Structures. In: Uustalu, T. (ed.) MPC 2006. LNCS, vol. 4014, pp. 115–139. Springer, Heidelberg (2006)
9. Desharnais, J., Möller, B., Struth, G.: Modal Kleene Algebra and applications a survey. Methods in Computer Science 1, 93–131 (2004)
10. Harwood, W., Cavalcanti, A.L.C., Woodcock, J.C.P.: A Model of Pointers for the Unifying Theories of Programming – Extended Version. Technical report, University of York, Department of Computer Science, UK (2008), www-users.cs.york.ac.uk/~alcc/publications/HCW08.pdf
11. Hoare, C.A.R., Jifeng, H.: Unifying Theories of Programming. In: Unifying Theories of Programming. Prentice-Hall, Englewood Cliffs (1998)
12. Hoare, C.A.R., Jifeng, H.: A trace model for pointers and objects. Programming methodology, 223 – 245 (2003)
13. Ishtiaq, S., O'Hearn, P.W.: BI as an assertion language for mutable data structures. In: POPL. ACM Press, New York (2001)
14. Liu, Z., He, J., Li, X.: rCOS: Refinement of Component and Object Systems. In: de Boer, F.S., Bonsangue, M.M., Graf, S., de Roever, W.-P. (eds.) FMCO 2004. LNCS, vol. 3657, Springer, Heidelberg (2005)
15. Meyer, B.: Eiffel: the language. Prentice-Hall, Englewood Cliffs (1992)
16. Meyer, B.: Towards practical proofs of class correctness. In: Bert, D., P. Bowen, J., King, S. (eds.) ZB 2003. LNCS, vol. 2651, pp. 359–387. Springer, Heidelberg (2003)
17. Milne, R., Strachey, C.: A Theory of Programming Language Semantics. Chapman and Hall, Boca Raton (1976)
18. Möller, B.: Calculating with pointer structures. In: IFIP TC 2 WG 2.1 International Workshop on Algorithmic Languages and Calculi, pp. 24–48. Chapman & Hall, Ltd, Boca Raton (1997)
19. Naumann, D.A.: Predicate Transformer Semantics of a Higher Order Imperative Language with Record Subtypes. SCP 41(1), 1–51 (2001)
20. O'Hearn, P., Reynolds, J., Yang, H.: Local reasoning about programs that alter data structures. In: Fribourg, L. (ed.) CSL 2001 and EACSL 2001. LNCS, vol. 2142, pp. 1–19. Springer, Heidelberg (2001)
21. Paige, R.F., Ostroff, J.S.: ERC – An object-oriented refinement calculus for Eiffel. Formal Aspects of Computing 16(1), 5 (2004)
22. Qin, S., Dong, J.S., Chin, W.N.: A Semantic Foundation for TCOZ in Unifying Theories of Programming. In: Araki, K., Gnesi, S., Mandrioli, D. (eds.) FME 2003. LNCS, vol. 2805, pp. 321–340. Springer, Heidelberg (2003)
23. Reynolds, J.: Separation logic: a logic for shared mutable data structures. In: IEEE Symposium on Logic in Computer Science, pp. 55–74. IEEE Press, Los Alamitos (2002)
24. Reynolds, J.C.: Intuitionistic reasoning about shared mutable data structure. In: Millenial Perspectives in Computer Science. Palgrave (2001)
25. Santos, T.L.V.L., Cavalcanti, A.L.C., Sampaio, A.C.A.: Object Orientation in the UTP. In: Dunne, S., Stoddart, B. (eds.) UTP 2006. LNCS, vol. 4010, pp. 18–37. Springer, Heidelberg (2006)
26. Smith, G.: The Object-Z Specification Language. Kluwer Academic Publishers, Dordrecht (1999)

Recasting Constraint Automata into Büchi Automata

Mohammad Izadi[1,3,4] and Marcello M. Bonsangue[1,2]

[1] LIACS - Leiden University, The Netherlands
[2] Centrum voor Wiskunde en Informatica (CWI), The Netherlands
[3] Dept. of Computer Engineering, Sharif University of Technology, Tehran, Iran
[4] Research Institute for Humanities and Cultural Studies, Tehran, Iran

Abstract. Constraint automata have been proposed as the operational semantics of Reo, a glue-code language for the exogenous composition and orchestration of components in a software system. In this paper we recast the theory of constraint automata into that of Büchi automata on infinite strings of records. We use records to express simultaneity constraints of I/O operations and show that every constraint automaton can be expressed as a Büchi automaton on an appropriate alphabet of records. Further, we give examples of component compositions that are expressible as Büchi automata but not as constraint automata. Finally, we show that the join composition operator for constraint automata and its counterpart for Büchi automata of records can be expressed as two basic operations on Büchi automata: alphabet extension and product.

1 Introduction

Component-based software development is concerned with software development by using pieces of software, the components, produced independently by each other [15]. Components are integrated into a functioning system using glue-code, another piece of software that is not intended to contribute to the functionality of the system, but instead serves to contribute to the data communications and to coordinate the control flow among the components.

A generic way to depict component-based systems is by blocks diagrams [10]. Blocks represent software components, that communicate with the environment solely through ports. Ports are related by a network of connectors that specifies the glue code. These connectors build together what is called the coordination system. Timed data streams [4] form an appropriate model for the specification of event-based communications through this network. A timed data stream for a port A is a pair of infinite streams of time and data. Each pair in a timed data stream denotes an *event*, that is, the occurrence of a data communication at the port A at a certain time. Two events are said to be *synchronous* when they occurs at the same time, otherwise they are *asynchronous*.

Constraint automata are acceptors of timed data streams [6], just like finite automata are models for recognizing finite strings [12]. Constraint automata are labeled transition systems where constraints label transitions and influence their

J.S. Fitzgerald, A.E. Haxthausen, and H. Yenigun (Eds.): ICTAC 2008, LNCS 5160, pp. 156–170, 2008.
© Springer-Verlag Berlin Heidelberg 2008

firing. There are two kinds of constraints: port constraints define those events that must happen synchronously when a transition is executed, whereas data constraints restrict the data that can flow through the ports involved in the transition.

Constraint automata have been introduced in [6] as models of Reo connector circuits. Reo is an exogenous glue-code language which is based on a calculus of channels [1]. By using Reo specifications, complex component connectors can be organized in a network of channels and build in a compositional manner. A channel is an abstract model for any kind of peer-to-peer communication: it has two channel ends, declared to be *sink* or *source* ends. At source ends data items enter the channel while they are delivered at sink ends. The behavior of a channel is user defined, and can be given, for example, by a constraint automata. Channel ends can be composed into a node by Reo's *join* operator. A node serves as routers selecting data from a source channel ends and copying it to all sink channel ends.

Although constraint automata are acceptor of timed data streams, there is an huge abstraction gap between the two models. Timed data streams are very concrete. They associate to each event not only the data communicated through a port, but also the precise time of its occurrence. On the other hand, constraint automata are much more abstract as they specify only the relative order of occurrence among events instead of their time. The concrete time-values play no role in the automata. This abstraction is enough for a compositional operational semantics of an important subset of the language Reo [6].

The main contribution of our work presented in this paper is a novel approach to specify the behavior of a network of components. We use records as data structures for modeling the simultaneous executions of events: ports in the domain of the record are allowed to communicate simultaneously the data assigned to them, while ports not in the domain of the record are blocked so that no communication can happen. The behavior of a network of components is given in terms of (infinite) sequences of records, so to specify the order of occurrence of the events. Standard operational models can be used to recognize such languages. For example, we use ordinary Büchi automata as operational devices for recognizing languages of streams of records.

Our main result is that every constraint automaton can be translated into an essentially equivalent Büchi automaton. The construction of the Büchi automaton is straightforward and the result may appear as not surprising at all. But beware! The languages recognized by the two type of automata have a different structure. In fact it is easy to embed a language on streams of records into a language of timed data streams, but not viceversa. Despite these structural differences, we show that the converse also holds without losing any information as far as constraint automata is concerned. An immediate consequence of this result is that, since Büchi automata enjoy closure properties that constraint automata do not have, our model is more expressive. In fact we give few concrete examples of realistic connectors (not considered in the Reo language until now) that can be specified in our model but not with constraint automata.

The main reason for having time information in the timed data streams is compositionality with respect to the Reo join operator. We introduce a join composition operator for Büchi automata on streams of records and show that it is correct with respect to the join operator for constraint automata. Finally, we presenting a method to recast this join operation using the standard product operator of Büchi automata.

Much work has been done on constraint automata for the verification of properties of Reo circuits through model-checking [5], to synthesize Reo circuits and executable code from constraint automata [2], and to automatically compose constraint automata. Further, several extensions of constraint automata have been defined to cover probabilities [7], real-time [5], and other quality of services of connectors [3]. On the other hand, since the definition of constraint automata [6], there has been no expressivity results with respect to existing automata models. In this paper we recast the theory of constraint automata into that of *ordinary* Büchi automata. The latter is especially important because many of the results, tools and extensions of actual interest for Reo and constraint automata have already been developed [11,16].

The remainder of this paper is organized as follows. In Section 2 we recall the basic theory of constraint automata as acceptors of timed data streams. We continue in Section 3, by introducing records as data structure for representing snapshots of a networks of components. Full behavior is represented as languages of streams of records, or, more operationally, by Büchi automata on streams of records. Our main result is that every constraint automaton is equivalent to a Büchi automaton on streams of records. In Section4 we introduce a novel composition operator for Büchi automata on streams of records, and we show its correctness with respect to the join of constraint automata. In Section 4.1, we recast the above composition operator in the theory of ordinary Büchi automata. In fact we show that it can be decomposed into two operators: record extension and ordinary Büchi automata product. We conclude in Section 5 with a discuss about the benefits of seing constraint automata as Büchi automata.

2   Basic Theory of Constraint Automata

Constraint automata are a formalism introduced in [6] for describing all possible data flow among the ports of an open components-based software system. For example, a compositional semantics for a large subset of the glue-code language Reo [1] can be given in terms of constraint automata [6]. In this section we present the basic theory of constraint automata as acceptors of timed data streams.

2.1   Timed Data Streams

To begin with, we recall the notion of *time data stream* presented in [4]. Let S be any set. The set of all finite sequences (words) over S is denoted by S^*. We define the set S^ω of all *streams* (infinite sequences) over S as the set of functions $w:\mathbb{N} \to S$. For a stream $w \in S^\omega$ we call $w(0)$ the initial value of w. The (stream) *derivative* w' of a stream w is defined as $w'(k) = w(k+1)$. We write $w^{(i)}$ for the i-th derivative of w which is defined by $w^{(0)} = w$ and $w^{(i+1)} = w^{(i)}{}'$. Note that $w^{(i)}(k) = w(i+k)$, for all $k, i \geq 0$. Now, let $\mathcal{N}$ be a fixed finite set of *port names* and $\mathcal{D}$ be a non-empty set of *data* that can be communicated through those ports. The set of all (infinite) *timed data streams* over $\mathcal{D}$ is given by:

$$TDS = \{\langle \alpha, a \rangle \in \mathcal{D}^\omega \times \mathbb{R}_+^\omega | \forall k \geq 0 \, [a(k) = \infty \vee (a(k) < a(k+1) \wedge \lim_{k \to \infty} a(k) = \infty)]\},$$

where $\mathbb{R}_+^\omega = [0, \infty]$ is the set of all positive real numbers including zero and infinity. Informally, a timed data stream consists of an infinite stream of data together with a time stamp consisting of increasing positive real numbers that go to infinity. The time stamp indicates for each data item $\alpha(k)$ the moment $a(k)$ at which it is communicated.

With each port $n \in \mathcal{N}$, we associate a timed data stream recording both the data communicated and the time when the communication happen. That is, we define $TDS^\mathcal{N}$ as the set of all TDS-tuples consisting of one timed data stream for each port in $\mathcal{N}$. We use a family-notation $\theta = (\theta|_n)_{n \in \mathcal{N}}$ for the elements of $TDS^\mathcal{N}$, where $\theta|_n$ stands for the projection of θ along the port n. A *TDS-language* for $\mathcal{N}$ is any subset of $TDS^\mathcal{N}$.

Simultaneous exchange of data between a set of ports can be detected by inspecting the time when communications happens. For this purpose, for $\theta \in TDS^\mathcal{N}$ we define $\theta.time$ to be a stream in $\mathbb{R}_+^\omega$ obtained by merging the streams $(\theta|_n)_r$ in increasing order. More formally,

$$\theta.time(0) \quad = min\{\pi_r(\theta|_n)(0) \mid n \in \mathcal{N}\}$$
$$\theta.time(i+1) = min\{\pi_r(\theta|_n)(k) \mid \pi_r(\theta|_n)(k) \rangle \theta.time(i), k \in \mathbb{N}, n \in \mathcal{N}\}.$$

Next we define the stream $\theta.N$ over $2^\mathcal{N}$ by setting

$$\theta.N(k) = \{n \mid \exists i \in \mathbb{N} : \pi_r(\theta|_n)(i) = \theta.time(k)\}.$$

Intuitively, the above set consists of all the ports exchanging a data item at time $\theta.time(k)$. We denote the data communicated by a port $n \in \theta.N(k)$ by

$$\theta.\delta(k)_n = \pi_l(\theta|_n)(i)$$

for the unique index i such that $\pi_r(\theta|_n)(i) = \theta.time(k)$.

2.2 Constraint Automata and Their Composition

A constraint automaton is a labeled transition system in which each transition label contains two parts: a set N of port names and a proposition g on the data. Both parts act as constraints: the set of ports N constraints which ports of the system should be active if the transition is taken, whereas the proposition g constraints the data that could be communicated through the ports in N.

The set $DC(\mathcal{N}, \mathcal{D})$ of *data constraint* over a finite set $\mathcal{N}$ of port names and a finite set $\mathcal{D}$ of data is defined by the following grammar:

$$g ::= true \mid d_A = d \mid g_1 \vee g_2 \mid \neg g \qquad d \in \mathcal{D}, \quad A \in \mathcal{N}.$$

Now we can define the notion of constraint automaton formally.

Definition 1. *A* constraint automaton *over finite data set* $\mathcal{D}$ *is a quadruple* $A = \langle Q, \mathcal{N}, \longrightarrow, Q_0 \rangle$ *where,* Q *is a set of states,* $\mathcal{N}$ *is a finite set of names,* $\longrightarrow \subseteq Q \times 2^{\mathcal{N}} \times DC(\mathcal{N}, \mathcal{D}) \times Q$ *is a set of transitions and* $Q_0 \subseteq Q$ *is a set of initial states.*

We write $p \xrightarrow{N,g} q$ *instead of* $(p, N, g, q) \in \longrightarrow$ *and call* N *the name set and* g *the guard of the transition. For every transition label* (N, g), *it is required that* $N \neq \emptyset$ *and* $g \in DC(N, Data)$.

A constraint automaton is said to be *finite* if its sets of states and transitions are finite, and to be *deterministic* if its set of initial states Q_0 is a singleton and for each state q, set of port names N and data assignment $\delta : N \to \mathcal{D}$ there is at most one transition $q \xrightarrow{N,g} q'$ with $\delta \models g$.

Like ordinary automata are acceptors of finite strings, constraint automata are acceptors of tuples of timed data streams. Informally, each element of the tuple is associated to a port of the system and corresponds to the streams of observed data communicated through this port together with the time when the data has been observed.

Definition 2. *Let* $A = \langle Q, \mathcal{N}, \longrightarrow, Q_0 \rangle$ *be a constraint automaton and* $\varphi \in TDS^{\mathcal{N}}$ *be a TDS-tuple.*

(i) An infinite computation *for* φ *in* A *is an infinite sequence of alternating states and transition labels* $\pi = q_0, (N_0, g_0), q_1, (N_1, g_1), ...,$ *in which, for all* i, $q_i \in Q$ *and* $q_i \xrightarrow{N_i, g_i} q_{i+1}$ *such that* $N_i = \varphi.N(i)$, $\varphi.\delta(i) \models g_i$. *Also,* π *is an* initial infinite computation, *if* $q_0 \in Q_0$.

(ii) A TDS-tuple φ *is* accepted *by* A *if and only if there is an initial infinite computation for* φ *in* A. *The language of constraint automaton* A *is*

$$\mathcal{L}(A) = \{\varphi \in TDS^{\mathcal{N}} \mid A \text{ accepts } \varphi\}.$$

Using the Rabin-Scott powerset construction as for finite automata, it is easy to see that for every constraint automaton A there is a deterministic constraint automaton A' such that $\mathcal{L}(A) = \mathcal{L}(A')$ [6]. Further, in a finite constraint automaton A all transitions with unsatisfiable guards can be removed without any effect on the TDS language accepted by A, where a guard g of a transition $p \xrightarrow{N,g} q$ is said to be semantically unsatisfiable for N if there is no data assignment for elements of N which satisfies g (take, for example, g to be $\neg true$). In the rest of this paper we assume without any loss of generality that all guards in a constraint automaton are satisfiable with respect to the set of names of the transition they belongs to.

Differently from finite and Büchi automata on languages, the simplicity of a constraint automaton is not reflected in the TDS language it recognizes. Consider for example the following constraint automaton on two ports A and B over a singleton data set:

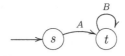

While the automaton describes only a *single* event happening at port A, a TDS-tuple θ accepted by the automaton consists a pair of two *infinite* sequence of events θ_A and θ_B, one describing the data flow at port A and the other the flow at port B, such that all events in θ_B happen between the first and the second event in θ_A. All event but the first in θ_A are not really relevant, yet one needs to describe them all.

Constraint automata can be composed by means of a join operator, the semantic counterpart of the join operator in Reo [6]. Differently from the ordinary product for finite automata, the composition of two constraint automata is allowed even if they have different alphabets. In fact, the resulting constraint automaton has transitions when data occur at the ports belonging to only one of the automaton, without involving the transitions or states that it inherits from the other automaton (because at that point in time, there is no data on any of its corresponding ports). More formally, the join operation for constraint automata is defined as follows:

Definition 3. *Let $A_1 = \langle Q_1, \mathcal{N}_1, \longrightarrow_1, Q_{01} \rangle$ and $A_2 = \langle Q_2, \mathcal{N}_2, \longrightarrow_2, Q_{02} \rangle$ be two constraint automata both over data set $\mathcal{D}$. The join of A_1 and A_2 produces a constraint automaton $A_1 \bowtie_C A_2 = \langle Q_1 \times Q_2, \mathcal{N}_1 \cup \mathcal{N}_2, \longrightarrow, Q_{01} \times Q_{02} \rangle$ in which transition relation $\longrightarrow$ is defined using the follow rules:*

$$\frac{s \xrightarrow{N_1,g_1}_1 s', t \xrightarrow{N_2,g_2}_2 t', N_1 \cap \mathcal{N}_2 = N_2 \cap \mathcal{N}_1}{\langle s, t \rangle \xrightarrow{N_1 \cup N_2, g_1 \wedge g_2} \langle s', t' \rangle},$$

$$\frac{s \xrightarrow{N_1,g_1}_1 s', N_1 \cap \mathcal{N}_2 = \emptyset}{\langle s, t \rangle \xrightarrow{N_1,g_1} \langle s', t \rangle}, \qquad \frac{t \xrightarrow{N_2,g_2}_1 t', N_2 \cap \mathcal{N}_1 = \emptyset}{\langle s, t \rangle \xrightarrow{N_2,g_2} \langle s, t' \rangle}.$$

The join of two constraint automata using the operation defined in Definition 3 induces the join of their accepted TDS-languages, where the join of two TDS-languages is basically the same as defined in the theory of relational data bases [6].

Constraint automata are, in general, not closed under complement. Informally this is due to the fact that constraint automata do not have "final" states. If we augment the definition of constraint automaton by a set of final states and use Büchi acceptance condition (a timed data stream is accepted if at least one of the correspondent runs for it contains one of the final states infinitely many times), we refer to the resulting automaton as a *Büchi constraint automaton*. Obviously, a constraint automaton is a Büchi constraint automaton in which all states are accepting. Its complement, however do not need to satisfy this property.

3   Büchi Automata of Record Languages

Constraint automata are acceptors of timed data streams. However, timed data streams are much more concrete than constraint automata because they record the actual times when communications happen, whereas constraint automata record just the temporal order of data communications and not their times. In this section, we introduce an alternative way to model temporal ordering of data occurrences using streams of records. After introducing the notion of record, we use Büchi automata to accept streams of records. We show that as far as we are interested in the temporal order of data communications, constraint automata are semantically equivalent to Büchi automata on streams of records.

3.1 Streams and Languages of Records

Let $\mathcal{N}$ be a finite nonempty set of (port) names and $\mathcal{D}$ be a finite nonempty set of data. We write $Rec_{\mathcal{N}}(\mathcal{D}) = \mathcal{N} \rightharpoonup \mathcal{D}$ for the set of *records* with entries from a set of data $\mathcal{D}$ and labels from a set of port name $\mathcal{N}$, consisting of all partial functions from $\mathcal{N}$ to $\mathcal{D}$. For a record $r \in Rec_{\mathcal{N}}(\mathcal{D})$ we write $dom(r)$ for the domain of r. Sometimes we use the more explicit notation $r \doteq [n_1 = d_1, \ldots, n_k = d_k]$ for a record $r \in Rec_{\mathcal{N}}(\mathcal{D})$, with $dom(r) = \{n_1, \ldots, n_k\}$ and $r(n_i) = d_i$ for $1 \leq i \leq k$. Differently from a tuple, the order of the components of a record is irrelevant and its size is not fixed a priori. We denote by τ the special record with empty domain, that is $dom(\tau) = \emptyset$.

We use records as data structures for modeling constrained synchronization of ports in $\mathcal{N}$. Following [14], we see a record $r \in Rec_{\mathcal{N}}(\mathcal{D})$ as carrying both positive and negative information: only the ports in the domain of r have the possibility to exchange the data assigned to them by r, while the other ports in $\mathcal{N} \setminus dom(r)$ are definitely constrained to *not* perform any communication. This intuition is formalized by the fact that only for ports $n \in dom(r)$ data can be retrieved, using *record selection* $r.n$. Formally, $r.n$ is just (partial) function application $r(n)$.

Further, positive information may increase by means of the *update* (and extension) operation $r[n := d]$, defined as the record with domain $dom(r) \cup \{n\}$ mapping the port n to d and remaining invariant with respect to all other ports. The *hiding* operator '\' is used to increase the negative information. For $n \in \mathcal{N}$, the record $r \setminus n$ hides the port n to the environment by setting $dom(r \setminus n) = dom(r) \setminus \{n\}$, and $(r \setminus n).m = r.m$.

Definition 4. *Let $r_1 \in Rec_{\mathcal{N}_1}(\mathcal{D})$ and $r_2 \in Rec_{\mathcal{N}_2}(\mathcal{D})$. We say that records r_1 and r_2 are compatible, if $dom(r_1) \cap \mathcal{N}_2 = dom(r_2) \cap \mathcal{N}_1$ and $\forall n \in dom(r_1) \cap dom(r_2):r_1.n = r_2.n$. The union of compatible records r_1 and r_2, denoted by $r_1 \cup r_2$, is a record over port names $\mathcal{N}_1 \cup \mathcal{N}_2$, such that, $\forall n \in dom(r_1):(r_1 \cup r_2).n = r_1.n$ and $\forall n \in dom(r_2):(r_1 \cup r_2).n = r_2.n$.*

Let us compare the expressiveness of TDS-languages with that of languages of streams of records. Given a TDS-language L for $\mathcal{N}$ we can abstract from its timing information to obtain a set of streams over $Rec_{\mathcal{N}}(\mathcal{D})$. For a TDS-tuple $\theta \in TDS^{\mathcal{N}}$, the idea is to construct a stream of records $\Upsilon(\theta) \in Rec_{\mathcal{N}}(\mathcal{D})^{\omega}$, where, for each k, the record $\Upsilon(\theta)(k)$ contains all ports and data exchanged at time $\theta.time(k)$. In fact, we define for each $n \in \theta.N(k)$ and $k \in \mathbb{N}$,

$$\Upsilon(\theta)(k).n = \theta.\delta(k)_n.$$

Note that $dom(\Upsilon(\theta)(k)) = \theta.N(k)$. As usual, we extend this construction to sets, namely, for every $L \subseteq TDS^{\mathcal{N}}$,

$$\Upsilon(L) = \bigcup \{\Upsilon(\theta) \mid \theta \in L\}.$$

Conversely, any stream of records $\rho \in Rec_{\mathcal{N}}(\mathcal{D})^{\omega}$ generates a TDS-language $\Theta(\rho)$ by *guessing* the time when data is exchanged so to respect the relative order of communication imposed by ρ. Formally,

$$\Theta(\rho) = \{\theta \mid \forall k \geq 0 : (\theta.N(k) = dom(\rho(k)) \text{ and } \forall n \in dom(\rho(k)) : \theta.\delta(k)_n = \rho(k).n)\}.$$

We extend Θ to languages $L \subseteq Rec_{\mathcal{N}}(\mathcal{D})^{\omega}$ by setting

$$\Theta(L) = \bigcup \{\Theta(\rho) \mid \rho \in L\}.$$

The function $\Theta : 2^{Rec_{\mathcal{N}}(\mathcal{D})^{\omega}} \to 2^{TDS^{\mathcal{N}}}$ is an embedding of languages over records into TDS-languages for $\mathcal{N}$.

Lemma 1. *For each* $L \subseteq Rec_{\mathcal{N}}(\mathcal{D})^{\omega}$, $L = \Upsilon(\Theta(L))$.

The counterpart of the above lemma for TDS-languages does not hold, because a tuple of time data stream $\theta \in TDS^{\mathcal{N}}$ may contain specific time information that get lost when mapped into a stream of record $\Upsilon(\theta)$. In the next section we will see that for constraint automata the information lost in the above translation is never used.

3.2   Büchi Automata of Records

Sets of streams of records are just languages of infinite strings, and as such some of them can be recognized by ordinary Büchi automata. Next we recall some basic definitions and facts on Büchi automata [16].

Definition 5. *A* Büchi automaton *is a tuple* $B = \langle Q, \Sigma, \Delta, Q_0, F \rangle$ *where,* Q *is a finite set of* states, Σ *is a finite nonempty set of symbols called* alphabet, $\Delta \subseteq (Q \times \Sigma \times Q)$ *is a transition relation,* $Q_0 \subseteq Q$ *is a nonempty set of* initial states *and* $F \subseteq Q$ *is a set of* accepting (final) states.

An *infinite computation* for a stream $\omega = a_0, a_1, \cdots \in \Sigma^{\omega}$ in B is an infinite sequence $q_0, a_0, q_1, a_1, ...,$ of alternating states and alphabet symbols in which $q_0 \in Q_0$ and $(q_i, a_i, q_{i+1}) \in \Delta$ for all i. The language accepted by a Büchi automaton B consists of all streams $\omega \in \Sigma^{\omega}$ such that there is an infinite computation for ω in B with at least one of the final states occurring infinitely often. The language of a Büchi automaton B, denoted by $L(B)$, is the set of all streams accepted by it. We say that two Büchi automata B_1 and B_2 are *language equivalent* if $L(B_1) = L(B_2)$.

In this paper we are interested in Büchi automata with as alphabet a subset of $Rec_{\mathcal{N}}(\mathcal{D})$, for some finite set of port names $\mathcal{N}$ and finite set of data $\mathcal{D}$. We refer to such an automaton as a *Büchi automaton (on streams) of records*.

In general, a Büchi automaton of records may contain transitions labeled by τ. These can be considered as internal actions, as no port of the system can be involved in a communication. Since they are externally invisible we may ignore them. However, if we remove all τ symbols from a stream of records ω, the resulting sequence need not to be infinite anymore. For example, removing all τ's from the stream consisting of only τ symbols will result in the empty (and hence finite) string.

Definition 6. *Let B be a Büchi automaton of records. The* visible language *of B is defined as:*

$$L_{vis}(B) = \{\rho \in Rec_{\mathcal{N}}(\mathcal{D})^{\omega} \mid \exists \omega \in L(B):\rho = vis(\omega)\},$$

where $vis(\omega)$ denote the sequence obtained by removing all τ symbols from ω. We say that automata B_1 and B_2 are visibly equivalent *if $L_{vis}(B_1) = L_{vis}(B_2)$.*

Note that $L_{vis}(B)$ contains only infinite sequences and therefore is a subset of the set of sequences obtained from removing the τ's from the streams in $L(B)$. Clearly, $L_{vis}(B) = L(B)$ if B does not have τ-transitions. By a simple generalization of the standard algorithm for eliminating the ϵ-transitions of an ordinary finite automaton over finite words [12], we can construct a Büchi automaton recognizing $L_{vis}(B)$.

Lemma 2. *For every Büchi automaton of records B there is a Büchi automaton of records B' (without τ-transition) such that, $L_{vis}(B) = L(B')$*

Now we show that for every constraint automaton A over name set $\mathcal{N}$ and data set $\mathcal{D}$ we can construct a Büchi automaton of records. The key observation is that for each transition labeled (N, g) in A, there is a set of (total) data assignments $\{\delta:N \to \mathcal{D} \mid \delta \models g\}$. Every data assignment in this set can be seen as a partial function from $\mathcal{N}$ to $\mathcal{D}$, with as domain $N \subseteq \mathcal{N}$, that is, it is a record in $Rec_N(\mathcal{D})$. We can thus construct a Büchi automaton of records $B(A)$ with the same (initial) states as A, with all states as final, and with transitions labeled by each of the above data assignment for every transition in A.

Definition 7. *For every constraint automaton $A = \langle Q, \mathcal{N}, \longrightarrow, Q_0 \rangle$ over finite data set $\mathcal{D}$ and finite name set $\mathcal{N}$, we define $B(A)$ to be the Büchi automaton of records $\langle Q, Rec_{\mathcal{N}}(\mathcal{D}), \Delta, Q_0, Q \rangle$, where*

$$\Delta = \{(q, r, q') \mid \exists q \xrightarrow{(N,g)} q', \exists \delta:N \to \mathcal{D}:\delta \models g, dom(r) = N \text{ } and \forall n \in N:r.n = \delta(n)\}.$$

For example, consider the constraint automaton depicted in Figure 1(a). It models a lossy synchronous communication channels between the ports A ad B: data in $\mathcal{D}$ either flows from the port A to the port B or it get lost after it is output by A. We used the data constraint $d_A = d_B$ as an abbreviation for $\vee_{d \in \mathcal{D}}(d_A = d \wedge d_B = d)$. Figure 1(b) shows the corresponding Büchi automaton on streams of records. To simplify the figure, we supposed that the data set is the singleton set $\mathcal{D} = \{d\}$ and used transition label A as a simplified expression for record $[A = d]$ and also AB for record $[A = d, B = d]$.

The following theorem shows that timed data streams are not different from streams of records, at least as for finite constraint automata is concerned.

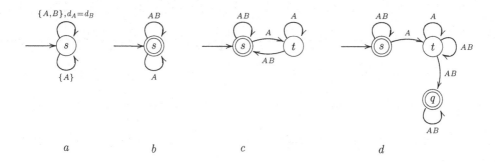

Fig. 1. Models of a lossy synchronous communication channel

Theorem 1. *For every finite constraint automaton* $A = \langle Q, \mathcal{N}, \longrightarrow, Q_0 \rangle$,

$$\Upsilon(\mathcal{L}(A)) = L(B(A)) \text{ and } \Theta(L(B(A)) = \mathcal{L}(A)).$$

It follows that Büchi automata of records are at least as expressive as constraint automata. They are actually more expressive, because Büchi automata of records are closed under complement while constraint automata are not.

As an example of a "realistic" connector between two ports A and B not expressible in ordinary constraint automata, consider the one modeled by the Büchi automaton of records depicted in Figure 1(c). It is a connector similar to the lossy synchronous channel depicted in (b), but with this extra property that it is not possible which all data can be lost. As a more realistic example, the Büchi automaton of records depicted in Figure 1(d) is also a lossy synchronous channel with the possibility of loosing only *finitely many* data at the port A.

Also, because Büchi automata of records are Büchi automata, we can express *unconditional fairness condition* [13]: in each infinite execution of the system, some actions should occur infinitely many times. For example, consider the *merger* connector among two with two source ports A and B and one sink port C (see Figure 2(a)). Intuitively, it transmits synchronously data item from either A or B to the port C. If both the source ports A and B are offering data at the same time than only one of them is chosen non-deterministically. The Büchi automaton of records corresponding to its constraint automaton model introduced in [6] is shown in Figure 2(b). Both models allow unfair executions where data from the same source is always preferred if both A and B are always offering data simultaneously. Figure 2(c) shows a Büchi automaton that disallows those unfair executions. It can be shown that this kind of fairness conditions cannot be expressed by ordinary constraint automaton as its author also say in [6].

4   Joining Büchi Automata on Streams of Records

In this section we define a join operator for Büchi automata of records and shows that it is correct with respect to the join of constraint automata. First let us

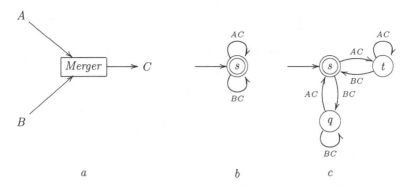

Fig. 2. Models of a merger connector

recall the definition of product of Büchi automata which, for simplicity, is given in terms of generalized Büchi automata [16].

A *generalized Büchi automaton* is a Büchi automaton $B = \langle Q, \Sigma, \Delta, Q_0, \mathcal{F} \rangle$ but for the set of final states, that now is a set of sets, that is, $\mathcal{F} \subseteq 2^Q$. A stream $\omega \in \Sigma^\omega$ is accepted by generalized Büchi automaton B if and only if there is an infinite computation π for ω in B such that for every $F \in \mathcal{F}$ at least one of the states in F occurs in π infinitely often. Clearly, every Büchi automaton is a generalized Büchi automaton with a singleton set of final states, containing the original set of of final states.

Definition 8. *Let $B_1 = \langle Q_1, \Sigma, \Delta_1, Q_{01}, F_1 \rangle$ and $B_2 = \langle Q_2, \Sigma, \Delta_2, Q_{02}, F_2 \rangle$ be two Büchi automata on the same alphabet. We define the product of B_1 and B_2 to be the generalized Büchi automaton:*

$$B_1 \times_B B_2 = \langle Q_1 \times Q_2, \Sigma, \Delta, Q_{01} \times Q_{02}, \{F_1 \times Q_2, Q_1 \times F_2\} \rangle$$

where $(\langle s, t \rangle, a, \langle s', t' \rangle) \in \Delta$ if and only if $(s, a, s') \in \Delta_1$ and $(t, a, t') \in \Delta_2$.

To obtain an ordinary Büchi automaton for the product, one can use the fact that for each generalized Büchi automaton B there is an ordinary Büchi automaton B' such that a stream $\omega \in \Sigma^\omega$ is accepted by B if and only if it is accepted by B'. For the construction of such an automaton we refer to [16]. The language of the product of two Büchi automata is the intersection of their respective languages [16].

Using the richer structure of the alphabet of Büchi automata of records, we can give a more general definition of product that works even if the alphabets of the two automata are different.

Definition 9. *Let $B_1 = \langle Q_1, Rec_{\mathcal{N}_1}(\mathcal{D}), \Delta_1, Q_{01}, F_1 \rangle$ and $B_2 = \langle Q_2, Rec_{\mathcal{N}_2}(\mathcal{D}), \Delta_2, Q_{02}, F_2 \rangle$ be two Büchi automata of records. We define the join of B_1 and B_2 to be the generalized Büchi automaton:*

$$B_1 \bowtie_B B_2 = \langle Q_1 \times Q_2, Rec_{\mathcal{N}_1 \cup \mathcal{N}_2}(\mathcal{D}), \Delta, Q_{01} \times Q_{02}, \{F_1 \times Q_2, Q_1 \times F_2\} \rangle$$

where the transition relation Δ is defined by the following rules:

1. *if $(s, r_1, s') \in \Delta_1$, $(t, r_2, t') \in \Delta_2$ and r_1 and r_2 are compatible then $(\langle s, t \rangle, r_1 \cup r_2, \langle s', t' \rangle) \in \Delta$;*
2. *if $(s, r_1, s') \in \Delta_1$ with $dom(r_1) \cap \mathcal{N}_2 = \emptyset$ then $(\langle s, t \rangle, r_1, \langle s', t \rangle) \in \Delta$;*
3. *dually, if $(t, r_2, t') \in \Delta_2$ with $dom(r_2) \cap \mathcal{N}_1 = \emptyset$ then $(\langle s, t \rangle, r_2, \langle s, t' \rangle) \in \Delta$.*

For Büchi automata without τ-transitions, the join operator coincides with the product in case both automata have the same alphabet. In this case, the language of the product is just the intersection.

Lemma 3. *Let B_1 and B_2 be two Büchi automata of records with the same alphabet and without τ-transitions. Then, $L(B_1 \bowtie_B B_2) = L(B_1) \cap L(B_2)$.*

This implies that our definition of join is correct with respect to the product of ordinary Büchi automata (up to τ-transitions). On the other hand, our definition of join is correct (even structurally, and not only language theoretically) also with respect to the join of constraint automata.

Theorem 2. *Let A_1 and A_2 be two constraint automata. Then,*

$$B(A_1) \bowtie_B B(A_2) = B(A_1 \bowtie_C A_2).$$

For example, Figure 3(a) shows the Büchi automaton of records model of a FIFO queue with a buffer of capacity one between ports A and B (using as data set $\mathcal{D} = \{d\}$) and (b) a FIFO1 between ports B and C over the same data set. The join of these automata obtained using definition 9 is shown in (c). In Figure 3(c) the generalized set of final states is $\{\{st, st'\}, \{st, s't\}\}$.

4.1   Splitting the Join

Next we give an alternative way to calculate the join of two Büchi automata of records. The idea is to use the standard product after we have extended the alphabets of the two automata to a minimal common alphabet. First of all we concentrate on how to extend a Büchi automata of records B with an extra port name, not necessarily present in the alphabet of B. If the port is new, the resulting automata will have to guess the right behavior non-deterministically, by allowing or not the simultaneous exchange of data with the other ports known by the automata.

Definition 10. *Let $B = \langle Q, Rec_{\mathcal{N}}(\mathcal{D}), \Delta, Q_0, F \rangle$ be a Büchi automaton of records and n be a (port) name. We define the extension of B with respect to n as the following Büchi automaton of records:*

$$B \!\uparrow\! n = \langle Q, Rec_{\mathcal{N} \cup \{n\}}(\mathcal{D}), \Delta', Q_0, F \rangle$$

where $\Delta' = \Delta$ if $n \in \mathcal{N}$ and otherwise

$$\Delta' = \Delta \cup \{(q, [n = d], q) | q \in Q, d \in \mathcal{D}\} \cup \{(q, r[n := d], q') | (q, r, q') \in \Delta, d \in \mathcal{D}\}.$$

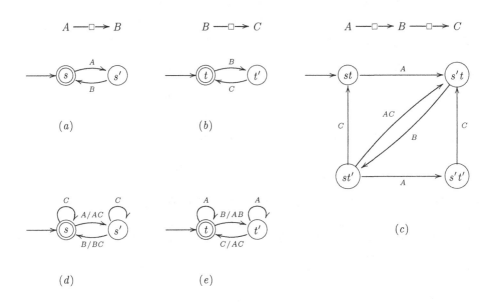

Fig. 3. Direct and indirect joining of two FIFO1 buffers

Intuitively, to extend Büchi automaton of records B using one extra port name n, we use the same structure of B and add only some new transitions to it representing the guesses of the new behavior of the automaton with respect to the new port n. There are three kind of guess: the environment does not use the name n in a communication (explaining why $\Delta \subseteq \Delta'$), or the environment use the name n for a communication but no other port of B is used (explaining the addition of a new loop transition on each state labeled by a record with n as the only name in the domain), or the environment use the name n in combination with the name constrained by B (corresponding to the new transitions of the form $(q,r[n:=d],q')$ in Δ'. Recall here that $r[n:=d]$ is the extension of record r by adding the new field $n = d$ to it).

For example, in Figure 3(d) we show the extension of the automaton has been shown in Figure 3(a) with respect to the new port name C. In this figure, $s \xrightarrow{A/AC} s'$ means that there are two transitions $s \xrightarrow{A} s'$ and $s \xrightarrow{AC} s'$. Also, Figure 3(e) is the extension of Figure 3(b) with A.

The operation of name extension is not sensible with respect to the order of different applications, in the sense that $(B{\uparrow}n){\uparrow}m = (B{\uparrow}m){\uparrow}n$, for two names n and m. Therefore we can define the extension of a Büchi automaton with respect to a finite set of name N, denoted by $B{\uparrow}N$ by inductively extending the automaton B by one name in N at a time.

Given two Büchi automata of records B_1 and B_2 we can extend each them with respect to the port names of the other, so that they become two Büchi automata over the same alphabet. We can thus take their ordinary product, obtaining as result the join of the two Büchi automata B_1 and B_2.

Theorem 3. *Let B_1 and B_2 be two Büchi automata of records over alphabet sets $Rec_{N_1}(\mathcal{D})$ and $Rec_{N_2}(\mathcal{D})$ respectively. Then,$B_1 {\uparrow} N_2 \times_B B_2 {\uparrow} N_1 = B_1 \bowtie_B B_2$.*

Therefore, to join two Büchi automata of records, one can first extend them to a common set of ports and then compose the resulting Büchi automaton using the standard Büchi product operation. Based on the previous theorem, the automata produced by both methods are structurally, and thus also language theoretically, the same.

For example, the join of the Büchi automata of records shown in Figures 3(a) and 3(b) is the automaton shown in 3(c). In 3(c) $F = \{\{st, st'\}, \{st, s't\}$. This automaton, in turn, is the product of the automata depicted in 3(d) and 3(e). The resulting automaton models a two-cells queue. Note that one of the diagonal transitions corresponds to the move of data from one cell to the other, while the other diagonal models the simultaneous consumption of data from port C and the insertion of a new data to the port A.

5   Concluding Remarks

In this paper, we introduced Büchi automata of records as an alternative operational semantics for component connectors. The model is at the same abstraction level of the language they recognize, a property satisfied by ordinary deterministic finite automata but unfortunately not by constraint automata. The model proposed is even more expressive than constraint automata. In fact every constraint automaton can be translated into a Büchi automaton on streams of records, but not viceversa. This generality asked for a novel definition of the join composition operator, that we have shown to be correct with respect to the original one for constraint automata. We have given also a new algorithm to calculate the join of Büchi automata that is based on the standard product of Büchi automata.

The main benefits of using Büchi automata for modeling networks of component connectors, like those specified by constraint automata and the Reo language, come from the area of model checking. We can use Büchi automata for expressing properties (directly or after translating from linear temporal logics [17,9]). Existing model checkers for Büchi automata, such as SPIN [11] and NuSMV [8], could be used directly for networks of connectors instead of reinventing similar tools for constraint automata. It is our plan to investigate this direction in the near future.

Another area of interest, that we leave for future work, is the study of how existing extensions of Büchi automata can be reflected in a specification language for component connectors. For example, one could use Büchi automata on streams of records with state labeled by sets of ports to model context sensitive connectors, like the lossy synchronous channel of Reo [1].

References

1. Arbab, F.: Reo: A Channel-based Coordination Model for Component Composition. Math. Struc. in Computer Science 14(3), 329–366 (2004)
2. Arbab, F., Baier, C., de Boer, F., Rutten, J., Sirjani, M.: Synthesis of Reo circuites for implementation of component-connector automata specifications. In: Jacquet, J.-M., Picco, G.P. (eds.) COORDINATION 2005. LNCS, vol. 3454, pp. 236–251. Springer, Heidelberg (2005)
3. Arbab, F., Chothia, T., Meng, S., Moon, Y.-J.: Component Connectors with QoS Guarantees. In: Murphy, A.L., Vitek, J. (eds.) COORDINATION 2007. LNCS, vol. 4467. Springer, Heidelberg (2007)
4. Arbab, F., Rutten, J.J.M.M.: A Coinductive Calculus of Component Connectors. In: Wirsing, M., Pattinson, D., Hennicker, R. (eds.) WADT 2003. LNCS, vol. 2755, pp. 35–56. Springer, Heidelberg (2003)
5. Arbab, F., Baier, C., de Boer, F., Rutten, J.: Models and temporal logics for timed component connectors. In: Proc. of the IEEE International Conference SEFM, pp. 198–207. IEEE Computer Society Press, Los Alamitos (2004)
6. Baier, C., Sirjani, M., Arbab, F., Rutten, J.: Modelling Component Connectors in Reo by Constraint Automata. Science of Computer Programming 61, 75–113 (2006)
7. Baier, C., Wolf, V.: Stochastic reasoning about channel-based component connectors. In: Ciancarini, P., Wiklicky, H. (eds.) COORDINATION 2006. LNCS, vol. 4038, pp. 1–15. Springer, Heidelberg (2006)
8. Cimatti, A., Clarke, E.M., Giunchiglia, E., Giunchiglia, F., Pistore, M., Roveri, M., Sebastiani, R., Tacchella, A.: NuSMV 2: An OpenSource Tool for Symbolic Model Checking. In: Brinksma, E., Larsen, K.G. (eds.) CAV 2002. LNCS, vol. 2404, pp. 359–364. Springer, Heidelberg (2002)
9. Clarke, E., Grumberg, O., Peled, D.: Model Checking. MIT Press, Cambridge (1999)
10. Hayes, J.P.: Computer Architecture and Organization, 2nd edn. McGraw Hill Publishing Company, New York (1998)
11. Holzmann, G.J.: The Model Checker SPIN. IEEE Transactions on software engineering 23(5), 279–295 (1997)
12. Hopcroft, J.E., Motwani, R., Ullman, J.D.: Introduction to Automata Theory, Languages, and Computation, 3rd edn. Addison-Wesley, Reading (2006)
13. Kupferman, O., Vardi, M.: Verification of Fair Transition Systems. In: Alur, R., Henzinger, T.A. (eds.) CAV 1996. LNCS, vol. 1102. Springer, Heidelberg (1996)
14. Remy, D.: Efficient representation of extensible records. In: Proc. ACM SIGPLAN Workshop on ML and its applications, pp. 12–16 (1994)
15. Szyperski, C., Gruntz, D., Murer, S.: Component Software: Beyond Object-Oriented Programming, 2nd edn. Addison-Wesley, Reading (2002)
16. Thomas, W.: Automata on Infinite Objects. In: van Leeuwen, J. (ed.) Handbook of Theoretical Computer Science, vol. B, pp. 133–191. Elsevier, Amsterdam (1990)
17. Vardi, M.: An Automata-Theoretic Approach to Linear Temporal Logic. In: Moller, F., Birtwistle, G. (eds.) Logics for Concurrency. LNCS, vol. 1043, pp. 238–266. Springer, Heidelberg (1996)

A Complete Realisability Semantics for Intersection Types and Arbitrary Expansion Variables

Fairouz Kamareddine[1], Karim Nour[2], Vincent Rahli[1], and J.B. Wells[1]

[1] ULTRA Group (Useful Logics, Types, Rewriting, and their Automation)
http://www.macs.hw.ac.uk/ultra/
[2] Université de Savoie, Campus Scientifique, 73378 Le Bourget du Lac, France
nour@univ-savoie.fr

Abstract. *Expansion* was introduced at the end of the 1970s for calculating *principal typings* for λ-terms in intersection type systems. *Expansion variables* (E-variables) were introduced at the end of the 1990s to simplify and help mechanise expansion. Recently, E-variables have been further simplified and generalised to also allow calculating other type operators than just intersection. There has been much work on semantics for intersection type systems, but only one such work on intersection type systems with E-variables. That work established that building a semantics for E-variables is very challenging. Because it is unclear how to devise a space of meanings for E-variables, that work developed instead a space of meanings for types that is hierarchical in the sense of having many degrees (denoted by indexes). However, although the indexed calculus helped identify the serious problems of giving a semantics for expansion variables, the sound realisability semantics was only complete when one single E-variable is used and furthermore, the universal type ω was not allowed. In this paper, we are able to overcome these challenges. We develop a realisability semantics where we allow an arbitrary (possibly infinite) number of expansion variables and where ω is present. We show the soundness and completeness of our proposed semantics.

1 Introduction

Expansion is a crucial part of a procedure for calculating *principal typings* and thus helps support compositional type inference. For example, the λ-term $M = (\lambda x.x(\lambda y.yz))$ can be assigned the typing $\Phi_1 = \langle (z : a) \vdash (((a \to b) \to b) \to c) \to c \rangle$, which happens to be its principal typing. The term M can also be assigned the typing $\Phi_2 = \langle (z : a_1 \sqcap a_2) \vdash (((a_1 \to b_1) \to b_1) \sqcap ((a_2 \to b_2) \to b_2) \to c) \to c \rangle$, and an expansion operation can obtain Φ_2 from Φ_1. Because the early definitions of expansion were complicated [4], E-variables were introduced in order to make the calculations easier to mechanise and reason about. For example, in System E [2], the above typing Φ_1 is replaced by $\Phi_3 = \langle (z : ea) \vdash (e((a \to b) \to b) \to c) \to c) \rangle$, which differs from Φ_1 by the insertion of the E-variable e at two places, and Φ_2 can be obtained from Φ_3 by substituting for e the *expansion term*:
$$E = (a := a_1, b := b_1) \sqcap (a := a_2, b := b_2).$$

J.S. Fitzgerald, A.E. Haxthausen, and H. Yenigun (Eds.): ICTAC 2008, LNCS 5160, pp. 171–185, 2008.

Carlier and Wells [3] have surveyed the history of expansion and also E-variables. Kamareddine, Nour, Rahli and Wells [13] showed that E-variables pose serious challenges for semantics. In the list of open problems published in 1975 in [6], it is suggested that an arrow type expresses functionality. Following this idea, a type's semantics is given as a set of closed λ-terms with behaviour related to the specification given by the type. In many kinds of semantics, the meaning of a type T is calculated by an expression $[T]_\nu$ that takes two parameters, the type T and a valuation ν that assigns to type variables the same kind of meanings that are assigned to types. In that way, models based on term-models have been built for intersection type systems [7,14,11] where intersection types (introduced to type more terms than in the Simply Typed Lambda Calculus) are interpreted by set-theoretical intersection of meanings. To extend this idea to types with E-variables, we need to devise some space of possible meanings for E-variables. Given that a type eT can be turned by expansion into a new type $S_1(T) \sqcap S_2(T)$, where S_1 and S_2 are arbitrary substitutions (or even arbitrary further expansions), and that this can introduce an unbounded number of new variables (both E-variables and regular type variables), the situation is complicated.

This was the main motivation for [13] to develop a space of meanings for types that is hierarchical in the sense of having many degrees. When assigning meanings to types, [13] captured accurately the intuition behind E-variables by ensuring that each use of E-variables simply changes degrees and that each E-variable acts as a kind of capsule that isolates parts of the λ-term being analysed by the typing.

The semantic approach used in [13] is realisability semantics along the lines in Coquand [5] and Kamareddine and Nour [11]. Realisability allows showing *soundness* in the sense that the meaning of a type T contains all closed λ-terms that can be assigned T as their result type. This has been shown useful in previous work for characterising the behaviour of typed λ-terms [14]. One also wants to show the converse of soundness which is called *completeness* (see Hindley [8,9,10]), i.e., that every closed λ-term in the meaning of T can be assigned T as its result type. Moreover, [13] showed that if more than one E-variable is used, the semantics is not complete. Furthermore, the degrees used in [13] made it difficult to allow the universal type ω and this limited the study to the λI-calculus. In this paper, we are able to overcome these challenges. We develop a realisability semantics where we allow the full λ-calculus, an arbitrary (possibly infinite) number of expansion variables and where ω is present, and we show its soundness and completeness. We do so by introducing an indexed calculus as in [13]. However here, our indices are finite sequences of natural numbers rather than single natural numbers.

In Section 2 we give the full λ-calculus indexed with finite sequences of natural numbers and show the confluence of β, $\beta\eta$ and weak head reduction on the indexed λ-calculus. In Section 3 we introduce the type system for the indexed λ-calculus (with the universal type ω). In this system, intersections and expansions cannot occur directly to the right of an arrow. In Section 4 we establish that subject reduction holds for $\vdash$. In Section 5 we show that subject β-expansion holds for $\vdash$ but that subject η-expansion fails. In Section 6 we introduce the realisability semantics and show its soundness for $\vdash$. In Section 7 we establish the completeness of $\vdash$ by introducing a special interpretation. We conclude in Section 8. Due to space limitations, we omit the details of the proofs. Full proofs however can be found in the expanded version of this article (currently at [12]) which will always be available at the authors' web pages.

2 The Pure $\lambda^{\mathcal{L}_{\mathbb{N}}}$-Calculus

In this section we give the λ-calculus indexed with finite sequences of natural numbers and show the confluence of β, $\beta\eta$ and weak head reduction.

Let n, m, i, j, k, l be metavariables which range over the set of natural numbers $\mathbb{N} = \{0, 1, 2, \ldots\}$. We assume that if a metavariable v ranges over a set s then v_i and v', v'', etc. also range over s. A binary relation is a set of pairs. Let rel range over binary relations. We sometimes write $x \; rel \; y$ instead of $\langle x, y \rangle \in rel$. Let $\mathrm{dom}(rel) = \{x \; / \; \langle x, y \rangle \in rel\}$ and $\mathrm{ran}(rel) = \{y \; / \; \langle x, y \rangle \in rel\}$. A function is a binary relation fun such that if $\{\langle x, y \rangle, \langle x, z \rangle\} \subseteq fun$ then $y = z$. Let fun range over functions. Let $s \to s' = \{fun \; / \; \mathrm{dom}(fun) \subseteq s \wedge \mathrm{ran}(fun) \subseteq s'\}$. We sometimes write $x : s$ instead of $x \in s$.

First, we introduce the set $\mathcal{L}_{\mathbb{N}}$ of indexes with an order relation on indexes.

Definition 1. *1. An index is a finite sequence of natural numbers $L = (n_i)_{1 \le i \le l}$.*
   We denote $\mathcal{L}_{\mathbb{N}}$ the set of indexes and $\oslash$ the empty sequence of natural numbers.
   We let L, K, R range over $\mathcal{L}_{\mathbb{N}}$.
 2. If $L = (n_i)_{1 \le i \le l}$ and $m \in \mathbb{N}$, we use $m :: L$ to denote the sequence $(r_i)_{1 \le i \le l+1}$
   where $r_1 = m$ and for all $i \in \{2, \ldots, l+1\}$, $r_i = n_{i-1}$.
   In particular, $k :: \oslash = (k)$.
 3. If $L = (n_i)_{1 \le i \le n}$ and $K = (m_i)_{1 \le i \le m}$, we use $L :: K$ to denote the sequence
   $(r_i)_{1 \le i \le n+m}$ where for all $i \in \{1, \ldots, n\}$, $r_i = n_i$ and for all $i \in \{n + 1, \ldots, n+m\}$, $r_i = m_{i-n}$. In particular, $L :: \oslash = \oslash :: L = L$.
 4. We define on $\mathcal{L}_{\mathbb{N}}$ a binary relation $\preceq$ by:
   $L_1 \preceq L_2$ (or $L_2 \succeq L_1$) if there exists $L_3 \in \mathcal{L}_{\mathbb{N}}$ such that $L_2 = L_1 :: L_3$.

Lemma 1. *$\preceq$ is an order relation on $\mathcal{L}_{\mathbb{N}}$.*

The next definition gives the syntax of the indexed calculus and the notions of reduction.

Definition 2. *1. Let $\mathcal{V}$ be a countably infinite set of variables. The set of terms $\mathcal{M}$, the set of free variables $\mathrm{fv}(M)$ of a term $M \in \mathcal{M}$, the degree function $d : \mathcal{M} \to \mathcal{L}_{\mathbb{N}}$ and the joinability $M \diamond N$ of terms M and N are defined by simultaneous induction as follows:*
   – If $x \in \mathcal{V}$ and $L \in \mathcal{L}_{\mathbb{N}}$, then $x^L \in \mathcal{M}$, $\mathrm{fv}(x^L) = \{x^L\}$ and $d(x^L) = L$.
   – If $M, N \in \mathcal{M}$, $d(M) \preceq d(N)$ and $M \diamond N$ (see below), then $M \, N \in \mathcal{M}$, $\mathrm{fv}(MN) = \mathrm{fv}(M) \cup \mathrm{fv}(N)$ and $d(M \, N) = d(M)$.
   – If $x \in \mathcal{V}$, $M \in \mathcal{M}$ and $L \succeq d(M)$, then $\lambda x^L.M \in \mathcal{M}$, $\mathrm{fv}(\lambda x^L.M) = \mathrm{fv}(M) \setminus \{x^L\}$ and $d(\lambda x^L.M) = d(M)$.

2. – Let $M, N \in \mathcal{M}$. We say that M and N are joinable and write $M \diamond N$ iff
    for all $x \in \mathcal{V}$, if $x^L \in \mathrm{fv}(M)$ and $x^K \in \mathrm{fv}(N)$, then $L = K$.
    – If $\mathcal{X} \subseteq \mathcal{M}$ such that for all $M, N \in \mathcal{X}, M \diamond N$, we write, $\diamond\mathcal{X}$.
    – If $\mathcal{X} \subseteq \mathcal{M}$ and $M \in \mathcal{M}$ such that for all $N \in \mathcal{X}, M \diamond N$, we write, $M \diamond \mathcal{X}$.
    The $\diamond$ property ensures that in any term M, variables have unique degrees.
    We assume the usual definition of subterms and the usual convention for
    parentheses and their omission (see Barendregt [1] and Krivine [14]). Note
    that every subterm of $M \in \mathcal{M}$ is also in $\mathcal{M}$. We let x, y, z, etc. range over $\mathcal{V}$
    and M, N, P range over $\mathcal{M}$ and use $=$ for syntactic equality.

3. The usual simultaneous substitution $M[(x_i^{L_i} := N_i)_n]$ of $N_i \in \mathcal{M}$ for all
    free occurrences of $x_i^{L_i}$ in $M \in \mathcal{M}$ is only defined when $\diamond\{M\} \cup \{N_i \ /$
    $i \in \{1, \ldots, n\}\}$ and for all $i \in \{1, \ldots, n\}$, $d(N_i) = L_i$. In a substitution,
    we sometimes write $x_1^{L_1} := N_1, \ldots, x_n^{L_n} := N_n$ instead of $(x_i^{L_i} := N_i)_n$. We
    sometimes write $M[(x_i^{L_i} := N_i)_1]$ as $M[x_1^{L_1} := N_1]$.

4. We take terms modulo α-conversion given by:
    $\lambda x^L.M = \lambda y^L.(M[x^L := y^L])$ where for all L, $y^L \notin \mathrm{fv}(M)$.
    Moreover, we use the Barendregt convention (BC) where the names of bound
    variables differ from the free ones and where we rewrite terms so that not
    both λx^L and λx^K co-occur when $L \neq K$.

5. A relation rel on $\mathcal{M}$ is compatible iff for all $M, N, P \in \mathcal{M}$:
    – If M rel N and $\lambda x^L.M, \lambda x^L.M \in \mathcal{M}$ then $(\lambda x^L.M)$ rel $(\lambda x^L.N)$.
    – If M rel N and $MP, NP \in \mathcal{M}$ (resp. $PM, PN \in \mathcal{M}$), then (MP) rel
    (NP) (resp. (PM) rel (PN)).

6. The reduction relation $\triangleright_\beta$ on $\mathcal{M}$ is defined as the least compatible relation
    closed under the rule: $(\lambda x^L.M)N \triangleright_\beta M[x^L := N]$ if $d(N) = L$

7. The reduction relation $\triangleright_\eta$ on $\mathcal{M}$ is defined as the least compatible relation
    closed under the rule: $\lambda x^L.(M \ x^L) \triangleright_\eta M$ if $x^L \notin \mathrm{fv}(M)$

8. The weak head reduction $\triangleright_h$ on $\mathcal{M}$ is defined by:
    $(\lambda x^L.M)NN_1 \ldots N_n \triangleright_h M[x^L := N]N_1 \ldots N_n$ where $n \geq 0$

9. We let $\triangleright_{\beta\eta} = \triangleright_\beta \cup \triangleright_\eta$. For $r \in \{\beta, \eta, h, \beta\eta\}$, we denote by $\triangleright_r^*$ the reflexive
    and transitive closure of $\triangleright_r$ and by $\simeq_r$ the equivalence relation induced by
    $\triangleright_r^*$.

The next theorem whose proof can be found in [12] states that free variables and
degrees are preserved by our notions of reduction.

Theorem 1. Let $M \in \mathcal{M}$ and $r \in \{\beta, \beta\eta, h\}$.

1. If $M \triangleright_\eta^* N$ then $\mathrm{fv}(N) = \mathrm{fv}(M)$ and $d(M) = d(N)$.
2. If $M \triangleright_r^* N$ then $\mathrm{fv}(N) \subseteq \mathrm{fv}(M)$ and $d(M) = d(N)$.

As expansions change the degree of a term, indexes in a term need to in-
crease/decrease.

Definition 3. Let $i \in \mathbb{N}$ and $M \in \mathcal{M}$.

1. We define M^{+i} by:
    $\bullet (x^L)^{+i} = x^{i::L}$ $\bullet (M_1 \ M_2)^{+i} = M_1^{+i} \ M_2^{+i}$ $\bullet (\lambda x^L.M)^{+i} = \lambda x^{i::L}.M^{+i}$
    Let $M^{+\oslash} = M$ and $M^{+(i::L)} = (M^{+i})^{+L}$.

2. If $d(M) = i :: L$, we define M^{-i} by:
   - $(x^{i::K})^{-i} = x^K$ $\bullet (M_1 \ M_2)^{-i} = M_1^{-i} \ M_2^{-i}$ $\bullet (\lambda x^{i::K}.M)^{-i} =$
   $\lambda x^K.M^{-i}$
   Let $M^{-\oslash} = M$ and if $d(M) \succeq i :: L$ then $M^{-(i::L)} = (M^{-i})^{-L}$.
3. Let $\mathcal{X} \subseteq \mathcal{M}$. We write $\mathcal{X}^{+i}$ for $\{M^{+i} \ / \ M \in \mathcal{X}\}$.

Normal forms are defined as usual.

Definition 4
1. $M \in \mathcal{M}$ is in β-normal form ($\beta\eta$-normal form, h-normal form resp.) if there is no $N \in \mathcal{M}$ such that $M \triangleright_\beta N$ ($M \triangleright_{\beta\eta} N$, $M \triangleright_h N$ resp.).
2. $M \in \mathcal{M}$ is β-normalising ($\beta\eta$-normalising, h-normalising resp.) if there is an $N \in \mathcal{M}$ such that $M \triangleright_\beta^* N$ ($M \triangleright_{\beta\eta} N$, $M \triangleright_h N$ resp.) and N is in β-normal form ($\beta\eta$-normal form, h-normal form resp.).

The next theorem states that all of our notions of reduction are confluent on our indexed calculus. For a proof see [12].

Theorem 2 (Confluence). Let $M, M_1, M_2 \in \mathcal{M}$ and $r \in \{\beta, \beta\eta, h\}$.

1. If $M \triangleright_r^* M_1$ and $M \triangleright_r^* M_2$, then there is M' such that $M_1 \triangleright_r^* M'$ and $M_2 \triangleright_r^* M'$.
2. $M_1 \simeq_r M_2$ iff there is a term M such that $M_1 \triangleright_r^* M$ and $M_2 \triangleright_r^* M$.

3   Typing System

This paper studies a type system for the indexed λ-calculus with the universal type ω. In this type system, in order to get subject reduction and hence completeness, intersections and expansions cannot occur directly to the right of an arrow (see $\mathbb{U}$ below).

The next two definitions introduce the type system.

Definition 5.   1. Let a range over a countably infinite set $\mathcal{A}$ of atomic types and let e range over a countably infinite set $\mathcal{E} = \{\bar{e}_0, \bar{e}_1, ...\}$ of expansion variables. We define sets of types $\mathbb{T}$ and $\mathbb{U}$, such that $\mathbb{T} \subseteq \mathbb{U}$, and a function $d : \mathbb{U} \to \mathcal{L}_\mathbb{N}$ by:
   - If $a \in \mathcal{A}$, then $a \in \mathbb{T}$ and $d(a) = \oslash$.
   - If $U \in \mathbb{U}$ and $T \in \mathbb{T}$, then $U \to T \in \mathbb{T}$ and $d(U \to T) = \oslash$.
   - If $L \in \mathcal{L}_\mathbb{N}$, then $\omega^L \in \mathbb{U}$ and $d(\omega^L) = L$.
   - If $U_1, U_2 \in \mathbb{U}$ and $d(U_1) = d(U_2)$, then $U_1 \sqcap U_2 \in \mathbb{U}$ and $d(U_1 \sqcap U_2) = d(U_1) = d(U_2)$.
   - $U \in \mathbb{U}$ and $\bar{e}_i \in \mathcal{E}$, then $\bar{e}_i U \in \mathbb{U}$ and $d(\bar{e}_i U) = i :: d(U)$.

   Note that d remembers the number of the expansion variables $\bar{e}_i$ in order to keep a trace of these variables.
   We let T range over $\mathbb{T}$, and U, V, W range over $\mathbb{U}$. We quotient types by taking $\sqcap$ to be commutative (i.e. $U_1 \sqcap U_2 = U_2 \sqcap U_1$), associative (i.e. $U_1 \sqcap (U_2 \sqcap U_3) = (U_1 \sqcap U_2) \sqcap U_3$) and idempotent (i.e. $U \sqcap U = U$), by assuming the distributivity of expansion variables over $\sqcap$ (i.e. $e(U_1 \sqcap U_2) = eU_1 \sqcap eU_2$) and by having ω^L as a neutral (i.e. $\omega^L \sqcap U = U$). We denote $U_n \sqcap U_{n+1} ... \sqcap U_m$ by $\sqcap_{i=n}^m U_i$ (when $n \leq m$). We also assume that for all $i \geq 0$ and $K \in \mathcal{L}_\mathbb{N}$, $\bar{e}_i \omega^K = \omega^{i::K}$.

2. *We denote $\bar{e}_{i_1} \ldots \bar{e}_{i_n}$ by e_K, where $K = (i_1, \ldots, i_n)$ and $U_n \sqcap U_{n+1} \ldots \sqcap U_m$ by $\sqcap_{i=n}^{m} U_i$ (when $n \leq m$).*

Definition 6

1. *A type environment is a set $\{x_1^{L_1} : U_1, \ldots, x_n^{L_n} : U_n\}$ such that for all $i, j \in \{1, \ldots, n\}$, if $x_i^{L_i} = x_j^{L_j}$ then $U_i = U_j$. We let Env be the set of environments, use Γ, Δ to range over Env and write $()$ for the empty environment. We define $\text{dom}(\Gamma) = \{x^L / x^L : U \in \Gamma\}$. If $\text{dom}(\Gamma_1) \cap \text{dom}(\Gamma_2) = \emptyset$, we write Γ_1, Γ_2 for $\Gamma_1 \cup \Gamma_2$. We write $\Gamma, x^L : U$ for $\Gamma, \{x^L : U\}$ and $x^L : U$ for $\{x^L : U\}$. We denote $x_1^{L_1} : U_1, \ldots, x_n^{L_n} : U_n$ by $(x_i^{L_i} : U_i)_n$.*
2. *If $M \in \mathcal{M}$ and $\text{fv}(M) = \{x_1^{L_1}, \ldots, x_n^{L_n}\}$, we denote env_M^ω the type environment $(x_i^{L_i} : \omega^{L_i})_n$.*
3. *We say that a type environment Γ is OK (and write $\text{OK}(\Gamma)$) iff for all $x^L : U \in \Gamma$, $d(U) = L$.*
4. *Let $\Gamma_1 = (x_i^{L_i} : U_i)_n, \Gamma_1'$ and $\Gamma_2 = (x_i^{L_i} : U_i')_n, \Gamma_2'$ such that $\text{dom}(\Gamma_1') \cap \text{dom}(\Gamma_2') = \emptyset$ and for all $i \in \{1, \ldots, n\}$, $d(U_i) = d(U_i')$. We denote $\Gamma_1 \sqcap \Gamma_2$ the type environment $(x_i^{L_i} : U_i \sqcap U_i')_n, \Gamma_1', \Gamma_2'$. Note that $\Gamma_1 \sqcap \Gamma_2$ is a type environment, $\text{dom}(\Gamma_1 \sqcap \Gamma_2) = \text{dom}(\Gamma_1) \cup \text{dom}(\Gamma_2)$ and that, on environments, $\sqcap$ is commutative, associative and idempotent.*
5. *Let $\Gamma = (x_i^{L_i} : U_i)_n$ We denote $\bar{e}_j \Gamma = (x_i^{j::L_i} : \bar{e}_j U_i)_n$. Note that $e\Gamma$ is a type environment and $e(G_1 \sqcap \Gamma_2) = e\Gamma_1 \sqcap e\Gamma_2$.*
6. *We write $\Gamma_1 \diamond \Gamma_2$ iff $x^L \in \text{dom}(\Gamma_1)$ and $x^K \in \text{dom}(\Gamma_2)$ implies $K = L$.*
7. *We follow [3] and write type judgements as $M : \langle \Gamma \vdash U \rangle$ instead of the traditional format of $\Gamma \vdash M : U$, where $\vdash$ is our typing relation. The typing rules of $\vdash$ are given on the left hand side of Figure 7. In the last clause, the binary relation $\sqsubseteq$ is defined on $\mathbb{U}$ by the rules on the right hand side of Figure 7. We let Φ denote types in $\mathbb{U}$, or environments Γ or typings $\langle \Gamma \vdash U \rangle$. When $\Phi \sqsubseteq \Phi'$, then Φ and Φ' belong to the same set ($\mathbb{U}$/environments/typings).*
8. *If $L \in \mathcal{L}_\mathbb{N}$, $U \in \mathbb{U}$ and $\Gamma = (x_i^{L_i} : U_i)_n$ is a type environment, we say that:*
   - *$d(\Gamma) \succeq L$ if and only if for all $i \in \{1, \ldots, n\}$, $d(U_i) \succeq L$ and $L_i \succeq L$.*
   - *$d(\langle \Gamma \vdash U \rangle) \succeq L$ if and only if $d(\Gamma) \succeq L$ and $d(U) \succeq L$.*

To illustrate how our indexed type system works, we give an example:

Example 1. Let $U = \bar{e}_3(\bar{e}_2(\bar{e}_1((\bar{e}_0 b \rightarrow c) \rightarrow (\bar{e}_0(a \sqcap (a \rightarrow b)) \rightarrow c)) \rightarrow d) \rightarrow (((\bar{e}_2 d \rightarrow a) \sqcap b) \rightarrow a))$ where $a, b, c, d \in \mathcal{A}$,
$$L_1 = 3 :: \oslash \preceq L_2 = 3 :: 2 :: \oslash \preceq L_3 = 3 :: 2 :: 1 :: \oslash \preceq L_4 = 3 :: 2 :: 1 :: 0 :: \oslash$$
and
$$M = \lambda x^{L_2}.\lambda y^{L_1}.(y^{L_1} (x^{L_2} \lambda u^{L_3}.\lambda v^{L_4}.(u^{L_3} (v^{L_4} v^{L_4})))).$$
We invite the reader to check that $M : \langle () \vdash U \rangle$.

Just as we did for terms, we decrease the indexes of types, environments and typings.

Definition 7

1. *If $d(U) \succeq L$, then if $L = \oslash$ then $U^{-L} = U$ else $L = i :: K$ and we inductively define the type U^{-L} as follows:*
   $$(U_1 \sqcap U_2)^{-i::K} = U_1^{-i::K} \sqcap U_2^{-i::K} \qquad (\bar{e}_i U)^{-i::K} = U^{-K}$$
   We write U^{-i} instead of $U^{-(i)}$.

$$\frac{}{x^\oslash : \langle (x^\oslash : T) \vdash T \rangle} \ (ax) \qquad\qquad \frac{}{\varPhi \sqsubseteq \varPhi} \ (ref)$$

$$\frac{}{M : \langle env_M^\omega \vdash \omega^{d(M)} \rangle} \ (\omega) \qquad\qquad \frac{\varPhi_1 \sqsubseteq \varPhi_2 \quad \varPhi_2 \sqsubseteq \varPhi_3}{\varPhi_1 \sqsubseteq \varPhi_3} \ (tr)$$

$$\frac{M : \langle \Gamma, (x^L : U) \vdash T \rangle}{\lambda x^L.M : \langle \Gamma \vdash U \to T \rangle} \ (\to_I) \qquad\qquad \frac{d(U_1) = d(U_2)}{U_1 \sqcap U_2 \sqsubseteq U_1} \ (\sqcap_E)$$

$$\frac{M : \langle \Gamma \vdash T \rangle \quad x^L \notin \mathrm{dom}(\Gamma)}{\lambda x^L.M : \langle \Gamma \vdash \omega^L \to T \rangle} \ (\to'_I) \qquad\qquad \frac{U_1 \sqsubseteq V_1 \quad U_2 \sqsubseteq V_2}{U_1 \sqcap U_2 \sqsubseteq V_1 \sqcap V_2} \ (\sqcap)$$

$$\frac{M_1 : \langle \Gamma_1 \vdash U \to T \rangle \quad M_2 : \langle \Gamma_2 \vdash U \rangle \quad \Gamma_1 \diamond \Gamma_2}{M_1 M_2 : \langle \Gamma_1 \sqcap \Gamma_2 \vdash T \rangle} \ (\to_E) \qquad \frac{U_2 \sqsubseteq U_1 \quad T_1 \sqsubseteq T_2}{U_1 \to T_1 \sqsubseteq U_2 \to T_2} \ (\to)$$

$$\frac{M : \langle \Gamma \vdash U_1 \rangle \qquad M : \langle \Gamma \vdash U_2 \rangle}{M : \langle \Gamma \vdash U_1 \sqcap U_2 \rangle} \ (\sqcap_I) \qquad\qquad \frac{U_1 \sqsubseteq U_2}{e U_1 \sqsubseteq e U_2} \ (\sqsubseteq_e)$$

$$\frac{M : \langle \Gamma \vdash U \rangle}{M^{+j} : \langle \bar{e}_j \Gamma \vdash \bar{e}_j U \rangle} \ (e) \qquad\qquad \frac{U_1 \sqsubseteq U_2}{\Gamma, y^L : U_1 \sqsubseteq \Gamma, y^L : U_2} \ (\sqsubseteq_c)$$

$$\frac{M : \langle \Gamma \vdash U \rangle \qquad \langle \Gamma \vdash U \rangle \sqsubseteq \langle \Gamma' \vdash U' \rangle}{M : \langle \Gamma' \vdash U' \rangle} \ (\sqsubseteq) \qquad \frac{U_1 \sqsubseteq U_2 \quad \Gamma_2 \sqsubseteq \Gamma_1}{\langle \Gamma_1 \vdash U_1 \rangle \sqsubseteq \langle \Gamma_2 \vdash U_2 \rangle} \ (\sqsubseteq_{\langle\rangle})$$

Fig. 1. Typing rules / Subtyping rules

2. If $\Gamma = (x_i^{L_i} : U_i)_k$ and $d(\Gamma) \succeq L$, then for all $i \in \{1, \ldots, k\}$, $L_i = L :: L_i'$ and $d(U_i) \succeq L$ and we denote $\Gamma^{-L} = (x_i^{L_i'} : U_i^{-L})_k$.
   We write Γ^{-i} instead of $\Gamma^{-(i)}$.
3. If U is a type and Γ is a type environment such that $d(\Gamma) \succeq K$ and $d(U) \succeq K$, then we denote $(\langle \Gamma \vdash U \rangle)^{-K} = \langle \Gamma^{-K} \vdash U^{-K} \rangle$.

The next lemma is informative about types and their degrees.

Lemma 2

1. If $T \in \mathbb{T}$, then $d(T) = \oslash$.
2. Let $U \in \mathbb{U}$. If $d(U) = L = (n_i)_{1 \le i \le m}$, then $U = \omega^L$ or $U = e_L \sqcap_{i=1}^p T_i$ where $p \ge 1$ and for all $i \in \{1, \ldots, p\}$, $T_i \in \mathbb{T}$.
3. Let $U_1 \sqsubseteq U_2$.
   (a) $d(U_1) = d(U_2)$.
   (b) If $U_1 = \omega^K$ then $U_2 = \omega^K$.
   (c) If $U_1 = e_K U$ then $U_2 = e_K U'$ and $U \sqsubseteq U'$.
   (d) If $U_2 = e_K U$ then $U_1 = e_K U'$ and $U \sqsubseteq U'$.
   (e) If $U_1 = \sqcap_{i=1}^p e_K(U_i \to T_i)$ where $p \ge 1$ then $U_2 = \omega^K$ or $U_2 = \sqcap_{j=1}^q e_K(U_j' \to T_j')$ where $q \ge 1$ and for all $j \in \{1, \ldots, q\}$, there exists $i \in \{1, \ldots, p\}$ such that $U_j' \sqsubseteq U_i$ and $T_i \sqsubseteq T_j'$.
4. If $U \in \mathbb{U}$ such that $d(U) = L$ then $U \sqsubseteq \omega^L$.

5. *If $U \sqsubseteq U_1' \sqcap U_2'$ then $U = U_1 \sqcap U_2$ where $U_1 \sqsubseteq U_1'$ and $U_2 \sqsubseteq U_2'$.*
6. *If $\Gamma \sqsubseteq \Gamma_1' \sqcap \Gamma_2'$ then $\Gamma = \Gamma_1 \sqcap \Gamma_2$ where $\Gamma_1 \sqsubseteq \Gamma_1'$ and $\Gamma_2 \sqsubseteq \Gamma_2'$.*

The next lemma says how ordering or the decreasing of indexes propagate to environments.

Lemma 3

1. $\mathrm{OK}(env_M^\omega)$.
2. *If $\Gamma \sqsubseteq \Gamma'$, $U \sqsubseteq U'$ and $x^L \notin \mathrm{dom}(\Gamma)$ then $\Gamma, (x^L : U) \sqsubseteq \Gamma', (x^L : U')$.*
3. *$\Gamma \sqsubseteq \Gamma'$ iff $\Gamma = (x_i^{L_i} : U_i)_n$, $\Gamma' = (x_i^{L_i} : U_i')_n$ and for every $1 \le i \le n$, $U_i \sqsubseteq U_i'$.*
4. *$\langle \Gamma \vdash U \rangle \sqsubseteq \langle \Gamma' \vdash U' \rangle$ iff $\Gamma' \sqsubseteq \Gamma$ and $U \sqsubseteq U'$.*
5. *If $\mathrm{dom}(\Gamma) = \mathrm{fv}(M)$ and $\mathrm{OK}(\Gamma)$ then $\Gamma \sqsubseteq env_M^\omega$*
6. *If $\Gamma \diamond \Delta$ and $d(\Gamma), d(\Delta) \succeq K$, then $\Gamma^{-K} \diamond \Delta^{-K}$.*
7. *If $U \sqsubseteq U'$ and $d(U) \succeq K$ then $U^{-K} \sqsubseteq U'^{-K}$.*
8. *If $\Gamma \sqsubseteq \Gamma'$ and $d(\Gamma) \succeq K$ then $\Gamma^{-K} \sqsubseteq \Gamma'^{-K}$.*
9. *If $\mathrm{OK}(\Gamma_1)$, $\mathrm{OK}(\Gamma_2)$ then $\mathrm{OK}(\Gamma_1 \sqcap \Gamma_2)$.*
10. *If $\mathrm{OK}(\Gamma)$ then $\mathrm{OK}(e\Gamma)$.*
11. *If $\Gamma_1 \sqsubseteq \Gamma_2$ then $(d(\Gamma_1) \succeq L$ iff $d(\Gamma_2) \succeq L)$ and $(\mathrm{OK}(\Gamma_1)$ iff $\mathrm{OK}(\Gamma_2))$.*

The next lemma shows that we do not allow weakening in $\vdash$.

Lemma 4

1. *For every Γ and M such that $\mathrm{OK}(\Gamma)$, $\mathrm{dom}(\Gamma) = \mathrm{fv}(M)$ and $d(M) = K$, we have $M : \langle \Gamma \vdash \omega^K \rangle$.*
2. *If $M : \langle \Gamma \vdash U \rangle$, then $\mathrm{dom}(\Gamma) = \mathrm{fv}(M)$.*
3. *If $M_1 : \langle \Gamma_1 \vdash U \rangle$ and $M_2 : \langle \Gamma_2 \vdash V \rangle$ then $\Gamma_1 \diamond \Gamma_2$ iff $M_1 \diamond M_2$.*

Proof 1. By ω, $M : \langle env_M^\omega \vdash \omega^K \rangle$. By Lemma 3.5, $\Gamma \sqsubseteq env_M^\omega$. Hence, by $\sqsubseteq$ and $\sqsubseteq_{\langle\rangle}$, $M : \langle \Gamma \vdash \omega^K \rangle$.
2. By induction on the derivation $M : \langle \Gamma \vdash U \rangle$.
3. If) Let $x^L \in \mathrm{dom}(\Gamma_1)$ and $x^K \in \mathrm{dom}(\Gamma_2)$ then by Lemma 4.2, $x^L \in \mathrm{fv}(M_1)$ and $x^K \in \mathrm{fv}(M_2)$ so $\Gamma_1 \diamond \Gamma_2$. Only if) Let $x^L \in \mathrm{fv}(M_1)$ and $x^K \in \mathrm{fv}(M_2)$ then by Lemma 4.2, $x^L \in \mathrm{dom}(\Gamma_1)$ and $x^K \in \mathrm{dom}(\Gamma_2)$ so $M_1 \diamond M_2$. □

The next theorem states that typings are well defined and that within a typing, degrees are well behaved.

Theorem 3

1. *The typing relation $\vdash$ is well defined on $\mathcal{M} \times Env \times \mathbb{U}$.*
2. *If $M : \langle \Gamma \vdash U \rangle$ then $\mathrm{OK}(\Gamma)$, and $d(\Gamma) \succeq d(U) = d(M)$.*
3. *If $M : \langle \Gamma \vdash U \rangle$ and $d(U) \succeq K$ then $M^{-K} : \langle \Gamma^{-K} \vdash U^{-K} \rangle$.*

Proof. We prove 1. and 2. simultaneously by induction on the derivation $M : \langle \Gamma \vdash U \rangle$. We prove 3. by induction on the derivation $M : \langle \Gamma \vdash U \rangle$. Full details can be found in [12]. □

Finally, here are two derivable typing rules that we will freely use in the rest of the article.

Remark 1. 1. The rule $\dfrac{M : \langle \Gamma_1 \vdash U_1 \rangle \qquad M : \langle \Gamma_2 \vdash U_2 \rangle}{M : \langle \Gamma_1 \sqcap \Gamma_2 \vdash U_1 \sqcap U_2 \rangle} \; \sqcap_I'$ is derivable.

2. The rule $\dfrac{}{x^{d(U)} : \langle (x^{d(U)} : U) \vdash U \rangle} \; ax'$ is derivable.

4 Subject Reduction Properties

In this section we show that subject reduction holds for $\vdash$. The proof of subject reduction uses generation and substitution. Hence the next two lemmas.

Lemma 5 (Generation for $\vdash$)

1. If $x^L : \langle \Gamma \vdash U \rangle$, then $\Gamma = (x^L : V)$ and $V \sqsubseteq U$.
2. If $\lambda x^L . M : \langle \Gamma \vdash U \rangle$, $x^L \in \mathrm{fv}(M)$ and $d(U) = K$, then $U = \omega^K$ or $U = \sqcap_{i=1}^{p} e_K (V_i \to T_i)$ where $p \geq 1$ and for all $i \in \{1, \ldots, p\}$, $M : \langle \Gamma, x^L : e_K V_i \vdash e_K T_i \rangle$.
3. If $\lambda x^L . M : \langle \Gamma \vdash U \rangle$, $x^L \notin \mathrm{fv}(M)$ and $d(U) = K$, then $U = \omega^K$ or $U = \sqcap_{i=1}^{p} e_K (V_i \to T_i)$ where $p \geq 1$ and for all $i \in \{1, \ldots, p\}$, $M : \langle \Gamma \vdash e_K T_i \rangle$.
4. If $M \, x^L : \langle \Gamma, (x^L : U) \vdash T \rangle$ and $x^L \notin \mathrm{fv}(M)$, then $M : \langle \Gamma \vdash U \to T \rangle$.

Lemma 6 (Substitution for $\vdash$). If $M : \langle \Gamma, x^L : U \vdash V \rangle$, $N : \langle \Delta \vdash U \rangle$ and $M \diamond N$ then $M[x^L := N] : \langle \Gamma \sqcap \Delta \vdash V \rangle$.

Since $\vdash$ does not allow weakening, we need the next definition since when a term is reduced, it may lose some of its free variables and hence will need to be typed in a smaller environment.

Definition 8. If Γ is a type environment and $\mathcal{U} \subseteq \mathrm{dom}(\Gamma)$, then we write $\Gamma \restriction_{\mathcal{U}}$ for the restriction of Γ on the variables of $\mathcal{U}$. If $\mathcal{U} = \mathrm{fv}(M)$ for a term M, we write $\Gamma \restriction_M$ instead of $\Gamma \restriction_{\mathrm{fv}(M)}$.

Now we are ready to prove the main result of this section:

Theorem 4 (Subject reduction for $\vdash$). If $M : \langle \Gamma \vdash U \rangle$ and $M \triangleright^*_{\beta\eta} N$, then $N : \langle \Gamma \restriction_N \vdash U \rangle$.

Proof. By induction on the length of the derivation $M \triangleright^*_{\beta\eta} N$. Case $M \triangleright_{\beta\eta} N$ is by induction on the derivation $M : \langle \Gamma \vdash U \rangle$. □

Corollary 1. 1. If $M : \langle \Gamma \vdash U \rangle$ and $M \triangleright^*_{\beta} N$, then $N : \langle \Gamma \restriction_N \vdash U \rangle$.
2. If $M : \langle \Gamma \vdash U \rangle$ and $M \triangleright^*_{h} N$, then $N : \langle \Gamma \restriction_N \vdash U \rangle$.

5 Subject Expansion Properties

In this section we show that subject β-expansion holds for $\vdash$ but that subject η-expansion fails.

The next lemma is needed for expansion.

Lemma 7. If $M[x^L := N] : \langle \Gamma \vdash U \rangle$ and $x^L \in \mathrm{fv}(M)$ then there exist a type V and two type environments Γ_1, Γ_2 such that:
$M : \langle \Gamma_1, x^L : V \vdash U \rangle \qquad N : \langle \Gamma_2 \vdash V \rangle \qquad \Gamma = \Gamma_1 \sqcap \Gamma_2$

Since more free variables might appear in the β-expansion of a term, the next definition gives a possible enlargement of an environment.

Definition 9. Let $m \geq n$, $\Gamma = (x_i^{L_i} : U_i)_n$ and $\mathcal{U} = \{x_1^{L_1}, ..., x_m^{L_m}\}$. We write $\Gamma\uparrow^{\mathcal{U}}$ for $x_1^{L_1} : U_1, ..., x_n^{L_n} : U_n, x_{n+1}^{L_{n+1}} : \omega^{L_{n+1}}, ..., x_m^{L_m} : \omega^{L_m}$. Note that $\Gamma\uparrow^{\mathcal{U}}$ is a type environment. If $\mathrm{dom}(\Gamma) \subseteq \mathrm{fv}(M)$, we write $\Gamma\uparrow^M$ instead of $\Gamma\uparrow^{\mathrm{fv}(M)}$.

We are now ready to establish that subject expansion holds for β (next theorem) and that it fails for η (Lemma 8).

Theorem 5 (Subject expansion for β). If $N : \langle \Gamma \vdash U \rangle$ and $M \rhd_\beta^* N$, then $M : \langle \Gamma\uparrow^M \vdash U \rangle$.

Proof. By induction on the length of the derivation $M \rhd_\beta^* N$ using the fact that if $\mathrm{fv}(P) \subseteq \mathrm{fv}(Q)$, then $(\Gamma\uparrow^P)\uparrow^Q = \Gamma\uparrow^Q$.   □

Corollary 2. If $N : \langle \Gamma \vdash U \rangle$ and $M \rhd_h^* N$, then $M : \langle \Gamma\uparrow^M \vdash U \rangle$.

Lemma 8 (Subject expansion fails for η). Let a be an element of $\mathcal{A}$. We have:

1. $\lambda y^\emptyset.\lambda x^\emptyset.y^\emptyset x^\emptyset \rhd_\eta \lambda y^\emptyset.y^\emptyset$
2. $\lambda y^\emptyset.y^\emptyset : \langle () \vdash a \to a \rangle$.
3. It is not possible that
   $\lambda y^\emptyset.\lambda x^\emptyset.y^\emptyset x^\emptyset : \langle () \vdash a \to a \rangle$.
   Hence, the subject η-expansion lemmas fail for $\vdash$.

Proof. 1. and 2. are easy. For 3., assume $\lambda y^\emptyset.\lambda x^\emptyset.y^\emptyset x^\emptyset : \langle () \vdash a \to a \rangle$. By Lemma 5.2, $\lambda x^\emptyset.y^\emptyset x^\emptyset : \langle (y : a) \vdash \to a \rangle$. Again, by Lemma 5.2, $a = \omega^\emptyset$ or there exists $n \geq 1$ such that $a = \sqcap_{i=1}^n(U_i \to T_i)$, absurd.   □

6   The Realisability Semantics

In this section we introduce the realisability semantics and show its soundness for $\vdash$.

Crucial to a realisability semantics is the notion of a saturated set:

Definition 10. Let $\mathcal{X}, \mathcal{Y} \subseteq \mathcal{M}$.

1. We use $\mathcal{P}(\mathcal{X})$ to denote the powerset of $\mathcal{X}$, i.e. $\{\mathcal{Y} \,/\, \mathcal{Y} \subseteq \mathcal{X}\}$.
2. We define $\mathcal{X}^{+i} = \{M^{+i} \,/\, M \in \mathcal{X}\}$.
3. We define $\mathcal{X} \rightsquigarrow \mathcal{Y} = \{M \in \mathcal{M} \,/\, M\,N \in \mathcal{Y} \text{ for all } N \in \mathcal{X} \text{ such that } M \diamond N\}$.
4. We say that $\mathcal{X} \wr \mathcal{Y}$ iff for all $M \in \mathcal{X} \rightsquigarrow \mathcal{Y}$, there exists $N \in \mathcal{X}$ such that $M \diamond N$.
5. For $r \in \{\beta, \beta\eta, h\}$, we say that $\mathcal{X}$ is r-saturated if whenever $M \rhd_r^* N$ and $N \in \mathcal{X}$, then $M \in \mathcal{X}$.

Saturation is closed under intersection, lifting and arrows:

Lemma 9.   1. $(\mathcal{X} \cap \mathcal{Y})^{+i} = \mathcal{X}^{+i} \cap \mathcal{Y}^{+i}$.
2. If $\mathcal{X}, \mathcal{Y}$ are r-saturated sets, then $\mathcal{X} \cap \mathcal{Y}$ is r-saturated.
3. If $\mathcal{X}$ is r-saturated, then $\mathcal{X}^{+i}$ is r-saturated.

4. *If $\mathcal{Y}$ is r-saturated, then, for every set $\mathcal{X}$, $\mathcal{X} \rightsquigarrow \mathcal{Y}$ is r-saturated.*
5. $(\mathcal{X} \rightsquigarrow \mathcal{Y})^{+i} \subseteq \mathcal{X}^{+i} \rightsquigarrow \mathcal{Y}^{+i}$.
6. *If $\mathcal{X}^{+i} \wr \mathcal{Y}^{+i}$, then $\mathcal{X}^{+i} \rightsquigarrow \mathcal{Y}^{+i} \subseteq (\mathcal{X} \rightsquigarrow \mathcal{Y})^{+i}$.*

We now give the basic step in our realisability semantics: the interpretations and meanings of types.

Definition 11. *Let $\mathcal{V}_1$, $\mathcal{V}_2$ be countably infinite, $\mathcal{V}_1 \cap \mathcal{V}_2 = \emptyset$ and $\mathcal{V} = \mathcal{V}_1 \cup \mathcal{V}_2$.*

1. *Let $L \in \mathcal{L}_{\mathbb{N}}$. We define $\mathcal{M}^L = \{M \in \mathcal{M} \ / \ d(M) = L\}$.*
2. *Let $x \in \mathcal{V}_1$. We define $\mathcal{N}_x^L = \{x^L N_1...N_k \in \mathcal{M} \ / \ k \geq 0\}$.*
3. *Let $r \in \{\beta, \beta\eta, h\}$. An r-interpretation $\mathcal{I} : \mathcal{A} \mapsto \mathcal{P}(\mathcal{M}^\oslash)$ is a function such that for all $a \in \mathcal{A}$:*
   - $\mathcal{I}(a)$ *is r-saturated*   *and*   • $\forall x \in \mathcal{V}_1. \ \mathcal{N}_x^\oslash \subseteq \mathcal{I}(a)$.
   We extend an r-interpretation $\mathcal{I}$ to $\mathbb{U}$ as follows:
   - $\mathcal{I}(\omega^L) = \mathcal{M}^L$ • $\mathcal{I}(\overline{e}_i U) = \mathcal{I}(U)^{+i}$
   - $\mathcal{I}(U_1 \sqcap U_2) = \mathcal{I}(U_1) \cap \mathcal{I}(U_2)$ • $\mathcal{I}(U \rightarrow T) = \mathcal{I}(U) \rightsquigarrow \mathcal{I}(T)$
   Let r-int $= \{\mathcal{I} \ / \ \mathcal{I}$ is an r-interpretation$\}$.
4. *Let $U \in \mathbb{U}$ and $r \in \{\beta, \beta\eta, h\}$. Define $[U]_r$, the r-interpretation of U by:*
   $[U]_r = \{M \in \mathcal{M} \ / \ M$ is closed and $M \in \bigcap_{\mathcal{I} \in r\text{-}int} \mathcal{I}(U)\}$

Lemma 10. *Let $r \in \{\beta, \beta\eta, h\}$.*

1. *(a) For any $U \in \mathbb{U}$ and $\mathcal{I} \in r\text{-}int$, we have $\mathcal{I}(U)$ is r-saturated.*
   (b) If $d(U) = L$ and $\mathcal{I} \in r\text{-}int$, then for all $x \in \mathcal{V}_1$, $\mathcal{N}_x^L \subseteq \mathcal{I}(U) \subseteq \mathcal{M}^L$.
2. *Let $r \in \{\beta, \beta\eta, h\}$. If $\mathcal{I} \in r\text{-}int$ and $U \sqsubseteq V$, then $\mathcal{I}(U) \subseteq \mathcal{I}(V)$.*

Here is the soundness lemma.

Lemma 11 (Soundness). *Let $r \in \{\beta, \beta\eta, h\}$, $M : \langle (x_j^{L_j} : U_j)_n \vdash U \rangle$, $\mathcal{I} \in r\text{-}int$ and for all $j \in \{1, ..., n\}$, $N_j \in \mathcal{I}(U_j)$. If $M[(x_j^{L_j} := N_j)_n] \in \mathcal{M}$ then $M[(x_j^{L_j} := N_j)_n] \in \mathcal{I}(U)$.*

Proof. By induction on the derivation $M : \langle (x_j^{L_j} : U_j)_n \vdash U \rangle$. $\square$

Corollary 3. *Let $r \in \{\beta, \beta\eta, h\}$. If $M : \langle () \vdash U \rangle$, then $M \in [U]_r$.* $\square$

Proof. By Lemma 11, $M \in \mathcal{I}(U)$ for any r-interpretation $\mathcal{I}$. By Lemma 4.2, $\text{fv}(M) = \text{dom}(()) = \emptyset$ and hence M is closed. Therefore, $M \in [U]_r$. $\square$

Lemma 12 (The meaning of types is closed under type operations).
Let $r \in \{\beta, \beta\eta, h\}$. On $\mathbb{U}$, the following hold:

1. $[\overline{e}_i U]_r = [U]_r^{+i}$
2. $[U \sqcap V]_r = [U]_r \cap [V]_r$
3. *If $\mathcal{I} \in r\text{-}int$ and $U, V \in \mathbb{U}$, then $\mathcal{I}(U) \wr \mathcal{I}(V)$.*

Proof. 1. and 2. are easy. 3. Let $d(U) = K$, $M \in \mathcal{I}(U) \rightsquigarrow \mathcal{I}(V)$ and $x \in \mathcal{V}_1$ such that for all L, $x^L \notin \text{fv}(M)$, then $M \diamond x^K$ and by lemma 10.1b, $x^K \in \mathcal{I}(V)$. $\square$

The next definition and lemma put the realisability semantics in use.

Definition 12 (Examples). *Let $a, b \in \mathcal{A}$ where $a \neq b$. We define:*

- $Id_0 = a \to a$, $Id_1 = \bar{e}_1(a \to a)$ and $Id_1' = \bar{e}_1 a \to \bar{e}_1 a$.
- $D = (a \sqcap (a \to b)) \to b$.
- $Nat_0 = (a \to a) \to (a \to a)$, $Nat_1 = \bar{e}_1((a \to a) \to (a \to a))$,
  and $Nat_0' = (\bar{e}_1 a \to a) \to (\bar{e}_1 a \to a)$.

Moreover, if M, N are terms and $n \in \mathbb{N}$, we define $(M)^n N$ by induction on n:
$(M)^0 N = N$ *and* $(M)^{m+1} N = M((M)^m N)$.

Lemma 13

1. $[Id_0]_\beta = \{M \in \mathcal{M}^\varnothing \;/\; M$ *is closed and* $M \triangleright_\beta^* \lambda y^\varnothing . y^\varnothing\}$.
2. $[Id_1]_\beta = [Id_1']_\beta = \{M \in \mathcal{M}^{(1)} \;/\; M$ *is closed and* $M \triangleright_\beta^* \lambda y^{(1)} . y^{(1)}\}$. *(Note that $Id_1' \notin \mathbb{U}$.)*
3. $[D]_\beta = \{M \in \mathcal{M}^\varnothing \;/\; M$ *is closed and* $M \triangleright_\beta^* \lambda y^\varnothing . y^\varnothing y^\varnothing\}$.
4. $[Nat_0]_\beta = \{M \in \mathcal{M}^\varnothing \;/\; M$ *is closed and* $M \triangleright_\beta^* \lambda f^\varnothing . f^\varnothing$ *or* $M \triangleright_\beta^* \lambda f^\varnothing . \lambda y^\varnothing . (f^\varnothing)^n y^\varnothing$ *where* $n \geq 1\}$.
5. $[Nat_1]_\beta = \{M \in \mathcal{M}^{(1)} \;/\; M$ *is closed and* $M \triangleright_\beta^* \lambda f^{(1)} . f^{(1)}$ *or* $M \triangleright_\beta^* \lambda f^{(1)} . \lambda x^{(1)} . (f^{(1)})^n y^{(1)}$ *where* $n \geq 1\}$.
6. $[Nat_0']_\beta = \{M \in \mathcal{M}^\varnothing \;/\; M$ *is closed and* $M \triangleright_\beta^* \lambda f^\varnothing . f^\varnothing$ *or* $M \triangleright_\beta^* \lambda f^\varnothing . \lambda y^{(1)} . f^\varnothing y^{(1)}\}$.

7 The Completeness Theorem

In this section we set out the machinery and prove that completeness holds for $\vdash$.
 We need the following partition of the set of variables $\{y^L / y \in \mathcal{V}_2\}$.

Definition 13

1. *Let $L \in \mathcal{L}_\mathbb{N}$. We define $\mathbb{U}^L = \{U \in \mathbb{U}/d(U) = L\}$ and $\mathcal{V}^L = \{x^L/x \in \mathcal{V}_2\}$.*
2. *Let $U \in \mathbb{U}$. We inductively define a set of variables $\mathbb{V}_U$ as follows:*
   - *If $d(U) = \varnothing$ then:*
     - $\mathbb{V}_U$ *is an infinite set of variables of degree $\varnothing$.*
     - *If $U \neq V$ and $d(U) = d(V) = \varnothing$, then $\mathbb{V}_U \cap \mathbb{V}_V = \emptyset$.*
     - $\bigcup_{U \in \mathbb{U}^\varnothing} \mathbb{V}_U = \mathcal{V}^\varnothing$.
   - *If $d(U) = L$, then we put $\mathbb{V}_U = \{y^L \;/\; y^\varnothing \in \mathbb{V}_{U-L}\}$.*

Lemma 14

1. *If $d(U), d(V) \succeq L$ and $U^{-L} = V^{-L}$, then $U = V$.*
2. *If $d(U) = L$, then $\mathbb{V}_U$ is an infinite subset of $\mathcal{V}^L$.*
3. *If $U \neq V$ and $d(U) = d(V) = L$, then $\mathbb{V}_U \cap \mathbb{V}_V = \emptyset$.*
4. $\bigcup_{U \in \mathbb{U}^L} \mathbb{V}_U = \mathcal{V}^L$.
5. *If $y^L \in \mathbb{V}_U$, then $y^{i::L} \in \mathbb{V}_{\bar{e}_i U}$.*
6. *If $y^{i::L} \in \mathbb{V}_U$, then $y^L \in \mathbb{V}_{U-i}$.*

Proof 1. If $L = (n_i)_m$, we have $U = \bar{e}_{n_1} \ldots \bar{e}_{n_m} U'$ and $V = \bar{e}_{n_1} \ldots \bar{e}_{n_m} V'$. Then $U^{-L} = U'$, $V^{-L} = V'$ and $U' = V'$. Thus $U = V$. 2. 3. and 4. By induction on L and using 1. 5. Because $(\bar{e}_i U)^{-i} = U$. 6. By definition. □

Our partition of the set $\mathcal{V}_2$ as above will enable us to give in the next definition useful infinite sets which will contain type environments that will play a crucial role in one particular type interpretation.

Definition 14

1. Let $L \in \mathcal{L}_{\mathbb{N}}$. We denote $\mathbb{G}^L = \{(y^L : U) \ / \ U \in \mathbb{U}^L \ and \ y^L \in \mathbb{V}_U\}$ and $\mathbb{H}^L = \bigcup_{K \succeq L} \mathbb{G}^K$. Note that $\mathbb{G}^L$ and $\mathbb{H}^L$ are not type environments because they are infinite sets.
2. Let $L \in \mathcal{L}_{\mathbb{N}}$, $M \in \mathcal{M}$ and $U \in \mathbb{U}$, we write:
   - $M : \langle \mathbb{H}^L \vdash U \rangle$ if there is a type environment $\Gamma \subset \mathbb{H}^L$ where $M : \langle \Gamma \vdash U \rangle$
   - $M : \langle \mathbb{H}^L \vdash^* U \rangle$ if $M \triangleright^*_{\beta\eta} N$ and $N : \langle \mathbb{H}^L \vdash U \rangle$

Lemma 15

1. If $\Gamma \subset \mathbb{H}^L$ then $\mathrm{OK}(\Gamma)$.
2. If $\Gamma \subset \mathbb{H}^L$ then $\overline{e}_i \Gamma \subset \mathbb{H}^{i::L}$.
3. If $\Gamma \subset \mathbb{H}^{i::L}$ then $\Gamma^{-i} \subset \mathbb{H}^L$.
4. If $\Gamma_1 \subset \mathbb{H}^L$, $\Gamma_2 \subset \mathbb{H}^K$ and $L \preceq K$ then $\Gamma_1 \sqcap \Gamma_2 \subset \mathbb{H}^L$.

Proof 1. Let $x^K : U \in \Gamma$ then $U \in \mathbb{U}^K$ and so $\mathrm{d}(U) = K$. 2. and 3. are by lemma 14. 4. First note that by 1., $\Gamma_1 \sqcap \Gamma_2$ is well defined. $\mathbb{H}^K \subseteq \mathbb{H}^L$. Let $(x^R : U_1 \sqcap U_2) \in \Gamma_1 \sqcap \Gamma_2$ where $(x^R : U_1) \in \Gamma_1 \subset \mathbb{H}^L$ and $(x^R : U_2) \in \Gamma_2 \subset \mathbb{H}^K \subseteq \mathbb{H}^L$, then $\mathrm{d}(U_1) = \mathrm{d}(U_2) = R$ and $x^R \in \mathbb{V}_{U_1} \cap \mathbb{V}_{U_2}$. Hence, by lemma 14, $U_1 = U_2$ and $\Gamma_1 \sqcap \Gamma_2 = \Gamma_1 \cup \Gamma_2 \subset \mathbb{H}^L$. $\square$

For every $L \in \mathcal{L}_{\mathbb{N}}$, we define the set of terms of degree L which contain some free variable x^K where $x \in \mathcal{V}_1$ and $K \succeq L$.

Definition 15. For every $L \in \mathcal{L}_{\mathbb{N}}$, let $\mathcal{O}^L = \{M \in \mathcal{M}^L \ / \ x^K \in \mathrm{fv}(M), x \in \mathcal{V}_1 \ and \ K \succeq L\}$. It is easy to see that, for every $L \in \mathcal{L}_{\mathbb{N}}$ and $x \in \mathcal{V}_1$, $\mathcal{N}_x^L \subseteq \mathcal{O}^L$.

Lemma 16

1. $(\mathcal{O}^L)^{+i} = \mathcal{O}^{i::L}$.
2. If $y \in \mathcal{V}_2$ and $(My^K) \in \mathcal{O}^L$, then $M \in \mathcal{O}^L$
3. If $M \in \mathcal{O}^L$, $M \diamond N$ and $L \preceq K = \mathrm{d}(N)$, then $MN \in \mathcal{O}^L$.
4. If $\mathrm{d}(M) = L$, $L \preceq K$, $M \diamond N$ and $N \in \mathcal{O}^K$, then $MN \in \mathcal{O}^L$.

The crucial interpretation $\mathbb{I}$ for the proof of completeness is given as follows:

Definition 16

1. Let $\mathbb{I}_{\beta\eta}$ be the $\beta\eta$-interpretation defined by: for all type variables a, $\mathbb{I}_{\beta\eta}(a) = \mathcal{O}^{\varnothing} \cup \{M \in \mathcal{M}^{\varnothing} \ / \ M : \langle \mathbb{H}^{\varnothing} \vdash^* a \rangle\}$.
2. Let $\mathbb{I}_{\beta}$ be the β-interpretation defined by: for all type variables a, $\mathbb{I}_{\beta}(a) = \mathcal{O}^{\varnothing} \cup \{M \in \mathcal{M}^{\varnothing} \ / \ M : \langle \mathbb{H}^{\varnothing} \vdash a \rangle\}$.
3. Let $\mathbb{I}_h$ be the h-interpretation defined by: for all type variables a, $\mathbb{I}_h(a) = \mathcal{O}^{\varnothing} \cup \{M \in \mathcal{M}^{\varnothing} \ / \ M : \langle \mathbb{H}^{\varnothing} \vdash a \rangle\}$.

The next crucial lemma shows that $\mathbb{I}$ is an interpretation and that the interpretation of a type of order L contains terms of order L which are typable in these special environments which are parts of the infinite sets of Definition 14.

Lemma 17. *Let $r \in \{\beta\eta, \beta, h\}$ and $r' \in \{\beta, h\}$*

1. *If $\mathbb{I}_r \in r\text{-int}$ and $a \in \mathcal{A}$ then $\mathbb{I}_r(a)$ is r-saturated and for all $x \in \mathcal{V}_1, \mathcal{N}_x^\emptyset \subseteq \mathbb{I}_r(a)$.*
2. *If $U \in \mathbb{U}$ and $d(U) = L$, then $\mathbb{I}_{\beta\eta}(U) = \mathcal{O}^L \cup \{M \in \mathcal{M}^L \ / \ M : \langle \mathbb{H}^L \vdash^* U \rangle\}$.*
3. *If $U \in \mathbb{U}$ and $d(U) = L$, then $\mathbb{I}_{r'}(U) = \mathcal{O}^L \cup \{M \in \mathcal{M}^L \ / \ M : \langle \mathbb{H}^L \vdash U \rangle\}$.*

Now, we use this crucial $\mathbb{I}$ to establish completeness of our semantics.

Theorem 6 (Completeness of $\vdash$). *Let $U \in \mathbb{U}$ such that $d(U) = L$.*

1. *$[U]_{\beta\eta} = \{M \in \mathcal{M}^L \ / \ M \text{ closed}, M \rhd_{\beta\eta}^* N \text{ and } N : \langle () \vdash U \rangle\}$.*
2. *$[U]_\beta = [U]_h = \{M \in \mathcal{M}^L \ / \ M : \langle () \vdash U \rangle\}$.*
3. *$[U]_{\beta\eta}$ is stable by reduction. I.e., If $M \in [U]_{\beta\eta}$ and $M \rhd_{\beta\eta}^* N$ then $N \in [U]_{\beta\eta}$.*

Proof. Let $r \in \{\beta, h, \beta\eta\}$.

1. Let $M \in [U]_{\beta\eta}$. Then M is a closed term and $M \in \mathbb{I}_{\beta\eta}(U)$. Hence, by Lemma 17, $M \in \mathcal{O}^L \cup \{M \in \mathcal{M}^L \ / \ M : \langle \mathbb{H}^L \vdash^* U \rangle\}$. Since M is closed, $M \notin \mathcal{O}^L$. Hence, $M \in \{M \in \mathcal{M}^L \ / \ M : \langle \mathbb{H}^L \vdash^* U \rangle\}$ and so, $M \rhd_{\beta\eta}^* N$ and $N : \langle \Gamma \vdash U \rangle$ where $\Gamma \subset \mathbb{H}^L$. By Theorem 1, N is closed and, by Lemma 4.2, $N : \langle () \vdash U \rangle$. Conversely, take M closed such that $M \rhd_\beta^* N$ and $N : \langle () \vdash U \rangle$. Let $\mathcal{I} \in \beta\eta\text{-int}$. By Lemma 11, $N \in \mathcal{I}(U)$. By Lemma 10.1, $\mathcal{I}(U)$ is $\beta\eta$-saturated. Hence, $M \in \mathcal{I}(U)$. Thus $M \in [U]$.
2. Let $M \in [U]_\beta$. Then M is a closed term and $M \in \mathbb{I}_\beta(U)$. Hence, by Lemma 17, $M \in \mathcal{O}^L \cup \{M \in \mathcal{M}^L \ / \ M : \langle \mathbb{H}^L \vdash U \rangle\}$. Since M is closed, $M \notin \mathcal{O}^L$. Hence, $M \in \{M \in \mathcal{M}^L \ / \ M : \langle \mathbb{H}^L \vdash U \rangle\}$ and so, $M : \langle \Gamma \vdash U \rangle$ where $\Gamma \subset \mathbb{H}^L$. By Lemma 4.2, $M : \langle () \vdash U \rangle$.
   Conversely, take M such that $M : \langle () \vdash U \rangle$. By Lemma 4.2, M is closed. Let $\mathcal{I} \in \beta\text{-int}$. By Lemma 11, $M \in \mathcal{I}(U)$. Thus $M \in [U]_\beta$.
   It is easy to see that $[U]_\beta = [U]_h$.
3. Let $M \in [U]_{\beta\eta}$ and $M \rhd_{\beta\eta}^* N$. By 1, M is closed, $M \rhd_{\beta\eta}^* P$ and $P : \langle () \vdash U \rangle$. By confluence Theorem 2, there is Q such that $P \rhd_{\beta\eta}^* Q$ and $N \rhd_{\beta\eta}^* Q$. By subject reduction Theorem 4, $Q : \langle () \vdash U \rangle$. By Theorem 1, N is closed and, by 1, $N \in [U]_{\beta\eta}$. $\square$

8   Conclusion

Expansion may be viewed to work like a multi-layered simultaneous substitution. Moreover, expansion is a crucial part of a procedure for calculating principal typings and helps support compositional type inference. Because the early definitions of expansion were complicated, expansion variables (E-variables) were introduced to simplify and mechanise expansion. The aim of this paper is to give a complete semantics for intersection type systems with expansion variables.

The only earlier attempt (see Kamareddine, Nour, Rahli and Wells [13]) at giving a semantics for expansion variables could only handle the λI-calculus, did not allow a universal type, and was incomplete in the presence of more than one expansion variable. This paper overcomes these difficulties and gives a complete semantics for an intersection type system with an arbitrary (possibly infinite) number of expansion variables using a calculus indexed with finite sequences of natural numbers.

References

1. Barendregt, H.P.: The Lambda Calculus: Its Syntax and Semantics. North-Holland, Amsterdam (revised edn.) (1984)
2. Carlier, S., Polakow, J., Wells, J.B., Kfoury, A.J.: System E: Expansion variables for flexible typing with linear and non-linear types and intersection types. In: Schmidt, D. (ed.) ESOP 2004. LNCS, vol. 2986. Springer, Heidelberg (2004)
3. Carlier, S., Wells, J.B.: Expansion: the crucial mechanism for type inference with intersection types: A survey and explanation. In: Proc. 3rd Int'l Workshop Intersection Types & Related Systems (ITRS 2004), July 19, 2005. The ITRS 2004 proceedings of Elec. Notes in Theoret. Comp. Sci., vol. 136 (2005)
4. Coppo, M., Dezani-Ciancaglini, M., Venneri, B.: Principal type schemes and λ-calculus semantics. In: Hindley, J.R., Seldin, J.P. (eds.) To H. B. Curry: Essays on Combinatory Logic, Lambda Calculus, and Formalism. Academic Press, London (1980)
5. Coquand, T.: Completeness theorems and lambda-calculus. In: Urzyczyn, P. (ed.) TLCA 2005. LNCS, vol. 3461. Springer, Heidelberg (2005)
6. Goos, G., Hartmanis, J. (eds.): λ - Calculus and Computer Science Theory. LNCS, vol. 37. Springer, Heidelberg (1975)
7. Hindley, J.R.: The simple semantics for Coppo-Dezani-Sallé types. In: Dezani-Ciancaglini, M., Montanari, U. (eds.) Programming 1982. LNCS, vol. 137. Springer, Heidelberg (1982)
8. Hindley, J.R.: The completeness theorem for typing λ-terms. Theoretical Computer Science 22 (1983)
9. Hindley, J.R.: Curry's types are complete with respect to F-semantics too. Theoretical Computer Science 22 (1983)
10. Hindley, J.R.: Basic Simple Type Theory. Cambridge Tracts in Theoretical Computer Science, vol. 42. Cambridge University Press, Cambridge (1997)
11. Kamareddine, F., Nour, K.: A completeness result for a realisability semantics for an intersection type system. Ann. Pure Appl. Logic 146(2-3) (2007)
12. Kamareddine, F., Nour, K., Rahli, V., Wells, J.B.: A complete realisability semantics for intersection types and infinite expansion variables (2008), http://www.macs.hw.ac.uk/~fairouz/papers/drafts/compsem-big.pdf
13. Kamareddine, F., Nour, K., Rahli, V., Wells, J.B.: Realisability semantics for intersection type systems and expansion variables. In: ITRS 2008 (2008), http://www.macs.hw.ac.uk/~fairouz/papers/conference-publications/semone.pdf
14. Krivine, J.: Lambda-Calcul : Types et Modèles. Etudes et Recherches en Informatique. Masson (1990)

Towards Efficient Verification of Systems with Dynamic Process Creation

Hanna Klaudel[1], Maciej Koutny[2], Elisabeth Pelz[3], and Franck Pommereau[3]

[1] IBISC, University of Evry, bd F. Mitterrand, 91025 Evry, France
`hanna.klaudel@ibisc.fr`
[2] SCS, Newcastle University, Newcastle upon Tyne, NE1 7RU, UK
`maciej.koutny@newcastle.ac.uk`
[3] LACL, University of Paris Est, 61 av. du général de Gaulle, 94010 Créteil, France
`{pelz,pommereau}@univ-paris12.fr`

Abstract. Modelling and analysis of dynamic multi-threaded state systems often encounters obstacles when one wants to use automated verification methods, such as model checking. Our aim in this paper is to develop a technical device for coping with one such obstacle, namely that caused by dynamic process creation.

We first introduce a general class of coloured Petri nets—not tied to any particular syntax or approach—allowing one to capture systems with dynamic (and concurrent) process creation as well as capable of manipulating data. Following this, we introduce the central notion of our method which is a marking equivalence that can be efficiently computed and then used, for instance, to aggregate markings in a reachability graph. In some situations, such an aggregation may produce a finite representation of an infinite state system which still allows one to establish the relevant behavioural properties. We show feasibility of the method on an example and provide initial experimental results.

Keywords: Petri nets, multi-threaded systems, marking symmetries, state-space generation.

1 Introduction

Multi-threading is a programming feature with an ever increasing presence due to its central role in a broad range of application areas, including web services, business computing, virtual reality, pervasive systems, and networks-on-a-chip. Given this and the widely acknowledged complexity of multi-threaded designs, there is a growing demand to provide methods supporting the highest possible confidence in their correctness. In a multi-threaded (or multi-process) programming paradigm, sequential code can be executed repeatedly in concurrent threads interacting through shared data and/or rendezvous communication. In this paper, we consider a Petri net model that captures such a scheme in a general fashion: programs are represented by Petri nets, and the active threads are identified by differently coloured tokens which use, in particular, thread identifiers. Such programs and their corresponding representation in coloured Petri

J.S. Fitzgerald, A.E. Haxthausen, and H. Yenigun (Eds.): ICTAC 2008, LNCS 5160, pp. 186–200, 2008.

nets may be obtained compositionally from algebras of Petri nets (*e.g.*, [19]) which ensures that several behavioural properties of the resulting nets may be validated automatically and/or syntactically (*i.e.*, by construction). The corresponding class of nets may also be characterised using a suitable combination of structural properties. The latter approach is used in this paper in order to avoid dealing with a concrete net algebra.

The presence of thread identifiers in net markings has the potential of accelerating the state space explosion, and so poses an additional threat for the efficiency of verification. However, thread identifiers are arbitrary (anonymous) symbols whose sole role is to ensure a consistent (*i.e.*, private or local) execution of each thread. The exact identity of an identifier is basically irrelevant, and what matters are the *relationships* between such identifiers, *e.g.*, being a thread created by another thread. As a result, (sets of) identifiers may often be swapped with other (sets of) identifiers without changing the resulting execution in any essential way. Moreover, an infinite state system can sometimes be reduced to a finite representation which in turn allows one to model check the relevant behavioural properties (*e.g.*, mutual exclusion or deadlock freeness). This leads to the problem of identifying symmetric executions, which must be addressed by any reasonable verification and/or simulation approach to multi-threaded programming schemes.

In this paper, we propose a method that contributes towards an efficient verification approach for multi-threaded systems modelled using a class of coloured Petri nets. At its core lies a marking equivalence that identifies global states which have essentially isomorphic future behaviour up to renaming of thread identifiers. The equivalence can be computed efficiently and then it may be used to aggregate nodes in a marking graph, or to find cut-offs during the unfolding of a Petri net [14]. The proposed method is complemented with a generation scheme for concrete values of thread identifiers that is both distributed and concurrent.

An important feature of the method is that it is parameterised by a set of operations that can be applied to thread identifiers. For instance, it may or may not be allowed to test whether one thread is a direct descendant of another thread, and the proposed method takes this into account.

Context and Related Works. The difficulty of reasoning about the behaviour of multiple threads operating on shared data has motivated the development of a variety of formalisms and methods for the modelling and detecting various kinds of errors, *e.g.*, data races, deadlocks and violations of data invariants.

In proof based methods, such as the recent approaches in [11,23], the model is described by means of axioms, and properties are theorems to be verified using a theorem prover. These techniques have the advantage of being applicable to infinite state systems, but the use of theorem provers can be a deeply technical task which is hard to automate.

As an alternative approach, model checking techniques (see [5]) allow one to achieve a high degree of confidence in system correctness in an essentially automatic way. This is done by exhaustively checking a finite system model for violations of a correctness requirement specified formally as, *e.g.*, a temporal logic formula [16]. However, this makes model checking sensitive to the state explosion problem, and so it may not be well suited to tackle real-life systems. A variety of methods (see, *e.g.*, [18] for a recent survey) address the state explosion problem by exploiting, for instance, symmetries in the system model, in order to avoid searching parts of the state space which are equivalent to those that have already been explored. Several techniques have been implemented in widely used verification tools, such as [3,13,17], and proved to be successful in the analysis of complex communication protocols and distributed systems.

When dealing with multi-threaded systems, model checking typically involves manual definition of models using low-level modelling means, such as pseudo programming languages, Petri nets or process algebras. Some recent methodologies (*e.g.* [24,6,1]) allow one to verify (Java or C) program invariants by combining model checking and abstract interpretation [8], while others (*e.g.* [9]) propose dedicated high-level input languages (a combination of multiset rewriting and constraints) allowing one to use verification techniques employing symbolic representations of infinite state spaces. In the domain of coloured Petri nets, extensive work has been conducted to make model checking efficient through the use of symbolic reachability graph constructions [4,25], and by exploiting various kinds of partial order reductions [10,14].

Being general purpose techniques rather than designed specifically for multi-threaded systems, the above approaches do not exploit explicitly symmetries related to thread identifiers. An example of work which addresses expressivity and decidability aspects of various extensions of P/T Petri nets allowing, in particular, fresh name generation and process replication is [22]. However, it only allows equality tests on process identifiers, and does not deal with aspects related to the efficiency of verification.

Outline of the Paper. After introducing basic concepts concerning thread identifiers, we present a class of Petri nets used to model multi-threaded systems and establish some relevant properties of their reachable markings. We then define an equivalence relation on markings abstracting from the identities of thread identifiers and discuss its main features. The paper ends with a procedure for checking the equivalence, supported by an example and some initial experimental results. All proofs and auxiliary results are provided in the technical report [15].

2   Process Identifiers

We denote by $\mathbb{D}$ the set of *data values* which, in particular, contains all integers. We then denote by $\mathbb{V}$ the set of variables such that $\mathbb{V} \cap \mathbb{D} = \varnothing$. The set $\mathbb{P}$, disjoint with $\mathbb{D} \cup \mathbb{V}$, is the set of *process identifiers*, (or *pids*) that allow one to distinguish different concurrent threads during an execution. We assume that there is a set $\mathbb{I} \subset \mathbb{P}$ of *initial* pids, *i.e.*, threads active at the system startup. To keep the formal treatment simpler, we assume throughout this paper that at the beginning there is just one active thread, and so $|\mathbb{I}| = 1$. This is a harmless restriction since any non-trivial initial marking (with several active threads) can be created from a restricted one by firing an initialisation transition.

Operations on Process Identifiers. It is possible to check whether two pids are equal or not since different threads must be distinguished. Other operations may also be applied to thread identifiers, in particular:

- $\pi \lessdot_1 \pi'$ checks whether π is the parent of π' (*i.e.*, thread π spawned thread π' at some point of its execution).
- $\pi \lessdot \pi'$ checks whether π is an ancestor of π' (*i.e.*, $\lessdot$ is $\lessdot_1^+$).
- $\pi \pitchfork_1 \pi'$ checks whether π is a sibling of π' and π was spawned immediately before π' (*i.e.*, after spawning π, the parent of π and π' did not spawn any other thread before spawning π').
- $\pi \pitchfork \pi'$ checks whether π is an elder sibling of π' (*i.e.*, $\pitchfork$ is $\pitchfork_1^+$).

Throughout the paper, we will denote by Ω_{pid} the set of the four relations introduced above, as yet informally, together with the equality. In particular, only the operators in Ω_{pid} can be used to compare pids in the annotations used in Petri nets. Crucially, it is not allowed to *decompose* a pid (to extract, for example, the parent pid of a given pid) which is considered as an atomic value (or black box), and no literals nor concrete pid values are allowed in Petri net annotations (*i.e.*, in guards and arc labels) involving the pids.

The resulting formalism is rich while still being decidable. Indeed, it can be shown that the monadic second order theory of $\mathbb{P}$ equipped with $\lessdot_1$ and $\pitchfork_1$ can be reduced to the theory of binary trees equipped with the left-child and right-child relation which, in turn, has been shown to be exactly as expressive as the tree automata [21]. Having said that, many simple extensions of the formalism based on pids (de)composition are undecidable.

Thread Implementation. We assume that there exists a function ν generating the i-th child of the thread identified by a pid π, and that there is no other way to generate a new pid. In order to avoid creating the same pid twice, each thread is assumed to maintain a count of the threads it has already spawned.

A possible way of implementing dynamic pids creation—adopted in this paper—is to consider them as finite strings of positive integers written down as dot-separated sequences. Then we take $\mathbb{I} \stackrel{\text{df}}{=} \{1\}$ and, for all π and i, we set $\nu(\pi, i-1) \stackrel{\text{df}}{=} \pi.i$ (*i.e.*, the i-th pid generated from π is $\pi.i$, and $i-1$ is the number of pids generated so far from π). With such a representation, the relations in Ω_{pid} other than equality are given by:

- $\pi \lessdot_1 \pi'$ iff $(\exists i \in \mathbb{N}^+)$ $\qquad\qquad\qquad$ $\pi.i = \pi'$
- $\pi \lessdot \pi'$ iff $(\exists n \geq 1)\,(\exists i_1, \ldots, i_n \in \mathbb{N}^+)$ $\pi.i_1.\cdots.i_n = \pi'$
- $\pi \pitchfork_1 \pi'$ iff $(\exists \pi'' \in \mathbb{P})\,(\exists i \in \mathbb{N}^+)$ $\pi = \pi''.i \ \wedge\ \pi' = \pi''.(i+1)$
- $\pi \pitchfork \pi'$ iff $(\exists \pi'' \in \mathbb{P})\,(\exists i < j \in \mathbb{N}^+)$ $\pi = \pi''.i \ \wedge\ \pi' = \pi''.j$

Such a scheme has several advantages: (i) it is deterministic and allows for distributed generation of pids; (ii) it is simple and easy to implement without re-using the pids; and (iii) it may be bounded by restricting, *e.g.*, the length of the pids, or the maximum number of children spawned by each thread.

3   Coloured Petri Nets

We start with a general definition of coloured Petri nets and their dynamic behaviour. More details about this particular formalism and, in particular, variable bindings and operations on multisets, can be found in [2].

Definition 1 (Petri net graph). *A Petri net graph is a tuple (S, T, ℓ) where S is a finite set of* places, *T is a finite set of* transitions *(disjoint from S), and ℓ is a* labelling *of places, transitions and arcs (in $(S \times T) \cup (T \times S)$) such that:*

- *For each place $s \in S$, $\ell(s)$ is a Cartesian product of subsets of pids and data, called the* type *of s.*
- *For each transition t, $\ell(t)$ is a computable Boolean expression, called the* guard *of t.*
- *For each arc α, $\ell(\alpha)$ is a finite set of tuples of values and/or variables.* ◇

Since we allow tuples as token values, it is possible to represent complex data structures in a flattened form (as Cartesian products). In what follows, the set of all finite tuples beginning with a value or variable x will be denoted by $\mathbb{T}_x$.

Definition 2 (Petri net and its behaviour). *A* marking *M of a Petri net graph (S, T, ℓ) is a mapping that associates with each $s \in S$ a finite multiset of values in $\ell(s)$. A* Petri net *is then defined as $N \stackrel{\mathrm{df}}{=} (S, T, \ell, M_0)$, where M_0 is the initial* marking.

A transition $t \in T$ is enabled *at a marking M if there exists a binding σ : $\mathbb{V} \to \mathbb{D}$ such that $\sigma(\ell(t))$ evaluates to true and, for all $s \in S$, $\sigma(\ell(s,t)) \leq M(s)$ and $\sigma(\ell(t,s))$ is a multiset over $\ell(s)$. (In other words, there are enough tokens in the input places, and the types of the output places are being respected.)*

An enabled t may fire *producing the marking M', defined for all $s \in S$ by $M'(s) \stackrel{\mathrm{df}}{=} M(s) - \sigma(\ell(s,t)) + \sigma(\ell(t,s))$. We denote this by $M[t, \sigma\rangle M'$.*

We also denote $M_0 \to^* M$ if M is produced from M_0 through the firing of a finite sequence of transitions, i.e., if the marking M is reachable *(from M_0).* ◇

We will use a specific family of Petri nets respecting structural restrictions detailed below. Throughout the rest of this section, N is as in definition 2.

Assumption 1 (places). *The set of places is partitioned into a unique* generator *place s_{gen}, a possibly empty set of* data *places S_{data}, and a nonempty set of* control-flow *places S_{flow}, i.e., $S \stackrel{\mathrm{df}}{=} \{s_{gen}\} \uplus S_{data} \uplus S_{flow}$. It is assumed that:*

1. *The generator place s_{gen} has the type $\mathbb{P} \times \mathbb{N}$.*
2. *Each control-flow or data place s has the type $\mathbb{P} \times \mathbb{P}^{k_s} \times \mathbb{D}_s$ where $\mathbb{D}_s \subseteq \mathbb{D}^{m_s}$, for some $k_s, m_s \geq 0$.* ◇

The typing discipline for places ensures that we can talk about each token $\langle \pi, \cdots \rangle$ being *owned* by a thread, the pid π of which is the first component of the token. A pid is *active* at a marking if it owns a token in the generator place.

Data places store, for different threads, tuples of data and/or pids owned by currently and previously active threads.

Control-flow places indicate where the control of active threads resides. When a control-flow place s is such that $k_s + m_s \geq 1$, the information following the pid of the owner provides the status of the execution; for instance, allowing one to find out whether an exception has been raised (like in [19]).

The generator place s_{gen} is needed by the underlying scheme for the dynamic creation of fresh pids. For each active thread π, it stores a *generator* token $\langle \pi, i \rangle$ where i is the number of threads already spawned by π. Thus the next thread to be created by π will receive the pid $\pi.(i + 1)$.

Assumption 2 (initial marking). *The initial marking is such that:*

1. *All data places are empty.*
2. *The generator place contains exactly one token, $\langle 1, 0 \rangle$.*
3. *There is exactly one control-flow place that is non-empty, its type is $\mathbb{P}$ and it contains exactly one token, $\langle 1 \rangle$.*   ◇

Firing a transition t captures a progression of one or several threads which meet at a rendezvous. Below, the threads entering the rendezvous belong to a finite non-empty set $\mathcal{E} \subset \mathbb{V}$. Some of them (in the set $\mathcal{X} \subseteq \mathcal{E}$) may exit the rendezvous, others may terminate (in $\mathcal{E} \setminus \mathcal{X}$), and new ones may be created (in the set $\mathcal{N}$). Each of the created threads is spawned by one of the threads entering the rendezvous. Without lost of generality, if all the entering threads terminate, we assume that at least one is created (in order to ensure that each transition has at least one output arc to a control-flow place).

Each thread e entering the rendezvous creates $k_e \geq 0$ children. Their pids are generated using the generator place s_{gen} that holds a counter $g \in \mathbb{N}$ for e (as for all active pids). This counter for e stored in s_{gen} is incremented by k_e when the transition fires, and the pids of the generated threads are $e.(g+1), \ldots, e.(g+k_e)$.

At the same time, e may access data using the *get* operation, which consumes a token from a data place, or the *put* operation, which produces a token and inserts it into a data place. If the tokens involved are owned by e, this corresponds to data management for e. For example, getting and putting the same value into the same data place corresponds to reading, while getting one value and putting another one into the same data place corresponds to an update (the computation of the new value may be expressed through the guard of t). If the tokens involved are not owned by e, this corresponds to asynchronous communication through shared variables. In such a case, the put operation corresponds to the sending of a message, while the get corresponds to the receiving of a value deposited by another thread.

The purely syntactic restrictions on arcs and guards given below ensure that pids are not treated as (transformable) data. Markings are not involved, and so each thread will be identified by the variable bound to an actual pid at firing time. This will not cause any confusion as each active pid will always appear only once in exactly one control-flow place.

Assumption 3 (transitions, arcs and guards). *For each transition $t \in T$, the following specifies all the arcs, arc annotations and guard components.*

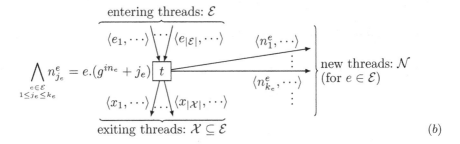

Fig. 1. Parts of the guard and the shape of arcs for assumption 3. In (a) the arcs are connected to the generator place, in (b) to control-flow places, and in (c) to data places. The a_i's and a'_j's are variables.

1. *The sets of threads $\mathcal{E}$, $\mathcal{X}$ and $\mathcal{N}$ are defined as:*

$$\mathcal{E} \stackrel{\mathrm{df}}{=} \{e \mid s \in S_{flow} \wedge \ell(s,t) \cap \mathbb{T}_e \neq \varnothing\},$$

$$\mathcal{X} \stackrel{\mathrm{df}}{=} \{x \mid s \in S_{flow} \wedge \ell(t,s) \cap \mathbb{T}_x \neq \varnothing\} \cap \mathcal{E},$$

$$\mathcal{N} \stackrel{\mathrm{df}}{=} \{n \mid s \in S_{flow} \wedge \ell(t,s) \cap \mathbb{T}_n \neq \varnothing\} \setminus \mathcal{E} = \biguplus_{e \in \mathcal{E}} \{n_1^e, \ldots, n_{k_e}^e\}.$$

It is assumed that $\mathcal{E}$, $\mathcal{X}$ and $\mathcal{N}$ are subsets of $\mathbb{V}$ and $\mathcal{E} \neq \varnothing \neq \mathcal{X} \cup \mathcal{N}$.

2. *t is connected to the control-flow places as shown in figure 1(b), where:*
   - *For each $e \in \mathcal{E}$, there exists exactly one control-flow place s such that $\ell(s,t) \cap \mathbb{T}_e \neq \varnothing$. Moreover, $|\ell(s,t) \cap \mathbb{T}_e| = 1$.*
   - *For each $x \in \mathcal{X}$, there exists exactly one control-flow place s such that $\ell(t,s) \cap \mathbb{T}_x \neq \varnothing$. Moreover, $|\ell(t,s) \cap \mathbb{T}_x| = 1$.*
   - *For each $n \in \mathcal{N}$, there exists exactly one control-flow place s such that $\ell(t,s) \cap \mathbb{T}_n \neq \varnothing$. Moreover, $|\ell(t,s) \cap \mathbb{T}_n| = 1$.*

3. *t is connected to the generator place s_{gen} as shown in figure 1(a), where:*
   - *For each $f \in \mathcal{E} \setminus \mathcal{X}$, $\ell(s_{gen},t) \cap \mathbb{T}_f = \{\langle f, g^{in_f} \rangle\}$ where $g^{in_f} \in \mathbb{V}$.*
   - *For each $n \in \mathcal{N}$, $\ell(t, s_{gen}) \cap \mathbb{T}_n = \{\langle n, 0 \rangle\}$.*

   – *For each $e \in \mathcal{E}$ with $k_e > 0$, $\ell(s_{gen}, t) \cap \mathbb{T}_e = \{\langle e, g^{in_e}\rangle\}$ and $\ell(t, s_{gen}) \cap$
   $\mathbb{T}_e = \{\langle e, g^{out_e}\rangle\}$ where $g^{in_e}, g^{out_e} \in \mathbb{V}$.*
   – *For each $e \in \mathcal{E}$ with $k_e = 0$, $\ell(s_{gen}, t) \cap \mathbb{T}_e = \ell(t, s_{gen}) \cap \mathbb{T}_e = \varnothing$.*

4. *There is no restriction on how t is connected to the data places. As illustrated in figure 1(c), each put operation corresponds to a tuple in the label of an arc from t to a data place while each get operation corresponds to a tuple in the label of an arc from a data place to t.*

5. *The variables occurring in the annotations of the arcs adjacent to t can be partitioned into pid variables and data variables, as follows: for each place $s \in S$ which has the type $\mathbb{P} \times \mathbb{P}^{k_s} \times D_1 \times \cdots \times D_{m_s}$, for each tuple $\langle x_0, x_1, \ldots, x_{k_s}, y_1, \ldots, y_{m_s}\rangle \in \ell(s, t) \cup \ell(t, s)$, the x_i's are pid variables and the y_j's are data variables. In other words, locally to each transition, a variable cannot be used simultaneously for pids and data.*

6. *The guard of t is a conjunction of the formulas corresponding to:*
   – *The creation of the new pids:* $\displaystyle\bigwedge_{e \in \mathcal{E}, 1 \le j_e \le k_e} n^e_{j_e} = e.(g^{in_e} + j_e).$
   – *The updating of counters of spawned threads:* $\displaystyle\bigwedge_{e \in \mathcal{E}} g^{out_e} = g^{in_e} + k_e.$
   – *A Boolean formula expressing a particular firing condition and data manipulation, where only the operations from Ω_{pid} are allowed on pid variables.*$\Diamond$

Finally, any N obeying the above assumptions is a *thread Petri net* (or *t-net*).

4   Properties of Reachable Markings

We want to capture some useful properties of t-net behaviours. First, we introduce control safeness and consistent thread configurations which will be used to characterise pids occurring in reachable t-net markings.

Definition 3 (control safe markings). *A t-net marking M is control safe if, for each pid $\pi \in \mathbb{P}$, one of the following holds:*

   – *There is exactly one token owned by π in the generator place and exactly one token owned by π in exactly one of the control-flow places (note that this unique place may contain tokens not owned by π).*
   – *Tokens owned by π (if any) appear only in the data places.* $\Diamond$

Control safeness ensures that each thread is sequential, and that there is no duplication of control-flow tokens.

Definition 4 (ct-configuration). *A consistent thread configuration (or ct-configuration) is a pair $ctc \stackrel{\mathrm{df}}{=} (G, H)$, where $G \subset \mathbb{P} \times \mathbb{N}$ and $H \subset \mathbb{P}$ are finite sets. Assuming that $pid_G \stackrel{\mathrm{df}}{=} \{\pi \mid \langle \pi, i\rangle \in G\}$ and $pid_{ctc} \stackrel{\mathrm{df}}{=} pid_G \cup H$, the following are satisfied, for all $\langle \pi, i\rangle \in G$ and $\pi' \in pid_{ctc}$:*

1. *$\langle \pi, j\rangle \notin G$, for every $j \neq i$.*
2. *If $\pi \lessdot \pi'$ then there is $j \le i$ such that $\pi.j = \pi'$ or $\pi.j \lessdot \pi'$.*

We also denote $nextpid_{ctc} \stackrel{\mathrm{df}}{=} \{\pi.(i+1) \mid \langle \pi, i \rangle \in G\}$. $\diamond$

Intuitively, G represents tokens held in the generator place, pid_G comprises pids of active threads, and H keeps record of all the pids that might occur in the data tokens of some reachable t-net marking.

Definition 5 (ctc of a marking). *Given a reachable t-net marking M, we define* $ctc(M) \stackrel{\mathrm{df}}{=} (M(s_{gen}), H)$, *where H is the set of all the pids occurring in the tokens held in the data and control-flow places at M.* $\diamond$

We can now characterise reachable markings of t-nets.

Theorem 1. *Let M be a reachable t-net marking.*

1. *M is control safe.*
2. *$ctc(M)$ is a ct-configuration.* $\diamond$

Knowing that all reachable t-net markings are control safe will allow us to identify those which admit essentially the same future behaviour. We start with an auxiliary definition at the level of ct-configurations (see [15] for its soundness).

Definition 6 (isomorphic ct-configurations). *Two ct-configurations, $ctc = (G, H)$ and $ctc' = (G', H')$, are h-isomorphic, denoted by $ctc \sim_h ctc'$, if there is a bijection $h : (pid_{ctc} \cup nextpid_{ctc}) \rightarrow (pid_{ctc'} \cup nextpid_{ctc'})$ such that:*

1. *$h(pid_G) = pid_{G'}$.*
2. *For all $\langle \pi, i \rangle \in G$ and $\langle h(\pi), j \rangle \in G'$, $h(\pi.(i+1)) = h(\pi).(j+1)$.*
3. *For $\prec$ in $\{\lhd_1, \lhd\}$ and $\pi, \pi' \in pid_{ctc}$: $\pi \prec \pi'$ iff $h(\pi) \prec h(\pi')$.*
4. *For $\curlywedge$ in $\{\pitchfork_1, \pitchfork\}$ and $\pi, \pi' \in pid_{ctc} \cup nextpid_{ctc}$: $\pi \curlywedge \pi'$ iff $h(\pi) \curlywedge h(\pi')$.* $\diamond$

We now can introduce the central notion of this paper.

Definition 7 (marking equivalence). *Let M and M' be reachable markings of a t-net such that $ctc(M) \sim_h ctc(M')$. Then M and M' are h-isomorphic if:*

- *For each control-flow or data place s, $M'(s)$ can be obtained from $M(s)$ by replacing each pid π occurring in the tuples of $M(s)$ by $h(\pi)$.*
- *$h(\{\pi \mid \langle \pi, i \rangle \in M(s_{gen})\}) = \{\pi' \mid \langle \pi', i \rangle \in M'(s_{gen})\}$.*

We denote this by $M \sim_h M'$ or simply by $M \sim M'$. $\diamond$

The equivalence $M \sim_h M'$ means that pids are related through h, and data in tokens in control-flow and data places remain unchanged. As far as the generator tokens are concerned, the only requirement is that they involve h-corresponding pids.

As shown in [15], $\sim$ is an equivalence relation. It follows from the next result that it captures a truly strong notion of marking similarity.

Theorem 2. *Let M and M' be h-isomorphic reachable markings of a t-net, and t be a transition such that $M[t, \sigma\rangle \widetilde{M}$. Then $M'[t, h \circ \sigma\rangle \widetilde{M'}$, where $\widetilde{M'}$ is a marking such that $\widetilde{M} \sim_{\widetilde{h}} \widetilde{M'}$ for a bijection $\widetilde{h}$ coinciding with h on the intersection of their domains.* $\diamond$

Moreover, the above result still holds if Ω_{pid} is restricted to any of its subsets that includes pid equality.

5   Checking Marking Equivalence

We check marking equivalence in two steps. First, markings are mapped to three-layered labelled directed graphs, and then the graphs are checked for isomorphism.

The three-layered graphs are constructed as follows. Layer-I nodes are labelled by places, layer-II by (abstracted) tokens and layer-III by (abstracted) pids. The arcs are of two kinds: those going from the container object toward the contained object (places contain tokens which in turn contain pids), and those between the vertices of layer-III reflecting the relationship between the corresponding pids through the comparisons in Ω_{pid} other than equality, denoted below as $\lhd_j$ (see figure 4).

Definition 8 (graph representation of markings). *Let M be a reachable marking of a t-net N. The corresponding graph representation*

$$R(M) \stackrel{\mathrm{df}}{=} (V; A, A_{\lhd_1}, \dots, A_{\lhd_\ell}; \lambda) \, ,$$

where V is the set of vertices, A, $A_{\lhd_1}$, ..., $A_{\lhd_\ell}$ are sets of arcs and λ is a labelling of vertices and arcs, is defined as follows:

1. *Layer-I: for each control-flow or data place s in N such that $M(s) \neq \varnothing$, s is a vertex in V labelled by s.*
2. *Layer-II: for each control-flow or data place s, and for each token $v \in M(s)$, v is a vertex in V labelled by $\lfloor v \rfloor$ (which is v with all pids replaced by epsilon's) and there is an unlabelled arc $s \longrightarrow v$ in A.*
   Note: separate copies of node v are created for different occurrences of v in case $M(s)(v) > 1$.
3. *Layer-III:*
   - *for each vertex v added at layer-II, for each pid π in v at the position n (in the tuple), π is an ε-labelled vertex in V and $v \xrightarrow{n} \pi$ an arc in A.*
   - *for each token $\langle \pi, i \rangle \in M(s_{gen})$, $\pi.(i+1)$ (that is, the potential next child of π) is a vertex in V labelled by ε.*
   - *for all vertices π, π' added at layer-III, for all $1 \leq j \leq \ell$, there is an arc $\pi \xrightarrow{\lhd_j} \pi'$ in $A_{\lhd_j}$ iff $\pi \lhd_j \pi'$ (that is, $A_{\lhd_j}$ defines the graph of the relation $\lhd_j$ on $V \cap \mathbb{P}$).*
4. *There is no other vertex nor arc in $R(M)$.*   ◇

To gain efficiency, $R(M)$ may be optimised by removing some vertices and arcs, e.g., each subgraph $\langle \pi \rangle \xrightarrow{0} \pi$ can be replaced by π.

Theorem 3. *Let M_1 and M_2 be two reachable markings of a t-net. $R(M_1)$ and $R(M_2)$ are isomorphic iff $M_1 \sim M_2$.*   ◇

5.1   Example

In order to illustrate the proposed approach, we consider a simple server system with a bunch of threads waiting for connections from clients (not modelled).

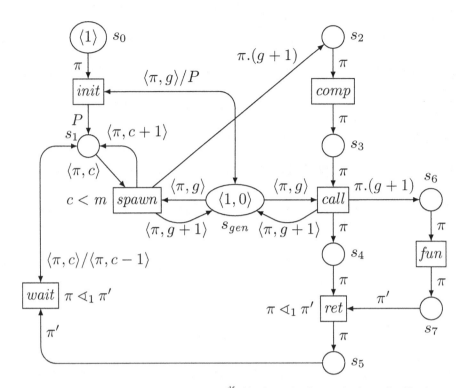

Fig. 2. The example Petri net, where $P \stackrel{\text{df}}{=} \{\langle \pi.(g+1), 0\rangle, \dots, \langle \pi.(g+k), 0\rangle\}$. An arc with an arrow at both sides and labelled by a/b denotes that a is consumed and b is produced. All places but s_{gen} are control-flow ones. Places s_{gen} and s_1 have type $\mathbb{P} \times \mathbb{N}$ and all the other places have type $\mathbb{P}$. The angle brackets around singletons and true guards are omitted. Finally, we may write an expression E on an output arc as a shorthand for a fresh variable y instead of E, together with the condition $y = E$ in the guard of the adjacent transition.

Whenever a new connection is made, a handler is spawned to process it. The handler performs some unspecified computation and then calls an auxiliary function. Terminated handlers are awaited for by the thread that spawned them. The example illustrates two typical ways of calling a subprogram: either asynchronously by spawning a thread, or synchronously by calling a function. In our setting, both ways result in creating a new thread, the only difference is that a function call is modelled by spawning a thread and immediately waiting for it. In order to simplify the presentation, data is not being modelled, only the control-flow. Moreover, for this particular example, we can take Ω_{pid} without the relations $\lhd$ and $\pitchfork$.

The whole system is modelled by the Petri net depicted in figure 2. The main process corresponds to the transitions *init*, *spawn* and *wait*:

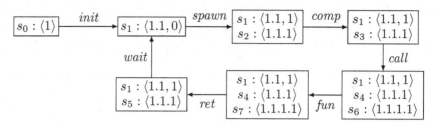

Fig. 3. The state graph of $N_{1,1}$ where the marking of s_{gen} has not been represented

- Upon firing *init*, the initial thread 1 terminates and creates k children that carry out the actual spawning/waiting for handler threads. The place s_1 holds pairs (pid, counter) in order to allow each thread to remember the number of handlers it has spawned.
- *spawn* creates one handler child and increments the counter. The maximum number of active children is bound by m due to the guard $c < m$.
- *wait* terminates one of the children (this is verified by the guard) and decrements the counter.

A handler process corresponds to the transitions *comp*, *call* and *ret*: *comp* models the computation performed by the handler; *call* creates one child in order to start an instance of the function; immediately after that *wait* awaits for its termination. The function itself is modelled by a single transition *fun*. The net is parameterised by two constants k and m, and so we denote it by $N_{k,m}$.

Bounding the Executions. Our approach allows to find a finite state space of the system by detecting loops in the behaviour, *i.e.*, parts of the execution that are repeated with new pids. This can be illustrated using $N_{1,1}$: its state space is infinite if we use the standard Petri net transition rule. But if we identify markings that are equivalent, it only has 7 states, as shown in figure 3.

The overall behaviour is clearly looping but, without using marking equivalence, there is no cycle in the state space. Indeed, the execution of *wait* produces the marking $\{s_1 : \langle 1.1, 0 \rangle; s_{gen} : \langle 1.1, 1 \rangle\}$ instead of $\langle 1.1, 0 \rangle$ in s_{gen} that was created by the firing of *init*. From here, a second execution of *spawn* would produce a new pid 1.1.2 instead of 1.1.1 that was used in the first loop. By incorporating the proposed marking equivalence, the exact values of pids are abstracted as well as the marking of the generator place, which allows to detect a state which is basically the same and thus to stop the computation.

Handling Symmetries. Another advantage of our approach can be illustrated using $N_{2,1}$: two main threads are started and each can have at most one active handler child. This system exhibits symmetric executions since the behaviour of both threads is concurrent but is interleaved in the marking graph. For instance, the state space has a diamond when the two threads spawn concurrently one child each. The markings corresponding to the intermediate states of the diamond are

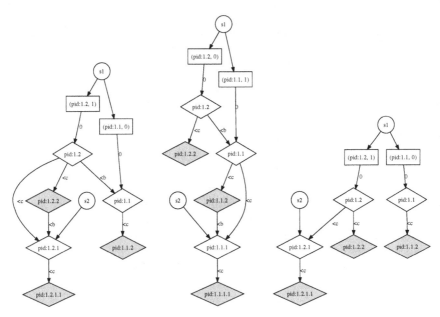

Fig. 4. Graph representations of states of $N_{2,1}$. On the right, the same states reduce to isomorphic ones when $\mathrel{\text{m}}_1$ is not taken into account (and so only one is depicted). The circle, square and diamond vertices depict respectively layer-I, layer-II and layer-III vertices. Gray vertices are those added on the basis of s_{gen}. $\lhd_1$ is depicted by **<c** and $\mathrel{\text{m}}_1$ by **<b**.

depicted in figure 4. Because the relation $\mathrel{\text{m}}_1$ has been taken into account, the two markings are clearly not equivalent. But, when this relation is not considered, the markings become equivalent, as shown on the right of figure 4. In the state spaces such diamonds are removed and only one interleaving preserved.

5.2 Experimental Results

We have implemented a prototype of the proposed method using SNAKES [20] and NetworkX [12], for the Petri net and graph part, respectively. The latter implements VF2 [7] that is considered to be one of the fastest algorithms for checking graph isomorphism. We have generated several state spaces, using various values of k and m and considering various Ω_{pid}'s. The global execution times are not relevant since our implementation is not yet optimised. However, we measured the time spent on computing the graph isomorphism (this part is implemented efficiently) with respect to the size of the graphs representing t-net markings (measured as the product of the number a of arcs and the number v of vertices in the union of the graphs being compared). The result shows a progression that appears to be linear (see figure 6 in [15]). This suggests that the heuristics in VF2 are efficient for the kind of graphs involved in the checking of marking equivalence. Considering that $a \leq v^2$, the experimentally observed performance appears to be at worst v^3 or, equivalently, $a^{3/2}$.

6   Conclusions

Working within the context of coloured Petri nets, we proposed a technical device for coping with dynamic and concurrent creation of processes capable of manipulating data encountered, *e.g.*, in multi-threaded systems. The method introduced in this paper defines and efficiently exploits an equivalence relation on markings with essentially isomorphic future behaviours. It can be used, in particular, to aggregate nodes in a state graph. As demonstrated by the initial experiments, this may produce efficiently a finite representation of an infinite state systems that is reduced with respect to symmetric executions.

Acknowledgements. We would like to thank Alexis Bes, Patrick Cegielski, Christian Laforest and Victor Khomenko for their comments on the earlier versions of this paper. This research was supported by NSFC Grant 60433010.

References

1. Ball, T., Chaki, S., Rajamani, S.K.: Parameterized Verification of Multithreaded Software Libraries. In: Margaria, T., Yi, W. (eds.) TACAS 2001. LNCS, vol. 2031, pp. 158–173. Springer, Heidelberg (2001)
2. Best, E., et al.: M-Nets: An Algebra of High-Level Petri Nets, with an Application to the Semantics of Concurrent Programming Languages. Acta Informatica 35, 813–857 (1998)
3. Bosnacki, D., Dams, D., Holenderski, L.: Symmetric Spin. International Journal on Software Tools for Technology Transfer 4, 92–106 (2002)
4. Chiola, G., Dutheillet, C., Franceschinis, G., Haddad, S.: A Symbolic Reachability Graph for Coloured Petri Nets. Theoretical Computer Science 176, 39–65 (1997)
5. Clarke, E., Grumberg, O., Peled, D.: Model Checking. MIT Press, Cambridge (2000)
6. Corbett, J.C., et al.: Bandera: Extracting Finite-state Models from Java Source Code. In: Proc. ICSE 2000, pp. 439–448. ACM, New York (2000)
7. Cordella, L.P., Foggia, P., Sansone, C., Vento, M.: A (Sub)Graph Isomorphism Algorithm for Matching Large Graphs. IEEE Transactions on Pattern Analysis and Machine Intelligence 26, 1367–1372 (2004)
8. Cousot, P., Cousot, R.: Abstract Interpretation: A Unified Lattice Model for Static Analysis of Programs by Construction or Approximation of Fixpoints. In: Proc. POPL 1977, pp. 238–252. ACM, New York (1977)
9. Delzanno, G.: Constraint-based Automatic Verification of Abstract Models of Multithreaded Programs. Journal of Theory and Practice of Logic Programming 7 (2007)
10. Evangelista, S.: High Level Petri Nets Analysis with Helena. In: Ciardo, G., Darondeau, P. (eds.) ICATPN 2005. LNCS, vol. 3536, pp. 455–464. Springer, Heidelberg (2005)
11. Flanagan, C., Freund, S.N., Qadeer, S., Seshia, S.A.: Modular Verification of Multithreaded Programs. Theoretical Computer Science 338, 153–183 (2005)
12. Hagberg, A., Schult, D., Swart, P.: NetworkX, High Productivity Software for Complex Networks, http://networkx.lanl.gov

13. Hendriks, M., et al.: Adding Symmetry Reduction to Uppaal. In: Larsen, K.G., Niebert, P. (eds.) FORMATS 2003. LNCS, vol. 2791, pp. 46–59. Springer, Heidelberg (2004)
14. Khomenko, V.: Model Checking Based on Prefixes of Petri Net Unfoldings. PhD Thesis, School of Computing Science, University of Newcastle (2003)
15. Klaudel, H., Koutny, M., Pelz, E., Pommereau, F.: Towards Efficient Verification of Systems with Dynamic Process Creation. LACL Technical Report (2008), http://lacl.univ-paris12.fr
16. Manna, Z., Pnueli, A.: The Temporal Logic of Reactive and Concurrent Systems Specification. Springer, Heidelberg (1991)
17. McMillan, K.: Symbolic Model Checking. Kluwer Academic Publishers, Dordrecht (1993)
18. Miller, A., Donaldson, A., Calder, M.: Symmetry in Temporal Logic Model Checking. ACM Comput. Surv. 38 (2006)
19. Pommereau, F.: Versatile Boxes, a Multi-Purpose Algebra of High-Level Petri Nets. In: DADS/SCSC 2007, SCS/ACM (2007)
20. Pommereau, F.: Quickly Prototyping Petri Net Tools with Snakes. In: Proc. PN-TAP 2008, ACM Digital Library (2008)
21. Rabin, M.O.: Decidability of Second-order Theories and Automata on Infinite Trees. Transactions of the American Mathematical Society 141 (1969)
22. Rosa-Velardo, F., de Frutos-Escrig, D.: Name Creation vs. Replication in Petri Net Systems. In: Kleijn, J., Yakovlev, A. (eds.) ICATPN 2007. LNCS, vol. 4546, pp. 402–422. Springer, Heidelberg (2007)
23. Stärk, R.F.: Formal Specification and Verification of the C# Thread Model. Theoretical Computer Science 343, 482–508 (2005)
24. Stoller, S.D.: Model-Checking Multi-threaded Distributed Java Programs. In: Havelund, K., Penix, J., Visser, W. (eds.) SPIN 2000. LNCS, vol. 1885, pp. 224–244. Springer, Heidelberg (2000)
25. Thierry-Mieg, Y., Dutheillet, C., Mounier, I.: Automatic Symmetry Detection in Well-Formed Nets. In: van der Aalst, W.M.P., Best, E. (eds.) ICATPN 2003. LNCS, vol. 2679, pp. 82–101. Springer, Heidelberg (2003)

An Observational Model for Transactional Calculus of Services Orchestration*

Jing Li, Huibiao Zhu, and Jifeng He

Software Engineering Institute
East China Normal University
Shanghai, China, 200062
{jli, hbzhu, jifeng}@sei.ecnu.edu.cn

Abstract. The notion of web services orchestration provides a mean to specify a process model governing business rules to provide a value-added service. The task of building orchestrations requires mechanisms to deal with business transactions so as to truly increase the consistency and reliability of services. Business transactions have distinguishable features from traditional transactions, such as autonomous and interactive, so that it is highly suggested to be constructed by compensable transactions. In this paper, we formally address the problem for orchestrating services, with particular attention to the transaction issue. We enhance our past work t-calculus by expanding the descriptions of basic actions which include data computations and communications. On the other hand, the enriched calculus is equipped with an observational semantics which is more suitable to characterize transactions with several behavioral aspects. Under this model, we are able to investigate the equivalence relation for justifying algebraic laws, as well as refinement relation for supporting stepwise service development.

1 Introduction

The notion of web services orchestration has been proposed to deal with web services composition so as to provide a value-added service composed by several existing services. Correspondingly, industrial consortia have developed several proposals for describing orchestration in the recent years, such as BPML, WSFL, XLANG and BPEL. The orchestration provides a mean to specify a process model governing business rules for gluing service operations together. These operations include both internal computations and externally visible interactions. Specifically, web services orchestration targets a variety of aspects, including interaction patterns, flow coordination, timing issues, session management and so on. In particular, specifying transactions is important as well so as to truly increase the reliability of business processes for composite services.

---
* Supported by National Basic Research Program of China (No.2005CB321904), National High Technology Research and Development Program of China (No.2007AA010302), National Natural Science Foundation of China (No.90718004) and Shanghai STCSM Project (No.067062017).

J.S. Fitzgerald, A.E. Haxthausen, and H. Yenigun (Eds.): ICTAC 2008, LNCS 5160, pp. 201–215, 2008.

Transaction processing techniques play a major role in preserving consistency in many types of applications. Likewise, web services orchestration requires to coordinate loosely coupled services into a unit of work performed as a business transaction to ensure a correct composition and a reliable execution. In the environment of web services, business transactions are accompanied by several distinct features. At first, they usually have long running duration which may cause severe performance problems. Secondly, services involved in a business transaction possibly belong to different and even competing companies, where security and inventory control policies prevent intentional locking of local resources. Lastly, communications between different services disable the outcome of interactions to be physically undone, where the pure rollback mechanism is not applicable at all. Therefore, the conventional automatic techniques to guarantee atomicity become infeasible for business transactions.

In this context, business transactions relax the degree of atomicity relying on the concept of compensation introduced by Sagas [7]. A compensation is a part of business logic so as to recover from failure in a semantic manner. In our former work, we proposed a transactional language t-calculus which provided a variety of ways to set up business transactions in terms of compensable transactions so as to enhance its flexibility and reliability. In fact, this calculus simply specifies transaction flow in a high level of granularity abstracting away from data states and service interactions, which hinders it from describing real case studies regarding service orchestration. From the semantic view, the algebraic and operational semantics for t-calculus have been studied [11,12]. However, these semantic models are good for optimization and simulation but not well suitable for verifying properties and bridging specifications and implementations.

In this paper, we propose a new transactional language TCOS which is an extension of t-calculus by expanding the descriptions of basic actions which include data computations and communications. Correspondingly, traditional constructs depending on data state like conditional choice and condition based iteration are actually included. In order to truly describe service behavior, we cannot just focus on high level transactions, we should also record data state and communication traces. For this purpose, an observational semantics is established which has its root to the seminal work of UTP [9]. Based on this model, the equivalence relation between compensable transactions is investigated formally. Thus all the algebraic laws derived before can be justified by strict proof in the case of involving low level details. Moreover, the refinement relation between compensable transactions is similarly explored, which is useful for reasoning properties and supporting stepwise service design.

This paper is organized as follows. The next section presents the syntax of TCOS and informally expresses the meaning for each construct. Section 3 introduces the semantic model with its ingredients and configurations to provide a complete semantic view. Further, the equivalence and refinement relations for compensable transactions are well defined. Afterwards, the observational semantics for this calculus is explored in Section 4, where each transactional construct is explained formally. Section 5 presents a set of algebraic laws with simple illustration on how to set up proof in this model. The last section draws conclusion with some points touching upon comparisons with some related work.

2 TCOS

We first introduce TCOS (Transactional Calculus for Orchestrating Services) which is an extension of t-calculus. The main syntactic categories are basic actions and compensable transactions. Its syntax is summarized below.

$$A, B ::= x := e \mid rec\ a\ x \mid sed\ a\ x \mid 0 \mid \Diamond$$
$$BT ::= A \div B \mid Skip \mid Abort \mid Fail$$
$$S, T ::= BT \mid b?S{:}T \mid S \sqcap T \mid b * T \mid S; T \mid S \| T \mid$$
$$S \otimes T \mid S \rightsquigarrow T \mid S \trianglerighteq T \mid S \triangleright T \mid S * T$$
$$TT ::= \{T\}$$

Basic actions in t-calculus are simply denoted by symbols which lack expressiveness of describing low level details. Here, basic actions are expanded in detail dealing with both internal computations and external communications. $x := e$ is an assignment which first evaluates the expression e and then sets the value to variable x. However, when the expression is unsuccessfully evaluated, the operation of assignment is aborted and its context is informed of this error. Services need to exchange messages with its partners so as to collaborate together for fulfilling a certain task. $rec\ a\ x$ denotes a message receipt through the channel a, where x here is a container to store the transmitted value. Contrarily, a sending message is represented by $sed\ a\ x$ which forwards the value of x via the channel a. However, network is an unstable environment under which the message may fail to transport, thus communicating operations cannot always succeed. Overall, basic actions are treated as *atomic transactions* which either succeed or abort during a short period. In particular, the two actions 0 and $\Diamond$ denote an always committed transaction and an aborted transaction respectively.

Compensable transactions are main blocks to build business transactions. A compensable transaction is different from traditional transactions. Its effect can be semantically removed even after it has committed. Basically, a compensable transaction is composed of two parts. One part is the forward behavior denoting the normal business logic required by applications. Another part is referred as the compensation behavior devised to reverse the effect of its associated forward behavior. The compensation behavior can only be activated on the successful completion of its forward behavior. Whenever some failure arises during normal flow, the compensation is enabled immediately to recover from this failure. The transactional pair $A \div B$ is the primary construct used to constitute a simple compensable transaction whose both parts are basic actions, where A denotes the forward behavior and B stands for its compensation behavior. In case of failure, completely successful compensation renders the whole transaction aborted since all the partial effects have been semantically undone. However, the compensation behavior may fail halfway so that some partial effects still exist, thus leading to an inconsistent state. We mark the inconsistent state produced by partial compensation as fail. Thus, compensable transactions have three distinct final states: committed, aborted and failed. There are three more variations ($Skip$, $Abort$ and $Fail$) corresponding to the three states separately.

Compensable transactions encourage composition so that a composite trans-action is still a compensable one on the basis of smaller ones. First of all, standard composition manners are supported, such as conditional choice $b?S:T$, nonde-terministic choice $S \sqcap T$, iteration $b * T$, sequential and parallel compositions. Particularly, the meaning for sequential and parallel compositions has been ex-tended to orchestrate compensations. For sequential composition $S; T$, the com-pensations of both branches are organized in a reverse order as opposed to their forward behavior. In case of failure, this arrangement for compensation helps to guarantee that the last exposed effect is first removed and the first exposed effect is last undone, similarly to operating stacks. As for parallel composition $S \parallel T$, both forward and compensation behavior are arranged in parallel. It is worth noting that, if one branch in parallel composition fails to complete, the other branch would not commit but terminates early by enabling its installed compen-sation immediately. This can be warranted by the underlying mechanisms. One mechanism is called *forced termination* which has been adopted by BPEL.

Apart from standard compositions, five more transaction featured operators have been investigated for building a whole business transaction (denoted as $\{T\}$) with a higher quality. First of all, flexibility is enforced by allowing users to provide functionally equivalent sub-transactions for a given objective. These equivalent transactions may have different or even priorities. Transactions with even priorities are arranged to run in parallel, denoted as $S \otimes T$. Otherwise, the transaction with higher priority is executed first and the one with lower priority is activated when the higher one is aborted, denoted as $S \rightsquigarrow T$. Secondly, reliability is enhanced by properly dealing with partial compensations. We have mentioned that half compensation flow will cause inconsistency for some partial effects have been not canceled yet. In order to keep consistency, the mechanism of *exception handling* ($S \unrhd T$ and $S \rhd T$) is introduced to offer further remedy. At last, specialization is added by offering specialized compensations for specific applications ($S * T$). Initially, the compensation of a composite transaction is constructed by the accumulation of those of its sub-transactions. Concerning the requirement of a concrete application, it is more satisfactory for developers to directly define an appropriate compensation according to specific business logic.

3   Semantic Model

This section presents the observational semantic model for TCOS. This model carefully selects several pairs of non-programmable variables to represent differ-ent behavioral aspects. Each pair of variables hold the initial and later values during the execution of a transactional service. This semantic model explores the relation between each pair of variables so as to reflect behavioral transformation.

First of all, the data state should be recorded in order to display the actual business information. Let Var be the set of data variables ranged over by x, y. Each data variable x has a counterpart x', where x and x' stand for the initial and final values for the same data item respectively. Data state is also important to control business flow. It decides branch selection with a condition and multiple execution within an iteration. Except for data variables, the trace variable is needed to register what happened between collaborating services. In other words, the sequence of communicating events is required to record for interactive systems. Hence, a pair of trace variables tr and tr' have been introduced. tr denotes the initial trace before a transaction starts, while tr' represents the final trace after the transaction ends. The element in a trace has the form of $a.v$ denoting that a value v is transmitted through the channel a.

In order to represent the execution state of a transaction, we use the pair of state variables st, st' to stand for its initial and final execution states. As mentioned before, when a compensable transaction finishes, it ends with one of three different states: committed, aborted and failed. $st' = cmt$ states that the current transaction has achieved its business target. $st' = abt$ says that the current transaction has encountered a failure but its compensation successfully undoes all the partial effects. $st' = fal$ tells that the compensation for the current transaction has been activated but it is unable to complete its compensation work by leaving some partial effects behind. Contrarily, different values of st denote distinct execution states of the previous transaction. Basic actions are treated as atomic transactions with two execution states: committed and aborted. Here, abortion for atomic transactions means nothing has really happened.

A transaction may perform infinite computations or interactions, thus making it divergent. To distinguish this chaotic behavior from terminated ones, we introduce boolean variables ok, ok' into the semantic model. $ok = false$ indicates the anterior transaction is divergent, thus it definitely disables the current transaction to start. While $ok' = true$ states the current transaction has terminated with either committed, aborted or failed outcome.

For compensable transactions, the compensation is useless when its related forward behavior does not commit. For some constructs, success of either branch leads to achievement of its objective. In this context, we need a manner to judge which branch is finally successful, thus the compensation for which can be determined to reserve. For this purpose, we introduce a pair of variables $trans$ and $trans'$ to separately record the initial and final set of completed transaction names. Given a transaction T, the function $\mathcal{N}(T)$ returns a unique name for this transaction. For instance, two transactions with same syntax but different locations should be assigned different names. Not all successful transaction names need to be recorded in this transaction list. Only those causing nondeterminacy for choosing compensation should be managed in this way. Whenever such type of transaction T succeeds, its name is put into the completed transaction list by doing this: $trans' = trans \cup \{\mathcal{N}(T)\}$. Different from other variables, this variable dose not represent a kind of behavior, thus this variable should be hidden when comparing transactions behavior.

In what follows, the observational semantics of atomic transactions is expressed in the following form:

$$true \vdash P, Q$$

The semantic configuration of compensable transactions is explicitly composed of two parts expressed as follows. The upper part $F \vdash P, Q, R$ denotes the forward behavior, denoted as $Fbeh(T)$. Whereas the lower part $F' \vdash P', Q', R'$ stands for the compensation behavior, denoted as $Cbeh(T)$.

$$\begin{pmatrix} F \vdash P, Q, R \\ F' \vdash P', Q', R' \end{pmatrix}$$

where

$$F \vdash P, Q \triangleq F \vdash (P \wedge st' = cmt) \vee (Q \wedge st' = abt)$$
$$F \vdash P, Q, R \triangleq F \vdash (P \wedge st' = cmt) \vee (Q \wedge st' = abt) \vee (R \wedge st' = fal)$$
$$F \vdash E \triangleq (F \wedge ok \Rightarrow E \wedge ok') \wedge Inv(tr, trans)$$
$$Inv(tr, trans) \triangleq tr \preceq tr' \wedge trans \subseteq trans'$$

Above, F is a predicate which only refers to initial values of variables. If F is not satisfied, the transaction may turn into divergence. P, Q, R do not mention any variable in $\{ok, ok', st', st\}$. They stand for committed behavior, aborted behavior, and failed behavior respectively. Besides, by attaching such an invariance $Inv(tr, trans)$, the transactional behavior guarantees that the final trace tr' cannot be shorten and the final value of $trans'$ can only be expanded. Here $tr \preceq tr'$ indicates that tr is a prefix of tr'.

At last, we define the equivalence and refinement relations for two arbitrary compensable transactions. Firstly, we define some new predicates:

$$\overline{P} \triangleq \exists_{trans, trans'} \bullet \qquad\qquad P{\downarrow} \triangleq P; (true \vdash true)$$
$$[P] \triangleq \forall_{x, y, \ldots} \bullet P \qquad\qquad P; Q \triangleq \exists_m \bullet (P[m/v'] \wedge Q[m/v])$$

The predicate $\overline{P}$ is used for hiding the pair of variables $trans, trans'$. $P{\downarrow}$ allows to change data variables to any values, but the invariance $Inv(tr, trans)$ still holds. While $[P]$ denotes universal quantification over all the variables in P. At last, $P; Q$ indicates that the final values of variables in P are passed to Q as the initial values of the corresponding variables. Thus, this predicate is used to model sequential composition. Besides, we stipulate that this boolean operator ; has a lower priority than other boolean operators, such as $\wedge, \vee, \Rightarrow$.

Definition 3.1 (Equivalence). *Two arbitrary transactions S, T are said to be equivalent (written as $S = T$) if and only if the following formula is satisfied.*

$$[\overline{Fbeh(S)} = \overline{Fbeh(T)}] \wedge [\overline{(true \vdash P_1){\downarrow}; Cbeh(S)} = \overline{(true \vdash P_2){\downarrow}; Cbeh(T)}]$$

where $Fbeh(S) = F_1 \vdash P_1, Q_1, R_1$, $Fbeh(T) = F_2 \vdash P_2, Q_2, R_2$

Two equivalent compensable transactions not only have equal forward behavior but also have equal compensation behavior. Specially, compensation is only activated after its forward behavior commits. However, the values of variables in its forward behavior may be changed by following programs before the control is passed to the compensation. Here, the predicate $(true \vdash P_1){\downarrow}; Cbeh(S)$

clearly manifests the execution dependence between forward behavior and its compensation. In addition, the pair of variables $trans, trans'$ has been hidden since this kind of variable does not represent any kind of behavior. Similarly, the refinement relation is defined below.

Definition 3.2 (Refinement). *S is said to be a refinement of T (written as $S \sqsupseteq T$) if and only if the following formula is satisfied.*

$$[\overline{Fbeh(S)} \Rightarrow \overline{Fbeh(T)}] \ \wedge \ [\overline{(true \vdash P_1)\downarrow; Cbeh(S)} \Rightarrow \overline{(true \vdash P_2)\downarrow; Cbeh(T)}]$$

where $Fbeh(S) = F_1 \vdash P_1, Q_1, R_1, \ Fbeh(T) = F_2 \vdash P_2, Q_2, R_2$

The refinement relation given above is quite useful for supporting stepwise service development since it builds a link between specifications and implementations.

4 Observational Semantics for TCOS

There are two types of transactions, i.e., atomic transactions and compensable transactions. For any transaction T, we use $[\![T]\!]$ to represent its observational semantics. Firstly, we define the exact behavior for atomic ones.

4.1 Atomic Transactions

Assignment $x := e$ is the primary way for internal computation. If the expression e is well defined, the value of variable x is updated while other variables remain unaltered. Otherwise, this operation is aborted with all the variables unchanged. The boolean function $D(e)$ is used to judge whether an expression is well defined or not. It returns $true$ if e is well defined, otherwise $false$ is returned.

$$[\![x := e]\!] \triangleq true \vdash x' = e \wedge \mathit{\Pi}(\{x\}) \wedge D(e), \mathit{\Pi} \wedge \neg D(e)$$

where

$$Col \triangleq Var \cup \{tr, trans\} \quad \mathit{\Pi} \triangleq \forall_{z \in Col} \bullet z' = z \quad \mathit{\Pi}(E) \triangleq \forall_{z \in Col-E} \bullet z' = z$$

Communications with other services are expressed as simple sending and receiving actions. The send action $sed \ a \ x$ delivers the message stored in x to its partner, either to invoke a remote operation or to respond upon a former request. The receive action $rec \ a \ x$ gets a message from its partner and stores this message in the variable x. This type of action contributes to a recent interactive event. Besides, the receive action changes the data state. However, an unfavorable environment of network will disable communications between services. $G(net)$ is a predicate to show the capability of network for interactions.

$$[\![sed \ a \ x]\!] \triangleq true \vdash tr' = tr \cdot \langle a.x \rangle \wedge \mathit{\Pi}(\{tr\}) \wedge G(net), \mathit{\Pi} \wedge \neg G(net)$$
$$[\![rec \ a \ x]\!] \triangleq true \vdash \exists_v \bullet (x' = v \wedge tr' = tr \cdot \langle a.v \rangle) \wedge \mathit{\Pi}(\{tr, x\}) \wedge G(net), \mathit{\Pi} \wedge \neg G(net)$$

where $s \cdot t$ denotes the concatenation for two traces s, t.

Finally, the two special actions 0 and $\Diamond$ stand for the committed and aborted transactions respectively. Thus, the aborted behavior for 0 is always $false$, and the committed behavior for $\Diamond$ is $false$ too.

$$[\![0]\!] \triangleq true \vdash \mathit{\Pi}, false \qquad [\![\Diamond]\!] \triangleq true \vdash false, \mathit{\Pi}$$

4.2 Compensable Transactions

The transactional pair $A \div B$ is the simplest form of compensable transactions. It is composed of two atomic transactions, provided that:

$$\llbracket A \rrbracket = true \vdash P_1, Q_1 \qquad \llbracket B \rrbracket = true \vdash P_2, Q_2$$

Since atomic transactions never fail, the failed behavior for the transactional pair is equal to $false$.

$$\llbracket A \div B \rrbracket \triangleq \begin{pmatrix} true \vdash P_1, Q_1, false \\ true \vdash P_2, Q_2, false \end{pmatrix}$$

Similarly, it is easy to give the behavioral definition for $Skip$ whose behavior is equivalent to $0 \div 0$.

$$\llbracket Skip \rrbracket \triangleq \llbracket 0 \div 0 \rrbracket = \begin{pmatrix} true \vdash II, false, false \\ true \vdash II, false, false \end{pmatrix}$$

As for $Abort, Fail$, they lead to the aborted and failed state respectively without changing anything. Thus, the relevant part of behavior is denoted as II and the irrelevant part is $false$.

$$\llbracket Abort \rrbracket \triangleq \begin{pmatrix} true \vdash false, II, false \\ true \vdash II, II, II \end{pmatrix} \qquad \llbracket Fail \rrbracket \triangleq \begin{pmatrix} true \vdash false, false, II \\ true \vdash II, II, II \end{pmatrix}$$

In fact, the compensation parts for $Abort$ and $Fail$ can be arbitrarily chosen, since their forward behavior has no chance to commit and the compensation will be never activated.

In the following, we consider composition constructs for compensable transactions. Suppose that the behavior for sub-transactions are given below:

$$\llbracket S \rrbracket = \begin{pmatrix} F_1 \vdash P_1, Q_1, R_1 \\ F_1' \vdash P_1', Q_1', R_1' \end{pmatrix} \qquad \llbracket T \rrbracket = \begin{pmatrix} F_2 \vdash P_2, Q_2, R_2 \\ F_2' \vdash P_2', Q_2', R_2' \end{pmatrix}$$

There are two kinds of selective structures, conditional choice and nondeterministic choice. The conditional $b?S:T$ chooses S to start if b is satisfied. Otherwise, it executes T instead. In addition, only the compensation for the successful branch is reserved by checking the completed transaction list.

$\llbracket b?S:T \rrbracket$

$$\triangleq \begin{pmatrix} (Fbeh(S); (III \lhd st \neq cmt \rhd Add(S))) \lhd b \rhd (Fbeh(T); (III \lhd st \neq cmt \rhd Add(T))) \\ Cbeh(S) \lhd Ck(S) \rhd Cbeh(T) \end{pmatrix}$$

$$= \begin{pmatrix} F_1 \lhd b \rhd F_2 \vdash P_S \lhd b \rhd P_T, Q_1 \lhd b \rhd Q_2, R_1 \lhd b \rhd R_2 \\ F_1' \lhd Ck(S) \rhd F_2' \vdash P_1' \lhd Ck(S) \rhd P_2', Q_1' \lhd Ck(S) \rhd Q_2', R_1' \lhd Ck(S) \rhd R_2' \end{pmatrix}$$

where

$$III \triangleq true \vdash II \land st' = st$$
$$P_S \triangleq P_1; trans' = trans \cup \{\mathcal{N}(S)\} \land II(\{trans\})$$
$$P_T \triangleq P_2; trans' = trans \cup \{\mathcal{N}(T)\} \land II(\{trans\})$$
$$Ck(S) \triangleq \mathcal{N}(S) \in trans$$
$$Add(S) \triangleq true \vdash trans' = trans \cup \{\mathcal{N}(S)\} \land II(\{trans\}), false, false$$
$$P \lhd b \rhd Q \triangleq (P \land b) \lor (Q \land \neg b)$$

Analogously, the semantics for nondeterministic choice is defined below.

$\llbracket S \sqcap T \rrbracket$

$$\triangleq \begin{pmatrix} (Fbeh(S); (III \lhd st \neq cmt \rhd Add(S))) \vee (Fbeh(T); (III \lhd st \neq cmt \rhd Add(T))) \\ Cbeh(S) \lhd Ck(S) \rhd Cbeh(T) \end{pmatrix}$$

$$= \begin{pmatrix} F_1 \wedge F_2 \vdash P_S \vee P_T, Q_1 \vee Q_2, R_1 \vee R_2 \\ F_1' \lhd Ck(S) \rhd F_2' \vdash P_1' \lhd Ck(S) \rhd P_2', Q_1' \lhd Ck(S) \rhd Q_2', R_1' \lhd Ck(S) \rhd R_2' \end{pmatrix}$$

For sequential composition $S; T$, T is activated when S has succeeded. The compensations for both branches are arranged in a reverse order. If T is aborted, S will be compensated instantly. In this case, the whole composition is aborted when the compensation of S completes, otherwise failed.

$\llbracket S; T \rrbracket$

$$\triangleq \begin{pmatrix} Fbeh(S); (III \lhd st \neq cmt \rhd (Fbeh(T); (III \lhd st \neq abt \rhd (Cbeh(S); ChSt)))) \\ Cbeh(T); (III \lhd st \neq cmt \rhd Cbeh(S)) \end{pmatrix}$$

$$= \begin{pmatrix} DSeq \vdash P_1; P_2, Q_1 \vee (P_1; Q_2; P_1'), R_1 \vee (P_1; R_2) \vee (P_1; Q_2; (Q_1' \vee R_1')) \\ F_2' \wedge \neg(P_2'; \neg F_1') \vdash P_2'; P_1', Q_2' \vee (P_2'; Q_1'), R_2' \vee (P_2'; R_1') \end{pmatrix}$$

where

$$DSeq \triangleq F_1 \wedge \neg(P_1; \neg F_2) \wedge \neg(P_1; Q_2; \neg F_1')$$
$$ChSt \triangleq (true \vdash st' = abt \wedge II) \lhd st = cmt \rhd (true \vdash st' = fal \wedge II)$$

The iteration is a combination of sequential and conditional composition. The forward behavior and compensation behavior of iteration are defined as the weakest fixed point of specific functions.

$$\llbracket b * T \rrbracket \triangleq \begin{pmatrix} \mu Y \bullet \mathcal{F}(Y) \\ \mu Y \bullet \mathcal{G}(Y) \end{pmatrix}$$

where

$$\mathcal{F}(Fbeh(X)) \triangleq Fbeh(b?(T; X) : Skip)$$
$$\mathcal{G}(Cbeh(X)) \triangleq Cbeh(b?(T; X) : Skip)$$

Here $\mu Y \bullet \mathcal{F}(Y)$ stands for the weakest fixed point of $\mathcal{F}$ in the set of solutions of the equation $Y = \mathcal{F}(Y)$.

Parallel composition $S \parallel T$ starts both branches concurrently. Two branches may exchange message with each other through shared channels. However, S and T do not share any data variables over Var. Likewise, their compensations are installed concurrently for later use. Notice that if one branch aborts or fails, the other branch is willing to disrupt its flow and yield to this failure. Hence, two branches must both commit or both not.

$$\llbracket S \parallel T \rrbracket \triangleq \begin{pmatrix} Fbeh(S) \parallel Fbeh(T) \\ Cbeh(S) \parallel Cbeh(T) \end{pmatrix}$$

$$= \begin{pmatrix} F_1 \wedge F_2 \vdash P_1 \parallel_\epsilon P_2, Q_1 \parallel_\epsilon Q_2, (Q_1 \parallel_\epsilon R_2) \vee (R_1 \parallel_\epsilon Q_2) \vee (R_1 \parallel_\epsilon R_2) \\ F_1' \wedge F_2' \vdash P_1' \parallel_\epsilon P_2', Q_1' \parallel_\epsilon Q_2', (Q_1' \parallel_\epsilon R_2') \vee (R_1' \parallel_\epsilon Q_2') \vee (R_1' \parallel_\epsilon R_2') \end{pmatrix}$$

where

$$(F_1 \vdash E_1) \| (F_2 \vdash E_2) \triangleq F_1 \wedge F_2 \vdash E_1 \|_M E_2$$

$$P \|_M Q \triangleq \exists_{\substack{tr'_1, tr'_2, st'_1, st'_2, \\ trans'_1, trans'_2}} \bullet \left(\begin{array}{l} (P[tr'_1/tr', st'_1/st', trans'_1/trans'] \wedge \\ Q[tr'_2/tr', st'_2/st', trans'_2/trans'] \wedge \\ tr' - tr \in (tr'_1 - tr) \|_C (tr'_2 - tr) \wedge \\ \exists_{s,s_1,s_2} \bullet (s = s_1 \cup s_2 \wedge trans'_1 = trans \cup s_1 \wedge \\ \quad trans'_2 = trans \cup s_2 \wedge trans' = trans \cup s) \wedge \\ st'_1 = cmt \wedge st'_2 = cmt \Rightarrow st' = cmt \wedge \\ st'_1 = abt \wedge st'_2 = abt \Rightarrow st' = abt \wedge \\ st'_1 = abt \wedge st'_2 = fal \Rightarrow st' = fal \wedge \\ st'_1 = fal \wedge st'_2 = abt \Rightarrow st' = fal \wedge \\ st'_1 = fal \wedge st'_2 = fal \Rightarrow st' = fal); \\ (st_1 = cmt \wedge st_2 = cmt \vee \\ \quad\quad\quad\quad st_1 \neq cmt \wedge st_2 \neq cmt)_\top \end{array} \right)$$

$$P \|_\epsilon Q \triangleq \exists_{tr'_1, tr'_2, trans'_1, trans'_2} \bullet \left(\begin{array}{l} P[tr'_1/tr', trans'_1/trans'] \wedge \\ Q[tr'_2/tr', trans'_2/trans'] \wedge \\ tr' - tr \in (tr'_1 - tr) \|_C (tr'_2 - tr) \wedge \\ \exists_{s,s_1,s_2} \bullet (s = s_1 \cup s_2 \wedge trans'_1 = trans \cup s_1 \\ \wedge trans'_2 = trans \cup s_2 \wedge trans' = trans \cup s) \end{array} \right)$$

Above, $s - t$ denotes the last part of s by cutting down its prefix t. $s \|_C t$ represents the set of all traces which are mergence of s and t with synchronization on shared channels. Here, C is the set of shared channels through which parallel branches exchange messages.

One more important concept is referred as **assurance** ($b_\top$) whose definition is given below:

$$b_\top \triangleq (II \wedge st' = st) \lhd b \rhd false$$

Hence, $((st_1 = cmt \wedge st_2 = cmt) \vee (st_1 \neq cmt \wedge st_2 \neq cmt))_\top$ warrants that branches in the parallel composition both commit or both not.

Speculative choice $S \otimes T$ arranges two functionally equivalent branches to run in parallel. However, only one branch is finally selected to fulfill its objective. When one branch commits successfully, the other cannot commit but aborts either internally or forcibly. Especially, if either branch fails halfway, the other should yield to this failure. Hence, the whole composition cannot end in the case that one branch is committed and another is failed. In addition, only the compensation for the finally completed branch is installed.

$$[\![S \otimes T]\!]$$
$$\triangleq \left(\begin{array}{l} Fbeh(S);(III \lhd st \neq cmt \rhd Add(S)) \otimes Fbeh(T);(III \lhd st \neq cmt \rhd Add(T)) \\ Cbeh(S) \lhd Ck(S) \rhd Cbeh(T) \end{array} \right)$$
$$= \left(\begin{array}{l} F_1 \wedge F_2 \vdash (P_S \|_\epsilon Q_2) \vee (Q_1 \|_\epsilon P_T), Q_1 \|_\epsilon Q_2, (Q_1 \|_\epsilon R_2) \vee (R_1 \|_\epsilon Q_2) \vee (R_1 \|_\epsilon R_2) \\ F'_1 \lhd Ck(S) \rhd F'_2 \vdash P'_1 \lhd Ck(S) \rhd P'_2, Q'_1 \lhd Ck(S) \rhd Q'_2, R'_1 \lhd Ck(S) \rhd R'_2 \end{array} \right)$$

where

$$(F_1 \vdash E_1) \otimes (F_2 \vdash E_2) \triangleq F_1 \wedge F_2 \vdash E_1 \otimes_M E_2$$

$$P \otimes_M Q \triangleq \exists_{\substack{tr_1', tr_2', st_1', st_2', \\ trans_1', trans_2'}} \bullet \begin{pmatrix} (P[tr_1'/tr', st_1'/st', trans_1'/trans'] \wedge \\ Q[tr_2'/tr', st_2'/st', trans_2'/trans'] \wedge \\ tr' - tr \in (tr_1' - tr) \|_C (tr_2' - tr) \wedge \\ \exists_{s,s_1,s_2} \bullet (s = s_1 \cup s_2 \wedge trans_1' = trans \cup s_1 \wedge \\ \quad trans_2' = trans \cup s_2 \wedge trans' = trans \cup s) \wedge \\ st_1' = cmt \wedge st_2' = abt \Rightarrow st' = cmt \wedge \\ st_1' = abt \wedge st_2' = cmt \Rightarrow st' = cmt \wedge \\ st_1' = abt \wedge st_2' = abt \Rightarrow st' = abt \wedge \\ st_1' = abt \wedge st_2' = fal \Rightarrow st' = fal \wedge \\ st_1' = fal \wedge st_2' = abt \Rightarrow st' = fal \wedge \\ st_1' = fal \wedge st_2' = fal \Rightarrow st' = fal); \\ (\neg(st_1 = cmt \wedge st_2 = cmt \vee \\ st_1 = cmt \wedge st_2 = fal \vee st_1 = fal \wedge st_2 = cmt))_\top \end{pmatrix}$$

Note that speculative choice is such a construct that behaves partially like parallel composition by allowing concurrent executions and partially like internal choice by choosing one branch to achieve the objective.

Alternative forwarding $S \rightsquigarrow T$ provides a forward recovery technique to recover from failure. The higher priority branch S is executed first and its backup T is activated when S aborts. The objective is realized when either branch is successful at last.

$$\llbracket S \rightsquigarrow T \rrbracket$$
$$\triangleq \begin{pmatrix} Fbeh(S);(III \triangleleft st \neq cmt \triangleright Add(S));(III \triangleleft st \neq abt \triangleright (Fbeh(T);(III \triangleleft st \neq cmt \triangleright Add(T)))) \\ Cbeh(S) \triangleleft Ck(S) \triangleright Cbeh(T) \end{pmatrix}$$
$$= \begin{pmatrix} F_1 \wedge \neg(Q_1; \neg F_2) \vdash P_S \vee (Q_1; P_T), Q_1; Q_2, R_1 \vee (Q_1; R_2) \\ F_1' \triangleleft Ck(S) \triangleright F_2' \vdash P_1' \triangleleft Ck(S) \triangleright P_2', Q_1' \triangleleft Ck(S) \triangleright Q_2', R_1' \triangleleft Ck(S) \triangleright R_2' \end{pmatrix}$$

Backward handling $S \trianglerighteq T$ is a construct that provides a backward handler T to remedy the failure thrown by S. The handler tries to undo all the remaining effects which are not covered by partial compensation of S. T is triggered on the failure of S, and the whole composition is treated as aborted when T is successful. Whether T is aborted or failed, the whole transaction is failed. In addition, the compensation for S will be remembered since only the success of S can lead to the success of the overall transaction.

$$\llbracket S \trianglerighteq T \rrbracket \triangleq \begin{pmatrix} Fbeh(S); (III \triangleleft st \neq fal \triangleright (Fbeh(T); ChSt)) \\ Cbeh(S) \end{pmatrix}$$
$$= \begin{pmatrix} F_1 \wedge \neg(R_1; \neg F_2) \vdash P_1, Q_1 \vee (R_1; P_2), R_1; (Q_2 \vee R_2) \\ F_1' \vdash P_1', Q_1', R_1' \end{pmatrix}$$

Forward handling $S \triangleright T$ is another manner to deal with partial compensation apart from backward handling. T is the forward handler to fix the failure thrown by S. Different from backward handling, this construct adopts the forward recovery technique trying to fulfil the business objective in the presence of failure. In other words, if the forward handler completes, the whole composition is regarded as success though some error has occurred previously. Likewise, this handler T is activated by the failure of S. Since the success of either branch makes the objective realized, the compensation of the successful branch is reserved.

$$\llbracket S \rhd T \rrbracket$$
$$\triangleq \left(\begin{array}{l} Fbeh(S);(I\!I\!I \lhd st \neq cmt \rhd Add(S));(I\!I\!I \lhd st \neq fal \rhd (Fbeh(T);(I\!I\!I \lhd st \neq cmt \rhd Add(T)))) \\ Cbeh(S) \lhd Ck(S) \rhd Cbeh(T) \end{array} \right)$$
$$= \left(\begin{array}{l} F_1 \wedge \neg(R_1; \neg F_2) \vdash P_S \vee (R_1; P_T), Q_1 \vee (R_1; Q_2), R_1; R_2 \\ F_1' \lhd Ck(S) \rhd F_2' \vdash P_1' \lhd Ck(S) \rhd P_2', Q_1' \lhd Ck(S) \rhd Q_2', R_1' \lhd Ck(S) \rhd R_2' \end{array} \right)$$

As for a composite transaction, developers sometimes need to program a new compensation so as to satisfy specific application requirements. The construct of $S * T$ is introduced to meet this demand. Here, T is the newly programmed compensation for S, while the original one is simply discarded.

$$\llbracket S * T \rrbracket \triangleq \left(\begin{array}{c} Fbeh(S) \\ Fbeh(T) \end{array} \right) = \left(\begin{array}{c} F_1 \vdash P_1, Q_1, R_1 \\ F_2 \vdash P_2, Q_2, R_2 \end{array} \right)$$

5   Algebraic Laws

Based on the equivalence definition for compensable transactions, we are able to verify a set of algebraic laws explored before. We will see that all these laws are still proved to be true while introducing data computations and communications. Due to space limitation, we only present two proofs for simple illustration.

Conditional choice is skew symmetric and associative. Nondeterministic choice is idempotent, commutative, associative and distributes through itself. Moreover, all the transactional operators distribute through it. The related algebraic laws are simply omitted.

Sequential composition is associative and has $Skip$ as its left unit, $Abort$ and $Fail$ as its left zeros.

$(;\text{-}1)\ Abort; T = Abort$ $(;\text{-}2)\ Fail; T = Fail$
$(;\text{-}3)\ Skip; T = T$ $(;\text{-}4)\ (T_1; T_2); T_3 = T_1; (T_2; T_3)$

Parallel composition is commutative and associative.

$(\|\text{-}1)\ S \| T = T \| S$ $(\|\text{-}2)\ (T_1 \| T_2) \| T_3 = T_1 \| (T_2 \| T_3)$

Speculative choice is commutative, associative and has $Abort$ as its unit.

$(\otimes\text{-}1)\ S \otimes T = T \otimes S$ $(\otimes\text{-}2)\ (T_1 \otimes T_2) \otimes T_3 = T_1 \otimes (T_2 \otimes T_3)$ $(\otimes\text{-}3)\ Abort \otimes T = T$

Proof of ($\otimes$ -3): Let $\llbracket T \rrbracket = \left(\begin{array}{l} F_1 \vdash P_1, Q_1, R_1 \\ F_1' \vdash P_1', Q_1', R_1' \end{array} \right)$

From the definitions of $[\![S \otimes T]\!]$ and $[\![Abort]\!]$, we get:

$[\![Abort \otimes T]\!]$

$$= \begin{pmatrix} true \wedge F_1 \vdash II \parallel_\epsilon (P_1; trans' = trans \cup \{\mathcal{N}(T)\} \wedge II(\{trans\})), II \parallel_\epsilon Q_1, II \parallel_\epsilon R_1 \\ true \triangleleft \neg Ck(T) \triangleright F_1' \vdash II \triangleleft \neg Ck(T) \triangleright P_1', II \triangleleft \neg Ck(T) \triangleright Q_1', II \triangleleft \neg Ck(T) \triangleright R_1' \end{pmatrix}$$

$\{II \parallel_\epsilon P = P, \ P \triangleleft b \triangleright Q = Q \triangleleft \neg b \triangleright P\}$

$$= \begin{pmatrix} F_1 \vdash P_1; trans' = trans \cup \{\mathcal{N}(T)\} \wedge II(\{trans\}), Q_1, R_1 \\ F_1' \triangleleft Ck(T) \triangleright true \vdash P_1' \triangleleft Ck(T) \triangleright II, Q_1' \triangleleft Ck(T) \triangleright II, R_1' \triangleleft Ck(T) \triangleright II \end{pmatrix}$$

According to Definition 3.1, we need to verify the following formula:

$$\frac{[\,\overline{Fbeh(Abort \otimes T)} = \overline{Fbeh(T)}\,] \wedge}{[\,\overline{(true \vdash P_1; trans' = trans \cup \{\mathcal{N}(T)\} \wedge II(\{trans\}))\downarrow; Cbeh(Abort \otimes T)} = \overline{(true \vdash P_1)\downarrow; Cbeh(T)}\,]}$$

Since $\overline{P}$ hides the variables $trans, trans'$, we easily have:

$$\overline{Fbeh(Abort \otimes T)} = \overline{Fbeh(T)}$$

Relying on definitions of $P\downarrow$ and $P; Q$, it is easy to derive that the value of $trans$ in $Cbeh(Abort \otimes T)$ has the element of $\mathcal{N}(T)$, that is, $Ck(T)$ is satisfied. Hence:

$$(true \vdash P_1; trans' = trans \cup \{\mathcal{N}(T)\} \wedge II(\{trans\}))\downarrow; Cbeh(Abort \otimes T)$$
$$= (true \vdash P_1; trans' = trans \cup \{\mathcal{N}(T)\} \wedge II(\{trans\}))\downarrow; Cbeh(T)$$

By using the hiding predicate again, we further have:

$$\overline{(true \vdash P_1; trans' = trans \cup \{\mathcal{N}(T)\} \wedge II(\{trans\}))\downarrow; Cbeh(Abort \otimes T)} = \overline{(true \vdash P_1)\downarrow; Cbeh(T)}$$

Therefore, $Abort \otimes T = T$ □

Alternative forwarding is associative and has $Skip$ and $Fail$ as its left zeros. Besides, $Abort$ is its left unit.

$(\rightsquigarrow$-1$)$ $Skip \rightsquigarrow T = Skip$ $(\rightsquigarrow$-2$)$ $Fail \rightsquigarrow T = Fail$
$(\rightsquigarrow$-3$)$ $Abort \rightsquigarrow T = T$ $(\rightsquigarrow$-4$)$ $(T_1 \rightsquigarrow T_2) \rightsquigarrow T_3 = T_1 \rightsquigarrow (T_2 \rightsquigarrow T_3)$

Exception handling has $Skip$ and $Abort$ as its left zeros. The handler is limited to the area which may raise failure. We use $\odot$ to stand for $\unrhd$ or $\rhd$.

$(\odot$-1$)$ $Skip \odot T = Skip$ $(\odot$-2$)$ $Abort \odot T = Abort$
$(\unrhd$-3$)$ $(Fail \unrhd S); T = Fail \unrhd S$ $(\rhd$-4$)$ $(Fail \rhd S); T = Fail \rhd (S; T)$
$(\unrhd$-5$)$ $T_1 \unrhd (T_2 * T_3) = T_1 \unrhd T_2$ $(\rhd$-6$)$ $(T_1 \rhd T_2) \rhd T_3 = T_1 \rhd (T_2 \rhd T_3)$

Programmable compensation has $Abort$ and $Fail$ as its left zeros. Moreover, it has several other interesting properties shown below.

$(*$-1$)$ $Abort * T = Abort$ $(*$-2$)$ $Fail * T = Fail$
$(*$-3$)$ $(T_1 * T_2) * T_3 = T_1 * T_3$ $(*$-4$)$ $T_1 * (T_2 * T_3) = T_1 * T_2$
$(*$-5$)$ $(T_1 \odot T_2) * T_3 = (T_1 * T_3) \odot (T_2 * T_3)$ $(*$-6$)$ $(T_1 \rightsquigarrow T_2) * T_3 = (T_1 * T_3) \rightsquigarrow (T_2 * T_3)$
$(*$-7$)$ $(T_1 * T_1'); (T_2 * T_2') = (T_1; T_2) * (T_2'; T_1')$ $(*$-8$)$ $(T_1 * T_1') \parallel (T_2 * T_2') = (T_1 \parallel T_2) * (T_1' \parallel T_2')$

Proof of (*-3): Based on the definition of $S * T$, we get that:

$$[\![T_1 * T_2]\!] = \begin{pmatrix} Fbeh(T_1) \\ Fbeh(T_2) \end{pmatrix}$$

$$[\![(T_1 * T_2) * T_3]\!] = \begin{pmatrix} Fbeh(T_1 * T_2) \\ Fbeh(T_3) \end{pmatrix} = \begin{pmatrix} Fbeh(T_1) \\ Fbeh(T_3) \end{pmatrix} = [\![T_1 * T_3]\!] \qquad \square$$

6   Conclusion

A key problem of orchestration is about the treatment of business transactions. In this paper, we continue our former works devoted to lay a formal foundation for orchestrating services, with particular attention to the transactional aspect. At first, we extend the transactional language by explicitly describing low level details which is essential to specify real case studies. Secondly, we establish a totally different semantic model from our previous work. Meanwhile, this semantic view is useful for describing transactional properties while several behavioral aspects are needed to consider. Under this model, the equivalence and refinement relations between them are formally investigated.

There are other works which exploit formal models to represent service orchestrations but not deal with transactional behavior. The calculus introduced in [10] called COWS allows modeling multiple start activities, receive conflicts and message routing. Orc [16] is an abstract orchestration language providing a basic programming model for structured orchestration of services, where service invocations are considered as function calls. As far as correlation sets exploited by BPEL are concerned, Viroli [17] proposed a formal framework for defining a business process as the concurrent behavior of several process instances. The work in [2] presented a name passing process calculus with explicit notions for service definition and session handling. SOCK [8] is a three-layered calculus aiming to cover different service features separately and orthogonally.

Recently, business transactions have been studied based on process algebra to provide a precise semantics. Bocchi [1] took the well known π-calculus [15] as a starting point and added to it a new construct to address the transactional issue. However, this new construct is relatively complex with some underlying operations in it. For example, the repository called *failure bag* to store enclosed compensations seems improper to appear in the syntax. An event based framework was suggested in [13] to provide a generic error handling mechanism. The event calculus is expressive enough to encode compensation handling at a low level description. However, it is inadequate to describe transactional structures and their properties. Danos [6] proposed a formalization of backtracking transactions using a variant of CCS [14]. Backtracking has similar effect to compensation, but compensation is more powerful by virtue of its programmable trait.

The line of our work has been inspired by Sagas Calculi [3] and cCSP [4,5] which have explicitly mentioned the notion of compensable transactions. On their basis, we go further intending to study more features of compensable transactions by investigating distinct compositional structures. Compensation itself is treated as a compensable transaction too, thus we are able to provide a uniform manner to manage both the forward and compensation behavior. In the future, the complete framework equipped with underlying mechanisms will be provided.

References

1. Bocchi, L., Laneve, C., Zavattaro, G.: A calculus for long-running transactions. In: Najm, E., Nestmann, U., Stevens, P. (eds.) FMOODS 2003. LNCS, vol. 2884, pp. 124–138. Springer, Heidelberg (2003)
2. Boreale, M., Bruni, R., Caires, L., De Nicola, R., Lanese, I., Loreti, M., Martins, F., Montanari, U., Ravara, A., Sangiorgi, D., Vasconcelos, V., Zavattaro, G.: SCC: a service centered calculus. In: Bravetti, M., Núñez, M., Zavattaro, G. (eds.) WS-FM 2006. LNCS, vol. 4184, pp. 38–57. Springer, Heidelberg (2006)
3. Bruni, R., Melgratti, H., Montanari, U.: Theoretical foundations for compensations in flow composition languages. In: Proc. of POPL 2005, pp. 209–220. ACM Press, New York (2005)
4. Butler, M., Hoare, T., Ferreira, C.: A trace semantics for long-running transaction. In: Abdallah, A.E., Jones, C.B., Sanders, J.W. (eds.) Communicating Sequential Processes. LNCS, vol. 3525, pp. 133–150. Springer, Heidelberg (2005)
5. Butler, M., Ripon, S.: Executable semantics for compensating CSP. In: Bravetti, M., Kloul, L., Zavattaro, G. (eds.) EPEW/WS-EM 2005. LNCS, vol. 3670, pp. 243–256. Springer, Heidelberg (2005)
6. Danos, V., Krivine, J.: Transactions in RCCS. In: Abadi, M., de Alfaro, L. (eds.) CONCUR 2005. LNCS, vol. 3653, pp. 398–412. Springer, Heidelberg (2005)
7. Garcia-Molina, H., Salem, K.: Sagas. In: Proc. of ACM SIGMOD 1987, pp. 249–259. ACM Press, New York (1987)
8. Guidi, C., Lucchi, R., Gorrieri, R., Busi, N., Zavattaro, G.: SOCK: A calculus for service oriented computing. In: Dan, A., Lamersdorf, W. (eds.) ICSOC 2006. LNCS, vol. 4294, pp. 327–338. Springer, Heidelberg (2006)
9. Hoare, C.A.R., He, J.: Unifying Theories of Programming. Prentice-Hall, Englewood Cliffs (1998)
10. Lapadula, A., Pugliese, R., Tiezzi, F.: A calculus for orchestration of web services. In: De Nicola, R. (ed.) ESOP 2007. LNCS, vol. 4421, pp. 33–47. Springer, Heidelberg (2007)
11. Li, J., Zhu, H., He, J.: Algebraic Semantics for Compensable Transactions. In: Jones, C.B., Liu, Z., Woodcock, J. (eds.) ICTAC 2007. LNCS, vol. 4711, pp. 306–321. Springer, Heidelberg (2007)
12. Li, J., Zhu, H., Pu, G., He, J.: A Formal Model for Compensable Transactions. In: Proc. of ICECCS 2007, pp. 64–73. IEEE Computer Society Press, Los Alamitos (2007)
13. Mazzara, M., Lucchi, R.: A framework for generic error handling in business processes. In: Proc. of WS-FM 2004. ENTCS, vol. 105, pp. 133–145. Elsevier, Amsterdam (2004)
14. Milner, R.: Communication and Concurrency. Prentice-Hall, Englewood Cliffs (1989)
15. Milner, R.: Communicating and Mobile Systems: the π-Calculus. Cambridge University Press, Cambridge (1999)
16. Misra, J., Cook, W.R.: Computation orchestration: A basis for wide-area computing. Journal of Software and Systems Modeling (May 2006)
17. Viroli, M.: Towards a formal foundation to orchestration languages. In: Proc. of WS-FM 2004. ENTCS 105, Elsevier, Amsterdam (2004)

Everything Is PSPACE-Complete
in Interaction Systems

Mila Majster-Cederbaum and Christoph Minnameier*

Institut für Informatik
Universität Mannheim, Germany
cmm@informatik.uni-mannheim.de

Abstract. We study complexity issues for interaction systems, a general model for component-based systems that allows for a very flexible interaction mechanism. We present complexity results for important properties of interaction systems such as local/global deadlock-freedom, progress and availability of components.

1   Introduction

First introduced by Sifakis et al. [GS03], *interaction systems* are a general model for component-based systems. Its main features can be summarized as follows. The description of a component is hidden to any other component, in particular a component does not refer to methods or operations of other components. Components offer ports for cooperation with other components. Components are put together by some kind of a (separate) gluing mechanism in a such way that the identity of each component is maintained. Components and the glue can thus be modified freely. The gluing is realized via connectors, that consist of ports of various components. Connectors can be of different size and each port can participate in more than one connector.

The model has been discussed in [GS03, Sif05, GS05, GGM+07]. In [GQ07] the model has been enriched by hierarchical connectors. A version including variables and value passing was implemented in the BIP-project [BBS06] and in the Prometheus-project [Goe06] and was used to implement and study a variety of component-based systems. The relevance of the model is also stressed by the fact that it is used as a common semantic framework in the European SPEEDS-project [GO07].

Interaction systems can be viewed as a generalization of interface automata [dAH01] as well as of input/output automata [LT89].

Given that interaction systems are a suitable and comfortable framework to model component-based systems it is interesting to investigate their properties.

Here, we study algorithmic properties of interaction systems, in particular reachability, local and global deadlock-freedom, progress and availability of components. These properties are defined on the global state space which is exponentially large in the number of components. We show that deciding either of

---

* Corresponding author.

J.S. Fitzgerald, A.E. Haxthausen, and H. Yenigun (Eds.): ICTAC 2008, LNCS 5160, pp. 216–227, 2008.
© Springer-Verlag Berlin Heidelberg 2008

the mentioned properties is PSPACE-complete. To do so we build on a connection between interaction systems and 1-safe Petri nets that was first presented in [MM08b] and yields PSPACE-hardness for reachability in interaction systems.

This paper is organized as follows. In Section 2 we give the basic definitions for interaction systems and the various properties we are going to discuss and point out the advantages of interaction systems over the closely-related models of 1-safe Petri nets. Section 3 presents the polynomial reductions that show that all discussed behavioral questions are PSPACE-complete. In Section 4 we give a short conclusion and discuss related work.

2   Interaction Systems

2.1   Syntax and Semantics

An ***interaction system*** is a tuple $Sys = (K, \{A_i\}_{i \in K}, C, Comp, \{T_i\}_{i \in K})$, where K is the set of ***components***. Often, we assume $K = \{1, \ldots, n\}$.

Each component $i \in K$ offers a finite, nonempty set of ***ports*** (resp. ***actions***) A_i for cooperation with other components. The ***port sets*** A_i are pairwise disjoint.

Cooperation is described by connectors and complete interactions. A ***connector*** is a finite, nonempty set of actions $c \subseteq \bigcup_{i \in K} A_i$, subject to the constraint that for each component i at most one action $a_i \in A_i$ is in c. A connector $c = \{a_{i_1}, \ldots, a_{i_k}\}$ with $a_{i_j} \in A_{i_j}$ describes the fact that the components $i_1, \ldots, i_j$ may cooperate via these ports. A ***connector set*** C is a finite set of connectors, s.t. every action of every component occurs in at least one connector and no connector contains any other connector. We define the set of ***interactions*** $Int := \{\alpha \mid \exists c \in C, \text{ s.t. } \alpha \subseteq c\}$. In some cases we want to allow that a connector is performed only partially, e.g. if not all components involved in a connector are ready to perform their respective action. For this we may designate certain interactions as ***complete interactions***. Let $Comp \subseteq Int$ be a designated set of complete interactions. $Comp$ has to be upwards-closed w.r.t. C, i.e. $\forall \alpha \in Comp \, \forall \alpha' \in Int : ((\alpha \subset \alpha') \Rightarrow \alpha' \in Comp)$.

The local behavior of each component i is described by $T_i = (Q_i, A_i, \rightarrow_i, q_i^0)$, where Q_i is a finite set of local states, $\rightarrow_i \subseteq Q_i \times A_i \times Q_i$ the local transition relation and $q_i^0 \in Q_i$ is the local starting state. We assume that the T_i's are non-terminating, i.e. each $q_i \in Q_i$ has at least one outgoing edge.

We call the class of all interaction systems ***IS***.

The ***global behavior*** $T_{Sys} = (Q, C \cup Comp, \rightarrow_{Sys}, q^0)$ of Sys (henceforth also referred to as the global transition system) is obtained from the behaviors of the individual components, given by the transition systems T_i, and the interactions in $C \cup Comp$ in a straightforward manner:

- $Q := \prod_{i \in K} Q_i$, the Cartesian product of the Q_i, which we consider to be order independent. We denote states by tuples $(q_1, \ldots, q_n)$ and call them global states.

- the relation $\to_{Sys} \subseteq Q \times (C \cup Comp) \times Q$, defined by
  $\forall \alpha \in (C \cup Comp) \; \forall q, q' \in Q \quad q = (q_1, \ldots, q_n) \xrightarrow{\alpha}_{Sys} q' = (q'_1, \ldots, q'_n)$ iff
  $\forall i \in K \; (q_i \xrightarrow{a_i}_i q'_i$ if $\alpha \cap A_i = \{a_i\}$ and $q'_i = q_i$ otherwise$)$.
- $q^0 := (q_1^0, \ldots, q_n^0)$ is the starting state for Sys.

Less formally, a transition labeled by α may take place in the global transition system when all ports occuring in α are offered by the respective components.

Example 1. The following interaction system $Count_{(3,4)}$ demonstrates the capability of interaction systems to synchronize with different numbers of participants. $Count_{(3,4)} = (\{1, 2, 3, 4\}, \{A_i\}_{1 \le i \le 4}, C, Comp, \{T_i\}_{1 \le i \le 4})$, where
$A_i = \{inc_i, dec_i\}$ $(1 \le i \le 3)$, $A_4 = \{inc_4, dummy_4\}$,
$C = \{\{inc_1, dummy_4\}, \{inc_2, dec_1\}, \{inc_3, dec_2, dec_1\}, \{inc_4, dec_3, dec_2, dec_1\}\}$,
$Comp = \{\{inc_1\}, \{inc_1, dummy_4\}\}$, and the T_i's are given in Figure 1.

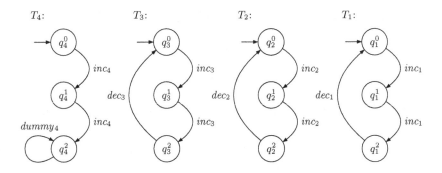

Fig. 1. The local transition systems for $Count_{(3,4)}$

The behavior[1] of our example system $Count_{(3,4)}$ is as follows: It performs a deterministic computation starting in $(q_1^0, q_2^0, q_3^0, q_4^0)$. The system describes a 3^4-counter that counts from 0 to $3^4-1=80$ and then cannot perform any further interaction.

We refer to the local transition system T_i of a component i of some previously defined system Sys by $T_i[Sys]$. The same notation is used for the other elements of the interaction system tuple. E.g. $Comp[Count_{(3,4)}] = \{\{inc_1\}, \{inc_1, dummy_4\}\}$. Whenever it is obvious by the context to which system we refer (as e.g. in the next subsection), we may simply write Q instead of $Q[Sys]$, etc. for ease of notation.

2.2 Properties of Interaction Systems

For the following definitions let $Sys \in IS$:

- For local states $q_i \in Q_i$ we define the set of **enabled actions** $ea(q_i) :=$
  $\{a_i \in A_i \mid \exists q'_i \in Q_i, \text{ s.t. } q_i \xrightarrow{a_i}_i q'_i\}$.

---

[1] Note that $dummy_4$ is introduced only to ensure that T_4 is non-terminating.

- For $q, q' \in Q$ we say that **there is a path from q to q'** if $q = q'$ or $\exists k \in \mathbb{N}_0 \; \exists q^1, \ldots, q^k \in Q \; \exists \alpha_0, \ldots, \alpha_k \in (C \cup Comp)$ s.t. $q \xrightarrow{\alpha_0}_{Sys} q^1 \xrightarrow{\alpha_1}_{Sys} \ldots \xrightarrow{\alpha_{k-1}}_{Sys} q^k \xrightarrow{\alpha_k}_{Sys} q'$. Such a transition sequence is called a path ϕ from q to q'.

- We call an infinite transition sequence $q \xrightarrow{\alpha_0}_{Sys} \ldots$ **a run ρ from q.**

- For a system $Sys \in IS$ and a global state $q \in Q$ we define **reach(q)** $:= \{q' \in Q \mid \exists$ a path ϕ from q to $q'\}$. Note that the existence of a run from q implies (together with the finiteness of the global transition system) the existence of a cycle that is reachable from q.

- We define the set of reachable states of Sys (with global starting state q^0) by **reach(Sys)** $:= reach(q^0)$.

- For $\alpha \in Int, k \in K$ we say that **k participates in α** if $k(\alpha) := \alpha \cap A_k \neq \emptyset$. If we have $k(\alpha) = \{a_k\}$ we say that k participates in α with a_k. Otherwise, we say that k does not participate in α.

- A global state **q enables an interaction α** $\in (C \cup Comp)$ if $\exists q' \in Q$: $q \xrightarrow{\alpha} q'$. We write $q \not\rightarrow$ if q does not enable any $\alpha \in (C \cup Comp)$.

- A global state **q enables a component k** $\in K$ if q enables some interaction α in which k participates. **q enables an action a_k** of some component $k \in K$ (resp. a_k is enabled in q) if q enables an interaction α in which k participates with a_k.

- Let $q = (q_1, \ldots, q_n) \in Q$ be a global state. We say that some non-empty set $\tilde{K} = \{j_1, j_2, \ldots, j_{|\tilde{K}|}\} \subseteq K$ of components **is in local deadlock in q** if
$$\forall i \in \tilde{K} \; \forall \alpha \in (C \cup Comp): (\alpha \cap ea(q_i) \neq \emptyset) \Rightarrow (\exists j \in \tilde{K} \; j(\alpha) \not\subseteq ea(q_j)).$$

- A **global deadlock** is a special case of a local deadlock, when $\tilde{K} = K$.

- For a system Sys that has no global deadlock, we define that **$k \in K$ does progress in Sys** if k occurs infinitely often in every run from q^0.

- For a system Sys that has no global deadlock, we define that **$k \in K$ is available in Sys** if k is enabled infinitely often in (states occuring in) every run from q^0.

We define in the following a list of decidability problems:

Reachability $:= \{(Sys, q) \mid Sys \in IS$ and $q \in reach(Sys)\}$.

LDIS $:= \{Sys \in IS \mid \exists q \in reach(Sys) \; \exists \tilde{K} \subseteq K$ s.t. $\tilde{K}$ is in local deadlock in $q\}$.

GDIS $:= \{Sys \in IS \mid \exists q \in reach(Sys),$ s.t. $q \not\rightarrow\}$.

Progress $:= \{(Sys, k) \mid Sys \in (IS \setminus GDIS)$ and $k \in K[Sys]$ does progress in $Sys\}$.

Availability $:= \{(Sys, k) \mid Sys \in (IS \setminus GDIS)$ and $k \in K[Sys]$ is available in $Sys\}$.

2.3   Interaction Systems and 1-Safe Petri Nets

In this subsection we give a short discussion of interaction systems versus 1-safe Petri-nets. As we showed in [MM08b] we can translate a 1-safe Petri net into an interaction system in time polynomial in the size of the input such that the property of reachability is preserved. This will be the basis for our PSPACE-hardness results. On the other hand one can show that there is no general translation from interaction systems to 1-safe Petri nets that yields bisimilarity for the global transition systems and that there is no polynomial translation that yields isomorphy even for the unlabeled versions of the global transition systems.

Still one might want to ask for further motivation why one should deal with interaction systems instead of using Petri nets.

Our first argument concerns the fact that we want to model and investigate component-based systems. In a component-based system it should be possible to freely combine components in a very flexible way, substitute a component by another one or change the glue code by which components are put together. As we argue interaction systems are a model that satisfies these needs.

There have been attempts to use Petri nets for the analysis of component-based systems. In [BB04, BB06] the model CompoNets based on colored Petri nets is proposed. In this model every component offers a set of ports. Its behavior is described by a Petri net. There is a set of syntactic rules that regulate how components are glued together via their port sets. However there is no formalism that allows to determine the behavior of the global system. Moreover when components are put together the identity of a component is lost and hence substituting one component for another one in the composed systems or asking for the liveness of a component is not feasible. Other approaches using Petri nets to model component-based systems can be found in [AS99, AS02, PK07, SVvdW]. General problems with Petri nets approaches are that Petri nets lack full compositionality and the loss of the identity of components in the composed system which is needed for reconfiguration of systems.

Given this situation one could think of modeling components systems by interaction systems and then transforming the interaction system by our translation into a 1-safe Petri net which could then be analyzed by a Petri net tools or submitted to a model checker. When however trying to translate an interaction system into a 1-safe Petri net one can show that there are simple interaction systems for which no bisimilar 1-safe Petri exists. In a context of model checking e.g. with respect to modal μ-calculus bisimilarity is however very important as two processes satisfy the same set of formulae if and only if they are bisimilar. Hence if we are interested in general properties as expressed by modal μ-calculus this approach does not work.

3   The Polynomial Time Reductions

In [MM08b], we gave a polynomial translation from 1-safe Petri nets to interaction systems, which yielded PSPACE-hardness for reachability in interaction systems. In this section, we give four polynomial reductions $f_1, \ldots, f_4$ that build a reduction chain as depicted in Figure 2. The chain allows us to derive the PSPACE-hardness result from reachability for all considered properties as well as PSPACE-solvability from availability for all properties in the chain. Hence we prove all problems in the chain to be PSPACE-complete. Although the reductions vary strongly in their degree of difficulty they also have some basic idea in common. In each of the reductions, we add a component *main* to the system. However, the local transition system of *main* will be a different one for each reduction.

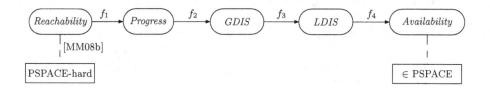

Fig. 2. The Polynomial Time Reductions f_i $(1 \leq i \leq 4)$

For each reduction, we present its formal definition followed by a short explanation. Explicit formal proofs have been omitted for better readability. The proofs for the reductions are sketched in the various following subsections and the verification of their logspace computability is left to the reader.

We will now give a short reasoning why *Availability* is in *PSPACE*:

Given an interaction system and one of its components k we want to decide whether from every reachable global state we will, - no matter in which way we continue our transition sequence - eventually reach a state that enables k.

Note that $\overline{Availability}$ is the question whether there exists a reachable global state q, from which q itself is reachable by a non-empty transition sequence $q \rightarrow q' \rightarrow \ldots \rightarrow q$ such that none of the global states $q, q', \ldots$ enables k.

To solve $\overline{Availability}$ we first guess our way from the global starting state q^0 to some q as described above. It is easy to verifiy in each step in polynomial space that we follow indeed an allowed edge in the global transition system. Next, once we reach q, we store it and guess the cycle described above back to q. It is possbile in polynomial space to verifiy that the cycle is non-empty, that none of the visited states enables k and that we do indeed reach q after all.

So $\overline{Availability}$ is in *NPSPACE* and thus *Availability* is in *co-NPSPACE* which equals *PSPACE* due to Savitch [Sav70].

3.1   *Reachability* Is Polynomially Reducible to *Progress*

Theorem 1. *Reachability is polynomially reducible to Progress*

Proof. Let $Sys \in IS$ and $q = (q_1, \ldots, q_n) \in Q[Sys]$. We associate with (Sys,q) an interaction system $f_1(Sys, q)$ (which is free of global deadlocks) s.t.
$$((Sys,q) \in Reachability) \Leftrightarrow ((f_1(Sys,q), main) \notin Progress).$$

Formal definition of f_1.
Let $Sys = \{K, \{A_i\}_{i \in K}, C, Comp, \{T_i\}_{i \in K}\}$, then
$f_1(Sys, q) = \{K', \{A'_i\}_{i \in K'}, C', Comp', \{T'_i\}_{i \in K'}\}$, where
$\quad\quad K' := K \cup \{main\}$,
For $i \in K: A'_i := A_i \cup \{run_i\}$,
$\quad\quad A'_{main} := \{dummy_{main}, check_{main}\}$,

For $i \in K$: $\boldsymbol{T_i'} := (Q_i, A_i', \rightarrow_i', q_i^0)$, where
$$\rightarrow_i' := \rightarrow_i \cup \{(q_i, run_i, q_i)\},$$
$$\boldsymbol{T_{main}'} := (\{q_{main}^0\}, A_{main}', \rightarrow_{main}', q_{main}^0), \text{ where}$$
$$\rightarrow_{main}' := \{(q_{main}^0, check_{main}, q_{main}^0), (q_{main}^0, dummy_{main}, q_{main}^0)\}.$$
$$\boldsymbol{C'} := \{c \cup \{check_{main}\} \,|\, c \in C\} \cup \{\{run_i \,|\, 1 \leq i \leq n\}\} \cup \{\{dummy_{main}\}\},$$
$$\boldsymbol{Comp'} := \{\alpha \cup \{check_{main}\} \,|\, \alpha \in Comp\}.$$

Explanation. We add a component $main$ whose local transition system consists of a single state with two loops. Also, for each local transition system T_i we add a loop in the state q_i labeled by run_i. Clearly $f_1(Sys, q) \in IS$ holds. The loop of $main$ labeled by $dummy_{main}$ can be performed independently (i.e. $\{dummy_{main}\}$ is a connector) and assures that $f_1(Sys,q) \notin GDIS$ (which is a precondition for asking for progress). The second loop is labeled by the action $check_{main}$, which is added to every interaction $\alpha \in C \cup Comp$. Hence, the only interaction in $C \cup Comp$ in which $main$ does not participate is $\{run_1, \ldots, run_n\}$.

This fact, together with the obvious observation that q is reachable in Sys iff q extended by q_{main}^0 is reachable in $f_1(Sys, q)$ allows us to conclude that in $f_1(Sys, q)$ there is a run from q in which $main$ does not participate iff q is reachable in Sys.

3.2 *Progress* Is Polynomially Reducible to *GDIS*

Preliminaries. The construction applied in Example 1 in Section 2.1 can easily be parameterized in order to build an interaction system for an m^n-counter, $m, n \in \mathbb{N}$:
$$Count_{(m,n)} = (\{n+1, \ldots, 2n\}, \{A_i\}_{n+1 \leq i \leq 2n}, C, Comp, \{T_i\}_{n+1 \leq i \leq 2n}),$$
where $A_i = \{inc_i, dec_i\}$ for $n+1 \leq i \leq 2n-1$ and $A_{2n} = \{inc_{2n}, dummy_{2n}\}$
$$C = \{\{inc_{n+1}, dummy_{2n}\}\} \cup \bigcup_{i=n+2}^{2n} \{c(inc_i)\}$$
$$\text{where } c(inc_i) = \{inc_i\} \cup \bigcup_{j=n+1}^{i-1} \{dec_j\},$$
$$Comp = \{\{inc_{n+1}\}, \{inc_{n+1}, dummy_{2n}\}\},$$
$$T_i = (Q_i, A_i, \rightarrow_i, q_i^0), \text{ where } Q_i = \{q_i^0, \ldots, q_i^{m-1}\} \text{ and}$$
$$\rightarrow_i = \begin{cases} \{(q_i^j, inc_i, q_i^{j+1}) \,|\, 0 \leq j \leq m-2\} \cup \{(q_i^{m-1}, dec_i, q_i^0)\} & ; n+1 \leq i \leq 2n-1 \\ \{(q_i^j, inc_i, q_i^{j+1}) \,|\, 0 \leq j \leq m-2\} \cup \{(q_i^{m-1}, dummy_{2n}, q_i^{m-1})\} & ; i = 2n \end{cases}$$

As already pointed out in Section 2.1, such a system behaves deterministically and simply performs $m^n - 1$ ("counting") interactions before stopping.

Theorem 2. *Progress is polynomially reducible to GDIS[2].*

Proof. Let $Sys \in (IS \setminus GDIS)$ and $k \in K[Sys]$. In case k participates in every $\alpha \in C \cup Comp$, k does progress[3]. Otherwise, we associate with (Sys,k) an interaction system $f_2(Sys, k)$ s.t.
$$((Sys,k) \in Progress) \Leftrightarrow (f_2(Sys,k) \notin GDIS).$$

In the following, let $m := max\{|Q_i| \,|\, i \in K[Sys]\}$.

---

[2] Please note that an alternative proof of PSPACE-hardness of GDIS is given in [MM08b]. Thus f_2 mainly serves to establish PSPACE-completeness.

[3] We have to consider this case explicitly because $f_2(Sys, k) \notin IS$ for such an input.

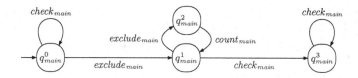

Fig. 3. The local transition system T'_{main}

Formal definition of f_2.
Let $Sys = \{K, \{A_i\}_{i \in K}, C, Comp, \{T_i\}_{i \in K}\}$, then
$f_2(Sys, k) = \{K', \{A'_i\}_{i \in K'}, C', Comp', \{T'_i\}_{i \in K'}\}$, where
$$K' := K \cup \{n+1, \ldots, 2n, main\},$$
For $i \in K$: $A'_i := A_i$,
For $i \in \{n+1, \ldots, 2n\}$: $A'_i := A_i[Count_{(m,n)}]$,
$$A'_{main} := \{check_{main}, exclude_{main}, count_{main}\},$$
For $i \in K$: $T'_i := T_i$,
For $i \in \{n+1, \ldots, 2n\}$: $T'_i := T_i[Count_{(m,n)}]$,
and T'_{main} is depicted in Figure 3.
$$C_{check} := \{c \cup \{check_{main}\} \mid c \in C\}$$
$$Comp_{check} := \{\alpha \cup \{check_{main}\} \mid \alpha \in Comp\}$$
$$C_{exclude} := \{c \cup \{exclude_{main}\} \mid c \in C \wedge k(c) = \emptyset\}$$
$$Comp_{exclude} := \{\alpha \cup \{exclude_{main}\} \mid \alpha \in Comp \wedge k(\alpha) = \emptyset\}$$
$$C_{counter} := \{c \cup \{count_{main}\} \mid c \in C[Count_{(m,n)}]\}$$
$$Comp_{counter} := \{\alpha \cup \{count_{main}\} \mid \alpha \in Comp[Count_{(m,n)}]\}$$
$$(= \{\{inc_{n+1}, count_{main}\}, \{inc_{n+1}, dummy_{2n}, count_{main}\}\})$$
$$C' := C_{check} \cup C_{exclude} \cup C_{counter}$$
$$Comp' := Comp_{check} \cup Comp_{exclude} \cup Comp_{counter}$$

Explanation. First, we observe that $f_2(Sys, k) \in IS$ holds. Sys is globally deadlock-free and we want to know whether it contains a run from q^0, in which k does not participate infinitely often. This amounts to the question, whether there is a reachable global state, that lies on a cycle that does not involve k. As m^n is an upper bound for the size of the global state space of Sys, this is equivalent to asking whether it is possible to perform m^n consecutive interactions in which k does not participate.

3.3 *GDIS* Is Polynomially Reducible to *LDIS*

Theorem 3. *GDIS is polynomially reducible to LDIS*

Proof. Let $Sys \in IS$. We associate with Sys an interaction system $f_3(Sys)$ s.t.
$$(Sys \in GDIS) \Leftrightarrow (f_3(Sys) \in LDIS).$$

Formal definition of f_3.
Let $Sys = \{K, \{A_i\}_{i \in K}, C, Comp, \{T_i\}_{i \in K}\}$, then
$f_3(Sys) = \{K', \{A'_i\}_{i \in K'}, C', Comp', \{T'_i\}_{i \in K'}\}$, where
$$\boldsymbol{K'} := K \cup \{main\},$$
For $i \in K$: $\boldsymbol{A'_i} := A_i \cup \{dummy_i\}$,
$$\boldsymbol{A'_{main}} := \{dummy_{main}, check_{main}\},$$
For $i \in K$: $\boldsymbol{T'_i} := (Q_i, A'_i, \rightarrow'_i, q_i^0)$, where
$$\rightarrow'_i := \rightarrow_i \cup \{(q_i, dummy_i, q_i) \mid q_i \in Q_i\}.$$
$$\boldsymbol{T'_{main}} := (\{q_{main}^0, q_{main}^1\}, A'_{main}, \rightarrow'_{main}, q_{main}^0), \text{ where}$$
$$\rightarrow'_{main} := \{(q_{main}^0, check_{main}, q_{main}^1), (q_{main}^1, dummy_{main}, q_{main}^0)\},$$
$$\boldsymbol{C'} := \{c \cup \{check_{main}\} \mid c \in C\} \cup \{\{dummy_1, \ldots, dummy_n, dummy_{main}\}\},$$
$$\boldsymbol{Comp'} := \{\alpha \cup \{check_{main}\} \mid \alpha \in Comp\}.$$

Explanation. Clearly, $f_3(Sys) \in IS$. We add an additional component $main$ which alternatingly accompanies orignal interactions of Sys in one step and then allows the system to perform a connector including all components in a second step. This preserves global deadlocks but resolves local ones.

3.4 *LDIS* Is Polynomially Reducible to *Availability*

Theorem 4. *LDIS is polynomially reducible to Availability*

Proof. Let $Sys \in IS$. We associate with Sys an interaction system $f_4(Sys)$ (which is free of global deadlocks) s.t.
$$(Sys \in LDIS) \Leftrightarrow ((f_4(Sys), main) \notin Availability).$$

Formal definition of f_4.
Let $Sys = \{K, \{A_i\}_{i \in K}, C, Comp, \{T_i\}_{i \in K}\}$,
then $f_4(Sys) = \{K', \{A'_i\}_{i \in K'}, C', Comp', \{T'_i\}_{i \in K'}\}$, where[4]
$$\boldsymbol{K'} := K \cup \{n+1\} \cup \{main\}$$
For $i \in K$: $\boldsymbol{A'_i} := A_i \cup \{\hat{a}_i \mid a_i \in A_i\} \cup \{lock_i, unlock_i, d_i, \overline{d}_i, clear_i\}$
$$\boldsymbol{A'_{n+1}} := \{dummy_{n+1}, lock_{n+1}, unlock_{n+1}\}$$
$$\boldsymbol{A'_{main}} := \{lock_{main}, unlock_{main}, clear_{main}, progress_{main}\}$$
For $i \in K$: $\boldsymbol{T'_i} := (Q'_i, A'_i, \rightarrow'_i, q_i^0)$, where
$$Q'_i := \bigcup_{q_i \in Q_i} \{q_i, \hat{q}_i, q_i^D, \hat{q}_i^D, q_i^{\overline{D}}, \hat{q}_i^{\overline{D}}, q_i^{clr}\}$$
$$\rightarrow'_i := \bigcup_{q_i \in Q_i} \{ (q_i, lock_i, \hat{q}_i), (\hat{q}_i, d_i, q_i^D), (q_i^D, unlock_i, \hat{q}_i^D), (\hat{q}_i, \overline{d}_i, q_i^{\overline{D}}),$$
$$(q_i^{\overline{D}}, unlock_i, \hat{q}_i^{\overline{D}}), (\hat{q}_i^D, \bigcup_{a_i \in ea(q_i)} \{a_i, \hat{a}_i\}, q_i^{clr}),$$
$$(\hat{q}_i^{\overline{D}}, A_i \cup \{all_i\}, \hat{q}_i^{\overline{D}}), (q_i^{clr}, clear_i, q_i^{clr})\}$$
$$\cup \rightarrow_i$$
$\boldsymbol{T'_{n+1}}$ and $\boldsymbol{T'_{main}}$ are given in Figure 5.

---

[4] For ease of notation we use sets of actions as edge labels in the definition of $\rightarrow'_i$ as well as in Figure 4. When we write $(q, A, q') \in \rightarrow'_i$ we mean $(q, a, q') \in \rightarrow'_i \ \forall a \in A$. Note that by $ea(q_i)$ we refer to the enabled actions of the local state q_i in Sys (not in $f_4(Sys)$).

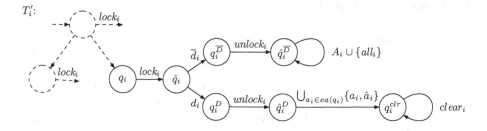

Fig. 4. The modification for a local state q_i in the local transition system T_i'

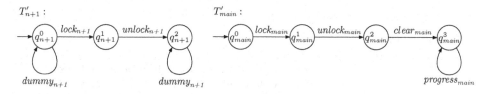

Fig. 5. The local transition system T_{main}'

The result of our modifications is sketched for a single state $q_i \in Q_i$ in Figure 4.

$$
\begin{aligned}
C' :=\ & \{\{dummy_{n+1}\}, \{lock_1, \ldots, lock_n, lock_{n+1}, lock_{main}\}\} \\
& \cup \{\{unlock_1, \ldots, unlock_n, unlock_{n+1}, unlock_{main}\}\} \\
& \cup \{\{d_1\}, \ldots, \{d_n\}, \{\overline{d}_1\}, \ldots, \{\overline{d}_n\}\} \\
& \cup \{\{all_1, \ldots, all_n, clear_{main}\}\} \\
& \cup \{\{clear_1, clear_{main}\}, \ldots, \{clear_n, clear_{main}\}\} \\
& \cup \{\{progress_{main}\}\} \\
& \cup C \cup C^{clear}, \text{ where} \\
C^{clear} :=\ & \{\{clear_{main}, \hat{a}\} \cup (c \setminus a) \mid a \in c \in C\} \\
Comp' :=\ & Comp \cup Comp^{clear}, \text{ where} \\
Comp^{clear} :=\ & \{\{clear_{main}, \hat{a}\} \cup (\alpha \setminus a) \mid a \in \alpha \in Comp\}
\end{aligned}
$$

Explanation. Clearly, $f_4(Sys) \in IS$ holds. Component $n+1$ guarantees $f_4(Sys) \notin GDIS$. The idea of our reduction is as follows: In the beginning *main* offers in any reachable state an action $lock_{main}$, which can participate in the *lock*-interaction which includes all components. As a result, *main* will always be enabled as long as this action is not performed. Now in any reachable state q of Sys we want to be able to check whether there is a local deadlock in q. For this purpose in any reachable state $(q_1, \ldots, q_n, q_{n+1}^0, q_{main}^0)$, the interaction $\{lock_1, \ldots, lock_n, lock_{n+1}, lock_{main}\}$ can be performed leading to a state where for every $i \in K$ a choice between d_i and $\overline{d}_i$ takes place. Those components j that select d_j form a subset $\tilde{K} \subseteq K$. If and only if $\tilde{K}$ is in local deadlock in $(q_1, \ldots, q_n)$ in Sys, the component *main* will not be able to participate in any further interaction.

4   Conclusion and Related Work

We give a complete complexity-theoretic characterization of the most relevant behavioral questions in interaction systems. Similar results have been proved for 1-safe Petri nets in [CEP93]. The PSPACE-hardness results motivate other approaches to guarantee the discussed properties. One approach is to establish conditions that can be tested in polynomial time and imply the desired properties [MMM07, MMM, IU01, BHH+06]. Another approach exploits compositionality [AB03, GGM+07]. Further, one may put restrictions on the communication structure of the interaction system [MM08a, BCD02]. The aim of all these approaches is to derive global properties from local information as much as possible.

References

[AB03]   Aldini, A., Bernardo, M.: A General Approach to Deadlock Freedom Verification for Software Architectures. In: Araki, K., Gnesi, S., Mandrioli, D. (eds.) FME 2003. LNCS, vol. 2805, pp. 658–677. Springer, Heidelberg (2003)

[AS99]   Aoumeur, N., Saake, G.: Towards an Object Petri Nets Model for Specifying and Validating Distributed Information Systems. In: Jarke, M., Oberweis, A. (eds.) CAiSE 1999. LNCS, vol. 1626, pp. 381–395. Springer, Heidelberg (1999)

[AS02]   Aoumeur, N., Saake, G.: A Component-based Petri Net Model for Specifying and Validating Cooperative Information Systems. Data Knowl. Eng. 42(2), 143–187 (2002)

[BB04]   Bastide, R., Barboni, E.: Component-based Behavioural Modelling with High-Level Petri Nets. In: Proceedings of MOCA 2004, pp. 37–46 (2004)

[BB06]   Bastide, R., Barboni, E.: Software Components: a Formal Semantics Based on Coloured Petri Nets. In: Proceedings of FACS 2005. ENTCS, vol. 160, pp. 57–73 (2006)

[BBS06]   Basu, A., Bozga, M., Sifakis, J.: Modeling Heterogeneous Real-time Components in BIP. In: Proceedings of SEFM 2006, pp. 3–12. IEEE Computer Society Press, Los Alamitos (2006)

[BCD02]   Bernardo, M., Ciancarini, P., Donatiello, L.: Architecting Families of Software Systems with Process Algebras. ACM Trans. on Software Engineering and Methodology 11, 386–426 (2002)

[BHH+06]   Baumeister, H., Hacklinger, F., Hennicker, R., Knapp, A., Wirsing, M.: A Component Model for Architectural Programming. In: Proceedings of FACS 2005. ENTCS, vol. 160, pp. 75–96 (2006)

[CEP93]   Cheng, A., Esparza, J., Palsberg, J.: Complexity Results for 1-safe Nets. In: Shyamasundar, R.K. (ed.) FSTTCS 1993. LNCS, vol. 761, pp. 326–337. Springer, Heidelberg (1993)

[dAH01]   de Alfaro, L., Henzinger, T.: Interface Automata. In: Matsui, M. (ed.) FSE 2001. LNCS, vol. 2355, pp. 109–120. Springer, Heidelberg (2002)

[GGM+07]   Goessler, G., Graf, S., Majster-Cederbaum, M., Martens, M., Sifakis, J.: Ensuring Properties of Interaction Systems. In: Reps, T., Sagiv, M., Bauer, J. (eds.) Wilhelm Festschrift. LNCS, vol. 4444, pp. 201–224. Springer, Heidelberg (2007)

[GO07]   Graf, S., Ober, I.: Modelling and Validation of Software and Architecture
            with Omega-UML and the IF Validation Toolbox. In: Genie Logiciel (to
            appear, 2007), http://www.speeds.eu.com
[Goe06]   Goessler, G.: Component-based Design of Heterogeneous Reactive Sys-
            tems in Prometheus. Technical report 6057, INRIA (December 2006)
[GQ07]   Graf, S., Quinton, S.: Contracts for BIP: Hierarchical Interaction Models
            for Compositional Verification. In: Derrick, J., Vain, J. (eds.) FORTE
            2007. LNCS, vol. 4574, pp. 1–18. Springer, Heidelberg (2007)
[GS03]   Goessler, G., Sifakis, J.: Component-based Construction of Deadlock-
            free Systems. In: Pandya, P.K., Radhakrishnan, J. (eds.) FSTTCS 2003.
            LNCS, vol. 2914, pp. 420–433. Springer, Heidelberg (2003)
[GS05]   Goessler, G., Sifakis, J.: Composition for Component-based Modeling. Sci.
            Comput. Program. 55(1-3), 161–183 (2005)
[IU01]   Inverardi, P., Uchitel, S.: Proving Deadlock Freedom in Component-Based
            Programming. In: Hussmann, H. (ed.) FASE 2001. LNCS, vol. 2029, pp.
            60–75. Springer, Heidelberg (2001)
[LT89]   Lynch, N.A., Tuttle, M.R.: An Introduction to Input/Output Automata.
            In: CWI-Quarterly, pp. 219–246 (1989)
[MM08a]   Majster-Cederbaum, M., Martens, M.: Compositional Analysis of Tree-
            Like Component Architectures (submitted for publication, 2008)
[MM08b]   Majster-Cederbaum, M., Minnameier, C.: Deriving Complexity Results
            for Interaction Systems from 1-safe Petri Nets. In: Geffert, V., Karhumäki,
            J., Bertoni, A., Preneel, B., Návrat, P., Bieliková, M. (eds.) SOFSEM
            2008. LNCS, vol. 4910, pp. 352–363. Springer, Heidelberg (2008)
[MMM]   Majster-Cederbaum, M., Martens, M., Minnameier, C.: Liveness in Inter-
            action Systems. In: Proceedings of FACS 2007. ENTCS (2007)
[MMM07]   Majster-Cederbaum, M., Martens, M., Minnameier, C.: A Polynomial-
            time Checkable Sufficient Condition for Deadlock-Freedom of Component-
            based Systems. In: van Leeuwen, J., Italiano, G.F., van der Hoek, W.,
            Meinel, C., Sack, H., Plášil, F. (eds.) SOFSEM 2007. LNCS, vol. 4362,
            pp. 888–899. Springer, Heidelberg (2007)
[PK07]   Padberg, J., Kuessel, U.: A Component-based Verification Approach based
            on Petri Net Components. In: Proceedings of FORMS/FORMAT 2007,
            pp. 40–50 (2007)
[Sav70]   Savitch, W.: Relationships between Nondeterministic and Deterministic
            Tape Complexities. Journal of Computer and System Sciences 4, 177–192
            (1970)
[Sif05]   Sifakis, J.: A Framework for Component-based Construction. In: Proceed-
            ings of the Third IEEE International Conference on Software Engineering
            and Formal Methods, pp. 293–300. IEEE Computer Society Press, Los
            Alamitos (2005)
[SVvdW]   Sidorova, N., Voorhoeve, M., van der Woude, J.C.S.P.: A Calculus of Petri
            Net Components. In: Proceedings of MOCA 2001, pp. 121–132 (2001)

A New Approach for the Construction of Multiway Decision Graphs

Y. Mokhtari[1], Sa'ed Abed[1], O. Ait Mohamed[1], S. Tahar[1], and X. Song[2]

[1] Dept. of ECE, Concordia University, Canada
{mokhtari,s_abed,ait,tahar}@ece.concordia.ca
[2] Dept. of ECE, Portland State University, USA
song@ee.pdx.edu

Abstract. Multiway Decision Graphs (MDGs) are a canonical representation of a subset of many-sorted first-order logic. It generalizes classical
BDDs with abstract data and uninterpreted functions. In this paper, we
describe a new MDG construction based on the Generalized-If-Then-Else
(GITE) operator. Consequently, we review the main algorithms used for
verification techniques i.e. relational product and pruning by subsumption. Unlike an earlier version of the MDG package, basic MDG algorithms
are defined uniformly through this single GITE operator which will lead
to a more efficient implementation. The new tool, called NuMDG, accepts
an extended SMV language, supporting abstract data sorts.

1 Introduction

Reduced and Ordered Binary Decision Diagrams (ROBDDs) [1] have been widely
studied due to their successful use in automated hardware verification. The key
of the success is a canonical representation and easy manipulation of Boolean
functions. Most BDD packages provide an efficient implementation based on
recursive operations using a three operand function commonly known as ITE.
Moreover, they provide many operations that are extensively used in automated
verification methods. However, these methods suffer from the drawback that
they require a binary representation of the circuit. Every individual bit of every
data signal must be encoded by a separate Boolean variable, while the size of
ROBDD grows, sometimes exponentially, with the number of variables. This
leads to a state explosion problem when ROBDD-based methods are applied to
circuits with complex datapath.

Multiway Decision Graphs (MDGs) [2] have been proposed to overcome this
limitation. MDGs are a canonical representation of a certain class of many-sorted
first-order logic formulae, where data values and operations are represented by
abstract variables and uninterpreted functions, respectively. Therefore, especially
for circuits having a complex datapath, MDGs are much more compact than
ROBDDs and enhance the capability to verify a broader range of circuits [3].
In MDG-based verification, abstract description of states machines (ASM) are
used for modeling systems. In contrast to ordinary Finite State Machines (FSM),
the ASM supports non-finite state machines as models in addition to their intended interpretations. The intent is to rise the abstraction level of automated

J.S. Fitzgerald, A.E. Haxthausen, and H. Yenigun (Eds.): ICTAC 2008, LNCS 5160, pp. 228–242, 2008.
© Springer-Verlag Berlin Heidelberg 2008

verification methods to approach those of interactive theorem proving methods without sacrificing automation. MDGs have been investigated from different angles and it culminated in a MDG tool providing Prolog-style MDG-HDL for modeling and different verification techniques including sequential and combinational equivalence checking, invariant checking and a subset of first-order LTL model checking [4,5].

The work presented here mainly reviews the previous work [2] in one respect. The set of basic operations on MDGs was implemented separately, while ROBDD operations are implemented using a single generic algorithm ITE. This is because the two edges that issue from an ROBDD node labeled x span the ranges of values $\{F, T\}$ that x can take, and this makes it possible to reason by case analysis. Consequently, MDGs do not enjoy this property due to abstract variables. The GITE operation can be considered to be a functionally complete three-input logic gate that implements the expression $GITE = (P \wedge Q) \vee (\neg P \wedge H)$. If P is an abstract variable, then there is no MDG representing the formula $\neg P$. In this paper, we claim that it is possible to use the GITE operation to produce an MDG R that is logically equivalent to $(P \wedge Q) \vee (\neg P \wedge H)$ except for some cases that will be discussed later. This leads to improve the efficiency of the existing basic MDG algorithms.

Finally, we provide an architecture for our new tool. The goal here is to build a robust model checking tool that accepts an extended SMV input language and supports an abstraction mechanism through abstract sorts and uninterpreted functions. Indeed, more work should be spent in implementing and developing the tool in order to enhance the performance.

The paper is organized as follows: Section 2 reviews the closest related work. Section 3 introduces a subset of many-sorted first-order logic that gives MDGs their meaning. Section 4 describes basic MDG algorithms, their optimization and their correctness proof. Section 5 introduces the architecture of NuMDG. Finally, Section 6 concludes our paper and presents the future work.

2   Related Work

Approaches that capture non-finite aspects of the system, by using uninterpreted functions or similar notion like first-order formulae with quantification, are more closely related work.

Burch and Dill [6] have proposed a verification method that uses uninterpreted functions to denote data operations and a decision procedure as a theorem-proving search method. Compared to MDG, their method does not support representation of a set of states, fixpoint calculation and the transition relation can be applied only a given number of times. Since then, uninterpreted functions have generated a considerable interest in two respects: integration into a symbolic model checkers [7,8] or developing BDD-based decision procedures [9,10].

More recently, Bryant et al. [11] translate a formula with uninterpreted functions to propositional formula within the theory of equality while preserving validity.

Therefore, the resulting formula can be checked efficiently either by a BDD or SAT solver. This reduction is based on Ackermann's approach [12] that consists of replacing each occurrence of a function with a new (domain) variable and adding functional consistency constraints in the formula. A similar approach is also proposed by Pnueli *et al.* [13] where the key differences are emphasized in [11].

These approaches are applicable when data operations can be viewed as blackboxes, i.e., the correctness of the system being modeled does not depend on the meaning of these operations. This is usually the form of RTL designs generated by high-level synthesis algorithms that schedule and allocate data operations without being concerned with the specific nature of the operations. However, ignoring properties of data operations leads sometimes to false negatives. For example, a multiplier can be abstracted away when one of its inputs is 0 or 1. In MDG, a simple rewriting system is used to deal with such cases. In [14], Velev combines rewriting rules and Burch and Dill's method [6] to verify out-of-order processors that have a Reorder Buffer.

3 Multiway Decision Graphs Overview

3.1 Sorted Signature

A sorted signature $\Sigma(\mathcal{V}, \mathcal{L}, \mathcal{S})$ consists of an infinite set of variables $\mathcal{V}$, partitioned into a set $\mathcal{V}_{abs}$ of abstract variables and a set $\mathcal{V}_{con}$ of concrete variables, a set of symbols $\mathcal{L}$, partitioned into a set $\mathcal{L}_{CO}$ of cross-operators and a set $\mathcal{L}_F$ of function symbols and a set of sort symbols $\mathcal{S}$, partitioned into a set $\mathcal{S}_{con}$ of concrete sorts and a set $\mathcal{S}_{abs}$ of abstract sorts. All these sets are disjoint. Furthermore there is:

- An arity function that associates to each symbol in $\mathcal{L}$ a natural number. Constant symbols are 0-ary function symbol.
- A function $\eta : \mathcal{V} \to \mathcal{S}$ which gives a sort to each variable symbol.
- A set of sort declarations for terms. A sort declaration for a term is a tuple $t : S$, where t is a non-variable term and $S \in \mathcal{S}_{abs}$ is a sort symbol. We sometimes abbreviate sort declaration $f(x_1, \ldots, x_n) : S$ as $f : S_1 \times \ldots \times S_n \to S$ where S_i is the sort of the variable x_i.
- A set of sort declaration for cross-operators. A sort declaration for a cross-operator is of the form $p : S_1 \times \ldots \times S_n \to S$ where the S_i are sorts and $S \in \mathcal{S}_{con}$

3.2 Well Sorted Terms

The set of well sorted terms $\mathcal{T}(\Sigma, S)$ of sort S in signature Σ is the smallest set such that:

- $x \in \mathcal{T}(\Sigma, S)$ if $x \in \mathcal{V}$ and $\eta(x) \in S$
- $f(t_1, \ldots, t_n) \in \mathcal{T}(\Sigma, S)$ if $t_i \in \mathcal{T}(\Sigma, S_i)$ for $i = 1, \ldots, n$ and $f : S_1 \times \ldots \times S_n \to S$ is a term sort declaration in Σ

The set $\mathcal{T}(\Sigma)$ of all well sorted terms is defined as the union $\bigcup \{\mathcal{T}(\Sigma, S) : S \in \mathcal{S}\}$. If $\mathcal{V} = \emptyset$, then $\mathcal{T}_G(\Sigma, S)$ denotes a set of ground terms i.e. terms that are not containing variables. A substitution σ is represented as a set $\{x_1 \mapsto t_1, \ldots, x_n \mapsto t_n\}$ where $\mathsf{Dom}(\sigma) = \{x_1, \ldots, x_n\}$ and is defined on terms as usual. Its extension by another substitution σ', written $\sigma \oplus \sigma'$, is another substitution such that:

- $\mathsf{Dom}(\sigma) \cap \mathsf{Dom}(\sigma') = \emptyset$ and
- for every variable $x \in \mathsf{Dom}(\sigma \oplus \sigma')$:

$$(\sigma \oplus \sigma')(x) = \begin{cases} \sigma(x) & \text{if } x \in \mathsf{Dom}(\sigma) \\ \sigma'(x) & \text{if } x \in \mathsf{Dom}(\sigma') \end{cases}$$

3.3   Well Formed Directed Formulae (DFs)

The set of well formed formulae $\mathcal{F}(\Sigma, S)$ of sort S in signature Σ is the smallest set such that:

- $x = t$ if $x \in \mathcal{T}(\Sigma, S)$, $t \in \mathcal{T}_G(\Sigma, S)$ and $S \in \mathcal{S}_{con}$.
- $x = t$ if $x, t \in \mathcal{T}(\Sigma, S)$ and $S \in \mathcal{S}_{abs}$.
- $p(t_1, \ldots, t_n) = t$ if $p : S_1 \times \ldots \times S_n \to S$ is a cross-operator declaration in Σ, either $t_i \in \mathcal{T}(\Sigma, S_i)$ and $S_i \in \mathcal{S}_{abs}$ or $t_i \in \mathcal{T}_G(\Sigma, S_i)$ and $S_i \in \mathcal{S}_{con}$ for $i = 1, \ldots, n$ and $t \in \mathcal{T}_G(\Sigma, S)$.
- $\neg P$ is a formula if $Vars(P) \cap \mathcal{V}_{abs} = \emptyset$.
- $P \wedge Q$ is a formula if $Vars(P) \cap Vars(Q) = \emptyset$.
- $P \vee Q$ is a formula if $Vars(P) \cap \mathcal{V}_{abs} = Vars(Q) \cap \mathcal{V}_{abs}$ and for each variable $x \in Vars(P)$ either it occurs as a primary or secondary occurrence but not both.
- $(\exists x : S)P$ is a formula where x can be both primary and secondary occurrence in P.

where further connectives like T F $\Rightarrow$, $\Leftrightarrow$ and $\forall$ are defined as the standard abbreviations. $Vars(P)$ denotes the variables occurring in P. The occurrence of the variable x in a LHS of the formula $x = t$ is called a *primary occurrence*, otherwise it is a *secondary occurrence*. Note that by our syntax definition, only abstract variables have secondary occurrences. We say a DF formula P is of type $U \to V$ iff (i) the set of abstract primary variables of P is equal to V_{abs}, (ii) the set of secondary abstract variables is a subset of U_{abs} and (iii) the concrete variables have occurrences in a set $U_{con} \cup V_{con}$. Intuitively, the set U represents the *independent variables* while V represents the *dependent variables*[1]. In the absence of abstract variables, the sets of variables U and V play symmetrical roles.

3.4   Semantics

A Σ-structure $\mathcal{M}$ consists of:

- $\mathcal{D}$ is a carrier set defined as the union of the denotations for each Sort S i.e. $\mathcal{D} = \bigcup\{\mathcal{D}_S : S \in \mathcal{S}\}$ such that if $S \in \mathcal{S}_{abs}$ then $\mathcal{D}_S$ is non-empty set and if $S \in \mathcal{S}_{con}$ then $\mathcal{D}_S = \{a_1, \ldots, a_n\}$ where $a_i \neq a_j$ for $1 \leq i < j \leq n$.

---

[1] The definition of dependent/independent notion is related to the case statement not with respect to classical function dependency.

- a n-ary function $\mathcal{M}(f) : \mathcal{D}^n \rightarrow \mathcal{D}$ for every n-ary function symbol f.
- a n-ary cross-operator $\mathcal{M}(p) : \mathcal{D}^n \rightarrow \mathcal{D}$ for every n-ary cross-operator symbol p.

We say a partial mapping $\phi : \mathcal{V} \rightarrow \mathcal{D}$ is a partial Σ-assignment iff $\phi(x) \in \mathcal{D}_{\eta(x)}$ for every variable $x \in \mathsf{Dom}(\phi)$. We assume that the structure $\mathcal{M}$ is fixed and the formal definition of the semantics relative to the mapping ϕ is:

$$[\![x]\!]^\phi = \phi(x) \quad \text{for } x \in \mathcal{V}$$
$$[\![f(t_1,\ldots,t_n)]\!]^\phi = \mathcal{M}(f)([\![t_1]\!]^\phi,\ldots,[\![t_n]\!]^\phi)$$
$$[\![x = t]\!]^\phi = tt \text{ iff } [\![x]\!]^\phi = [\![t]\!]^\phi$$
$$[\![p(t_1,\ldots,t_n)]\!]^\phi = tt \text{ iff } \mathcal{M}(p)([\![t_1]\!]^\phi,\ldots,[\![t_n]\!]^\phi) = tt$$
$$[\![\neg P]\!]^\phi = tt \text{ iff } [\![P]\!]^\phi = f\!f$$
$$[\![P \wedge Q]\!]^\phi = tt \text{ iff } [\![P]\!]^\phi = tt \text{ and } [\![Q]\!]^\phi = tt$$
$$[\![(\exists x : S)P]\!]^\phi = tt \text{ iff } [\![P]\!]^{\phi[c/x]} = tt$$
$$\text{for some } c \in \mathcal{D}_S$$
$$\text{such that } \phi[c/x] \text{ is like } \phi$$
$$\text{but maps } x \text{ to } c$$

The remaining logical connectives are interpreted as usual.

3.5   MDG Structure

An *MDG* of type $U \rightarrow V$ is a directed acyclic graph (DAG) G with one root and ordered edges, such that:

1. Every leaf node is labeled by the formula T, except if G has a single node, which may be labeled T or F.
2. For every internal node N, either
   (a) N is labeled by $\mathcal{T}(U \cup V_{con}, \mathcal{L}_{CO}, \mathcal{S})$ and the edges that issue from N are labeled by $\mathcal{T}_G(\mathcal{S}_{con})$, or
   (b) N is labeled by a variable in V_{abs} and the edges that issue from N are labeled by $\mathcal{T}(U_{abs}, \mathcal{L}_F, \mathcal{S})$

MDG is a canonical representation of DFs and therefore must be *reduced* and *ordered* like ROBDD [1]. Consequently, DFs must obey a set of well-formedness conditions given in [2]. Some of them are already stated above. Intuitively, these conditions represent pre-conditions for some basic MDG algorithms which are mainly disjunction, relational product and pruning by subsumption. We will investigate these algorithms in next Section. In order to illustrate the above definitions, we consider the following example DF of type $\{u_1, u_2\} \rightarrow \{v_1, v_2\}$, where u_1 and v_1 are variables of a concrete sort *bool* with enumeration $\{0, 1\}$ while u_2 and v_2 are variables of an abstract sort α, g is an abstract function symbol of type $\alpha \rightarrow \alpha$ and f is a cross-operator of type $\alpha \rightarrow bool$. The MDG of this formula is as follows:

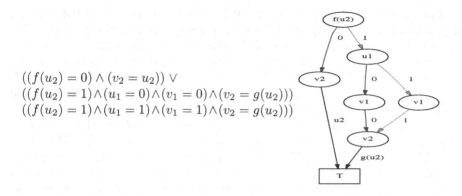

$$((f(u_2) = 0) \wedge (v_2 = u_2)) \vee$$
$$((f(u_2) = 1) \wedge (u_1 = 0) \wedge (v_1 = 0) \wedge (v_2 = g(u_2)))$$
$$((f(u_2) = 1) \wedge (u_1 = 1) \wedge (v_1 = 1) \wedge (v_2 = g(u_2)))$$

4   MDG Construction

Let P be an MDG of the form:

$$\text{MDG}(x, \{a_1, \dots, a_m\}, \{l_1, \dots, l_n\}, \{m_1, \dots, m_n\})$$

then $\mathsf{top}(P)$ denotes the root node x, $\mathsf{arg}(P)$ denotes the set $\{a_1, \dots, a_m\}$ (eventually empty) of the cross-operator arguments, $\mathsf{edges}(P)$ denotes a non-empty set $\{l_1, \dots, l_n\}$ of labels (edges), and $\mathsf{childs}(P)$ denotes a non-empty set $\{m_1, \dots, m_n\}$ of sub-MDGs.

In a ROBDD, Boolean variables are used to encode the enumerated types. This can be done by simply using a recursive function that divides the values into two subsets of roughly equal size, creates a variable to distinguish between them, and then recurses on the two subsets. It results in an Algebraic Decision Diagram (ADD) [16] that extends BDD's by allowing values from arbitrary finite domain to be associated with the terminal nodes. Then this ADD is translated to ROBDD. Due to the presence of abstract sorts, this approach cannot be used for MDG. Therefore, an equation (atomic formula with equality) is used to represent directly the MDG without encoding the concrete domains. We will use the notation $Eq(x, \{a_1, \dots, a_n\}, l)$ to denote an MDG such that (i) the root node is labeled with x and the (eventually empty) set $\{a_1, \dots, a_n\}$ (ii) the edge is labeled with l and (iii) the terminal node is labeled with T.

4.1   Generalized-If-Then-Else (GITE)

Given a ROBDD b, a boolean function f represented by b is recursively defined by:

$$f = (\neg x \wedge f_{x=0}) \vee (x \wedge f_{x=1})$$

where x is the variable in b's root node and the cofactor function $f_{x=0}$ is defined by the reachable subgraph of b's 0-branch child. Similarly, $f_{x=1}$ is recursively defined by the reachable subgraph of b's 1-branch child. Therefore a ROBDD node can be naturally represented by an If-Then-Else statement, i.e. $\mathsf{ITE}(x, f_{x=1}, f_{x=0})$.

Given a variable ordering and three ROBDDs f, g and h, the ROBDD result of f, g and h is easily constructed by Shannon's expansion in the depth-first manner. This expansion process repeats recursively following the given variable order for the Boolean variables in f, g, and h. The base case (also called the terminal case) is when f, g or h are representing a terminal node (i.e. T or F node). For example, $\mathsf{ITE}(\mathsf{T}, g, h)$ can be trivially evaluated to g. The recursive process will terminate because restricting all the variables of functions produces constant functions T or F. At the end of the expansion phase, the uniqueness of ROBDD representation is ensured by reducing expressions like $\mathsf{ITE}(x, f, f)$ to f. This bottom-up reduction phase is performed in the reverse order of the expansion phase. Finally, since all the boolean connectives can be expressed as If-Then-Else statement, this construction provides a uniform way to build arbitrary Boolean functions.

Similarly, our goal is to provide the same construction for MDGs. The definition of the cofactor function is made upon the following observation. Assuming that x ranges over $\{0, 1, 3\}$ and that there could be, say, only three edges issuing from the root, as in the following graph:

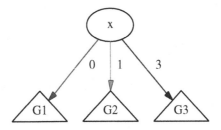

and G_1, G_2 and G_3 represent the formulae P_1, P_2 and P_3 respectively, then this MDG could represent the formula

$$(x = 0 \land P_1) \lor (x = 1 \land P_2) \lor (x = 3 \land P_3)$$

When x denotes 2, this formula is simply a false sentence. Therefore, the cofactor $P_{x=l,\mathsf{arg}(x)}$ with respect to a (concrete or abstract) variable x restricted to label l and a set of the cross-operator arguments $\mathsf{arg}(x)$ (possibly empty) is defined as follows:

$$P_{x=l,\mathsf{arg}(x)} = \begin{cases} P & \text{if } x < \mathsf{top}(P) \\ m_i & \text{if } \exists i (l = l_i) \land (\mathsf{arg}(P) = \mathsf{arg}(x)) \\ \mathsf{F} & \text{otherwise} \end{cases}$$

While concrete sorts have enumerations, abstract sorts do not. To overcome this problem, we can collect all the labels of the abstract variable x from the MDGs involved in the construction. This task is achieved by the function enum which is defined as:

$$\mathsf{enum}(x, P) = \begin{cases} S_{con} & \text{if } x \in S_{con} \text{ and } \mathsf{top}(P) = x \\ \mathsf{edges}(P) & \text{if } x \in S_{abs} \text{ and } \mathsf{top}(P) = x \end{cases}$$

This function exploits the variable ordering, hence there is no need to traverse all the children of P to collect the edges. The generalization of this function to a set of MDGs is defined as usual. Moreover, we assume that the set of edges are ordered.

Our GITE algorithm takes as input three MDGs P, Q and H of type $U_i \rightarrow V_i$ for $i = 1..3$ respectively and produces an MDG $R = GITE(P, Q, H)$ of type $\bigcup_{1 \leq i \leq 3} U_i \rightarrow \bigcup_{1 \leq i \leq 3} V_i$ such that $\models R \Leftrightarrow (P \wedge Q) \vee (\neg P \wedge H)$. Such MDG R does not always exist due to abstract variables. For example, let x be an abstract variable and a be an abstract generic constant. Let P be $x = a$ (i.e., an MDG with a root node labeled x and a single edge labeled a leading to T), then there is no MDG representing the formula $\neg(x = a)$. Thus there can be no algorithm for *general negation*. On the other hand, it is easy to compute a formula logically equivalent to $\neg P$ that has no nodes labeled by abstract variables. Similarly, there does not always exist an MDG R such that $\models R \Leftrightarrow (P \vee Q)$. For example, let x and y be distinct abstract variables, and a and b distinct abstract generic constants, then there exists no well-formed MDG representing the formula $x = a \vee y = b$. Finally, it may be impossible to compute the conjunction of two MDGs whose root nodes have the same label, if that label is an abstract variable (i.e., $x = a \wedge x = b$). Note all these formulae are not DFs since they do not respect the syntax constraints defined in Section 3. Moreover, we claim that the logical equivalence between R and $(P \wedge Q) \vee (\neg P \wedge H)$ can be shown independent of the negation of P, particularly when the top symbol of P is an abstract variable. For example, it is easy to show that $\models (x = a \vee x = b) \Leftrightarrow (x = a \wedge T) \vee (\neg(x = a) \wedge x = b)$ in classical logic. The detailed algorithm is given below:

$GITE(P, Q, H)$
```
1.   if (terminal case) then
2.         return (R = trivial result);
3.   else
4.         if (computed table has entry {(P, Q, H), R}) then
5.               return R from computed table ;
6.         else
7.               x = top variables of P, Q and H;
8.               S = enum(x, P, Q, H);
9.               a = arg(x);
10.              l, m = ∅;
11.              for (each s s.t. s ∈ S) do
12.                    R = GITE(P_{x=s,a}, Q_{x=s,a}, H_{x=s,a});
13.                    if (R ≠ F) then
14.                          append(l,s); append(m,R);
15.                    endif
16.              endfor
17.              if(l = ∅) then (R = F);
18.              else R = find_or_add_unique(x, a, l, m);
19.              endif
20.              insert (P, Q, H, R) in the computed table
```

21.   return R;
22.   endif
23. endif

The result MDG is constructed by recursively performing Shannon's expansion. This recursive expansion ends when a terminal node is reached (lines 1 and 2) or when it is found in the computed table (line 4 and 5). A computed table stores previously computed results to avoid repeating work that was done previously. Line 7 determines the top variable of P, Q and H. Line 8 extracts a set of labels (edges) S according to the top variable sort. When this sort is concrete, then S is equal to the enumeration of this sort. Otherwise, we collect the labels from the MDGs involved in the construction. Line 9 and 10 extract eventually the arguments if the top variable is a cross-operator and initialize the new set of labels and MDGs to be constructed. Lines 11 to 16 recursively perform Shannon's expansion on the cofactor in respect to S and computes the new edges and MDGs by discarding the elements of S that result in a terminal MDG F. At the end of the expansion (line 17), either the resulting MDG is F or the reduction step and uniqueness of the resulting MDG are performed (line 18). The reduction step is applied only on the concrete sorts. Therefore a node is redundant if all the edges are in the enumeration of the concrete sort and the corresponding MDGs are the same.

Theorem 1. *The GITE algorithm is correct and terminates*[2].

4.2   Relational Product (RelP)

The relational product combines conjunction and existential quantification in one step. We provide an algorithm that extends the ROBDD relational product. It takes the conjunction of two MDGs having disjoint sets of abstract primary variables and existentially quantifies with respect to some abstract or concrete variables that have primary occurrence in at least one of the MDGs. The primary occurrence of an abstract variable in one MDG can be a secondary occurrence in the other MDG. For this reason, we have introduced a substitution that includes those variables during the construction (i.e., the secondary variables are implicitly quantified). The substitution is applied in the reverse order of the expansion phase on the edges labeled with secondary occurrence variables and cross-operators arguments. However, while the ordering variable cannot be preserved in case of cross-operators, there may exist redundant or contradictory MDG result during intermediate steps. For example, let $x < m < M$ be an ordering variables and let P be $leq(x, m) = 1 \land leq(x, M) = 0$ where x, m and M are secondary abstract variables that having primary occurrences in another MDG, say, Q, and $\sigma = \{x \mapsto x\#3, m \mapsto x\#2, M \mapsto x\#1\}$, then the resulting MDG $leq(x\#3, x\#2) = 1 \land leq(x\#3, x\#1)) = 0$ does not preserve the order[3]. Therefore, we will distinguish the case of the cross-operator and provide a special construction for it.

---

[2] The correctness proof of all the algorithms is included in a technical report[19].

[3] The variable $x\#i$ serves as a symbolic value of x at the ith step and $i < j \Rightarrow x\#i < x\#j$.

Let E be the set of quantified variables, our algorithm takes two MDGs P, Q of type $U_i \to V_i$ for $i = 1..2$ and a substitution σ with $\mathsf{Dom}(\sigma) = E$ and returns an MDG $R = \mathsf{RelP}(P, Q, E, \sigma)$ of type $(\bigcup_{1 \le i \le 2} U_i \setminus \bigcup_{1 \le i \le 2} V_i) \to (\bigcup_{1 \le i \le 2} V_i \setminus \bigcup_{1 \le i \le 2} U_i)$ such that $\models R \Leftrightarrow \exists E(P \wedge Q)$.

$\mathsf{RelP}(P, Q, E, \sigma)$
1. if (terminal case) then
2.   return ($R = $ trivial result);
3. else
4.   if (computed table has entry $\{(P, Q, E, \sigma), R\}$) then
5.   return R from computed table ;
6.   else
7. $x = $ top variables of P, Q
8. $S = \mathsf{enum}(x, P, Q)$;
9. $a = \mathsf{arg}(x)$;
10. $l, m = \emptyset$;
11.   for (each s s.t. $s \in S$) do
12. $R = \mathsf{RelP}(P_{x=s,a}, Q_{x=s,a}, E, Extend(\sigma, x, s, E))$;
13.   if ($R \ne \mathsf{F}$) then
14.   append(l,s); append(m,R);
15.   endif
16.   endfor
17.   if($l = \emptyset$) then ($R = \mathsf{F}$);
18.   else
19.   if($x \in E$) then
20. $R = Or(m)$
21.   else
22.   if($a = \emptyset$) then
23. $R = \mathsf{find\_or\_add\_unique}(x, a, \sigma(l), m)$;
24.   else
25. $R = \mathsf{F}$
26.   for (each $l_i \in l$ and $m_i \in m$)
27. $R = Or(R, And(Eq(x, \sigma(a), l_i), m_i))$
28.   endfor
29.   endif
30.   endif
31.   endif
32.   insert (P, Q, E, σ, R) in the computed table
33.   return R
34. endif
35. endif

Like ROBDD relational product algorithm, RelP uses a result cache. If the entry (P, Q, E, σ) is in the cache, then it means that a previous call to $\mathsf{RelP}(P, Q, E, \sigma)$ returned R as result. Lines 7 and 16 apply recursively the relational product with respect to a top symbol x where $Extend(\sigma, x, s, E)$ returns $\sigma \oplus \{s/x\}$ if $x \in E$

otherwise it returns σ. Lines 19 to 31 apply either quantification or conjunction depending whether the variable x occurs in E or not. As explained above, we distinguish the cross-operators case (lines 25 to 28), where we construct a new MDG that respects the ordering variable, thus avoiding any contradictions.

Theorem 2. *The* RelP *algorithm is correct and terminates.*

4.3   Pruning by Subsumption (PbyS)

The pruning by subsumption algorithm approximates the difference of sets represented by MDGs (i.e. DFs). We propose a new algorithm which uses restricted operators and builds an MDG in a similar manner as GITE does. The proposed algorithm improves the original one in many ways. First, the expansion is done only on the first argument i.e., P rather than on P and Q. Indeed, we can view each disjunct of DF as a state description. Without loss of generality, we can assume that P and Q contain only one disjunct. Then, we can say that P is subsumed by Q if and only if there exists a substitution σ such that the state description of $Q\sigma$ is a subset of the state description of P. Therefore the size of P should be at least equal to the size of Q. Next, when the top variable of Q is less than the top variable of P, it is obvious that the state description of Q is not a subset of P. Hence, the cofactor of Q should be F, which improves drastically the original algorithm. Finally, when P and Q have the same top symbol cross-operator but there is a mismatch either on the edges or on the arguments, the cofactor of Q is Q itself and we discard the substitution if any resulting from the unification of their arguments. These observations lead to a new restricted operator defined as follows.

Given an MDG Q, the restriction of Q with respect to a variable x, an edge l, a set of cross-operator arguments $\mathsf{arg}(x)$ and a substitution σ, written $Q|_{x=l,\mathsf{arg}(x),\sigma}$, returns a pair of MDG-substitution $\langle m, \sigma' \rangle$ as:

$$\begin{cases} \langle Q, \sigma \rangle & \text{if } x < \mathsf{top}(Q) \\ \langle F, \sigma \rangle & \text{if } \mathsf{top}(Q) < x \\ \langle m_i, \sigma' \rangle & \text{if } (\exists i)(l = l_i \sigma') \wedge \mathsf{arg}(Q) = \mathsf{arg}(x) = \emptyset \\ \langle Q, \sigma \rangle & \text{if } (\not\exists i)(l = l_i \sigma') \wedge \mathsf{arg}(Q) = \mathsf{arg}(x) = \emptyset \\ \langle m_i, \sigma'' \rangle & \text{if } \exists i (l = l_i \sigma'') \wedge (\mathsf{arg}(Q)\sigma'' = \mathsf{arg}(x)) \\ \langle Q, \sigma \rangle & \text{if } \not\exists i (l = l_i \sigma'') \vee (\mathsf{arg}(Q)\sigma'' \neq \mathsf{arg}(x)) \\ \langle F, \sigma \rangle & \text{otherwise} \end{cases}$$

where $\sigma' = \sigma \oplus \{l_i \mapsto l\}$ and $\sigma'' = \sigma \oplus \{\mathsf{arg}(Q) \mapsto \mathsf{arg}(x)\}$.

Our PbyS algorithm takes two MDGs P and Q of type $U \rightarrow V_1$ and $U \rightarrow V_2$ and a substitution σ initially equal to the identity and produces an MDG P' of type $U \rightarrow V_1$ such that P' is derivable from P by *pruning* some paths such that $\models P \vee (\exists U)Q \equiv P' \vee (\exists U)Q$. The paths that are removed from P are subsumed by Q, hence the name of the algorithm. If $P' = F$ then, we can view P' as a logical difference of P and $(\exists U)Q$ i.e. $\models P \Rightarrow (\exists U)Q$. The detailed algorithm is given below:

PbyS(P, Q, σ)
1.   if (terminal case) then return (P' = trivial result);
2.   else if (pbys table has entry $\{(P, Q, \sigma), P'\}$) then
3.   return P' from pbys table ;
4.   else
5. $x = \mathsf{top}(P); l, m = \emptyset; a = \mathsf{arg}(P);$
6.   for (each $s \in \mathsf{edges}(P)$) do
7. $P' = P_{x=s,a};$
8.   stack $= Q|_{x=s,a,\sigma};$
9.   while stack is not empty;
10. $\langle m', \sigma' \rangle =$ pop stack;
11. $P' = \mathsf{PbyS}(P', m', \sigma');$
12.   if ($P' = \mathsf{F}$) break;
13.   endwhile;
14.   if($P' \neq \mathsf{F}$) then
15.   append(l,s); append(m,P');
16.   endif
17.   endfor;
18.   if($l = \emptyset$) then ($P' = \mathsf{F}$);
19.   else $P' = $ find_or_add_unique$(x, a, l, m);$
20.   update pbys table $(\{(P, Q, \sigma), P'\})$;
21.   return P';
22. endif

The result MDG is constructed by recursively performing the restricted operators introduced on P and Q until a terminal node is reached (line 1) or when it is found in the pbys table (line 2). Line 5 determines the top variable of P and the cross-operator arguments (if possible) and initializes the new edges and children to be constructed. Then from each edge issuing from the node x (line 6), we extract the cofactors of P and Q where the cofactors of Q are pairs of MDG-substitution stored in a stack. Lines 9 to 13 check whether the cofactors of P, written P', is subsumed by one of the Q paths. If so (line 12) then there is no need to try the other cofactors of Q and therefore we continue with the remaining cofactors of P and we discard P'. Otherwise, the edge and this cofactor are added to the corresponding table (lines 14-16). When we have processed all the cofactors of P (line 18) either all the paths of P are subsumed by P and thus the result MDG is F, or the reduction step and uniqueness of the resulting MDG are performed (line 20) with all or some paths of P that not subsumed.

Theorem 3. *The* PbyS *algorithm is correct and terminates.*

5   NuMDG Structure

A high level description of NuMDG is given in Figure 1. In the future, we will provide an open source tool with many functionalities independent of the model checking engine used. Like NuSMV [17], the tool will be able to process files

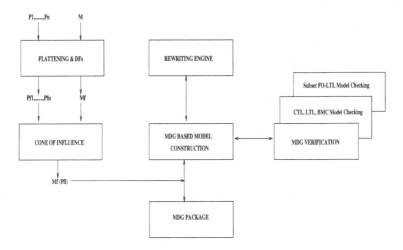

Fig. 1. Internal structure of NuMDG

written in an extension of the SMV language with abstract sort and uninterpreted functions. In this language, finite state machines are described by using instantiation mechanism of modules and processes, corresponding to synchronous and asynchronous composition respectively. The requirements are written in CTL, LTL or in a first-order subset of temporal logic.

An (extended) SMV file is processed in several phases. The first phase analyzes the input file with different layers in order to construct an internal representation of the model. The construction starts from modular description of a model M and of a set of properties $P_1, \ldots P_n$. The flattening step consists of eliminating modules and processes and producing a synchronous flat model, where each variable is given an absolute name. The second step, called DF, maps each expression in the flat model to a directed formula, thus obtaining the corresponding flattened directed model M_f. Compared to SMV-based tools, there is no boolean encoding. Hence, some interpreted predicates and arithmetic functions are not supported in a straightforward manner. The same reduction is applied to the properties P_i, thus obtaining the corresponding flattened directed formula P_{if}. By cone of influence, we restrict the analysis of each property to the relevant parts of the model $M_f(P_{if})$.

After the preprocessing phase, the user can choose the model checking engine to be used for verification. The choice is restricted by the nature of the model being described i.e. whether it supports abstract sorts and uninterpreted functions or not. In the absence of the latter, NuMDG is acting like NuSMV and should provide the same facilities including MDG-based, SAT-based model checking and different partitioning methods. For the time being, MDG-based verification includes reachability analysis and fair CTL model checking.

The rewriting engine is used during the MDG-verification if necessary when the reachability analysis does not terminate due to the presence of abstract sort and uninterpreted functions. In this case we can interpret partially some functions or predicates in order to cope with this non termination [18]. The input language supports a rewriting layer which is extracted and feeded to the rewriting engine. Currently, we are working to complete the infrastructure shown in Figure 1.

6   Conclusion and Future Work

We have described the basic MDG algorithms that incorporated many optimizations that will yield further improvements in the performance of MDG package. The efficiency is achieved through the use of the generalization of the If-Then-Else (ITE) operator defined in the BDD package. Consequently, we have redefined the main algorithms on which the MDG verification techniques are based, i.e, relational product and pruning by subsumption. These new algorithms descriptions are based mainly on the ROBDD ones and lifted to the realm of abstract sorts and uninterpreted functions.

We have also presented the internal architecture of the NuMDG tool and identified a number of open issues and future work directions. We need to complete the implementation and confirm that NuMDG can be used to check SMV specifications. However, the effect of cache and the garbage collection should be characterized according to a rigorous evaluation methodology. Also case studies and experiments are required to check the new tool and compare the results with SMV.

References

1. Bryant, R.E.: Graph-based Algorithms for Boolean Function Manipulation. IEEE Transactions on Computers 35(8), 677–691 (1986)
2. Corella, F., Zhou, Z., Song, X., Langevin, M., Cerny, E.: Multiway Decision Graphs for Automated Hardware Verification. Formal Methods in System Design 10(2), 7–46 (1997)
3. Tahar, S., Song, X., Cerny, E., Zhou, Z., Langevin, M., Ait Mohamed, O.: Modeling and Verification of the Fairisle ATM Switch Fabric using MDGs. IEEE Transactions on CAD of Integrated Circuits and Systems 18(7), 956–972 (1999)
4. Xu, Y., Cerny, E., Song, X., Corella, F., Ait Mohamed, O.: Model Checking for A First-Order Temporal Logic using Multiway Decision Graphs. The Computer Journal 47(1), 71–84 (2004)
5. Zhou, Z.: Mutliway Decision Graphs and Their Applications in Automatic Formal Verification of RTL Designs, PhD thesis, Montréal University (1997)
6. Burch, J.R., Dill, D.L.: Automatic Verification of Pipelined Microprocessor Control. In: Dill, D.L. (ed.) CAV 1994. LNCS, vol. 818, pp. 68–80. Springer, Heidelberg (1994)
7. Damm, W., Pnueli, A., Ruah, S.: Herbrand Automata for Hardware Verification. In: Sangiorgi, D., de Simone, R. (eds.) CONCUR 1998. LNCS, vol. 1466, pp. 67–83. Springer, Heidelberg (1998)
8. Berezin, S., Biere, A., Clarke, E.M., Zhu, Y.: Combining Symbolic Model Checking with Uninterpreted Functions for Out-of-Order Processor Verification. Formal Methods in Computer Aided Design 1522, 187–201 (1998)

9. Hojati, R., Kuehlmann, A., German, S., Brayton, R.K.: Validity Checking in the Theory of Equality with Uninterpreted Functions using Finite Instantiations. In: The International Workshop on Logic Synthesis (1997)

10. Goel, A., Sajid, K., Zhou, H., Aziz, A., Singhal, V.: BDD based Procedures for A Theory of Equality with Uninterpreted Functions. In: Y. Vardi, M. (ed.) CAV 1998. LNCS, vol. 1427, pp. 244–255. Springer, Heidelberg (1998)

11. Bryant, R.E., German, S., Velev, M.N.: Processor Verification Using Efficient Reductions of the Logic of Uninterpreted Functions to Propositional Logic. ACM Transactions on Computational Logic 2(1), 93–134 (2001)

12. Ackermann, W.: Solvable Cases of the Decision Problem. North-Holland Pub. Co., Amsterdam (1954)

13. Pnueli, A., Rodeh, Y., Shitrichman, O., Siegel, M.: Deciding Equality Formulas by Small Domain Instantiations. In: Halbwachs, N., Peled, D.A. (eds.) CAV 1999. LNCS, vol. 1633, pp. 455–469. Springer, Heidelberg (1999)

14. Velev, M.N.: Using Rewriting Rules and Positive Equality to Formally Verify Wide-issue Out-of-Order Microprocessors with Reorder Buffer. In: Proc. of DAC, pp. 28–35 (2002)

15. Clocksin, W., Mellish, C.: Programming in Prolog, 3rd edn. Springer, Heidelberg (1987)

16. Bahar, R., Frohm, E., Gaona, C., Hatchel, G., Macii, E., Pardo, A., Sommenzi, F.: Algebraic Decision Diagrams and their Applications. In: Proc. of International Conference on Computer-Aided Design, pp. 188–191 (1993)

17. Cimatti, A., Clarke, E., Giunchiglia, E., Giunchiglia, F., Pistore, M., Roveri, M., Sebastiani, R., Tacchella, A.: NuSMV Version 2: An OpenSource Tool for Symbolic Model Checking. In: Brinksma, E., Larsen, K.G. (eds.) CAV 2002. LNCS, vol. 2404, Springer, Heidelberg (2002)

18. Ait Mohamed, O., Song, X., Cerny, E.: On the Non-termination of MDG-based Abstract State Enumeration. Theoretical Computer Science 300, 161–179 (2003)

19. Mokhtari, Y., Abed, S., Ait Mohamed, O., Tahar, S., Song, X.: A New Approach for the Construction of Multiway Decision Graphs. Technical Report 2008-3-Abed, ECE Department, Concordia University, Montreal, Canada (June 2008)

Congruence Results of Scope Equivalence for a Graph Rewriting Model of Concurrent Programs

Masaki Murakami

Mathematical Science and Electronic Technology,
Graduate School of Natural Science and Technology, Okayama University
3-1-1 Tsushima-Naka, Okayama, 700-0082, Japan
murakami@momo.cs.okayama-u.ac.jp

Abstract. This paper presents a formal model of concurrent systems based on graph rewriting to represent scopes of communication channel names precisely. A bipartite directed acyclic graph represents a concurrent system consists of a number of processes and messages. Each process or message corresponds to a source node of the graph. Names of communication channel in the system are sink nodes. The edges of the graph represent the scopes of the names in the system. The operational semantics of the system is given as a labeled transition system. The model presented here makes it possible to represent local names that their scope are not nested. We define an equivalence relation that two systems are equivalent not only in their behavior but in extrusions of scopes of names. We show that the equivalence relation is a congruence relation wrt prefix, new-name, replication and composition.

1   Introduction

A number of formal models of concurrent systems that are based on communication using channel names such as [5,10,12] are reported. Operations to restrict the scopes of channel names such as ν-operations[10] are introduced many of them. It is essential to describe which process is in *the scope of each name* in the system for models of distributed systems.

However, as we reported in [6,8], it is difficult to represent the scopes of names of communication channels using models based on process algebra. In many existing models based on process algebra, the scope of a name is represented using a binary operation as the ν-operation[10]. Thus the scope of a name is a subterm of an expression representing a system. For example, in a π-calculus term: $\nu a_2(\nu a_1(b_1|b_2)|b_3)$, the scope of the name a_2 is the subterm $(\nu a_1(b_1|b_2)|b_3)$ and the scope of the name a_2 is the subterm $(b_1|b_2)$. However, this method has problems as followings.

For example, consider a system **S** consisting of a server and two clients. A client b_1 communicates with the server b_2 using a channel a_1 whose name is known only by b_2 and oneself, and a client b_3 communicates with b_2 using a channel a_2 that is known only by b_2 and oneself. In this system a_1 and a_2 are local names. As b_2 and b_1 knows the name a_1 but b_3 does not, then the scope of a_1 includes b_1 and b_2 and the scope of a_2 includes b_3 and b_2. Thus the scopes of a_1 and a_2 are not nested as shown in Fig.1.

J.S. Fitzgerald, A.E. Haxthausen, and H. Yenigun (Eds.): ICTAC 2008, LNCS 5160, pp. 243–257, 2008.

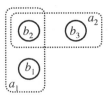

Fig. 1. Scopes of names in **S**

The method denoting local names as bound names using ν-operator cannot represent the scopes of a_1 and a_2 precisely because the scope of a name is a sub-term of a term and then the scopes of bound variable are nested (or disjoint) in any π-calculus term. In order to represent the situation above using ν-operator, the scopes must be 'encoded' into the nested scopes. For example, we must denote the above example as $\nu a_1(b_1|\nu a_2(b_2|b_3))$ or $\nu a_2(b_3|\nu a_1(b_1|b_2))$. Then we require a number of inferences to 'decode' the system using the structural congruence rules to see the scope for each name. And we must regard $\nu a_1(b_1|\nu a_2(b_3|b_2))$ and $\nu a_2(b_3|\nu a_1(b_1|b_2))$ equivalent because both of them represents the same system **S** shown in Fig.1. Then it is impossible to represent scopes of a_1 and a_2 with just one expression precisely.

Furthermore, it is sometimes impossible to represent the scope even for one name precisely with ν-operator. Consider the example, $\nu a(\bar{v}a.P) \mid v(x).Q$ where x does not occur in Q. In this example, a is a local name and its scope is $\bar{v}a.P$. The scope of a is extruded by communication with prefixes $\bar{v}a$ and $v(x)$. Then the result of the action is $\nu a(P|Q)$ and Q is in the scope of a. However, as a does not occur in Q, it is equivalent to $(\nu aP)|Q$ by the rules of the structural congruence. We cannot see the fact that a is 'leaked' to Q from the resulting expression: $(\nu aP)|Q$. Thus we must keep the trace of communication for the analysis of scope extrusion. This makes difficult to analyze extrusions of scopes of names by executions.

We presented a model based on graph rewriting[6,8] instead of process algebra as a solution for the problem on representation of scopes of names and defined an equivalence relation *scope equivalence* in that two systems are equivalent not only in their behavior but extrusions of scopes of names. And we presented examples that are equivalent in their behavior but not scope equivalent. We reported the congruence results of the bisimulation equivalence relation on the model[7]. This paper presents congruence results for of the scope equivalence.

Congruence results on bisimilarity based on graph rewriting models are reported in [1,11]. Those studies adopts graph transformation approach for proof techniques. In this paper, graph rewriting is introduced to extend the model for the representation of name scopes.

2   Basic Idea

The model presented here is based on graph rewriting system such as [4,5,9,12]. We represent a concurrent program consists of a number of processes (and

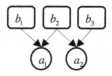

Fig. 2. Bipartite Directed Acyclic Graph

Fig. 3. A Message Node

messages on the way) using a bipartite directed acyclic graph. A bipartite graph is a graph whose nodes are decomposed into two disjoint sets: source nodes and sink nodes such that no two graph nodes within the same set are adjacent. Every edge is directed from a source node to a sink node. The system **S** shown in Fig.1. is represented with a graph as Fig.2.

Processes and messages on the way are represented with source nodes. We call source nodes as *behaviors*. In Fig. 2., b_1, b_2 and b_3 are behaviors. A behavior node has a nested structure in general. Namely, a behavior has a graph structure of a program inside. Then the structure of a program is a recursive graph. Scopes of names are represented edges of the graph.

Message. A behavior node that represents a message is a node labeled with a name of the recipient n (it is called the subject of the message) and the object of the message o (Fig.3). The object of the message is a name.

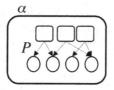

Fig. 4. A Process Node

Message receiving. A message is received by a receiver process. A process that receives a message execute an input action and then continue the execution. We denote such receiver process with a node consists of its *epidermis* that denotes the first input action and its *content* that denotes the continuation. For example, a receiver that executes an input action α and then become a program P (denoted as $\alpha.P$ in CCS term), it is denoted with the epidermis labeled with α and the content P (Fig.4). As the continuation P is a concurrent program, then it has a graph structure inside of the node. Thus the receiver process also has the nested structure.

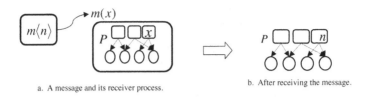

a. A message and its receiver process.

b. After receiving the message.

Fig. 5. Message Receiving

Fig. 6. Message Sending

Message receiving is represented as follows. Consider a message to send an name n to a recipient with name m and the receiver of the message(Fig.5. a). The execution of the input action is represented by "peeling" the epidermis of the receiver process node. When the message is received then it vanishes and the epidermis of the receiver is removed and the content is exposed (Fig.5. b). Now the continuation P is activated. The received name n is substituted to the name x in the content P.

Message sending. In asynchronous π-calculus, message sending is represented in the same way to process activation. We adopt the similar idea. Consider an example that executes an input action α and send a message m (Fig.6. left). When the action α is executed, then the epidermis is peeled and the message m is exposed as Fig.6. right. Now the message m is transmitted and m can be received by the receiver. And the execution of Q continues.

Scopes of names. Names of communication channel in the system are sink nodes of the graph in this model. We represent the scopes of the local names using edges of the graph. Consider a system consists of three processes (behaviors) b_1, b_2 and b_3 and two names a_1 and a_2 as in Fig.1. Let b_1 and b_2 be in the scope of a_1 and b_2 and b_3 be in the scope of a_2. We represent such system with a directed acyclic graph (DAG) such as Fig.2. A process (or a message) is inside of the scope of a name if and only if there is an edge to the name from the process in the DAG. In Fig.2., as a_1 is reachable from b_1 and b_2, then b_1 and b_2 are in the scope of a_1, and b_2 and b_3 are in the scope of a_2 as the sink node a_2 is reachable from b_2 and b_3. It is possible to represent local names that their scope are not nested with the model. It is difficult to represent this situation precisely with restriction operation, which is commonly used in models based on process algebra.

3   Formal Definitions

3.1   Programs

First, a countably-infinite set of *names* is presupposed as other formal models based on process algebra.

Definition 3.1 (program, behaviours) Let $a_1, \ldots, a_k$ are distinct names.

(i) A *program* is a a bipartite directed acyclic graph with source nodes $b_1, \ldots, b_m$ and sink nodes $a_1, \ldots, a_k$ such that

- Each source node $b_i (1 \leq i \leq m)$ is a behaviour. Multiple occurrences of the same behavior are allowed.
- Each sink node is a name $a_j (1 \leq j \leq k)$. All a_j's are distinct.
- Each edge is directed from a source node to a sink node. Namely, an edge is an ordered pair (b_i, a_j) of a source node and a name. For any source node b_i and a name a_j there is at most one edge from b_i to a_j.

For a program P, we denote the multiset of all source nodes of P as $\mathrm{src}(P)$, the set of all sink nodes as $\mathrm{snk}(P)$ and the set of all edges as $\mathrm{edge}(P)$. Note that the empty graph $\mathbf{0}$ such that $\mathrm{src}(\mathbf{0}) = \mathrm{snk}(\mathbf{0}) = \mathrm{edge}(\mathbf{0}) = \emptyset$ is a program, that represents an inactive program just like $\mathbf{0}$ in π-calculus.

(ii) A *behavior* is a message or a node consists of *the epidermis* and *the content* defined as follows. In the following of this definition, we assume that any element of $\mathrm{snk}(P) \cup \{x\}$ occurs only in P and does not occur anywhere else in the programs.

1. A node labeled with a tuple of names n (called *the subject of the message*) and o (called *the object of the message*) is *a message* and denoted as $n\langle o \rangle$.
2. A node whose epidermis is labeled with ! and the content is a program P is *a replication*, and denoted as $!P$.
3. *An input prefix* is a node (denoted as $a(x).P$) that the epidermis is labeled with a tuple of a name a and a variable x and the content is a program P.
4. A τ-*prefix* is a node (denoted as $\tau.P$) that the epidermis is labeled with a silent action τ and the content is a program P.

The assumption for the elements of $\mathrm{snk}(P) \cup \{x\}$ is from the idea that these names are "private names" on P and they can be renamed if necessary. Note that this assumption is assumed for the contents of some behaviours (input prefixes, τ-prefixes or replications) in a program but not assumed for the whole of the program.

Definition 3.2 (free name, bound name)

1. For a behavior b, *the set of free names of b* : $\mathrm{fn}(b)$ is defined as follows.
   - $\mathrm{fn}(a\langle o \rangle) = \{a, o\}$,

- $\text{fn}(!P) = \text{fn}(P)$,
- $\text{fn}(\tau.P) = \text{fn}(P)$ and
- $\text{fn}(a(x).P) = (\text{fn}(P) \setminus \{x\}) \cup \{a\}$.

2. For a program P where $\text{src}(P) = \{b_1, \ldots, b_m\}$, $\text{fn}(P) = \bigcup_i \text{fn}(b_i) \setminus \text{snk}(P)$.

The set of *bound names* of P (denoted as $\text{bn}(P)$) is the set of all names that occur in P (including elements of $\text{snk}(P)$ even if they do not occur in any element of $\text{src}(P)$) but not in $\text{fn}(P)$. We can rename bound names as the case of π-calculus. Renaming operation is defined as follow.

Definition 3.3 (renaming). For a program P, $n \in \text{bn}(P)$ and a flesh name n' that does not occur in P, *renaming n with n'* is the operation replacing all occurrences of n in $\text{src}(P), \text{snk}(P)$ and $\text{edge}(P)$ with n'.

Definition 3.4 (locality condition). A program P is *local* if for any input prefix $c(x).Q$ that occurs in P, no input prefix in Q has the form of $x(y).R$.

Definition 3.5 (normal program). A program P is *normal* if for any program Q occur in $b \in \text{src}(P)$, for any $b' \in \text{src}(Q)$ for any $n \in \text{fn}(b') \cap \text{snk}(Q)$, $(b', n) \in \text{edge}(Q)$.

It is quite natural to assume the normality for a program, because anyone must know the name to use it. The locality condition says that "anyone cannot use the name given from other one as the name of itself to receive messages". Though this condition affects the expressive power of the model, in many practical examples, transfer of receiving capability is implemented with transfer of sending capability. We do not consider that this restriction seriously damages the expressive power. So in this paper, we consider local and normal programs only. Theoretical motivations of this restriction are discussed in [10].

Definition 3.6 (composition). Let P and Q be programs and $\text{src}(P) \cap \text{src}(Q) = \emptyset$. *The composition $P \| Q$ of P and Q* is the program such that:

- $\text{src}(P \| Q) = \text{src}(P) \cup \text{src}(Q)$.
- $\text{snk}(P \| Q) = \text{snk}(P) \cup \text{snk}(Q)$.
- $\text{edge}(P \| Q) = \text{edge}(P) \cup \text{edge}(Q)$.

Intuitively, $P \| Q$ is the parallel composition of P and Q. Note that we do not assume $\text{snk}(P) \cap \text{snk}(Q) = \emptyset$. Obviously $P \| Q = Q \| P$ and $((P \| Q) \| R) = (P \| (Q \| R))$ for any P, Q and R from the definition. The empty graph **0** is the unit of "$\|$". Note that $\text{src}(P) \cup \text{src}(Q)$ and $\text{edge}(P) \cup \text{edge}(Q)$ denote the multiset unions while $\text{snk}(P) \cup \text{snk}(Q)$ denotes the set union.

Definition 3.7 (N-closure). For a normal program P and a set of names N such that $N \cap \text{bn}(P) = \emptyset$, *the N-closure $\nu N(P)$* is the program such that:

$$\mathrm{src}(\nu N(P)) = \mathrm{src}(P)$$
$$\mathrm{snk}(\nu N(P)) = \mathrm{snk}(P) \cup N$$
$$\mathrm{edge}(\nu N(P)) = \mathrm{edge}(P) \cup \{(b,n)|b \in \mathrm{src}(P), n \in N\}$$

Intuitively, N-closure corresponds to the the ν-operation of π-calculus.

Definition 3.8 (deleting a behaviour). For a normal program P and $b \in \mathrm{src}(P)$, $P \setminus b$ is a program that is obtained by deleting a node b and edges that are connected with b from P. Namely,

$$\mathrm{src}(P \setminus b) = \mathrm{src}(P) \setminus \{b\}$$
$$\mathrm{snk}(P \setminus b) = \mathrm{snk}(P)$$
$$\mathrm{edge}(P \setminus b) = \mathrm{edge}(P) \setminus \{(b,n)|(b,n) \in \mathrm{edge}(P)\}$$

Note that $\mathrm{src}(P) \setminus \{b\}$ and $\mathrm{edge}(P) \setminus \{(b,n)|(b,n) \in \mathrm{edge}(P)\}$ denote the multiset subtractions.

Definition 3.9 (context). Let P be a program and $b \in \mathrm{src}(P)$ where b is an input prefix, τ-prefix or a replication and the content of b is $\mathbf{0}$. A *simple context* is a graph $P[\ ]$ such that the contents $\mathbf{0}$ of b is replaced with a *hole* "$[\ ]$". We call a simple context as a *τ-context*, an *input context* or *replication context* if the hole is the contents of a τ-prefix, of an input prefix or of a replication respectively.

A *context* is a simple context or the graph $P[Q[\_]]$ that is obtained by replacing the hole of a simple context $P[\ ]$ replacing with a context $Q[\ ]$ (with some renaming of the names occur in Q if necessary).

For a context $P[\ ]$ and a program Q, $P[Q]$ is a program obtained by replacing the hole in $P[\ ]$ by Q (with some renaming of the names occur in Q if necessary).

3.2   Operational Semantics

We define the operational semantics with a labeled transition system.

Definition 3.10 (substitution). *The substitution* of a name to a program or to a behaviour is defined recursively as follows. Let p be a behavior or a program. For a name a, we assume that $a \in \mathrm{fn}(p)$. The substitution of a name $o (\notin \mathrm{bn}(p))$ to name a in p is denoted as $p[o/a]$ and defined as follows.

- for a name c, $c[o/a] = \begin{cases} o & \text{if } c = a \\ c & \text{otherwise} \end{cases}$
- $(m\langle n\rangle)[o/a] = m[o/a]\langle n[o/a]\rangle$,
- $(!P)[o/a] =!(P[o/a])$,
- $(c(x).P)[o/a] = c(x).(P[o/a])$,
- $(\tau.P)[o/a] = \tau.(P[o/a])$ and
- for a program P and $a \in \mathrm{fn}(P)$, $P[o/a] = P'$ where P' is a program such that

$$\mathrm{src}(P') = \{b[o/a]|b \in \mathrm{src}(P)\},$$
$$\mathrm{snk}(P') = \mathrm{snk}(P) \text{ and}$$
$$\mathrm{edge}(P') = \{(b[o/a],n)|(b,n) \in \mathrm{edge}(P)\}.$$

For the case of input prefix, note that we can assume $x \neq a$ because $a \in$ $\text{fn}(c(x).P)$ without losing generality. (We can rename x if necessary.) We can also assume $a \neq c$ from the locality condition as substitutions are applied only for the contents of input prefixes. We can also assume that $o \notin \text{snk}(P)$ because we consider only the case that P is the contents of a input prefix (from the definition of a program, elements of $\text{snk}(P)$ do not occur in elsewhere as o).

Note that substitutions work only for the occurrences of names in $\text{src}(P)$. The elements of $\text{snk}(P)$ are not affected by substitutions. On the other hand, renameings affect elements of $\text{snk}(P)$.

Definition 3.11 (action). *An action* is *a silent action* τ, an output action or an input action. For a name a and o, *an input action* is a tuple $a(o)$ and *an output action* is a tuple $a\langle o \rangle$.

Definition 3.12 (labeled transition). For an action α, $\overset{\alpha}{\rightarrow}$ is the least binary relation on normal programs that satisfies the following rules.

Input: if $b \in \text{src}(P)$ and $b = a(x).Q$, then $P \overset{a(o)}{\rightarrow} (P \setminus b) \| \nu\{n|(b,n) \in \text{edge}(P)\} \nu o Q[o/x]$

τ-Action: if $b \in \text{src}(P)$ and $b = \tau.Q$, then $P \overset{\tau}{\rightarrow} (P\setminus b) \| \nu\{n|(b,n) \in \text{edge}(P)\}Q$

Replication 1: $P \overset{\alpha}{\rightarrow} P'$ if $!Q \in \text{src}(P)$, and $P\|\nu\{n|(!Q,n) \in \text{edge}(P)\}Q' \overset{\alpha}{\rightarrow} P'$, where Q' is a program obtained from Q by renaming all names in $\text{snk}(R)$ to distinct fresh names that do not occur in anywhere else, for all R's where each R is a program that occur in Q (including Q itself).

Replication 2: $P \overset{\tau}{\rightarrow} P'$ if $!Q \in \text{src}(P)$ and $P\|\nu\{n|(!Q,n) \in \text{edge}(P)\}(Q'_1\|Q'_2) \overset{\tau}{\rightarrow} P'$, where each $Q'_i (i = 1,2)$ is a program obtained from Q by renaming all names in $\text{snk}(R)$ to distinct fresh names that do not occur in anywhere else, for all R's where each R is a program that occur in Q (including Q itself).

Output: if $b \in \text{src}(P), b = a\langle v \rangle$ then, $P \overset{a\langle v \rangle}{\rightarrow} P \setminus b$

Communication: if $b_1, b_2 \in \text{src}(P)$, $b_1 = a\langle o \rangle$, $b_2 = a(x).Q$ then, $P \overset{\tau}{\rightarrow} ((P \setminus b_1) \setminus b_2) \| \nu\{n|(b_2, n) \in \text{edge}(P)\} \nu o Q[o/x]$

The following propositions are straightforward from the definitions.

Proposition 3.1. For any programs P, P' and any action α such that $P \overset{\alpha}{\rightarrow} P'$,

1. If P is local then P' is local.
2. If P is normal then P' is normal.

Proposition 3.1. arrows us to assume that every program is normal and local if we start with such one.

Proposition 3.2. For any normal programs P, P' and Q, and any action α if $P \xrightarrow{\alpha} P'$ then $P\|Q \xrightarrow{\alpha} P'\|Q$.

Proposition 3.3. For any programs P, P', an action α and a set of names such that $N \cap \mathrm{bn}(P) = \emptyset$, if $\nu N P \xrightarrow{\alpha} P'$ then there exists $P"$ such that $P \xrightarrow{\alpha} P"$ and $\nu N P" = P'$.

From **Proposition 3.2** to **3.3** correspond to the rules of restriction and parallel composition of the structural operational semantics of π-calculus respectively.

Proposition 3.4. For any programs P, P', an action α and a set of names such that $N \cap \mathrm{bn}(P) = \emptyset$, if $P \xrightarrow{\alpha} P'$ the $\nu N P \xrightarrow{\alpha} \nu N P'$.

Definition 3.13. For an action α and a substitution $[o/x]$, $\alpha[o/x]$ is the action defined as follows.

$$\alpha[o/x] = \begin{cases} \tau & \text{if } \alpha = \tau \\ a[o/x](n)[o/x] & \text{if } \alpha = a(n) \\ a[o/x]\langle n\rangle[o/x] & \text{if } \alpha = a\langle n\rangle \end{cases}$$

Proposition 3.5. For a program P, an action α and a name $o \notin \mathrm{bn}(P)$, if $P[o/x] \xrightarrow{\alpha} P'$, then there exists $P"$ such that $P \xrightarrow{\alpha'} P"$, $\alpha'[o/x] = \alpha$ and $P"[o/x] = P'$ or exists $P"$ such that $P \xrightarrow{a\langle n\rangle b(m)} P"$, $a[o/x] = b[o/x]$, $n[o/x] = m[o/x]$ and $P"[o/x] = P'$.

Proposition 3.6. For a program P, an action α and a name $o \notin \mathrm{bn}(P)$, if $P \xrightarrow{\alpha} P'$ then $P[o/x] \xrightarrow{\alpha[o/x]} P'[o/x]$.

Proposition 3.7. For a program P, an output action α, an input action β and a substitution $[o/x]$ such that $\alpha[o/x] = a\langle n\rangle$, $\beta[o/x] = a(n)$ and $o \notin \mathrm{bn}(P)$, if $P \xrightarrow{\alpha\,\beta} P'$, then $P[o/x] \xrightarrow{\tau} P'[o/x]$.

From **Proposition 3.5** to **3.7** will be used for showing congruence results of behavioural equivalence wrt substitution. The proofs are analogues of those of corresponding results in π-calculus.

4 Behavioral Equivalence

As usual, we denote $P \xRightarrow{\alpha} P'$ if $P \xrightarrow{\tau} \cdots \xrightarrow{\tau}\xrightarrow{\alpha}\xrightarrow{\tau} \cdots \xrightarrow{\tau}\xrightarrow{\tau} P'$. And we denote $P \xRightarrow{\hat{\alpha}} P'$ if $P \xRightarrow{\alpha} P'$ when $\alpha \neq \tau$ and $P \xRightarrow{\hat{\tau}} P'$ if $P \xrightarrow{\tau} \cdots \xrightarrow{\tau} P'$. The definition of weak bisimulation is as usual.

Definition 4.1 (weak bisimulation) A binary relation $\mathcal{R}$ on normal programs is *a weak bisimulation* if: for any $(P, Q) \in \mathcal{R}$, for any α and P' if $P \xrightarrow{\alpha} P'$ then there exists Q' such that $Q \xRightarrow{\hat{\alpha}} Q'$ and $(P', Q') \in \mathcal{R}$ and vice versa.

Definition 4.2 (weak bisimilarity). Weak bisimulation equivalence is defined as follows.

$$\simeq = \bigcup\{\mathcal{R}|\mathcal{R} \text{ is a weak bisimulation}\}$$

It is easy to show $\simeq$ is an equivalence relation.

We can show that congruence property of $\simeq$ wrt composition from the definitions of "$\|$" and bisimilarity.

Proposition 4.1. For any program R, if $P \simeq Q$ then $P\|R \simeq Q\|R$.

We have the following propositions for the congruence results of $\simeq$[7].

Proposition 4.2. For any P and Q such that $P \simeq Q$ and for any τ-context $R[\ ]$, $R[P] \simeq R[Q]$.

Proposition 4.3. If $!Q \in \mathrm{src}(P)$ then, $P\|Q' \simeq P$ where each Q' is a program obtained from Q by renaming a name in $\mathrm{snk}(Q)$ to a fresh name.

From **Proposition 4.3, 4.1** and the transitivity of $\simeq$, we have the following congruence result wrt replication.

Proposition 4.4. For any P and Q such that $P \simeq Q$ and for any replication context $R[\ ]$, $R[P] \simeq R[Q]$.

From **Proposition 3.5, 3.6** and **3.7**, we have the following proposition.

Proposition 4.5. For any P and Q such that $P \simeq Q$ and a name $o \notin \mathrm{bn}(P) \cup \mathrm{bn}(Q)$, $P[o/x] \simeq Q[o/x]$.

From **Proposition 4.5**, we have the following proposition.

Proposition 4.6. For any P and Q such that $P \simeq Q$ and for any input context $R[\ ]$, $R[P] \simeq R[Q]$.

From **Proposition 4.1** $\sim$ **4.6**, we have the following theorem.

Theorem 4.1[7]. For any P and Q such that $P \simeq Q$ and for any context $R[\ ]$, $R[P] \simeq R[Q]$.

We considered the context consists of composition, prefix and replication for congruence results. In asynchronous π-calculus[10], the congruence result wrt name restriction "$P \simeq Q$ implies $\nu x P \simeq \nu x Q$" is also reported. We can show the corresponding result from **Proposition 4.2**. Consider a τ- context $R[\ ]$ that is obtained from R such that $\mathrm{src}(R) = \{\tau.\mathbf{0}\}, \mathrm{snk}(R) = \{x\}, \mathrm{edge}(R) = \{(\tau.\mathbf{0}, x)\}$. From **Proposition 4.2**, $P \simeq Q$ implies $R[P] \simeq R[Q]$. Then for P' such that

$R[P] \xrightarrow{\tau} P'$, there exists Q' such that $R[Q] \xrightarrow{\tau} Q'$ and $P' \simeq Q'$. From τ-rule, P' is $\nu\{x\}P$. Similarly, only possible Q' reachable with "$\xrightarrow{\tau}$" is $\nu\{x\}Q$. Thus we have that two programs $\nu\{x\}P$ and $\nu\{x\}Q$ are weak bisimilar. This implies the congruence result wrt the closure operation.

Proposition 4.7. For any P and Q and a set of names N such that $N \cap (\mathrm{bn}(P) \cup \mathrm{bn}(Q)) = \emptyset$, if $P \simeq Q$ then $\nu N P \simeq \nu N Q$.

5   Scope Equivalence

5.1   Equivalence Relation

This section presents an equivalence relation on programs which ensures that two systems are equivalent in their behavior and in the scopes of names. We introduce preliminary notions first.

Definition 5.1 For a program P and a name n such that $n \in \mathrm{snk}(P)$, P/n is the program defined as follows:

$\mathrm{src}(P/n) = \{b | b \in \mathrm{src}(P), (b, n) \in \mathrm{edge}(P)\}$
$\mathrm{snk}(P/n) = \mathrm{snk}(P) \setminus \{n\}$
$\mathrm{edge}(P/n) = \{(b, a) | b \in \mathrm{src}(P/n), a \in \mathrm{snk}(P/n), (b, a) \in \mathrm{edge}(P)\}$

Intuitively P/n is the subsystem of P that consists of behaviors which are in the scope of n. Let P be an example of Fig.2., P/a_1 is a subgraph of Fig.2. obtained by removing the node of b_3. (and the edge from b_3 to a_2) and a_1 (and the edges to a_1) as shown in Fig.7. It consists of behaviour nodes b_1 and b_2 and name nodes a_1 and a_2.

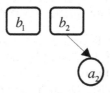

Fig. 7. The graph P/a_1

The following propositions are straightforward from the definitions. These propositions are commutativity of $/n$ and other operations on programs. We will refer to these propositions in the proof of congruence results wrt to the scope equivalence that will be defined below.

Proposition 5.1. For any P, Q and $n \in \mathrm{snk}(P) \cup \mathrm{snk}(Q)$,

$$(P\|Q)/n = P/n\|Q/n.$$

Proposition 5.2 . For a program P, a set of names N such that $N \cap \mathrm{bn}(P) = \emptyset$ and a name $n \in \mathrm{snk}(P)$,

$$(\nu N\ P)/n = \nu N(P/n).$$

Proposition 5.3. Let $R[\ ]$ be a context and P be a program. For any name $m \in \mathrm{snk}(R)$,

$$(R[P])/m = R/m[P].$$

Proposition 5.4. For a program P, a name o such that $o \notin \mathrm{bn}(P)$, a name $x \in \mathrm{fn}(P)$ and a name $m \in \mathrm{snk}(P)$,

$$P[o/x]/m = (P/m)[o/x].$$

Definition 5.2 (scope bisimulation). A binary relation $\mathcal{R}$ on programs is *scope bisimulation* if for any $(P, Q) \in \mathcal{R}$,

1. $\mathrm{src}(P/n) = \emptyset$ iff $\mathrm{src}(Q/n) = \emptyset$ for any $n \in \mathrm{snk}(P) \cap \mathrm{snk}(Q)$,
2. $P/n \simeq Q/n$ for any $n \in \mathrm{snk}(P) \cap \mathrm{snk}(Q)$ and
3. $\mathcal{R}$ is a weak bisimulation.

It is easy to show that the union of all scope bisimulations is a scope bisimulation and it is the unique largest scope bisimulation.

Definition 5.3 (scope equivalence). The largest scope bisimulation is *scope equivalence* and denoted as $\perp$.

It is obvious from the definition that $\perp$ is an equivalence relation. The motivation and the background of the definition of $\perp$ is reported in [6,8].As $\perp$ is a weak bisimulation from **Definition 5.2**. 3., $P \perp Q$ implies $P \simeq Q$.

Definition 5.4 (scope bisimulation up to $\perp$). A binary relation $\mathcal{R}$ on programs is *scope bisimulation up to* $\perp$ if for any $(P, Q) \in \mathcal{R}$,

1. $\mathrm{src}(P/n) = \emptyset$ iff $\mathrm{src}(Q/n) = \emptyset$ for any $n \in \mathrm{snk}(P) \cap \mathrm{snk}(Q)$,
2. $P/n \simeq Q/n$ for any $n \in \mathrm{snk}(P) \cap \mathrm{snk}(Q)$ and
3. $\mathcal{R}$ is a weak bisimulation up to $\perp$, namely for any $(P, Q) \in \mathcal{R}$, for any P' such that $P \overset{\alpha}{\to} P'$, there exists Q' such that $Q \overset{\alpha}{\Rightarrow} Q'$ and $P' \perp \mathcal{R} \perp Q'$ and vice versa.

Proposition 5.5. If $\mathcal{R}$ is a weak bisimulation up to $\perp$, then $\perp \mathcal{R} \perp$ is a scope bisimulation.

5.2   Congruence Results

The next proposition says that $\perp$ is a congruence relation wrt $\|$.

Proposition 5.6. If $P \perp Q$ then $P\|R \perp Q\|R$.

Proof(outline). We can show that the following relation is a scope bisimulation from the definitions and **Proposition 3.2** and **5.1**.

$$\{(P\|R, Q\|R)|P \perp Q\}$$

The following proposition is also straightforward from the definitions.

Proposition 5.7. For any program P and Q, let P' and Q' be programs obtained from P and Q respectively by renaming $n \in \text{snk}(P) \cap \text{snk}(Q)$ to a fresh name n'. If $P \perp Q$ then $P' \perp Q'$.

Proposition 5.8. For any P and Q and a set of names N such that $N \cap (\text{bn}(P) \cup \text{bn}(Q)) = \emptyset$, if $P \perp Q$ then $\nu NP \perp \nu NQ$.
proof(outline): We show that the following relation is a scope bisimulation:

$$\{(\nu NP, \nu NQ)|P \perp Q\}.$$

It is straightforward from the definition to show **Definition 5.2 1.**. 2. is from **Proposition 5,2** and **Proposition 4.7**. 3. is from **Proposition 3.3** and **3.4**.

Remember that the congruence result of $\simeq$ wrt closure operation is implied from the congruence wrt τ-context (**Proposition 4.7**). However we do not use the similar argument here because we use **Proposition 5.8** to prove the congruence of $\perp$ wrt τ-context.

Proposition 5.9. For any P and Q such that $P \perp Q$ and for any τ-context $R[\ ]$, $R[P] \perp R[Q]$.
Proof (outline). We have the result by showing that the following relation is a scope bisimulation.

$$\{(R[P_1], R[P_2])|P_1 \perp P_2, R[\ ] \text{ is a } \tau\text{-context.}\} \cup \perp .$$

To show **Definition 5.2**, 1. is straightforward from the definitions. 2. is from **Proposition 5.3** and **Proposition 4.2**. 3. is from **Definition 3.12**, τ-rule and **Proposition 5.6** and **5.8**.

Proposition 5.10. For any P and Q such that $P \perp Q$ and for any replication context $R[\ ]$, $R[P] \perp R[Q]$.
Proof (outline) We can show the result with **Proposition 5.5** by showing the following relation is a scope bisimulation up to $\perp$.

$$\{(R[P_1], R[P_2])|P_1 \perp P_2, R[\ ] \text{ is a replication context.}\} \cup \perp .$$

To show **Definition 5.4**, 1. is straightforward from the definitions. 2. is from **Proposition 5.3** and **Proposition 4.4**. 3. is by the induction on the number of the replication rules to derive $R[P_1] \xrightarrow{\alpha} R'$ and **Proposition 5.6** and **5.7**.

Proposition 5.11. For any P and Q such that $P \perp Q$ and a name $o \notin \mathrm{bn}(P) \cup \mathrm{bn}(Q)$, $P[o/x] \perp Q[o/x]$.

Proof (outline). We have the result by showing that the following relation is a scope bisimulation.

$$\{(P_1[o/x], P_2[o/x]) | P_1 \perp P_2, o \notin \mathrm{bn}(P_1) \cup \mathrm{bn}(P_2)\}$$

To show **Definition 5.2**, 1. is straightforward from the definitions. 2. is from **Proposition 4.5** and **Proposition 5.4**. 3. is similar to the proof of **Proposition 4.5** as $\perp$ is a weak bisimulation.

Proposition 5.12. For any P and Q such that $P \perp Q$ and for any input context $R[\ ]$, $R[P] \perp R[Q]$.

Proof (outline). We have the result by showing that the following relation is a scope bisimulation.

$$\{(R[P_1], R[P_2]) | P_1 \perp P_2, R[\ ] \text{ is a input context.}\} \cup \perp.$$

Showing **Definition 5.2** 1. is similar to the case of τ-prefix. 2. is from **Proposition 4.6** and **5.3**. 3. is from **Proposition 5.11, 5.8** and **5.6**.

From **Proposition 5.9** $\sim$ **5.12**, we have the following result.

Theorem 5.1. For any P and Q such that $P \perp Q$ and for any context $R[\ ]$, $R[P] \perp R[Q]$.

6   Conclusions

We presented a model of concurrent system based on graph rewriting. The model can represent the scopes of channel names of programs precisely. We defined the equivalence relation for the scopes programs that are equivalent in their behaviour but not in their scopes of names. The equivalence relation make it possible to distinguish programs that are equivalent in their behaviour but not equivalent on their treatment of the scopes of names.

This paper presented congruence results of scope equivalence wrt composition, τ-context, input context and replication. Congruence properties of the equivalence relation make it possible to verify if a program satisfies the given specification in compositional way. Thus we can discuss how a program treats the scopes of names by discussing for each component of a system.

References

1. Ehrig, H., König, B.: Deriving Bisimulation Congruences in the DPO Approach to Graph Rewriting with Borrowed Contexts. Mathematical Structures in Computer Science 16(6), 1133–1163 (2006)
2. Gadducci, F.: Term Graph rewriting for the π-calculus. In: Ohori, A. (ed.) APLAS 2003. LNCS, vol. 2895, pp. 37–54. Springer, Heidelberg (2003)

3. König, B.: A Graph Rewriting Semantics for the Polyadic π-Calculus. In: Proc. of GT-VMT 2000 Workshop on Graph Transformation and Visual Modeling Techniques, pp. 451–458 (2000)
4. Lafont, Y.: Interaction Nets. In: Proc. of POPL 1990, pp. 95–108. ACM, New York (1990)
5. Milner, R.: Bigraphical Reactive Systems. In: Larsen, K.G., Nielsen, M. (eds.) CONCUR 2001. LNCS, vol. 2154, pp. 16–35. Springer, Heidelberg (2001)
6. Murakami, M.: A Formal Model of Concurrent Systems Based on Bipartite Directed Acyclic Graph. Science of Computer Programming 61, 38–47 (2006)
7. Murakami, M.: Congruence Results of Behavioral Equivalence for A Graph Rewriting Model of Concurrent Programs. In: Proc. of ICITA 2008 (to appear, 2008)
8. Murakami, M.: A Graph Rewriting Model of Concurrent Programs with Higher-Order Communication. In Proc. of TMFCS 2008 (to appear, 2008)
9. Odersky, M.: Functional Nets. In: Smolka, G. (ed.) ESOP 2000. LNCS, vol. 1782. Springer, Heidelberg (2000)
10. Sangiorgi, D.: Asynchronous Process Calculi: The First- and Higher-order Paradigms. Theoretical Computer Science 253, 311–350 (2001)
11. Sassone, V., Sobociński, P.: Reactive systems over cospans. In: Proc. of LICS 2005, pp. 311–320. IEEE, Los Alamitos (2005)
12. Ueda, K., Kato, N.: Programming with Logical Links: Design of the LMNtal language. In: Proc. of PPL 2003. JSSST, pp. 20–31 (2003)

Guided Test Generation from CSP Models

Sidney Nogueira[1,2], Augusto Sampaio[1], and Alexandre Mota[1]

[1] Centro de Informática, Universidade Federal de Pernambuco
Caixa Postal 7851 - 50732-970 - Recife/PE - Brazil
[2] Mobile Devices R&D Motorola Industrial Ltda,
Rod SP 340 - Km 128, 7 A - 13820 000 - Jaguariuna/SP - Brazil

Abstract. We introduce an approach for the construction of feature test models expressed in the CSP process algebra, from use cases described in a controlled natural language. From these models, our strategy automatically generates test cases for both individual features and feature interactions, in the context of an industrial cooperation with Motorola Inc., where each feature represents a mobile device functionality. The test case generation can be guided by test purposes, which allow selection based on particular traces of interest. More generally, we characterise a testing theory in terms of CSP: test models, test purposes, test cases, test execution, test verdicts and soundness are entirely defined in terms of CSP processes and refinement notions. We have also developed a tool, ATG, which mechanises the entire generation process.

1 Introduction

Some of the main problems of effective testing is the selection of a good set of test cases and its automation [6], aiming at making the process more agile, less susceptible to errors and less dependent on human interaction. Formal notations like Finite State Machines (FSM) and Labelled Transition Systems (LTS) can provide accurate models for software that can be processed by tools that automatise the test design activity. There are several test generation approaches that use such models, as, for instance, [4,21].

While LTS and FSM are the main models used as basis to automate test generation, they are very concrete models and often adopted as the operational semantics of more abstract process algebras like CSP [15], CCS [11] and LOTOS [10]. Contrasting with operational models, process algebra models can naturally evolve to incorporate additional requirements; the operators of a process algebra also allow complex models to be built from simpler ones, compositionally. Test generation can take advantage of this modular structure, and can be formalised in terms of the process algebra semantic models.

Particularly, CSP is the standard formalism of the Brazil Test Center (BTC) research project [16], a cooperation between the Federal University of Pernambuco and Motorola Inc., in the context of testing embedded software that run over mobile phones. The rich repertoire of CSP operators are used to model individual features (mobile device functionalities) as well as several patterns of

J.S. Fitzgerald, A.E. Haxthausen, and H. Yenigun (Eds.): ICTAC 2008, LNCS 5160, pp. 258–273, 2008.

feature interaction. The CSP models are automatically constructed [2] from use cases described in a domain specific language [18,8] (a small subset of English with a fixed grammar) for mobile applications.

The main contribution of this paper is a uniform strategy for generating test cases from CSP models. Instead of devising explicit generation algorithms (for instance, to deal separately with individual features and with feature interaction), our approach is based on using the CSP model checker (FDR) [9] in background. Test scenarios are incrementally generated as counter-examples of refinement verifications using FDR. Test selection is captured by CSP processes that describe the properties of interest, based on the concept of test purpose [7]; writing test purposes can also benefit from the expressiveness of CSP. The refinement relations submitted to FDR involves the original model and an annotated model obtained from the parallel composition of the original model and the test purposes.

In our testing theory, we consider as test hypothesis that the class of implementations to be tested can be specified by some CSP process [3]. We introduce an implementation relation, **cspio**, which defines the set of observations considered in testing: the implementation must produce a subset of the outputs for the inputs that are specified; although CSP does not differentiate input and output events, we make this distinction using separate input and output alphabets. Moreover, assuming that implementations are input enabled (accept all inputs from the alphabet) and output available (always produce an output for a given input), we prove that test cases are sound in the sense that they do not reject correct implementations according to **cspio**. All the elements of our approach are entirely characterised in terms of CSP processes and refinement notions.

Some previous approaches have addressed test generation [13,17,3] in the context of CSP. The focus of [17] is the formalisation of conformance relations, while [13,3] also consider the generation of infinite test sets. Nevertheless, these works do not distinguish input and output events nor address test purposes as selection criteria.

Section 2 presents our application domain (mobile device software). Section 3 shows how CSP is used to construct test models, both for individual features and for feature interaction. Section 4 addresses test scenario generation based on process refinement, and test selection based on test purposes is the subject of Section 5. Section 6 introduces our CSP characterization of conformance testing and shows how to obtain sound test cases from a set of test scenarios. The final section considers related and future work.

2 Application Domain

The development process of mobile phone software follows an iterative approach, where sets of functionalities (known as features) are incrementally considered in each development cycle. An example of a feature is the set of requirements for sending a multimedia message. In general, new features are developed and tested, firstly, in isolation, and later integrated with other features, giving rise to feature interactions.

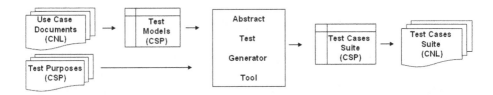

Fig. 1. Test automation workflow

Figure 1 presents an overview of the automatic test generation approach in the BTC project. The main inputs are use case documents that describe the behaviour of the features to be tested, and selection criteria defined in terms of test purposes; the output is a test case suite suitable for manual execution. Input and output templates obey a Controlled Natural Language (CNL) standard [18,8] that can be translated to and from CSP. We have developed a tool, Abstract Test Generator (ATG), which plays a central role in the automation flow; ATG takes as input a test model (which is generated [2] from use cases in CNL) and a set of test purposes. Internally, the tool generates a set of test scenarios that satisfy the test purposes; the user can inform the number of scenarios to be generated. The test scenarios are then used to generate sound test cases (still expressed as CSP processes). Finally, the test cases are translated back to CNL [18], yielding the test case suite.

In what follows, we overview the use case documents, see Figures 2 and 3.

From Step: START
To Step: END

Step Id	User Action	System State	System Response
1M	Go to Message Center.		"Important Messages" folder is displayed.
2M	Go to "Inbox".		All Inbox Messages are displayed.
3M	Scroll to a message.		Message is highlighted.
4M	Go to Context Sensitive Menu.		"Move to Important Messages" option is displayed.
5M	Select "Move to Important Messages" option.	Message storage is not full.	"Message moved to Important Messages folder" is displayed.

Fig. 2. Main flow

From Step: 5M
To Step: END

Step Id	User Action	System State	System Response
1A	Select "Move to Important Messages" option.	Message storage is full.	"Message storage is full" is displayed. "Clean Up request" is displayed.
2A	Perform clean up.		"Message moved to Important Messages folder" is displayed.

Interaction Point: 2M

Step Id	User Action	System State	System Response
1I	Select store status option information.		Storage status dialog is displayed.
2I	Dismiss the storage status dialog.		Storage status dialog is closed.

Fig. 3. Alternative and interaction flows

Feature Use Cases. A feature use case has a set of interconnected flows (main, alternative and exception); each flow is a sequence of steps, and each step has an identifier (Id) that is used for referencing (use cases can be shared by different features and documents). Features and use cases also have unique identifiers. The complete reference for a step has the form FEATURE_ID#UC_ID#STEP_ID. Moreover, each flow step specifies an user input action (User Action column), the expected system output in the System Response column, and the (optional) condition required to produce the expected system output (System State column). Figure 2 shows the main flow of the use case of the Important Messages Feature. Such a flow specifies the sequence of actions that the user must perform to move a message from the Inbox to the Important Messages Folder. For instance, in step 5M, to get a message dialog that confirms the success of moving a message, the memory storage must not be full.

The fields 'From Step' and 'To Step' are used to indicate the set of steps from where the flow must start and to where it must continue. As a default, the main flow uses the constants START (no previous step) and END (no subsequent step) for these fields. Alternative flows are simply defined by characterising where (From Step) they can assume control and where they must resume (To Step), with respect to the flows they are referencing. Figure 3 (top) shows a possible alternative flow for the Important Messages use case. It specifies that, after step 4M of the Feature main flow, if the memory storage is full, the selected message is not moved because a clean up action is requested. After the clean up the message is moved to the Important Messages Folder and the alternative flow finalizes. The exception flows are similar to alternative flows, except for representing exceptional behaviours.

Feature Interaction. Feature interactions are extensions of feature use cases by introducing interaction points. Using the field Interaction Point one can indicate a set of steps from which the interactive flow can assume and resume control to the next step in the original flow. Figure 3 (bottom) shows the specification of a flow that can interact after step 1M of the main flow. This interaction specifies that after the main action "Go to Message Center", the feature can continue its main flow or verify the message storage status (interaction flow), and then continue the main flow from step 2M.

3   Test Models as CSP Processes

A process is the central element of a CSP specification. Processes can offer events from Σ (the set of possible events) to establish communication with the environment or with other processes. The alphabet of a CSP process, say P, is the set of events it can communicate, say α_P, where $\alpha_P \subseteq \Sigma$. Furthermore, the primitive process *Stop* specifies a broken process (deadlock), and the primitive *Skip* a process that communicates an event $\checkmark$ and terminates successfully.

Although there is no semantic distinction between input and output events in CSP, we consider that Σ is split into three disjoint sets of events: inputs Σ_i, outputs Σ_o and conditionals Σ_c. In our application domain, input events represent user actions, the output events model system responses, and conditional events abstract the system internal state. Then, $\Sigma = \Sigma_i \cup \Sigma_o \cup \Sigma_c$. Similarly, the alphabets of the processes follow the same structure: $\alpha_P = \alpha_{Pi} \cup \alpha_{Po} \cup \alpha_{Pc}$.

The rest of this section shows how CSP operators are used to build test models for our application domain. The operators are introduced by demand.

Modelling Individual Features. Basic CSP operators as prefix and external choice are suitable to model feature use cases. The CSP prefix operator $P = ev \rightarrow Q$ specifies that event ev is communicated by P, which then behaves as the process Q. The external choice operator $P = Q \square R$ indicates that the process P can behave as Q or R; the choice is made by the environment.

As an example, applying the translation approach presented in [2] to the main and alternative flows of the use case of Important Messages Feature (Figures 2 and 3) we obtain the model specified as follows. For conciseness, we abbreviate the event names that represent the elements of the use case templates.

$$UC_1 = goToMsgCenter \rightarrow IMFolderIsDisp \rightarrow goToInbox \rightarrow inboxMsgsDisp \rightarrow$$
$$scrollToAMsg \rightarrow msgHighlighted \rightarrow goToCSM \rightarrow moveToIMOptDisp \rightarrow$$
$$selMoveToIMOpt \rightarrow (UC_{11} \square UC_{12})$$
$$UC_{11} = msgStoIsNotFull \rightarrow msgMovedToIMDisp \rightarrow Skip$$
$$UC_{12} = msgStoIsFull \rightarrow cleanUpReqDisp \rightarrow$$
$$performCleanUp \rightarrow msgMovedToIMDisp \rightarrow Skip$$

The process UC_1 specifies the main use case flow (Figure 2) up to Step $4M$ (event $selMoveToIMOpt$). From this point, it behaves as the choice $UC_{11} \square UC_{12}$. The process UC_{11} specifies Step $5M$ of the main flow, and UC_{12} the behaviour of the alternative flow (Figure 3). Both main and alternative flows finish with success (behave as $Skip$).

Modelling Feature Interactions. Now we show an approach to capture feature interactions using CSP, by combining the CSP processes that specify interaction flows with the processes that specify main, alternative and exception flows.

Consider the CSP notation $P \setminus s$ that defines a process which behaves like P communicates all its events, except the events that belong to s, which become internal (invisible): $\setminus$ stands for the hiding operator. The process $P \,[\![X]\!]\, Q$ stands for the generalised parallel composition of the processes P and Q with synchronisation set X. This expression states that P and Q must synchronize on events that belong to X. Each process can evolve independently for events that are not in X.

Figures 4 and 5 give a graphical overview on how to model feature interaction by using CSP parallel composition. The top of Figure 4 represents the use cases process UC_1 modified with the insertion of one interaction point (the events $beginI.1$ and $endI.1$ are control events). The bottom of the same figure illustrates the interaction process for the interaction flow of Figure3. Finally, putting these processes in parallel with synchronization set $\{beginI.1, endI.1\}$ and hiding this set, we obtain the model exhibited in Figure 5. The transition labelled as $\_tau$ in Figure 5 denotes invisible event and appears in the resulting model to allow the interaction to occur optionally.

The rest of this section materializes the graphical modelling of interaction shown in Figures 4 and 5 motivated above in terms of CSP. Consider the indexed external choice construction of CSP $\square x : A \bullet F(x)$, where x can be a value or an event from set A, and $F(x)$ any CSP term involving x. This construction behaves as the external choice $F(x_1) \square F(x_2) \square ... \square F(x_n)$ for $A = \{x_1, x_2, ..., x_n\}$.

We define the auxiliary process $InteractionPoint$ that is used to introduce control points in the use case processes that are affected by interactions.

$$InteractionPoint(indices) = Skip \square (\square i : indices \bullet beginI.i \rightarrow endI.i \rightarrow Skip)$$

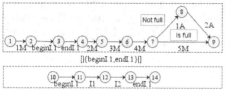
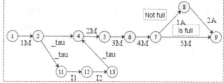

Fig. 4. Marked use case and interaction   **Fig. 5.** Feature interaction model

The parameter *indices* is a set of interaction identifiers used to characterise which interactions are allowed in the same point of a given use case. The events from *IntControl* = {*beginI.i*, *endI.i*} are used to specify such points. For each $i \in indices$ the process *InteractionPoint* offers a choice with the prefix $begin.i \rightarrow end.i \rightarrow Skip$. Furthermore, the external choice with *Skip* allows the original flow to perform without any interaction.

Consider the CSP process $P; Q$ that behaves like P until it terminates successfully, when the control passes to Q. The process UC_1' in Figure 4 (top) is the process UC_1 from the previous section modified by the insertion of an interaction point after the step 1M. In UC_1' the processes UC_{11} and UC_{12} remain unchanged because there are no interactions for them.

$$UC_1' = goToMsgCenter \rightarrow IMFolderIsDisp \rightarrow Skip; \ InteractionPoint(\{1\});$$
$$goToInbox \rightarrow inboxMsgsDisp \rightarrow scrollToAMsg \rightarrow msgHighlighted \rightarrow$$
$$goToCSM \rightarrow moveToIMOptDisp \rightarrow selMoveToIMOpt \rightarrow (UC_{11} \ \square \ UC_{12})$$

The parameter {1} for the process *InteractionPoint* above is the index for the interaction in Figure 3 whose CSP specification is the process

$$STORAGE\_STATUS = selStoStaOpt \rightarrow stoStaDiaDisp \rightarrow$$
$$dismStoStaDia \rightarrow stoStaDiaClosed \rightarrow Skip$$

In addition, we define the auxiliary process I that is similar to *InteractionPoint* except that it handles a unique control point (instead of a set), and between the *beginI.index* and *endI.index* events it includes the interaction flow itself.

$$I(index, interaction) = Skip \ \square \ (beginI.index \rightarrow interaction; \ endI.index \rightarrow Skip)$$

Finally, the CSP interaction specification of the use case flows of Figures 2 and 3 is

$$UC_1\_I = (UC_1' \,\|[\,IntControl\,]\| \,I(1, STORAGE\_STATUS)) \setminus IntControl$$

where the process $I(1, STORAGE\_STATUS)$ (represented in Figure 4, at bottom) allows the flow $STORAGE\_STATUS$ to occur in the point where *Interaction Point*({1}) is included in UC_1'. The events of *IntControl* are hidden from the model since they only play the role of control events. Figure 5 shows a graphical view of the process UC_1_I. Note that the original flow can be interrupted at point 2, where the subflow demarcated by 11, 12 and 13 is the interruption behaviour.

The notation $\mu X.F(X)$ stands for a nameless recursive CSP process. For the general case, the CSP process below specifies the feature interaction model for a set of independent feature model processes $\{UC'_1, ..., UC'_N\}$ with a set of independent interactions $\{I(1, int_i), ..., I(n, int_n)\}$ that can occur in any point of the feature models.

$$UC\_I = (\,\square\, k : \{1..N\} \bullet UC'_k \,[\![\, IntControl \,]\!]\,|$$
$$\mu X.\,\square\, i : \{1..n\} \bullet I(i, int_i);\ X) \setminus IntControl$$

On the left-hand side of the parallelism, the use cases are modelled as the external choice of the respective processes; each process UC'_k ($1 \leq k \leq N$) stands for the use case UC_k modified with the insertion of interaction points. On the right-hand side, there is a choice among the possible interactions $I(i, int_i)$ ($1 \leq i \leq n$) that recurs after successful termination. This recursion allows the run of any interaction whenever the respective interaction points are reached in the use cases.

A more elaborate model of feature interaction can be achieved using the interleaving operator of CSP. We can define that the occurrences of the process $I(i, int_i)$ are interleaved, and that each occurrence is itself recursive. Similarly, the use case models can as well be combined using interleaving. This allows multiple interactions to occur simultaneously, and is useful in the context of concurrent features.

Semantic Models for CSP. Trace semantics is the simplest model for a CSP process. The traces of a process P, given by $traces(P)$, correspond to the set of all possible sequences (even infinite) of events P can communicate. For the process $Stop$, $traces(Stop) = \{\langle\rangle\}$, and for $Skip$, $traces(Skip) = \{\langle\rangle, \langle\checkmark\rangle\}$, where $\checkmark \notin \Sigma$. For prefix, $traces(a \rightarrow P) = (\{\langle\rangle, \langle a\rangle\}) \cup traces(P)$. Let $P1$ and $P2$ be two CSP processes, then $traces(P1\ \square\ P2) = traces(P1) \cup traces(P2)$. For the sequential composition, $traces(P;\ Q) = (traces(P) \cap \Sigma^*) \cup \{s\ \frown\ t \mid s\ \frown\ \langle\checkmark\rangle \in traces(P) \wedge t \in traces(Q)\}$. A complete definition for all CSP operators can be found in [15].

It is possible to compare the traces semantics of two processes by refinement verification using the FDR [9] tool. A process Q refines the process P in the traces model, say $P \sqsubseteq_\tau Q$, if and only if $traces(P) \supseteq traces(Q)$. Otherwise, FDR yields a trace (the shortest counter-example), say ce, such that $ce \in traces(Q)$ but $ce \notin traces(P)$. For instance, $UC_{11}\ \square\ UC_{12} \sqsubseteq_\tau UC_{12}$ holds, since $traces(UC_{11}\ \square\ UC_{12}) \supseteq traces(UC_{12})$. However, the relation $Skip \sqsubseteq_\tau Skip;\ accept.1 \rightarrow Stop$ does not, since $\langle accept.1\rangle \in traces(accept.1 \rightarrow Stop)$ but $\langle accept.1\rangle \notin traces(Skip)$. Thus, the trace $\langle accept.1\rangle$ is a counter-example.

Structuring the process UC_I as explained previously, we have that $UC\_I \sqsubseteq_\tau UC$ holds: the traces of the use case model without interactions is included in the traces of the interaction model. For instance, $UC_1\_I \sqsubseteq_\tau UC_1$ holds.

Other more elaborate semantic models of CSP are the failures and the failures-divergences models. The former captures deadlock situations, whereas the latter captures livelocks as well. See [15] for further details.

4   Test Scenario Generation

Given a test model S and a safety property Φ, we can obtain the traces of S that satisfy Φ (e.g. traces from S that lead to a successful termination). We call these traces test scenarios, say ts, when Φ describes some test selection criteria. A test scenario is the central element used to construct a CSP test case. This Section shows how to generate test scenarios as the counter-examples of refinement verifications.

Consider the set $MARK = \{accept.n\}$ for $n \in \mathbb{N}$, the alphabet of mark events used in our test generation approach. Let S be the process that specifies the model we want to select tests from, then we define S' to be S with the addition of mark events after test scenarios that satisfies Φ. The idea is to perform refinement verifications of the form $S \sqsubseteq_\tau S'$ that generate the test scenarios as counter-examples. Consider that $s_1 \frown s_2$ indicates the concatenation of sequences s_1 and s_2, and $\langle ev \rangle$ a sequence containing the element e. Then, S' is defined in such a way that for all test scenarios $ts \in traces(S)$ that satisfies Φ, there is a trace $ts \frown \langle m \rangle \in traces(S')$, such that $m \in MARK$ and $MARK \cap \alpha_S = \emptyset$. As a consequence $ts \frown \langle m \rangle \notin traces(S)$, so the relation $S \sqsubseteq_\tau S'$ does not hold and the counter-examples are traces of the form $ts \frown \langle m \rangle$. The shortest test scenario, say ts_1, is retrieved by FDR when $S \sqsubseteq_\tau S'$ does not hold.

To illustrate the proposed test scenario generation approach, we show how to generate a set of test scenarios ($ts \in traces(S)$) that lead the test model to successful termination. Consider the process $ACCEPT(id) = accept.id \rightarrow Stop$ that is used to mark test scenarios by communicating the mark event $accept.id$ ($accept.id \in MARK$). Thus, we define S' as the process (S; $ACCEPT(i)$). This process inserts marks ($accept.i$) after each successful termination of S. As a consequence, the verification of relation ($S \sqsubseteq_\tau S'$) yields as counter-examples the test scenarios that lead the specification to successful termination (if they exist).

For example, checking the relation $UC_1 \sqsubseteq_\tau UC_1$; $ACCEPT(1)$ using FDR results in the shortest counter-example, as displayed below.

$UC_1\_ts_1 = \langle goToMsgCenter, IMFolderIsDisp, goToInbox, inboxMsgsDisp,$
$scrollToAMsg, msgHighlighted, goToCSM, moveToIMOptDisp, selMoveToIMOpt,$
$msgStoIsNotFull, msgMovedToIMDisp, accept.1 \rangle$

The above trace (ignoring the marking event $accept.1$) is the shortest successful termination test scenario to UC_1. It corresponds to the main use case flow of the Important Messages Feature (Figure 2).

To obtain from S subsequent test scenarios lengthier than a test scenario ts_1, we use the function $Proc$ that receives as input a sequence of events and generates a process whose maximum trace corresponds to the input sequence. For instance, $Proc(\langle a, b, c \rangle)$ yields the process $a \rightarrow b \rightarrow c \rightarrow Stop$. The reason for using $Stop$, rather than $Skip$, is that $Stop$ does not generate any visible event in the traces model, while $Skip$ generates the event $\checkmark$.

The second counter-example is generated from S using the previous refinement, but the process formed by the counter-example ts_1 ($Proc(ts_1)$) as an alternative to S on the left-hand side. The second test scenario can then be generated as the counter-example to the refinement $S \,\square\, Proc(ts_1) \sqsubseteq_\tau S'$. As $traces(S \,\square\, Proc(ts_1))$ is equivalent to $traces(S) \cup ts_1$, ts_1 cannot be a counter-example of the second refinement iteration. Thus, if the refinement does not hold again, then we have ts_2 as the counter-example.

The iterations can be repeated until the desired set of test scenarios is obtained (for instance, a fixed number of tests is generated). In general, the $n + 1^{th}$ test scenario can be generated as a counter-example of the following refinement.

$$S \,\square\, Proc(ts_1) \,\square\, Proc(ts_2) \,\square\, ... \,\square\, Proc(ts_n) \sqsubseteq_\tau S' \qquad (1)$$

Continuing the selection of successful termination traces of UC_1, checking the relation $UC_1 \,\square\, Proc(UC_1\_ts_1) \sqsubseteq_\tau UC_1; \; ACCEPT(1)$ yields a second counter-example.

$UC_1\_ts_2 = \langle goToMsgCenter, IMFolderIsDisp, goToInbox, inboxMsgsDisp,$
$scrollToAMsg, msgHighlighted, goToCSM, moveToIMOptDisp, selMoveToIMOpt,$
$msgStoIsFull, cleanUpReqDisp, performCleanUp, msgMovedToIMDisp, accept.1\rangle$

The above trace is another successful termination test scenario for UC_1. It corresponds to the alternative flow of the Important Messages (Figure 3). Finally, since there is no more successful termination scenarios to generate from UC_1, the following refinement $UC_1 \,\square\, Proc(UC_1\_ts_1) \,\square\, Proc(UC_1\_ts_2) \sqsubseteq_\tau UC_1; \; ACCEPT(1)$ holds.

This strategy applies both to feature models and to feature interaction models, introduced in the previous section.

5   Test Scenario Selection

Although successful termination can itself be used as a selection criteria, as illustrated in the previous section, this section shows a more flexible strategy for selecting a set of test scenarios from a test model S based on the concept of a test purpose TP, described as a CSP process. A CSP test purpose is based on the notion introduced in [7]: a test purpose is a partial specification describing the characteristics of the desired tests. The definition below formalizes the concept.

Definition 1. *Let TP and S be CSP processes. The process TP is a test purpose for S if it has deterministic behaviour and $\forall ts \,^\frown\, \langle m \rangle : traces(TP) \bullet ts \in traces(S) \wedge m \in MARK$.*

A TP must be deterministic to avoid the selection of inconsistent test scenarios. The other relevant property of a TP is that its traces (excluding the mark event) must be traces of the specification model. To ease the task of writing TP in CSP following Definition 1, we provide a set of primitive processes that can be combined to design possibly complex test purposes.

The primitive $ANY(evset, next) = \square \; ev : evset \bullet ev \rightarrow next$ performs basic selection. It selects the events offered by the specification that belong to $evset$. If any of these events can occur, it behaves as $next$. Otherwise, it deadlocks.

Consider the process $RUN(s) = \square\, ev : s \bullet ev \rightarrow RUN(s)$ that continuously offers the events from the set s, and $P \triangle Q$ which indicates that Q can interrupt the behaviour of P if an event offered by Q is communicated. The process $UNTIL(\alpha_S, evset, next) = RUN(\alpha_S - evset) \triangle ANY(evset, next)$ selects all sequences offered by the specification events until it engages on some event that belongs to $evset$. In [12] one can find a comprehensive list of primitives.

The following is an example of a test purpose TP_1 that is used to select scenarios from UC_1. The objective of TP_1 is to select from UC_1 test scenarios whose final output is a message confirming that the selected important message is moved to the folder ($msgMovedToIMDisp$), and at some point before the user has performed a cleanup action ($performCleanUp$).

$$TP_1 = UNTIL(\alpha_{UC_1}, \{performCleanUp\},$$
$$UNTIL(\alpha_{UC_1}, \{msgMovedToIMDisp\}, ACCEPT(1)))$$

The process TP_1 offers the events of α_{UC_1} until it engages on $performCleanUp$. Next, it offers the events of α_{UC_1} until it engages on $msgMovedToIMDisp$, when it behaves as $ACCEPT(1)$ that inserts the mark event $accept.1$.

Based on the test scenario generation approach from the previous section, one can select test scenarios for a given CSP test purpose TP by defining the process S' (here referred to as $PP(S, TP)$) as the *parallel product* of S with a test purpose TP with synchronisation set α_S: $PP(S, TP) = S\,|[\,\alpha_S\,]|\,TP$. The process TP synchronises in all events offered by S until the test purpose that follows Definition 1 matches a test scenario, when TP communicates an event $mark \in MARKS$. At this point, the process TP deadlocks, and consequently $PP(S, TP)$ deadlocks as well. This makes the parallel product to produce traces $ts \,^\frown\, \langle mark \rangle$, where ts are the test scenarios. If S does not contain scenarios specified by TP, no mark event is communicated, the parallel product does not deadlock and the relation $S \sqsubseteq_\tau PP(S, TP)$ holds.

Considering again our example, the shortest test scenario from UC_1 that matches TP_1 is obtained from a counter-example of the relation $UC_1 \sqsubseteq_\tau PP$ (UC_1, TP_1), where $PP(UC_1, TP_1) = UC_1\,|[\,\alpha_{UC_1}\,]|\,TP_1$. The counter-example is given below.

$UC_1\_TP1\_ts_1 = \langle goToMsgCenter, IMFolderIsDisp, goToInbox, inboxMsgsDisp,$
$scrollToAMsg, msgHighlighted, goToCSM, moveToIMOptDisp, selMoveToIMOpt,$
$msgStoIsFull, cleanUpReqDisp, performCleanUp, msgMovedToIMDisp, accept.1\rangle$

Further test scenarios that satisfy a given test purpose can be generated incrementally as explained in the previous section.

6   Constructing Sound Test Cases

In conformance testing, the minimum requirement for the generated test cases is that they do not reject correct implementations; they must be *sound*. In this section we show that our test case generation strategy always produces sound test cases.

CSP Input-Output Conformance. To obtain soundness, conformance testing [20] requires the definition of an implementation relation between the domain of specifications and the domain of implementations. In our work elements of such domains are expressed as CSP processes. Thus, to present our definition for such a relation we assume as *test hypothesis* [3] that there is a CSP process which specifies an implementation under test (IUT), say IUT_{CSP}.

We also assume that implementations are always able to accept any input from the alphabet (input enabled), and always produce some output after a given input (output available). These properties are formalized by the two following definitions. An implementation is input enabled when the inputs communicated after each of its traces equals its input alphabet.

Definition 2. *Let IUT_{CSP} be an implementation model. It is input enabled iff*
$$\forall t : traces(IUT_{CSP}) \bullet \{e : \alpha_{IUT_{CSP}i} \mid t ^\frown \langle e \rangle \in traces(IUT_{CSP})\} = \alpha_{IUT_{CSP}i}$$

An implementation is output available when we can always find an output event immediately after each input event.

Definition 3. *Let IUT_{CSP} be an implementation model. It is output available iff* $\forall t : traces(IUT_{CSP}); i : \alpha_{IUT_{CSP}i} \bullet$
$$t ^\frown \langle i \rangle \in traces(IUT_{CSP}) \Rightarrow (\exists o : \alpha_{IUT_{CSP}o} \bullet t ^\frown \langle i, o \rangle \in traces(IUT_{CSP}))$$

From now on we assume that any implementation model IUT_{CSP} is both input enabled and output available.

Our implementation relation **cspio** (CSP Input-Output Conformance), formalised in Definition 4, is the basis for our generation of sound CSP test cases. Consider that $initials(P) = \{a \mid \langle a \rangle \in traces(P)\}$ yields the initial events offered by the process P, and the function $out(P, s)$ gives the set of output events of P after the trace s. More precisely, $out(P, s) =$ if $s \in traces(P)$ then $initials(P/s) \cap \alpha_{Po}$ else $\emptyset$. The relation **cspio** establishes that any output event observed in an implementation model IUT_{CSP} is also observed in the specification S, after any trace of S. In this case, IUT_{CSP} **cspio** S.

Definition 4. *Let IUT_{CSP} be an implementation model, and S a specification, such that $\alpha_{Sc} = \emptyset$, $\alpha_{Si} \subseteq \alpha_{IUT_{CSP}i}$, $\alpha_{So} \subseteq \alpha_{IUT_{CSP}o}$. Then,*

$$IUT_{CSP} \ \textbf{cspio} \ S \Leftrightarrow \forall s : traces(S) \bullet out(IUT_{CSP}, s) \subseteq out(S, s)$$

Consider the notation $P \mid\mid\mid Q$ represents the interleaving between the processes P and Q. In such a composition both processes communicate any event freely (no synchronisation). The following theorem captures **cspio** using process refinement.

Theorem 1. *Let IUT_{CSP} be an implementation model, and S a specification, such that $\alpha_{Sc} = \emptyset$, $\alpha_{Si} \subseteq \alpha_{IUT_{CSP}i}$ and $\alpha_{So} \subseteq \alpha_{IUT_{CSP}o}$. The relation IUT_{CSP} **cspio** S holds iff the following refinement holds.*

$$S \sqsubseteq_\tau (S \mid\mid\mid RUN(\alpha_{IUT_{CSP}o})) \mid [\alpha_{IUT_{CSP}}] \mid IUT_{CSP} \qquad (2)$$

The intuition for this theorem is as follows. Consider an input event that occurs in IUT_{CSP}, but not in S. On the right-hand side of the refinement, the parallel composition cannot progress through this event, so it is refused. Because refused events are ignored in the traces model, new IUT_{CSP} inputs are allowed by the above refinement. The objective of the interleaving with the process $RUN(\alpha_{IUT_{CSP}o})$ is to avoid that the right-hand process refuses output events that the implementation can perform but S cannot. Thus, $RUN(\alpha_{IUT_{CSP}o})$ allows that such outputs be communicated to IUT_{CSP}. Finally, if IUT_{CSP} can perform such output events, then they appear in the traces of the right-hand side process, which falsifies the traces refinement.

In summary, the expression on the right-hand side captures new inputs performed by IUT_{CSP} generating deadlock from the trace where the input has occurred, in such a way that any event that comes after is allowed. Also, it keeps in the traces all the output events of IUT_{CSP} for the inputs from S, allowing a comparison in the traces models. The proof of the previous theorem and of the following ones can be found in [12].

If we know IUT_{CSP} we can verify if IUT_{CSP} **cspio** S by checking (using FDR) the relation (2) directly. This is equivalent to generating all the traces of S and exercising them against the implementation according to **cspio**. However, in general we do not know IUT_{CSP} and the number of traces of S is infinite. Therefore, we need to exercise the implementation with a selected subset of test cases and look for possible violations of IUT **cspio** S during the test execution.

Test Case and Successful Test Execution. We need to state what is the meaning of a test execution and the verdicts it can produce. The execution of a test TC against an implementation IUT_{CSP}, named $EX(IUT_{CSP}, TC)$, is the parallel composition $IUT_{CSP} \,|[\, \alpha_{IUT_{CSP}} \,]|\, TC$. Such an execution must yield a verdict event $v \in VER = \{pass, fail, inc\}$, which does not belong to $\alpha_{IUT_{CSP}}$. To check this in CSP, we need these verdict elements expressed as CSP processes. Thus, we use process $PASS = pass \rightarrow Stop$ to express when the test passes in the execution. Similarly $INC = inc \rightarrow Stop$ for an inconclusive execution, and $FAIL = fail \rightarrow Stop$ for a failed execution.

A test execution $EX(IUT_{CSP}, TC)$ for a given implementation IUT_{CSP} and a test case TC must always be successful. This is captured by the following definition.

Definition 5. *Let TC be a test case process, IUT_{CSP} an implementation model and $T = traces(EX(IUT_{CSP}, TC))$. The execution of TC against IUT_{CSP} is a successful test execution if the following holds.*

$$\forall t : T \mid (\neg \exists t' : T \mid t \neq t' \bullet t \leq t') \bullet last(t) \in \{pass, inc, fail\}$$

where $last(s)$ yields the last element of the sequence s.

The above definition states that the last element of each execution trace, which is not a prefix of any other execution trace, is a verdict event.

Constructing Sound Test Cases. To construct a test case from a test scenario ts, first we create an *output complete* sequence lt that contains pairs $(ev_i, outs_i)$ such that ev_i is the ith element of ts and $outs_i$ is the set of output events after the specification performs the trace $\langle ev_1, ..., ev_{i-1} \rangle$. Formally, $outs_i =$

$out(S, \langle ev_i, ..., ev_{i-1}\rangle)$, for $1 \le i \le \#ts$, and $lt = \langle (ev_1, outs_1), ..., (ev_{\#ts}, outs_{\#ts})\rangle$, where $\#s$ yields the size of the sequence s.

The function $TC\_BUILDER(lt)$ defines how a sound test case can be constructed from a test scenario.

$TC\_BUILDER(\langle\rangle) = PASS$

$TC\_BUILDER(\langle(ev_i, outs_i)\rangle \frown tail) = SUBTC((ev_i, outs_i)); \ TC\_BUILDER(tail)$

where

$$SUBTC((ev_i, outs_i)) = if \ (ev_i \in \alpha IUT_{CSP i}) \ then \ ev \to \ Skip$$
$$else \ (ev_i \to Skip \ \Box \ ANY(outs_i - \{ev_i\}, INC)$$
$$\Box \ ANY(\alpha IUT_{CSP o} - outs_i, FAIL))$$

The process $TC\_BUILDER(lt)$ recursively applies the process $SUBTC$ for each pair $(ev_i, outs_i)$ of lt and yields the process $PASS$ when the last element of lt is reached. The goal of the process $SUBTC$ is to create the body of the test, inserting the verdicts fail and inconclusive at intermediate points of the test case according to the following.

If the event ev_i is an input, the test case communicates this event to the implementation, and finishes the verification of this test fragment successfully $(Skip)$. Otherwise, if ev_i is an output, the test must be ready to synchronise with any output response of the IUT_{CSP} (output completeness), including ev_i. If IUT_{CSP} communicates ev_i, the test synchronises on this event and ends with success $(Skip)$. Case the IUT_{CSP} communicates an event that belongs to $outs_i - \{ev_i\}$, the test reaches the verdict inconclusive since the IUT_{CSP} response is not exactly the one expected by the test scenario (ev_i), but it is a behaviour foreseen by the specification. Otherwise, if the IUT_{CSP} communicates an event not foreseen by the specification the test reaches the verdict fail.

Before we address soundness of a test case, the following theorem states that a test case constructed from $TC\_BUILDER$ terminates successfully when executed against an implementation model.

Theorem 2. *Let IUT_{CSP} be an implementation model, S a specification, ts a test scenario from S, such that $\alpha_{Sc} = \emptyset$, $\alpha_{Si} \subseteq \alpha IUT_{CSP i}$ and $\alpha_{So} \subseteq \alpha IUT_{CSP o}$. If lt is an output complete sequence of ts and $TC = TC\_BUILDER(lt)$, then the execution of TC against IUT_{CSP} is a successful test execution.*

Soundness is stated as: if the test execution leads to a fail verdict then the implementation does not conform to the specification. A CSP test execution of a test TC with an implementation IUT_{CSP} fails when the test execution $EX(IUT_{CSP}, TC)$ has the event *fail* as part of at least one of its traces.

Definition 6. *Let IUT_{CSP} be an implementation process, S the specification and TC a test case process. Then TC is a sound test case if the following holds.*

$$\langle fail \rangle \in traces(EX(IUT_{CSP}, TC) \setminus \alpha IUT_{CSP}) \Rightarrow \neg(IUT_{CSP} \ \textbf{cspio} \ S)$$

A CSP test suite is sound if all its tests are also sound. The following theorem states that a test case constructed from $TC\_BUILDER$ is sound.

Theorem 3. *Let S be a specification, ts a test scenario from S and IUT_{CSP} an implementation model, such that $\alpha_{Sc} = \emptyset$, $\alpha_{Si} \subseteq \alpha_{IUT_{CSP}i}$ and $\alpha_{So} \subseteq \alpha_{IUT_{CSP}o}$. If lt is an output complete sequence of ts, then $TC\_BUILDER(lt)$ is a sound test case.*

To exemplify the construction of a sound test case, we assume the test scenario $UC_1\_ts_1$ and build the process $TC_1 = TC\_BUILDER(lt\_ts_1)$, where $lt\_ts_1 = \langle(goToMsgCenter, \emptyset), (IMFolderIsDisp, \{IMFolderIsDisp\}), (goToInbox, \emptyset), (inboxMsgsDisp, \{inboxMsgsDisp\}), (scrollToAMsg, \emptyset), (msgHighlighted, \{msgHighlighted\}), (goToCSM, \emptyset), (moveToIMOptDisp, \{moveToIMOptDisp\}), (selMoveToIMOpt, \emptyset), (msgMovedToIMDisp, \{msgMovedToIMDisp\})\rangle$. The resulting process is

$TC_1 = goToMsgCenter \rightarrow Skip;$
$(IMFolderIsDisp \rightarrow Skip \;\square\; ANY(\alpha_{UC1o} - \{IMFolderIsDisp\}, FAIL));$
$goToInbox \rightarrow Skip;$
$(inboxMsgsDisp \rightarrow Skip \;\square\; ANY(\alpha_{UC1o} - \{inboxMsgsDisp\}, FAIL));$
$scrollToAMsg \rightarrow Skip;$
$(msgHighlighted \rightarrow Skip \;\square\; ANY(\alpha_{UC1o} - \{msgHighlighted\}, FAIL));$
$goToCSM \rightarrow Skip;$
$(moveToIMOptDisp \rightarrow Skip \;\square\; ANY(\alpha_{UC1o} - \{moveToIMOptDisp\}, FAIL));$
$selMoveToIMOpt \rightarrow Skip;$
$(msgMovedToIMDisp \rightarrow PASS \;\square\; ANY(\alpha_{UC1o} - \{moveToIMOptDisp\}, FAIL));$

According to Theorem 3 TC_1 is a sound test case.

7   Conclusions

The main contribution of this paper is a uniform strategy for generating sound test cases, based on the **cspio** conformance relation, from test scenarios extracted from CSP test models. All the elements of our approach are entirely characterised in terms of CSP processes and refinement notions. We have shown how to specify test models both for individual features and for feature interaction, from use case documents that are written in a controlled natural language (CNL). Test scenarios are incrementally generated from the test models as counter-examples of refinement verifications using the FDR tool; test selection is captured by CSP processes based on the concept of test purpose.

Tretmans [20,21,19] outlines a formal testing theory and tool that is based on IOLTS (Input-Output LTS) models and on the implementation relation named **ioco**. Our relation **cspio** is similar to **ioco**; both use input and output events to define conformance. However **ioco** is formulated in terms of IOLTS, while **cspio** is defined in terms of the CSP denotational semantics. The relation **ioco** considers quiescence behaviours, that we currently forbid by assuming that implementations are both input enabled and output available; we plan to allow quiescence in a future work. Based on the **ioco** relation, Jard and Jéron [5] present the TGV tool that is able to select test cases based on test purposes and uses a test generation approach that is close to ours, but based on IOLTS.

Expressing test models (particularly feature interaction) and test purposes in a process algebra has proved very convenient in our application domain.

Andrade et al. [1] made an alternative effort to capture the mobile devices application domain based on LTS. This has demanded a strategy to deal with individual features and a separate one to capture feature interaction. Our approach does not need explicit generation algorithms, and deals uniformly with features and (flexible patterns of) interactions.

Cavalcanti and Gaudel [3] stated the testability hypothesis for CSP and proposed a characterization of a test generation approach proved to be complete with respect to their implementation relation that is based on traces and failures refinement of CSP. However, they do not address test purposes; also, their work does not distinguish inputs and outputs, and does not propose an automatic approach to test generation.

Peleska and Siegel [13] present some implementation relations based on the semantic models of CSP. Their definitions are based on several refinement relations that define the observations of testing; however, unlike our approach, input and output are not observations. Schneider [17] defines a partition that classifies refusable and non-refusable events, and high-level and low-level events, for specifying fault-tolerance systems with CSP. He defines two conformance relations and refinement is used to check whether conformance holds, but no approach for test generation is proposed.

Based on our results on the formal composition of components and frameworks [14] we plan to explore compositional test generation, which avoids the retesting of already assembled components. We believe that this kind of application will emphasise the distinguishing nature of our approach entirely based on a process algebra, where we can make explicit the application architecture, including the interaction patterns among components, unlike more operational models based on LTS or FSM.

Acknowledgements

We would like to thank the feedback from the IFIP WG 2.3, from the UK Motorola Labs, and from the members of the CIn-BTC Research Project. Also, we want to thank Lars Frantzen for feedbacks in an earlier draft, and Jim Woodcock for having suggested to us the relation (1).

References

1. Andrade, W., et al.: Interruption Test Case Generation for Mobile Phone Applications (in Portuguese). In: XXV Brazilian Symposium in Computer Networks and Distributed Systems (2007)
2. Cabral, G., Sampaio, A.: Formal Specification Generation from Requirement Documents. Electron. Notes Theor. Comput. Sci. 195, 171–188 (2008); Best Paper Award

3. Cavalcanti, A., Gaudel, M.-C.: Testing for Refinement in CSP. In: Butler, M., Hinchey, M.G., Larrondo-Petrie, M.M. (eds.) ICFEM 2007. LNCS, vol. 4789, pp. 151–170. Springer, Heidelberg (2007)
4. Hierons, R.: Checking states and transitions of a set of communicating finite state. Microprocessors and Microsystems, Special Issue on Testing and testing techniques for real-time embedded software systems 24(9), 443–452 (2001)
5. Jard, C., Jéron, T.: TGV: theory, principles and algorithms: A tool for the automatic synthesis of conformance test cases for non-deterministic reactive systems. Int. J. Softw. Tools Technol. Transf. 7(4), 297–315 (2005)
6. Bogdanov, K., et al.: Working together: Formal Methods and Testing. ACM Computing Surveys (December 2003)
7. Ledru, Y., et al.: Test Purposes: Adapting the Notion of Specification to Testing. In: ASE 2000, p. 127 (2001)
8. Leitão, D., Torres, D., Barros, F.A.: Nlforspec: Translating natural language descriptions into formal test case specifications. In: SEKE, Knowledge Systems Institute Graduate School, pp. 129–134 (2007)
9. Formal Systems. Failures-Divergence Refinement - FDR2 User Manual. Formal Systems (Europe) Ltd (June 2005)
10. ISO 8807:1989. LOTOS: A formal description technique based on the temporal ordering of observational behaviour. ISO (1989)
11. Milner, R.: Communication and Concurrency. Prentice-Hall, Englewood Cliffs (1989)
12. Nogueira, S., Sampaio, A., and Mota, A. Guided Test Generation from CSP Models. Tech. rep., CIn-UFPE (July 2007), http://www.cin.ufpe.br/~scn/reports/TR-Mar08.pdf
13. Peleska, J., Siegel, M.: Test automation of safety-critical reactive systems. South African Computer Journal 19, 53–77 (1997)
14. Ramos, R., Sampaio, A., Mota, A.: Framework composition conformance via refinement checking. In: SAC 2008: Proceedings of the, ACM symposium on Applied computing, vol. 23, pp. 119–125 (2008)
15. Roscoe, A.W., Hoare, C.A.R., Bird, R.: The Theory and Practice of Concurrency. Prentice Hall PTR (1997)
16. Sampaio, A., et al.: Software test program: a software residency experience. In: ICSE 2005, pp. 611–612. ACM Press, New York (2005)
17. Schneider, S.: Abstraction and testing. In: Wing, J.M., Woodcock, J.C.P., Davies, J. (eds.) FM 1999. LNCS, vol. 1708, pp. 738–757. Springer, Heidelberg (1999)
18. Torres, D., Leitão, D., Barros, F.A.: Motorola SpecNL: A Hybrid System to Generate NL Descriptions from Test Case Specifications. HIS 0, 45 (2006)
19. Tretmans, J.: Test Generation with Inputs, Outputs and Repetitive Quiescence. Software—Concepts and Tools 17(3), 103–120 (1996)
20. Tretmans, J.: Testing concurrent systems: A formal approach. In: Baeten, J.C.M., Mauw, S. (eds.) CONCUR 1999. LNCS, vol. 1664, pp. 46–65. Springer, Heidelberg (1999)
21. Tretmans, J., Belinfante, A.: Automatic testing with formal methods. In: EuroSTAR 1999: 7th European Int. Conference on Software Testing, Analysis & Review, November 8–12, pp. 8–12 (1999)

Relaxing Goodness Is Still Good

Gordon J. Pace[1] and Gerardo Schneider[2]

[1] Dept. of Computer Science and AI, University of Malta, Msida, Malta
[2] Dept. of Informatics, University of Oslo, Oslo, Norway
gordon.pace@um.edu.mt, gerardo@ifi.uio.no

Abstract. Polygonal hybrid systems (SPDIs) are planar hybrid systems, whose dynamics are defined in terms of constant differential inclusions, one for each of a number of polygonal regions partitioning the plane. The reachability problem for SPDIs is known to be decidable, but depends on the *goodness* assumption — which states that the dynamics do not allow a trajectory to both enter and leave a region through the same edge. In this paper we extend the decidability result to *generalised SPDIs* (GSPDI), SPDIs not satisfying the goodness assumption, and give an algorithmic solution to decide reachability of such systems.

1 Introduction

A hybrid system is one in which discrete and continuous behaviours interact. Some systems are inherently hybrid — consider a robot, with differential equations determining its speed, together with an embedded computer taking discrete decisions based on the continuous input values coming from sensors. In other cases, a system consisting only of continuous behaviour, can be *hybridised,* introducing discrete behaviour in order to facilitate the analysis. For example, exact solutions can be difficult to obtain for a non-linear differential equation, making a qualitative and approximative analysis necessary.

A class of hybrid systems for which the reachability question is known to be decidable, are Polygonal Hybrid Systems (SPDIs) — a subclass of hybrid systems on the plane whose dynamics is defined by constant differential inclusions [ASY01, ASY07]. Informally, an SPDI consists of a partition of the plane into polygonal regions, each of which enforces different dynamics given by two vectors determining the possible directions a trajectory might take; a simple SPDI is depicted in Fig. 1-(a). A constructive proof for deciding reachability on SPDIs can be found in [ASY07]. The proof is restricted to SPDIs satisfying the so-called *goodness* assumption — the dynamics of any region of the SPDI do not allow a trajectory to traverse any edge of the polygonal region in opposite directions. An SPDI without the goodness assumption is called a *Generalised SPDI* (GSPDI).

Fig. 1-(b) shows an example of a good and a 'bad' region (here 'bad' indicates that the region does not satisfy the goodness criterion). In the figure on the left we can see a good region, where the two vectors **a** and **b** make it impossible for a trajectory to enter and leave the region P through the same edge of the polygon

J.S. Fitzgerald, A.E. Haxthausen, and H. Yenigun (Eds.): ICTAC 2008, LNCS 5160, pp. 274–289, 2008.
© Springer-Verlag Berlin Heidelberg 2008

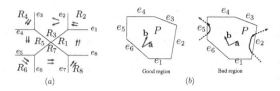

Fig. 1. (a) Example of an SPDI; (b) Good and bad regions

delimiting the region. On the other hand, the figure on the right shows a bad region: Both e_2 and e_5 can be crossed in both directions by a trajectory entering and leaving P. The algorithm presented in [ASY07] for deciding reachability on SPDI depends on pre-processing of trajectory segments and a qualitative analysis to guarantee that it is possible to review the behaviour of all the possible *signatures*[1], by looking at only a finite set of abstract signatures. Informally, this is achieved as follows: (1) Trajectory segments are simplified — it is sufficient to look at trajectories made up of straight segments across regions, and which do not cross themselves; (2) Trajectory segments are abstracted into signatures, based on the *Poincaré map* that relates n-dimensional continuous-time systems with $(n-1)$-dimensional discrete-time systems; (3) It is shown that it is sufficient to look at signatures which consist only of sequences of edges and simple cycles; (4) Such signatures can be abstracted into *types of signatures* — signatures which do not take into account the number of times each simple cycle is iterated.

Many of the lemmas for proving that the above guarantee the finiteness of types of signatures critically depend on the goodness assumption, which propagate this dependency to the constructive proof given for deciding reachability of SPDIs.

The restriction to "good" SPDIs is not justified by applications or inherent interest, it was just a technical condition to facilitate the application of certain techniques and prove decidability. In fact restricting oneself only to SPDIs satisfying the goodness assumption makes it very difficult to model real-life examples. Unfortunately, extending the SPDI model in most ways, such as allowing jumps with resets (from one edge to another remote one), increasing the number of dimensions and allowing non-linear differential inclusions, have been shown to make the model undecidable (see [AS02, MP05] and references therein).

A potentially interesting and useful application of SPDIs is that of the approximation and analysis of two-dimensional non-linear differential equations. By splitting the plane into polygons, and by setting the dynamics of each polygon to be over-approximations of the non-linear differential equation in that region, one can ask reachability questions about the equation, and obtain answers accordingly. When over-approximating the dynamics, a negative reachability answer implies a negative answer in the exact equation. Using more and smaller polygons enables more precise approximations.

The problem with using this approach is that for most differential equations, using a fixed partition breaks the goodness assumption, since some edges will

---

[1] We call *signature* the sequence of traversed edges by the trajectory. A more formal definition will be given in a later section.

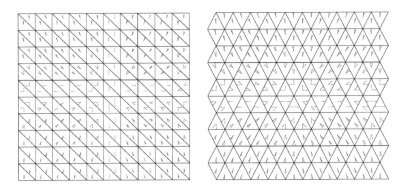

Fig. 2. Approximating a non-linear differential equation using different partitioning of the plane

lie within the differential inclusion of that region. One solution would be to try to derive an intelligent partition which maintains goodness, but which may be impossible, or by extending the SPDI analysis algorithms to relax the goodness assumption, thus enabling the modelling of non-linear differential equations in a straightforward manner.

As a simple example, consider a pendulum with friction coefficient k, mass M, pendulum length R and gravitational constant g. If θ is the angle subtended with the vertical, the behaviour of the pendulum follows the differential equation: $MR^2\ddot{\theta} + k\dot{\theta} + MgR\sin\theta = 0$. Taking $x = \theta$, and $y = \dot{\theta}$, we get $\dot{x} = y$ and $\dot{y} = -\frac{ky}{MR^2} - \frac{g\sin(x)}{R}$. Using these formulae, SPDIs expressing these constraints can be constructed, possibly with different plane partitions. Fig. 2 gives two such partitions for $k = 1$, $R = 10$, $M = 10$, and $g = -10$. Visual inspection shows that various polygons are not good. By presenting an algorithm to decide GSPDI reachability, we can automatically analyse such systems.

In this paper we present an algorithm for solving the reachability problem for GSPDIs, contributing towards the narrowing of the undecidability frontier of low dimension hybrid systems [AS02, MP05], and enabling the use of GSPDIs to approximate planar non-linear differential equations.

In the next section we outline definitions and results about SPDIs, and then extend them to enable the analysis of GSPDIs in section 3.

2 Polygonal Hybrid Systems (SPDIs)

In this section we recall the main definitions and concepts required in the rest of the paper, and give an outline of the results for SPDIs, upon which the results presented in this paper are built. For a more detailed presentation see [ASY07]. In what follows, we will use $\mathbf{a} = (a_1, a_2)$ and $\mathbf{x} = (x_1, x_2)$ to represent 2-dimensional vectors $(\mathbf{a}, \mathbf{x} \in \mathbb{R}^2)$. An *angle* $\angle_{\mathbf{a}}^{\mathbf{b}}$ on the plane, defined by two non-zero vectors $\mathbf{a}$ and $\mathbf{b}$ is the set of all positive linear combinations $\mathbf{x} = \alpha\,\mathbf{a} + \beta\,\mathbf{b}$, with $\alpha,\ \beta \geq 0$, and $\alpha + \beta > 0$. We can always assume that $\mathbf{b}$ is situated in the counter-clockwise direction from $\mathbf{a}$.

Definition 1. *A polygonal hybrid system (SPDI) is a pair* $\mathcal{H} = \langle \mathbb{P}, \mathbb{F} \rangle$*, where* $\mathbb{P}$ *is a finite partition of the plane (each* $P \in \mathbb{P}$ *being a convex polygon), called the* regions *of the SPDI, and* $\mathbb{F}$ *is a function associating a pair of vectors to each polygon:* $\mathbb{F}(P) = (\mathbf{a}_P, \mathbf{b}_P)$*. In an SPDI every point on the plane has its dynamics defined according to which polygon it belongs to: if* $\mathbf{x} \in P$*, then* $\dot{\mathbf{x}} \in \angle_{\mathbf{a}_P}^{\mathbf{b}_P}$*.* ∎

Example 1. Consider the SPDI illustrated in Fig. 1-(a), with eight regions $R_1, R_2, \ldots, R_8$. A pair of vectors $(\mathbf{a}_i, \mathbf{b}_i)$ is also associated to each region R_i: $\mathbf{a}_1 = \mathbf{b}_1 = (1,5)$, $\mathbf{a}_2 = \mathbf{b}_2 = (-1, \frac{1}{2})$, $\mathbf{a}_3 = (-1, \frac{11}{60})$ and $\mathbf{b}_3 = (-1, -\frac{1}{4})$, $\mathbf{a}_4 = \mathbf{b}_4 = (-1, -1)$, $\mathbf{a}_5 = \mathbf{b}_5 = (0, -1)$, $\mathbf{a}_6 = \mathbf{b}_6 = (1, -1)$, $\mathbf{a}_7 = \mathbf{b}_7 = (1, 0)$, $\mathbf{a}_8 = \mathbf{b}_8 = (1, 1)$. ∎

We define $E(P)$ to be the set of edges of region P. We say that an edge e ($e \in E(P)$) is an *entry-only* of P if for all $\mathbf{x} \in e$ and for all $\mathbf{c} \in \angle_{\mathbf{a}_P}^{\mathbf{b}_P}$, $\mathbf{x} + \mathbf{c}\epsilon \in P$ for some $\epsilon > 0$. We say that e is an *exit-only* of P if the same condition holds for some $\epsilon < 0$. Intuitively, an entry-only (exit-only) edge of a region P allows at least a trajectory in P starting (terminating) on edge e, but allows no trajectories in P terminating (starting) on edge e. We write $In(P)$ ($In(P) \subseteq E(P)$) to denote the set of all entry-only edges of P and $Out(P)$ ($Out(P) \subseteq E(P)$) to denote the set of exit-only edges of P. From the definition, it follows immediately that no edge can be both an entry-only and an exit-only edge of a region: $In(P) \cap Out(P) = \emptyset$.

A region P is said to be *good*, if all the edges of that region are either entry-only or exit-only: $E(P) = In(P) \cup Out(P)$. An SPDI is said to be *good*, or satisfy the *goodness* assumption, if it consists of only good regions: $\forall P \in \mathbb{P} \cdot E(P) = In(P) \cup Out(P)$.

Example 2. In Fig. 1-(b), the region P shown on the left is good since all edges are either entry-only or exit-only. The region depicted on the right shows a region that is not good, since neither edge e_2 nor edge e_5 are in $In(P) \cup Out(P)$. ∎

Note that though the definition of SPDIs does not exclude the possibility of having dynamics with $\mathbf{a}$ and $\mathbf{b}$ co-linear (i.e., $\mathbf{a} = -\mathbf{b}$), this is excluded under the goodness assumption. In what follows, 'SPDI' will always denote a good SPDI, unless specified otherwise.

We will use the notation $e_\circlearrowright^P$ to indicate the directed edge e such that it follows a clockwise direction around region P, and similarly $e_\circlearrowleft^P$ to indicate the directed edge e following an anti-clockwise direction around region P. Given a directed edge e, its inverse will be written as e^{-1}.

Definition 2. *The set of directed edges of an SPDI* $\mathcal{H}$ *with partition* $\mathbb{P}$*, written* $E_d(\mathcal{H})$*, is defined to be:* $E_d(\mathcal{H}) = \{e_\circlearrowright^P \mid P \in \mathbb{P}, e \in In(P)\} \cup \{e_\circlearrowleft^P \mid P \in \mathbb{P}, e \in Out(P)\}$*. Similarly, we define* $In_d(P)$ *and* $Out_d(P)$ *to correspond to* $In(P)$ *and* $Out(P)$ *but with directed edges.* ∎

Since an edge appears in two adjacent regions, the direction induced in the two regions may be different. However, it is easy to see that edges which are entry-only in one region, and exit-only in the other, result in matching induced directions: $e \in E_d(\mathcal{H})$ or $e^{-1} \in E_d(\mathcal{H})$, but not both [ASY01,MP93]. In an SPDI the only case where one can have both e and e^{-1} in a signature is when e is an entry-only (or exit-only) edge in both adjacent regions it belongs to.

A *trajectory segment* of an SPDI $\mathcal{H}$, is a continuous and almost-everywhere (everywhere except on finitely many points) differentiable function $\xi \in [0,T] \to \mathbb{R}^2$ such that for all $t \in [0,T]$, if $\xi(t) \in P$ and $\dot{\xi}(t)$ is defined then $\dot{\xi}(t) \in \angle_{\mathbf{a}_P}^{\mathbf{b}_P}$. The *signature* of a trajectory segment ξ, written $\mathsf{Sig}(\xi)$, is the sequence of edges traversed by the trajectory, that is, $e_1, e_2, \ldots e_n$ resulting from $\xi \cap E_d(\mathcal{H})$, where edges are arranged in the order they are "visited" by ξ.

One important result is that the behaviour of any trajectory is equivalent, with respect to reachability, to the behaviour of some trajectory which does not cross itself and follows straight-line segments within regions.

Lemma 1 ([ASY07]). *Given a trajectory segment $\xi \in [0,T] \to \mathbb{R}^2$, there exists another trajectory segment $\xi' \in [0,T'] \to \mathbb{R}^2$ starting and finishing at the same points as ξ ($\xi(0) = \xi'(0)$ and $\xi(T) = \xi'(T')$) such that (i) ξ' does not cross itself (ξ is injective); and (ii) ξ' follows straight-line segments inside regions.* $\square$

Though in general the reachability problem for an SPDI $\mathcal{H}$ may be considered for region-to-region, for simplicity of presentation we define it as the following predicate: $Reach(\mathcal{H}, \mathbf{x}_0, \mathbf{x}_f) \equiv \exists \xi \exists t \geq 0 \; . \; (\xi(0) = \mathbf{x}_0 \wedge \xi(t) = \mathbf{x}_f)$. Lemma 1 shows that to decide reachability, it is sufficient to look at non-self-crossing trajectories consisting of straight-line segments. In the rest of the discussion, we will restrict our use of trajectory to mean 'a non-self-crossing trajectory composed of straight-line segments between edges'. Similarly, the term signature will be used to indicate the signature of a trajectory with these constraints.

As usual in reachability analysis we need to compute successors, which are built upon special kind of multi-valued functions introduced in what follows.

Truncated Affine Multi-Valued Functions. An *affine* function $f \in \mathbb{R} \to \mathbb{R}$ is such that $f(x) = ax + b$. If $a > 0$ we say that f is *positive affine*, and if $a < 0$ we say that f is *negative affine*; we call this the parity of the affine function.

An *affine multivalued* function (AMF) $F \in \mathbb{R} \to 2^{\mathbb{R}}$, written $F = \langle f_l, f_u \rangle$, is defined by $F(x) = \langle f_l(x), f_u(x) \rangle$ where f_l and f_u are positive affine and $\langle \cdot, \cdot \rangle$ denotes an interval. For notational convenience, we do not make explicit whether intervals are open, closed, left-open or right-open, unless required for comprehension. For an interval $I = \langle l, u \rangle$ we have that $F(\langle l, u \rangle) = \langle f_l(l), f_u(u) \rangle$. An *inverted affine multivalued* function $F \in \mathbb{R} \to 2^{\mathbb{R}}$, is defined by $F(x) = \langle f_u(x), f_l(x) \rangle$ where f_l and f_u are both negative affine and $\langle \cdot, \cdot \rangle$ denotes an interval.

Given an AMF F and two intervals $S \subseteq \mathbb{R}^+$ and $J \subseteq \mathbb{R}^+$, a *truncated affine multivalued* function (TAMF) $\mathcal{F}_{F,S,J} \in \mathbb{R} \to 2^{\mathbb{R}}$ is defined as follows: $\mathcal{F}_{F,S,J}(x) = F(x) \cap J$ if $x \in S$, otherwise $\mathcal{F}_{F,S,J}(x) = \emptyset$. In what follows we will write $\mathcal{F}$ instead of $\mathcal{F}_{F,S,J}$ whenever no confusion may arise. Moreover, in the rest of the paper F will always denote an AMF and $\mathcal{F}$ a TAMF. For convenience we write $\mathcal{F}(x) = F(\{x\} \cap S) \cap J$ instead of $\mathcal{F}(x) = F(x) \cap J$ if $x \in S$. We overload the application of a TAMF on an interval I: $\mathcal{F}(I) = F(I \cap S) \cap J$. We say that $\mathcal{F}$ is *normalised* if $S = \mathsf{Dom}(\mathcal{F}) = \{x \mid F(x) \cap J \neq \emptyset\}$ and $J = \mathsf{Im}(\mathcal{F}) = \mathcal{F}(S)$.

As in the case of affine multivalued functions, an *inverted truncated affine multivalued* function (inverted TAMF) is similar to a TAMF, but defined in terms of an inverted affine multivalued function as opposed to a normal one. An important result is that normal TAMFs are closed under composition.

Theorem 1 ([ASY07]). *The functional composition of two normal TAMFs* $\mathcal{F}_1(I) = F_1(I \cap S_1) \cap J_1$ *and* $\mathcal{F}_2(I) = F_2(I \cap S_2) \cap J_2$, *is the TAMF* $(\mathcal{F}_2 \circ \mathcal{F}_1)(I) = \mathcal{F}(I) = F(I \cap S) \cap J$, *where* $F = F_2 \circ F_1$, $S = S_1 \cap F_1^{-1}(J_1 \cap S_2)$ *and* $J = J_2 \cap F_2(J_1 \cap S_2)$. □

The following new corollary extends the above result.

Corollary 1. *The composition of two inverted TAMFs gives a normal TAMF. Conversely, the composition of one normal and one inverted TAMF (in either order) gives an inverted TAMF.* □

To avoid having to reason about the length of every edge, we normalise every edge e such that its TAMF has the domain $[0, 1]$ (that is, the normalised version of e has length 1, with 0 corresponding to the starting point of the directed edge, and 1 to the end point).

Successors. Given an SPDI, we fix a one-dimensional coordinate system on each edge to represent points lying on edges. For notational convenience, we will use e to denote both the directed edge and its one-dimensional representation. Accordingly, we write $\mathbf{x} \in e$ and $x \in e$, to mean "point $\mathbf{x}$ lies on edge e" and "coordinate x in the one-dimensional coordinate system of e" respectively. The same convention applied to sets of points of e represented as intervals (for example, $\mathbf{x} \in I$ and $x \in I$, where $I \subseteq e$) and to trajectories (for example, "ξ starting at x" or "ξ starting at $\mathbf{x}$").

Consider a polygon $P \in \mathbb{P}$, with $e_0 \in In_d(P)$ and $e_1 \in Out_d(P)$. For $I \subseteq e_0$, $\mathsf{Succ}_{e_0 e_1}(I)$ is defined to be the set of all points lying on e_1 reachable from some point in I by a trajectory segment $\xi \in [0, t] \to \mathbb{R}^2$ in P (that is, $\xi(0) \in I \wedge \xi(t) \in e_1 \wedge \mathsf{Sig}(\xi) = e_0 e_1)$. Given $I = [l, u]$, $\mathsf{Succ}_{e_0 e_1}(I) = F(I \cap S_{e_0 e_1}) \cap J_{e_0 e_1}$, where $S_{e_0 e_1}$ and $J_{e_0 e_1}$ are intervals, $F([l, u]) = \langle f_l(l), f_u(u) \rangle$ and f_l and f_u are positive affine functions. Successors are thus normal TAMFs.

Qualitative analysis of simple edge-cycles. In what follows a sequence of edges in parenthesis, $\sigma = (e_1 \ldots e_k)$, will denote a simple edge-cycle – that is, a signature that can be repeated at least once, and such that all edges are distinct ($e_i \neq e_j$ for all $1 \leq i < j \leq k$). Given an SPDI, its topology determines when a sequence of edges may form a simple cycle [ASY07]. Let $\mathsf{Succ}_\sigma(I) = F(I \cap S_\sigma) \cap J_\sigma$ with $F = \langle f_l, f_u \rangle$, and S_σ and J_σ computed as in theorem 1.

We assume that neither of the two functions f_l, f_u is the identity function. The following analysis, taken from [ASY01], allows us to calculate the behaviour of cycles provided that the path along the cycle has a normal (not inverted) TAMF. Since, in SPDIs, the TAMF between a pair of edges is normal, and the composition of two normal TAMFs is itself a normal TAMF, this approach is universally applicable as long as the goodness assumption holds.

Let σ be a simple cycle, and l^* and u^* be the fix-points[2] of f_l and f_u, respectively, and $S_\sigma \cap J_\sigma = \langle L, U \rangle$. It can be shown that σ is of one of the following kinds: **STAY:** The cycle is not abandoned neither by the leftmost nor the rightmost trajectory, that is, $L \leq l^* \leq u^* \leq U$. **DIE:** The rightmost trajectory exits the cycle through the left (consequently the leftmost one also exits) or the leftmost trajectory exits the cycle through the right (consequently the rightmost one also exits), that is, $u^* < L \vee l^* > U$. **EXIT-BOTH:** The leftmost trajectory exits the cycle through the left and the rightmost one through the right, that is, $l^* < L \wedge u^* > U$. **EXIT-LEFT:** The leftmost trajectory exits the cycle (through the left) but the rightmost one stays inside, that is, $l^* < L \leq u^* \leq U$. **EXIT-RIGHT:** The rightmost trajectory exits the cycle (through the right) but the leftmost one stays inside, that is, $L \leq l^* \leq U < u^*$.

The classification above provides useful information about the qualitative behaviour of trajectories. Any trajectory that enters a cycle of kind DIE will eventually leave it after a finite number of turns. In a cycle of kind STAY, all trajectories that happen to enter it will keep turning inside it forever. In all other cases, some trajectories will turn for a while and then exit, and others will continue turning forever. This information is crucial for solving the reachability problem for SPDIs. Also note that the above analysis gives us a non-iterative solution of cycle behaviour for most cycles; the theoretical algorithm [ASY07] as well as the tool SPeeDI [Spe] uses such acceleration techniques. An important result to prove the decidability of SPDIs is that any valid signature can be expressed in a normal form, consisting of alternating sequential paths and simple cycles:

Theorem 2 ([ASY07]). *Given an SPDI with the goodness assumption, any edge signature $\sigma = e_1 \ldots e_p$ can be written as $\sigma_{\mathcal{A}} = r_1 s_1^{k_1} \ldots r_n s_n^{k_n} r_{n+1}$, where for any $1 \leq i \leq n+1$, r_i is a sequence of pairwise different edges and for all $1 \leq i \leq n$, s_i is a simple cycle (no edges are repeated within s_i).* □

Let $\sigma = e_1 \ldots e_p$ be an edge signature and $\sigma_{\mathcal{A}} = r_1 s_1^{k_1} \ldots r_n s_n^{k_n} r_{n+1}$ be its representation as in the above theorem. Then we define the *type of a signature* σ as $\mathsf{type}(\sigma) = r_1, s_1, \ldots, r_n, s_n, r_{n+1}$. We say that a signature σ is *feasible* if and only if there exists a trajectory segment ξ with signature σ, i.e., $\mathsf{Sig}(\xi) = \sigma$.

Types of signatures have the following properties:

Lemma 2 ([ASY07]). *Given an SPDI, let $\sigma = e_0 \ldots e_p$ be a feasible signature, then its type, $\mathsf{type}(\sigma) = r_1, s_1, \ldots, r_n, s_n, r_{n+1}$ satisfies the following properties: (i) every $1 \leq i < j \leq n+1$, r_i and r_j are disjoint; (ii) every $1 \leq i < j \leq n$, s_i and s_j are different.* □

The finiteness of types of signatures is the basis of the proof of decidability of (good) SPDI reachability, and of the termination of the reachability algorithm (together with acceleration results for simple cycles).

Theorem 3 ([ASY07]). *Point-to-point, interval-to-interval and region-to-region reachability for SPDIs is decidable.* □

---

[2] The fix-point x^* is the solution of $f(x^*) = x^*$, where $f(\cdot)$ is positive affine. The existence and computation of such fix-points are detailed in [ASY07].

3   Relaxing Goodness: Generalised SPDIs

The original proof of the decidability of the reachability question for SPDIs, depended on the concept of monotonicity of TAMFs and their composition. Before starting the analysis, the algorithm fixed the direction of the edges separating regions. An interesting result guaranteed that the orientation of the edges resulted in each polygon split into two contiguous sequences of edges — one being entry-only edges, the other being exit-only edges. Furthermore, the orientation of an edge in one region is guaranteed to match the orientation of the same edge in the adjacent region[3], as shown in Fig. 3-(a). When one moves on to GSPDIs, *inout* edges (those that may be traversed in both directions) break this result, since the direction of an edge when considered as an input edge clashes with the direction it is given when used as an output edge in the same region. The previous result however, still guaranteed that the entry-only edges and the exit-only edges can be assigned in one fixed direction (see Fig. 3-(b)).

To solve this problem, we use directed edges, and differentiate between the edge used as an input, and when it is used as an output, just as though they were two different edges in the GSPDI. Fig. 3-(c) shows how an inout edge can be seen in this manner. Note that depending on in which direction the trajectory traverse the inout edge e_1, it is an input edge in region R_1, but an output edge in region R_2, and similarly, e_1^{-1} is an output edge in region R_1 and an input edge in region R_2; that is why we did not draw the direction vector in the picture. In other words, any path passing through the edge such as $\sigma = e_0 e_1 e_2 \ldots e_3 e_1^{-1} e_4$ (see Fig. 3-(d)) can be analysed as before, and through monotonicity, one can deduce that Succ_σ is a positive TAMF. e_1 and e_1^{-1} are considered distinct edges, and the above path contains no cycle.

It can be seen that the standard analysis for SPDIs works well for such cases. However, paths can now 'bounce' off an edge. Recall that any pair of edges $e_0 e_1$ is part of a path if e_0 is an input edge of a region, and e_1 is an output edge of the same region. One can calculate the TAMF for such a trajectory. However, ee^{-1} can now be a valid path, whose behaviour cannot be expressed as a normal TAMF. This breaks the analysis used in SPDIs, to accelerate the analysis of simple cycles. The standard SPDI analysis thus needs to be extended to handle such 'bounces' in paths.

3.1   Preliminary Results

The *goodness* assumption was originally introduced to simplify treatment of trajectories and to guarantee that each region can be partitioned into *entry-only* and *exit-only* edges in an ordered way, a fact used in the proof of decidability of the reachability problem. In this section, we will introduce further background, and provide new results concerning GSPDIs, needed to prove our decidability result.

---

[3] There are special cases when an edge is an entry-only to a region and an exit-only to an adjacent region. From the reachability point of view this does not cause any problem as these cases can be identified and treated accordingly.

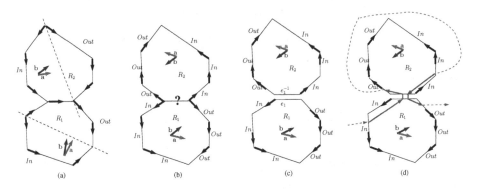

Fig. 3. (a) An SPDI with matching order of edges; (b) a GSPDI showing that the order breaks the contiguity of the edge directions; (c) a GSPDI with a duplicated inout edge; (d) a path through the GSPDI using edge e_1 in both directions

Definition 3. *An edge $e \in P$ is an inout edge of P if e is neither an entry-only nor an exit-only edge of P.* ∎

An SPDI without the goodness assumption is called a *Generalised SPDI (GSPDI)*. Thus, in GSPDIs there are three kinds of edges: inouts, entry-only and exit-only.

Self-crossing of trajectory (segments) of SPDIs can be eliminated, which allows us to consider only non-crossing trajectory (segments). Standard algebraic manipulation of vector suffices to show that lemma 1 [ASY07]) also applies to GSPDIs. Therefore, in what follows, we will consider only trajectory segments without self-crossings. Note that on GSPDIs, a trajectory can "intersect" an edge at an infinite number of points by *sliding* along it. A trace is thus no longer a sequence of points, but rather, a sequence of intervals.

Definition 4. *The trace of a trajectory ξ is the sequence $\mathsf{trace}(\xi) = I_0 I_1 \ldots I_n$ of the intersection intervals of ξ with the set of edges: $I_i \subseteq \xi \cap E_d(\mathcal{H})$.* ∎

In Fig. 4-(a) we show a trajectory segment ξ, such that $\mathsf{trace}(\xi) = I_0 I_1 I_2 \ldots I_3 I_4 I_5$ where I_1, I_2, I_3, I_4 and I_5 are points.

Definition 5. *An edge signature (or simply a signature) of a GSPDI is a sequence of edges. The edge signature of a trajectory ξ, $\mathsf{Sig}(\xi)$, is the sequence of traversed edges by the trajectory segment, that is, $\mathsf{Sig}(\xi) = e_0 e_1 \ldots e_n$, with $\mathsf{trace}(\xi) = I_0 I_1 \ldots I_n$ and $I_i \subseteq e_i$.* ∎

In Fig. 4-(a) the signature of the trajectory segment ξ is $\mathsf{Sig}(\xi) = e e' e'' \ldots e''^{-1} e'^{-1} e'''$ (to simplify the picture we do not draw the "duplicated" edges e''^{-1} and e'^{-1}).

Note that, in many cases, the intervals of a trace are in fact points. We say that a trajectory with edge signature $\mathsf{Sig}(\xi) = e_0 e_1 \ldots e_n$ and trace $\mathsf{trace}(\xi) = I_0 I_1 \ldots I_n$ *interval-crosses* edge e_i if I_i is not a point. Given a trajectory segment, we will distinguish between *proper inout* edges and *sliding* edges.

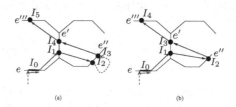

(a)   (b)

Fig. 4. (a) A sliding trajectory with a proper inout edge; (b) A sliding trajectory with a proper inout edge and a bounce

Definition 6. *Let ξ be a trajectory segment from point $\mathbf{x}_0 \in e_0$ to $\mathbf{x}_f \in e_f$, with edge signature $\mathsf{Sig}(\xi) = e_0 \ldots e_i \ldots e_n$, and $e_i \in E(P)$ be an edge of P. We say that e_i is a sliding edge of P for ξ if ξ interval-crosses e_i, otherwise e is said to be a proper inout edge of P for ξ.* ∎

We say that a trajectory segment ξ *slides* along an edge e, if e is a sliding edge of P for ξ, and that ξ is a *sliding trajectory* if it contains at least one sliding edge. Fig. 4-(a) shows a sliding trajectory, where e is a sliding edge while e' and e'' are proper inout edges. The following is a useful property of inout edges.

Proposition 1. *If e is an inout edge, then any trajectory reaching the edge can always slide on the edge (in one or the other direction, or both).* □

Since inout edges may appear in different situations, we need to explain our strategy to deal with them, for which we need some preliminaries. For a region P let us say that a vector $\mathbf{c}$ is *compatible* with the orientation of P if $\mathbf{c}$ is a positive combination of vectors $\mathbf{a}$ and $\mathbf{b}$ associated with P.

Let e be an edge separating two polygons P_1 and P_2. There are the following four new cases in addition to those from [ASY07]: (1) e is an inout edge in P_1 and an entry-only edge in P_2; (2) e is an inout edge in P_1 and an exit-only edge in P_2; (3) e is an inout edge in P_1 and also an inout edge in P_2[4]; (4) e is an inout edge in P_1 and also an inout edge in P_2 like in the previous case[5]. In all these cases a trajectory may slide on the edge if at least one of the dynamics on the region allows it. For instance, in case (4), the trajectory may slide in both directions. The above cases are included in our reachability analysis.

As for SPDIs, we have the following property of Succ: for any edge signatures σ_1 and σ_2 and edge e: $\mathsf{Succ}_{e\sigma_1} \circ \mathsf{Succ}_{\sigma_2 e} = \mathsf{Succ}_{\sigma_2 e \sigma_1}$.

The following lemma shows that the edge-to-edge successor function is a normal TAMF whenever the two edges are not the inverse of each other. It follows

---

[4] If $\mathbf{c}_1$ is a vector compatible with the orientation of P_1 and $\mathbf{c}_2$ a vector compatible with the orientation of P_2 (see definition above) such that $\mathbf{c}_1$ and $\mathbf{c}_2$ are parallel to edge e then both vectors are oriented in the same direction.

[5] In this case if $\mathbf{c}_1$ is a vector compatible with the orientation of P_1 and $\mathbf{c}_2$ a vector compatible with the orientation of P_2 such that both $\mathbf{c}_1$ and $\mathbf{c}_2$ are parallel to edge e then $\mathbf{c}_1$ and $\mathbf{c}_2$ are oriented in the opposite directions.

directly from the similar result for SPDIs [ASY07], which makes no assumption regarding goodness.[6]

Lemma 3. *For any two edges e_0 and e_1, $\mathsf{Succ}_{e_0 e_1}$ is always a normal TAMF, whenever $e_1 \neq e_0^{-1}$.*   □

Besides sliding, the signatures that we will be analysing in GSPDIs may include subsequences of the form ee^{-1}. The behaviour between such edges does not correspond to a normal TAMF, and thus has to be analysed separately. A *bounce* is a part of a trajectory which crosses an edge twice in immediate succession. More formally:

Definition 7. *Given a signature $\sigma = e_0 e_1 \ldots e_n$, a pair of edges $e_i e_{i+1}$ is said to be a bounce if $e_{i+1} = e_i^{-1}$. We say that a signature $e_0 e_1 \ldots e_n$ contains m bounces, if there are exactly m distinct indices $I = \{i_1, i_2, \ldots i_m\}$ such for every $i \in I$, $e_i = e_{i+1}^{-1}$.*   ∎

Fig. 4-(b) shows a sliding trajectory $\mathsf{Sig}(\xi) = ee'e''e''^{-1}e'^{-1}e'''$. There is only one bounce, namely $e''e''^{-1}$.

Let $\mathsf{Flip}[l, u] = [1 - u, \ 1 - l]$ be an interval function. The following result establishes that the successor function for bounces can be defined in terms of the Flip function. It is easy to prove that $\mathsf{Succ}_{ee^{-1}} = \mathsf{Flip}$.

One of the useful properties of SPDIs is that the successor function of any given signature is a normal TAMF. For GSPDIs, however, we need to take into account bounces, and hence analyse the composition of normal TAMFs with Flip:

Lemma 4. *Composing Flip with an inverted TAMF gives a normal TAMF and an inverted TAMF if we compose it with a normal TAMF.*   □

The parity of the number of bounces occurring in a given signature influences the form of the underlying TAMF, as shown in the following result, whose proof follows immediately by induction on the number of bounces.

Corollary 2. *Any signature with an even number of bounces has its behaviour characterised by a normal TAMF, while a signature with an odd number of bounces is characterised by an inverted TAMF.*   □

Recall that the analysis of simple cycle behaviour given for SPDIs depends only on the assumption that the TAMF of the cycle body is a normal one. From the previous result, it thus follows that whenever the number of bounces is even on a given cyclic signature, the composed TAMF is a normal one, so the analysis of simple cycles can be conducted as for SPDIs:

Lemma 5. *Given a simple cycle σ containing an even number of bounces, its iterated behaviour can be calculated as for SPDIs.*   □

---

[6] Note that the underlying AMFs are not necessarily positive affine whenever applied to an inout edge, since the leftmost (rightmost) function may give $-\infty$ ($+\infty$). However, this is not a problem for successors, as in this case the underlying TAMFs are of the form $[0, ax + b]$ or $[ax + b, 1]$ due to sliding.

Since a trajectory slides only along inout edges, and can only bounce off inout edges, we can prove that simple cycles which include at least one bounce are never STAY cycles. This gives us the advantage of the use of acceleration techniques already used for SPDIs.

Lemma 6. *Simple cycles which include bounces are not STAY cycles.*   □

From lemma 5 we have that only simple cycles with an odd number of bounces need to be analysed. Considering the case when a bounce appears as the first pair of elements of a simple cycle body, we can accelerate the analysis by running through the simple cycle only once. The proof follows from the fact that the initial bounce enables a slide, thus allowing us to identify the limits through only one application of the simple cycle body:

Lemma 7. *Given a signature* $\sigma = e_0(e_1 e_1^{-1} e_2 \ldots e_n)^k e_1$ *(i) with only one simple cycle; (ii) with* $k > 0$; *(iii) with an odd number of bounces; and (iv) starts with a bounce; its behaviour is equivalent to following the simple cycle only once* $\sigma' = e_0 e_1 e_1^{-1} e_2 \ldots e_n e_1$. *In other words:* $\mathsf{Succ}_\sigma = \mathsf{Succ}_{\sigma'}$.   □

Based on the above lemma, we can prove that any simple cycle containing an odd number of bounces can be accelerated. The proof works by unwinding the simple cycle body to push the first bounce to the beginning, and then applying the previous lemma:

Lemma 8. *Given a simple cycle* s *with an odd number of bounces, we can calculate the limit of its iterated behaviour without iterating.*   □

Therefore, we can now analyse any type of signature in GSPDIs using the results from lemma 3 (to deal with inout edges), and lemmas 5 and 8 (to deal with bounces). Given a simple cycle s, let s^+ be the cycle iterated one or more times.

Theorem 4. *We can (constructively) compute the behaviour of a signature* $r_1 s_1^+$ $r_2 s_2^+ \ldots r_n$.   □

3.2   Decidability Results

The following lemma guarantees that it is sufficient to consider simple cycles which occur in a type of signature with certain patterns. Any type of signature containing two occurrences of the same simple cycle can be reduced to another type of signature where the simple cycle s occurs only once, provided the cycle with the edges in reverse order does not occur between them. The proof is based on the fact that, assuming the trajectory does not cross itself, between two instances of a repeated simple cycle, one can always find either the reverse of the cycle or a bounce, in which case, the bounce can be eliminated to avoid leaving the simple cycle.

Lemma 9. *Given a GSPDI, and assuming only trajectories without self-crossing, if there is a type of signature where a simple cycle* $s = (e_0, e_1, \ldots, e_n)$ *appears twice, i.e.* $\mathsf{type}(\mathsf{Sig}(\xi)) = \sigma' \sigma'' \sigma'''$ *with* $\sigma'' = s^k \ldots s^{k''}$, *then if there is no reverse(s) between the two occurrences of* s, *then* $\mathsf{type}(\mathsf{Sig}(\xi)) = \sigma' s^{k'''} \sigma'''$.   □

We also prove that a trajectory which takes a simple cycle (any number of times), then takes it again (any number of times) but in reverse order, and finally takes it a number of times in the forward direction, can be simulated by another trajectory which simply takes the simple cycle a number of times. The proof is based on the fact that whichever direction the first edge of the simple cycle under consideration allows sliding in, it is possible to obtain a type of signature preserving reachability without such a pattern.

Lemma 10. *Given a GSPDI, if there is a trajectory segment* $\xi : [0, T] \to \mathbb{R}^2$, *with* $\xi(0) = \mathbf{x}$ *and* $\xi(t) = \mathbf{x}'$ *for some* $t > 0$, *such that* $\mathsf{type}(\mathsf{Sig}(\xi)) = r_1 s_1^{k_1} r_2 s_2^{k_2} r_3 s_3^{k_3} r_4$, *with* $s_2 = s_1^{-1}$ *and* $s_3 = s_1$, *then it is always possible to find a trajectory segment* $\xi' : [0, T] \to \mathbb{R}^2$ *such that* $\xi'(0) = \mathbf{x}$ *and* $\xi'(t) = \mathbf{x}'$ *for some* $t > 0$, *and* $\mathsf{type}(\mathsf{Sig}(\xi)) = r_1 s_1^{k'_1} r_4$. $\qquad\square$

Based on the above, we can conclude that for GSPDIs we can always transform a type of signature into one where simple cycles are not repeated.

Corollary 3. *Given a GSPDI, an edge signature* σ *can be written as* $\sigma_{\mathcal{A}} = r_1 s_1^{k_1} \ldots r_n s_n^{k_n} r_{n+1}$, *where for any* $1 \leq i \leq n + 1$, s_i *is a simple cycle (no repetition of edges), and for every* $1 \leq i < j \leq n$, s_i *and* s_j *are different.* $\qquad\square$

We can define the notion of *type of signature* as for SPDIs, abstracting the number of times simple cycles are iterated on signatures of the kind shown on the above corollary. Note that the statement of corollary 3 is weaker than the corresponding result for SPDIs (theorem 2 and lemma 2) since it does not have any restriction on the sequences of edges r_i. However, the result is enough to prove that there is only a finite number of types of signatures for a given GSPDI.

Corollary 4. *A GSPDI has finitely many different types of signatures.* $\qquad\square$

Given a type of signature σ where each edge is traversed in exactly one direction, let $\mathbf{Reach}_\sigma(\mathbf{x}_0, \mathbf{x}_f)$ be the SPDI reachability algorithm from [ASY07]. The reachability algorithm for a GSPDI $\mathcal{H}$, $\mathbf{Reach}(\mathcal{H}, \mathbf{x}_0, \mathbf{x}_f)$, works as follows: (1) Generate the finite set of types of signatures $\Sigma = \{\sigma_0, \ldots, \sigma_n\}$ (taking into account e and e^{-1} as different edges), and such that the simple cycles are all distinct; (2) Apply $\mathbf{Reach}_{\sigma_i}(\mathbf{x}_0, \mathbf{x}_f)$ for each $\sigma_i \in \Sigma$; (3) Answer Yes if and only if for some $\sigma_i \in \Sigma$, $\mathbf{Reach}_{\sigma_i}(\mathbf{x}_0, \mathbf{x}_f) = \mathsf{Yes}$.

In step 2 we apply Succ progressively on the abstract signature, using lemmas 5 and 8 to compute the successor of a simple cycle with bounces, and the Succ function as in the case of SPDIs for the rest. Based on these results, it is possible to show termination, correctness and completeness of GSPDI reachability. From this, the main theoretical result follows immediately:

Theorem 5. $\mathbf{Reach}(\mathcal{H}, \mathbf{x}_0, \mathbf{x}_f)$ *is a sound and complete algorithm calculating GSPDI reachability. The reachability problem for GSPDIs is decidable.* $\qquad\square$

4   Final Remarks

We have proved that the reachability question for GSPDIs is decidable. The proof is constructive, extending the algorithm for SPDIs [ASY07]. The key lies in showing that the previous analysis works in all cases except when a simple cycle contains an odd number of bounces. The algorithm is extended to deal with such cases, considering now inout edges which enable sliding, but the overall effect is to accelerate the analysis of an SPDI, since at least one end of the edge is immediately covered once the edge is reached.

Concerning complexity, the algorithm presented here has the same worst-case space complexity as for SPDIs, with the only extra additional drawback of eventually doubling the number of edges due to duplication of inout edges. Concerning time complexity, the reachability algorithm developed for SPDIs makes massive use of acceleration techniques, reducing the practical complexity of the analysis. For GSPDIs acceleration is used even in more cases: every simple cycle containing an inout edge can be accelerated. Overall, if compared with SPDI reachability analysis, we have a slight increase on the size of the search state-space, but a faster way of analysing simple cycles. Furthermore, we conjecture that the techniques presented in [PS06b] for reducing the search state-space as well as the compositional analysis introduced in [PS06a] for SPDIs could be applied without further development for GSPDIs.

The main contribution of our paper is interesting in a theoretical sense since it extends the class of decidable hybrid systems, narrowing further the gap between what is known to be be decidable and what is known to be undecidable [AS02, MP05]. The result is also interesting in a practical sense, since it provides a good foundation to approximate planar non-linear differential equations, complementing other works using piecewise linear hybrid systems.

Reachability analysis of GSPDIs is not easy. An early (unsuccessful) attempt to prove decidability of GSPDI reachability was presented in [Sch08] — in which it is shown that no structure-preserving reduction of GPSDI reachability into SPDI reachability is possible. Instead, a semi-test algorithm, which reduces reachability of GSPDI into reachability of an exponential number of SPDIs was developed. The main idea behind this algorithm is that in most cases reachability is preserved when fixing inout edges as entry-only or exit-only edges, and considering all possible permutations of SPDIs generated from this pre-processing, reducing then the problem to SPDI reachability. However, there are cases where it is not possible to eliminate inout edges while preserving reachability. Moreover, the proposed algorithm introduces an extra exponential blow-up to the analysis. The decidable algorithm presented in the present paper for GSPDIs follows a completely different approach than the semi-test presented in [Sch08].

Reachability analysis over SPDIs converges in various cases in which semi-algorithms for general n-dimensional hybrid systems diverge (eg. see [APSY02] for a comparative analysis with HyTech [HHW95]) This extends for GSPDI analysis. Decidability of low-dimensional hybrid systems is addressed in [AS02, MP05]. In particular, in [AS02] it was shown that by slightly modifying PCDs to obtain 2-dimensional linear hybrid automata, the reachability problem becomes undecidable, showing that GSPDIs really lies on the edge of decidability. The relation between GSPDIs and rectangular hybrid automata [HM00] restricted to 2-dimensional systems, is that not all GSPDIs can be reduced into a rectangular automaton, but on the other hand, no resets are allowed in GSPDIs — making them incomparable.

Multi-affine functions have also been used in [KB06], in which the reachability problem is translated into an abstract discrete system resulting in an over-approximation. The notion of trace and edge signatures has also been used in [BMRT04] to build a bisimulation relation for o-minimal hybrid systems [LPS00] — GSPDIs are not o-minimal systems since the flow is nondeterministic.

Further comparison of other work with GSPDIs can be induced from their comparison to SPDIs [ASY07]. A full version of this paper can be found in [PS08].

References

[APSY02]   Asarin, E., Pace, G., Schneider, G., Yovine, S.: SPeeDI: a verification tool for polygonal hybrid systems. In: Brinksma, E., Larsen, K.G. (eds.) CAV 2002. LNCS, vol. 2404, Springer, Heidelberg (2002)

[AS02]   Asarin, E., Schneider, G.: Widening the boundary between decidable and undecidable hybrid systems. In: Brim, L., Jančar, P., Křetínský, M., Kucera, A. (eds.) CONCUR 2002. LNCS, vol. 2421. Springer, Heidelberg (2002)

[ASY01]   Asarin, E., Schneider, G., Yovine, S.: On the decidability of the reachability problem for planar differential inclusions. In: Di Benedetto, M.D., Sangiovanni-Vincentelli, A.L. (eds.) HSCC 2001. LNCS, vol. 2034. Springer, Heidelberg (2001)

[ASY07]   Asarin, E., Schneider, G., Yovine, S.: Algorithmic Analysis of Polygonal Hybrid Systems. Part I: Reachability. TCS 379(1-2), 231–265 (2007)

[BMRT04]   Brihaye, T., Michaux, C., Rivière, C., Troestler, C.: On o-minimal hybrid systems. In: Alur, R., Pappas, G.J. (eds.) HSCC 2004. LNCS, vol. 2993, pp. 219–233. Springer, Heidelberg (2004)

[HHW95]   Henzinger, T.A., Ho, P.-H., Wong-Toi, H.: Hytech: The next generation. In: Proc. IEEE Real-Time Systems Symposium RTSS 1995 (1995)

[HM00]   Henzinger, T.A., Majumdar, R.: Symbolic model checking for rectangular hybrid systems. In: Schwartzbach, M.I., Graf, S. (eds.) TACAS 2000. LNCS, vol. 1785, pp. 142–156. Springer, Heidelberg (2000)

[KB06]   Kloetzer, M., Belta, C.: Reachability analysis of multi-affine systems. In: Hespanha, J.P., Tiwari, A. (eds.) HSCC 2006. LNCS, vol. 3927, pp. 348–362. Springer, Heidelberg (2006)

[LPS00]   Lafferriere, G., Pappas, G.J., Sastry, S.: O–Minimal hybrid systems. Mathematics of control, signals and systems 13, 1–21 (2000)

[MP93]   Maler, O., Pnueli, A.: Reachability analysis of planar multi-linear systems. In: Courcoubetis, C. (ed.) CAV 1993. LNCS, vol. 697. Springer, Heidelberg (1993)

[MP05]   Mysore, V., Pnueli, A.: Refining the undecidability frontier of hybrid automata. In: Ramanujam, R., Sen, S. (eds.) FSTTCS 2005. LNCS, vol. 3821. Springer, Heidelberg (2005)

[PS06a]   Pace, G.J., Schneider, G.: A compositional algorithm for parallel model
            checking of polygonal hybrid systems. In: Barkaoui, K., Cavalcanti, A.,
            Cerone, A. (eds.) ICTAC 2006. LNCS, vol. 4281. Springer, Heidelberg
            (2006)
[PS06b]   Pace, G.J., Schneider, G.: Static analysis for state-space reduction of
            polygonal hybrid systems. In: Asarin, E., Bouyer, P. (eds.) FORMATS
            2006. LNCS, vol. 4202. Springer, Heidelberg (2006)
[PS08]   Pace, G.J., Schneider, G.: Relaxing Goodness is Still Good for SPDIs.
            Technical Report 372, Dept. of Informatics, Univ. of Oslo, Norway (Feb-
            ruary 2008)
[Sch08]   Schneider, G.: Reachability analysis of Generalized Polygonal Hybrid Sys-
            tems. In: ACM SAC-SV 2008, March 2008, pp. 327–332. ACM Press, New
            York (2008)
[Spe]   SpeeDI$^+$, http://www.cs.um.edu.mt/speedi/

Benchmarking Model- and Satisfiability-Checking on Bi-infinite Time[*]

Matteo Pradella[1], Angelo Morzenti[2], and Pierluigi San Pietro[2]

[1] IEIIT, Consiglio Nazionale delle Ricerche, Milano, Italy
[2] Dipartimento di Elettronica e Informazione, Politecnico di Milano, Italy
{pradella,morzenti,sanpietr}@elet.polimi.it

Abstract. Model checking techniques traditionally deal with temporal logic languages and automata interpreted over ω-words, i.e., where time is infinite in the future but finite in the past. This is motivated by the study of reactive systems, which are typically nonterminating: system termination may be abstracted away by allowing an infinite future. In the same way, if time is infinite also in the past one is allowed to ignore the complexity of system initialization. Specifications may then be simpler and more easily understandable, because they do not necessarily include the description of operations (such as configuration or installation) typically performed at system deployment time. In this paper, we investigate the feasibility of bounded model checking and bounded satisfiability checking when dealing with bi-infinite automata and logics. We present a tool and we discuss its application to a set of case studies, arguing that bi-infinite time does not entail significant penalties in verification time and space.

Keywords: Bounded model checking, bi-infinite words and automata, metric temporal logic.

1 Introduction

Temporal logics and automata models used in specification and verification usually consider time to be finite in the past, i.e., with a "first" time instant. The reason is both pragmatical and historical: finite automata and temporal logic were applied to model programs or hardware, where often there is an initialization step. Hence, automata and temporal logics (the latter also extended with past operators) on ω-words seemed adequate for modeling and verification. The only concession to infinity was in the future: a reactive system does not necessarily have a final state (i.e., it may not terminate). It has been widely argued that allowing time to be infinite in the future is very convenient when describing reactive systems and studying their properties (such as liveness and fairness), even though obviously all real systems have to terminate, sooner or later. For instance, the controller of a railroad crossing may be considered as nonterminating, since one might simply not want to model explicitly the case when the controller is stopped for failures, maintenance or replacement. Nontermination is only an abstraction, useful to write simpler models that avoid explicit consideration of the final disposal of the analyzed system, and to verify and analyze properties that essentially refer to infinite behaviors, such as fairness.

---

[*] Work partially supported by *FME Small Project*.

J.S. Fitzgerald, A.E. Haxthausen, and H. Yenigun (Eds.): ICTAC 2008, LNCS 5160, pp. 290–304, 2008.

However, philosophers and logicians such as Prior have always considered that time may be bi-infinite, i.e., infinite both in the future and in the past. Also Automata Theory has considered bi-infinite computations [10,22]. Actually, bi-infinity may be a useful abstraction, too. Analogously to the mono-infinite case where termination may be ignored, bi-infinite time is convenient for modeling systems where initialization may be ignored. One can write specifications that are simpler and more easily understandable, because they do not include the description of the operations (such as configuration, installation, ...) typically performed at system deployment time. For instance, for reactive systems embedded into devices that continuously monitor or control some process, one may often focus only on regime behavior, ignoring initialization. As an example, consider a simple mutual exclusion problem, where, say, three processes may need to gain exclusive access to a shared resource R. A resource allocator might have a policy, in case of conflicting resource requests, to allocate R first to the process, among those that are currently requesting R, that accessed the resource least recently. This fairness property may be formalized more easily by assuming that every request by a process is preceded by a previous request by some other process, i.e., that the sequence of requests extends indefinitely in the past (a property similar to this one will be formalized in Section 5).

Recent developments in the research on Bounded Model Checking (**BMC**), a verification technique originally defined only for Linear Time Temporal Logic (LTL) [2], have extended its applicability also to PLTL (LTL with Past time operators) [1,14]. In these works, however, the time domain is infinite in the future only, so that the asymmetrical definition of past and future in PLTL actually complicates the translation of PLTL into a boolean formula. In our work [23] we presented a novel, bi-infinite encoding of PLTL for bounded model checking, which is significantly simpler than the previous ones, because we consider past and future as completely symmetrical. Furthermore, we introduced a variant of bounded model checking where both the system under analysis and the property to be checked are expressed in a single uniform notation as formulae of temporal logic, without any reference to operational components. In this novel setting, which we called bounded *satisfiability* checking (**BSC**), the system under analysis is modeled through the set of all its fundamental properties as a formula ϕ (that in all non-trivial cases would be of significant size) and the additional property to be checked (e.g. a further desired requirement) is expressed as another (usually much smaller) formula ψ. Aim of the verification activity is then to prove that any implementation of the system under analysis possessing the assumed fundamental properties ϕ would also ensure the additional property ψ; in other terms, the verification tool would prove that the formula $\phi \to \psi$ is valid, or equivalently that its negation is not satisfiable (hence the term satisfiability checking).

The present paper provides two more contributions. First, the above outlined method of satisfiability checking is generalized by permitting, also for the case of a bi-infinite time, the more customary operation of bounded *model* checking, where the system under analysis is modeled by means of a finite state automaton: to this end we provide the definition of automata on bi-infinite strings and the encoding of the automaton on bi-infinite time structures. Second, we validate our approach and the tool implemented to support it by comparing the performance figures obtained on mono- and bi-infinite

time structures, by performing either model or satisfiability checking on a set of selected case studies. The results allow us to state that the bi-infinite approach is feasible
and can be applied with no significant penalty, also when considering a mono-infinite
specification. Since bi-infinite time is also more natural and more expressive, we argue
that one may use a bi-infinite approach to specification and verification, even when the
system to be modeled is mono-infinite.

The paper is structured as follows: Section 2 provides definitions of bi-infinite words,
automata and logic, while Section 3 motivates the usefulness of a bi-infinite semantics.
Section 4 briefly describes a toolkit, called Zot, extended with the new encoding, translating models and formulae into boolean logic. Section 5 presents experimental results,
using Zot and MiniSat solver, comparing mono-infinite and bi-infinite verifications of
a set of case studies, showing the feasibility of bi-infinite bounded model checking.
Finally, Section 6 draws some conclusions.

2   Automata and Logics on Bi-infinite Words

Given a finite alphabet Σ, Σ^* denotes the set of finite words over Σ. A bi-infinite word
w over Σ (also called a $\mathbb{Z}$-word) is a function $w : \mathbb{Z} \longrightarrow \Sigma$. Hence, $w(j) \in \Sigma$ for every
j. Word w is also denoted as $\dots w(-1)w(0)w(1)\dots$ and each $w(j)$ also as w_j. The
set of all bi-infinite words over Σ is denoted by $\Sigma^{\mathbb{Z}}$. An ω-word over Σ is a function
from $\mathbb{N} \to \Sigma$, i.e., it has the form $w(0)w(1)\dots$. The shift function $\sigma : \Sigma^{\mathbb{Z}} \to \Sigma^{\mathbb{Z}}$ is
defined for every $w \in \Sigma^{\mathbb{Z}}$ and for every $n \in \mathbb{Z}$, by $\sigma(w)(n) = w(n-1)$. Given a
language $L \subseteq A^{\mathbb{Z}}$, $\sigma(L) = \{\sigma(w) \mid w \in L\}$. L is said to be shift invariant if $L = \sigma(L)$.
Shift invariance basically means that the instant 0 (the "origin" for ω-words) has no
special role. Finite automata and linear temporal logic may only define shift invariant
languages.

2.1   Automata on Bi-infinite Words

An automaton A is a five-tuple (Q, Σ, T, I, F), where Q is a finite set of *states*, $T \subseteq
Q \times \Sigma \times Q$ is the set of *transitions*, $I \subseteq Q$ is the set of *initial* states and $F \subseteq Q$ is the set
of *final* states. Two transitions (q, a, q'), (p, b, p') are consecutive if $q' = p$. A *bi-infinite
path* of A is a bi-infinite sequence of consecutive transitions. A path is *successful* if
$q_n \in I$ for infinitely many $n \leq 0$, and if $q_n \in F$ for infinitely many $n \geq 0$. For a
path $\dots (q_{-1}, a_{-1}, q_0)(q_0, a_0, q_1)(q_1, a_1, q_2)\dots$, define its label as the bi-infinite word
$\dots a_{-1}a_0a_1\dots$. The language $L(A)$ of A is the set of labels of successful bi-infinite
paths of A. It is easy to see that $L(A)$ is shift-invariant.

A bi-infinite run is a bi-infinite word $\dots q_{-1}q_0q_1q_2\dots$ on $Q^{\mathbb{Z}}$ such that there exists
a bi-infinite path $\dots (q_{-1}, a_{-1}, q_0)(q_0, a_0, q_1)(q_1, a_1, q_2)\dots$ of A. The run is successful if it corresponds to a successful path. In this paper, we are rarely interested in the
language of A, but rather we remove the input alphabet and add both a finite set Ap
of boolean propositions and an evaluation function $S : Q \to 2^{Ap}$. T is then a subset
of $Q \times Q$. S indicates the set of propositions that are true in a state. For simplicity,
we still call this structure (Q, Ap, S, T, I, F) a bi-infinite automaton (although it is
a Kripke structure with bi-infinite fairness constraints). This form is especially convenient for model checking. Given a run $\dots q_{-1}q_0q_1q_2\dots$, the corresponding sequence of

assignments $\ldots S(q_{-1})S(q_0)S(q_1)S(q_2)\ldots$ is denoted with $\ldots S_{-1}S_0S_1S_2\ldots$. For simplicity, each S_i may also be called a *state* of the automaton. No confusion can arise since one can always assume, by extending Ap, that $S(q) = S(q')$ if, and only if, $q = q'$.

2.2 A Temporal Logic on Bi-infinite Time

We define here Linear Temporal Logic with past operators (PLTL), in the version first introduced by Kamp [12]. However, rather than using more traditional ω-words, semantics will be defined on $\mathbb{Z}$-words.

Syntax of PLTL. The alphabet of PLTL includes: a finite set Ap of propositional letters; two propositional connectives $\neg, \vee$ (from which other traditional connectives such as $\top, \bot, \neg, \vee, \wedge, \rightarrow, \ldots$ may be defined); four temporal operators (from which other temporal operators can be derived): the "until" operator $\mathcal{U}$, the "next-time" operator $\circ$, the "since" operator $\mathcal{S}$ and the "past-time" (or Yesterday) operator, $\bullet$. Formulae are defined in the usual inductive way: a propositional letter $p \in Ap$ is a formula; $\neg\phi, \phi \vee \psi, \phi\mathcal{U}\psi, \circ\phi, \phi\mathcal{S}\psi, \bullet\phi$, where ϕ, ψ are formulae, are formulae; nothing else is a formula.

The traditional eventually and globally operators may be defined as: $\Diamond\phi$ is $\top\mathcal{U}\phi$, $\Box\phi$ is $\neg\Diamond\neg\phi$. Their past counterparts are: $\blacklozenge\phi$ is $\top\mathcal{S}\phi$, $\blacksquare\phi$ is $\neg\blacklozenge\neg\phi$. Another useful operator for PLTL is the Always operator $\mathcal{A}lw$, which can be defined by $\mathcal{A}lw\ \phi := \Box\phi \wedge \blacksquare\phi$. The intended meaning of $\mathcal{A}lw\ \phi$ is that ϕ must hold in every instant in the future and in the past. Its dual is the Sometimes operator $\mathcal{S}om\ \phi$ defined as $\neg\mathcal{A}lw\neg\phi$.

Semantics of PLTL. The semantics of PLTL may be defined on $\mathbb{Z}$-words. For all PLTL formulae ϕ, for all $w \in (2^{Ap})^{\mathbb{Z}}$, for all integer numbers i, the satisfaction relation $w, i \models \phi$ is defined as follows.

$w, i \models p, \Longleftrightarrow p \in w(i)$, for $p \in Ap$

$w, i \models \neg\phi \Longleftrightarrow w, i \not\models \phi$

$w, i \models \phi \vee \psi \Longleftrightarrow w, i \models \phi \text{ or } w, i \models \psi$

$w, i \models \circ\phi \Longleftrightarrow w, i+1 \models \phi$

$w, i \models \phi\mathcal{U}\psi \Longleftrightarrow \exists k \geq 0 \mid w, i+k \models \psi, \text{ and } w, i+j \models \phi\ \forall 0 \leq j < k$

$w, i \models \bullet\phi \Longleftrightarrow w, i-1 \models \phi$

$w, i \models \phi\mathcal{S}\psi \Longleftrightarrow \exists k \geq 0 \mid w, i-k \models \psi, \text{ and } w, i-j \models \phi\ \forall 0 \leq j < k$

2.3 A Bi-infinite Encoding

In [23] we defined how PLTL formulae may be encoded into boolean formulae. The encoding includes additional information on the finite structure over which a PLTL formula is interpreted, so that the resulting boolean formula is satisfied in the finite structure if and only if the original PLTL formula is satisfied in a finite or possibly bi-infinite structure. Our encoding is essentially a bi-infinite generalization of a classical mono-infinite BMC encoding (see e.g. [3]). The interested reader can find its complete description in [23].

The idea on which the encoding is based is graphically depicted in Figure 1(b). A ultimately-periodic bi-infinite structure has a finite representation that includes a non-periodic portion, and two periodic portions corresponding to two cycles that are encoded

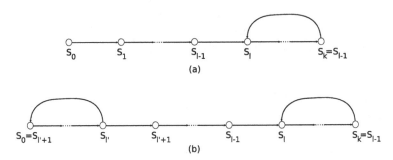

Fig. 1. a) Mono-infinite and b) bi-infinite bounded paths

by having two pairs of equal states in the sequence: when the interpreter of the formula (in our case, a SAT solver), needs the truth value of a subformula at a state beyond the last state S_k, it follows a "backward link" (resp., "forward link") and considers the states S_l, S_{l+1}, ... as the states following S_k. Analogously, when it is necessary to evaluate a subformula before the first state S_0, then the interpreter follows a "forward link" and considers the states $S_{l'}$, $S_{l'-1}$, ... as the states preceding S_0.

Coming to the automaton encoding, to perform bounded *model* checking, we represent symbolically the transition relation of the system M as a propositional formula, where the states are represented as bit vectors. The k-times unrolling of the transition relation represents all the finite paths of length k:

$$|[M]|_k \iff \bigwedge_{0 \le i < k} T(S_i, S_{i+1})$$

where T is a total transition relation predicate. Notice that, being M a bi-infinite automaton, there is no initial state predicate.

2.4 Metric Temporal Operators

PLTL can also be extended by adding metric operators, on discrete time. Metric operators are very convenient for modeling hard real time systems, whose requirements include quantitative time constraints. We call the resulting logic Metric PLTL, although it does not actually extend the expressive power of PLTL.

Metric PLTL extends the alphabet of PLTL with a *bounded until* operator $\mathcal{U}_{\sim c}$ and a *bounded since* operator $\mathcal{S}_{\sim c}$, where $\sim$ represents any relational operator (i.e., $\sim \in \{\le, =, \ge\}$), and c is a natural number. Also, we allow n-ary predicate letters (with $n \ge 1$) and the $\forall, \exists$ quantifiers as long as their domains are finite. Hence, one can write, e.g., formulae of the form: $\exists p \, gr(p)$, with p ranging over $\{1, 2, 3\}$ as a shorthand for $\bigvee_{p \in \{1,2,3\}} gr_p$.

The bounded globally and bounded eventually operators are defined as follows: $\Diamond_{\sim c} \phi$ is $\top \mathcal{U}_{\sim c} \phi$, $\Box_{\sim c} \phi$ is $\neg \Diamond_{\sim c} \neg \phi$. The past versions of the bounded eventually and globally operators may be defined symmetrically to their future counterparts: $\blacklozenge_{\sim c} \phi$ is $\top \mathcal{S}_{\sim c} \phi$, $\blacksquare_{\sim c} \phi$ is $\neg \blacklozenge_{\sim c} \neg \phi$.

In the following, as a useful shorthand, we will use also the versions of the bounded operators with a strict bound. For instance, $\phi \mathcal{U}_{>0} \psi$ stands for $\circ(\phi \mathcal{U}_{\geq 0} \psi)$, and similarly for the other ones.

The semantics of Metric PLTL may be defined by a straightforward translation τ of its operators into PLTL:

$$\begin{aligned}
&\tau(\phi_1 \mathcal{U}_{\leq 0} \phi_2) := \phi_2 \\
&\underline{\tau(\phi_1 \mathcal{U}_{\leq t} \phi_2) := \phi_2 \vee \phi_1 \wedge \circ\tau(\phi_1 \mathcal{U}_{\leq t-1} \phi_2), \text{ with } t > 0} \\
&\tau(\phi_1 \mathcal{U}_{\geq 0} \phi_2) := \phi_1 \mathcal{U} \phi_2 \\
&\underline{\tau(\phi_1 \mathcal{U}_{\geq t} \phi_2) := \phi_1 \wedge \circ\tau(\phi_1 \mathcal{U}_{\geq t-1} \phi_2), \text{ with } t > 0} \\
&\tau(\phi_1 \mathcal{U}_{=0} \phi_2) := \phi_2 \\
&\tau(\phi_1 \mathcal{U}_{=t} \phi_2) := \phi_1 \wedge \circ\tau(\phi_1 \mathcal{U}_{=t-1} \phi_2), \text{ with } t > 0
\end{aligned}$$

and symmetrically for the operators in the past.

Hence, in what follows we will consider Metric PLTL as a syntactically-sugared, but considerably more succinct, version of PLTL.

3 Bi-infinite Time: A Short Motivation

It is widely recognized that allowing past operators in temporal logic, as in PLTL, makes it possible to write specifications that are easier, shorter, and, in some significant cases even exponentially more succinct than LTL specifications [16]. However, the ω-word semantics of PLTL is asymmetric: past is treated differently from future. Asymmetry in itself may seem a minor glitch, but it entails a problem: only a conventional value is returned when the evaluation of past operators requires time instants before the origin. For instance, consider the $\bullet$ operator: in a mono-infinite time domain, when $\bullet\phi$ is evaluated at instant $i > 0$, it returns the value of ϕ at instant $i - 1$; if $i = 0$, $\bullet\phi$ is conventionally evaluated to false. This ω-word semantics may easily lead to subtle specification errors, since natural, "expected" properties of the temporal operators are violated. These problems are usually "fixed" by allowing two dual forms of the $\bullet$ operator, the second one being defined to the default value true when its argument cannot be evaluated. This issue is even worsened when considering metric time operators, to be used for specifying real-time systems, since they may very easily refer to non-existent time instants in the past. For example, one may describe a system having a fixed cycle of operation of m time units by the formula $\square(shutdown \leftrightarrow \blacklozenge_{=m} startup)$ (i.e., a shutdown occurs if and only if a startup took place m time units before), which could be rewritten (e.g., as a consequence of some automatic transformation performed by some tool that analyzes it) in the following, supposedly equivalent form:

$$\square \left(\begin{array}{c} (\neg shutdown \vee \blacklozenge_{=m} startup) \\ \wedge \\ (shutdown \vee \blacklozenge_{=m} \neg startup) \end{array} \right).$$

Unfortunately, this latter, simple specification is unsatisfiable on a mono-infinite time domain, because in the first $m-1$ instants of the domain, both $shutdown$ and $\neg shutdown$ must be true, since both $\blacklozenge_{=m} startup$ and $\blacklozenge_{=m} \neg startup$ are (conventionally) false. This effect is dependent on the syntax used: for instance, if the lower subformula $(shutdown \lor$ $\blacklozenge_{=m} \neg startup)$ is written in the apparently equivalent form: $shutdown \lor \neg \blacklozenge_{=m} startup$, then the behavior becomes the intended one, because in this case the conventional false value for $\blacklozenge_{=m}$ makes $shutdown \lor \neg \blacklozenge_{=m} startup$ true in the first $m-1$ instants. Clearly, these subtle semantics issues may easily escape notice in a more complex specification.

By adopting bi-infinite time, where event sequences may extend indefinitely in the past, past operators have a simple semantics that is symmetrical to that of the corresponding future-time operators: they are always defined and there is no need to use conventional values. Notice that the usage of bi-infinite time does not rule out the explicit modeling of the initial state of a system, and hence it incurs in no loss of expressive power (e.g., just use a propositional symbol $Start$, with the additional constraint that $Start$ must occur exactly once). Hence, one may use a convenient bi-infinite semantics even when specifying a mono-infinite system.

Throughout our past research, we have heavily dealt with temporal logic specifications and their application to industrial, critical real-time systems [5,20,17,4]. Our approach has focused on using TRIO (a first order, linear-time temporal logic with a quantitative metric on time) for requirements specifications, without relying on machine models such as automata. One of the main features of TRIO is its ability to deal with different time domains: dense or discrete, finite or infinite [18]. In particular, most TRIO specifications adopt a bi-infinite time domain, using both future and past time operators. The application of the BMC techniques to a decidable fragment of TRIO was one of our original motivations for dealing with bi-infinity.

4   The Zot Toolkit

Zot is an agile and easily extendible bounded model and satisfiability checker, which can be downloaded at http://home.dei.polimi.it/pradella/, together with the case studies and results described in Section 5.

The tool supports different logic languages through a multi-layered approach: its core uses PLTL, and on top of it a decidable predicative fragment of TRIO [9] is defined (essentially, equivalent to Metric PLTL). An interesting feature of Zot is its ability to support different encodings of temporal logic as SAT problems by means of plugins. This approach encourages experimentation, as plugins are expected to be quite simple, compact (usually around 500 lines of code), easily modifiable, and extendible. At the moment, a few variants of some of the encodings presented in [3] are supported, a dense-time variant of MTL [8], and the bi-infinite encoding presented in [23].

Zot offers three basic usage modalities:

1. *Bounded satisfiability checking (BSC)*: given as input a specification formula, the tool returns a (possibly empty) history (i.e., an execution trace of the specified system) which satisfies the specification. An empty history means that it is impossible to satisfy the specification.
2. *Bounded model checking (BMC)*: given as input an operational model of the system, the tool returns a (possibly empty) history (i.e., an execution trace of the specified system) which satisfies it.

3. *History checking and completion (HCC)*: The input file can also contain a partial (or complete) history H. In this case, if H complies with the specification, then a completed version of H is returned as output, otherwise the output is empty.

The provided output histories have temporal length $\leq k$, the bound given by the user, but may represent infinite behaviors thanks to the loop selector variables, marking the start of the periodic sections of the history. The BSC/BMC modalities can be used to check if a property *prop* of the given specification *spec* holds over every periodic behavior with period $\leq k$. In this case, the input file contains spec $\wedge \neg$prop, and, if prop indeed holds, then the output history is empty. If this is not the case, the output history is a counterexample, explaining why prop does not hold.

The tool and its plugins were validated on mono-infinite examples, such as the Mutex examples included in the distribution of NuSMV. The results were exactly the same as those obtained by using NuSMV [6] with the same encoding. On one hand, Zot is in general slower than NuSMV, but being quite small and written in *Common Lisp* is quite flexible, and promotes experimentation with different encodings and logic languages. On the other hand, in practice its performances are usually acceptable, because for non-trivial verifications the bottleneck typically resides in the SAT solver rather than in the translator.

Zot supports the model checkers MiniSat [7], zChaff, [21], and the recent multi-threaded MiraXT solver [15].

5 Case Studies and Experiments

To assess the actual feasibility of our approach, we applied it to some significant case studies, illustrated in the following sections. For all examples we apply the tool with reference to both mono- and bi-infinite structure, and then compare the results by computing the ratio of the various (time and memory) figures obtained in the two cases. We point out that some of the following case studies are framed as bounded *satisfiability* checking problems (because the analyzed system is described by means of a set of PLTL formulas without any constraint on their structure, and in particular on the nesting of their temporal operators): this is the case of the In/out channel, the Kernel Railway Crossing, and the Fischer's protocol. Three case studies are instead expressed as bounded *model* checking problems (the analyzed system is modeled through a set of PLTL formulae that are at all similar to a finite state automaton, because they relate the system current state with its next state): the In/Out channel (the only one to be considered in both ways), the simple mutual exclusion protocol, and the Real-time allocator.

5.1 A Simple In/Out Channel

The simplest example on which we tested the tool is that of a transmission line where any message entering at one end (represented by the predicate letter in) at any time is emitted at the other end (predicate out) after k time units. No message is lost nor is generated spuriously, so the transmission line is described by the formula:

$$Alw(in \leftrightarrow \Diamond_{=k} out).$$

We considered two possible values for the delay k, namely, 5 and 15 time units. Moreover, to allow for bounded *model* checking, besides the above "descriptive" formalization, we used also a different, "operational" characterization of the transmission line system, composed of constraints that refer only to "current" and the "next" time instants. This requires the introduction of a counter to, which starts at value k when in holds, and is then decremented at each successive time instant, until out holds. In the tables reporting the experimentation results four versions of this examples are considered, corresponding to the descriptive or state-based style (suffix "d" or "s") and to the time bounds (5 or 15). For this simplest example the tool was only used to generate a possible trace of execution, as opposed to the other examples, for which we also carried out the proof of a few selected properties.

5.2 Kernel Railway Crossing

The Railway Crossing problem is a standard benchmark in real time systems verification [11]. It considers a railway crossing composed of a sensor, a gate and a controller. When a train is sensed to approach the crossing, a signal is sent to the controller. The controller then sends a command to the gate, closing the railway crossing to cars. The system operates in real time, ensuring safety (when the train is inside the railway crossing then the bar gate is closed) while maximizing utility (the bar should be open as long as possible). To this goal, there are various assumptions on the minimum and maximum speed of trains (e.g., the minimum time it takes for a train to enter the crossing after being sensed) and on the bar speed (the time it takes for the bar to be moved up or down). The Kernel Railroad crossing problem is a simplified version, where there is only one track and hence only one train at a time may enter the crossing. The goal of the KRC specification is twofold: a formal definition of the KRC system, and the proof of the safety and utility properties.

KRC is a toy example per se, but in this case we are completely defining it with a temporal logic specification, thus obtaining a logic formula much bigger and more complex than those used in traditional model checking, where the KRC is defined with an automaton and short temporal logic formulae are used only to model safety or utility properties.

In our example we studied the KRC problem with two different sets of constants, calling the two cases KRC1 and KRC2. Satisfiability of the specification, a safety property and a utility property were considered for the experiments. A complete specification, composed of a dozen axioms, of KRC1 and KRC2 and their properties can be found in [19].

5.3 Fischer's Protocol

As a third case study, we consider Fischer's algorithm [13]. Fischer's is a timed mutual exclusion algorithm that allows a number of timed processes to access a shared resource. These processes are usually described as timed automata, and are often used as a benchmark for timed automata verification tools.

We considered a pure-logic description of the system in two variants. The first one, called Fischer1, considers 2 processes with a delay after the request of 3 time units. The second one, called Fischer2, considers 5 processes with a delay after the request of 6 time units.

We used the tool to check the safety property of the system (*safety-m* and *safety-b* in the tables of the following section), i.e. it is never possible that two different processes enter their critical sections at the same time instant.

As a last test for this system, we added a constraint to generate a behavior where there is always at least an alive process (*alive-m* and *alive-b* in the tables).

5.4   Simple Mutual Exclusion Protocol

The fourth case study is a simple Mutual exclusion protocol for two processes, originally found in the distribution of NuSMV, which is called Mutex1. This was also extended to consider mutual exclusion with three processes, a model called Mutex2. Both examples have been defined with an automaton model.

For Mutex1 we considered the following property (where, quite naturally, turn $= i$ means that it is the turn of process i):

$$Alw \left(\begin{array}{l} (\text{turn} = 1 \rightarrow \Diamond(\text{turn} = 2)) \wedge \\ (\text{turn} = 2 \rightarrow \Diamond(\text{turn} = 1)) \end{array} \right).$$

This is the variant of the previous property that we considered for Mutex2:

$$Alw \left(\begin{array}{l} (\text{turn} = 1 \rightarrow \Diamond(\text{turn} = 2 \vee \text{turn} = 3)) \wedge \\ (\text{turn} = 2 \rightarrow \Diamond(\text{turn} = 1 \vee \text{turn} = 3)) \wedge \\ (\text{turn} = 3 \rightarrow \Diamond(\text{turn} = 2 \vee \text{turn} = 3)) \end{array} \right).$$

5.5   Real-Time Allocator

The last case study consists of a real-time allocator which serves a set of client processes, competing for a shared resource. The system is a purely operational version of the one presented in [23].

Each process p requires the resource by issuing the message rq(p), by which it identifies itself to the allocator. Requests have a time out: they must be served within T_{req} time units, or else be ignored by the allocator. If the allocator is able to satisfy p's request within the time-out, then it grants the resource to p by a gr(p) signal. Once a process is assigned the resource by the allocator, it releases the resource, by issuing a rel signal, within a maximum of T_{rel} time units. The allocator grants the request to processes according to a FIFO policy, considering only requests that are not timed out yet and in a timely manner, i.e., no process will have to wait for the resource while it is not assigned to any other process.

Two cases were considered in the following experiments: Alloc1 is the allocator model with two processes and $T_{rel} = 2$ and $T_{req} = 3$. Alloc2 is the allocator model with two processes and $T_{rel} = 4$ and $T_{req} = 5$.

Two hard real time properties $p1$ and $p2$ of Alloc1 and Alloc2 are considered in the experiments.

The first is a simple fairness property $p1$. If a process that does not obtain the resource always requests it again immediately after the request is expired, then if it requests the resource it will eventually obtain it:

$$(p1): \frac{\mathcal{A}lw\left(\mathrm{rq}(p) \wedge \square_{\leq T_{req}} \neg \mathrm{gr}(p) \rightarrow \Diamond_{=T_{req}} \mathrm{rq}(p)\right)}{\mathcal{A}lw\left(\mathrm{rq}(p) \rightarrow \Diamond \mathrm{gr}(p)\right)}$$

A second, more complex property may be intuitively described as a sort of "conditional fairness". Let us first define the notion of "unconstrained rotation" among processes: a process will require the resource only after all other ones have requested and obtained it. Notice that this requirement does not impose any precise ordering among the requests made by the processes (though, once requests take place in a given order, the order remains unchanged from one round among processes to the next one). This property is described by the following formula:

$$\mathcal{A}lw\left(\forall q \left(q \neq p \rightarrow \neg \mathrm{rq}(p)\mathcal{S}\left(\begin{array}{c}\mathrm{rq}(p) \rightarrow \\ \mathrm{rq}(q) \wedge \\ \Diamond_{\leq T_{req}} \mathrm{gr}(q)\end{array}\right)\right)\right)$$

Under this assumption of "unconstrained rotation" the allocator system is fair for all processes: if a process, when it requests the resource and does not obtain it, always requests it again after the request is expired, then, when it requests the resource, it will eventually obtain it. If for brevity we symbolically indicate the property of "unconstrained rotation" as *UNROT*, this *conditional fairness* property $p2$ may be stated as:

$$(p2): \mathrm{UNROT} \rightarrow \left(\frac{\mathcal{A}lw(\mathrm{rq}(p) \wedge \square_{\leq T_{req}} \neg \mathrm{gr}(p) \rightarrow \Diamond_{>0} \mathrm{rq}(p))}{\mathcal{A}lw(\mathrm{rq}(p) \rightarrow \Diamond_{>0} \mathrm{gr}(p))}\right)$$

By careful inspection, however, it can be found that in the mono-infinite case $p2$ is only *vacuously true*, i.e., it corresponds to a run where no event occurs. In fact, the property of unconstrained rotation, in the simple form of the above UNROT formula, implies that any nonempty sequence of request events (and corresponding grant and release) goes back indefinitely towards the past. Therefore it can be satisfied non vacuously (i.e., with reference to behaviors that effectively include some events) only over a structure which is infinite in the past.

5.6 Summary of Experimental Results

We report here and comment on the results of applying the tool to the selected benchmarks and case studies. The experiments were run on a PC equipped with AMD Athlon 64 X2 4600+, 2 GB RAM, Linux OS. The SAT solver was MiniSat [7], version 2, along with SAT2CNF, part of the Alloy Analyzer (http://alloy.mit.edu).

For most examples we considered both a mono-infinite and a bi-infinite time structure, trying various bounds T on the size of the structure: 30, 60, 120, and 240 time units. For every example, the first basic experiment is checking satisfiability (non-emptiness) of the specification, without considering any property. This operation is useful as a sort of "sanity check" for a temporal logic specification, since it ensures that at least the formula is not contradictory. For all examples, except for the simplest In/Out channel, we

Table 1. Summary of collected experimental data

Case	Prop	Translation time (s)				Ratio b/m		SAT time (s)				Ratio b/m		SAT memory (MB)				Ratio b/m		Kilo-Clauses (#)				Ratio b/m	
		T=30	T=60	T=120	T=240	AVER	STDEV	T=30	T=60	T=120	T=240	AVER	STDEV	T=30	T=60	T=120	T=240	AVER	STDEV	T=30	T=60	T=120	T=240	AVER	STDEV
Io5d	sat-m	0.84	0.95	2.32	9.10	2.07	0.81	0.06	0.18	0.52	1.70	2.63	0.35	5.71	9.22	16.89	31.78	1.73	0.09	22.5	44.7	89.0	177.5	1.88	0.00
	sat-b	0.83	1.84	6.28	24.26			0.15	0.41	1.30	5.20			9.15	16.35	28.99	57.48			42.2	83.9	167.3	334.1		
Io5s	sat-m	0.93	1.77	6.71	27.13	1.86	0.38	0.15	0.38	1.20	4.29	2.10	0.21	8.39	13.95	26.49	51.04	1.64	0.08	37.7	74.7	148.8	296.9	1.67	0.00
	sat-b	1.24	3.82	14.35	48.39			0.27	0.80	2.54	10.07			12.84	23.58	43.11	86.63			62.9	125.0	249.2	497.6		
Io15d	sat-m	0.78	1.80	7.40	27.43	2.91	0.48	0.14	0.40	1.78	5.32	2.76	0.39	8.26	13.81	26.34	50.80	2.05	0.17	37.2	73.8	146.9	293.0	2.20	0.01
	sat-b	1.81	6.29	21.83	78.81			0.38	1.17	3.95	16.61			14.98	28.36	56.43	111.55			81.6	162.3	323.7	646.5		
Io15s	sat-m	2.63	9.93	38.72	151.28	1.95	0.09	0.52	1.66	6.07	27.10	2.32	0.17	17.25	30.59	59.58	121.95	1.69	0.07	90.4	179.0	356.3	710.7	1.71	0.00
	sat-b	5.40	19.72	71.73	286.63			1.12	3.72	14.88	67.02			27.44	53.78	103.29	205.52			154.1	306.2	610.4	1218.8		
KRC1	sat-m	11.17	41.45	154.87	649.42	2.24	0.05	2.11	8.48	30.95	134.37	2.46	0.25	40.29	78.69	151.80	301.27	1.61	0.03	210.9	420.3	837.2	1670.8	1.61	0.00
	sat-b	25.14	90.70	356.96	1433.83			4.79	18.77	82.36	359.66			63.91	125.57	243.41	497.14			341.4	678.2	1351.9	2699.2		
	safety-m	11.98	41.39	153.15	605.17	2.25	0.13	0.17	0.36	0.66	1.39	na		42.95	85.96	170.70	416.45	na		215.0	426.5	849.5	1695.3	na	
	safety-b	25.00	91.74	363.32	1408.93			0.27	1.04	2.39	1582.58			u.p.	u.p.	u.p.	u.p.			346.8	689.0	1373.4	2742.3		
	utility-m	28.43	105.39	411.40	1658.37	2.30	0.09	5.54	23.37	91.67	397.14	2.49	0.50	69.07	135.78	271.64	525.52	1.51	0.17	367.1	729.4	1454.0	2903.1	1.58	0.00
	utility-b	46.60	174.97	697.04	2425.10			7.74	33.47	133.44	588.03			u.p.	u.p.	u.p.	u.p.			415.9	824.9	1643.0	3279.2		
KRC2	sat-m	42.11	161.26	622.03	2425.10	2.51	0.02	22.35	83.45	365.99	1044.31	2.49	0.50	78.11	151.51	304.27	610.79	1.49	0.40	706.2	1403.4	2797.8	5586.6	1.70	0.00
	sat-b	106.67	402.95	1555.55	6110.06									133.29	250.52	516.16	543.24								
	safety-m	41.89	155.59	600.79	2365.76	2.58	0.02	0.38	0.70	1.43	2.81	na		u.p.	u.p.	u.p.	u.p.	na		419.0	831.1	1655.3	3303.8	na	
	safety-b	107.30	404.06	1563.68	6098.64			0.56	1.14	2.34	2.75			58.74	116.37	225.58	450.66			711.7	1414.3	2819.4	5629.7		
	utility-m	51.72	185.95	731.44	2873.39	2.55	0.03	10.52	44.93	201.68	1628.47	1.92	0.77	86.20	172.32	337.07	686.50	1.44	0.41	465.6	923.8	1840.4	3673.5	1.66	0.00
	utility-b	129.53	478.12	1887.22	7360.83			26.73	430.40	430.40	1297.75			142.22	283.35	568.61	568.61			770.7	1531.6	3053.3	6096.7		
Fischer1	sat-m	11.52	38.11	150.29	565.13	2.06	0.11	2.12	6.72	27.77	114.49	2.36	0.26	35.30	66.98	132.55	271.89	1.54	0.01	194.9	386.2	768.9	1534.1	1.59	0.00
	sat-b	21.91	79.54	314.89	1227.55			4.18	16.78	68.79	285.19			53.93	103.33	205.23	421.84			302.6	600.7	1196.9	2389.4		
	safety-m	11.39	41.26	154.91	612.97	2.18	0.07	0.17	0.34	0.66	1.38	na		58.74	116.37	225.58	450.66	na		208.4	413.0	822.2	1640.6	na	
	safety-b	24.02	88.45	348.48	1361.90			4.76	18.29	78.31	333.12			58.74	116.37	225.58	450.66			323.1	641.4	1277.9	2551.0		
	alive-m	11.39	42.80	156.82	625.52	2.12	0.06	2.04	7.29	30.25	125.93	2.39	0.11	38.02	74.49	143.47	286.62	1.53	0.01	205.5	407.2	810.7	1617.5	1.56	0.00
	alive-b	24.04	87.52	344.21	1338.79			4.54	17.26	74.43	312.82			57.78	113.88	220.54	440.45			320.0	635.4	1266.0	2527.4		
Fischer2	sat-m	98.47	373.82	1447.75	5793.60	2.30	0.03	19.11	77.60	339.66	431.07	1.98	0.91	113.47	220.43	346.37	465.79	1.40	0.36	639.5	1267.3	2522.9	5034.2	1.59	0.00
	sat-b	100.65	867.98	3342.28	13130.04			48.68	192.61	212.68	971.33			177.14	346.37	378.32	752.75			1017.8	2020.8	4026.7	8038.7		
	safety-m	238.81	387.13	1513.45	5944.03	2.34	0.02	0.55	1.09	2.20	3.04	na		52.54	363.19	386.17	809.12	na		663.6	1315.0	2617.9	5223.7	na	
	safety-b	98.39	908.40	3518.50	13884.41			52.54	212.86	516.70	2223.07			117.71	229.44	461.21	474.39			1053.5	2091.7	4168.1	8320.8		
	alive-m	98.39	393.15	1578.25	6030.94	2.29	0.06	23.69	84.98	348.01	1077.19	1.72	0.75	181.88	356.96	394.31	805.50	1.41	0.39	655.3	1298.6	2585.3	5158.7	1.60	0.00
	alive-b	231.08	905.03	3483.97	13779.06			51.77	199.56	234.09	1814.90			181.88	356.96	394.31	805.50			1045.0	2075.0	4134.8	8254.5		
Mutex1	sat-b	0.61	1.09	2.71	8.91	1.17	0.08	0.07	0.17	0.45	1.38	1.33	0.07	6.07	9.83	17.09	33.07	1.15	0.05	29.0	57.6	114.9	229.5	1.22	0.00
	safety-m	0.65	1.30	3.23	11.16			0.08	0.22	0.61	1.92			6.66	11.42	20.72	36.99			35.3	70.2	140.2	280.1		
	safety-b	0.84	1.78	6.14	22.96	1.49	0.10	0.11	0.31	0.98	3.42	1.67	0.09	9.45	16.96	30.54	59.73	1.31	0.06	45.5	90.4	180.3	359.9	1.35	0.00
Mutex2	sat-b	1.14	2.63	9.84	34.85	1.16	0.04	0.18	0.51	1.62	6.10			12.00	21.07	40.48	82.95			61.4	122.2	243.8	486.9		
	safety-m	1.49	4.57	16.58	59.62			0.41	1.13	3.36	12.27	0.94	0.42	12.70	34.02	64.37	123.90	1.16	0.04	79.2	157.4	313.9	626.9	1.18	0.00
	safety-b	0.90	1.94	5.52	19.63	1.48	0.11	0.24	0.64	8.16	38.34			11.77	22.00	41.35	82.94			47.8	95.1	189.7	379.0		
Alloc1	sat-m	1.08	2.27	6.35	21.62	1.02	0.03	0.25	0.87	4.66	22.70	1.53	0.32	13.23	25.63	49.86	94.80	1.13	0.03	56.4	112.5	224.6	448.7	1.05	0.02
	sat-b	1.37	3.43	12.67	46.75			0.90	3.54	15.85	121.80			80.61	164.05	338.28	633.13			329.0	656.4	1311.1	2620.7		
	p1-m	1.86	5.51	19.19	67.86	1.47	0.16	0.90	7.82	55.68	164.06	1.60	1.45	91.18	179.94	365.02	733.25	1.13	0.03	386.2	770.7	1539.7	3077.6	1.17	0.00
	p1-b	2.72	9.09	31.75	118.62			1.02	6.50	23.69	184.39			88.73	173.63	352.50	688.97			373.2	744.3	1486.5	2970.9		
	p2-m	9.04	20.25	55.21	152.30	1.54	0.13	3.38	6.50	69.10	139.18	2.25	0.66	100.05	203.07	800.21	800.21	1.15	0.00	443.9	885.3	1768.2	3533.9	1.19	0.00
	p2-b	9.06	21.14	55.11	159.94			3.15	5.17	14.63	35.58			74.32	142.14	289.20	587.30			292.3	583.8	1166.8	2332.9		
Alloc2	sat-m	10.45	29.10	83.05	268.08	1.02	0.05	2.26	5.17	12.78	45.91	1.00	0.07	77.89	151.51	298.32	608.94	1.02	0.00	306.3	611.9	1223.2	2445.8	1.03	0.00
	sat-b	13.37	41.75	126.56	445.51			17.25	118.30	130.66	333.55	1.60		176.34	348.55	356.57	557.92			360.6	656.4	1311.1	2620.7		
	p1-m	13.52	38.95	123.12	428.37	1.39	0.15	16.45	55.68	164.06	1242.65	2.25	0.65	183.03	362.61	753.39	599.47	1.08	0.02	750.2	1498.5	1642.8	6564.7	1.10	0.00
	p1-b	18.52	59.22	195.62	721.61			3.06	7.82	23.69	81.61			196.53	398.84	800.46	660.96			822.5	1642.8	3283.4	6564.7		
	p2-m	20.35	42.66	102.33	264.48	1.02	0.00	4.70	14.49	69.10	219.49			190.95	382.60	738.41	533.55	1.09	0.03	791.6	1580.8	3159.2	6315.9	1.10	0.00
	p2-b	34.23	64.36	135.29	600.01	1.48	0.11	10.58	31.25	114.95	962.54	4.90	6.25	202.80	411.22	824.39	597.55			872.4	1742.0	3481.2	6959.5		

also proved a few selected properties: the property holds if and only if the tool answers UNSAT when applied to the specification conjoined with the negation of the property.

The entire collection of results is displayed in Table 1, which includes: translation time (dominated by the conjunctive normal form translation performed by SAT2CNF), SAT time and SAT memory (time and space taken by the SAT solver only), and the number of clauses in the formula generated by SAT2CNF. Translation time, closely related to the size of the original specification, changes in a quite regular way, and in our experiments it appears to be quadratically related to the bound T. SAT time is much less regular and predictable, as it may depend, in a very involved way, on the semantics of the specification and of the property being checked and on the details of the solver algorithms.

Certain data in Table 1 are denoted by **u.p.**. In these cases, MiniSat is able to determine unsatisfiability already during the parsing phase, using so-called unit propagation technique. SAT memory in this case cannot be computed, since the SAT solver has not really started a computation, and also SAT time is not very meaningful (it corresponds only to parsing time, which is negligible and only related to the size of the boolean formula fed to the solver). In two experiments, unit propagation occurred for both the bi-infinite and the mono-infinite case; in one experiment it occurred only in the mono-infinite case.

Table 1 also contains four columns labeled "ratio b/m", which are more closely focused on the comparison between the figures for the mono and the bi-infinite case: for each pair of such data (for the same example and the same property) it reports the average, over the four values of T, of the ratio between the bi-infinite figure and the corresponding mono-infinite one, together with its standard deviation.

A few values were left out of these columns, since they correspond to cases where the comparison is not possible or would give misleading results:

- The property safety-b-b for both Mutex1 and Mutex2 is bi-infinite only, since it does not hold on a mono-infinite domain (and hence it is difficult to be compared).
- All occurrences of unit propagation were ignored for SAT time and SAT memory, since no meaningful measure can be used to make a comparison.

Also, Property $p2$ for the Allocator, as already pointed out, is only vacuously true on a mono-infinite structure, so the SAT-solver can very easily prove unsatisfiability. This explains the relatively large b/m ratio for SAT time.

As one can notice, standard deviations are typically small for all measures except SAT time, which, as expected, shows more volatility. Hence, for all measures, except for SAT time, the ratio is close to be a constant for the same case study, when considering different bounds.

Overall, results are satisfactory. All measures, including SAT time, show a ratio between 1 and 3, except in the above reported special cases. SAT time shows more volatility than other measures, but it is still bounded and occasionally the ratio can even go below 1, with 2 being the most typical value. Also, there does not appear to be any significant difference in the ratios between cases where the specification is purely operational (Allocator, Mutex, io5d, io15d) or purely logical (Fischer, KRC, io5s, io15d).

6 Conclusions

In this paper we have argued that bi-infinite time in specifications is a useful abstraction, allowing one to ignore the complexity of system initialization, and to express fairness properties also in the past.

Bi-infinite time has certainly been used before in specification. For instance, our own requirement specifications of industrial systems using TRIO temporal logic language [9] most often adopted bi-infinite time. However, we are not aware of any other work extending model checking to deal with bi-infinity, apart from our encoding of automata and PLTL formulae [23] that includes additional information to represent bi-infinite structures by means of finite ones having two cycles of states, one that unfolds in the future and one for the past.

Our Zot tool incorporates the bi-infinite encoding and, by relying on standard satisfiability checkers, supports a variety of analysis and verification activities.

This paper investigated the tool and its application to many case studies, ranging from simple to complex, in order to assess the feasibility of the approach, by comparing the performance of the same case when using a mono-infinite and a then a bi-infinite structure. The experimental results show that, on these examples, tool performance on bi-infinite structures is comparable to that on mono-infinite ones, suggesting that adopting a bi-infinite notion of time does not impose very significant penalties to the efficiency of bounded model checking and bounded satisfiability checking. On the other hand, bi-infinite time is more natural than mono-infinite time in many cases and it avoids subtle semantics problem with PLTL formulae.

Further work might consider various optimizations, such as incremental encodings, and also deal with completeness issues [24,3]. These were ignored in this paper, where we applied a standard, relatively simple encoding technique, since we were mainly interested in comparing the performance of mono- and bi-infinite model checking.

References

1. Benedetti, M., Cimatti, A.: Bounded model checking for past LTL. In: Garavel, H., Hatcliff, J. (eds.) TACAS 2003. LNCS, vol. 2619, pp. 18–33. Springer, Heidelberg (2003)
2. Biere, A., Cimatti, A., Clarke, E., Zhu, Y.: Symbolic model checking without BDDs. In: Cleaveland, W.R. (ed.) TACAS 1999. LNCS, vol. 1579, pp. 193–207. Springer, Heidelberg (1999)
3. Biere, A., Heljanko, K., Junttila, T., Latvala, T., Schuppan, V.: Linear encodings of bounded LTL model checking. Logical Methods in Computer Science 2(5), 1–64 (2006)
4. Capobianchi, R., Coen-Porisini, A., Mandrioli, D., Morzenti, A.: A framework architecture for supervision and control systems. ACM Comput. Surv. 32(1es), 26 (2000)
5. Ciapessoni, E., Mirandola, P., Coen-Porisini, A., Mandrioli, D., Morzenti, A.: From formal models to formally based methods: An industrial experience. ACM Trans. Softw. Eng. Methodol. 8(1), 79–113 (1999)
6. Cimatti, A., Clarke, E.M., Giunchiglia, E., Giunchiglia, F., Pistore, M., Roveri, M., Sebastiani, R., Tacchella, A.: NuSMV 2: An opensource tool for symbolic model checking. In: Brinksma, E., Larsen, K.G. (eds.) CAV 2002. LNCS, vol. 2404, pp. 359–364. Springer, Heidelberg (2002)

7. Eén, N., Sörensson, N.: An extensible SAT-solver. In: Giunchiglia, E., Tacchella, A. (eds.) SAT 2003. LNCS, vol. 2919, pp. 502–518. Springer, Heidelberg (2004)
8. Furia, C.A., Pradella, M., Rossi, M.: Dense-time MTL verification through sampling. In: Cuellar, J., Maibaum, T.S.E. (eds.) FM 2008. LNCS, vol. 5014. Springer, Heidelberg (2008)
9. Ghezzi, C., Mandrioli, D., Morzenti, A.: TRIO: A logic language for executable specifications of real-time systems. Journal of Systems and Software 12(2), 107–123 (1990)
10. Gire, F., Nivat, M.: Langages algébriques de mots biinfinis. Theoret. Comput. Sci. 86(2), 277–323 (1991)
11. Heitmeyer, C., Mandrioli, D.: Formal Methods for Real-Time Computing. John Wiley & Sons, Inc., New York (1996)
12. Kamp, J.A.W.: Tense Logic and the Theory of Linear Order (Ph.D. thesis). University of California at Los Angeles (1968)
13. Lamport, L.: A fast mutual exclusion algorithm. ACM TOCS-Transactions On Computer Systems 5(1), 1–11 (1987)
14. Latvala, T., Biere, A., Heljanko, K., Junttila, T.: Simple is better: Efficient bounded model checking for past LTL. In: Cousot, R. (ed.) VMCAI 2005. LNCS, vol. 3385, pp. 380–395. Springer, Heidelberg (2005)
15. Lewis, M., Schubert, T., Becker, B.: Multithreaded SAT solving. In: 12th Asia and South Pacific Design Automation Conference (2007)
16. Lichtenstein, O., Pnueli, A., Zuck, L.D.: The glory of the past. In: Proceedings of the Conf. on Logic of Programs, London, UK, pp. 196–218. Springer, Heidelberg (1985)
17. Morasca, S., Morzenti, A., San Pietro, P.: A case study on applying a tool for automated system analysis object oriented logic specification of time-critical systems. Based on modular specifications written in TRIO. Autom. Softw. Eng. 7(2), 125–155 (2000)
18. Morzenti, A., Mandrioli, D., Ghezzi, C.: A model parametric real-time logic. ACM Trans. Program. Lang. Syst. 14(4), 521–573 (1992)
19. Morzenti, A., Pradella, M., San Pietro, P., Spoletini, P.: Model-checking TRIO specifications in SPIN. In: Araki, K., Gnesi, S., Mandrioli, D. (eds.) FME 2003. LNCS, vol. 2805, pp. 542–561. Springer, Heidelberg (2003)
20. Morzenti, A., San Pietro, P.: Object-oriented logical specification of time-critical systems. ACM Trans. Softw. Eng. Methodol. 3(1), 56–98 (1994)
21. Moskewicz, M.W., Madigan, C.F., Zhao, Y., Zhang, L., Malik, S.: Chaff: engineering an efficient SAT solver. In: DAC 2001: Proceedings of the 38th Conf. on Design automation, pp. 530–535. ACM Press, New York (2001)
22. Perrin, D., Pin, J.-É.: Infinite Words. Pure and Applied Mathematics, vol. 141. Elsevier, Amsterdam (2004)
23. Pradella, M., Morzenti, A., San Pietro, P.: The symmetry of the past and of the future: Bi-infinite time in the verification of temporal properties. In: Proc. of The 6th joint meeting of the European Software Engineering Conference and the ACM SIGSOFT Symposium on the Foundations of Software Engineering ESEC/FSE, Dubrovnik, Croatia (September 2007)
24. Sheeran, M., Singh, S., Stålmarck, G.: Checking safety properties using induction and a SAT-solver. In: Johnson, S.D., Hunt Jr., W.A. (eds.) FMCAD 2000. LNCS, vol. 1954, pp. 108–125. Springer, Heidelberg (2000)

Formal Analysis of Workflows Using UML 2.0 Activities and Graph Transformation Systems

Vahid Rafe and Adel T. Rahmani

Department of Computer Engineering
Iran University of Science and Technology
Tehran, Iran
{rafe,rahmani}@iust.ac.ir

Abstract. Graph transformation has recently become more and more popular as a general visual language to formally state the dynamic semantics of the designed models. Using this technique, we present a highly understandable yet precise approach to formally model the behavioral semantics of UML 2.0 Activity diagrams. Automated formal verification and analysis of UML Activities is the main advantage of our approach. In our proposal, AGG toolset is used to design Activities, then using our previous approach to model checking graph transformation systems, designers can verify and analyze designed Activity diagrams. One of the main application areas of the Activities is workflow modeling; hence to illustrate our approach, we use our proposed semantics for modeling and verification of workflows.

Keywords: Activity Diagram, Workflow, Graph Transformation, Verification, Dynamic Semantics.

1 Introduction

UML Activity diagrams are suitable means to model dynamic parts of a system. They allow modeling of complex and large processes or specifying workflows [1]. They can be used to model the behavior of a system or to specify the global behavior of a web service conversation [2]. Oftentimes, however, modeling must be complemented with suitable analysis capabilities to let the user understand whether the designed model fulfills the stated requirements. To have a precise analysis in an automated way, design models like Activities should be stated with a formal language (i.e. a language with a precise semantics).

Since the past decade, Unified Modeling Language (UML) has been a standard modeling language to express models in a software development process. The major drawback of UML and similar modeling languages are that they only define syntax for modeling without a precise formal semantics. Formal methods are crucial in automated software engineering. But the problem of formal methods is that they are difficult to be understood by designers because there is a complex mathematics behind them. Hence, our aim is to implement a precise semantics –based on UML 2.0 specification [3]-yet easily understandable for UML 2.0 Activities using graph transformation systems [4,5].

J.S. Fitzgerald, A.E. Haxthausen, and H. Yenigun (Eds.): ICTAC 2008, LNCS 5160, pp. 305–318, 2008.

Graph transformation has recently become more and more popular as a general formal modeling language. Many of the artifacts which software engineers are used to deal with are nothing but suitable annotated graphs. Software architectures, class diagrams, and version histories are only a few well-known examples in which graphs have proven their usefulness in everyday software engineering. These models, and many others, can easily be described by means of suitable graph transformation systems to formalize their syntax and define the formal semantics of used notations [6]. Hence, graph transformation is a natural formalism for languages which basically are graphs and this motivates us to choose graph transformation as a semantic background for modeling Activities.

To analyze Activities –modeled by graph transformation system- we use model checking. For doing so, based on our defined semantics, the *transition system* must be generated. In the generated transition system *states* are graphs representing the current state of the activity. Then it is possible to check specified properties of the model (e.g. via temporal logics interpreted on the transition system). To implement semantics of UML 2.0 Activity diagrams, we use AGG[1] toolset [7]. AGG supports attributed typed graphs and layered graph transformation systems. It is also possible to define desired constraints using *atomic constraints* in AGG. As AGG cannot generate transition systems, we use our previous approach to generate transition systems and to do model checking [8]. We translate graph transformation systems designed in AGG to BIR (Bandera Intermediate Language) –the input language of Bogor[2] model checker [9]-. Bogor generates the transition system and checks desired properties stated by LTL (Linear Temporal Logic). This translation is done automatically and designers can use this approach without any knowledge about the BIR or Bogor.

As it was mentioned before, one of the main application areas of the Activities is "workflow modeling". Hence, we use our proposed semantics of UML 2.0 Activity diagrams for modeling workflows. To verify the correctness of workflows, we consider several crucial properties of Activities modeling workflows. We describe how our proposed semantics can be used automatically to verify workflows. In contrast to previous approaches [10,11], our proposed semantics supports concepts defined in UML 2.0 Activities (e.g. Petri-like semantics and traverse-to-completion). Furthermore, our approach can cover more elements of Activities (e.g. exception handling and events) for modeling than [12] and it has more flexibility to check user defined properties on the Activities. As we use traditional graph transformation systems (in contrast to [12] which uses a new concept named rule invocation) it is easier for designers to use our approach because the existing environments for modeling graph transformation systems (e.g. AGG) do not support directly rule invocation.

The paper is organized as follows. Section 2 surveys the related work. Section 3 briefly introduces graph transformation systems. Section 4 describes our approach to define a formal semantics for Activities. Section 5 shows our approach to verify modeled workflows and section 6 concludes the paper.

2 Related Work

There is much research done about definition of formal semantics for Activity diagrams using different formal languages. In [13], Hausmann defines a concept named

---

[1] http://tfs.cs.tu-berlin.de/agg/

[2] http://bogor.projects.cis.ksu.edu/

Dynamic Meta Modeling (DMM) using graph transformation systems. He extends the traditional graph rules by defining a new concept named rule invocation. In DMM there are two kinds of rules: big-step and small-step rules. Big-step rules act as traditional rules but small-step rules should be invoked by big-step rules. Hausmann then defines semantics for Activity diagrams using concept of DMM. Engels et al. [14] use DMM and semantics defined by Hausmann for modeling and verification of workflows. For verification, they use GROOVE [15], but as GROOVE does not support attributed typed graphs and rule invocation, they change the rules to be verifiable by GROOVE. They check deadlock freeness and action reachability properties on the modeled workflows. In contrast to this work, our approach has more flexibility to support user defined properties. Furthermore, event and exception modeling can be supported by our approach. Additionally, the extension defined by Hausmann (small/big step rules and rule invocation) cannot be modeled directly in existing graph transformation tools; hence it is not so easy for designers to use this approach.

Störrle et al. [16] use Petri-nets as the semantic background for the UML 2.0 Activities. They examine Activities as described in the UML version 2.0 standard by defining denotational semantics. It covers basic control flow and data flow, expansion nodes and exception handling. They show that some of the constructs proposed in the standard are not so easily formalized. Due to the traverse-to-completion semantics in UML 2.0, they conclude that it is not possible to use Petri nets for this purpose. Although we only consider control flow in our approach, but using graph transformation we are capable to define many semantics which have been described in UML 2.0 standard.

Eshuis [17] defines a statechart-like semantics for UML 1.5 Activity diagrams. He defines a property called strong fairness (the model should not have any infinite loops) to verify functional requirements of the model. This approach uses NuSMV [18] model checker to check the strong fairness property stated in LTL expression. He defines two levels of formalisms: requirements level that is easy to analyze but somewhat abstract and implementation level that is difficult to analyze but has an accurate representation. This approach and others [11,19] do not treat UML 2.0 Activities, but its 1.5 predecessor.

Baldan et al. [20] use hyper graphs to show the behavior of a model (instance graph) by using UML Activities (rather than to define semantics for Activities). They use instance graph to show the static model of a system, then by defining a rule for each Action in the Activity and using synchronized hypergraph rewriting, they control the application of the rules. They present a variant of monadic second-order logic to verify hyper graphs. But they do not introduce any tools to implement their ideas. Furthermore, they do not use semantics defined by UML 2.0 (e.g token flow) to implement their proposal.

3 Attributed Typed Graph Transformation Systems

The mathematical foundation of graph transformation systems returns to thirty years ago in reaction to shortcomings in the expressiveness of classical approaches to rewriting (e.g. Chomsky grammars), to deal with non-linear grammars. In this subsection, we describe graph transformation briefly, as a modeling means. For more information about theoretical background and semantics of graph transformation, interested readers can refer to [4,5].

Graph transformation is a pattern and rule based formalism for the manipulation of graph models. The abstract syntax of a modeling language is defined by a metamodel. It can be represented formally as a **type graph**. The instance model or **host graph** is a well-formed instance of the metamodel and describes concrete systems defined in the modeling language. On **rule** application, a graph is transformed by replacing a part of it by another graph. With the definition of a metamodel and a set of rules over that metamodel the dynamic changes of an initial model can be described.

An attributed typed graph transformation system is a triple $AGT=(TG,HG,R)$, where TG is the type graph, HG is the host graph and R is the set of rules. Each type graph is a pair $TG=(NT, ET)$, NT is a set of node types and ET is a set of edge types. Each node n in NT is a triple $\{Mult, Attr, O\}$, where $Mult$ is the multiplicity of the node, $Attr$ is the set of its attributes and O is the set of its outgoing edges (associations) with corresponding multiplicity and destination node. Host graph $H=(N, E)$ is an instance graph typed over TG. N is the set of nodes, typed over NT and E is the set of edges, typed over ET. Each rule r in R is a triple $R=(LHS, NAC, RHS)$ where LHS, NAC and RHS are graphs typed over TG. In a graph transformation rule LHS is the left-hand side graph, RHS is the right-hand side graph and NAC is the negative application condition graphs. The LHS and the NAC graphs are together called as the precondition of the rule R.

The application of a rule to a host graph H (which is instance model of the metamodel or type graph) replaces a matching of the LHS in H by an image of the RHS (formally there is graph morphism between the LHS and the instance model H). This is performed by (1) finding a matching of LHS in H, (2) checking the negative application conditions NACs (which prohibit the presence of certain objects and links) (3) removing a part of the host graph (that can be mapped to LHS but not to RHS) yielding the context model, and (4) gluing the context model with an image of the RHS together by adding new objects and links (that can be mapped to the RHS but not to the LHS) and obtaining the derived model H'.

By recursively applying all enabled graph transformation rules to the start (host) graph, a transition system can be generated. Transition systems are frequently used to represent the behavior semantics of software systems. They divide the runtime evolution of a system into discrete *states* and use a binary *transition relation* to define possible state changes. In the case of graph transition systems, one considers graphs as representations of system states. If used as operational model of a graph transformation model, its state space contains all reachable graphs of the transformation model. If the resulting state space of the graph transition system is finite, we can easily check different properties (e.g. reachability, safety, liveness, etc.), even for unrestricted forms of graph transformation systems, by searching the state space.

We have proposed an innovative approach based on Bogor to model check AGG-like graph transformation systems. We use AGG, because it supports attributed typed graph transformation systems, hence we can analyze models that are rich enough to render complex types (in contrast to GROOVE). We rely on Bogor to tackle dynamic systems, i.e. systems whose nodes are added/deleted by transformation rules while the system evolves (in contrast to CheckVML [21]).

4   Modeling Workflows

To ease modeling of workflows we only use a subset of UML 2.0 Activities, since using this subset suffices to model many types of workflows. As our approach focuses mainly on control flow perspective; therefore, to model workflows we consider these parts of Activity diagrams: *Init* node, *Final* node, *Action* node, *Fork* node, *Join* node, *Merge* node, *Decision* node and *AcceptEvent* node (to support event modeling in workflows). Before we present our defined semantics for workflow modeling, we need to show a basic idea of that. According to the UML 2.0 specification [3] "Activities have a Petri-like semantics", i.e., the semantics is based on token flow. Before an Activity is executed, only *Init* node has a token. Then based on our defined rules, this token routed through the Activity.

Taking the semantics described above into account, we need to define an accurate syntax for the models under design. For doing so, we define some constraints on the models. These constraints are as following:

1- Each activity diagram must have exactly one *Init* node and one *Final* node.
2- *Init* node has no incoming edge and *Final* node has no outgoing edge.
3- Each *Fork* and *Decision* node should have exactly two outgoing edges. Note that it is possible to have these nodes with more outgoing edges by cascading them. Therefore, it has no restriction on our models.
4- Each *Action*, *Merge*, *Init* and *Join* node must have exactly one outgoing edge.
5- The source and target node of each edge should not be identical. (There must not be any self-edge in the graphs.)
6- Each *Final*, *Action*, *Fork*, *Decision* node should have only one incoming edge.
7- Each *Join* and *Merge* node should have exactly two incoming edges. Note that it is possible to have these nodes with more incoming edges by cascading them.
8- Each *Action* node can have some outgoing edges to some different *Accept Event* node and each *Accept Event* node should have exactly one outgoing edge to an *Action* node (this kind of edges is different with other edges).

Note that in practice, constraints 1,3 and 7 do not restrict the modeler: more than one *Init* node can be modeled equivalently by one *Init* node and one or more *Fork* node(s). (*Final* and *Join* nodes accordingly). *Fork* (or *Decision*) nodes with more than two outgoing edges can be modeled equivalently by cascading two or more *Fork* (*Decision*) nodes. (We use the same way for *Join* and *Merge* nodes). We have proposed these constraints to have models with precise syntax and it is possible to draw many of UML 2.0 Activities using these constructs[3].

The class diagram shown in figure 1 represents a portion of UML 2.0 Activity diagrams' metamodel [22]. This metamodel can be formally considered as an attributed typed graph. As it mentioned in sec. 3, the abstract syntax of a modeling language is defined by a metamodel and it can be represented formally as a type graph. Since UML 2.0 specification stipulates that activities "use a Petri-like semantics" [22], we will use token-flow semantics in our graphs. Therefore; to show tokens we add an

---

[3] We do not consider labels or guards on the edges because it has not any effect on our approach for verification.

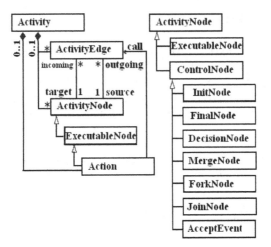

Fig. 1. A small portion of UML 2.0 metamodel [22]

attribute to each node, named "token" with "boolean" type. Figure 2 shows the proposed type graph for Activity diagrams.

Figure 2 shows the designed type graph based on mentioned constraints. This type graph and other parts of proposed graph transformation system are designed in AGG toolset. AGG checks automatically that each host graph (i.e. Activity diagram) and rules should be consistent with its type graph and other constraints. Therefore, when we model an Activity in AGG, we are sure it is syntactically consistent with type graph and other constraints.

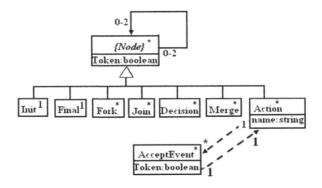

Fig. 2. Proposed type graph for UML 2.0 Activity diagram

The proposed type graph consists of one abstract type (i.e. *Node*), the star (*) sign on the top right corner shows the multiplicity of these nodes in the models. Other nodes (except *AcceptEvent*) have inherited it. It means all nodes have the *Token* field. As it is shown, for *Init* and *final* nodes the multiplicity is one. Additionally, there are two different kinds of edges, only *Action* nodes can use dashed edges with *AcceptEvent* nodes and vice versa. We will use this kind of edge to support exception handling. Each Action node may raise an exception and a handler node is needed for this purpose. The dashed edge is used to show the handler node for an *Action* node which can raise an exception.

The multiplicities of edges show the minimum and maximum edges that each node can have as incoming or outgoing edges. This type graph does not satisfy all the above constraints. Therefore, we need some more constraints besides this type graph. For example, based on this type graph, it is possible to have host graphs (Activity diagrams) with some *Action* nodes that have not any outgoing edge or incoming edge. In AGG, using *atomic graph constraint* and *formula constraint*, we can define desired constraints on the model. As an example consider figure 3.

It consists of two *atomic graph constraints* which have been described by two rules. One of them depicts each *Decision* node should have exactly two outgoing edges with different target nodes (the different numbers before *Node* show they are different. These numbers are generated automatically by AGG). The other states the same meaning for *Fork* nodes. Then the *formula constraint:* (1 && 2) shows that all the host graphs (Activities) should follow these two constraints.

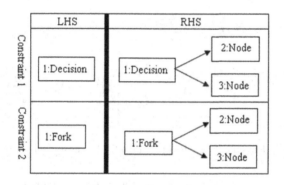

Fig. 3. Two atomic graph constraints

After adding other constraints to the graph transformation system, the static part (metamodel) of the proposed formal semantics is completed. Now we can model workflows (or Activities) directly as a host graph in graph transformation system. Figure 4 shows a sample workflow modeled by an Activity diagram [3]. Dashed region shows the area that the event *"Cancel Order Request"* can be activated. All *Action* nodes in this area can activate this event. We will use this Activity diagram as a running example for the rest of this paper. It describes the processing of orders in a company. The meaning of this diagram is supposed as follows:

When an order arrives, it might be accepted or rejected (the *Decision* node with two guards shows this fact). In the case of acceptance, action *Fill Order* must be done. Then to speed up the process, two actions *Ship Order* and *Send Invoice* are performed in parallel. When either these two actions are terminated or in the case of rejection, *Order Close* action is performed. Finally either by reaching the *Final* node or raising the exception *Cancel Order Request*, the process is terminated.

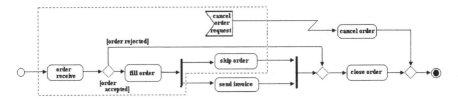

Fig. 4. A sample activity diagram [3]

This Activity diagram can be modeled as the host graph in figure 5. As it is shown, this host graph is consistent with the type graph and constraints. Note that we have modeled workflows directly as a host graph (Activity) in AGG, but it is possible to draw the Activity in a desired UML editor. Then using a one to one mapping between UML and AGG constructs, we can implement a transformer to automatically transform Activities which have been designed in UML editor to host graphs in AGG. The benefit is that non-expert designers do not need to learn graph transformation or to work with AGG.

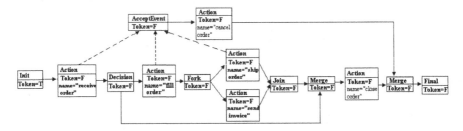

Fig. 5. The sample activity diagram in fig 4 as host graph in AGG

Most of the constraints formulated above put restrictions more on the syntax of Activities rather than semantics. Since syntax restrictions are usually easy to verify, their verifications will not be discussed further. The dynamic semantics are more important. To verify them, at first we need a formal semantics of the behavior of Activity diagrams. Hence, the next step is designing the dynamic semantics of the model by defining graph transformation rules. The proposed rules show the token flow in the host graphs. To define these rules we consider these definitions for token flow:

- In each workflow, at first, only the *Init* node has the token, i.e., the *Token* attribute of *Init* node is true and this attribute is false for other nodes.
- Tokens can not get stuck on nodes, it means as soon as there is a suitable way, the token should be routed. This is compliance with the UML specification which states the traverse-to-completion semantics for tokens.
- The flow of tokens will be terminated when *Token* attribute of all nodes are true, or when there is not any way for tokens to be routed (i.e. there is not any rule to be applicable on the model). It means, it is possible that token reaches the *Final* node before reaching to some other nodes. Therefore; our rules should be designed in a way that consider this fact.

Based on these definitions and the desired behavior of Activity diagrams, we have proposed 24 graph transformation rules as dynamic semantics for Activities. Due to the lack of space, we can not explain all of them here, but we briefly describe some of them. We have implemented the token flow semantics in a simple way: as soon as a node receives the token, it offers the token to its following node(s) and the following node(s) (except *Join* node) accepts the token. Figure 6 shows two example rules implementing the semantics of the *Init* node. We have designed two rules to show this semantics. NAC (Negative Application Condition) and LHS (Left Hand Side) describe the preconditions while RHS (Right Hand Side) shows the post-conditions of the rules. We have used notation defined by AGG to show the rules. Rule (a) of figure 6 simply depicts that if *Init* node has the token but its following node has not the token, token must be routed to its following node. The NAC of this rule states that the following node can not have any other predecessor node, i.e. the following node must not be a *Join* node or *Merge* node because only these two kinds of nodes can have two incoming edges. The main goal of this NAC is preventing the application of this rule for cases that the following node of the *Init* node is a *Join* node, because the semantics of *Join* nodes are different. We have designed other rules to show the semantics of the *Join* nodes.

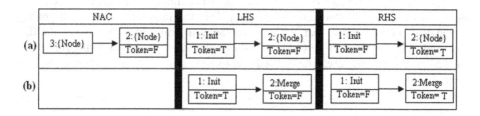

Fig. 6. Rules showing the semantics of *Init* node

Rule (b) in figure 6 shows the token flow from *Init* node to a *Merge* node. Note that the NAC of rule (a) prevents this rule to be applicable for *Merge* nodes, hence we have defined rule (b) for this purpose.

Figure 7 shows two another rules. Rule (a) of figure 7 shows a portion of semantics for *Join* nodes. It has not any NAC; the only precondition for this rule is that both predecessors of *Join* node must have the token; in this case the token will be routed to the *Join* node.

Rule (b) of figure 7 shows a portion of semantics for *Decision* nodes. The NAC of this rule states that both of the following nodes must not be *Join* or *Merge* nodes (it is similar to NAC of rule (a) in figure 6). We have different rules for cases that the following nodes are *Join* or *Merge* nodes. The LHS shows the precondition of this rule. If *Decision* node has the token and both of the following nodes have not any token, then this rule can be applied on the model and token will be routed to only one of the following nodes. As it is shown, the RHS says that token must be routed to only one of the following nodes. Hence in the cases that there is a matching for this rule, application of it will add two new different states on the transition system (because there are two different situations for the following nodes to receive the token).

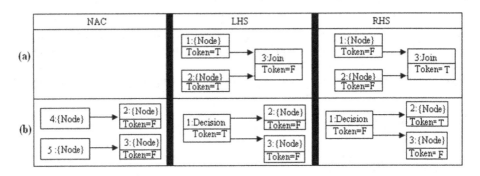

Fig. 7. Rule (a) shows a portion of semantics for *Join* nodes, Rule (b) shows a portion of semantics for *Decision* nodes

Figure 8 illustrates this process. Left rectangle shows a part of host graph (Activity diagram) as a state in the transition system ("state i" in this case) which token has arrived to the *Decision* node. It shows the matching of the LHS for rule (b) of figure 7. There are two matching for this rule. In one case "Action1" is the image of "node2" and "Action2" is the image of "node3" of rule (b) in figure 7. In the other case, "Action1" is the image of "node3" and "Action2" is the image of "node2". Right top rectangle ("state j") shows that Activity after applying rule (b) of figure 7 in the first case and right down rectangle ("state k") shows the Activity after applying rule (b) of figure 7 in the second case. The derived graphs represent two new generated states in the transition system.

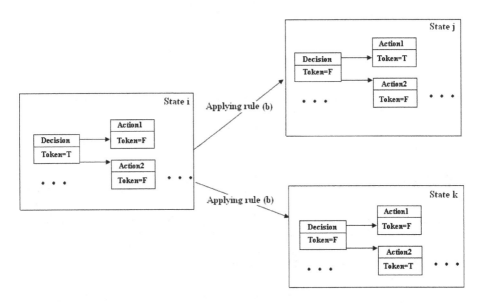

Fig. 8. A portion of transition system generated by applying rule (b) of figure 7

Applying all enabled rules to initial state (the Activity diagram which only its *Init* node has the token) will result a transition system. This resulting transition system represents the complete behavior of the Activity under consideration. It will be the basis for analysis of the Activity, using model checking. In the next section, we show our approach to verify an Activity using its transition system.

5 Verification and Validation

To analyze designed Activities we use our previous approach to verify graph transformation systems [8]. Our verification approach gets the graph transformation system (type graph, host graph and rules) and properties as input. The graph transformation system should be designed in AGG. Also properties should be defined by some special rules. Then it gets a LTL expression with name of rules as atoms. These rules that show the properties have the identical LHS and RHS. These kinds of rules do not change the model (i.e. its application do not change the state, hence do not change the transition system) and only represent the properties which must be checked on the model (we mimic both GROOVE and CheckVML to state properties). In cases which designers are expert in graph transformation, they can model directly workflows by graph transformation (rather than UML), using rules to state properties has this advantage that designers do not need to learn any other formal method, and they can state properties by the same formalisms that they model the system (i.e. graph transformation). In cases which designers are not familiar with graph transformation, they can model workflows by UML Activities[4] (rather than graph transformation), in this case, they do not need define any rules for verification, because we have designed some fixed properties, it means designers only model the workflow, and then verification is done via our fixed designed properties automatically (without intervention of designers). In addition, it is possible to define new properties by expert designers (designers which are expert in graph transformation).

First, recall from section 4, which for an Activity to be supposed sound, a token must finally arrive at the *Final* node. It means the Activity must be deadlock free. In other words, there must not be any hanging path in the Activity. To verify this property we should check that for all possible executions of the Activity *Final* node is reachable. To state this property we have designed two rules: *FinalWithoutToken* and *FinalWithToken*. Figure 9 shows these rules. They have not any NAC and as we mentioned in the beginning of this section, their LHS and RHS are identical. If a rule matches a state, we know that the preconditions of that rule hold within the state. The only precondition of *FinalWithoutToken* is that the Final node must be without token (in contrast to *FinalWithToken*). Hence, we can state this property as the following LTL expression: $\Box(FinalWithoutToken \rightarrow \Diamond(FinalWithToken))$, where symbol "$\Box$" means *always*, "$\Diamond$" means *finally* and symbol "$\rightarrow$" shows the *implication*. The result of checking this property on the transition systems is true if in every possible execution of the Activity, there is a state in a path in which *FinalWithoutToken* is satisfied (the token attribute of *Final* node is false) and then eventually there is a state in the

---

[4] In this case, a transformer needed (as we referred to it in section 4) to automatically transform UML Activities to graph transformation.

postfix of that path, in which the token attribute of the *Final* node is true (i.e. *Final-WithToken* is satisfied). It means always the token must arrive at *Final* node. As an example which this property is satisfied by the Activity, consider Activity of figure 4. In this Activity token always arrive at *Final* node. But as an example which the mentioned property is not satisfied consider Activity in figure 10 (a). This Activity shows a workflow which contains a deadlock. In this diagram, there is a *Join* node immediately after *Init* node and it prevents token to be propagated from *Init* node. Therefore, token never reaches to *Final* node and it causes a deadlock. Hence, the mentioned property is never satisfied for this Activity.

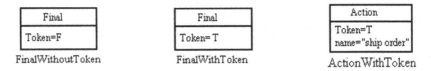

Fig. 9. Rules *FinalWithoutToken*, *FinalWithToken* and *ActionWithToken*

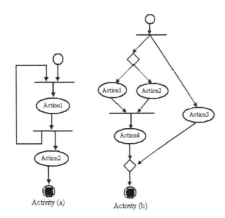

Fig. 10. Two faulty Activities. (a) contains a deadlock. (b) contains an unreachable action node.

Another property which should hold for a sound workflow is that there must not be any useless work (action) in it, i.e. for each *Action* node there should be at least one execution which the token arrives at that node. In other words, each *Action* in a sound workflow must be reachable. We can state this property as the following: each specified Action must be reachable, it means we should design a rule for each Action (using its name) to check this property, figure 9 shows a rule (*ActionWithToken*) to state that the Action *"Ship Order"* in the Activity of figure 4 is reachable. The following LTL expression states this property: ¬□(¬*ActionWithToken*), this property is satisfied on the Activity of figure 4. This LTL expression means that there must be an execution of the Activity which the specified *Action* node (*"Ship Order"* in this case) has the token (i.e. it is reachable). Now consider the Activity of figure 10 (b), if we replace the name of Action node in figure 9 (*ActionWithToken*) with "Action4", then check the property, it is not satisfied. Because there is a *Decision* node before *"Action1"* and *"Action2"*, according to the semantics of *Decision* nodes, token is routed to only one of them, hence in all execution of this Activity, only one token will arrive at *Join* node before *"Action4"*. Based on the semantics of *Join* nodes, token will never reach to the *"Action4"*. Therefore, we can conclude that this property never is satisfied for this workflow. We can state this kind of property in a more general way by ignoring the name of Action. In this case, checking the property only says that is there any unreachable Action in the Activity or not, and it does not determine the unreachable Action.

6   Conclusions and Future Work

In this paper we have presented an approach to formally define a semantics for UML 2.0 Activities. We have defined this semantics based on "token flow" and "traverse-to-completion" using graph transformation systems. To define static semantics, we have defined a type graph and all Activities are modeled as a host graph. The host graph must confirm to the type graph. To define dynamic semantics, we have defined some graph transformation rules. We have used our previous approach to verify graph transformations. As workflows are a typical modeling domain for UML 2.0 Activities, so we have illustrated our proposed verification approach to verify workflows by defining some quality criterion. Non-expert designers can use our approach without any knowledge about underlying formalisms (i.e. BIR and Bogor).

However, further research is required to model other required elements (e.g. Action calls). We have a plan to model other elements and define semantics for them as some graph transformation rules.

Acknowledgments. This research was partially done while the first author was in university of Politecnico di Milano (Italy) as a visiting researcher and would like to thank the supports provided by Professor Luciano Baresi and Dr. Paola Spoletini.

References

1. Eshuis, R., Jansen, D., Andwieringa, R.: Requirements-level Semantics and Model Checking of Object-Oriented Statecharts. Requirements Eng. J. 7, 243–263 (2002)
2. Alonso, G., Casati, F., Kuno, H., Machiraju, V.: Web Services: Concepts, Architectures and Applications. Springer, Heidelberg (2004)
3. Object Management Group: UML Specification V2.0. (2005), http://www.omg.org/technology/documents/modelingspeccatalog.htm
4. Baresi, L., Heckel, R.: Tutorial Introduction to Graph Transformation: A Software Engineering Perspective. In: Corradini, A., Ehrig, H., Kreowski, H.-J., Rozenberg, G. (eds.) ICGT 2002. LNCS, vol. 2505, pp. 402–429. Springer, Heidelberg (2002)
5. Ehrig, H., Engels, G., Kreowski, H.j., Rozenberg, G. (eds.): Handbook on Graph Grammars and Computing by Graph Transformation. Applications, Languages and Tools, vol. 2. World Scientific, Singapore (1999)
6. Kuske, S.: A Formal Semantics of UML State Machines Based on Structured Graph Transformation. In: Gogolla, M., Kobryn, C. (eds.) UML 2001. LNCS, vol. 2185. Springer, Heidelberg (2001)

7. Beyer, M.: AGG1.0 – Tutorial. Technical University of Berlin, Department of Computer Science (1992)
8. Baresi, L., Rafe, V., Rahmani, A.T., Spoletini, P.: An Efficient Model Checking Approach for Graph Transformation Systems. In: Proc. of 3th International Workshop on Graph Transformation for Verification and Concurrency (GT-VC 2007)
9. Robby, D.M., Hatcliff, J.: Bogor: An Extensible and Highly-Modular Software Model Checking Framework. In: Proc. of the 9th European software engineering Confference, pp. 267–276 (2003)
10. Eshuis, R.: Semantics and Verification of UML Activity Diagrams for Workflow Modelling, Ph.D. Thesis, University of Twente, Netherlands (2005)
11. Bolton, C., Davies, J.: On Giving a Behavioural Semantics to Activity Graphs. In: Evans, A., Kent, S., Selic, B. (eds.) UML 2000. LNCS, vol. 1939. Springer, Heidelberg (2000)
12. Soltenborn, C.: Analysis of UML Workflow Diagrams with Dynamic Meta Modeling Techniques, Master's Thesis, University of Paderborn, Germany (2006)
13. Hausmann, J.H.: Dynamic Meta Modeling: A Semantics Description Technique for Visual Modeling Languages, Ph.D. Thesis, University of Paderborn, Germany (2005)
14. Engels, G., Soltenborn, C., Wehrheim, H.: Analysis UML Activities Using Dynamic Meta Modeling. In: Bonsangue, M.M., Johnsen, E.B. (eds.) FMOODS 2007. LNCS, vol. 4468, pp. 76–90. Springer, Heidelberg (2007)
15. Rensink, A.: The GROOVE Simulator: A Tool for State Space Generation, In Applications of Graph Transformations with Industrial Relevance (AGTIVE). In: Pfaltz, J.L., Nagl, M., Böhlen, B. (eds.) AGTIVE 2003. LNCS, vol. 3062, pp. 479–485. Springer, Heidelberg (2004)
16. Störrle, H., Hausmann, J.H.: Towards a Formal Semantics of UML 2.0 Activities. In: Liggesmeyer, P., Pohl, K., Goedicke, M. (eds.) Software Engineering. LNI., GI, vol. 64, pp. 117–128 (2005)
17. Eshuis, R.: Symbolic Model Checking of UML Activity Diagrams. ACM Transaction on Software Engineering Methodology 15(1), 1–38 (2006)
18. Cimatti, A., Clarke, E., Giunchiglia, F., Roveri, M.: NuSMV: A New Symbolic Model Checker. International Journal on Software Tools for Technology Transfer 2(4), 410–425 (2000)
19. Börger, E., Cavarra, A., Riccobene, E.: An ASM Semantics for UML Activity Diagrams. In: Rus, T. (ed.) AMAST 2000. LNCS, vol. 1816, pp. 293–308. Springer, Heidelberg (2000)
20. Baldan, P., Corradini, A., Gadducci, F.: Specifying and Verifying UML Activity Diagrams via Graph Transformation. In: Priami, C., Quaglia, P. (eds.) GC 2004. LNCS, vol. 3267, pp. 18–33. Springer, Heidelberg (2005)
21. Schmidt, Á., Varró, D.: CheckVML: A tool for model checking visual modeling languages. In: Stevens, P., Whittle, J., Booch, G. (eds.) UML 2003. LNCS, vol. 2863, pp. 92–95. Springer, Heidelberg (2003)
22. Störrle, H.: Semantics of Control-Flow in UML 2.0 Activities. In: N.N. (ed.) Proc. IEEE Symposium on Visual Languages and Human-Centric Computing (VL/HCC) (2004)

Testing Concurrent Objects with Application-Specific Schedulers*

Rudolf Schlatte [1,2], Bernhard Aichernig [1,2], Frank de Boer [3],
Andreas Griesmayer [1], and Einar Broch Johnsen [4]

[1] International Institute for Software Technology, United Nations University
(UNU-IIST), Macao S.A.R., China
{agriesma,bka,rschlatte}@iist.unu.edu
[2] Institute for Software Technology, Graz University of Technology, Austria
aichernig@ist.tugraz.at
[3] CWI, Amsterdam, Netherlands
frb@cwi.nl
[4] Department of Informatics, University of Oslo, Norway
einarj@ifi.uio.no

Abstract. In this paper, we propose a novel approach to testing executable models of concurrent objects under application-specific scheduling regimes. Method activations in concurrent objects are modeled as a composition of symbolic automata; this composition expresses all possible interleavings of actions. Scheduler specifications, also modeled as automata, are used to constrain the system execution. Test purposes are expressed as assertions on selected states of the system, and weakest precondition calculation is used to derive the test cases from these test purposes. Our new testing technique is based on the assumption that we have full control over the (application-specific) scheduler, which is the case in our executable models under test. Hence, the enforced scheduling policy becomes an integral part of a test case. This tackles the problem of testing non-deterministic behavior due to scheduling.

1 Introduction

In this paper we address the problem of testing executable high-level behavioral models of concurrent objects. In contrast to multi-threaded execution models for object-oriented programs such as, e.g., the Java model for the parallel execution of threads, we consider in this paper a model of object-oriented computation which describes a method call in terms of the generation of a corresponding process in the callee. The concurrent execution of objects then naturally arises from asynchronous method calls, which do not suspend while waiting for the return value from the method calls. Objects execute their internal (encapsulated) processes in parallel. In this setting, the scheduling of the internal processes of an object directly affects its behavior (both its functional and non-functional

---

* This research was carried out as part of the EU FP6 project *Credo*: Modeling and analysis of evolutionary structures for distributed services (IST-33826).

J.S. Fitzgerald, A.E. Haxthausen, and H. Yenigun (Eds.): ICTAC 2008, LNCS 5160, pp. 319–333, 2008.

behavior). Therefore, a crucial aspect of the analysis of concurrent objects is the analysis of the intra-object scheduling of processes. In contrast to scheduling on the operating-system level, the object-level scheduling policies will be fine-tuned according to the application requirements. We call this *application-specific scheduling*. In this paper we introduce a novel testing technique for concurrent objects under application-specific scheduling regimes.

We develop a testing technique for concurrent objects in the context of Creol [9,4], a high-level modeling language which allows for the abstraction from implementation details related to deployment, distribution, and data types. The semantics of this language is formalized in rewriting logic [11] and executes on the Maude platform [3]. As such the Creol modeling language also allows for the simulation, testing, and verification of properties of concurrent object models, based on execution on the Maude platform as described by formal specifications. One of the main contributions of this paper is a formal testing technique for this language which integrates formal specifications of application-specific scheduling regimes at an abstraction level which is *at least as high as that of the modeling language*. The novelty of this approach is that it takes the scheduling policy as an integral part of a test case in order to control its execution.

In order to specify test cases in our formal testing technique, we first develop suitable behavioral abstractions of the mechanisms for synchronizing the processes within an object, as featured by the modeling language. The integration of these behavioral abstractions and the formal specification of a particular scheduling regime provides the formal basis for the generation of test cases. For the formal specification of test purposes we use assertions which express required properties of the object state (or a suitable abstraction thereof). Test cases are then generated by applying a weakest precondition calculus in order to find an abstract behavior which satisfies the assertions [8]. The execution of a test case on the Maude platform requires instrumenting the Maude interpreter of Creol's operational semantics such that it will enforce the embodied scheduling policy on the processes of the particular concurrent object which is considered by the test case. Particular test cases address the behavior of the concurrent object model under a given, formally defined scheduling regime. If such a test case fails to reach its goal (test purpose), this might indicate a problem with the given scheduling policy. Hence, the relevance of this contribution for modeling object-oriented systems in general is that it also allows the specification and analysis of scheduling issues in an early stage of design, as an integral part of the high-level models. However, in the following discussion we focus on the important aspect of controlling test-case execution by enforcing a scheduling regime.

Paper overview. The rest of this paper is organized as follows: Section 2 introduces the Creol language and executable modeling. Section 3 gives a high-level overview and scope for our approach to testing. Section 4 explains the modelling approach used, including the high-level specification of scheduling policies. Section 5 discusses the details of test case generation and execution. Finally, Section 6 discusses related work and Section 7 concludes the paper.

$$sr ::= s \mid s; \textbf{return } e \qquad L ::= \textbf{class } C(\overline{v}) \; \{\overline{T \; f}; \overline{M}\}$$
$$v ::= f \mid x \qquad\qquad M ::= T \; m \; (\overline{T \; x}) \; \{\overline{T \; x}; sr\}$$
$$b ::= \textbf{true} \mid \textbf{false} \mid v \quad e ::= v \mid \textbf{new } C(\overline{v}) \mid e.\textbf{get} \mid e!m(\overline{e}) \mid \textbf{null} \mid \textbf{this} \mid \textbf{caller}$$
$$T ::= C \mid \textbf{Bool} \mid \textbf{Void} \quad s ::= v := e \mid \textbf{await } g \mid \textbf{skip} \mid s; s$$
$$g ::= b \mid v? \mid g \wedge g \qquad\qquad\quad \mid \textbf{if } g \textbf{ then } s \textbf{ fi} \mid \textbf{release}$$

Fig. 1. The language syntax. Variables v are fields (f) or local variables (x), and C is a class name.

2   Creol and Executable Modeling

In the design of component-based or object-oriented systems, it may be desirable to introduce a separation of concerns between business code, dealing with the functionality of the software unit, and synchronization code, dealing with the local scheduling of different computing activities. Creol is a high-level executable modeling language for concurrent objects in which such scheduling may be left underspecified [9]. The language has a formal semantics defined in rewriting logic [11] and executes on the Maude platform [3]. This allows various analysis techniques to be developed and applied to the Creol models, including, e.g., pseudo-random simulation and breadth-first search through the execution space.

In contrast to, e.g., Java, each Creol object encapsulates its state; i.e., all external manipulation of the object state happens through calls to the object's methods. Each process corresponds to the activation of one of the object's methods. In addition, objects execute concurrently: each object has a processor dedicated to executing the processes of that object, so processes in different objects execute in parallel. In Creol, method calls are asynchronous and assigned to so-called futures [4]. Only one process may be active in an object at a time; the other processes in the object are *suspended*. We distinguish between *blocking* a process and *releasing* a process. Blocking causes the execution of the process to stop, but does not let a suspended process resume. Releasing a process suspends the execution of that process and lets another (suspended) process resume. Thus, if a process is blocked there is no execution in the object, whereas if a process is released another process in the object may execute. Although processes need not terminate, the execution of several processes within an object may be combined using *release points* within method bodies. Release points may include polling operations on futures, to check for the arrival of replies to asynchronous method calls. At a release point, the active process may be released and *some* suspended process may resume.

Syntax. The language syntax of the subset of Creol used in this paper is presented in a Java-like style in Fig. 1. For the purpose of this paper, we emphasize the differences with Java and focus on the specification of a single class. At present, we omit some features of Creol, including inheritance and method calls. *Expressions* e are standard apart from the asynchronous method call $e!m(\overline{e})$, the (blocking) read operation $v.\textbf{get}$, and the pseudo-variable **caller** which refers to the caller of the current method activation. *Statements* s are standard apart

```
class batch_queue(Nat x) {
  Nat wc, batch, comein // waiting clients, barrier size
  Seq[Object] display // queue of registered client objects

  Void batch_queue() { batch := x; wc := 0; comein := 0 }

  Void register() {
    wc := wc+1;
    if wc ≥ batch then comein := batch fi;
    await comein > 0;
    comein := comein - 1;
    wc := wc-1;
    display := (display;caller);
  }
}
```

Fig. 2. Motivating example: The batch_queue class

from release points **await** g and **release**. *Guards* g are conjunctions of Boolean expressions b and polling operations $v?$ on futures v. When the guard in an **await** statement evaluates to *false*, the statement becomes a **release**, otherwise a **skip**. A **release** statement suspends the active process and another suspended process may be rescheduled.

Example. We consider a version of barrier synchronization given by the class batch_queue in Fig. 2.. In a batch_queue object, clients are processed in batches (of size batch, the parameter x to the constructor sets the size of the batches). A client which registers must wait until enough clients have registered before getting assigned slot in the queue. For simplicity, we represent the queue as a local variable display, which is a sequence of clients (semicolon is the append operator on sequences). Before any call to register will return, the object will contain batch processes. When enough calls are waiting to be registered, the next batch of processes may proceed by assigning the value of batch to display. It is easy to see that the order in which callers are added to the display sequence depends on the internal scheduling of processes in the object.

Once more, we mention that only a subset of Creol is presented in this paper; the interested reader is referred to e.g. [9].

3   Testing and Testing Methodology

The executable formal semantics of the Creol language allows the application of different analysis techniques. In this section we briefly sketch our proposed methodology for testing Creol applications on the Maude platform.

Our methodology focuses on testing run-time properties of Creol objects. By the very nature of Creol objects, of particular interest is to test run-time properties of the object state under different possible interleavings of its processes.

In order to specify and execute such tests we need an appropriate abstraction of processes which focuses on their interleavings as described by the control structure of their release points. We do so by modeling the internal flow of control within a process between its release points into atomic blocks consisting of sequences of assignments. The release points of a process themselves then can be represented by the states of a finite automaton, also called a *method automaton* (because processes are generated by method calls). The transitions of a method automaton involve the assignments and a guard on the object state which specifies the enabling condition of the corresponding atomic block. We assume given a finite set of internal processes in an object, reflecting the message queue of incoming method calls for the object. The possible interleavings of this initially given finite set of processes is thus abstracted into the interleavings of their automata representations.

Scheduler automata further constrain the possible interleavings by means of abstract representations of the enabling conditions of the method automata. The automatically generated *scheduled system automaton* representing the possible interleavings of the method automata and the scheduler automaton is instrumented with test purposes, expressed as Boolean conditions over the method automata's state variables, that are attached to states.[1]

To compute test cases for a test purpose we search for paths that reach and fulfill the test purpose. We generate a set of such test cases by computing a test "harness" describing all paths in the model that will reach the test purpose. To this end, we use weakest precondition computation to propagate the conditions to the initial state of the system. The condition at the initial state describes the values that state variables can take for executing that test case, reflecting the actual parameters to the method calls in the message queue. Each possible path that reaches the condition(s) is its own test case.

The execution of a test on the Maude platform then checks whether the particular interleaving of the method automata described by the path in the system automaton can be realized by the Maude implementation of the Creol object such that it satisfies the conditions.

4   Combining Method Automata and Scheduling Policies

In this section, we present the symbolic transition system construction used to specify the system's behavior. We adapt the symbolic transition systems of [13], using shared variables for communication instead of input/output actions.

Syntax. A Symbolic Transition System is a tuple $\langle Q, q_0, T, V \rangle$, where:

- Q is a finite set of locations $q_i, i \geq 0$
- $q_0 \in Q$ is the initial location
- V is a set of variables

---

[1] Computing test cases that reach a certain condition in the program can be done with conditions that are simply *true*.

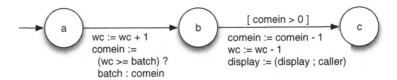

Fig. 3. Method Automaton of the `register()` method

- T is a set of transitions of the form $\langle q, g, S, q' \rangle$, where
  - $q \in Q$ is the source location
  - g is a Boolean *guard expression* over V
  - S is a sequence of *assignment statements* changing the value of some $v \in V$
  - $q' \in Q$ is the target location

Semantics. A *state* is a pair $\langle q, v \rangle$ consisting of a location q and a valuation v for the variables. For the initial state, $q = q_0$. Let *eval* be the function mapping an expression and a valuation to a result[2]. Then, for a state $\langle q, v \rangle$, *executing* a transition $\langle q, g, S, q' \rangle$ results in a new state $\langle q', v' \rangle$ where the new valuation v' is the result of evaluating all assignment statements in S, using *eval* with the former valuation v to calculate new values for the affected variables, provided that $eval(g, v) = true$.

4.1 Modeling Method Invocations: Method Automata

Invocations of methods on Creol objects are modeled by *Method Automata*, a slight extension of the symbolic transition systems described above.

A method automaton is a tuple $\langle m, Q_m, q_0^m, T_m, V_m, Val_m \rangle$ so that m is a unique identifier, Q is a set of locations q_i^m etc. Other than the systematic renaming of locations, the semantics are the same as for symbolic transition systems. Additionally, Val_m is a mapping $v \in V_m \mapsto x$ giving initial values x to all variables v. (Conceptually, Val_m models parameters passed to the method as well as initial values of local variables.)

A Creol method without release points is modeled as a method automaton with only beginning and end state. Each release point is modeled as an intermediate state where execution can switch to another running method.

By convention, the names of the local variables in a method automaton are prefixed with the unique identifier m of the automaton, so that the names are unique in the presence of multiple instances of the automaton. This approach is sufficient since each invocation of a Creol method is modeled by its own automaton. Names of instance variables, such as `wc` and `display` in Fig. 3 are not prefixed in this way, since every method automaton has access to the same instance variables.

---

[2] In this paper, we use expressions over the integer and Boolean domains with the usual operations and semantics.

4.2 Modeling Parallelism: The System Automaton

A configuration of multiple method invocations running in parallel is modeled as a symbolic transition system as well. We shall refer to such an automaton as a *system automaton*.

Definition 1. *Let* $A_i = \langle m_i, Q_{m_i}, q_0^{m_i}, T_{m_i}, V_{m_i}, Val_{m_i} \rangle$ *be method automata (for* $1 \leq i \leq n$*). Define the composition of* $A_1, \ldots, A_n$ *as a system automaton* $A = \langle Q, q_0, T, V, Val \rangle$ *such that*

$$Q = \{\langle m_i, q^{m_1}, \ldots, q^{m_n} \rangle \mid \forall 0 < j \leq n : q^{m_j} \in Q_{m_j}\}$$
$$q_0 = \langle m_1, q_0^{m_1}, \ldots, q_0^{m_n} \rangle$$
$$T = \left\{ \langle q, g, S, q' \rangle \middle| \begin{array}{l} q = \langle m_l, q^{m_1}, \ldots, q^{m_i}, \ldots, q^{m_n} \rangle \wedge \\ q' = \langle m_i, q'^{m_1}, \ldots, q'^{m_i}, \ldots, q'^{m_n} \rangle \wedge \\ \langle q^{m_i}, g, S, q'^{m_i} \rangle \in T_{m_i} \wedge \forall j \neq i : q'^{m_j} = q^{m_j} \end{array} \right\}$$
$$V = \bigcup_{0 < i \leq n} V_{m_i}$$
$$Val = \bigcup_{0 < i \leq n} Val_{m_i}$$

The semantics of executing a transition of the system automaton is that of executing the transition of *one* of the participating method automata ($q^{m_i} \rightsquigarrow q'^{m_i}$), leaving the state of all other method automata invariant ($q'^{m_j} = q^{m_j}$). Further note that the first element of the system automaton's state designates the method automaton which did the previous transition (for the initial state, it is arbitrarily set to m_1). Because of this, the transitions of the system automaton can be attributed back to a particular method automaton; this will become important in scheduling.

4.3 Modeling Schedulers: The Scheduler Automata

The system automaton as defined in Section 4.2 does not place restrictions on which method automaton executes at each step beyond the guards of the method automata transition themselves. We use a *scheduler automaton* to express additional restrictions on method automata execution in the system automaton.

A scheduler automaton is modeled as a labeled transition system. It is used to strengthen the guards on the transitions of a system automaton composed of method automata $m_1 \ldots m_n$, and hence, restrict which method(s) are allowed to run.

Definition 2. *Let* A *be a system automaton for methods* $m_1, \ldots, m_n$. *Define a scheduler for* A *as an automaton* $S = \langle Q, q_0, T \rangle$ *such that*

$$Q = \{m_i \mid 1 \leq i \leq n\}$$
$$q_0 = m_1$$
$$T = \{\langle q, g, q' \rangle \mid q \in Q \wedge q' \in Q \wedge g \in G(A)\}$$

The transitions on a scheduler automaton have guards $g \in G(A)$ in the form of *readiness predicates* that are defined in the following way: Given a system automaton A for methods $m_1, \ldots, m_n$, $G(A)$ is defined inductively by $ready(m_i) \in$

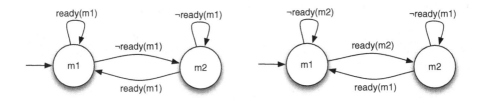

Fig. 4. Example scheduler automata: priority (left), round-robin (right)

$G(A)$ and $\neg ready(m_i) \in G(A)$ for $1 \leq i \leq n$, and $g_1 \wedge g_2 \in G(A)$ and $g_1 \vee g_2 \in G(A)$ if $g_1, g_2 \in G(A)$. The expression $ready(m_i)$ denotes a predicate which is *true* whenever the method automaton m_i has at least one *enabled transition* (i.e., whose guard evaluates to *true*) in the current state of A.

The scheduler automaton has n states, one for each method automaton in the system automaton. Each scheduler state is labeled with one method automaton's unique identifier m_i. The label on the current state of the scheduler automaton names the method automaton that executed the most recent transition of the system automaton. By definition, m_1 is the scheduler automaton's initial state.

Figure 4 shows two scheduling automata, both for a system automaton with two method automata m_1 and m_2: a simple priority scheduler that always gives preference to m_1 over m_2, and a round-robin scheduler.

4.4 Integration of the Scheduler and the System Automaton

The scheduling of tasks in a system automaton according to the policy expressed by a specific scheduler automaton is done in the following way:

For each state $q = \langle m_k, \ldots \rangle$ of the system automaton, find the corresponding state m_k of the scheduler automaton. For each transition $t = \langle q, g, S, q_1 \rangle$ in the system automaton, take the scheduler automaton's transition that enables t, i.e. the transition that leads to the scheduler state m_i if $q_1 = \langle m_i, \ldots \rangle$. If there is no such scheduler transition, remove the transition from the system automaton (since the scheduler does not allow the method automaton m_i to run after m_k). Otherwise, strengthen the guard on the transition t by the guard expression on the scheduler transition from m_k and m_i, replacing all sub-expressions $ready(m_x)$ with the disjunction of the guards on all transitions of method automaton m_x in its current state.

We refer to a system automaton which is scheduled by a scheduler automaton as a *scheduled system automaton*. Formally, we define the expansion of readiness predicates for specific states of a system automaton and a scheduled system automaton as follows.

Definition 3. *Let $A = \langle Q, q_0, T, V, Val \rangle$ be a system automaton for the methods $m_1, \ldots, m_n$. For a state $q \in Q$ and a scheduler guard $g \in G(A)$, scheduler guard expansion is a function $[\![g]\!]_q$, inductively defined as follows:*

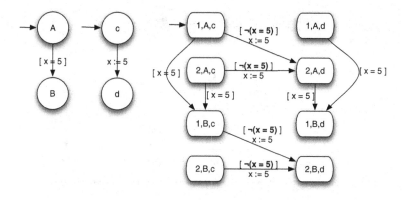

Fig. 5. Two simple method automata and a system automaton consisting of the two automata running in parallel under the priority scheduler of Figure 4 (guards in bold added by the scheduler)

$$[ready(m_i)]_q = \bigvee\{g \mid \langle q, g, S, q_1 \rangle \in T \wedge q_1 = \langle m_i, q^{m_1}, \ldots, q^{m_n} \rangle\}$$
$$[\neg ready(m_i)]_q = \neg[ready(m_i)]_q$$
$$[g_1 \vee g_2]_q = [g_1]_q \vee [g_2]_q$$
$$[g_1 \wedge g_2]_q = [g_1]_q \wedge [g_2]_q$$

In the first part of Definition 3, we use the disjunction on a set to denote the disjunction of all the elements in the set.

Definition 4. *Let* $A = \langle Q_A, q_0^A, T_A, V_A \, Val_A \rangle$ *be a system automaton for methods* $m_1, \ldots, m_n$ *and let* $S = \langle Q_S, q_0^S, T_S \rangle$ *be a scheduler. Define a scheduled system as an automaton* $SA = \langle Q, q_0, T, V, Val \rangle$ *such that*

$$Q = Q_A$$
$$q_0 = q_0^A$$
$$T = \left\{ \langle q, g, S, q' \rangle \; \middle| \; \begin{array}{c} q = \langle m_l, q^{m_1}, \ldots, q^{m_n} \rangle \wedge q' = \langle m_i, q'^{m_1}, \ldots, q'^{m_n} \rangle \\ \wedge \langle q, g', S, q' \rangle \in T_A \wedge \langle m_l, g'', m_i \rangle \in T_S \wedge g = (g' \wedge [g'']_q) \end{array} \right\}$$
$$V = V_A$$
$$Val = Val_A$$

For example, if the transition guard on the scheduler is $[\neg ready(m)]$ and automaton m in its current state has two transitions with the guards $[x <= 5]$ and $[x > 5]$, then relevant guards on the transitions in the system automaton will be strengthened with $\neg(x <= 5 \vee x > 5)$. Transitions whose guards reduce to *false* (as in this example) can be eliminated from the system automaton.

5   Test Case Generation with WP and Schedulers

We use a scheduled system automaton SA (see Definition 4) to test the Creol object it represents. SA contains all runs an object can perform for a given

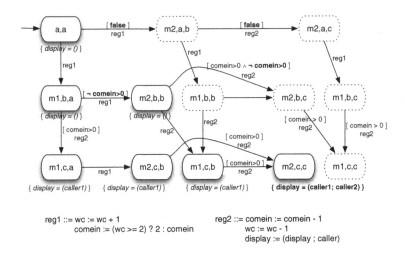

Fig. 6. A scheduled system automaton with two method automata for the `register` method, under priority scheduling and with batch size 2. Guard terms in bold are added by the scheduler, states that are unreachable under priority scheduling are dashed.

initial message queue and scheduler. In the following, we give an approach to computing test cases of interest from this automaton.

Specifically, we define how to compute the weakest precondition (WP) for a scheduled system automaton and use this technique to generate test cases according to a *test purpose*.

The intention of the test cases to generate is captured by *test purposes*, which are abstract specifications of actual test cases. In conformance testing, the notion of a test purpose has been standardized [7]:

Definition 5 (Test purpose, general). *A description of a precise goal of the test case, in terms of exercising a particular execution path or verifying the compliance with a specific requirement.*

In our setting, these requirements are expressed by assert statements in a system automaton. The condition p of an assert has to be fulfilled in all possible runs leading to the assert. (For simplicity, we will use p to refer to the assertion and its condition synonymously.) To compute test cases for a test purpose, we search for paths that reach and comply with all its assert statements. Intuitively, this corresponds to computing the *weakest precondition* for p. In the following we will, without loss of generality, concentrate on test purposes that can be specified with a single assertion. Conditions for the general case are computed by combining the results from the single conditions.

Figure 6 shows the graph of a system automaton that models two invocations of the `register` method and `batch` size 2, scheduled with the priority scheduler from Figure 4. This scheduler removes the edge from the initial state (a,a) to (m2,a,b) because both processes are enabled (with m1 having priority).

Consequently, a portion of the state space of the system automaton becomes unreachable in the scheduled system automaton and can be removed.

Figure 6 also shows the additional conditions from scheduling on the edges. E.g., in state (m1,b,a) process m2 is only enabled if *comein* is not > 0. The test purpose is to compute test cases to reach state (m2,c,c) with *display* = (*caller1*; *caller2*). We constrain ourselves to only illustrate the WP computation for the *display* variable, whose computed value is depicted in curly brackets. Computing the WP to the initial state results in an empty *display* variable, for which all paths reach the desired state[3]. The actual implementation must not block for this input and must satisfy the assertion.

To test the intermediate and final assertions on the Creol model, we create a *test harness H*. The harness is constructed from the system automaton A as $H = \langle Q_A, q_0^A, T_A, V_A, c(Q_A) \rangle$, with Q_A, q_0^A, T_A and V_A reflecting the system automaton, and $c(Q_A)$ a condition defined for each location of A, representing those valuations in a location that only occur in runs that eventually will reach and comply with p. Thus, for every valuation in $c(Q_A)$ two properties hold: (1) there is a transition such that the destination is again in $c(Q_A)$ and (for determinism) (2) there is no transition such that the destination is not in $c(Q_A)$. Using standard weakest-precondition predicate transformers wp for our simple statements S (assignments and sequential composition only), we have:

$$c_p(q) = \bigvee_{\forall \langle q, g, S, q' \rangle \in T} wp\left(S, c(q')\right) \wedge g \tag{1}$$

$$c_{\neg p}(q) = \bigvee_{\forall \langle q, g, S, q' \rangle \in T} wp\left(S, \neg c(q')\right) \wedge g \tag{2}$$

$$c(q) = c_p(q) \wedge \neg c_{\neg p}(q) \tag{3}$$

We compute $c(Q_A)$ iteratively by setting $c_0(q) = p$ for $q = q_p$ and $c_0(q) = false$ for all other locations. The first iteration will result in all states that reach p in one step, then those with distance two and so forth. The iteration steps are sound: each iteration results in valuations that give valid test cases. This is an important observation because although this process always results in a fixed point for finite state systems (cf. CTL model checking of **AF** p [2]), the state space for STS is infinite and the iteration might not terminate. Soundness allows us to stop computation after a certain bound or amount of time even if no fixed point is reached yet. Any initial state in $c(q_0)$ gives valid test cases even if no fixed point can be computed.

The test case for the scenario of Figure 6 consists of the following:

- A list of method invocations $(\langle m_1, \texttt{register()} \rangle, \langle m_2, \texttt{register()} \rangle)$
- The priority scheduler from Figure 4
- The initial value () for the instance variable `display`
- The test harness H, giving verdicts at each scheduling decision point

---

[3] The representation is strongly simplified, exact computation will give more conditions on the states and unveils that only the path using the edge (m1,b,a)(m2,b,b) is feasible.

5.1   Test Case Execution

The test driver in Creol uses the scheduler to guide the Creol model and the test harness H to arrive at test verdicts. The initial values and method parameters are chosen such that condition $c(q_0)$ is fulfilled, at each release point of the Creol object, the conditions on the harness are checked. At each release point, the scheduler chooses among the enabled processes to continue the execution. There are two different ways of arriving at a test verdict of *Fail*:

- If the Creol object does not fulfill the current condition of the harness, the implementation of the last executed basic block violates the specification by the method automaton.
- If the condition is fulfilled but no process is enabled (the test process deadlocks), the implementation fails to handle all the valuations that are required by the model.

If the test harness arrives at the terminating state and the condition is fulfilled, a test verdict of *Success* is reached.

Strengthening the Guards of the Harness. The computation as shown above uses the weakest precondition to reach the test purpose p, or, in other words, the set of initial states that reach the test purpose in every legal run. Input values that might miss p due to non-determinism are ignored. To achieve optimal test coverage, however, it is desirable to search for all input values that *can* fulfill the test purpose and add enough information to H for the test driver to guide the run to the desired state. In other words, instead of computing those initial states that will reach p in every run, we want to compute states for which a run *exists*.

The annotated automaton provides us with a simple mechanism to achieve this goal. For the necessary adjustments we have a second look at the computation of $c(Q_A)$. Formula (1) represents the states that can reach p, while those states that can avoid p are removed using Formula (2). If we don't consider $c_{\neg p}$ in Formula (3), we compute all valuations for which a run to p *exists*, but the test driver has to perform the run on a trial an error basis: executing a statement and checking if the result still can reach p, backtracking otherwise. To avoid this overhead, we add new guards g' to H to restrict the runs to those valuations that always can reach p:

$$g'(< q, g, S, q' >) = g \wedge wp(S, c(q'))$$

Using g' for the computation of $c(Q_A)$ results in all states for which a run to p exists, which easily can be seen by inserting g with $g \wedge wp(S, c(q'))$ in formulae (1) and (2):

$$c'_p(q) = \bigvee_{\forall \langle q,g,S,q' \rangle \in T} wp\left(S, c(q')\right) \wedge g \wedge wp\left(S, c(q')\right) = c_p(q)$$

$$c'_{\neg p}(q) = \bigvee_{\forall \langle q,g,S,q' \rangle \in T} wp\left(S, \neg c(q')\right) \wedge g \wedge wp\left(S, c(q')\right) = \mathit{false}$$

$$c'(q) = c'_p(q)$$

Using g' as guards for the test driver excludes all transitions to states that cannot reach p. This allows to avoid unnecessary backtracking while examining all paths that can be extended to reach the test purpose, resulting in a larger variety of possible runs and better coverage. The approach does not come without obstacles though, g' only points to states that *can* reach p — the test driver needs to be able to detect loops to make sure to finally reach it. Furthermore, a path to p might not be available in the implementation. If the only available path avoids p, the test driver has to backtrack to find a path to p.

6   Related Work

With the growing dependency on distributed systems and the arrival of multicore computers, concurrent object-oriented programs form a research topic of increasing importance. Automata-based approaches have previously been used to model concurrent object-oriented systems; for example, Kramer and Magee's FSP [10] use automata to represent both threads and objects, abstracting from specific synchronization mechanisms. However, they do not address the issue of representing specific scheduling policies that we consider in this paper. Schönborn and Kyas [14] use Streett Automata to model fair scheduling policies of external events, with controlled scheduler suspension for configurations that deadlock the scheduler.

A lot of work is done in the area of schedulability which mainly deals with the question if a scheduler exists which is able to meet certain timing constraints (e.g., [12, 6]), but does not look into the functional changes imposed by different application-level scheduling policies. Established methods for testing object-oriented programs like unit-testing, on the other hand, deal with the functionality on a fine grained level, but fail to check for the effects of different schedulers (see e.g., [18]). Instead, the main challenge for testing concurrent programs is to show that the properties of interest hold independent of the used scheduler. In contrast, the approach we have taken in this paper is to test properties of a program under a specific scheduling regime.

Stone [15] was the first proposing the manipulation of the schedules to isolate failure causes in concurrent programs. Her idea was to reduce the nondeterminism due to scheduling by inserting additional break points at which a process waits for an event of another process. In Creol, this could be achieved by inserting additional await-statements. However, dealing with a modeling language, we prefer the more explicit restriction of non-determinism by modeling the scheduling policy directly. More recently, Edelstein et al. [5] manipulated the scheduler in order to gain higher test coverage of concurrent Java programs. They randomly seeded *sleep*, *yield* or *priority* statements at selected points in order to alter the scheduling during testing. This approach is based on the observation that a given scheduler behaves largely deterministic under constant operating conditions; by running existing tests under other scheduling strategies, additional timing-related errors are uncovered. Choi and Zeller [1] change schedules of a program to show the cause of a problem for a failing test case. They use DEJAVU, a capture/replay tool that records the thread schedule and allows the replay of a concurrent Java program in a deterministic way. Delta-debugging is used to systematically narrow down the difference between a passing and failing thread schedule. This approach helps in order to check if programs work under different schedules, but unlike the method shown in this paper do not help in the actual generation of the test case.

Jasper et al. [8] use weakest precondition computation to generate test cases especially tailored for a complex coverage criterion in single threaded ADA programs. Rather than augmenting the model, they generate axioms describing the program and use a theorem prover to compute its feasibility. More recently, [17] use weakest precondition to identify cause-effect chains in failing test cases to localize statements responsible for the error (fault localization). WP computation is furthermore used in several abstraction algorithms to identify relevant predicates for removing infeasible paths in abstract models. In [16], Tillmann and Schulte introduce "parametrized unit tests", which serve as specifications for object oriented programs. They use symbolic execution to generate the input values for the actual test cases. However, none of these approaches use WP computation for test case generation in concurrent systems.

7   Conclusion and Future Work

This paper presents an approach to generating test cases for concurrent, object-oriented programs with application-specific schedulers. The scheduling policy becomes part of the test case in order to control its execution. We therefore introduce an automaton approach for specifying the behavior of both the system and the scheduler, as well as its composition and extension to a harness for a test driver. Enforcing a scheduling regime limits the non-deterministic interleavings of behavior, a well-known problem in testing and debugging of concurrent systems. A further important aspect is that the separation of concerns between functionality and scheduling allows scheduling issues, which are crucial in concurrent programs, to be specified and tested at the abstraction level of the executable modeling language.

In this paper, we expect the method automata and scheduler to be given as specifications, and check for compliance with a given Creol implementation. A natural extension for future work is to automatically construct the method automata from the Creol code and check against different schedulers for compliance. The test driver will be implemented within the Maude interpreter for Creol, which allows the test driver to influence the scheduling.

Further future work comprises the extension to schedulers with internal state to express more involved scheduling strategies and to extend our approach with further features of object-oriented languages.

References

1. Choi, J.-D., Zeller, A.: Isolating failure-inducing thread schedules. In: International Symposium on Software Testing and Analysis, pp. 210–220. ACM Press, New York (2002)
2. Clarke, E.M., Grumberg, O., Peled, D.A.: Model Checking. The MIT Press, Cambridge (1999)
3. Clavel, M., Durán, F., Eker, S., Lincoln, P., Martí-Oliet, N., Meseguer, J., Quesada, J.F.: Maude: Specification and programming in rewriting logic. Theoretical Computer Science 285, 187–243 (2002)
4. de Boer, F.S., Clarke, D., Johnsen, E.B.: A complete guide to the future. In: De Nicola, R. (ed.) ESOP 2007. LNCS, vol. 4421, pp. 316–330. Springer, Heidelberg (2007)
5. Edelstein, O., Farchi, E., Nir, Y., Ratzaby, G., Ur, S.: Multithreaded Java program test generation. IBM Systems Journal 41(1), 111–125 (2002)
6. Fersman, E., Krcál, P., Pettersson, P., Yi, W.: Task automata: Schedulability, decidability and undecidability. Information and Computation 205(8), 1149–1172 (2007)
7. ISO/IEC 9646-1: Information technology - OSI - Conformance testing methodology and framework - Part 1: General Concepts (1994)
8. Jasper, R., Brennan, M., Williamson, K., Currier, B., Zimmerman, D.: Test data generation and feasible path analysis. In: Proceedings of the International symposium on Software testing and analysis (ISSTA 1994), pp. 95–107. ACM Press, New York (1994)
9. Johnsen, E.B., Owe, O.: An asynchronous communication model for distributed concurrent objects. Software and Systems Modeling 6(1), 35–58 (2007)
10. Magee, J., Kramer, J.: Concurrency: State Models & Java Programs, 2nd edn. Wiley, Chichester (2006)
11. Meseguer, J.: Conditional rewriting logic as a unified model of concurrency. Theoretical Computer Science 96, 73–155 (1992)
12. Nigro, L., Pupo, F.: Schedulability analysis of real time actor systems using coloured petri nets. In: Agha, G.A., De Cindio, F., Rozenberg, G. (eds.) APN 2001. LNCS, vol. 2001, pp. 493–513. Springer, Heidelberg (2001)
13. Rusu, V., du Bousquet, L., Jéron, T.: An approach to symbolic test generation. In: Grieskamp, W., Santen, T., Stoddart, B. (eds.) IFM 2000. LNCS, vol. 1945, pp. 338–357. Springer, Heidelberg (2000)
14. Schönborn, J., Kyas, M.: A theory of bounded fair scheduling. In: Fitzgerald, J., Haxthausen, A. (eds.) International Colloquium on Theoretical Aspects of Computing (ICTAC). LNCS, vol. 5160, pp. 334–348. Springer, Heidelberg (2008)
15. Stone, J.M.: Debugging concurrent processes: A case study. In: Proceedings SIGPLAN Conference on Programming Language Design and Implementation (PLDI 1988), June 1988, pp. 145–153. ACM Press, New York (1988)
16. Tillmann, N., Schulte, W.: Parameterized unit tests. In: Proceedings of the 10th European Software Engineering Conference / 13th ACM SIGSOFT Symposium on the Foundations of Software Engineering (ESEC/FSE 2005), pp. 253–262. ACM Press, New York (2005)
17. Wang, C., Yang, Z., Ivancic, F., Gupta, A.: Whodunit? Causal analysis for counterexamples. In: Graf, S., Zhang, W. (eds.) ATVA 2006. LNCS, vol. 4218, pp. 82–95. Springer, Heidelberg (2006)
18. Weyuker, E.J.: Testing component-based software: A cautionary tale. IEEE Software, pp. 54–59 (September 1998)

A Theory of Bounded Fair Scheduling

Jens Schönborn[1,*] and Marcel Kyas[2,**]

[1] Christian-Albrechts-Universität zu Kiel, Germany
jes@informatik.uni-kiel.de,
http://www.informatik.uni-kiel.de/~refism/refism.html
[2] Department of Informatics, University of Oslo, Norway
kyas@ifi.uio.no,
http://credo.cwi.nl

Abstract. Modeling languages like UML use asynchronous communication but do not specify the order in which messages are received. A simple language for specifying such orders declaratively is proposed that ensures fair and bounded fair scheduling. Such scheduling specifications are then translated to Streett automata that accept only and all infinite runs satisfying the specification. Using the automaton as a scheduler guarantees fairness and allows to analyze schedulability using standard automata-theoretic algorithms. The formalism is extended to the case of an uncooperative environment by "fall-back" scheduling specifications when events required for progress are not provided by the environment.

1 Introduction

UML has become the standard modeling language for object-oriented systems. UML state machines are among the most important constituents of UML, because they are widely used for modeling the reactive behavior of objects. The UML 2.x standards give an informal semantics of UML state machines [1]: The description assumes an *event pool*, where all incoming messages are stored. Then a message is selected from that pool and processed for execution. Just the exact mechanism for selecting the event is left unspecified in the UML standard.

We present a language that allows to specify, among others, in which order events can be selected from the event pool in Sect. 2. The selection is intended to be *fair*. Because general fairness cannot be implemented, the language is designed with a focus on *bounded fairness*. Rules are the conjunction of clauses of the form "at most k events from set F before any event from set E".

Common fairness is robust (independent of the granularity of transitions) and simple (abstracts complicated time bounds), but suffers from two major drawbacks: First, it cannot be observed in finite time, though it is a mathematically

---

* J. Schönborn's work has been supported by DFG-project FE 942/1-1 RO 1122/12-2 *refism*.
** M. Kyas' work has been supported by EU-project IST-33826 *CREDO: Modeling and analysis of evolutionary structures for distributed services*.

J.S. Fitzgerald, A.E. Haxthausen, and H. Yenigun (Eds.): ICTAC 2008, LNCS 5160, pp. 334–348, 2008.

appealing assumption. Still, fairness proofs have to be conducted hands on. Second, the time until good events happen may be unbounded, whereas we often desire that such events happen within a bounded number of steps.

In Sect. 3 we show how one can compute a *scheduler* from these specifications. The scheduler is a *Streett automaton* [2] that accepts exactly those infinite words that satisfy our scheduling specifications.

Consistency properties and progress properties are decidable, because each specification can be represented as a Streett automaton. These results are collected in Sect. 4. The most important properties are consistency, which is equivalent to emptiness of the language accepted by the automaton, and absence of possible deadlock. The absence of possible deadlock implies that a system can always proceed with an event in any state. Such schedulers can select events without concern for the event pools content and will guarantee progress.

As the final and most important contribution, we extend the specification language towards *modal specifications,* because we cannot assume that all events will be provided by the environment. Since our formalism is untimed we need to have other mechanisms of ensuring reasonable progress of the system, which we achieve by a change of scheduling policies in situations where the system is considered stuck. The details are described in Sect. 5.

Related Work. We are confident that modal specifications are of great importance, since they allow us to specify and implement scheduling strategies in the presence of non-cooperating environments.

We have good hopes that our formalism can be used in a very wide context. Other languages leave exact details of the order of event handling unspecified, e.g., the experimental modeling language Creol [3]. Our scheduling automata can be used to reduce the non-determinism exhibited by random scheduling and to enable black-box testing.

Fair and bounded scheduling, which is called *finitary fairness* by R. Alur and T.A. Henzinger, is especially important for the verification of distributed algorithms with failures. They write about [4].: "This is illustrated by the celebrated result of Fischer, Lynch, and Paterson that, under the standard fairness assumption, processes cannot reach agreement in an asynchronous distributed system if one process fails." [5].

The use of fairness by means of explicit scheduling in program verification was already suggested by K. Apt and E.-R. Olderog [6]. Their proposal uses a program transformation to ensure that non-deterministic branches of a guarded-command program are chosen fairly.

Bounded fairness plays an important role in telecommunication applications and cryptographic protocols. Kang and Wilbur consider the scheduling of handovers in cellular networks. They suggest time-bounds as one means to enforce fairness of bandwidth allocation [7].

Tidwell et.al. suggest to enforce cyclic behavior of their schedulers to enforce fairness [8]. Such cyclic structures have also been proposed by Ramanujam and Lodaya [9] to prove fairness in programs. The latter paper inspired us to use

Streett automata as a semantic model: Streett acceptance can be decided by finding cycles in the automaton (as one necessary conditions).

Another application area are cryptographic protocols. For example, Backes et.al. introduce *polynomial fairness* and *polynomial liveness* is introduced as a means that good events will be scheduled after at most polynomial many steps [10]. They justify the importance of polynomial fairness in cryptographic protocols but fail to explain how polynomial fairness is to be achieved. Here, scheduling specifications can be applied.

Our use of Streett automata is very similar to the use of *edge Streett Automata* [11]. Instead of selecting particular edges into the fairness sets, the symbol and the specification decide on the edges in the fairness set. Using edge Streett automata does therefore not offer any advantage in our setting.

2   Fair Scheduling

Let Σ be an alphabet of events, e.g., messages which are processed by some component. Possible sequences, in which the components processes these events, are from the ω-regular set Σ^ω. These general infinite words do not capture a notion of fairness. For example, given the alphabet $\{a, b\}$, the input sequence ab^ω can be served by the sequence b^ω, and never selecting a. Instead, constrains need to be imposed on the way events are selected, such that application dependent fairness properties are satisfied.

For any $w \in \Sigma^\omega$ we write w_k for the kth element of w, $w_{k,m}$ for the sub-word from k to m, $|w|$ for the length of the word w with $|w| = \omega$ if w is infinite, and $w^A \triangleq \sum_{k<|w|} \sum_{a \in A} \delta(w_k, a)$, where $\delta(a, b) = 1$ if $a = b$ and $\delta(a, b) = 0$ otherwise, for the number of occurrences of elements of $A \subseteq \Sigma$ in w, where $w^A \triangleq \infty$ if these elements occur infinitely often. Note that $\sum_{a \in \emptyset} \delta(w_k, a) = 0$ for all w and therefore $w^\emptyset = 0$. Note that $A \subseteq B$ implies $w^A \leq w^B$ for all w. Infinite words may be viewed as the concatenation of a finite word w and an infinite word w', where we write that concatenation as juxtaposition ww'.

Definition 1. *Let Σ be an alphabet of events and I a finite set of indexes. A scheduling specification is an indexed set $\{(E_i, F_i, L_i) \mid i \in I\}$ of constraints (E_i, F_i, L_i), where $E_i \subseteq \Sigma$, $F_i \subseteq \Sigma$, and $L_i \in \mathbb{N} \cup \{\infty\}$.*

The intuitive semantics of such a specification is, that for each $i \in I$ with $L_i \in \mathbb{N}$ at most L_i occurrences of F_i occur before an occurrence of E_i. If $L_i = \infty$, the constraint means that if F_i occurs infinitely often, so must E_i.

Example 1. Consider a street crossing, where we specify a traffic light that allows at most n_p pedestrians cross before each car and at most n_c cars before each pedestrian. The scheduling specification is $P \triangleq \{(\{p\}, \{c\}, n_c), (\{c\}, \{p\}, n_p)\}$, where c resp. p represent a car resp. a pedestrian and the alphabet is $\Sigma = \{c, p\}$.

Definition 2. *Let* $S = \{(E_i, F_i, L_i) \mid i \in I\}$ *be a scheduling specification. A word* $w \in \Sigma^\omega$ *satisfies* S, *written* $w \models S$, *if and only if:*

$$\forall i \in I : \left(L_i = \infty \wedge w^{F_i} = \infty \implies w^{E_i} = \infty\right) \wedge$$

$$, \left(L_i \neq \infty \implies \forall m < \omega : \forall k \leq m : w_{k,m}^{F_i} > L_i \implies w_{k,m}^{E_i} > 0\right).$$

Remark 1. Let S be a scheduling specification that includes a constraint of the form $(E, F, 0)$. Then for all words that satisfy S no event of F is observed before any event of E, that is *no* event of F occurs in w.

Example 2. Consider the specification in Example 1 with $n_c = 1$ and $n_p = 2$. The sequence of events $(cpp)^\omega$ satisfies the specification P. The sequence $ppp(cpp)^\omega$ does not: Choose $m = 2$ and $k = 0$. Then $(ppp)^{\{p\}} = 3 > 2$ but $(ppp)^{\{c\}} = 0$.

Specifications can be written in many ways. The following lemmas describes when specifications are semantically equivalent and how they can be simplified.

Definition 3. *Let* S *and* T *be two specifications. We say that* S *is* semantically equivalent *(or just* equivalent*) to* T, *written* $S \equiv T$, *if and only if* $\forall w \in \Sigma^\omega$: $w \models S \iff w \models T$.

Lemma 1. *Let* $S = \{(E_i, F_i, L_i) \mid i \in I\}$ *be a scheduling specification. Let* $i \in I$ *such that* $F_i = \emptyset$. *Then* S *is equivalent to* $S \setminus \{(E_i, F_i, L_i)\}$.

Proof. Since $w^{F_i} = w^\emptyset$ and $w^\emptyset = 0$, we neither have $w^{F_i} = \infty$ nor $w^{F_i} > L_i$. Then the constraint i is trivially valid according to Def. 2. □

Lemma 2. *Let* $S = \{(E_i, F_i, L_i) \mid i \in I\}$ *be a scheduling specification. Let* $i, j \in I$ *such that* $i \neq j$, $E_i \subseteq E_j$, $F_j \subseteq F_i$, *and* $L_i \leq L_j$. *Then* S *is equivalent to* $S \setminus \{(E_j, F_j, L_j)\}$ *and we say constraint* i dominates *constraint* j.

Proof. Let $S = \{(E_i, F_i, L_i) \mid i \in I\}$, $i, j \in I$ such that $i \neq j$, $E_i \subseteq E_j$, $F_j \subseteq F_i$, and $L_i \leq L_j$ and $S' = S \setminus \{(E_j, F_j, L_j)\}$. Let $w \models S$. Then from Def. 2 and the fact that $S' \subseteq S$ it obviously follows that $w \models S'$. Let $w \models S'$. Case $L_j = \infty$. Let $w^{F_j} = \infty$. From $F_j \subseteq F_i$ conclude $w^{F_i} = \infty$ and with $E_i \subseteq E_j$ therefore $\infty = w^{E_i} = w^{E_j}$. Thus $w \models S$. Case $L_j < \infty$. Let $k \leq m < \infty$ such that $w_{k,m}^{F_j} > L_j$. From $F_j \subseteq F_i$ conclude $w_{k,m}^{F_i} \geq w_{k,m}^{F_j} > L_j \geq L_i$. From $E_i \subseteq E_j$ conclude $0 < w_{k,m}^{E_i} \leq w_{k,m}^{E_j}$. Thus $w \models S$. □

Lemma 3. *Let* $S = \{(E_i, F_i, L_i) \mid i \in I\}$ *be a scheduling specification and* $T = \{(E_i, F_i \setminus E_i, L_i) \mid i \in I\}$. *Then* S *is equivalent to* T.

Proof. Let $w \in \Sigma^\omega$ such that $w \models S$. We show $w \models T$. Let $i \in I$. By Def. 2 we need to consider two cases. Assume $L_i = \infty$ and assume $w^{F_i} = \infty$. If $w^{F_i \setminus E_i} = \infty$, then $w^{E_i} = \infty$ holds, because $w \models S$. Otherwise, if $w^{F_i \setminus E_i} \neq \infty$, then still $w^{E_i} = \infty$. Now assume $L_i \neq \infty$. Let $m < \omega$ and $k < m$. Then, $w_{k,m}^{F_i} > L_i$ implies $w_{k,m}^{E_i} > 0$ because $w \models S$. If $w_{k,m}^{F_i \setminus E_i} \leq L_i$, then there is nothing to prove. So assume $w_{k,m}^{F_i \setminus E_i} > L_i$. But $w_{k,m}^{E_i} > 0$ still holds. In any case we have $w \models T$.

To show the opposite direction, let $w \in \Sigma^\omega$ such that $w \models T$. Let $i \in I$. If $L_i = \infty$ and $w^{F_i \setminus E_i} = \infty$, then $w^{E_i} = \infty$. But we also have $w^{F_i} = \infty$, because $F_i \setminus E_i \subseteq F_i$ for all E_i. And we also still have $w^{E_i} = \infty$. If $w^{F_i \setminus E_i} \neq \infty$ but $w^{F_i} = \infty$, then $w^{F_i \cap E_i} = \infty$ and $F_i \cap E_i \subseteq E_i$ implies $w^{E_i} = \infty$. Now let $L_i \neq \infty$ and $m < \omega$ and $k < m$. If $w_{k,m}^{F_i \setminus E_i} > L_i$ then we also have $w_{k,m}^{F_i} > L_i$, and $w \models T$ implies $w_{k,m}^{E_i} > 0$. If $w_{k,m}^{F_i \setminus E_i} \leq L_i$ and $w_{k,m}^{F_i} > L_i$, then $w_{k,m}^{F_i \cap E_i} > 0$. But because $F_i \cap E_i \subseteq E_i$ we have $w_{k,m}^{E_i} > 0$. In any case, we have $w \models S$.   □

Lemma 4. *Let $S = \{(E_i, F_i, L_i) \mid i \in I\}$ be a scheduling specification. Let $i \in I$ such that $F_i \subseteq E_i$. Then S is equivalent to $S \setminus (E_i, F_i, L_i)$ and we say that the constraint i is* vacuously satisfied.

Proof. Follows from Lemma 3 and Lemma 1 by observing that $F_i \setminus E_i = \emptyset$.   □

These lemmas allow us to define a *normal form* for specifications. These normal forms allow us to simplify the following technical presentation.

Definition 4. *A specification $\{(E_i, F_i, L_i) \mid i \in I\}$ is in* normal form *if:*

- *For all $i \in I$ we have $F_i \neq \emptyset$*
- *For all $i \in I$ we have $E_i \cap F_i = \emptyset$*
- *For all $i \in I$ and all $j \in I \setminus \{i\}$ with $E_i \subseteq E_j$, $F_j \subseteq F_i$ we have $L_i > L_j$.*

Theorem 1. *For each specification S there exists a unique (modulo permutations of indexes) specification S' which is in normal form.*

Proof. With applying Lemma 3, Lemma 1, and Lemma 2 any specification can be converted to a specification in normal form.   □

Example 3. The specification $S = \{(\{a\}, \emptyset, 2), (\{a, b\}, \{b\}, 1), (\{b\}, \{a, b\}, 2)\}$ is not in normal form. The specification $T = \{(\{b\}, \{a\}, 2)\}$ is. Moreover, $S \equiv T$.

Henceforth we will assume, that all specifications are in normal form, because we can convert all specifications into ones in normal form.

The next lemma shows that specifications are "shift-invariant": when we remove the first letter of a word that satisfies the specification, then the remainder of the word still satisfies the specification. This lemma will be used to prove the correctness of the automata construction in the following section.

Lemma 5. *Let $S = \{(E_i, F_i, L_i) \mid i \in I\}$ be a scheduling specification and $w' \in \Sigma^\omega$ and $a \in \Sigma$ with $(aw') \models S$. Then $w' \models S$.*

Proof. Assume $(aw') \models S$ and let $i \in I$. If $L_i = \infty$ and $(aw')^{F_i} = \infty$, then $aw^{E_i} = \infty$. But we also have $w'^{F_i} = \infty$ and $w'^{E_i} = \infty$. Now assume $L_i \neq \infty$ and prove $\forall m < \omega : \forall k \leq m : w'^{F_i}_{k,m} > 0 \implies w'^{E_i}_{k,m} > 0$. Let $m < \omega$ and $k \leq m$. Observe $\forall A : (aw')^A_{k+1, m+1} = w'^A_{k,m}$, from which we conclude the claim.   □

3   From Scheduling Specifications to Streett Automata

In the previous section we have introduced *scheduling specifications* and defined their formal semantics. We continue to define automata which accept all infinite words that satisfy a scheduling specification. We chose *Streett automata* [2], because their acceptance conditions closely resemble the structure of our specifications. We recall the definition of Streett automata.

Definition 5. *A Streett automaton $\mathcal{A}$ is a tuple $(Q, q_0, \Sigma, \rho, \Omega)$, where Q is a non-empty, finite set of states, $q_0 \in Q$ the initial state, Σ an alphabet, ρ : $Q \times \Sigma \to 2^Q$ a transition function, and Ω an indexed set $\{(E_i, F_i) \mid i \in I\}$ called acceptance condition. A trajectory τ of the Streett automaton $\mathcal{A}$ is a sequence $(s_i, \lambda_i)_{i<\omega}$ of states such that $s_0 = q_0$ and $s_{i+1} \in \rho(s_i, \lambda_i)$ for all $i < \omega$. The word of that trajectory is the sequence $\mathrm{Word}(\tau) \triangleq (\lambda_i)_{i<\omega}$. The set of states that occur infinitely often in that trajectory, $\mathrm{Inf}(\tau) \triangleq \{s \mid \forall i < \omega : \exists j > i : s = s_j\}$. A Streett automaton $\mathcal{A}$ accepts a word w, if and only if $\mathrm{Word}(\tau) = w$ and: $\forall i \in I : \mathrm{Inf}(\tau) \cap E_i = \emptyset \implies \mathrm{Inf}(\tau) \cap F_i = \emptyset$. In this case we call τ an accepting trajectory. The language accepted by a Streett automaton $\mathcal{A}$ is called $\mathcal{L}(\mathcal{A})$. We write $w \in \mathcal{L}(\mathcal{A})$ if $\mathcal{A}$ accepts the word $w \in \Sigma^\omega$.*

For any scheduling specification we can build a Streett automaton that accepts all infinite words which satisfy the scheduling specification. From that we can conclude, that all scheduling specifications have a finite model.

Definition 6. *Let S be a scheduling specification in normal form over the alphabet Σ and let $\sharp \notin \Sigma$ and $\flat \notin \Sigma$, i.e., $\sharp$ and $\flat$ cannot occur in any scheduling specification. The closure $C(S)$ of a specification S is the smallest set that satisfies the following conditions:*

1. *$S \in C(S)$.*
2. *If $S' \in C(S)$ and $(E, F, L) \in S'$ for $L \neq \infty$ and $L > 0$, then $S' \cup \{(E, F, L - 1)\} \setminus \{(E, F, L)\} \in C(S)$.*
3. *If $S' \in C(S)$. $(E, F, \infty) \in S'$ then $S' \cup \{(E, F \cup \{\sharp\}, \infty)\} \setminus \{(E, F, \infty)\} \in C(S)$ and $S' \cup \{(E, F \cup \{\flat\}, \infty)\} \setminus \{(E, F, \infty)\} \in C(S)$.*

The closure characterizes the possible states of the automaton. The initial state is the specification itself.

The second item decrements the limit of events from F down by one. Such a state will be reached if an event of F is observed, and decrementing indicates, that from now on the automaton is only allowed to observe one event of F less until reset.

Finally, the last item covers the case of events which occur infinitely often. The acceptance condition for constraints of the form (E, F, ∞) is very similar to the Streett acceptance condition, only that the Streett acceptance condition refers to states and not to labels. We encode the condition on labels as follows: Whenever we take a transition with a symbol in F, we visit a state containing the symbol $\sharp$. Whenever we take a transition with a symbol in E, we visit a state containing the symbol $\flat$. Our intuition is, that infinitely many symbols from F will cause the automaton to visit a state with the $\sharp$ label infinitely often. Since the automaton accepts, it must visit a state labeled with $\flat$ infinitely often, which are only visited by using a symbol of E. This intuition will be formalized in Def. 7 below.

Example 4. Let $\Sigma = \{a, b, c\}$ and $S = \{(\{a\}, \{b\}, 1), (\{b\}, \{c\}, \infty)\}$. Then the closure $C(S)$ is:

$$C(S) = \{S, \{(\{a\}, \{b\}, 0), (\{b\}, \{c\}, \infty)\}, \{(\{a\}, \{b\}, 1), (\{b\}, \{c\}, \infty)\},$$
$$\{(\{a\}, \{b\}, 0), (\{b\}, \{c, \sharp\}, \infty)\}, \{(\{a\}, \{b\}, 1), (\{b\}, \{c, \sharp\}, \infty)\},$$
$$\{(\{a\}, \{b\}, 0), (\{b\}, \{c, \flat\}, \infty)\}, \{(\{a\}, \{b\}, 1), (\{b\}, \{c, \flat\}, \infty)\},$$
$$\{(\{a\}, \{b\}, 0), (\{b\}, \{c, \flat, \sharp\}, \infty)\}, \{(\{a\}, \{b\}, 1), (\{b\}, \{c, \flat, \sharp\}, \infty)\}\} \quad .$$

Remark 2. Constraints of the form (E, F, ∞) with $\{\flat, \sharp\} \subseteq F$ are only reachable if E and F are not disjoint. Thus the specification is not in normal form. If specifications are in normal form, we can remove these from the closure.

Definition 7. *Let* $S = \{(E_i, F_i, L_i) \mid i \in I\}$ *be a scheduling specification in normal form. We define a* Streett *automaton* $\mathcal{A}(S)$ *for the specification* S *by defining the set of states to be* $Q \triangleq C(S)$, *the initial state by* $q_0 \triangleq S$, *the transition function by:*
$\rho(\{(E_i, F_i, L'_i) \mid i \in I\}, e)$ *undefined if there exists* $m \in I$ *where* $e \in F_m$ *and* $L'_m = 0$ *and otherwise:*

$$\rho(\{(E_i, F_i, L'_i) \mid i \in I\}, e) \triangleq \{\{(E_i, F_i, L_i) \mid i \in I \wedge e \in E_i \wedge L_i \neq \infty\} \cup$$
$$\{(E_i, (F_i \cup \{\flat\}) \setminus \{\sharp\}, L_i) \mid i \in I \wedge e \in E_i \wedge L_i = \infty\} \cup$$
$$\{(E_i, F_i, L'_i - 1) \mid i \in I \wedge e \in F_i \wedge L'_i \neq \infty\} \cup$$
$$\{(E_i, (F_i \cup \{\sharp\}) \setminus \{\flat\}, L'_i) \mid i \in I \wedge e \in F_i \wedge L'_i = \infty\} \cup$$
$$\{(E_i, F_i \setminus \{\sharp, \flat\}, L'_i) \mid i \in I \wedge e \notin E_i \cup F_i\}\} \quad .$$

Finally, the acceptance condition is defined to be $\Omega \triangleq \{(\hat{E}_i, \hat{F}_i) \mid i \in I \wedge L_i = \infty\}$, *where* $\hat{E}_i \triangleq \{S' \in C(S) \mid (E_i, F_i \cup \{\flat\}, \infty) \in S'\}$ *and* $\hat{F}_i \triangleq \{S' \in C(S) \mid (E_i, F_i \cup \{\sharp\}, \infty) \in S'\}$.

Example 5. Reconsider Example 4 with the alphabet $\{a, b, c\}$ and the specification $\{(\{a\}, \{b\}, 1), (\{b\}, \{c\}, \infty)\}$.

The resulting automaton is displayed in Fig. 1, where the events are elided from the state label and only reachable states are depicted. Only the limits $0, 1$ or whether a marker $\sharp, \flat$ is part of the state is shown. For example, the label $0, \sharp$ refers to the state labeled $\{(\{a\}, \{b\}, 0), (\{b\}, \{c, \sharp\}, \infty)\}$. The acceptance condition of the corresponding Streett automaton is:

$$\{(\{\{(\{a\}, \{b\}, 1), (\{b\}, \{c, \flat\}, \infty)\}, \{(\{a\}, \{b, \}, 0), (\{b\}, \{c, \flat\}, \infty)\}\},$$
$$\{\{(\{a\}, \{b\}, 1), (\{b\}, \{c, \sharp\}, \infty)\}, \{(\{a\}, \{b\}, 0), (\{b\}, \{c, \sharp\}, \infty)\}\}\})\} \quad .$$

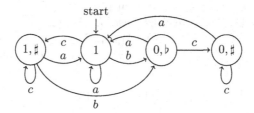

Fig. 1. Streett automaton for Example 5

Note that the state labeled $\{\{(\{a\}, \{b\}, 1), (\{b\}, \{c, b\}, \infty)\}$ is not reachable from the initial state.

A soundness proof of our construction follows. First, we establish a "shift-invariance" property similar to Lemma 5 for the language accepted by the Streett automaton.

Lemma 6. *Let S be a scheduling specification in normal form, $\mathcal{A}(S)$ its Streett automaton, $a \in \Sigma$, and $w' \in \Sigma^\omega$. If $(aw') \in \mathcal{L}(\mathcal{A}(S))$ then $w' \in \mathcal{L}(\mathcal{A}(S))$.*

Proof (sketch). Let $S = \{(E_i, F_i, L_i) \mid i \in I\}$ be a scheduling specification, $a \in \Sigma$ and $w' \in \Sigma^\omega$ such that $(aw') \in \mathcal{L}(\mathcal{A}(S))$, $(\lambda_t)_{t<\omega} = (aw')$, and $(S_t, \lambda_t)_{t<\omega}$ an accepting trajectory. Define a function $\xi : \Sigma \times \Sigma^* \times Q \to Q$ as:

$$\xi(a, \lambda_{1,t+1}, S_{t+1}) \triangleq$$
$$\{(E_i, F_i, L'_i) \mid (E_i, F_i, L'_i) \in S_{t+1} \wedge (\lambda_0 \notin F_i \vee L'_i = \infty \vee \lambda_{1,t+1}^{E_i} > 0)\} \cup$$
$$\{(E_i, F_i, L'_i + 1) \mid (E_i, F_i, L'_i) \in S_{t+1} \wedge \lambda_0 \in F_i \wedge L'_i \neq \infty \wedge \lambda_{1,t+1}^{E_i} = 0\} \quad .$$

Let $S'_0 = S$ and $S'_t = \xi(\lambda_0, \lambda_{1,t+1}, S_{t+1})$ for all $0 < t < \omega$. We show $w' \in \mathcal{L}(\mathcal{A}(S))$ by proving that $(S'_t, \lambda_{t+1})_{t<\omega}$ is an accepting trajectory on the word w'. Apparently, $w = (\lambda_{t+1})_{t<\omega}$.

We show $\xi(\lambda_0, \lambda_{1,t+1}, S_{t+1}) \in \rho(S'_t, \lambda_{t+1})$ with help of $S_{t+1} \in \rho(S_t, \lambda_t)$. Let $t < \omega$ and $(E_i, F_i, L'_i) \in S'_t$.

1. Case $\lambda_0 \in F_i \wedge L'_i \neq \infty \wedge \lambda_{1,t+1}^{E_i} = 0$. Then $(E_i, F_i, L'_i - 1) \in S_t$.
   (a) If $\lambda_t \in E_i$ then $(E_i, F_i, L_i) \in S_{t+1}$. From $\lambda_{1,t+2}^{E_i} > 0$ follows $(E_i, F_i, L_i) \in \xi(\lambda_0, \lambda_{1,t+1}, S_{t+1})$.
   (b) If $\lambda_t \in F_i$ then $(E_i, F_i, L'_i - 2) \in S_{t+1}$. Then $\lambda_{1,t+2}^{E_i} = 0$ holds and we conclude $(E_i, F_i, L'_i - 1) \in \xi(\lambda_0, \lambda_{1,t+1}, S_{t+1})$.
   (c) If $\lambda_t \notin F_i \cup E_i$, then $(E_i, F_i, L'_i - 1) \in S_{t+1}$. Then $\lambda_{1,t+2}^{E_i} = 0$ holds and we conclude $(E_i, F_i, L'_i) \in \xi(\lambda_0, \lambda_{1,t+1}, S_{t+1})$.
2. Case $\lambda_0 \notin F_i \vee L_i = \infty \vee \lambda_{1,t+1}^{E_i} > 0$. Then $(E_i, F_i, L'_i) \in S_t$.
   (a) Assume $\lambda_t \in E_i$. If $L_i = \infty$ then $(E_i, F_i \cup \{b\}, L_i) \in S_{t+1}$. Otherwise $(E_i, F_i, L_i) \in S_{t+1}$. In either case $\lambda_0 \notin F_i \vee L_i = \infty \vee \lambda_{1,t+1}^{E_i} > 0$ holds and therefore $(E_i, F_i \cup \{b\}, L_i) \in \xi(\lambda_0, \lambda_{1,t+1}, S_{t+1})$ respectively $(E_i, F_i, L_i) \in \xi(\lambda_0, \lambda_{1,t+1}, S_{t+1})$.

(b) Assume $\lambda_t \in F_i$. If $L_i = \infty$ then $(E_i, F_i \cup \{\sharp\}, L_i) \in S_{t+1}$. Otherwise $(E_i, F_i, L'_i - 1) \in S_{t+1}$. In either case $(E_i, F_i \cup \{\sharp\}, L_i) \in \xi(\lambda_0, \lambda_{1,t+1}, S_{t+1})$ respectively $(E_i, F_i, L'_i) \in \xi(\lambda_0, \lambda_{1,t+1}, S_{t+1})$.

(c) If $\lambda_t \notin F_i \cup E_i$ then $(E_i, F_i, L'_i) \in S_{t+1}$ and consequently $(E_i, F_i, L'_i) \in \xi(\lambda_0, \lambda_{1,t+1}, S_{t+1})$.

Now we proceed to show acceptance. Let $\Xi \triangleq \bigcup_{(\hat{E}_i, \hat{F}_i) \in \Omega} \{\hat{E}_i, \hat{F}_i\}$. First we show:

$$\forall \hat{X} \in \Xi : \mathrm{Inf}((S_t, \lambda_t)_{t<\omega}) \cap \hat{X} \neq \emptyset \iff \mathrm{Inf}((S'_t, \lambda_{t+1})_{t<\omega}) \cap \hat{X} \neq \emptyset . \quad (1)$$

Let $\hat{X} \in \Xi$. Case $\mathrm{Inf}((S_t, \lambda_t)_{t<\omega}) \cap \hat{X} \neq \emptyset \implies \mathrm{Inf}((S'_t, \lambda_{t+1})_{t<\omega}) \cap \hat{X} \neq \emptyset$. Let $X \in (\mathrm{Inf}((S_t, \lambda_t)_{t<\omega}) \cap \hat{X})$. Let $t < \omega$. Then $\xi(\lambda_0, \lambda_{1,t}, X) \in \mathrm{Inf}((S'_t, \lambda_{t+1})_{t<\omega})$ and since ξ does not change (E_i, F_i, L_i) when $L_i = \infty$ we have $\xi(\lambda_0, \lambda_{1,t}, X) \in \hat{X}$.

Case $\mathrm{Inf}((S'_t, \lambda_{t+1})_{t<\omega}) \cap \hat{X} \neq \emptyset \implies \mathrm{Inf}((S_t, \lambda_t)_{t<\omega}) \cap \hat{X} \neq \emptyset$. Let $t < \omega$, $X' \in \mathrm{Inf}((S'_t, \lambda_{t+1})_{t<\omega}) \cap \hat{X}$ and X such that $X' = \xi(\lambda_0, \lambda_{1,t}, X)$. Then $X \in \mathrm{Inf}((S_t, \lambda_t)_{t<\omega})$ and since ξ does not change (E_i, F_i, L_i) when $L_i = \infty$ we have $X \in \hat{X}$.

By (1) and $\mathrm{Inf}((S_t, \lambda_t)_{t<\omega})_{t<\omega}) \cap \hat{E}_i \neq \emptyset$ implies $\mathrm{Inf}((S'_t, \lambda_{t+1})_{t<\omega}) \cap \hat{E}_i \neq \emptyset$. Consequently, $(S'_t, \lambda_{t+1})_{t<\omega}$ is accepting.

Conversely, if $\mathrm{Inf}((S_t, \lambda_t)_{t<\omega})_{t<\omega}) \cap \hat{E}_i = \emptyset$, then $\mathrm{Inf}((S'_t, \lambda_{t+1})_{t<\omega}) \cap \hat{E}_i = \emptyset$ by (1). But $\mathrm{Inf}((S_t, \lambda_t)_{t<\omega})_{t<\omega}) \cap \hat{F}_i = \emptyset$ holds, $\mathrm{Inf}((S'_t, \lambda_{t+1})_{t<\omega})_{t<\omega}) \cap \hat{F}_i = \emptyset$ also holds by (1). In any case, $(S'_t, \lambda_{t+1})_{t<\omega}$ is accepting. $\qquad\square$

We can now prove the soundness of the construction with the help of that property.

Definition 8. *An event e is called* permitted *by specification* $S = \{(E_i, F_i, L_i) \mid i \in I\}$ *if and only if* $\forall i \in I : e \in F_i \implies L_i > 0$.

Theorem 2. *The language accepted by the Street automaton $\mathcal{A}(S)$ is the same as the language characterized by S.*

Proof. The proof is by co-induction. Let $(aw') \in \Sigma^\omega$. Assume $(aw') \models S \iff (aw') \in \mathcal{L}(\mathcal{A}(S))$. Define

$$\theta(S, S', e) = \{\{(E_i, F_i, L''_i) \mid (E_i, F_i, L_i) \in S \wedge (E_i, F_i, L'_i) \in S' \wedge L'_i > 0 \wedge$$
$$(L'_i = \infty \implies L''_i = \infty) \wedge (e \in E_i \implies L''_i = L_i) \wedge$$
$$(e \in F_i \implies L''_i = L'_i - 1) \wedge (e \notin E_i \cup F_i \implies L''_i = L'_i)\}\} .$$

By computation, we conclude that $\theta(S, S, a) = \{(E, F \setminus \{\flat, \sharp\}, L) \mid (E, F, L) \in \rho(S, a)\}$. From Lemmas 5 and 6 we conclude $w' \models S \iff w' \in \mathcal{L}(\mathcal{A}(S))$. $\qquad\square$

With this theorem, we have established that the construction of the automaton is correct. We will now look at the complexity of our construction. We prove that the size of the automaton is exponential in the number of constraints.

Lemma 7. *The size of the Streett automaton $\mathcal{A}(S)$ which corresponds to a scheduling specification $S = \{(E_i, F_i, L_i) \mid i \in I\}$ in normal form is $|Q| \in O(L^{|I|})$, where $L = \max (\{L_i + 1 \mid i \in I \wedge L_i \neq \infty\} \cup \{3 \mid i \in I \wedge L_i = \infty\})$.*

Proof. Since $Q \triangleq C(S)$ we show $|C(S)| \in O(L^{|I|})$. If $I = \emptyset$, then the automaton has one state. Otherwise, Def. 6 implies that for every tuple in S there is exactly one corresponding tuple in every element of $C(S)$. At most L variations of each tuple in S. Enumerating all solutions, we have $\prod_{i \in I} L$ as the upper bound. $\square$

4   Consistency of Specifications

The automata model allows us to decide many properties of the scheduling specifications. Here, the most important properties are shown.

Lemma 8. *A scheduling specification S is* consistent, *if there exists $w \in \Sigma^\omega$ with $w \models S$. Whether S is consistent is decidable.*

Proof. A scheduling specification is consistent, if the language accepted by $\mathcal{A}(S)$ is not empty. The language emptiness problem is decidable [12]. $\square$

Finally, given finite state transition systems, like UML state machines, we can decide schedulability of these machines by a scheduling specification.

Lemma 9. *For finite state transition systems, the schedulability problem is decidable.*

Proof. Let P be a finite state process. That process can be represented by a Streett automaton $\mathcal{A}(P)$. Let S be a scheduling specification. Schedulability becomes $L(\mathcal{A}(p) \parallel \mathcal{A}(S)) \stackrel{?}{=} \emptyset$, where $\parallel$ is the standard synchronous product. $\square$

Scheduling specifications may admit deadlocks, as Example 6 below shows. To formalize the possibility of deadlocks, let the set of *forbidden* events Forb(S) and the set of *permitted* events Perm(S) for states S be defined as:

$$\mathrm{Forb}(\{(E_i, F_i, L_i') \mid i \in I\}) \triangleq \bigcup_{i \in I \wedge L_i' = 0} F_i$$

$$\mathrm{Perm}(\{(E_i, F_i, L_i') \mid i \in I\}) \triangleq \Sigma \setminus \mathrm{Forb}(\{(E_i, F_i, L_i') \mid i \in I\})$$

Example 6. Consider the specification $S = \{(\{a\}, \{b, c\}, 1), (\{b\}, \{a, c\}, 1)\}$ over $\Sigma = \{a, b, c\}$. With S, infinite schedules involving only $\{a, b\}$ are feasible. Any occurrence of c moves $\mathcal{A}(S)$ into the state $S' = \{(\{a\}, \{b, c\}, 0), (\{b\}, \{a, c\}, 0)\}$ in which no event is permitted, because Forb(S) $= \Sigma$. The automaton $\mathcal{A}(S)$ is displayed in Fig. 2, where the deadlock state is labelled $0, 0$.

These deadlocks cannot be avoided, but they can be detected automatically. Although these deadlocks states are reachable it is still possible that they are never reached in real applications. Also, the approach described in Sect. 5 allows us dealing with deadlocks.

Definition 9. *We define function $D(S)$ that yields all deadlocking states reachable in scheduling automaton $\mathcal{A}(S)$.*

$$D(S) = \{S' \mid \mathrm{Perm}(S') = \emptyset \wedge S' \text{ reachable from } S\}   .$$

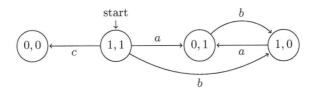

Fig. 2. Streett automaton for Example 6

Remark 3. Since automata states are closely related to the corresponding specifications, they only differ in markers, $D(S)$ also describes the deadlocking specifications reachable from specification S.

The set $D(S)$ of deadlock states can be easily computed by first constructing
the scheduler automaton and then searching for all reachable states which do
not have outgoing transitions. Using breadth-first-search we can even determine
the shortest sequence of events leading to such a state. Breadth-first-search is
linear in the number of transitions and the number of states.

5   Suspending the Scheduler

So far we have assumed that the environment provides at least the events required for the inspected trajectories. In this section we drop this assumption.
    To formalize the input of the environment we assume that each scheduling
automaton has access to an *event pool P*, or *pool* for short, that contains all
events currently available for scheduling. The pool is a *multiset* of events, i.e.,
$P \in \mathbb{N}^{\Sigma}$.[1] The environment may add new events to be scheduled to the pool,
whereas the scheduling automaton will consume these events from the pool. The
automaton may choose any event, which is *permitted* in the current state of
scheduling. The set of events of pool P that are enabled in state S is defined by:

$$\mathrm{Enab}(S, P) \triangleq \{a \in \Sigma \mid a \in \mathrm{Perm}(S) \land P(a) > 0\}$$

In real situations we cannot assume that all events needed for the system to
progress are provided by the environment. Nevertheless we want that the system
will progress, i.e., it should not wait for any event which might never occur.

Example 7. Recall Example 1. We would consider this specification to be *unreasonable* towards pedestrians on days on which no car crosses the street. Naturally,
pedestrians cross the traffic light if no car is in sight contrary to the red signal.

The formulation of that example assumes a notion of time: *on days*. We want to
suspend scheduling only *temporarily*. However, the formalism we present assumes
an untimed setting. We want that pedestrians cross the street as long as no car is

---
[1] The notation $\mathbb{N}^{\Sigma}$ represents the set of all functions of Σ into $\mathbb{N}$ and is isomorphic
to the set of all multisets over Σ.

in sight (in the pool). The arrival of the first car shall indicate that the intended scheduling is resumed. More formal: The question is, what the automaton does, if $\text{Enab}(S, P) = \emptyset$, meaning that currently no permitted event is available in the pool, especially if $\text{Perm}(S) \neq \emptyset$?

First, the automaton may wait until the environment will provide a necessary event. Such a strategy will lead us into assumption-commitment style reasoning. In principle, the system should be allowed to assume that it is always the case that in every state a transition will eventually be enabled. However, this assumption-commitment style reasoning is outside the scope of this paper. Here, we want to focus on the situation that the environment is "demonic". It need not happen that it will provide one of the permitted events and the scheduler needs to choose an event contrary to its defining specification in order to make progress. This is done by suspending the scheduling automaton in these situations and switching to some different scheduling automaton. In terms of assumption-commitment violation, our situation refers to the violation of the assumption that the environment always provides necessary events (in time). Then the scheduling automaton need not commit to anything.

The situation where no event at all is allowed in the current state of scheduling, already addresses in the previous Sect. 4, can be handled by the approach described in this section.

If we prioritize the scheduling automaton, we may on the other hand starve other sub-specifications.

We have two cases:

1. Choosing one event may reset one of the limits and by this enable more events in the next step. This causes a change of state in the automaton.
   (a) $a \notin \text{Perm}(S)$ implies $a \in \text{Forb}(S)$ and the situation is handled in the preceding section.
   (b) $a \in \text{Perm}(S)$ but then $P(a) > 0$, then $a \in \text{Enab}(S, P)$, in contradiction to our assumption.
2. Choosing one event does not reset one of the limits of the automaton, because it does not change the state.

Definition 10. *A* modal specification *is a set of* guarded and extended *specifications of the form* $\phi \implies (S, U)$, *where* ϕ *is generated by the grammar* $\phi ::= \top \mid a \mid \neg\phi \mid \phi \wedge \phi \mid \phi \vee \phi$, *where* $a \in \Sigma$, S *is a specification following Def. 1 and* $U \subseteq \Sigma$ *is called* exit-set.

A pool satisfies a condition (written $P \models \phi$), *if and only if:*

1. $P \models \top$.
2. $P \models a$ *if* $P(a) > 0$
3. $P \models \neg\phi$ *if not* $P \models \phi$.
4. $P \models \phi \wedge \phi'$ *if* $P \models \phi$ *and* $P \models \phi'$.
5. $P \models \phi \vee \phi'$ *if* $P \models \phi$ *or* $P \models \phi'$.

Modal specifications are used to define how scheduling shall continue ($P \models \phi$) when it is required (there exists an event in the exit-set U which is in the pool), once a policy cannot progress.

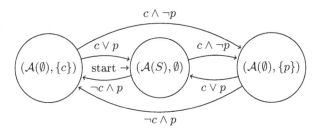

Fig. 3. Automaton for Example 8

Example 8. A possible modal specification of the pedestrian/car scheduler is:

$$c \vee p \implies (\{(\{c\}, \{p\}, l_p), (\{p\}, \{c\}, l_c)\}, \emptyset)$$
$$c \wedge \neg p \implies (\emptyset, \{p\})$$
$$\neg c \wedge p \implies (\emptyset, \{c\}) \quad .$$

The resulting scheduling automaton is displayed in Fig. 3 where the histories are not considered.

We refine the definition of enabledness for exit-sets:

$$\text{Enab}(S, U, P) \triangleq \begin{cases} \emptyset & \text{if } \exists a : P(a) > 0 \wedge a \in U \\ \{a \in \Sigma \mid a \in \text{Perm}(S) \wedge P(a) > 0\} & \text{otherwise.} \end{cases}$$

Now we can capture the intuition of scheduler suspension: if $\text{Enab}(S, U, P) = \emptyset$ and $\exists l \in L : P \models \phi_l$, then we continue with the scheduling policy defined by element l of the modal specification.

Definition 11. *Let L be a finite set of indexes and $\{(\phi_l \implies (S_l, U_l)) \mid l \in L\}$ a modal specification. We define the corresponding modal scheduling automaton as follows: The set of states is in $\{(\mathcal{A}_l, U_l, H) \mid l \in L \wedge H \subseteq C(S)\}$, where $\mathcal{A}(S_l)$ as defined in Def. 7. The initial state is defined to be $(S : \mathcal{A}(S), \emptyset)$ and the transition function with respect to states $(\mathcal{A}_j, U_j, H)$ is defined as follows:*

1. *If $\exists a : P(a) > 0$, $\text{Enab}(S, U_j, P) = \emptyset$, $P \models \phi_l$, $Q_l \cap H = \{S'\}$, then $(S : \mathcal{A}_j, U_j, H) \to (S' : \mathcal{A}_l, U_l, (H \setminus \{S'\}) \cup \{S\})$,*
2. *If $\exists a : P(a) > 0$, $\text{Enab}(S, U_j, P) = \emptyset$, $P \models \phi_l$, $\forall k \in \{l \mid P \models \phi_l\} : Q_k \cap H = \emptyset$, then $(S : \mathcal{A}_j, U_j, H) \to (S^0 : \mathcal{A}_k, U_k, H \cup \{S\})$, and*

Where $\mathcal{A}_l$ denotes the automaton corresponding to modal specification l and Q_l denotes the states the automaton, where $S : \mathcal{A}$ denotes that execution continues in state S and where $S^0 : \mathcal{A}$ continuation in the initial state of automaton $\mathcal{A}$.

Observe that U_j defines those events, which, when present in the pool, cause a change of the scheduling mode. Thus we should have some distinguished modal specification with $U_l = \emptyset$. This mode describes a *normal mode* of execution. By condition $\text{Enab}(S, U, P) = \emptyset$ in every of the above cases we ensure that scheduling automaton transitions have priority over modal scheduling automaton transitions. Thus maximal progress in normal mode is ensured by $U = \emptyset$.

Example 9. We consider some special right-hand sides of modal specifications.

1. $(\emptyset, \emptyset)$ is the universal specification. It will never be changed and allows every scheduling.
2. $(S, \emptyset)$ for a non-empty scheduling specification S describes a scheduling policy which is only suspended if $\text{Enab}(S, \emptyset, P)$.
3. $(\emptyset, U)$ where $U \neq \emptyset$ describes a universal scheduling policy which allows any event to be scheduled as long as there is no event of U in the pool.

Let us return to Example 8. The initial scheduling, which we already described in Example 1 is maintained as long as we can choose events from the pool. Once only events are available in the pool which are forbidden in the current configuration, say cars c, a transition from the normal mode to the suspension mode $(\emptyset, \{p\})$ is permitted. When should we change back? During the universal behavior, car events may be scheduled *unless a pedestrian p is in the pool*, because the exit set is $\{p\}$. The behavior with which the scheduling will resume depends on the content of the pool:

1. If a car c is in the pool, then the automaton must resume with the initial scheduling, because the guard $p \vee c$ holds and the guard $p \wedge \neg c$ does not hold.
2. If no car c is in the pool, then the automaton may *choose* between resuming the initial specification or $(\emptyset, \{c\})$, because both guards $p \vee c$ and $p \wedge \neg c$ hold.

Finally, the modal specification automata can be flattened to flat extended transition systems with Streett fairness assumptions. The transition system uses condition on event pools in addition to the currently scheduled event. The exact details of that construction are standard and not described in this paper.

6   Conclusions and Future Work

We have described a simple language for specifying bounded and fair scheduling constraints. We described a formal semantics for that language and showed how we can obtain a Streett automaton that accepts only and all schedules that satisfy the specification.

These automata can then be composed with a system, and if there are only bounded requirements in the Street acceptance it is sufficient to examine the composition of the system and the automaton, which is finite, in order to show that the system is fair, i.e. fairness can then be proved automatically.

Finally, we addressed the issue of uncooperative environments. If the environment does not send expected messages, scheduling may be suspended until the expected message arrives. We define a semantics of these transition systems.

Concerning future work, we point out that the presentation of this paper was mostly focused on the semantics of our language. We will develop a concrete syntax as a next step, probably based on a variant of UML state machines, whose hierarchicy looks well suited different modes of a specification.

Game based methods may provide more efficient means for finding possible deadlocks, because the automaton need not be constructed completely. It may even be possible to decide consistency and possible deadlocks statically.

The properties of modal scheduling will be investigated in the future.

Finally, we plan to integrate this language into the modeling language Creol, which allows us to specify the scheduling of method activations. Similar to [13] it may facilitate testing. Our notation is simpler, because we only order events, but we believe that it is therefore more accessible.

Acknowledgments. We thank H. Fecher for pointing out the possibility of deadlocks, H. Fecher and H. Schmidt for valuable insight provided during fruitful discussions, and thank the anonymous reviewers for their valuable suggestions.

References

1. Object Management Group: UML 2.1.2 Superstructure Specification (2007), http://www.omg.org/cgi-bin/docs/formal/2007-11-02.pdf
2. Streett, R.S.: Propositional dynamic logic of looping and converse is elementary decidable. Information and Control 54(1/2), 121–141 (1982)
3. Johnsen, E.B., Owe, O., Yu, I.C.: Creol: A type-safe object-oriented model for distributed concurrent systems. TCS 365(1–2), 23–66 (2006)
4. Fischer, M.J., Lynch, N.A., Paterson, M.: Impossibility of distributed consensus with one faulty process. J. ACM 32(2), 374–382 (1985)
5. Alur, R., Henzinger, T.A.: Finitary fairness. ACM Trans. Program. Lang. Syst. 20(6), 1171–1194 (1998)
6. Apt, K.R., Olderog, E.R.: Proof rules dealing with fairness. In: Kozen, D. (ed.) Logic of Programs, vol. 131, pp. 1–8. Springer, Heidelberg (1982)
7. Kang, M., Wilbur, S.: A fair guaranteed down-link sharing scheme for cellular switched networks. In: GLOBECOM 1997, Phoenix, AZ, USA, vol. 2, pp. 1006–1010. IEEE Computer Society Press, Los Alamitos (1997)
8. Tidwell, T., Gill, C., Subramonian, V.: Scheduling induced bounds and the verification of preemptive real-time systems. Technical Report 2007-34, Washington University in St.Louis, Department of Computer Science & Engineering (2007)
9. Ramanujam, R., Lodaya, K.: Proving fairness of schedulers. In: Parikh, R. (ed.) Logic of Programs 1985. LNCS, vol. 193, pp. 284–301. Springer, Heidelberg (1985)
10. Backes, M., Pfitzmann, B., Steiner, M., Waidner, M.: Polynomial fairness and liveness. In: CSFW, pp. 160–174. IEEE Computer Society, Los Alamitos (2002)
11. Hojati, R., Singhal, V., Brayton, R.K.: Edge-streett/ edge-rabin automata environment for formal verification using language containment. Memorandum ERL-94-12, University of California at Berkeley, Berkeley, CA, USA (1994)
12. Thomas, W.: Automata on infinite objects. In: van Leeuwen, J. (ed.) Handbook of Theoretical Computer Science, pp. 165–191. MIT Press, Cambridge (1990)
13. Schlatte, R., Aichernig, B., de Boer, F., Griesmayer, A., Johnsen, E.B.: Testing concurrent objects with application-specific schedulers. In: Fitzgerald, J., Haxthausen, A., Yenigün, H. (eds.) ICTAC. LNCS, vol. 5160, pp. 318–332. Springer, Heidelberg (2008)

Fair Exchange Is Incomparable to Consensus

Simona Orzan[1] and Mohammad Torabi Dashti[2]

[1] Technical University of Eindhoven, The Netherlands
[2] ETH Zürich, Switzerland

Abstract. In asynchronous systems where processes are prone to crash failures, we show that fair exchange is incomparable to distributed consensus. By incomparability we mean there exist failure detector classes that solve fair exchange and not distributed consensus, and vice versa. Remarkably, this is in contrast to the folklore belief that solving fair exchange is generally harder than solving distributed consensus.

1 Introduction

Distributed consensus (DC) is an essential building block for fault-tolerant distributed computing (e.g. see [27]). Fair exchange (FE) is a fundamental problem in computer security, upon which various contract signing, certified email, and non-repudiation protocols are built [5,14,1,28]. There are remarkable similarities between these two problems, as observed by Tygar [38] and Pagnia and Gärtner [30]. The goal of this paper is to give a formal comparison between FE and DC in asynchronous multiparty settings. A clear picture of this relation has two immediate benefits: (1) from a practical point of view, this would help in translating efficient solutions of one to the other, as much research has been done independently on these two problems so far, and (2) from a theoretical point of view, this can give us a better understanding of the limits of *solvability* of FE, as solvability for DC is to a great extent well understood.

(Un)solvability criteria for DC, such as [18,9,8], virtually define the boundaries of *what is possible* in fault-tolerant distributed computing, and have therefore been subject to intense research. Below, we give a chronological overview on work dealing with solvability of FE (in deterministic systems):

In synchronous systems, Even and Yacobi [15] (1980), and independently Rabin [34] (1981), informally argue that two processes cannot fairly exchange secrets, when one of them is prone to Byzantine failure. This negative result has been later on formalized by DeMilo, Lynch and Merritt [12]. However, in fully connected network topologies, the completeness theorems of Ben-Or, Goldwasser and Wigderson [4] (independently derived in [10]) show that, in the presence of t Byzantine processes, any secure n party computation, including FE and DC, can be solved when $t < \frac{n}{3}$.

In asynchronous systems, Pagnia and Gärtner show that when one process is prone to crash failure, DC between two processes is reducible to FE, which entails that FE is *harder* than DC [30]. This, along with the impossibility of DC in such settings [18], establish the unsolvability of FE. It is worth noticing that

J.S. Fitzgerald, A.E. Haxthausen, and H. Yenigun (Eds.): ICTAC 2008, LNCS 5160, pp. 349–363, 2008.
© Springer-Verlag Berlin Heidelberg 2008

the unsolvability result of [15] (and [34,12]) is based on the malicious act of with-holding (parts of) information, whereas in [30], inability to decide termination in asynchronous systems when processes may crash is used to imply unsolvability of FE. These, thus, establish their results based on orthogonal difficulties in solving FE, and neither of them immediately follows from the other.

A natural question at this point is: Can we conclude that FE is solvable only in the settings in which DC is solvable? In other words, is solving FE harder than solving DC? The answer turns out to be negative, as we contend in this paper.

We show that the reduction of DC to FE in [30] is bound to two processes, and does not hold in general. We prove that in asynchronous systems where partic-ipating processes are prone to crash failures, while a majority of the processes are correct, FE is *incomparable* to DC. That is, there exist failure detector classes that solve FE and not DC, and vice versa. This is in contrast to the folklore belief that solving FE is harder than solving DC (e.g. see [30,16]). To prove this re-sult, we build upon Guerraoui's work on incomparability of non-blocking atomic commit (NBAC) to DC [25]. As a side note, we describe why in the special case of only two participating processes, FE is indeed harder than DC, hence com-ing to terms with the previous result of Pagnia and Gärtner [30]. We use an LTL [33] formalization to define the DC, NBAC and FE problems. This removes doubts about what textual requirements for FE, often found in the literature, might mean. The LTL formulas are interpreted in the well-accepted finite state machine model, widely used in the distributed computing literature (e.g. [9]). This neatly places the FE security problem into a framework often used to reason about distributed computing. Other approaches to formal definition of the FE requirements, such as game theory, have been investigated in [32,30,31,6,22].

Our incomparability result is stated in asynchronous models, where processes may *crash*. The choice of this model has certain implications: (1) It follows that in more sophisticated models where faulty processes are allowed to misbehave beyond benign crashes (such as crash-recovery, or Byzantine failure models), FE and DC remain incomparable. Therefore, our result draws an incomparability line in stronger failure models as well. (2) In practical terms, crash failures are usually considered to be simplistic for design and analysis of security protocols. Although this weakens the relevance of our result to some practical scenarios, we point out that recent advances in trusted computing devices, and their use in security protocols, allow for more restricted hostile environment models. In particular, in section 4, we discuss how our model is related to the existing literature on practical realizations of FE using *guardians* and *TrustedPals*.

Road map. We start with introducing the notions and notations used in the paper in section 2. In section 3 we present our incomparability result. Section 4 discusses related work, while section 5 concludes the paper.

2   Preliminaries

We consider the asynchronous message passing model of [18], plus the failure detector abstraction of [9]. A brief description of this model follows.

The System Model. We consider n processes, $\Omega = \{p_1, \cdots, p_n\}$, sitting on the nodes of a fully connected communication graph. No bound is assumed on their clock drifts, or the time needed to complete a local instruction. The bidirectional channels that connect these processes are *asynchronous*, i.e. they guarantee to eventually deliver sent messages, but no time bounds or specific ordering is enforced. The processes are prone to *crash failures*, i.e. a failed process ceases to act from the point of crash onwards. A process that does not crash is *correct*.

We assume a discrete global clock, which is not accessible to the participating processes. The range of the clock, denoted Φ, is the set of natural numbers.

A *failure pattern* is a non-decreasing function $F : \Phi \to 2^{\Omega}$, where $F(t)$ contains the set of crashed processes at time t. An *environment* E is a set of failure patterns. Although processes do not have direct access to F, each process has a local *failure detector module* which gives hints about the processes that are *suspected* of crash. Failure detector modules can in general make mistakes. A *failure detector* is intuitively such a distributed oracle. A *failure detector history* is a function $H : \Omega \times \Phi \to 2^{\Omega}$. Intuitively, $H(p, t)$ characterizes the output of the failure detector module hosted in process p, at time t. A failure detector class **D** is a function that maps any failure pattern to a set of failure detector histories.

An *algorithm* assigns a finite state machine to each $p \in \Omega$. At time $t \in \Phi$, three tasks are performed atomically: (1) p picks a message non-deterministically from the set of buffered incoming messages, or receives the null message λ, (2) p gets the value of $H(p, t)$ from its local failure detector module, (3) p performs a computation based on the values from (1) and (2) and its current state, selects a next state, and sends out a message (possibly none) to another process $q \in \Omega$.

A *configuration* is a pair (P, M), where P is the Cartesian product of the states of elements of Ω, and M is a multiset of messages, containing the messages buffered for delivery. The *initial* configuration is $(P_0, \emptyset)$, where P_0 is the Cartesian product of the initial states of the elements of Ω. A *transition* is a triple $\theta = (p_i, m, d)$, where p_i is the process that takes the transition, m is the message that p_i receives, and d is the value that p_i reads off its local failure detector module. Clearly, θ is applicable to (P, M) only if $m \in M \cup \{\lambda\}$. The unique configuration resulted is denoted $\theta((P, M))$.

The *Kripke structure* resulting from the asynchronous interleaving of the transitions of processes in Ω, is a triple $(C, \hat{c}_0, R)$, where C is a countable set of configurations, $\hat{c}_0 = (P_0, \emptyset)$, and $R \subseteq C \times C$ is defined as: $(c, c') \in R$ iff $c' = \theta(c)$, for an applicable θ. $c \in C$ is *reachable* iff $(\hat{c}_0, c) \in R^*$, the reflexive transitive closure of R. We only consider reachable configurations. A *trace* in $K = (C, \hat{c}_0, R)$ is an infinite sequence of configurations $\gamma = c_0, c_1, \ldots$, such that $\forall i \geq 0.\ (c_i, c_{i+1}) \in R$. We say γ is *rooted* iff $c_0 = \hat{c}_0$. When $T = t_0, t_1, \ldots$ is an increasing sequence of natural numbers and γ is rooted, $\sigma = (\gamma, T)$ is an *execution* in K. For $\sigma = (\gamma, T)$, we abuse the notation and write $F(\sigma) = \cup_{t \in T} F(t)$.

The LTL Logic. We use a subset of LTL [33] for describing properties of Kripke structures. For a finite set of atomic propositions AP,

- If $a \in AP$, then a is an LTL formula.
- If ϕ and ϕ' are LTL formulas, then so are $\neg\phi$, $\phi \vee \phi'$ and $\Diamond\phi$.

As shorthands, we write $\phi \wedge \phi'$ for $\neg(\neg\phi \vee \neg\phi')$, and $\Box\phi$ for $\neg\Diamond(\neg\phi)$.

Given a Kripke structure $K = (C, \hat{c}_0, R)$, a *labeling* function $[\cdot] : C \to 2^{AP}$ assigns propositions to the configurations. Intuitively, for a configuration c, the set $[c]$ is the set of atomic propositions (elements of AP) true at c. For example, $(y_p \neq y_q) \in [c]$ iff the value of y_p is different from y_q at configuration c. Other propositions are likewise interpreted in the natural way.

Kripke structures are models of LTL formulas. We say K satisfies formula ϕ iff for all rooted traces γ in K, $\gamma \models \phi$. For γ being a trace in K, and ϕ an LTL formula, the relation $\gamma \models \phi$ is defined below. We let $\gamma = c_0, \cdots, c_n, c_{n+1}, \ldots$, and write $\gamma^n = c_n, c_{n+1}, \ldots$.

- $\gamma \models a$, with $a \in AP$, iff $a \in [c_0]$.
- $\gamma \models \neg\phi$, iff $\neg(\gamma \models \phi)$.
- $\gamma \models \phi \vee \phi'$, iff $\gamma \models \phi$ or $\gamma \models \phi'$.
- $\gamma \models \Diamond(\phi)$, iff $\exists n \geq 0.\ \gamma^n \models \phi$.

Intuitively, $\Diamond$ expresses eventual reachability, while $\Box$ is used for invariants.

Problem Definitions. We now specify the requirements of the DC, NBAC and FE problems using LTL formulas. As a syntactic shorthand, we use quantifiers inside the formulas. Since Ω is finite, existential ($\exists$) and universal ($\forall$) quantifiers over elements of Ω can be rewritten into a finite number of disjunctions and conjunctions, respectively. Therefore, these formulas remain inside LTL.

Definition 1 (DC). *Consider a set of items $V = \{0, 1\}$. Each process $p \in \Omega$ starts with a pair (x_p, y_p), where $x_p \in V$ is its input item, and $y_p \in V \cup \{b\}$ is a write-once buffer containing the process's output item. We assume $\forall p \in \Omega.\ y_p = b$ at the initial state. An algorithm is said to solve DC using a failure detector class $\mathbf{D}$ for environment E, iff, for any crash failure pattern $F \in E$ and any $H \in \mathbf{D}(F)$, every rooted execution $\sigma = (\gamma, T)$ in the Kripke structure resulting from the algorithm satisfies the following properties:*

- *Termination: $\forall p \notin F(\sigma).\ \Diamond(y_p \neq b)$.* [1]
- *Agreement: $\forall p, q \notin F(\sigma).\ \Box((y_p \neq b \wedge y_q \neq b) \Rightarrow y_p = y_q)$.*
- *Validity: $\forall p \notin F(\sigma).\ \Box(y_p = b \vee (\exists q \in \Omega.\ y_p = x_q))$.* [2]

Definition 2 (NBAC). *Consider a set of items $V = \{0, 1\}$. Each process $p \in \Omega$ starts with a pair (x_p, y_p), where $x_p \in V$ is its input item (also called vote), and $y_p \in V \cup \{b\}$ is a write-once buffer containing the process's output item. We assume $\forall p \in \Omega.\ y_p = b$ at the initial state. An algorithm is said to solve NBAC using a failure detector class $\mathbf{D}$ for environment E, iff, for any crash failure pattern $F \in E$ and any $H \in \mathbf{D}(F)$, every rooted execution $\sigma = (\gamma, T)$ in the Kripke structure resulting from the algorithm satisfies the following properties:*

---

[1] At configuration c, $y_p \neq b$ holds (i.e. $(y_p \neq b) \in [c]$) iff process p has assigned a value to its local y_p that is different from b, and similarly for other propositions.

[2] This variant of the validity condition is sometimes called *uniform validity* [9].

- *Termination:* $\forall p \notin F(\sigma).\ \Diamond(y_p \neq b)$.
- *Agreement:* $\forall p, q \notin F(\sigma).\ \Box((y_p \neq b \wedge y_q \neq b) \Rightarrow y_p = y_q)$.
- *A-validity:* $(\exists q \in \Omega.\ x_q = 0) \Rightarrow \forall p \notin F(\sigma).\ \Box(y_p \neq b \Rightarrow y_p = 0)$.
- *C-validity:* $(F(\sigma) = \emptyset \wedge \forall q \in \Omega.\ x_q = 1) \Rightarrow \forall p \in \Omega.\ \Box(y_p \neq b \Rightarrow y_p = 1)$.

Intuitively, in NBAC processes aim for output 1. Each process has however a right to veto the outcome, by voting 0. We note that when every process votes 1, and then one crashes, A-validity and C-validity enforce no particular outcome for the NBAC problem. Thus, in such cases, both 0 and 1 are legitimate outcomes.

Now, we turn to the requirements of FE. Fair exchange aims at exchanging items in a *fair* manner. Informally, fair means that either all the participants receive a desired item in exchange for their own, or none of them does so. In the literature, there are various definitions for multiparty FE, depending on which topology is chosen, whether one unit or more are exchanged, etc., see [21,29].

Below, we focus on *ring exchange patterns* [21], where processes are sitting in a ring and each process p receives its desired item from its predecessor and sends its item to its successor. The underlying communication network is nonetheless a fully connected graph. Since any permutation can be decomposed into disjoint cycles [21], this pattern can capture any exchange situation in which each process has one unit of item to offer and expects one unit of item in exchange.

The '+' and '-' operators on indexes of Ω are calculated modulo n, the size of Ω. We confine the items exchanged to single bits. Our results can naturally be extended to the case in which arbitrary strings of bits are subject to exchange.

Definition 3 (FE). *Consider a set of items $V = \{0, 1\}$. Each process $p \in \Omega$ starts with a pair (x_p, y_p), where $x_p \in V$ is its input item, and $y_p \in V \cup \{b, \bot\}$ is a write-once buffer containing the process's output item. We assume $\forall p \in \Omega.\ y_p = b$ at the initial state. An algorithm is said to solve FE using a failure detector class $\mathbf{D}$ for environment E, iff, for any crash failure pattern $F \in E$ and any $H \in \mathbf{D}(F)$, every rooted execution $\sigma = (\gamma, T)$ in the Kripke structure resulting from the algorithm satisfies the following properties:*

- *Soundness:* $\forall p \notin F(\sigma).\ \Box(y_p \neq b \Rightarrow (y_p = \bot \vee y_p = x_{p-1}))$.
- *Timeliness:* $\forall p \notin F(\sigma).\ \Diamond(y_p \neq b)$.
- *Effectiveness:* $F(\sigma) = \emptyset \Rightarrow \forall p \in \Omega.\ \Box(y_p \neq b \Rightarrow y_p = x_{p-1})$.
- *Fairness:* $\forall p \notin F(\sigma).\ \Box((y_{p+1} = x_p \wedge y_p \neq b) \Rightarrow y_p = x_{p-1})$.
- *Consistency:* $\forall p, q \notin F(\sigma).\ \Box((y_p = \bot \wedge y_q \neq b) \Rightarrow y_q = \bot)$.

Intuitively, $\bot$ is the mark of *unsuccessful* exchanges. The soundness requirement enforces that all unsuccessful correct processes assign $\bot$ to their output buffer. Since we are in the crash failure model, when p receives an item from $p - 1$, it can be sure that the received item is indeed x_{p-1}. In the presence of Byzantine failures, in order to recognize the right item, p is usually assumed to have a *description* of x_{p-1}, which characterizes x_{p-1} "with enough precision" [1].

Timeliness forces termination of non-faulty processes. Effectiveness is a sanity check, ensuring that if every process is correct, the exchanges are indeed successful. A weaker variant of effectiveness is used in [7], where if $F(\sigma) = \emptyset$, then only one (as opposed to all) execution of the algorithm is required to satisfy $\forall p \in \Omega.\ \square(y_p \neq b \Rightarrow y_p = x_{p-1})$. Fairness states that if a non-faulty process reveals its item to its successor, it will certainly receive the item of its predecessor. The consistency condition guarantees that either all the non-faulty processes terminate successfully, or none of them do so. In some applications, the consistency requirement is deemed unnecessary for FE, e.g. fair certified email protocols typically allow some of the correct processes being excluded from the exchange, while the rest exchange their items, cf. [23]. However, some protocols, such as fair contract signing protocols, explicitly rely on consistency, cf. [24].

Note that if a crash occurs (i.e. $F(\sigma) \neq \emptyset$), the FE requirements do not enforce the exchange to be unsuccessful (or to be successful). This is because crashes may occur after faulty processes have sent out their items to the corresponding processes, thus potentially allowing correct process to terminate successfully.

Remark 1. If a process p crashes after it has completed its role in an execution σ, i.e. it has assigned a value to y_p, formally we have $p \in F(\sigma)$. It is however unreasonable to allow the behavior of p after it has left the protocol to affect the algorithm (and the requirements of the problem). Therefore for any execution σ, if p assigns a value to y_p at time t and $p \notin F(t)$, we assume $p \notin F(\sigma)$.

Solvability and Comparability. We say that a failure detector class **D** solves problem B in environment E, iff there exists an algorithm using **D** and its execution in E results in a Kripke structure that satisfies B's specification. A problem B_1 is *harder* than problem B_2 for E, denoted by $E \vdash B_2 \rightarrow B_1$, iff any failure detector class **D** that solves B_1 in E, also solves B_2 in E. [3] When $\neg(E \vdash B_1 \rightarrow B_2)$ and $\neg(E \vdash B_2 \rightarrow B_1)$, we say B_1 and B_2 are *E-incomparable*. Problems B_1 and B_2 are *incomparable* if they are *E-incomparable* for some environment E. When $E \vdash B_1 \rightarrow B_2$ and $E \vdash B_2 \rightarrow B_1$, B_1 and B_2 are *E-equivalent*.

A failure detector class $\mathbf{D}_1$ is said to be *weaker* than failure detector class $\mathbf{D}_2$ in environment E, denoted $E \vdash \mathbf{D}_1 \preceq \mathbf{D}_2$, iff there exists a distributed algorithm that, given the information provided by $\mathbf{D}_2$, can emulate $\mathbf{D}_1$ in E.

Failure Detector Classes $\Diamond\mathcal{S}$, $\mathcal{P}$ and $\mathcal{B}$. Of particular interest in this paper are the *eventually strong* failure detector class $\Diamond\mathcal{S}$, the *perfect* failure detector class $\mathcal{P}$ and the *stillborn* failure detector class $\mathcal{B}$. The brief description below is mainly borrowed from [37]. For extensive discussions we refer to [9,37,25].

A failure detector class **D** is *strongly complete* if every crashed process is eventually suspected by (failure detector modules at) every correct process, that is for each execution $\sigma = (\gamma, T)$, we have $\exists t.\forall t' \geq t.\forall p \in F(\sigma), q \notin F(\sigma).\ p \in H(q, t')$. The class **D** is *strongly accurate* if no process is ever suspected if it has not crashed. More precisely, if for each execution $\sigma = (\gamma, T)$, we have $\forall t.\forall p, q \notin F(t).\ p \notin H(q, t)$. The class **D** is *eventually weakly accurate* if there exist a time and a correct process that is not suspected after that time. More precisely, if for each execution $\sigma = (\gamma, T)$, we have $\exists t.\exists p \notin F(\sigma).\forall t' \geq t.\forall q \notin F(\sigma).\ p \notin H(q, t')$.

---

[3] To be precise, *harder* here stands for *at least as hard as*.

Eventually strong detectors ($\Diamond\mathcal{S}$) are the class of strongly complete and eventually weakly accurate failure detectors. Perfect detectors ($\mathcal{P}$) are the class of strongly complete and strongly accurate failure detectors. The stillborn detectors ($\mathcal{B}$), originally introduced in [25], behave as perfect detectors $\mathcal{P}$ if no process initially crashes, i.e. $F(0) = \emptyset$. However, if $F(0) \neq \emptyset$, then every failure detector module at every correct process permanently "suspects" its own host process. More precisely, we have $\forall t.\forall p \notin F(t).\ H(p, t) = \{p\}$. This is a way to inform the correct processes that *some other* process has initially crashed.

From a practical point of view, as noted in [25], $\mathcal{B}$ and $\mathcal{P}$ effectively require the same underlying synchronization mechanism. However, $\mathcal{B}$ is formally weaker than $\mathcal{P}$, and can serve as a technical means to differentiate between synchrony requirements of FE and DC, as shown below.

3   FE and DC Are Incomparable

We show that DC and FE are incomparable in asynchronous environments, where a majority of processes are correct (that is, $|F(\sigma)| < \frac{n}{2}$ for each execution σ), while at least two processes can crash. Below, the symbol **E** is fixed to refer to such an environment.[4]

Theorem 1. FE *is incomparable to* DC.

Proof. To prove this theorem, it is shown that DC and FE are **E**-incomparable. We follow the proof technique of [25]. The proof consists of two parts:

1. To establish $\neg(\mathbf{E} \vdash \mathsf{FE} \rightarrow \mathsf{DC})$, it is enough to prove that the failure detector class $\Diamond\mathcal{S}$ does not solve FE in **E**, as lemma 1 below shows. It is a well-known result that $\Diamond\mathcal{S}$ does solve DC in **E**, see [9].
2. To establish $\neg(\mathbf{E} \vdash \mathsf{DC} \rightarrow \mathsf{FE})$, we make use of the stillborn failure detector $\mathcal{B}$. Lemma 2 below proves that $\mathcal{B}$ does solve FE. As shown in [25] (lemma 3.4), $\neg(\mathbf{E} \vdash \Diamond\mathcal{S} \preceq \mathcal{B})$. Since $\Diamond\mathcal{S}$ is the weakest failure detector that solves DC [8], i.e. $\Diamond\mathcal{S}$ can be emulated by any failure detector that solves DC, hence $\mathcal{B}$ does not solve DC in **E**.

This completes the proof. $\square$

Lemma 1. FE *is not solvable using* $\Diamond\mathcal{S}$ *in* **E**.

Proof. We prove this lemma by showing that $\mathbf{E} \vdash \mathsf{NBAC} \rightarrow \mathsf{FE}$. As NBAC cannot be solved in **E** using $\Diamond\mathcal{S}$ (see [25], lemma 3.1), it follows that FE can also not be solved using $\Diamond\mathcal{S}$ in **E**.

Algorithm 1 (specified for process p, which as input receives (x_p, y_p), where x_p is the initial vote of the process) solves NBAC, given that a black-box procedure to solve FE is available to the processes. Translating this pseudo-code to a finite state machine (cf. section 2) is straightforward. The proposed construct asserts $\mathbf{E} \vdash \mathsf{NBAC} \rightarrow \mathsf{FE}$.

---

[4] The condition that at least two processes can crash in **E** is required to ensure the validity of $\neg(\mathbf{E} \vdash \Diamond\mathcal{S} \preceq \mathcal{B})$, needed in the proof of theorem 1.

Algorithm 1. E ⊢ NBAC → FE

```
 1: let i_p := x_p;
 2: for cntr_p := 1 to n − 1 do
 3:     let o_p := b;
 4:     FE(i_p, o_p);
 5:     if o_p = ⊥ then
 6:         let y_p := 0;
 7:         quit;
 8:     else if o_p ≠ ⊥ then
 9:         let i_p := i_p × o_p;
10:     end if
11: end for
12: let y_p := i_p;
13: quit;
```

Intuitive description of algorithm 1: We think of the processes who want to perform NBAC as being placed on a ring (conforming to the ring exchange pattern of the FE procedure available to the processes). The algorithm consists of $n − 1$ rounds, where $n = |\Omega|$. In each round, each process receives the vote of its predecessor, and sends its vote to its successor, both using the FE procedure available to it. Each process updates its vote to the product of its vote and the value it receives from its predecessor (here, we could in effect use the *min* function instead of product).

If no failure occurs, after $n − 1$ rounds, the initial vote of each process is propagated through the entire ring. Finally, for each p, y_p is assigned with $\Pi_{q \in \Omega} x_q = x_{p_1} \times \cdots \times x_{p_n}$. If $\forall q \in \Omega.\ x_q = 1$, then each y_p is assigned with 1. However, if there exists a process whose initial vote is 0, then $\Pi_{q \in \Omega} = 0$, resulting in $y_p = 0$ for all $p \in \Omega$.

Correctness of algorithm 1:

- (termination) The termination of this algorithm relies on the timeliness property of FE. Note that the only possible blocking point in the code is the call to FE; the rest of the code is executed purely locally. However, from timeliness of FE (see definition 3) we know that $\forall p \notin F(\sigma).\ \Diamond(o_p \neq b)$, i.e. in each FE call, any correct process p eventually assigns a value to o_p.

- (agreement) Let $\sigma = (\gamma, T)$ be an execution of the algorithm. We distinguish two possibilities for σ: (1) $F(\sigma) = \emptyset$, (2) $F(\sigma) \neq \emptyset$. In case (1), due to effectiveness of FE, all the processes assign $y_p := \Pi_{q \in \Omega}\ x_q$, thus $y_p = y_q$ for any two processes p and q for which $y_p \neq b$ and $y_q \neq b$. Agreement is therefore satisfied in this case.

  In case (2), let us assume the first crash happens at time t. We distinguish three cases for t: (a) t is before the last (i.e. the $n − 1^{th}$) call to FE occurs, (b) t is placed in the time interval in which the last call to FE has started, but has not finishes yet, (c) the last call to FE has completed before t.

  In case (a), observe that all correct processes will assign $y_p := 0$. This is because of fairness and consistency of FE that any $p \notin F(\sigma)$ will receive

$o_p = \perp$ in its next FE call, which is definitely forthcoming. In case (b), both outcomes $o_p = \perp$ and $o_p \neq \perp$ are possible. However, the outcome would in any event be consistent, due to consistency of FE. Therefore, in both these situations, $y_p = y_q$ for any two processes $p, q \notin F(\sigma)$ for which $y_p \neq b$ and $y_q \neq b$. In case (c), all the correct processes will assign $y_p := \Pi_{q \in \Omega}\, x_q$, hence meeting agreement. This is due to effectiveness of FE that any process receives $o_p \neq \perp$. We remark that a crash after the last call to FE is not observed by the FE procedure (cf. remark 1). Agreement is thus satisfied in case (2) as well.

- (A-validity) Consider an execution in which no process crashes and a correct process votes 0. Then, due to effectiveness of FE, clearly $\Pi_{q \in \Omega}\, x_q = 0$, hence follows $\Box(y_p \neq b \Rightarrow y_p = 0)$ for any p. This proves A-validity. For the case (at least) a process crashes, we reuse the proof of the agreement property above. We note that for correct processes two outcomes are possible: (1) all the correct processes assign $y_p := 0$, thus meeting A-validity, or (2) all the correct processes assign $y_p := \Pi_{q \in \Omega}\, x_q$. In the latter case, if there is a process q with $x_q = 0$, then clearly y_p is assigned with 0 for all correct p, thus satisfying A-validity. If there is no process who has voted 0 initially, then the antecedent of the A-validity condition (i.e. $\exists q \in \Omega.\ x_q = 0$) is false. A-validity holds for such an execution automatically.

- (C-validity) To check C-validity we only need to consider executions in which $F(\sigma) = \emptyset \wedge \forall q \in \Omega.\ x_q = 1$. Observe that if no process crashes and $\forall q \in \Omega.\ x_q = 1$, then $\Pi_{q \in \Omega}\, x_q = 1$ due to effectiveness of FE, thus $\Box(y_p \neq b \Rightarrow y_p = 1)$ for any p. The C-validity condition follows from this.

This completes the proof of the correctness of algorithm 1.   □

Below, we use $\mathsf{send}_{\to p}(m)$ and $\mathsf{recv}_{\leftarrow p}(v)$ actions to indicate sending message m to process p and receiving a message from process p and assigning the local variable v with the received content, respectively. Since there is a designated communication channel between every two processes (recall that the communication graphs are fully connected, section 2), no confusion may arise regarding the source or destination of the messages exchanged using these actions.

Lemma 2. FE *is solvable using* $\mathcal{B}$ *in* **E**.

Proof. We prove this lemma by showing that $\mathbf{E} \vdash \mathsf{FE} \to \mathsf{NBAC}$.[5] As NBAC can be solved in **E** using $\mathcal{B}$ (see [35], and lemma 3.3 in [25]), it follows that FE can also be solved in **E** using $\mathcal{B}$.

To solve FE, algorithm 2 is executed by each process $p \in \Omega$. Note that this algorithm assumes access to a black-box procedure for solving NBAC. Translating this pseudo-code to a finite state machine (cf. section 2) is straightforward.

---

[5] A reduction of FE to the *biased consensus* problem is given in [2], for synchronous systems. We note that this reduction cannot be used here, because of asynchrony in our model. In particular, recv actions may see only empty messages for an arbitrary (though not infinite) number of times.

Algorithm 2. $\mathbf{E} \vdash \mathsf{FE} \to \mathsf{NBAC}$

```
 1: send_→p+1(x_p);
 2: let w_p := 1; let v_p := λ;
 3: repeat
 4:     recv_←p−1(v_p);
 5:     if v_p = λ then
 6:         let i_p := 0;
 7:     else
 8:         let i_p := 1;
 9:     end if
10:     if local time out is reached then
11:         let w_p := 0;
12:     end if
13: until w_p = 0 ∨ i_p = 1
14: let z_p := b;
15: NBAC(i_p, z_p);
16: if z_p = 1 then
17:     let y_p := v_p;
18: else
19:     let y_p := ⊥;    % in case z_p = 0
20: end if
21: quit;
```

Intuitive description of algorithm 2: Any correct process sends its item to its successor, and waits to receive the item of its predecessor. If a process p does not receive its desired item within a certain time interval, locally specified by p itself, it will time out and stop waiting, reflected in the code by letting $w_p := 0$ (over asynchronous channels, messages may be delivered with an arbitrary finite delay). Any correct process, therefore, will eventually exit its **repeat** loop.

The call to the NBAC procedure, available to the processes, is meant to ensure that if a correct process p has not received x_{p-1}, then every correct process q will respect fairness and consistency, and set $y_q := \perp$.

Notice that it cannot occur that a correct process p assigns λ to y_p. This is because if "let $y_p := v_p$;" (line 17 of the code) is executed by p, then p must have set $i_p := 1$, due to A-validity of NBAC. This, in turn, implies $v_p \neq \lambda$.

If no failure or time-out occurs, eventually all the items reach their destinations, and only then does the call to NBAC return $z_p := 1$ for all $p \in \Omega$. This lets all the participants assign the received items to their output buffers, and quit.

Correctness of algorithm 2: Below, we argue for the correctness criteria from the view point of a correct process, called p. The arguments can naturally be used for other correct processes as well.

- (soundness) Since y_p is assigned only with either of $\perp$ or v_p, which contains x_{p-1}, the soundness requirement of FE is met. We emphasize that in the crash failure model, the value sent by $p-1$ to p, if it ever arrives, is x_{p-1}. This is simply because a faulty process in this model, by definition, does not tamper with data.

- (timeliness) Timeliness for p hinges on the termination condition for NBAC. Note that except for the NBAC call, all the actions (including setting a definite time out) performed by p are local. From definition 2, we know that $\Diamond(z_p \neq b)$, i.e. p will eventually receive a value for z_p. Process p would then assign the proper value to y_p, and quit the exchange. Therefore, $\gamma \models \Diamond(y_p \neq b)$ in all $\sigma = (\gamma, T)$, where $p \notin F(\sigma)$ (recall that $F(\sigma) \in \mathbf{E}$).

- (effectiveness) We only need to consider executions σ for which $F(\sigma) = \emptyset$. When no process crashes and messages are delivered in a timely manner [6], there is a point in time at which all the correct processes have received their desired items. Then, any such correct process p calls the NBAC procedure by letting $i_p := 1$. Therefore, we have $\forall q \in \Omega. \ i_q = 1$. This, and $F(\sigma) = \emptyset$, according to C-validity of NBAC, guarantee $z_p \neq b \Rightarrow z_p = 1$, for all $p \in \Omega$. Since y_p will be assigned with v_p in this case, we have $\forall p \in \Omega. \ \Box(y_p \neq b \Rightarrow y_p = x_{p-1})$.

- (fairness) To check fairness for process p, we need to consider only executions $\sigma = (\gamma, T)$ in which $p \notin F(\sigma)$. Now consider any configuration c on γ such that $(y_{p+1} = x_p) \in [c]$ (i.e. process $p + 1$ has assigned x_p to y_{p+1} in configuration c). According to remark 1 we get $p + 1 \notin F(\sigma)$. Two cases are then possible:

  1. $(y_p \neq b) \in [c]$: This is the case in which p has assigned some value to y_p. According to soundness (see above), we have $(y_p = \bot) \in [c]$ or $(y_p = x_{p-1}) \in [c]$. The latter situation would immediately imply fairness. However, the situation $(y_p = \bot) \in [c]$ can only happen if $(z_p = 0) \in [c]$. According to agreement of NBAC, this implies $(z_{p+1} = 0) \in [c]$. Consulting algorithm 2, this shows that process $p+1$ should have assigned $y_{p+1} := \bot$, contradicting the assumption that $y_{p+1} = x_p$. Hence, the situation $(y_p = \bot) \in [c]$ cannot happen.

  2. $(y_p = b) \in [c]$: This is the case p has not yet assigned any value to y_p. We split this into two cases: (a) p has received x_{p-1}, (b) p has not received x_{p-1}. Note that since $p + 1$ has $y_{p+1} = x_p$, $\text{NBAC}(i_p, z_p)$ should have returned $z_p = 1$ (a result of the agreement property of NBAC). Now, in case (a), p can (and according to timeliness will eventually do) assign $y_p := v_p$, where $v_p = x_{p-1}$. This shows that $\gamma \models \Box(y_p \neq b \Rightarrow y_p = x_{p-1})$, hence attaining fairness. In case (b), since p has not received x_{p-1}, clearly p has set $i_p := 0$ in its call to NBAC. Since $p + 1 \notin F(\sigma)$, according to A-validity of NBAC, $\gamma \models \Box(z_{p+1} \neq b \Rightarrow z_{p+1} = 0)$. This contradicts $(y_{p+1} = x_p) \in [c]$, as $z_{p+1} = 0$ enforces $y_{p+1} = \bot$ in algorithm 2.

  This shows that the algorithm achieves fairness.

- (consistency) To check consistency, we confine to executions $\sigma = (\gamma, T)$ in which $p, q \notin F(\sigma)$, and $y_p \neq b, y_q \neq b$. Towards a contradiction, assume there

---

[6] Although needed in this step of our proof, we note that effectiveness in definition 3 places no conditions on processes not timing out, or messages being delivered timely. In general, if processes want to abandon the exchange, e.g. by early time-outs, no protocol can achieve its goals. This is indeed reflected in the definition of effectiveness given by Asokan (see page 9 in [1]). We feel putting the timeout condition in the formal definition of FE would, however, unnecessarily clutter the presentation, and make the definition rather low-level.

is a configuration c on γ, in which $(y_p = \bot) \in [c]$ and $(y_q \neq \bot) \in [c]$. According to soundness, $(y_q = x_{q-1}) \in [c]$. Therefore, q should have received $z_q = 1$ in its NBAC call. The agreement property of NBAC, nevertheless, states that $z_p = 1$ as well. Now, we distinguish two cases: (1) If $(i_p = 0) \in [c]$, then the A-validity condition of NBAC has been violated by returning $z_p = 1$, thus reaching a contradiction. (2) If $(i_p = 1) \in [c]$, then p must have received x_{p-1}. From the argument above, we know $(z_p = 1) \in [c]$. Therefore, p would, according to algorithm 2, set $y_p := x_{p-1}$ in this situation, contradicting the assumption that $(y_p = \bot) \in [c]$. This shows no such configuration c can belong to γ.

This completes the proof of the correctness of algorithm 2.   □

Remark 2. Suppose some process q crashes in algorithm 2, while all other processes are correct. If q crashes *after* sending its item to $q+1$, the item may arrive at $q + 1$ in time. We note that even if everything goes well with all the other processes in this scenario (i.e. they all vote 1 by letting $i_p := 1$), the outcome of the NBAC call is not guaranteed to be 1 nor 0, because q has crashed, no correct process has voted 0, while q could have voted 0 or 1. This may (wrongly) seem to violate effectiveness of FE, since despite all the correct processes receiving their desired items, the exchange may still terminate unsuccessfully (in case NBAC returns $z_{q+1} = 0$). We remark that because $F(\sigma) \neq \emptyset$ in this scenario, the effectiveness condition does not enforce a successful exchange.

The following corollary is straightforward, hence we omit the proof.

Corollary 1. FE *and* NBAC *are* **E**-*equivalent.*

The connection between FE and NBAC has been noticed in previous studies, such as [38] and [26]. These however rely only upon informal arguments.

4   Related Work

In this section we discuss how our incomparability result relates to the existing literature on FE and DC.

The incomparability of FE to DC (theorem 1) may wrongly seem to contradict the result of [30], where it is shown that in any asynchronous system of two processes, while one process is prone to crash failure, FE is harder than DC (that is DC $\rightarrow$ FE). The fact that theorem 1 assumes a majority of correct processes should clarify this discrepancy from a technical point of view.

To give an intuitive reason for this distinction, let us proceed with considering a scenario in which one process crashes, and then all the correct processes, using failure detectors, learn that this process has crashed. In FE, these correct processes can all safely return $\bot$ and quit the exchange, while in DC, they still need to reach a consensus on what value they would return (they cannot all return 0, because it would violate the validity condition if they all had proposed 1, and so forth). An interesting special case is when only two processes are engaged in the protocol, while one process is prone to crash: The aforementioned difficulty in DC does not arise, as *the* correct process can simply output its own input value. This is exactly why the reduction given in [30] works for two processes (and not more), when one process is prone to the crash failure.

The fair exchange problem in the security literature is usually studied in the Dolev-Yao hostile environment model [13]. In this model, the attacker is a (cryptographically bounded) Byzantine process, sitting in the center of a star-like network. All the correct processes therefore communicate *via* the attacker. The network connectivity [7] in such graphs is therefore 1. This implies DC and FE are not solvable in such environment, as the attacker can simply drop all the transmitted messages, preventing termination, cf. [36]. [8]

A conventional way to circumvent this difficulty in deterministic systems [9] is to assume trusted parties which are connected to other processes via *resilient channels*. A resilient channel guarantees to eventually deliver all the messages submitted through it. Note that adding resilient channels to the system weakens the Dolev-Yao model, in the sense that the attacker node cannot indefinitely delay (or completely suppress) certain messages. For more on this approach see, e.g., [1].

Another way to weaken the Dolev-Yao intruder is via introducing trusted computing devices at each user node, in contrast to a central trustee. These devices can then be used to perform distributed tasks, such as DC or FE. Although these trusted devices are operated by non-trusted malicious entities, it is assumed that they can establish secure channels between themselves, e.g. using encryption. In case the trusted devices are stateful, once the attacker drops a message destined to one of them, the device will behave as if it has crashed (i.e. does not receive or send any message or do any internal computation, unless that particular message arrives). The model used in this paper potentially represents such environments. Practical implementations of such distributed systems have recently attracted much interest; for instance see the literature on using *guardians* [3,2] and *TrustedPals* [19,11] to realize FE.

5   Concluding Remarks

In this paper, we establish that solving the fair exchange problem is in general not harder than reaching consensus in a distributed system. The model used for proving this result consists of processes connected via asynchronous reliable channels, while processes are assumed to be prone to crash failures. As a side result, it is also shown that in this model, fair exchange is equivalent to the non-blocking atomic commit problem, i.e. any failure detector class that solves fair exchange, also solves non-blocking atomic commit in this model, and vice versa.

---

[7] A network has connectivity c iff at least c nodes need to be removed to disconnect the network.

[8] To solve DC in synchronous systems in presence of f Byzantine processes, the network connectivity needs to be at least $2f + 1$, e.g. see [17].

[9] Probabilistic protocols were indeed among the first solutions proposed for the FE problem, e.g. see [5,14]. These are however beyond the scope of this paper; the reader is instead referred to [20] for a comprehensive survey.

As future research, it must be interesting to explore the practical implications of our incomparability result for solving FE. A related uninvestigated question pertains to the existence of models in which fair exchange can be differentiated from non-blocking atomic commit.

Acknowledgment. We are grateful to Wan Fokkink and Felix Freiling for many helpful discussions. M. Torabi Dashti was partially supported by the FP7-ICT-2007-1 Project no. 216471, "AVANTSSAR: Automated Validation of Trust and Security of Service-oriented Architectures".

References

1. Asokan, N.: Fairness in electronic commerce. PhD thesis, University of Waterloo, Canada (1998)
2. Avoine, G., Gärtner, F., Guerraoui, R., Vukolić, M.: Gracefully degrading fair exchange with security modules. In: Dal Cin, M., Kaâniche, M., Pataricza, A. (eds.) EDCC 2005. LNCS, vol. 3463. Springer, Heidelberg (2005)
3. Avoine, G., Vaudenay, S.: Optimal fair exchange with guardian angels. In: Chae, K.-J., Yung, M. (eds.) WISA 2003. LNCS, vol. 2908. Springer, Heidelberg (2004)
4. Ben-Or, M., Goldwasser, S., Wigderson, A.: Completeness theorems for non-cryptographic fault-tolerant distributed computation. In: STOC 1988, pp. 1–10. ACM Press, New York (1988)
5. Blum, M.: Three applications of the oblivious transfer: Part I: Coin flipping by the telephone; part II: How to exchange secrets; part III: How to send certified electronic mail. Technical report, Dept. EECS, UC Berkeley (1981)
6. Buttyán, L., Hubaux, J., Capkun, S.: A formal model of rational exchange and its application to the analysis of Syverson's protocol. Journal of Computer Security 12(3-4), 551–587 (2004)
7. Chadha, R., Kanovich, M., Scedrov, A.: Inductive methods and contract-signing protocols. In: CCS 2001, pp. 176–185. ACM Press, New York (2001)
8. Chandra, T., Hadzilacos, V., Toueg, S.: The weakest failure detector for solving consensus. J. ACM 43(4), 685–722 (1996)
9. Chandra, T., Toueg, S.: Unreliable failure detectors for reliable distributed systems. J. ACM 43(2), 225–267 (1996)
10. Chaum, D., Crépeau, C., Damgard, I.: Multiparty unconditionally secure protocols. In: STOC 1988, pp. 11–19. ACM Press, New York (1988)
11. Cortiñas, R., Freiling, F., Ghajar-Azadanlou, M., Lafuente, A., Larrea, M., Draque Penso, L., Soraluze Arriola, I.: Secure failure detection in TrustedPals. In: Masuzawa, T., Tixeuil, S. (eds.) SSS 2007. LNCS, vol. 4838. Springer, Heidelberg (2007)
12. DeMillo, R., Lynch, N., Merritt, M.: Cryptographic protocols. In: STOC 1982, pp. 383–400. ACM Press, New York (1982)
13. Dolev, D., Yao, A.: On the security of public key protocols. IEEE Trans. on Information Theory IT-29(2), 198–208 (1983)
14. Even, S., Goldreich, O., Lempel, A.: A randomized protocol for signing contracts. Commun. ACM 28(6), 637–647 (1985)
15. Even, S., Yacobi, Y.: Relations among public key signature systems. Technical Report 175, Computer Science Dept., Technion, Haifa, Isreal (March 1980)
16. Ezhilchelvan, P., Shrivastava, S.: A family of trusted third party based fair-exchange protocols. IEEE Trans. Dependable and Secure Computing 2(4) (2005)

17. Fischer, M., Lynch, N., Merritt, M.: Easy impossibility proofs for distributed consensus problems. Distrib. Comput. 1(1), 26–39 (1986)
18. Fischer, M., Lynch, N., Paterson, M.: Impossibility of distributed consensus with one faulty process. J. ACM 32(2), 374–382 (1985)
19. Fort, M., Freiling, F., Draque Penso, L., Benenson, Z., Kesdogan, D.: TrustedPals: Secure multiparty computation implemented with smart cards. In: Gollmann, D., Meier, J., Sabelfeld, A. (eds.) ESORICS 2006. LNCS, vol. 4189. Springer, Heidelberg (2006)
20. Franklin, M., Galil, Z., Yung, M.: An overview of secure distributed computing. Technical Report TR CUCS-008-92, Columbia University (March 1992)
21. Franklin, M., Tsudik, G.: Secure group barter: Multi-party fair exchange with semi-trusted neutral parties. In: Hirschfeld, R. (ed.) FC 1998. LNCS, vol. 1465. Springer, Heidelberg (1998)
22. Garbinato, B., Rickebusch, I.: A topological condition for solving fair exchange in byzantine environments. In: Ning, P., Qing, S., Li, N. (eds.) ICICS 2006. LNCS, vol. 4307. Springer, Heidelberg (2006)
23. Gomila, J., Capellà, M., Rotger, L.: A realistic protocol for multi-party certified electronic mail. In: Chan, A.H., Gligor, V.D. (eds.) ISC 2002. LNCS, vol. 2433. Springer, Heidelberg (2002)
24. González-Deleito, N., Markowitch, O.: Exclusion-freeness in multi-party exchange protocols. In: Chan, A.H., Gligor, V.D. (eds.) ISC 2002. LNCS, vol. 2433. Springer, Heidelberg (2002)
25. Guerraoui, R.: Non-blocking atomic commit in asynchronous distributed systems with failure detectors. Distributed Computing 15(1), 17–25 (2002)
26. Liu, P., Ning, P., Jajodia, S.: Avoiding loss of fairness owing to failures in fair data exchange systems. Decision Support Systems 31(3), 337–350 (2001)
27. Lynch, N.: Distributed Algorithms. Morgan Kaufmann, San Francisco (1996)
28. Micali, S.: Simple and fast optimistic protocols for fair electronic exchange. In: PODC 2003, pp. 12–19. ACM Press, New York (2003)
29. Mukhamedov, A., Kremer, S., Ritter, E.: Analysis of a multi-party fair exchange protocol and formal proof of correctness in the strand space model. In: S. Patrick, A., Yung, M. (eds.) FC 2005. LNCS, vol. 3570. Springer, Heidelberg (2005)
30. Pagnia, H., Gärtner, F.: On the impossibility of fair exchange without a trusted third party. Technical Report TUD-BS-1999-02, Department of Computer Science, Darmstadt University of Technology, Germany (March 1999)
31. Pagnia, H., Vogt, H., Gärtner, F.: Fair exchange. Comput. J. 46(1), 55–75 (2003)
32. Pfitzmann, B., Schuner, M., Waidner, M.: Optimal efficiency of optimistic contract signing. In: PODC 1998, pp. 113–122. ACM Press, New York (1998)
33. Pnueli, A.: The temporal logic of programs. In: FOCS 1977. IEEE, Los Alamitos (1977)
34. Rabin, M.: How to exchange secrets with oblivious transfer. Technical Report TR-81, Harvard University (May 1981)
35. Skeen, D.: Nonblocking commit protocols. In: SIGMOD Conference on Management of Data, pp. 133–142. ACM Press, New York (1981)
36. Syverson, P.: A different look at secure distributed computation. In: CSFW 1997, pp. 109–115. IEEE Computer Society Press, Los Alamitos (1997)
37. Tel, G.: Introduction to distributed algorithms, 2nd edn. Cambridge University Press, Cambridge (2000)
38. Tygar, J.: Atomicity in electronic commerce. In: PODC 1996, pp. 8–26. ACM Press, New York (1996)

Automatic Generation of CSP ∥ B Skeletons from xUML Models

Edward Turner, Helen Treharne, Steve Schneider[1], and Neil Evans[2]

[1] Department of Computing, University of Surrey
[2] AWE plc Aldermaston

Abstract. CSP ∥ B is a formal approach to specification that combines CSP and B. In this paper we present our tool that automatically translates a subset of executable UML (xUML) models into CSP ∥ B, for the purpose of verification and increased validation at the early stages of a software engineering development lifecycle. The tool is being developed for our industrial collaborators, AWE plc, in order to strengthen their software engineering process which uses xUML. As part of this process, AWE and Kennedy Carter Ltd. have built an xUML to SPARK Ada code generator, which is also employed to contribute a higher level of safety assurance at the latter stages of the lifecycle. Our tool is based on a model-text transformation strategy that uses the xUML meta-model to map to CSP and B constructs. The tool generates machine readable CSP and B; we present a simple example to demonstrate the transformation strategy, and the analysis of the resulting specification.

1   Introduction

In this paper we discuss our approach to providing formal reasoning support for UML platform-independent models. The approach is being developed as part of a collaborative project with AWE plc. The application domain of interest is safety critical and therefore it is essential to achieve a high level of assurance in the safety of the models, i.e., they adhere to desirable behavioural properties and are deadlock-free. Current industrial practice involves validating UML models by examining and/or running numerous simulations. Our aim is to automatically generate CSP ∥ B [1] specifications, from executable UML (xUML) models [2], which can be formally analysed. The challenge is to identify an appropriate translation mapping with tool support so that a specifier's effort is spent on conducting formal analysis rather than on defining formal models.

The project will consider two different routes for developing a *CSP ∥ B specification generator*. Firstly, we will develop a specification generator using the xUML toolset provided by Kennedy Carter Ltd. (KC). The toolset offers the capability of code generation into C, C++ or Java from platform independent models. AWE have been working alongside Kennedy Carter to develop SPARK Ada translators from xUML. Thus, our tool will enable formal analysis support to fit into the AWE software development life cycle. Secondly, we will also investigate building a model generator using the Epsilon [3] toolset developed

J.S. Fitzgerald, A.E. Haxthausen, and H. Yenigun (Eds.): ICTAC 2008, LNCS 5160, pp. 364–379, 2008.
© Springer-Verlag Berlin Heidelberg 2008

at York University. The contribution of this paper is a description of the first tool that we are currently building. The paper also demonstrates the need to develop an analysis framework so that added value can be gained from generating the formal CSP || B specification. The analysis framework is the way the specifications are verified for deadlock freedom and consistency. The process of generating the specifications themselves is also valuable because it forces us to think about ambiguities within an xUML model and resolves what are often implicit assumptions in xUML models.

We have chosen CSP || B as the underlying formalism because it provides a clean separation between control (in CSP [4]) and state (in B [5]). Moreover, its decompositional verification framework [1,6] will be particularly relevant when it comes to analysing large xUML models. Much research exists on developing formal tool support for UML, including [7,8]. Nonetheless, few focus on what else needs to be included in formalising large xUML models.

The paper begins with an overview of xUML and CSP || B. Section 2.1 illustrates a small running example. In Section 4 we present our tool which implements a model-text transformation strategy from xUML models to CSP || B specifications. It takes as input an xUML model written using the KC toolset, it is then invoked from within that toolset, and the output is a machine readable CSP || B specification. The strategy covers a large subset of concrete xUML and throughout the paper we identify restrictions on this subset. In Section 5 we discuss what analysis framework could be appropriate for the generated CSP || B specifications and Section 6 concludes with related work.

2   Executable UML

xUML is a coherent subset of UML 2.0 and supports six diagrams: Use Case, Domain Models, Sequence Diagrams, Class Diagrams, Collaboration Diagrams, and State Charts. In this paper we focus on class diagrams and state charts, since these are the main diagrams that are used when constructing xUML models using the Kennedy Carter toolset. We will refer to an xUML model comprising the class diagram and associated state charts as the *model* throughout the paper, and the corresponding CSP || B specification as the *specification*.

We also restrict ourselves to examining one domain within a model. Class diagrams enable the classes of a model to be defined together with the relationships between them. We currently support associations in xUML, which are binary by definition, but we do not handle generalisations. Class diagrams can have at most one state chart. The behaviour of instances (objects) of classes are described using state charts, each of which consists of a set of states and signals. Each state can define an entry action, whereas exit actions are not permitted. An action is defined by a sequence of statements described using the Action Specification Language (ASL) [9], which is a more low level language than OCL [10], and whose statements have no side effects and execute immediately. ASL statements can change the state of a system, be grouped into blocks, and execute concurrently. Hence, state actions can interleave their statements.

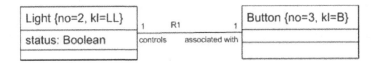

Fig. 1. Class diagram of the Lighting System

The ASL can be categorised into statements that perform object management, relationship management, state chart communication, sequential logic and assignments. The ASL we use in this paper is given as follows: `create` and `delete`, are used to create new instances and delete existing ones, respectively; `link` and `unlink`, are used to link and unlink instances over a specified association, respectively; `->` (pronounced *'navigate via'*), is used to retrieve instance handles over an association; `generate`, is used to send signals to a specified instance; and `<instance handle>.<attribute list> = <value list>` is used for writing to attributes of objects. We do not support ASL statements that deal with timers and access to methods from other domains.

Methods of class diagrams are also defined in terms of ASL. Currently, our work allows only for the definition of object scoped methods, and we must restrict the ASL they use, since methods will be mapped to B operations. For example, ASL for-loops are not permitted in methods and attribute values can only be written to once within an ASL block.

Traversing between states is achieved by processing signals on a queue, details of which are given in Section 4.3. A signal emerging from an action cannot be processed until the action has completed its execution (also known as *run to completion*). To ensure a complete description of behaviour for a state chart, xUML requires the specifier to define one of three effects of receiving any signal in any state: a signal can cause a *transition* between states and the execution of the entry action of the successor state; a signal can be *ignored*; or it may cause a run-time error (denoted a *cannot happen* effect).

2.1 Running Example

Consider an example lighting system consisting of two classes representing buttons and lights, shown in Figure 1. A button instance is paired with one light instance, and vice-versa, such that when a button is switched on, its attached light illuminates. Similarly, when a button is turned off, its light also turns off. Larger examples provided by KC have also been examined.

The only data we model explicitly is the boolean attribute, `status`, in the Light class, which denotes whether or not a light is illuminated. No object scoped methods are defined (however, our tool does support generating operations corresponding to object scoped methods and attribute accessor methods as shown in Section 4). The desired behaviour of button and light instances is captured by the state charts given in Figures 2 and 3, respectively.

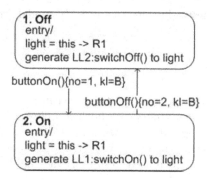

buttonOn(){no=1, kl=B}

buttonOff(){no=2, kl=B}

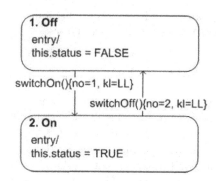

switchOn(){no=1, kl=LL}

switchOff(){no=2, kl=LL}

Fig. 2. State chart for Buttons

Fig. 3. State chart for Lights

Table 1. Effects of Button Signals

State	buttonOn	buttonOff
Off	On	Ignore
On	Ignore	Off

Table 2. Effects of Light Signals

State	switchOn	switchOff
Off	On	Ignore
On	Ignore	Off

We now describe the interaction of these state charts, so that lights can be turned on and off. Consider an instance of both classes in their `Off` states. To turn on the light, we must send a `buttonOn` signal to the button. In our model, this task is neither the responsibility of buttons or lights; instead, it is externally generated. Receipt of this signal by the button triggers transition to its `On` state, and the execution of the defined entry action. Accordingly, we first obtain an instance handle to the attached light through the ASL navigation statement: `light = this -> R1`; where `this` refers to the instance handle of the button and `R1` is the name of the association being navigated. Subsequently, a `switchOn` signal is sent to the light, using the signal generation statement: `generate LL1:switchOn() to light`[1]. The attached light can process this signal and move to its own `On` state even if the button was still processing any remaining ASL statements (in this case there are none). The actions in this state then sets `status` to `TRUE`, to denote the light has been successfully illuminated. The procedure for turning off a light follows a similar pattern, but where the trigger is the `buttonOff` signal, which is also external.

Tables 1 and 2 show the effects of signals in particular states of our model. For example, we define in Table 1 that when a button is in the `Off` state and it processes a `buttonOff` signal, the signal should be ignored and discarded. Similarly, we ignore all unexpected signals.

Typical object scenarios are described in initialisation segments, e.g., to set up linked lights and buttons. Test methods can then be defined to generate

---

[1] Identifiers of signals and methods are made unique by the KC tool using automatically generated prefixes. Therefore, **switchOn** and **switchOff** signals are denoted by **LL1:switchOn()** and **LL2:switchOff()**.

signals to evolve system behaviour. Both these additions to an xUML model are achieved using ASL statements.

3   CSP ∥ B

CSP ∥ B is an approach that combines an event-based notation with a state-based notation to facilitate the specification of systems with both complex flows of control and structured data. A degree of separation between the CSP [4] and B [5] aspects is maintained so that we can retain the use of existing tool support. The FDR model checker [11] and ProB [12] are both used to support the analysis and verification of CSP ∥ B specifications.

CSP process expressions can be constructed from several operators, the ones used in this paper are: event sequencing ($\rightarrow$), (indexed) external choice ($\Box$), (indexed) interleaving ($\interleave$), (indexed) alphabetised parallel composition ($\parallel$), and interface parallel ($P \parallel_S Q$ where S is the synchronisation set). We also use conditional expressions (if then else) and local definitions (let within).

The failures of a process P consists of all (tr, X) where tr is a trace and X is a set of events P can refuse (see [13,14]). A trace tr is said to be a trace of a process P if the process can perform the sequence of events in tr. The refinement relation in the failures model is denoted by $\sqsubseteq_F$. The refinement relation in the traces model is denoted by $\sqsubseteq_T$.

B specifications are structured using *machines*. Each machine contains some *state* describing the objects of interest, and *operations* to manipulate the state. A B machine also contains an *invariant* that declares properties of the state variables, and specifies what must be preserved by the execution of operations. Functions and relations are used to model complex state, e.g., R^{-1}, gives the relational inverse of a relation R and, given a set U, the relational image $R[U]$ is the set of objects (in the range of R) related to the elements of U.

A B operation takes the form **PRE** P **THEN** S **END** where P is a predicate and S represents the statements that update variables. In CSP ∥ B we are particularly interested in operations without guards. The kind of B machines that we define are referred to as *non-blocking*. Hence, any deadlock in a CSP ∥ B specification is as a result of the CSP processes deadlocking.

In CSP ∥ B, the events of a CSP process trigger operation calls of a B machine, and the process is said to 'control' the B machine because its events cause state updates within the B machine via the operation calls. We refer to CSP processes as *controllers*. Structured events are used to pass values between the controller process and the B machine. For example, an event $e!x?y$, that outputs a value x and binds the variable y to an input value, corresponds to an operation call $y \longleftarrow e(x)$ that inputs x and outputs a value y. These events can contain a number of inputs/outputs or none. Our previous work has justified that it is meaningful to combine CSP processes and B machines [1]. We combine collections of controller/machine pairs using the architecture identified in [15] and shown in Figure 4. The association machine $ASSOC$ is controlled by the synchronising events of two processes P and Q. These processes define the

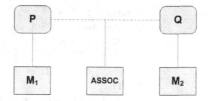

Fig. 4. Overview of CSP || B architecture

collections of controllers representing the behaviour of instances of classes and the machines, M_1 and M_2, record and update the instances' attribute information. The *ASSOC* machine tracks the associations that exist between instances.

4   Automatic Generator

The overall architecture of our tool is given in Figure 5. By importing an xUML model into our tool, we populate a suite of meta-models describing various aspects of the system. Our tool primarily relies on two of these; the representation of entities of the imported system, such as the classes and state charts used (part of the xUML meta-model), and the ASL used by system entities (stored within the ASL meta-model). The pattern for generating CSP and B then comprises a procedure that initiates a guided traversal of these meta-models, to access certain data, and the application of our transformation rules to obtain the elements of the formal specifications. The following sections discuss the steps for generating CSP and B from the meta-models.

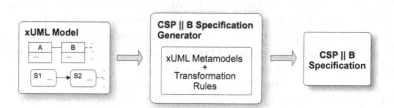

Fig. 5. The main components of our tool

4.1   Translating ASL to Skeleton B Machines

A B machine is created for each class in the class diagram of the xUML system. Figure 6 presents the B machine generated by our tool for the light class. A set, *llIH*, is used to specify the instance handles of the class, a subset of which, *llObj*, captures the current light instances in the system. The approach we use

MACHINE
  LIGHT_MCH
SEES
  Bool_TYPE
SETS
  lllH = { *ll0* , *ll1* }
VARIABLES
  llObj , *status*
INVARIANT
  llObj ⊆ *lllH* ∧
  status ∈ *llObj* → *BOOL*
INITIALISATION
  llObj := ∅ ∥
  status := ∅

OPERATIONS
  LL_create (*ih*) ≙
    PRE *ih* ∈ *lllH* ∧ *ih* ∉ *llObj*   **THEN**
      llObj := *llObj* ∪ { *ih* } ∥
      status (*ih*) := *false*
    END ;
  vv ⟵ **LL_default_get_status** (*ih*) ≙
    PRE *ih* ∈ *llObj*   **THEN**
      vv := *status* (*ih*)
    END ;
  LL_default_set_status (*ih* , *val*) ≙
    PRE *ih* ∈ *llObj* ∧ *val* ∈ *BOOL*   **THEN**
      status (*ih*) := *val*
    END
END

Fig. 6. Skeleton machine for the Light class

link_R1 (*ll_ih* , *b_ih*) ≙
PRE *ll_ih* ∈ *llObj* ∧ *b_ih* ∈ *bObj*
  ll_ih ∉ dom (*R1*) ∧ *b_ih* ∉ ran(*R1*)
THEN
  R1 := *R1* ∪ { *ll_ih* ↦ *b_ih* }
END

ll_ih ⟵ **navigate_R1_from_B** (*b_ih*) ≙
PRE *b_ih* ∈ *bObj* ∧ *b_ih* ∈ ran (*R1*)
THEN
  ll_ih := $R1^{-1}$ (*b_ih*)
END

Fig. 7. Example B operations for managing the *R1* association

resembles the B style, presented in [7], for modelling objects and continues our previous work developed in [16]. Attributes are represented by functions, and simple operations are generated to query or modify their values. In addition, operations are provided to support the dynamic creation of objects. For example, **LL_create** creates a light instance and explicitly sets the *status* variable. In general, other methods of a class are transformed to skeleton B operations that specify the typing of input and output variables.

A single B machine is used to capture all the relationships used within an xUML model. For our example, a machine called *ASSOC* is generated, which defines the variable, *R1*, and its invariant representing the relationship between *llObj* and *bObj* (current button instances), as follows:

$$R1 \in llObj \leftrightarrow bObj$$

The relation can be specified in terms of the *llObj* and *bObj* variables since they are accessible via the **USES** structuring mechanism within the B-Method. The multiplicity constraints of *R1* need to be maintained throughout the lifetime of the objects but the constraints are not discharged until we consider model consistency in Section 5.2. The *ASSOC* machine defines **link_R1** and **unlink_R1** operations linking/unlinking lights and buttons, and **navigate_R1_from_LL** and **navigate_R1_from_B** to traverse the association from either side, two of which are given in Figure 7.

4.2   Translating ASL to CSP

The general procedure for generating CSP for object behaviour is outlined in Algorithm 1. For each class c in an xUML system we define a controller process. Thus, for the button class, $\langle c \rangle\_CTRLS$ is instantiated as B_CTRLS, to represent the behaviour of all button instances, shown in Figure 8, where B denotes the class key letter and b denotes the instance handle to which it applies. This interleaving process means that all buttons instances act independently and only interact via the signal queues. In general, instances may be composed in parallel; the synchronising events would be those corresponding to creation/deletion methods, object scoped methods and attribute accessor methods. For all instances a create event initially occurs and the subsequent behaviour is defined using the B_CTRL parameterised process. For example, $B\_create!b1$, where $b1$ is a particular button instance, is a create event which triggers the corresponding B operation so that a new object is added, i.e., $b1$ is added to $bObj$. The

---

Algorithm 1. An outline for generating CSP for object lifecycles

for all c **in** classes of xUML model m **do**
  if c has a state chart **then**
    $\langle c \rangle_SCTRL(ih) = $ **let** /* state chart behaviour for instance handle ih */
    for all states, s **in** sc **do**
      $\langle c \rangle_\langle s \rangle_ENTRY = $ sequence entry actions ending in $\langle c \rangle\_\langle s \rangle\_STATE$
      $\langle c \rangle\_\langle s \rangle\_STATE = \Box_{se \in \{signal\ effects\}}\ se \rightarrow \langle c \rangle\_\langle s \rangle\_STATE$
    end for
    within /* initial _STATE process */
  end if
  if c has a state chart **then**
    if c has no attributes and no methods (excluding create/delete) **then**
      $\langle c \rangle\_CTRL(ih) = \langle c \rangle\_SCTRL(ih) \triangle (\langle c \rangle\_delete.ih \rightarrow STOP)$
    else
      $\langle c \rangle\_CTRL(ih) = (\langle c \rangle\_SCTRL(ih) \triangle (\langle c \rangle\_delete!ih \rightarrow STOP))$
      $\qquad\qquad \|_{\{\langle c \rangle\_delete.ih\}}\ \langle c \rangle\_DOPS(ih)$
    end if
  else
    if c has no attributes and no methods (excluding create/delete) **then**
      $\langle c \rangle\_CTRL(ih) = \langle c \rangle\_delete!ih \rightarrow STOP$
    else
      $\langle c \rangle\_CTRL(ih) = \langle c \rangle\_DOPS(ih)$
    end if
  end if
  where $\langle c \rangle\_DOPS(ih) = (\Box_{o \in O}\ o \rightarrow \langle c \rangle\_DOPS(ih)) \Box (\langle c \rangle\_delete!ih \rightarrow STOP)$
  and O is the set of methods and attribute accessor methods
  /* composition of all instances in $\langle c \rangle\_INSTANCES$, e.g., in simple case: */
  $\langle c \rangle\_CTRLS = |||_{ih \in \langle c \rangle\_INSTANCES}\ \langle c \rangle\_create!ih \rightarrow \langle c \rangle\_CTRL(ih)$
  $\alpha \langle c \rangle_CTRLS = $ /* set of events in $\langle c \rangle\_CTRLS$ */
end for

$B_SCTRL(b) = $ let
$\quad B\_Off\_ENTRY = navigate\_R1\_from\_B!b?ih \rightarrow$
$\qquad\qquad\qquad\qquad generate!ih!b!LL2\_switchOffSignal \rightarrow B\_Off\_STATE$
$\quad B\_Off\_STATE =$
$\qquad remove!b?\_!B1\_buttonOnSignal \rightarrow B\_On\_ENTRY$
$\qquad \square \; /* \text{ branch representing ignored signals } */$
$\quad B\_On\_ENTRY = navigate\_R1\_from\_B!b?ih \rightarrow$
$\qquad\qquad\qquad\qquad generate!ih!b!LL1\_switchOnSignal \rightarrow B\_On\_STATE$
$\quad B\_On\_STATE =$
$\qquad remove!b?\_!B2\_buttonOffSignal \rightarrow B\_Off\_ENTRY$
$\qquad \square \; /* \text{ branch representing ignored signals } */$
within B_Off_STATE
$B\_CTRL(b) = B\_SCTRL(b) \; \triangle \; (B\_delete!b \rightarrow STOP)$
$B\_CTRLS = \big|\big|\big|_{b \in B\_INSTANCES} B\_create!b \rightarrow B\_CTRL(b)$

Fig. 8. Generated CSP for the Button state chart

creation of an object must make explicit all its initial attribute values and set the state machine into a particular state. This information is required by the corresponding B operation and the CSP *within* clause respectively. Currently, we do not support state charts containing an explicit initialisation state.

The B_CTRL process is responsible for describing the behaviour of the state chart associated with class B, defined in B_SCTRL. The B_CTRL process also ensures that when a deletion event is performed the state chart behaviour terminates. In general, any object scoped methods and attribute accessor methods of an object must be offered at all times while that object exists. An instantiation of process $\langle c \rangle\_DOPS$ would provide this behaviour.

The pattern for the B_SCTRL process comprises two process equations for each state. The first process models the execution of ASL statements in the state's entry action. In B_Off_ENTRY this corresponds to obtaining the light to which the button is attached via $R1$, and generating a $LL2\_switchOffSignal$ communication. In LL_On_ENTRY, defined in Figure 9, we set the **status** attribute which means calling the operation corresponding to the communication along $LL\_default\_set\_status$[2].

The second process defined for a state captures the effects of a signal in that state. e.g., LL_On_STATE. Our transformation rules for signal effects are described in Table 3. Signals that cause a transition to another state are removed from one of the object's signal queues via *remove*, after which the successor's entry action is performed. We ensure signals with the *ignored* effect have no consequence and are removed from the signal queue, before returning to the same process; and *cannot happen* signals give rise to a *msg.ih.cannot_happen* event, where *ih* is an instance handle.

---

[2] In general, we need to distinguish between object a's methods of class A being called by a itself and by other objects. Synchronisation must only occur between the methods in $A\_DOPS(a)$ and their occurrence in other $SCTRL$ processes, and not between those found in any of a's $\_ENTRY$ processes.

$L\_SCTRL(ll) = \ldots$
$LL\_On\_ENTRY = LL\_default\_set\_status!ll!true \rightarrow LL\_On\_STATE$
$LL\_On\_STATE =$
    $remove!ll?\_!LL2\_switchOffSignal \rightarrow LL\_Off\_ENTRY$
    $\square$
    $remove!ll?\_!LL2\_switchOnSignal \rightarrow msg.ll.ignore \rightarrow LL\_On\_STATE$

Fig. 9. Fragment of generated CSP for the Light state chart

Table 3. Transformation rules for signal effects

Description	CSP Translation
Transition from *state* to successor *succ* on occurrence of signal, *sig*	$remove!ih?\_!sig \rightarrow \langle c \rangle\_\langle succ \rangle\_ENTRY$
Ignored signals, *igs*, are consumed	$\square_{sig \in igs}\ remove!ih?\_!sig \rightarrow$ $msg.ih.ignore \rightarrow \langle c \rangle\_\langle state \rangle\_STATE$
Cannot happen signals, *chs*, trigger cannot happen events	$\square_{sig \in chs}\ remove!ih?\_!sig \rightarrow$ $msg.ih.cannot\_happen \rightarrow \langle c \rangle\_\langle state \rangle\_STATE$

4.3   Generating the Execution Environment

In order to analyse the generated CSP ∥ B specifications we must consider their execution environment. We presented our original version in [16] but the model presented was not general enough. Consider the following:

$$P1 = generate!i1!i3!s1 \rightarrow generate!i1!i2!s2 \rightarrow STOP$$
$$P2 = remove!i2?s \rightarrow generate!i2!i3!s \rightarrow STOP$$
$$P3 = remove!i3?s1 \rightarrow remove!i3?s2 \rightarrow STOP$$

Assuming no other processes, $P2$ will only generate its signal after it has received $P1$'s $s2$ signal. Hence, using our original definition of the queues, $P3$ will necessarily receive $P1$'s $s1$ signal before $P2$'s $s2$ signal, but this is too deterministic. The rules stated in Mellor & Balcer [2] do not enforce this: there is nothing to prevent $P3$ getting $P2$'s signal before $P1$'s. Our solution was to change the queuing model: for each instance i there is a queue, SQ, to handle self generated signals and also a queue, Q, for each instance j that is different from i, and which describes the behaviour of i with respect to the signals generated from j to i. Furthermore, queues must only associated with active objects. Thus, all the queues can be collectively defined as *SignalQueues* (renaming create/delete omitted) and are initially empty as follows:

$$\vertiii{}_{i \in INSTANCE}\ create.i \rightarrow ((SQ(i, \langle \rangle)\ \underset{\{|remove.i|\}}{\parallel} (\vertiii{}_{j \in (INSTANCE - \{i\})} Q(i, j, \langle \rangle)))$$
$$\triangle\ (delete.i \rightarrow STOP))$$

4.4   Translating Supporting ASL to Enable Animation

Besides the CSP processes representing the state charts of classes, our tool also generates initialisation segments and test methods as processes, e.g., *InitSegment*

and *TestMethod*. This enables us to define an animation scenario in terms of the
following:

$$((SYSTEM \quad \underset{\{|externalGenerate|\}}{\|} \quad TestMethod) \| InitSegment)$$

where *SYSTEM* represents the controllers of the specification and the signal
queues, and the *externalGenerate* channel enables the test method to invoke signals that are externally visible from within the model. For example, a *TestMethod*
defined as $externalGenerate.b1.ext0.B1\_buttonOnSignal \rightarrow STOP$ generates a
$B1\_buttonOnSignal$ from the external instance $ext0$ to the button instance $b1$.
Our tool creates a specified number of animation scenarios for each model.

5   Towards an Analysis Framework

The contributions of this paper beyond that of the original transformation strategy presented in [16] are the mapping of the creation and deletion of objects, the
correction and generalisation in the queuing model, the inclusion of classes that
do not have state charts, initialisation segments and test methods. These were
described in the last section and are implemented in our tool. In this section we
discuss an analysis framework that is work in progress. We identify three kinds
of analysis of interest: model consistency checking, deadlock freedom checking,
and the verification of the Effects table. In the KC tool validation takes place
via simulation, which will only expose bad behaviour if the right animation scenario is provided. Our framework aims to verify that under no circumstances
such bad behaviour is possible. We have yet to consider other system properties
that could be specified using LTL formulae in ProB and also CSP specifications.
For example, verifying that if the button is switched on the corresponding light
status is eventually on could be achieved by observing the signal event and then
checking the status attribute value.

5.1   Analysis of the Effects Table

This first analysis is straightforward; we define the following specification:

$$NoCannotHappens = \square_{s\in(\Sigma-\{|nomsg|\})} s \rightarrow NoCannotHappens$$

where $\{|$ *nomsg* $|\}$ is the set of all messages involving *cannot_happen*. If the
following check holds:

$$NoCannotHappens \sqsubseteq_T ((SYSTEM \quad \underset{\{|externalGenerate|\}}{\|} \quad ExternalSignals)$$

where *ExternalSignals* represents a recursive choice over all externally generated signals for active objects, then we can be confident that *cannot_happen*
communications are not possible in specification. It only makes sense to label
cannot_happen messages on internal signals. The refinement is trivially false if
external signals are labelled *cannot_happen* since they can be invoked in any
state.

5.2 Model Consistency

Model consistency means checking that a model preserves its multiplicities at certain execution points. Instances can be created independently and a subsequent explicit link statement sets up the association between them. Thus, for example, a 1..1 association would not be preserved until after the link statement has been executed. However, the validity of the association is only important at the point a navigation occurs. Otherwise, an action may attempt to navigate to an invalid instance.

Associations are dynamic since object and relationship management ASL statements can be used within entry actions, and so model consistency needs to be checked throughout the execution of a system. Our current work is investigating a rely/guarantee style for consistency checking, which spans across state charts and initialisation segments and will be based upon our work on *decompositional verification* in CSP || B [6]. This is where we see a benefit of explicitly modelling association information in the *ASSOC* machine.

The way to proceed is to identify for each state action A_i in each state machine P the predicate that needs to be guaranteed in order to prevent model inconsistency. This predicate is then attached to all the incoming signals of A_i as a *blocking assertion* (which is a rely condition). We then find appropriate associated state actions $Q_1 \ldots Q_n$ which ensure that the assertions are guaranteed, and decorate the relevant generate signals with *diverging assertions* (which are guarantee conditions). We would need to demonstrate, using our weakest precondition control loop invariant (*CLI*) technique, that the process expressions related to each A_i's entry action in P's CSP controller is model consistent with respect to P_MCH and *ASSOC*. That is, $(P\_A_i\_Entry \parallel P\_MCH \parallel ASSOC)$ is divergence-free meaning the guarantees have fulfilled the rely conditions. In general, it is not the case that diverging assertions and their corresponding blocking assertions are on the same signal, and in some cases the rely/guarantee conditions are contained and fulfilled within a single entry action [6].

In our example, there is only one state action that contains behaviour which could result in the model being inconsistent: the On state action of the *Button* state chart. Thus, we can identify from the **navigate_R1_from_B** operation the predicate $b \in \mathsf{ran}(R_1)$ as the *blocking assertion* on the *buttonOn* signal. (We would need to be careful how variables were quantified, i.e., $b \in B\_INSTANCES$.) Normally, we would find the corresponding generating signals and attach *diverging assertions*, provided that the signal was generated internally by the model. Decorating signal channels with assertions and their associated proofs ensures that the pair of instances exists when the signal is generated. Subsequently, when we retrieve the light instance in the On state it is a valid instance. In our example the signal generation of *buttonOn* is externally controlled, and therefore, the blocking assertion becomes an assumption of the external environment; and anyone using this xUML model would need to discharge it. As we have seen, the *buttonOn* signal can be invoked after the initialisation segment. Therefore, we would need to demonstrate that all operation sequences resulting from the *InitSegment* ‖ *BUTTON_MCH* ‖ *LIGHT_MCH* ‖ *ASSOC* establishes the identified predicate.

Only a single predicate needs to be relied upon in our example. However, this need not be the case in general; it can be a conjunctive predicate identified from propagating all the conditions which need to be relied upon within a state action. Thus, we may be required to demonstrate that more than one complementary action or external method ensures that such predicates are preserved to ensure model consistency.

5.3   Deadlock Freedom Checking

Deadlock checking means that the model does not deadlock with respect to the processing of signals in active objects. For example, we need to check that:

$$((SYSTEM \underset{\{|externalGenerate|\}}{\|} ExternalSignals) \| InitSegment)$$

is deadlock-free. It follows a similar pattern to an animation scenario but here the *ExternalSignals* process replaces a particular test method in order to allow always the availability of externally generated signals for active objects. However, this only gives us assurance that the system does not deadlock in the context of a particular object initialisation. We need to provide confidence that the system does not deadlock given an arbitrary valid collection of active objects. This means that we need mechanisms for generating collections of objects that preserve the consistency of multiplicities described in the class diagram, using the same notion of consistency as above. It makes no sense to check for deadlocks when the multiplicities are not preserved at certain execution points. We have developed *multiplicity templates* for all the association types supported in xUML.

Recall that button instances in our example are uniquely related to light instances via the $R1$ association. Therefore, before a button instance can perform a communication along the channel *navigate_R1_from_B*, in order to find its corresponding light instance, it must have been associated with it via a *link* event. Furthermore, button instances cannot be related to other instances unless they have first been unlinked; instances can only be deleted if they are no longer connected to other instances. Figure 10 provides a CSP definition of a process which constrains button instances to link to precisely one light instance (in order to identify the 1 multiplicity at the light end of $R1$ association in Figure 1). A similar template is needed for light instances and together they provide the overall multiplicity constraint.

We then construct a parallel process, *CONSTRAINED_CTRLS*, which is the combination of the button and light controllers constrained by their multiplicity templates:

$$(BUTTONOBJECTS\_R1 \| B\_CTRLS) \| (LIGHTOBJECTS\_R1 \| LL\_CTRLS)$$

The final system, *SYSTEM*2, is the parallel composition of these constrained controllers, together with their signal queues, and the process which enables external signals to be generated, defined as follows (renaming has been omitted):

$ButtonMT\_R1(b) =$
  let $ButtonMT\_1 = B\_create!b \rightarrow link\_R1?a!b \rightarrow ButtonMT\_2(\{a\})$
    $ButtonMT\_2(\varnothing) =$
        $(B\_delete!b \rightarrow ButtonMT\_1) \; \Box$
        $link\_R1?a!b \rightarrow ButtonMT\_2(\{a\})$
    $ButtonMT\_2(S) =$
        $unlink\_R1?a \in S!b \rightarrow ButtonMT\_2(S - \{a\}) \; \Box$
        $navigate\_R1\_from\_B!b?a \in S \rightarrow ButtonMT\_2(S)$
  within $ButtonMT\_1$
$BUTTONOBJECTS\_R1 = (\; \big\|\big|\big| \; b \in Button\_INSTANCES \bullet ButtonMT\_R1(b))$

Fig. 10. Button Multiplicity Template for $R1$

$$CONSTRAINED\_CTRLS \quad \| \quad SignalQueues \quad \| \quad ExternalSignals$$
$$\{|create, delete, generate, remove|\} \qquad \{|create, delete, externalGenerate|\}$$

Without the inclusion of the *ExternalSignals* process the system would not be able to evolve the behaviour of the button and light state charts.

Finally, we define a specification, *SPEC*, which is a composition of the *ExternalsSignals* process and processes which represent conditional deadlocks for both buttons and lights. An object cannot deadlock when it is active. The form of such a process for a button i is as follows:

$$B\_CD(i) = (B\_create.i \rightarrow B\_CDF(i)) \sqcap STOP$$
$$B\_CDF(i) = (B\_delete.i \rightarrow B\_CD(i)) \sqcap (\textstyle\bigsqcap_{b \in B(i)} b \rightarrow B\_CDF(i))$$

where $B(i)$ is the set of all events that the active object i can engage in. If $SPEC \sqsubseteq_F SYSTEM2$ holds then the specification is shown to be deadlock-free. The theoretical foundations of CSP ‖ B [1] allow us to deduce that if the controllers of a specification are deadlock-free then the whole specification is deadlock-free. Hence, the above deadlock check allows us to conclude that $SYSTEM2 \; \| \; (LIGHT\_MCH \; \| \; BUTTON\_MCH \; \| \; ASSOC)$ is deadlock-free. We anticipate that in order to extend this to apply to several relations for each class we will define a separate multiplicity template for each association of a class and the $CONSTRAINED\_CTRLS$ process will be the composition of each controller and all its associated multiplicities. The controllers themselves can already support manipulating several associations. The open research issue is whether will we need to develop decomposition arguments in order to make the model checking tractable.

6   Conclusions

This paper outlined our tool that produces CSP ‖ B specifications and which is integrated into the KC toolset. The specifications are based on transformation rules that are invoked during the traversal of the xUML meta-model using particular xUML classes and any associated state charts. The tool can translate the structure of class diagrams and state charts with limited object manipulation. We have documented assumptions and other forms of restrictions on the xUML input models. More work is needed to identify what datatype definitions cannot be supported and this issue is also identified in [17] as a potential weakness. The subset we use will need to be sufficiently wide ranging so that the translated models can be verified using tool support.

There is a significant body of work relating UML and formal methods, including [7,8]. The action language in Snook and Butler's UML-B tool is more abstract than ASL, and guards are used within Event-B to provide the control instead of CSP. The emphasis of the UML-B tool is to provide a graphical interface to Event-B rather than analysing the integrity of a UML model. As far as we know, they do not provide support for instrumenting a formal model with animation scenarios based on initialisation segments and test methods. Larsen's work [8] on mapping VDM++ from UML is very pragmatic. The specifier is able to add to the VDM++ produced and these additions are preserved, even if the specification is re-generated. Furthermore, errors from the VDM++ can be mapped back to the UML and this is an important feature in order to provide backwards traceability.

References

1. Schneider, S., Treharne, H.: CSP theorems for communicating B machines. Formal Asp. Comput. 17(4), 390–422 (2005)
2. Mellor, S.J., Balcer, M.J.: Executable UML, A Foundation for Model-Driven Architecture. Addison-Wesley, Reading (2002)
3. Kolovos, D.S., Paige, R.F., Polack, F.A.C.: Epsilon development tools for Eclipse. In: Eclipse Summit (2006)
4. Hoare, C.A.R.: Communicating Sequential Processes. Prentice-Hall, Englewood Cliffs (1985)
5. Abrial, J.R.: The B-Book: Assigning Programs to Meanings. Cambridge University Press, Cambridge (1996)
6. Schneider, S.A., Treharne, H., Evans, N.: Chunks: Component verification in CSP ‖ B. In: Romijn, J.M.T., Smith, G.P., van de Pol, J. (eds.) IFM 2005. LNCS, vol. 3771, pp. 89–108. Springer, Heidelberg (2005)
7. Snook, C., Butler, M.: UML-B: Formal modeling and design aided by UML. ACM Trans. Softw. Eng. Methodol. 15(1), 92–122 (2006)
8. Group, T.V.T.: The Rose-VDM++ link. Technical report, CSK Systems (2008)
9. Wilkie, I., King, A., Clarke, M., Weaver, C., Raistrick, C., Francis, P.: UML ASL Reference Guide (ASL language level 2.5). Kennedy Carter Ltd (2003)
10. Object Management Group: UML 2.0 OCL Specification (2003)
11. Formal Systems Oxford: FDR 2.83 manual (2007)
12. Leuschel, M., Butler, M.: ProB: A Model Checker for B. In: Araki, K., Gnesi, S., Mandrioli, D. (eds.) FME 2003. LNCS, vol. 2805, pp. 855–874. Springer, Heidelberg (2003)
13. Schneider, S.: Concurrent and Real-Time Systems: the CSP Approach. Wiley, Chichester (1999)
14. Roscoe, A.W.: The theory and practice of concurrency. Prentice-Hall, Englewood Cliffs (1998)

15. Evans, N., Treharne, H., Laleau, R., Frappier, M.: Applying CSP || B to information systems. Software and System Modeling 7(1), 85–102 (2008)
16. Treharne, H., Schneider, S., Grant, N., Evans, N., Ifill, W.: A step towards merging xUML and CSP || B. In: Dagstuhl workshop on Rigorous Methods for Software Construction and Analysis (to appear)
17. Anastasakis, K., Bordbar, B., Georg, G., Ray, I.: UML2Alloy: A challenging model transformation. In: Engels, G., Opdyke, B., Schmidt, D.C., Weil, F. (eds.) MODELS 2007. LNCS, vol. 4735, pp. 436–450. Springer, Heidelberg (2007)

Bounded Model Checking for Partial Kripke Structures

Heike Wehrheim

Universität Paderborn, Institut für Informatik
33098 Paderborn, Germany
wehrheim@uni-paderborn.de

Abstract. Partial Kripke structures model incomplete state spaces with unknown parts. The evaluation of temporal logic formulae on partial Kripke structures is thus based on three-valued interpretations; the additional truth value $\perp$ stands for "unknown whether property true or false". There are existing model checking algorithms as well as tools employing this three-valued interpretation.

In this paper we study the applicability of *bounded model checking* techniques to partial Kripke structures. To this end, we generalise the translation of Kripke structure and temporal logic formula to propositional logic as to include the value $\perp$, and define a new notion of satisfiability for propositional formulae containing $\perp$ as constants. We show that a check for this kind of satisfiability can be reduced to two checks for ordinary two-valued satisfiability, thus allowing for the use of standard SAT solvers.

1 Introduction

Temporal logic model checking [CGP99] is used for checking whether certain properties specified in temporal logic hold in system specifications (models of hardware or software). Since its invention in the late '80ties, a lot of progress has been made, in particular with respect to the size of systems which can be verified by model checking. Nevertheless, the so-called state-explosion problem remains an issue, and today research in verification is still mainly devoted to managing large state spaces. Two landmark developments in this area are the introduction of *symbolic model checking* [BCM+92], using binary decision diagrams for representing state spaces, and the development of *bounded model checking* [BCC+03]. The latter reduces the model checking problem for temporal logic to propositional satisfiability. Recent advances in SAT solving technology have made this approach feasible, also for large systems [PBG05].

Model checking techniques usually assume the system to be *completely* known. This general assumption fails to hold for some classes of systems, for instance for certain kinds of self-* systems (e.g. self-organising, self-adapting, self-healing). Self-organising systems [KM07] can adapt to changing system states (e.g. failures) or environmental conditions, and thus may dynamically evolve over time reaching initially unknown states. This adaption may lead to system models

J.S. Fitzgerald, A.E. Haxthausen, and H. Yenigun (Eds.): ICTAC 2008, LNCS 5160, pp. 380–394, 2008.
© Springer-Verlag Berlin Heidelberg 2008

or specifications, which are only partially known. Inconsistencies are another, different source of uncompleteness: in a system specification with multiple viewpoints these might be contradictory and thus lead to a certain imprecision in the model. And third, *abstractions* naturally lead to partially known systems as the abstract system only partially resembles the information in the original system (for examples see [GC06]).

Multi-valued model checking [BG99, CDEG03] has been developed as to cope with such incomplete specifications. Multi-valued model checking is usually based on system models given by *partial Kripke structures*. In partial Kripke structures labellings of states with atomic propositions as well as transitions can take values out of some many-valued logic. The interpretation of temporal logic formulae on partial Kripke structures therefore also takes values out of the multi-valued domain. Several results have shown that multi-valued model checking can be reduced to a number of standard model checking runs [GC03, KP02, BG00]. Multi-valued model checkers however usually do not follow this approach and use specialised techniques like MBTDDs or MDDs instead [CDEG03]. Bounded model checking for partial Kripke structures has - to the best of the author's knowledge - only be considered in [AY04], which however *first* encodes the multi-valued model checking problem into a "layered" binary one, where the layers represent boolean encodings of the multi-valued setting. This layered model is then the starting point of standard bounded model checking.

In this paper we develop a technique for bounded model checking of *three-valued* partial Kripke structures which keeps the third truth value $\perp$ during the translation to a propositional formula. The translation generalises the definitions in [BCCZ99] to the many-valued case. The satisfiability check, however, then needs to be able to treat propositional formulae with $\perp$ as constant. For this type of formulae we define a new notion of satisfiability (which can give three types of answers: yes, no and unknown), and show that - alike the corresponding results for model checking - testing for this type of satisfiability can be reduced to two ordinary binary satisfiability checks. This allows for the use of standard SAT solvers. We moreover prove correctness of the translation with respect to this new type of satisfiability.

The paper is structured as follows. We start with a short review of partial Kripke structures and the three-valued interpretation of LTL formulae. Then alike [BCCZ99] we define a bounded semantics for LTL and show its relationship to the non-bounded semantics in our three-valued setting. Section 4 defines the translation to 3-valued propositional logic and the new kind of satisfiability. It furthermore shows the correctness of our approach. The reduction of this type of satisfiability checking to two two-valued satisfiability checks is shown in Section 5, the last section concludes.

2   Background

We start with briefly reviewing partial Kripke structures, the evaluation of temporal logic formulae on them and some known results about the relationship between model checking partial and complete Kripke structures. Let AP be a set of atomic propositions.

Definition 1. *A partial Kripke structure over a set of atomic propositions AP is a tuple $M = (S, S_0, R, L)$ such that*

- S *is a finite set of states,*
- $S_0 \subseteq S$ *is a set of initial states,*
- $R \subseteq S \times S$ *is a total transition relation, i.e.* $\forall s \exists s' : (s, s') \in R$, *and*
- $L : S \times P \to \{true, \bot, false\}$ *is a labelling function telling us whether an atomic proposition is true, false or unknown in a particular state.*

A Kripke structure is complete *if $L(s, p) \subseteq \{true, false\}$ for all $s \in S, p \in AP$.*

A partial Kripke structure thus has some unknown parts: we might be unsure as to whether an atomic proposition is true or not in a particular state. A more generalised notion of partiality might also take transitions to be unknown [LT88] or use values of arbitrary multi-valued lattices (see e.g. [CED01]). Unknown values might arise out of inconsistencies in a system specification or just unknown components which contribute to the overall semantics.

A *path* of M is a finite or infinite sequence of states $s_0 s_1 \ldots s_k \ldots$ such that $s_0 \in S_0$ and $(s_i, s_{i+1}) \in R$; $\pi(i)$ denotes the state s_i and π^i the sequence $s_i s_{i+1} \ldots$. Paths are considered when evaluating linear time properties of Kripke structures. Here, we use the temporal logic LTL [MP92] to specify such properties. LTL formuale are built over atomic propositions from AP using the boolean operators $\neg$, $\vee$, $\wedge$ and the temporal operators $\square$ (always), $\Diamond$ (eventually), X (next) and U (until).

In contrast to ordinary complete Kripke structure, the evaluation of an LTL formula on a Kripke structure can yield three values: *true* (if the properties holds), *false* (if the property does not hold) or $\bot$ (if it is unknown whether the property is true or false). Thus we have to use a three-valued logic (here Kleene's logic $\mathcal{L}_3$ [Fit94]) for the evaluation. Figure 1 gives the truth tables for conjunction, disjunction and negation in $\mathcal{L}_3$. It can be seen that conjunction computes the *minimal* value of its arguments and disjunction the *maximal* value using the *truth ordering false $\leq \bot \leq$ true*.

The validity of an LTL formula on a partial Kripke structure can thus be inductively defined as follows.

$\wedge$	*true*	$\bot$	*false*
true	*true*	$\bot$	*false*
$\bot$	$\bot$	$\bot$	*false*
false	*false*	*false*	*false*

$\vee$	*true*	$\bot$	*false*
true	*true*	*true*	*true*
$\bot$	*true*	$\bot$	$\bot$
false	*true*	$\bot$	*false*

$\neg$	
true	*false*
$\bot$	$\bot$
false	*true*

Fig. 1. Truth tables for $\mathcal{L}_3$

Definition 2. *Let M be a Kripke structure, π a path of M and φ an LTL formula. The value of φ in M, $[M \models \varphi]$, is defined as*

$$[M \models \varphi] = \bigwedge_{\pi, \pi \text{ infinite path of } M} [\pi \models \varphi]$$

where

$$[\pi \models p] = L(\pi(0), p)$$
$$[\pi \models \neg \varphi] = \neg [\pi \models \varphi]$$
$$[\pi \models \varphi_1 \wedge \varphi_2] = [\pi \models \varphi_1] \wedge [\pi \models \varphi_2]$$
$$[\pi \models \varphi_1 \vee \varphi_2] = [\pi \models \varphi_1] \vee [\pi \models \varphi_2]$$
$$[\pi \models X \varphi] = [\pi^1 \models \varphi]$$
$$[\pi \models \square \varphi] = \bigwedge_{i \in \mathbb{N}} [\pi^i \models \varphi]$$
$$[\pi \models \lozenge \varphi] = \bigvee_{i \in \mathbb{N}} [\pi^i \models \varphi]$$
$$[\pi \models \varphi_1 \ U \ \varphi_2] = \bigvee_{j \in \mathbb{N}} [\pi \models \varphi_1 \ U_j \ \varphi_2]$$

with $[\pi \models \varphi_1 \ U_j \ \varphi_2] = [\pi^j \models \varphi_2] \wedge \bigwedge_{i < j} [\pi^i \models \varphi_1]$

This looks completely standard. The unknown values only come into play when evaluating atomic propositions on states, and are then propagated on the higher level of a formula by means of conjunction and disjunction. Figure 2 shows a Kripke structure M over $AP = \{p, q\}$ with three states. Here, we have $[M \models \square p] = \bot$ and $[M \models \lozenge q] = \bot$, whereas $[M \models \lozenge p] = true$ and $[M \models X \neg p] = false$. Note also that in particular both $\square(q \vee \neg q)$ and $\square(q \wedge \neg q)$ evaluate to $\bot$ in the structure. The evaluation of a formula might yield $\bot$, although the formula is – on complete Kripke structures – universally valid or unsatisfiable. A semantics which does not have this property (sometimes also called the *thorough* semantics) can be found in [BG00]. The complexity of model checking wrt. this thorough semantics is however much higher (and the semantics does not enjoy a natural inductive definition). Most of the work on model checking partial Kripke structures sticks to the semantics given here, in particular also the many-valued model checker χChek [CDEG03].

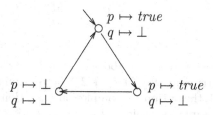

Fig. 2. A partial Kripke structure

In the following, we will only use a positive form of LTL formula, LTL$^+$. LTL$^+$ formulae contain no negations at all. They are evaluated on *complement-closed* Kripke structures [BG00]. In complement-closed structure every atomic proposition p has a complementary proposition $\bar{p}$ such that $L(s, p) = \neg L(s, \bar{p})$. Instead of at least allowing negations on atomic propositions (as in negation normal form), we replace $\neg p$ with $\bar{p}$ in every LTL formula. Thus $\Box(q \wedge \neg q)$ becomes $\Box(q \wedge \bar{q})$. The corresponding complement-closed structure for M is given in Figure 3.

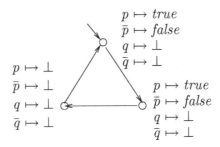

Fig. 3. A complement-closed Kripke structure

The semantics we use here has the interesting property that the model checking problem for partial Kripke structures can be reduced to two model checking problems for complete Kripke structures.

Definition 3. *Given a partial Kripke structure M, we define K^o, the* optimistic completion *of M, as (S, S_0, R, L^o) and K^p, the* pessimistic completion *of M, as (S, S_0, R, L^p) with*

$$L^o(s, p) = \begin{cases} true & if\ L(s, p) = \bot \\ L(s, p) & else \end{cases}$$
$$L^p(s, p) = \begin{cases} false & if\ L(s, p) = \bot \\ L(s, p) & else \end{cases}$$

From [BG00] we get the following result (where $M \models \varphi$ stands for the standard LTL semantics on complete Kripke structures). Similar results relating multi-valued to two-valued model checking can be found in [KP02, GC03].

Theorem 1. *Let M be a partial Kripke structure and φ an LTL$^+$ formula. Then*

$$[M \models \varphi] = \begin{cases} true & if\ M^p \models \varphi \\ false & if\ M^o \not\models \varphi \\ \bot & else \end{cases}$$

This property is consistent with the above observed fact that $\Box(q \wedge \neg q)$ evaluates to $\bot$ in the Kripke structure M of Figure 2. The pessimistic completion assigns *false* to both q and $\bar{q}$, the optimistic completion *true*. Hence, evaluating $\Box(q \wedge \bar{q})$ on the pessimistic completion yields *false*, on the optimistic completion we get *true*. Later, we will develop a similar result for satisfiability checking.

3 Bounded Semantics

Instead of checking whether a formula is true on all paths, bounded model checking tries to find one path on which the *negation* of the formula is *not* true. Intuitively, the idea is to try to find a counterexample to the universal validity of a formula. A universal problem is thus transfered into an existential validity check.

Definition 4. *The* universal value *of an LTL formula* φ *in a Kripke structure* M *is* $[M \models_A \varphi] := [M \models \varphi]$, *its* existential value *is*

$$[M \models_E \varphi] = \bigvee_{\pi,\pi \text{ infinite paths of } M} [\pi \models \varphi]$$

Thus, instead of checking for instance $[M \models_A \square p]$, we check $[M \models_E \Diamond \neg p]$. A witness for this property can then serve as a counterexample to $[M \models_A \square p]$. Bounded model checking tries to find witnesses by only looking at a *finite prefix* of a path. The prefix' length is bound by some number k, which is progressively increased during the model checking runs. For some fixed k, the existence of a witness with length k is checked by testing a propositional formula for satisfiability. The propositional formula is obtained by a translation of the Kripke structure and the LTL formula. Here, we aim at extending this technique to partial Kripke structures with three-valued interpretations.

We start with the basic idea of transfering a universal into an existential problem. Alike the two-valued case, we get the following correspondence between universal and existential validity:

Proposition 1. *Let* M *be a partial Kripke structure,* φ *an LTL formula.*

$$[M \models_A \varphi] = \neg[M \models_E \neg\varphi]$$

Next, we have to define the bounded semantics for LTL formula. This semantics defines the value of an LTL formula on a path of length k. Intuitively, a finite prefix can also represent an infinite path, namely if the prefix contains a loop (definition from [BCCZ99]).

Definition 5. *A path* π *has a* $(k, l) - loop, l \leq k$, *if* $(\pi(k), \pi(l)) \in R$ *and* $\pi = u \cdot v^\omega$ *with* $u = \pi(0) \ldots \pi(l-1)$ *and* $v = \pi(l) \ldots \pi(k)$. π *has a* k-loop *if there is some* l *such that* π *has a* (k, l)-loop.

The bounded semantics (and the translation of Kripke structure and formula to propositional logic) has to distinguish between paths with and without loops.

Definition 6. *Let* φ *be an* LTL^+ *formula,* π *a path of a complement-closed Kripke structure without k-loop,* $k \in \mathbb{N}$ *the bound (length of prefix) and* $i \in \mathbb{N}$ *a number denoting the current position in the path. The bounded semantics of* φ *is inductively defined by*

$$[\pi \models_k^i p] = L(\pi(i), p)$$
$$[\pi \models_k^i \bar{p}] = L(\pi(i), \bar{p})$$

$$[\pi \models_k^i \varphi_1 \wedge \varphi_2] = [\pi \models_k^i \varphi_1] \wedge [\pi \models_k^i \varphi_2]$$

$$[\pi \models_k^i \varphi_1 \vee \varphi_2] = [\pi \models_k^i \varphi_1] \vee [\pi \models_k^i \varphi_2]$$

$$[\pi \models_k^i X \varphi] = i < k \wedge [\pi \models_k^{i+1} \varphi]$$

$$[\pi \models_k^i \square \varphi] = false$$

$$[\pi \models_k^i \Diamond \varphi] = \bigvee_{j=i}^{k} [\pi \models_k^j \varphi]$$

$$[\pi \models_k^i \varphi_1 U \varphi_2] = \bigvee_{j \leq k} [\pi \models_k^i \varphi_1 U_j \varphi_2]$$

$$[\pi \models_k^i \varphi_1 U_j \varphi_2] = [\pi \models_k^j \varphi_2] \wedge \bigwedge_{i \leq n < j} [\pi \models_k^n \varphi_1]$$

If π has a k-loop, then $[\pi \models_k^i \varphi] := [\pi^i \models \varphi]$.
Finally, $[M \models_{E,k} \varphi] := \bigvee_{\pi, \pi \text{ infinite path of } M} [\pi \models_k^0 \varphi]$.

This bounded semantics approximates the existential semantics with respect to the truth ordering: whenever we get the value $[M \models_{E,k} \varphi]$ for a particular k, we know that the value for $[M \models_E \varphi]$ can only be "better" (in the truth ordering).

Theorem 2. *Let φ be an LTL^+ formula, M a complement-closed Kripke structure. For all $k \in \mathbb{N}$ we get*

$$[M \models_E \varphi] \geq [M \models_{E,k} \varphi]$$

Proof. For the three-valued logic we get $[M \models_E \varphi] = \bigvee_{k \in \mathbb{N}} [M \models_{E,k} \varphi]$. This holds since on a finite Kripke structure all infinite paths eventually contain loops. The above theorem is a corollary of this fact, since disjunction amounts to computing the maximum of truth values.   □

Thus, when $[M \models_{E,k} \varphi]$ becomes $\perp$ for some k, we already know that $[M \models_E \varphi]$ will either yield $\perp$ or *true*. As an example, consider the Kripke structure in Figure 4 and assume we want to check $[M \models_A \square p]$. Transferring this to an existential problem we need to check $[M \models_E \Diamond \bar{p}]$. For the bounded semantics we get

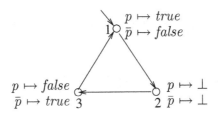

Fig. 4. Checking $[M \models_E \Diamond \bar{p}]$

$$[M \models_{E,0} \Diamond \bar{p}] = \mathit{false}$$
$$[M \models_{E,1} \Diamond \bar{p}] = \bot$$
$$[M \models_{E,2} \Diamond \bar{p}] = \mathit{true}$$

For bound $k = 1$ we already see that $[M \models_E \Diamond \bar{p}]$ cannot become *false* anymore, i.e. we have already found a counterexample to $[M \models_A \Box p] = \mathit{true}$.

4   Translation to Propositional Logic

In the next step, the bounded model checking problem is reduced to propositional satisfiability. For a Kripke structure M, a bound k and an LTL formula φ, a propositional formula $F = [M, \varphi]_k$ is constructed such that F is satisfiable if and only if $M \models_{E,k} \varphi$. This is the two-valued setting. Here, we aim at a similar result: we also translate M, k, φ into a propositional formula $[M, \varphi]_k$ with the translation differing in the treatment of atomic propositions (where we now might get $\bot$), define a notion of satisfiability sat_3 which has three possible outcomes (*true, false,* $\bot$) and show the following:

$$[[M, \varphi]_k \, sat_3] = [M \models_{E,k} \varphi]$$

The next section will then show that this 3-valued satisfiability testing can - like 3-valued model checking - be reduced to two normal satisfiability checks. Thus we can employ standard SAT solvers.

The definitions of $[M]_k$ and $[\varphi]_k$ in this section closely follow [BCCZ99]. The translation to propositional logic consists of two parts: the translation of the Kripke structure (which guarantees that only valid paths of M can be taken) and the translation of the LTL formula. We start with the former. First, we have to encode states as boolean formulas. To this end we take n atoms $Atoms = \{A, B, \ldots\}$ such that $2^{n-1} < |S| \leq 2^n$. Let $L(Atoms)$ be the set of propositional formulae over $Atoms$ and the boolean constants *true, false* using negation, conjunction and disjunction; $L^\bot(Atoms)$ additional includes $\bot$ as constant. A *valuation* is a mapping $\mathcal{A} : Atoms \to \{true, false\}$, $\mathcal{A}(F)$ is the evaluation of F under a given $\mathcal{A}$. Note that valuations $\mathcal{A}$ never assign the truth value $\bot$ to atoms.

Definition 7. *An* encoding *of states of a Kripke structure is an injective mapping* $c : S \to L(Atoms)$ *such that* $c(s)$ *is a conjunction of literals. Alternatively,* $c(s)$ *can be seen as a valuation mapping atoms to true or false.*

For the Kripke structure in Figure 4 we could for instance use the encoding $c(1) = \neg A \wedge \neg B$, $c(2) = \neg A \wedge B$ and $c(3) = A \wedge \neg B$. For a propositional formula F we write F_i to stand for $F[A, B, \ldots / A_i, B_i, \ldots]$, e.g. $((A \wedge \neg B) \vee C)_i = (A_i \wedge \neg B_i) \vee C_i$. The Kripke structure M is now translated into a formula $[M]_k$ which exactly characterises the k-prefixes of paths.

Definition 8. *Let* $M = (S, S_0, R, L)$ *be a partial Kripke structure. Define* $Init$ *to be the predicate* $\bigvee_{s \in S_0} c(s)$ *characterising initial states and* $T_{i,i+1} = \bigvee_{(s,s') \in R} c(s)_i \wedge c(s')_{i+1}$ *to be a predicate for transitions. Then*

$$[M]_k := Init_0 \wedge \bigwedge_{i=0}^{k-1} T_{i,i+1}$$

For the Kripke structure of Figure 4 we get

$$Init = \neg A_0 \wedge \neg B_0$$
$$T_{i,i+1} = (\neg A_i \wedge \neg B_i \wedge \neg A_{i+1} \wedge B_{i+1})$$
$$\vee (\neg A_i \wedge B_i \wedge A_{i+1} \wedge \neg B_{i+1})$$
$$\vee (A_i \wedge \neg B_i \wedge \neg A_{i+1} \wedge \neg B_{i+1})$$

The formula $[M]_k$ is satisfiable (since there are valid paths in the Kripke structure) and the satisfying valuation exactly characterises a path. For a (prefix) of a path $\pi = s_0 s_1 s_2 \ldots s_k$, the valuation $\mathcal{A}_\pi : \{A_0, B_0, \ldots, A_k, B_k, \ldots\} \rightarrow \{true, false\}$ is defined as $\mathcal{A}(A_i) = c(s_i)(A)$. A satisfying assignment for $[M]_k$ is a valuation $\mathcal{A}_\pi$ for some path prefix π.

Proposition 2. *Let M be a Kripke structure, $k \in \mathbb{N}$, $[M]_k$ the translation. Then*

1. *for all paths π of M, $\mathcal{A}_\pi([M]_k) = true$, and*
2. *all valuations $\mathcal{A}$ such that $\mathcal{A}([M]_k) = true$ denote k-prefixes of paths.*

The second part of the translation concerns the LTL formula. Here, we need to distinguish between paths with and without loops. The basic idea for the translation of the temporal logic formula is to encode all possibilities for a formula to become true into the propositional formula. For instance, if the LTL formula is $\varphi = \Diamond p$, we are currently at position i in a prefix and the prefix has length k, then φ becomes true if p holds at position i or $i + 1$ or ... until position k. The difference in the 3-valued case is that proposition p holding at position j can now take three different values: $true, false$ or $\bot$. The translation of atomic propositions p (and their complements) thus is the disjunction over all states with their encodings conjoined with the value of p in the state.

Definition 9. *Translation without a loop.*
Let φ be an LTL^+ formula and $k, i \in \mathbb{N}, i \leq k$.

$$[p]_k^i = \bigvee_{s \in S} c(s)_i \wedge L(s, p)$$

$$[\bar{p}]_k^i = \bigvee_{s \in S} c(s)_i \wedge L(s, \bar{p})$$

$$[\varphi_1 \wedge \varphi_2]_k^i = [\varphi_1]_k^i \wedge [\varphi_2]_k^i$$
$$[\varphi_1 \vee \varphi_2]_k^i = [\varphi_1]_k^i \vee [\varphi_2]_k^i$$
$$[\Box \varphi]_k^i = false$$

$$[\Diamond \varphi]_k^i = \bigvee_{j=i}^{k} [\varphi]_k^j$$

$$[X \varphi]_k^i = \text{if } i < k \text{ then } [\varphi]_k^{i+1} \text{ else } false$$

$$[\varphi_1 U \varphi_2] = \bigvee_{j=i}^{k} ([\varphi_2]_k^j \wedge \bigwedge_{n=i}^{j-1} [\varphi_1]_k^n)$$

Considering again Figure 4, $[p]_2^1 = (\neg A_1 \wedge \neg B_1 \wedge \textit{true}) \vee (\neg A_1 \wedge B_1 \wedge \bot) \vee (A_1 \wedge \neg B_1 \wedge \textit{false})$. Note that $[\bar{p}]_k^i$ is in general not equivalent to $\neg[p]_k^i$, e.g. $\neg(A_i \wedge B_i \wedge \bot) \neq (A_i \wedge B_i \wedge \neg\bot)$. Here, we thus need our complement-closed structures. In contrast to $[M]_k$, we have the constant $\bot$ in these formulae, i.e. $[\varphi]_k^i \in L^{\bot}(\textit{Atoms})$. As mentioned before, valuations of atoms will however still only take values out of $\{\textit{true}, \textit{false}\}$. For such a valuation $\mathcal{A}$ and a propositional formula $F \in L^{\bot}(\textit{Atoms})$, $\mathcal{A}(F) \in \{\textit{true}, \textit{false}, \bot\}$.

Next, we take a look at the correctness of this translation, i.e. the relationship between the bounded model checking problem and the valuation of the propositional formula. The translation ensures the following property: for a valuation $\mathcal{A}$ describing a path π, the evaluation of the propositional formula with respect to $\mathcal{A}$ takes exactly the same value as the interpretation of the LTL formula on the path π.

Lemma 1. *Let $\pi = s_0 s_1 \ldots$ be a path without a k-loop, φ an LTL^+ formula, $\mathcal{A}_\pi$ the valuation for $A_0, B_0, \ldots, A_k, B_k, \ldots$ as fixed by π. Then*

$$[\pi \models_k^i \varphi] = \mathcal{A}_\pi([\varphi]_k^i)$$

Proof. Induction on the structure of φ. We only present some cases.

– Atomic propositions: $\varphi = p$ (same for complements)

$$[\pi \models_k^i p] = L(\pi(i), p))$$
$$\mathcal{A}_\pi([p]_k^i) = \mathcal{A}_\pi(\bigvee_{s \in S} c(s)_i \wedge L(s, p))$$
$$= L(s_i, p) = L(\pi(i), p)$$

– Temporal operator *globally*: $\varphi = \square \varphi_1$
  $[\pi \models_k^i \square \varphi_1] = \textit{false} = \mathcal{A}(\textit{false}) = \mathcal{A}([\square \varphi_1]_k^i)$.
– Temporal operator *eventually*: $\varphi = \Diamond \varphi_1$

$$[\pi \models_k^i \Diamond \varphi_1] = \bigvee_{j=i}^{k} [\pi \models_k^j \varphi_1]$$
$$= \bigvee_{j=i}^{k} \mathcal{A}_\pi([\varphi_1]_k^j)$$
$$= \mathcal{A}_\pi(\bigvee_{j=i}^{k} [\varphi_1]_k^j)$$
$$= \mathcal{A}_\pi([\Diamond \varphi_1]_k^i)$$

$\square$

This so far give us a treatment of paths without loops. The translation for loops is similar. Below k is the bound, i the current position and l the starting position of the loop.

Definition 10. *Translation with a loop.*
Let φ be an LTL^+ formula and $k, i, l \in \mathbb{N}, l, i \leq k$.

$$\iota[p]_k^i = \bigvee_{s \in S} c(s)_i \wedge L(s, p)$$

$$\iota[\bar{p}]_k^i = \bigvee_{s \in S} c(s)_i \wedge L(s, \bar{p})$$

$$\iota[\varphi_1 \wedge \varphi_2]_k^i = \iota[\varphi_1]_k^i \wedge \iota[\varphi_2]_k^i$$

$$\iota[\varphi_1 \vee \varphi_2]_k^i = \iota[\varphi_1]_k^i \vee \iota[\varphi_2]_k^i$$

$$\iota[\square \varphi]_k^i = \bigwedge_{j=min(i,l)}^{k} \iota[\varphi]_k^j$$

$$\iota[\diamond \varphi]_k^i = \bigvee_{j=min(i,l)}^{k} \iota[\varphi]_k^j$$

$$\iota[X \varphi]_k^i = \iota[\varphi]_k^{succ(i)}$$

$$\iota[\varphi_1 \ U \ \varphi_2] = \bigvee_{j=i}^{k}(\iota[\varphi_2]_k^j \wedge \bigwedge_{n=i}^{j-1} \iota[\varphi_1]_k^n) \vee$$

$$\bigvee_{j=l}^{i-1}(\iota[\varphi_2]_k^j \wedge \bigwedge_{n=i}^{k} \iota[\varphi_1]_k^n \wedge \bigwedge_{n=l}^{j-1} \iota[\varphi_1]_k^n)$$

Here, $succ(i)$ is either $i+1$ or, in case of $i = k$, l. Alike the translation without loops, we get a result relating a specific path-valuation of the formula and the validity of an LTL formula.

Lemma 2. *Let $\pi = s_0 s_1 \ldots$ be a path with a (k, l)-loop, φ an LTL^+ formula, $\mathcal{A}_\pi$ the valuation for $A_0, B_0, \ldots, A_k, B_k, \ldots, A_{k+1}, B_{k+1}, \ldots$ as fixed by π. Then*

$$[\pi \models_k^i \varphi] = \mathcal{A}_\pi(\iota[\varphi]_k^i)$$

Proof. The proof again proceeds by induction on the structure of φ. The main argument here, which differs from the case of paths without loops, is the following: if π contains a (k, l)-loop, then $\forall j \geq l : [\pi \models_k^j \varphi] = [\pi \models_k^{j+(k-l)+1} \varphi]$. $\square$

The general translation of the formula now needs to take both cases into account. For this, [BCCZ99] uses a loop condition.

Definition 11. *For $k, l \in \mathbb{N}$, we define $_l L_k = T_{k,k+1}$ and $L_k = \bigvee_{l=0}^{k} {}_l L_k$.*

Proposition 3. *Let π_1 be a path without a k-loop and π_2 a path with a (k, l)-loop. Then $\mathcal{A}_{\pi_1}(L_k) = false$ and $\mathcal{A}_{\pi_2}(L_k) = true$.*

The overall translation now combines the translation of the Kripke structure with the translation of the formula.

Definition 12. *Let M be a partial Kripke structure, $k \in \mathbb{N}$ a bound and φ an LTL^+ formula.*

$$[M, \varphi]_k = [M]_k \wedge \left((\neg L_k \wedge [\varphi]_k^0) \vee \bigvee_{l=0}^{k} ({}_l L_k \wedge {}_l [\varphi]_k^0) \right)$$

Finally, we need a test for satisfiability. The essential difference to ordinary satisfiability is the presence of the constant $\perp$ in our propositional formulae. Valuations should however still take only values from $\{true, false\}$. The overall goal is to define a notion of $[F \ sat_3]$, $F \in L^{\perp}(Atoms)$, such that

$$[[M, \varphi]_k \, sat_3] = [M \models_{E,k} \varphi]$$

holds. The following definition is a non-standard generalisation of 2-valued satisfiability: a formula is satisfiable if some valuation can make it true, it is unsatisfiable if all valuations make it false, and its satisfiability is unknown otherwise. Note that this does not coincide with ordinary multi-valued satisfiability and thus we cannot use multi-valued SAT solvers like CAMA [LKM03].

Definition 13. *Sat_3 Let $F \in L^{\perp}(Atoms)$ be a 3-valued propositional formula.*

$$[F \ sat_3] = \begin{cases} true & \text{if } \exists \mathcal{A} : \mathcal{A}(F) = true \\ false & \text{if } \forall \mathcal{A} : \mathcal{A}(F) = false \\ \perp & \text{else} \end{cases}$$

Then we get the following correctness result for our translation which is a direct corollary of Lemmas 1 and 2 and Propositions 2 and 3.

Corollary 1. *Let M be a partial Kripke structure, $k \in \mathbb{N}$ a bound and φ an LTL^+ formula.*

$$[[M, \varphi]_k \, sat_3] = [M \models_{E,k} \varphi]$$

For the example in Figure 4 and $k = 1$, we get the following formulae: $[M]_1 = (\neg A_0 \wedge \neg B_0) \wedge ((\neg A_0 \wedge \neg B_0 \wedge \neg A_1 \wedge B_1) \vee (\neg A_0 \wedge B_0 \wedge A_1 \wedge \neg B_1) \vee (A_0 \wedge \neg B_0 \wedge \neg A_1 \wedge \neg B_1))$ and $[\Diamond \bar{p}]_1^0 = [\bar{p}]_1^0 \vee [\bar{p}]_1^1$ which (leaving out conjunctions with *false*) is $(\neg A_0 \wedge B_0 \wedge \perp) \vee (A_0 \wedge \neg B_0 \wedge true) \vee (\neg A_1 \wedge B_1 \wedge \perp) \vee (A_1 \wedge \neg B_1 \wedge true)$. There is no valuation which makes $[M]_1 \wedge [\Diamond \bar{p}]_1^0$ true, but one which makes it $\perp$, namely $\mathcal{A} : A_0 \mapsto false, B_0 \mapsto false, A_1 \mapsto false, B_1 \mapsto true$. Thus $[([M]_1 \wedge [\Diamond \bar{p}]_1^0) \ sat_3] = \perp$ which coincides with $[\pi \models_1^0 \varphi]$ for 1-loop-free paths π.

5 Checking Sat_3

Having defined a new notion of satisfiability we have to see how this can actually be checked. The feasibilty of bounded model checking crucially depends on fast SAT solvers, only the recent advances in SAT solving have made bounded model checking a success.

Fortunately, we can also make use of existing SAT solvers here. We use a trick similar to the one used in model checking partial Kripke structures: a satisfiability test on a pessimistic and an optimistic completion of our three-valued propositional formula is all we need. The pessimistic completion replaces all $\perp$'s with *false* ($F^p = F[\perp/false]$), the optimistic completion with *true* ($F^o = F[\perp/true]$). We let $[F\ sat_2]$ denote standard two-valued satisfiability yielding *true* if F is satisfiable and *false* otherwise.

Theorem 3. *Let $F \in L^\perp(Atoms)$ be a propositional formula with negation in front of atoms only. Then*

$$[F\ sat_3] = \begin{cases} true & if\ [F^p\,sat_2] = true \\ false & if\ [F^o\,sat_2] = false \\ \perp & else \end{cases}$$

The check for our 3-valued satisfiability can hence be reduced to two checks for standard 2-valued satisfiability using standard SAT solvers. This result requires the formula to be in a kind of *negation normal form*, in particular no negations are allowed in front of $\perp$. This is a neccessary requirement, which is however indeed fulfilled by the formula $[\![\varphi]\!]_k$. The proof of the above theorem is a direct consequence of the following lemma:

Lemma 3. *Let $F \in L^\perp(Atoms)$ be a propositional formula with negation in front of atomic propositions only, and let $\mathcal{A} : Atoms \to \{true, false\}$ be a valuation. Then*

$$\mathcal{A}(F) = \begin{cases} true & if\ \mathcal{A}(F^p) = true \\ false & if\ \mathcal{A}(F^o) = false \\ \perp & else \end{cases}$$

Proof: The proof follows by induction on the structure of F. For instance, for $F = \perp$ we get $\mathcal{A}(F) = \perp$ (for every $\mathcal{A}$) and $\mathcal{A}(\perp^p) = \mathcal{A}(false) = false$, $\mathcal{A}(\perp^o) = \mathcal{A}(true) = true$. The other cases are similar. The result fails to hold if negations occur in front of $\perp$: $\mathcal{A}(\neg\perp) = \perp$ whereas $\mathcal{A}((\neg\perp)^p) = \mathcal{A}(\neg false) = true$. $\qquad\square$

We have thus found a way of using standard SAT solvers (like e.g. Chaff [MMZ+01]) for bounded model checking of partial Kripke structures.

6 Conclusion

In this paper we have presented a technique for bounded model checking of three-valued Kripke structures. It employs a variation of the standard technique for translating Kripke structure and temporal logic formula into propositional logic. A new notion of satisfiability for propositional formulae with third truth value $\perp$ as constants has been developed and shown to be adequate for bounded model checking. An implementation of the technique could reuse much from existing bounded model checkers, only the translation of three-valued satisfiability to ordinary satisfiability needs to be added.

We conjecture that the technique presented here can naturally be extended to arbitrary multi-valued Kripke structures, even those having multi-valued transitions. This could be achieved by reducing satisfiability checks for formulae with constants out of the multi-valued domain to an appropriate number of standard satisfiability checks along the lines done here for the three-valued case.

The implementation of this approach remains as future work. This would also give us a more precise comparison with [AY04]. As [AY04] requires a transformation on the level of the specification (viz. the abstract description of the Kripke structure) translating program variables and expressions, while our approach only needs to rename constants in propositional formulae ($\perp$ to *true* or *false*), we expect our approach to favourably compare to theirs.

References

[AY04]   Andrade, J.O., Yonezawa, T.: Multi-valued bounded model checking. Technical report, Department of Computer Science, University of Tsukuba, Japan (2004)

[BCC⁺03]   Biere, A., Cimatti, A., Clarke, E.M., Strichman, O., Zhu, Y.: Bounded model checking. Advances in Computers 58, 118–149 (2003)

[BCCZ99]   Biere, A., Cimatti, A., Clarke, E.M., Zhu, Y.: Symbolic Model Checking without BDDs. In: Cleaveland, W.R. (ed.) TACAS 1999. LNCS, vol. 1579, pp. 193–207. Springer, Heidelberg (1999)

[BCM⁺92]   Burch, J.R., Clarke, E.M., McMillan, K.L., Dill, D.L., Hwang, L.J.: Symbolic Model Checking: 10^{20} States and Beyond. Inf. Comput. 98(2), 142–170 (1992)

[BG99]   Bruns, G., Godefroid, P.: Model checking partial state spaces with 3-valued temporal logics. In: Halbwachs, N., Peled, D.A. (eds.) CAV 1999. LNCS, vol. 1633, pp. 274–287. Springer, Heidelberg (1999)

[BG00]   Bruns, G., Godefroid, P.: Generalized Model Checking: Reasoning about Partial State Spaces. In: Palamidessi, C. (ed.) CONCUR 2000. LNCS, vol. 1877, pp. 168–182. Springer, Heidelberg (2000)

[CDEG03]   Chechik, M., Devereux, B., Easterbrook, S.M., Gurfinkel, A.: Multi-valued symbolic model-checking. ACM Trans. Softw. Eng. Methodol. 12(4), 371–408 (2003)

[CED01]   Chechik, M., Easterbrook, S.M., Devereux, B.: Model checking with multi-valued temporal logics. In: ISMVL, pp. 187–192 (2001)

[CGP99]   Clarke, E., Grumberg, O., Peled, D.: Model checking. MIT Press, Cambridge (1999)

[Fit94]   Fitting, M.: Kleene's three valued logics and their children. Fundam. Inform. 20(1/2/3), 113–131 (1994)

[GC03]   Gurfinkel, A., Chechik, M.: Multi-valued model checking via classical model checking. In: Amadio, R., Lugiez, D. (eds.) CONCUR 2003. LNCS, vol. 2761, pp. 263–277. Springer, Heidelberg (2003)

[GC06]   Gurfinkel, A., Chechik, M.: Why waste a perfectly good abstraction? In: Hermanns, H., Palsberg, J. (eds.) TACAS 2006. LNCS, vol. 3920, pp. 212–226. Springer, Heidelberg (2006)

[KM07]   Kramer, J., Magee, J.: Self-Managed Systems: an Architectural Challenge. In: ICSE 2007 - Future of Software Engineering Track. ACM Press, New York (2007)

[KP02]   Konikowska, B., Penczek, W.: Reducing Model Checking from Multi-valued CTL* to CTL*. In: Brim, L., Jančar, P., Křetínský, M., Kucera, A. (eds.) CONCUR 2002. LNCS, vol. 2421, pp. 226–239. Springer, Heidelberg (2002)

[LKM03]   Liu, C., Kuehlmann, A., Moskewicz, M.: CAMA: A Multi-Valued Satisfiability Solver. In: International Conference on Computer Aided Design, pp. 326–333. IEEE/ACM (November 2003)

[LT88]   Larsen, K.G., Thomsen, B.: A modal process logic. In: LICS, pp. 203–210. IEEE Computer Society, Los Alamitos (1988)

[MMZ⁺01]   Moskewicz, M.W., Madigan, C.F., Zhao, Y., Zhang, L., Malik, S.: Chaff: Engineering an Efficient SAT Solver. In: DAC, pp. 530–535. ACM, New York (2001)

[MP92]   Manna, Z., Pnueli, A.: The Temporal Logic of Reactive and Concurrent Systems: Specification. Springer, Heidelberg (1992)

[PBG05]   Prasad, M.R., Biere, A., Gupta, A.: A survey of recent advances in SAT-based formal verification. STTT 7(2), 156–173 (2005)

Verification of Linear Duration Invariants by Model Checking CTL Properties*

Miaomiao Zhang[1], Dang Van Hung[2], and Zhiming Liu[3]

[1] School of Software Engineering,
Tongji University, Shanghai, China
`miaomiao@mail.tongji.edu.cn`
[2] College of Technology,
Vietnam National University, Hanoi, Vietnam
`dvh@vnu.edu.vn`
[3] International Institute of Software Technology,
United Nations University, Macau, China
`Z.Liu@iist.unu.edu`

Abstract. Linear duration invariants (LDI) are important safety properties of real-time systems. They can be easily formulated in terms of a class of chop-free formulas in the Duration Calculus (DC). Compared to other temporal logics, the specification in DC is simpler, neater and more importantly easier to understand. However, directly model checking them is more difficult than model checking properties formulated in the computation tree logic (CTL). In this paper, we present a technique for the verification of the satisfaction of a LDI $\mathcal{D}$ by a timed automaton $\mathcal{A}$ by model checking a CTL property. For this, we construct an untimed automaton G from $\mathcal{A}$, and prove that $\mathcal{A}$ satisfies $\mathcal{D}$ iff $\mathcal{D}$ is is satisfied by the set of all paths of G. To Verify that all paths of G satisfy $\mathcal{D}$, we construct a CTL formula ψ and simply check if G satisfies ψ. By this, we convert the problem of verification of the LDI to the problem of model checking CTL formula. As a result, the CTL model checking techniques and tools, such as UPPAAL, can be used for verification of LDI specified in the DC.

1 Introduction

Linear constraints on the durations of states are important properties of real-time systems. Such a property can be easily formalized as a *chop-free formula* in the Duration Calculus (DC) [11] of the form

$$A \leq \ell \leq B \Rightarrow \sum_{s \in S} c_s \int s \leq M \qquad (1)$$

where S is a finite set of system states, $\int s$ is the duration of state s, ℓ denotes the length of the reference time interval, and A, B, and c_s are constants. This class was

---

* Research supported by the project of National Natural Science Foundation of China (No.60603037) and HTTS project funded by Macau Science and Technology Development Fund.

J.S. Fitzgerald, A.E. Haxthausen, and H. Yenigun (Eds.): ICTAC 2008, LNCS 5160, pp. 395–409, 2008.

first introduced and called *linear duration invariants* (LDI) in [12]. The duration $\int s$ of a state s and the length ℓ are mappings from time intervals to reals. For an observation time interval $[b, e]$, $\int s$ defines the accumulated time for the presence of state s over $[b, e]$ and ℓ is the length $e - b$ of the interval. A LDI $A \leq \ell \leq B \Rightarrow \sum_{s \in S} c_s \int s \leq M$ simply says that for any observation time interval $[b, e]$, if the length ℓ of the interval satisfies the constraint $A \leq \ell \leq B$ then the durations of the system states over that interval should satisfy the linear constraint $\sum_{s \in S} c_s \int s \leq M$.

Since timed automata are good models of real-time systems and linear duration invariants are important properties of real-time systems [12], an important problem is weather the verification of a LDI of a timed automaton can be done automatically.

To solve this problem, several algorithms are proposed in the literature, but they have high complexity and they only work with various restrictions either on the timed automata or on the LDIs [6,12,7,3]. For improving the complexity the algorithms proposed in [10,8,9] are restricted to the class of the so-called *discretisable properties*. A property is discretisable iff it is satisfied by all the behaviors of a timed automaton exactly when it is satisfied by the *integral behaviors* of the automaton (i.e behavior in which transitions take place only at integer time). Furthermore, to the best of our knowledge, there are no existing implementations of these algorithms.

Another popular logic for specification and verification of real-time systems is the *computation tree logic* (CTL)[5]. Effective techniques and tools [14,15] have been developed for checking real-time systems modeled by timed automata [1,2] against properties specified in CTL. This motivates our interest in this paper to study the possibility of reducing the problem of verification of a LDI of a timed automaton to an equivalent problem of model checking a CTL property of an automaton. The goal is that, instead of directly checking a LDI $\mathcal{D}$ for a timed automata using the techniques in [10,8,9], we check a CTL property for a translated model G, using popular model checker, such as UPPAAL.

Our technique following the idea proposed in [9] for checking $\mathcal{D}$ for an automaton $\mathcal{A}$, we construct a *reachability graph* $\mathcal{RG}$. We then optimize $\mathcal{RG}$ to derive a graph G. However, different in technique from [9] that uses extra sub-vertices to record the duration that the system stays in a node of $\mathcal{RG}$, we use an integer variable n to denote the duration that the system stays in a vertex v of $\mathcal{RG}$ together with a self-loop transition of v. This makes our model much simpler and thus easier for model checking. Also, we use a variable gc to bind the value of observation time, and another variable d to bind the value of duration of system states. The value of n is bounded because we remove infinite edges in $\mathcal{RG}$. In achieving these, our graph is constructed carefully in different ways depending on whether the constant B in formula (1) is finite or not.

We use $\mathcal{P}(G)$ to denote the set of all paths of the graph G constructed from $\mathcal{A}$. We then prove that $\mathcal{D}$ is satisfied by $\mathcal{A}$ iff $\mathcal{D}$ is satisfied by the paths $\mathcal{P}(G)$, i.e. $\mathcal{A} \models \mathcal{D}$ if and only if $\mathcal{P}(G) \models \mathcal{D}$. Finally, we define a CTL formula ψ for G, and prove that $\mathcal{P}(G) \models \mathcal{D}$ iff $G \models \psi$.

The rest of the paper is organized as follows. Section 2 recalls some basic notions of timed automaton and Duration Calculus. It also introduces the integral reachability graph of timed automaton. The main technical contribution is presented in Section 3. There, we introduce two kinds of graphs respectively for the cases when B is finite and when B is infinite, and prove the main theorems. We then show an algorithm for checking an CTL of a graph of the automaton. A case study is given in Section 4 to illustrate our technique. Conclusions are discussed in Section 5.

2   Preliminary

We introduce the notions that we need in this paper. These include *timed automata*, *region graphs*, and Linear Duration Invariants (LDI) defined in DC.

2.1   Timed Automata

We first recall the definition of timed automata given in in [1,2] and explain their behavior. For this, we use $\mathbf{R}^{\geq 0}$ and $\mathbf{N}$ to denote the sets of nonnegative real numbers and natural numbers, respectively.

A timed automaton is a finite state machine equipped with a set of clocks. We use a set X of real value variables to resents the clocks and let $\Phi(X)$ be the set of clock constraints on X, which are conjunctions of the formulas of the form $x \leq c$ or $c \leq x$, where $x \in X$ and $c \in \mathbf{N}$.

Definition 1. *A timed automaton $\mathcal{A}$ is a tuple $\langle L, s_0, \Sigma, X, E, I \rangle$, where*

- *L is a finite set of locations,*
- *$s_0 \in L$ is the initial location,*
- *Σ is a finite set of symbols (action names),*
- *X is a finite set of clocks,*
- *I is a mapping that assigns each location $s \in L$ with a clock constraint $I(s) \in \Phi(X)$ called the invariant of location s. Intuitively, the timed automaton only stays at s when the values of the clocks satisfy the invariant $I(s)$.*
- *$E \subseteq L \times \Phi(X) \times \Sigma \times 2^X \times L$ is a set of switches. A switch $\langle s, \varphi, a, \lambda, s' \rangle$ represents a transition from location s to location s' with event a, where φ is a clock constraint over X that specifies the enabling condition of the switch, and $\lambda \subseteq X$ is the set of clocks to be reset to 0 by this switch.*

A clock interpretation ν is a mapping that assigns a nonnegative real value to each clock in X. For $\delta \in \mathbf{R}^{\geq 0}$, let $\nu + \delta$ denote the clock interpretation which maps every clock $x \in X$ to the value $\nu(x) + \delta$. For $\lambda \subseteq X$, let $\nu[\lambda := 0]$ denote the clock interpretation which assigns 0 to each $x \in \lambda$ and agrees with ν over the rest of the clocks.

A state of automaton $\mathcal{A}$ is a pair (s, ν) where s is a location of $\mathcal{A}$ and ν is a clock interpretation which satisfies the invariant $I(s)$. State (s_0, ν_0) is the initial state where s_0 is the initial location of $\mathcal{A}$ and ν_0 is the clock interpretation for which $\nu_0(x) = 0$ for all clocks x. Here we should note that $I(s_0)$ is always assumed to be satisfied by ν_0 to make the automaton A operate.

2.2   Linear Duration Invariants and Duration Properties

Duration Calculus. DC [11] is a logic for reasoning about about durations of states of real-time systems of real-time systems. A comprehensive introduction to DC is given in the monograph by Zhou and Hansen [13]. In DC, a state s is *interpreted* as a function from the time domain $\mathbf{R}^{\geq 0}$ to the boolean values $\{1, 0\}$, and s is 1 at time t if the system is in state s and 0 otherwise. Therefore, a model of DC formula consists of an interpretation $\mathcal{I}$ of the states and a time interval $[b, e]$. It represents an observation of the behavior of the system in term of presence and absence of the states in the interval of time. Given an interpretation $\mathcal{I}$, the duration of a state s over the time interval $[b, e]$ is defined as the integral $\int_b^e \mathcal{I}_s(t)dt$, which is exactly the accumulated present time of s in the interval $[b, e]$ under the interpretation $\mathcal{I}$.

We consider the set of DC models that express all the observations of the behaviors of a timed automaton. Each behavior $\rho = (s_0, t_0)(s_1, t_1) \dots$ of timed automaton $\mathcal{A}$ defines an interpretation $\mathcal{I}$ of the DC formulas about the states of $\mathcal{A}$: for any state s of $\mathcal{A}$, $\mathcal{I}_s(t) = 1$ iff $\exists i \bullet (s_i = s \wedge t \in [t_i, t_{i+1}))$. We also denote such $\mathcal{I}$ by $(\bar{s}, \bar{t})$ where $\bar{s} = (s_0, s_1, \dots)$ and $\bar{t} = (t_0, t_1, \dots)$ are respectively the sequence of states s_i and the sequence of time stamps t_i from the behavior ρ. Hence, $(\bar{s}, \bar{t}, [b, e])$ is also considered as a DC model representing the observation of $\mathcal{A}$ in the time interval $[b, e]$, which is a possible observation of the timed automaton $\mathcal{A}$ over interval $[b, e]$. For this reason, we also call $(\bar{s}, \bar{t}, [b, e])$ an $\mathcal{A}$-model of DC.

Let $\mathcal{M}(\mathcal{A})$ denote the set of $\mathcal{A}$ Models of DC. For a given timed automaton $\mathcal{A}$, the following three classes of $\mathcal{A}$ models of DC are identified and studied in [9]:

1. the set of all $\mathcal{A}$ models that start from time 0 and end at any time point

$$\mathcal{M}_0(\mathcal{A}) \stackrel{\frown}{=} \{\sigma \mid \sigma = (\bar{s}, \bar{t}, [0, T]) \in \mathcal{M}(\mathcal{A}), \ T \geq 0\}$$

2. the models representing the observations starting and ending at those time points at which the automaton $\mathcal{A}$ switches from one location to another location:

$$\mathcal{M}_d(\mathcal{A}) \stackrel{\frown}{=} \{\sigma \mid \sigma = (\bar{s}, \bar{t}, [t_u, t_v]) \in \mathcal{M}(\mathcal{A}), \ t_u, t_v \text{ occur in } \bar{t} \text{ and } t_u \leq t_v\}$$

3. the models with integral observation intervals

$$\mathcal{M}_I(\mathcal{A}) \stackrel{\frown}{=} \{\sigma \mid \sigma = (\bar{s}, \bar{t}, [b, e]) \in \mathcal{M}(\mathcal{A}) \text{ and } b, e \in \mathbf{N}, b \leq e\}$$

Linear Duration Properties and Linear Duration Invariants. A *linear duration invariant (LDI)* of a timed automaton $\mathcal{A} = \langle L, s_0, \Sigma, X, E, I \rangle$ is a DC formula $\mathcal{D}$ of the form

$$A \leq \ell \leq B \Rightarrow \sum_{s \in L} c_s \int s \leq M$$

where c_s, A, B and M are real numbers, $A \leq B$ (B may be ∞), the DC term $\int s$ denotes the duration of location s, and the DC term ℓ the length of the interval. A LDI $\mathcal{D}$ is evaluated in an $\mathcal{A}$ model $(\mathcal{I}, [b, e])$ to tt, denoted by $(\mathcal{I}, [b, e]) \models \mathcal{D}$, iff $A \leq e - b \leq B \Rightarrow \sum_{s \in L} c_s \int_b^e \mathcal{I}_s(t)dt \leq M$ holds. $\mathcal{D}$ is satisfied by $\mathcal{A}$, denoted by $\mathcal{A} \models \mathcal{D}$, if $(\mathcal{I}, [b, e]) \models \mathcal{D}$ holds for any model $(\mathcal{I}, [b, e]) \in \mathcal{M}(\mathcal{A})$. We use $\Sigma(\mathcal{D})$ to denote the the sum of the durations $\sum_{s \in L} c_s \int s$.

A LDI $\mathcal{D}$ of a timed automaton $\mathcal{A}$ is said to be *discretisable* with respect to $\mathcal{A}$ iff $\mathcal{A} \models \mathcal{D}$ exactly when $\mathcal{M}_I(\mathcal{A}) \models \mathcal{D}$. We have the following theorem [9].

Theorem 1. *Let* $\mathcal{D} \hat{=} A \leq \ell \leq B \Rightarrow \sum_{s \in L} c_s \int s \leq M$ *be a LDI of a timed automaton* $\mathcal{A}$. *It is discretisable with respect to* $\mathcal{A}$ *if* A *and* B *are integers. Here we consider* ∞ *as an integer.*

2.3 Integral Reachability Graph of Timed Automata

An integral reachability graph $\mathcal{RG} = (V_R, E_R)$ of a timed automaton $\mathcal{A}$ is constructed as follows. Each vertex $v \in V_R$ will be a pair $\langle s, \pi \rangle$, where s is a state of $\mathcal{A}$, and π is an integral region of $\mathcal{A}$, i.e. the restriction on the set of integers of a clock region of $\mathcal{A}$ (see [9] for more detailed definition). E_R is initialized to $\emptyset$, and V_R is initialized to $\{\langle s_0, \pi_0 \rangle\}$, where s_0 is initial location of $\mathcal{A}$ and π_0 is the integral region containing the assignment that assigns 0 to all clocks, i.e. π_0 contains only the assignment that assigns 0 to all clocks. Then, V_R is expanded as follows. If a vertex $\langle s, \pi \rangle \in V_R$ has a successor $\langle s', \pi' \rangle$, i.e. there exist $d \geq 0$ and a transition $e = \langle s, \varphi, a, \lambda, s' \rangle$ such that $(s, \nu) \xrightarrow{d,a} (s', \nu')$, then $\langle s', \pi' \rangle$ is added into V_R and $e = (\langle s, \pi \rangle, \langle s', \pi' \rangle)$ is an edge in E_R. $[l(e), u(e)]$, where $l(e)$ and $u(e)$ are the minimal and maximal integer time delay that the automaton can stay at location s before it transits into location s'. $l(e)$ and $u(e)$ are defined as:

$$l(e) = \inf \left\{ d \geq 0 \mid d \in \mathbf{N}, \langle s, \pi \rangle \xrightarrow{d,a} \langle s', \pi' \rangle \right\},$$
$$u(e) = \sup \left\{ d \geq 0 \mid d \in \mathbf{N}, \langle s, \pi \rangle \xrightarrow{d,a} \langle s', \pi' \rangle \right\}.$$

A detailed description of the algorithm are given in [10,9]. From the definition of $\langle s, \pi \rangle$ and $\langle s', \pi' \rangle$, we have $l(e) \leq u(e)$ and it is possible that $u(e) = \infty$. We call e an infinite edge if $u(e) = \infty$. We will label an edge e by $(v, v', [l(e), u(e)])$.

There is a clear correspondence relation between the paths of the graph and the $\mathcal{A}$ models of DC [9]. Let $p = v_1 v_2 \ldots v_m$ be a path in $\mathcal{RG}$ and $\overline{d} = d_1, d_2, \ldots, d_{m-1}$ a sequence of integers, where $d_i \in [l(v_i, v_{i+1}), u(v_i, v_{i+1})]$, for $i = 1..m-1$. We call the sequence $\wp = v_1 d_1 v_2 d_2 \ldots v_{m-1} d_{m-1} v_m$ (written as $\wp = (p, \overline{d})$ for short) *weighted interpretation* of p.

We define the following

- the *length* of $\wp$: $l(\wp) \hat{=} \sum_{i=1}^{m-1} d_i$
- the *cost* of $\wp$: $\theta(\wp) \hat{=} \sum_{i=0}^{m-1} c_{v_i} d_i$ where c_{v_i} is the coefficient c_{s_i} in LDI $\mathcal{D}$ when s_i is the location of v_i.
- a weighted interpretation $\wp$ is said to satisfy $\mathcal{D}$, denoted by $\wp \models \mathcal{D}$, iff

$$A \leq l(\wp) \leq B \Rightarrow \theta(\wp) \leq M$$

- a graph $\mathcal{RG}$ is said to satisfy LDI $\mathcal{D}$, denoted by $\mathcal{RG} \models \mathcal{D}$, iff $\wp \models \mathcal{D}$ for all weighted interpretations $\wp$ of $\mathcal{RG}$.

The fact that $\mathcal{M}_d(\mathcal{A}) \models \mathcal{D}$ iff $\mathcal{RG} \models \mathcal{D}$ can be derived from relation in the following lemma between the models in $\mathcal{M}_d(\mathcal{A})$ and the weighted interpretations of $\mathcal{RG}$.

Lemma 1. *For any model* $\sigma \in \mathcal{M}_d(\mathcal{A})$, *there exists a weighted interpretation* $\wp$ *of* $\mathcal{RG}$ *such that* $l(\sigma) = l(\wp)$ *and* $\theta(\sigma) = \theta(\wp)$, *and vice versa.*

Case analysis is needed when checking a region graph with infinite edges. This is done following the two lemmas below, in which $A \leq \ell \leq B$ is the premise of the LDI $\mathcal{D}$ of concern. For a node $v = \langle s, \pi \rangle$ we simply write c_v for the coefficient c_s in the LDI $\mathcal{D}$.

Lemma 2. *Assume that* $e = (v, v', [l(e), \infty))$ *is an infinite edge of a region graph* $\mathcal{RG}$. $\mathcal{RG} \not\models \mathcal{D}$ *if* $B = \infty$ *and* $c_v > 0$.

Lemma 3. *Assume that* $e = (v, v', [l(e), \infty))$ *is an infinite edge of* $\mathcal{RG}$. *Then the label* $[l(e), \infty)$ *can be replaced as follows without affecting the result of checking* $\mathcal{RG} \models \mathcal{D}$.

  – *If* $B = \infty$ *and* $c_v \leq 0$, *replace* $[l(e), \infty)$ *by* $[l(e), u(e)]$ *with* $u(e) = \max\{l(e), A\}$.
  – *If* $B < \infty$, *replace* $[l(e), \infty)$ *by* $[l(e), u(e)]$ *with* $u(e) = \max\{l(e), B\}$.

Therefore, to verify $\mathcal{M}_d(\mathcal{A}) \models \mathcal{D}$, lemma 2 allows us to conclude with $\mathcal{M}_d(\mathcal{A}) \not\models \mathcal{D}$ immediately if the conditions of the lemma hold, otherwise we can use lemma 3 to translate the graph to one without infinite edges. In the rest of the paper, we assume that $\mathcal{RG}$ does not contain infinite edges.

3 Technique to Check LDI Using CTL

We now present our technique to reduce the verification of the satisfaction of a LDI by a timed automaton to checking a CTL formula of timed automaton. From the discussion in the previous section, we only need to construct a graph G with variables from a reachability graph $\mathcal{RG}$ (without infinite edges) and a CTL formula ψ such that $\mathcal{RG} \models \mathcal{D}$ if and only if $G \models \psi$. We distinguish two cases of the constant B in the premise of $\mathcal{D}$: 1) B is finite, 2) B is infinite.

3.1 When B Is finite

We first introduce integer variables n, gc and d

  – n is used to count the number of time units that $\mathcal{RG}$ stays in a vertex v before moving to another vertex,
  – gc is used to record the time length of an observation interval (corresponding to a path in $\mathcal{RG}$), and
  – d records the sum of durations of states.

All of the variables are initialized to 0. For the reachability graph $\mathcal{RG} = (V_R, E_R)$, an untimed graph $G = (V, E)$ with integer variables n, gc and d is constructed by a procedure.

For the description of the procedure, we need the following normalization function for variable gc.

Definition 2. *($B + 1$-normalization)*

$$norm_{B+1}(gc) = \begin{cases} gc + 1, & \text{if } gc \leq B \\ B + 1, & \text{if } gc > B \end{cases}$$

The intuitive intention is that gc records the length of the current observation interval, and the LDI $\mathcal{D}$ is satisfied trivially when it exceeds the constant B in premise of $\mathcal{D}$. Hence, we do not need to record every value of gc that bigger than B. It is sufficient to record $B + 1$ when the length of the observation time exceeds B. The procedure for construction $G = (V, E)$ from $\mathcal{RG} = (V_R, E_R)$ is given as follows. In the construction, we introduce an extra vertice v_0 as the single initial node to set the initial value of data variavles. Note that with data variables, a CTL formula is not a state formula in our system graph because with different histories leading to a node, a data variable might have different values.

Step 1. $V := V_R \cup \{v_0\}$, $E := E_R \cup \{(v_0, v)|v \in V_R\}$, where v_0 is a fresh node and is also considered as an initial node in G.

1. Let $u(v)$ be the maximum time units that $\mathcal{RG}$ stays in v. In the edge (v_0, v), we have the guard $n \leq u(v)$.
2. Let $T = \max \{u(v)|v \in V_R\}$. In v_0 there is a self-loop transition that nondeterministically select the value of n between $[0, T]$. In UPPAAL, this can be described by a select language $n : \text{int}[0, T]$.

Starting with the initial node v_0 and the initial values $gc, n, d := 0, 0, 0$, the above two conditions imply that gc starts to count time from the first enter of any node v; and the system can stay the node v for any n time units provided that $n \leq u(v)$.

Step 2. For each edge $e = ((v_i, v_j), [l(e), u(e)]) \in E_R$

1. $E := E \setminus \{e\}$,
2. $E := E \cup E1 \cup E2$, where

   - $E1 := \{(v_i, v_i)\}$, and for this edge we have the guard $\varphi : n < u(e)$ and the multiple assignment λ :
     - $n := n + 1$,
     - $gc := (gc \leq B?gc + 1 : B + 1)$,
     - $d := (gc \leq B?d + c_{v_i} : 0)$
     The second assignment assigns gc the value of $gc + 1$ if $gc \leq B$ and the value $B + 1$ otherwise, i.e. it is the implementation of the $B + 1$ normalization. Similarly, the third assignment assigns d the value of $d + c_{v_i}$ if $gc \leq B$ and 0 otherwise.
   - $E2 := \{(v_i, v_j)\}$, and for this edge we have the guard $\varphi : n \geq l(e)$ and the assignment $\lambda : n := 0$,

Notice that precisely speaking an edge in G is labeled with a guard and a set of assignments. There can be different edges between the same pair of nodes but with different labels. We call G constructed by this procedure the *untimed graph* of $\mathcal{A}$ for $\mathcal{D}$.

Roughly speaking, G is built by adding self-loop edges in vertex v_i and the edges between v_i and v_j. By assigning 0 to d when $gc > B$, the value of variable d is finite. Besides, gc is bounded by $B + 1$. Since $\mathcal{RG}$ does not contain infinite edges, the value of n is bounded. This construction is much simpler than the one in paper [9], which "splitting" each edge $e = (v, v', [l(e), u(e)])$ of $\mathcal{RG}$ into $u(e)$ small edges with the length (weight) 1 by adding $u(e) - 1$ sub-vertices. Figure 1 gives an example how to build the graph G from the graph $\mathcal{RG}$.

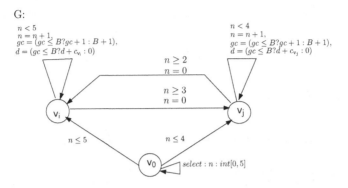

Fig. 1. "Discretising" graph when B is finite

The corresponding CTL formula. We now define the CTL ψ_1 formula corresponding to the LDI $\mathcal{D}$ of a timed automaton $\mathcal{A}$

$$\psi_1 \,\hat{=}\, \texttt{A[]} \ \texttt{not} \ A \leq gc \leq B \wedge d > M \tag{2}$$

We call ψ_1 the *CTL-version* of $\mathcal{D}$ for $\mathcal{A}$.

Lemma 4. *Let $\mathcal{D}$ be a LDI of a timed automaton $\mathcal{A}$, G the untimed graph of $\mathcal{A}$ for $\mathcal{D}$, and ψ_1 the CTL-version of $\mathcal{D}$ for $\mathcal{A}$. Then there exists a path $\mathsf{p} \in \mathcal{P}(\mathsf{G})$ such that $\mathsf{p} \not\models \psi_1$ iff there exists an integral model $\sigma \in \mathcal{M}_I(\mathcal{A})$ such that $\sigma \not\models \mathcal{D}$.*

Proof. From the construction procedure for G, there is an obvious one-to-one correspondence between a path ρ of $\mathcal{RG}$ and a path ρ_g of G starting from the node v_0, that represents an observation of the system in the two models. Let $\ell(\rho)$ be the length of ρ, which represents the time of the observation, and $last(\rho_g)$ be the last node of ρ_g.

1. When $\ell(\rho) \leq B$, the value of gc at $last(\rho_g)$ equals $\ell(\rho)$, and the value of d at $last(\rho_g)$ is the value of the sum $\Sigma(\mathcal{D})$.
2. When $\ell(\rho) > B$, the value of gc at $last(\rho_g)$ is $B + 1$.

Consequently, the lemma follows immediately from the definition of the satisfaction relations $\models$ for LDI and CTL formulas.   □

From this lemma and the discretisability of LDI, we have to check only integer models of the automaton $\mathcal{A}$. Hence we can restrict ourselves to the integral region graph. The theorem below follows straightforward.

Theorem 2. *When B is finite, the verification of a LDI $\mathcal{D}$ by a timed automaton $\mathcal{A}$ is equivalent to the verification of the satisfaction of CTL-version of $\mathcal{D}$ for $\mathcal{A}$ by the set of paths $\mathcal{P}(\mathsf{G})$, i.e. $\mathcal{A} \models \mathcal{D}$ if and only if $\mathcal{P}(\mathsf{G}) \models \psi_1$.*

We can use a model checker for CTL, such as UPPAAL, to verify $\mathcal{P}(\mathsf{G}) \models \psi_1$.

3.2   When B Is Infinite

In terms of the graph constructed as above, for the case that B is infinite, gc can increase infinitely and d can take an arbitrary value. This case makes it impossible to check the property $\mathcal{D}$ using the technique presented in the previous section. To bind the value of gc we will use "A-normalization" as follows in the graph construction, where A is the other constant in the premise of the LDI.

Definition 3. *(A-normalization)*

$$norm_A(gc) = \begin{cases} gc + 1, & \text{if } gc < A \\ A, & \text{if } gc \geq A \end{cases}$$

Intuitively, the A normalization is dual to the B-normalization. The variable gc is still used for the length of the observation. Therefore with this normalization, for checking LDI $\mathcal{D}$ when gc equals A, we only need to check whether there exists a path along which the value of $\Sigma(\mathcal{D})$ is bigger than M. Now we introduce a number to bound the value of d.

Definition 4. *Let V^+ be the set of all nodes v_p in $\mathcal{RG}$ for which $c_{v_p} > 0$. Then we call the value $Q = \sum_{v_p \in V^+}(c_{v_p} \cdot u(v_p))$ the maximum increment of $\mathcal{RG}$.*

The intended meaning for the number Q is that in case there is no loop in a path of $\mathcal{RG}$, the value of d along that path can increase at most Q. In other words, if the value of d along a path increases more than Q, then there must be a positive loop in the path. The graph $G^+ = (V, E)$ is constructed from $\mathcal{RG} = (V_R, E_R)$ in a way similar to the case that B is finite by the following procedure. For any $v \in V$, we make variable d bounded by updating it differently depending on whether the coefficient c_v in $\Sigma(\mathcal{D})$ is negative or not.

The Procedure for Constructing G^+.

Step 1. This step is the same as that in the construction of G.
Step 2. For each edge $e = ((v_i, v_j), [l(e), u(e)]) \in E_R$, where v_i has a non-negative coefficient c_{v_i}, do the following:

1. $E := E \setminus \{e\}$,
2. $E := E \cup E1 \cup E2$, where
   - $E1 := \{(v_i, v_i)\}$, and in this edge we have the guard $\varphi : n < u(e)$ and the multiple assignment λ :
     - $n := n + 1$,
     - $gc := (gc < A?gc + 1 : A)$,
     - $d := (gc \geq A \wedge d > M?M + 1 : d + c_{v_i})$
   - $E2 := \{(v_i, v_j)\}$, and in this edge we have the guard $\varphi : n \geq l(e)$ and the assignment $\lambda : n := 0$.

Step 3. For each edge $e = ((v_i, v_j), [l(e), u(e)]) \in E_R$, where v_i has a negative coefficient c_{v_i}, do the following:

1. $E := E \setminus \{e\}$,
2. $E := E \cup E1 \cup E2$, where
   - $E1 := \{(v_i, v_i)\}$, and in this edge we have the guard $\varphi : n < u(e)$ and the assignment $\lambda :$
     - $n := n + 1$,
     - $gc := (gc < A?gc + 1 : A)$,
     - $d := (gc \geq A \wedge d < M - Q?d : d + c_{v_i})$
   - $E2 := \{(v_i, v_j)\}$, and in this edge we have the guard $\varphi : n \geq l(e)$ and the assignment $\lambda : n := 0$,

In case of c_{v_i} is non-negative, when $gc \geq A$ and $d > M$, by setting d to $M+1$, the value of d is finite. Moreover, when $gc \geq A$, gc remains as A, so gc is a bounded variable. Since the states that satisfy $gc \geq A \wedge d = M + 1$ imply $\mathcal{P}(G^+) \not\models \mathcal{D}$, it is obvious that the update does not change the verification result.

When c_{v_i} is negative, the edge of the graph from v_i to v_i is the same as that of the non-negative one, except that the value update of d is $d := (gc \geq A \wedge d < M - Q?d : d + c_{v_i})$. It is not hard to see why we set d to $d + c_{v_i}$ if $\neg(gc \geq A \wedge d < M - Q)$: we have to evaluate the value of d precisely when we do not have enough information for verifying if $\mathcal{D}$ is satisfied. Now we prove that if $gc \geq A \wedge d < M - Q$, the value of d remaining unchanged does not alter the checking result of the LDI. To do so, we define another graph $G^\bullet$ that is the same as G^+ except that if $gc \geq A \wedge d < M - Q$ the assignment for d is $d := d + c_{v_i}$.

Similar to the case that B is finite, we define a CTL-version of $\mathcal{D}$, denoted by ψ_2, for a timed automaton $\mathcal{A}$.

$$\psi_2 : A[] \ not \ \ gc \geq A \wedge d > M. \tag{3}$$

Lemma 5. *There exists a path $\rho \in \mathcal{P}(G^+)$ such that $\rho \not\models \psi_2$ if and only if there exists a path $\rho' \in \mathcal{P}(G^\bullet)$ such that $\rho' \not\models \psi_2$.*

Proof. Notice that the topological structure of G^+ and $G^\bullet$ are the same. Each path $\rho = v_0^+, \ldots, v_m^+$ in G^+ corresponds to exactly one path $\rho^\bullet = v_0^\bullet, \ldots, v_m^\bullet$ in $G^\bullet$. Let v_i^+ and $v_i^\bullet$ be any two corresponding nodes respectively in ρ and $\rho^\bullet$. Then the value of gc at vertex v_i^+ is the same as the value of that at vertex $v_i^\bullet$. Due to the different updates of d in ρ and $\rho^\bullet$ for the negative coefficient of a vertex, we know that at vertex v_i^+, the value of d is bigger than or equal to the value of d at $v_i^\bullet$. Hence, a path $\rho' = \rho^\bullet$ in $G^\bullet$ that does not satisfy ψ_2 then its corresponding path ρ in G^+ does not satisfy ψ_2.

To prove the other direction, let ρ in G^+ be such that $\rho \not\models \psi_2$ and ρ starts from the initial node v_0. If $\rho^\bullet \not\models \psi_2$, we are done. Otherwise, we need to show that there will be a "positive cycle" in ρ, i.e. there is a cycle such that going along the cycle will increase the value of d properly by at least 1. We now give the illustration for the case $\rho \not\models \psi_2 \wedge \rho^\bullet \models \psi_2$. This case denotes that the values of d on ρ and on $\rho^\bullet$ are different and there should be a first node v_j^+ along ρ where the condition $gc \geq A \wedge d < M - Q \wedge c_{v_j} < 0$ holds. Thus, from v_j^+, the value of d is increased by at least $Q + 1$ to make $\rho \not\models \psi_2$.

From the definition of Q, in ρ there must be a "positive cycle" along which d will be increased by at least 1. From the correspondence relation between ρ and $\rho^\bullet$, $\rho^\bullet$ must also have a positive cycle $\mathcal{C}$. Thus ρ' is formed by increasing the number of repetition of the cycle $\mathcal{C}$ in $\rho^\bullet$, such that $\rho' \not\models \psi_2$. $\qquad\square$

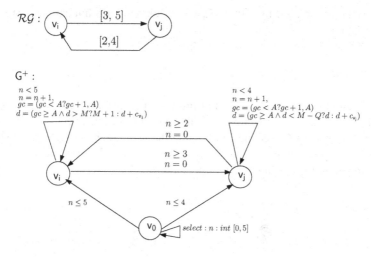

Fig. 2. "Discretising" graph when B is infinite and c_{v_i} is non-negative, c_{v_j} is negative

Therefor we conclude that d is a bounded integer variable. Figure 2 gives an example how to build the graph G^+ from the graph $\mathcal{RG}$ when c_{v_i} is non-negative and c_{v_j} is negative. The lemma bellow follows from the definitions of relations $\models$ for $\mathcal{D}$ and ψ_2.

Lemma 6. *Given a timed automaton $\mathcal{A}$ and a LDI $\mathcal{D}$. Then there exists a path $\rho \in \mathcal{P}(G^+)$ such that $\rho \not\models \psi_2$ iff there exists an integral model $\sigma \in \mathcal{M}_I(\mathcal{A})$ such that $\sigma \not\models \mathcal{D}$.*

Now we have our main theorem for the case when B is infinite.

Theorem 3. *When B is infinite, the verification of a LDI $\mathcal{D}$ by a timed automaton $\mathcal{A}$ is equivalent to the verification of the satisfaction of CTL-version ψ_2 of $\mathcal{D}$ for $\mathcal{A}$ by the set of paths $\mathcal{P}(G^+)$, i.e. $\mathcal{A} \models \mathcal{D}$ if and only if $\mathcal{P}(G^+) \models \psi_2$.*

3.3   Verification in UPPAAL

The model checking tool-UPPAAL that is available at www.uppaal.com, is an integrated tool environment for formal specification, validation and verification of real time systems modeled as networks of timed automata. UPPAAL uses a simplified version of CTL to express the requirement specification. The query language consists of path formulas and state formulate. State formulate describe individual states, whereas path formula quantify over paths or traces of the model. Path formula can be classified into reachability, safety and liveness.

The properties ψ_1 and ψ_2 in our checking algorithm are safety properties. This implies that on one hand, we can draw the graph in UPPALL and just click the "check" button to verify the safety property ψ_1 or ψ_2 from the extra vertex v_0. And this is done automatically. On the other hand, since we use the same modeling language and the same query language used by UPPAAL, the checking algorithm can be easily implemented in UPPAAL.

4   Case Study

In [11], the Duration Calculus is used to prove that a gas burner does not leak excessively. That is, the accumulated time of leakage is at most one twentieth of the time in any interval of at least 60 seconds. Following the techniques in Section 3, using UP-PAAL, we have checked that the LDI property is satisfied. We now use a more general model $\mathcal{A}$ shown in Fig 3 to illustrate our techniques.

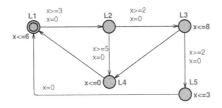

Fig. 3. A Model $\mathcal{A}$

The LDI properties to be checked are:

1. $D_1 : 10 \leq \ell \leq 30 \rightarrow (-2 \times \int L2 + \int L3 + 3 \times \int L5) \leq 30$.
2. $D_2 : 10 \leq \ell \leq \infty \rightarrow (-2 \times \int L2 + \int L3 + 3 \times \int L5) \leq 30$.

Let e_1, e_2 be the infinite edges from $L2$ respectively to $L3$ and $L4$. To check whether or not D_1 is satisfied, we first use the methods of removing infinite edge in subsection 2.3, to translate e_1 and e_2 to finite edges. We thus have $l(e_1) = 2$, $l(e_2) = 5$, $u(e_1) = u(e_2) = 30$. Also, in this case we have $A = 10$, $B = 30$, $M = 30$. The CTL formula C_1 for D_1 is:

$$C_1 : \text{A[] not } (gc >= 10 \text{ \&\& } gc <= 30 \text{ \&\& } d > 30)$$

In terms of the technique in subsection 3.2, we construct the graph $\mathcal{A}'$ shown in Fig.4 that is used in UPPAAL as a model to check C_1. The checking result shows that $\mathcal{A}' \models C_1$. Therefore, we have $\mathcal{A} \models D_1$.

We now check D_2 and construct the model $\mathcal{A}''$ shown in Fig 5. In this case, $u(e_1) = u(e_2) = 10$, $A = 10$, $B = \infty$, $M = 30$, $Q = 8 + 3 \times 3 = 17$. The CTL logic C_2 for D_2 is:

$$C_2 : \text{A[] not } (gc >= 10 \text{ \&\& } d > 30)$$

We have checked with UPPAAL, and the checking result is that $\mathcal{A}'' \not\models C_2$. Thus $\mathcal{A} \not\models D_2$.

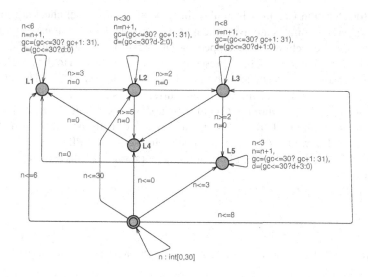

Fig. 4. "Disretising" graph $\mathcal{A}'$

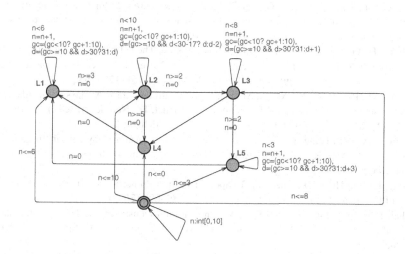

Fig. 5. "Disretising" graph $\mathcal{A}''$

5 Conclusion

The examples in the paper show that the DC formulation of Linear Duration Constraints is simpler, neater and easier to understand than those in LTL and CTL. The automata that are given for the DC specification are simpler than those that would be constructed for a LTL or CTL specification. However, the existing algorithms for model checking Linear Duration Calculus invariants are complex and have not been implemented. A lot of works have been done recently [16,17,18] for the development of model checking tools for Duration Calculus formulas. In spite of some model checking tools for Duration Calculus formulas are available now, to our knowledge, compared with other temporal logics, the techniques developed for DC are still not widely applicable in industrial fields. In this paper, we have presented a different approach to the problem. Our approach is to reduce the verification of a LDI to model checking CTL. This allows us to use or easily extend the techniques in the current tools for CTL, such as UPPAAL and SMV, to check linear Duration Calculus Invariant of real-time embedded systems. Furthermore, since the CTL formulas ψ_1 and ψ_2 can directly be specified in the linear time logic LTL, we thus can use the model checkers like SPIN to check the LDI. We believe that this technique will help to make Duration Calculus more applicable in industry field.

References

1. Alur, R., Dill, D.L.: A Theory of Timed Automata. Theoretical Computer Science, 183–235 (1994)
2. Alur, R.: Timed Automata. In: Halbwachs, N., Peled, D.A. (eds.) CAV 1999. LNCS, vol. 1633, pp. 8–22. Springer, Heidelberg (1999)
3. Braberman, V.A., Van Hung, D.: On Checking Timed Automata for Linear Duration Invariants. In: Proceedings of the 19th Real-Time Systems Symposium RTSS 1998, pp. 264–273. IEEE Computer Society Press, Los Alamitos (1998)
4. Clarke, E., Grumberg, O., Peled, D.: Model Checking. The MIT Press, Cambridge (1999)
5. Emerson, E.A., Halpern, J.Y.: "Sometimes" and "Not Never" Revisited: On Branching versus Linear Time Temporal Logic. Journal of the ACM 33(1), 151–178 (1986)
6. Kesten, Y., Pnueli, A., Sifakis, J., Yovine, S.: Integration Graphs: A Class of Decidable Hybrid Systems. In: Grossman, R.L., Ravn, A.P., Rischel, H., Nerode, A. (eds.) HS 1991 and HS 1992. LNCS, vol. 736, pp. 179–208. Springer, Heidelberg (1993)
7. Dong, L.X., Van Hung, D.: Checking Linear Duration Invariants by Linear Programming. In: Jaffar, J., Yap, R.H.C. (eds.) ASIAN 1996. LNCS, vol. 1179, pp. 321–332. Springer, Heidelberg (1996)
8. Yong, L., Van Hung, D.: Checking Temporal Duration Properties of Timed Automata. Journal of Computer Science and Technology 17(6), 689–698 (2002)
9. Thai, P.H., Van Hung, D.: Verifying Linear Duration Constraints of Timed Automata. In: Liu, Z., Araki, K. (eds.) ICTAC 2004. LNCS, vol. 3407, pp. 295–309. Springer, Heidelberg (2005)
10. Jianhua, Z., Van Hung, D.: Checking Timed Automata for Some Discretisable Duration Properties. Journal of Computer Science and Technology 15(5), 423–429 (2000)
11. Chaochen, Z., Hoare, C.A.R., Ravn, A.P.: A calculus of durations. Information Processing Letters 40(5), 269–276 (1991)
12. Zhou, C.: Linear Duration Invariants. In: Langmaack, H., de Roever, W.-P., Vytopil, J. (eds.) FTRTFT 1994 and ProCoS 1994. LNCS, vol. 863, pp. 86–109. Springer, Heidelberg (1994)
13. Chaochen, Z., Hansen, M.R.: Duration Calculus. A Formal Approach to Real-Time Systems. Springer, Heidelberg (2004)
14. Yovine, S.: KRONOS: A Verification Tool for Real-Time Systems. STTT 1(1-2), 123–133 (1997)
15. Behrmann, G., David, A., Larsen, K.G.: A tutorial on Uppaal. In: Bernardo, M., Corradini, F. (eds.) SFM-RT 2004. LNCS, vol. 3185, pp. 200–236. Springer, Heidelberg (2004)

16. Pandya, P.K.: Interval Duration Logic: Expressiveness and Decidability. ENTCS 65(6) (2002)
17. Meyer, R., Faber, J., Rybalchenko, A.: Model Checking Duration Calculus: A Practical Approach. In: Barkaoui, K., Cavalcanti, A., Cerone, A. (eds.) ICTAC 2006. LNCS, vol. 4281, pp. 332–346. Springer, Heidelberg (2006)
18. Fränzle, M., Hansen, M.R.: Deciding an Interval Logic with Accumulated Durations. In: Grumberg, O., Huth, M. (eds.) TACAS 2007. LNCS, vol. 4424, pp. 201–215. Springer, Heidelberg (2007)

Exact Response Time Scheduling Analysis of Accumulatively Monotonic Multiframe Real Time Tasks

Areej Zuhily[1] and Alan Burns[2]

[1] RTS Group, Department of Computer Science, University of York, York, UK
ehar@cs.york.ac.uk
[2] RTS Group, Department of Computer Science, University of York, York, UK
burns@cs.york.ac.uk

Abstract. An exact schedulability test of *Accumulatively Monotonic (AM) multi-frame* tasks executing on a uniprocessor according to the fixed priority scheduling scheme is presented in this paper. The test is given as an analysis of the worst case response time of each AM multiframe task. This analysis is given in two stages, firstly we give the basic formula of the worst case response time of an AM multiframe task. Secondly, we extend this formula to include blocking time. An evaluation of this analysis is given as a comparison between this exact schedulability analysis and the most recent published, but non-optimal, schedulability analysis.

1 Introduction

A real-time *multiframe* task is a generalized real-time task whose worst-case execution time is different from one phase to another of its execution, for instance, a task that executes with worst-case execution times of 10ms and 5ms is said to have two frames. Another example, often found in industrial applications [5], is a periodic task that does a small amount of data collection in each period consuming a small execution time, but then summaries and stores this data every n cycles using a much more expensive algorithm that consumes a larger execution time. A further example is found within the MPEG coding standard where there are three types of video frames (usually represented by the letters I, P and B). The I frame usually takes much more decoding than the others, but may occur only every 10 frames. The assumption of all frames being I frames leads to poor utilization and the system could be deemed unschedulable whilst in reality it is schedulable. We therefore wish to present the decoder task as a multiframe task. Other examples of the multiframe tasks can be found in practical systems.

Mok and Chen [12,13] were the first who introduced the multiframe concept as a generalisation of the classic Liu and Layland model [10]. They proposed a utilization based schedulability test, for fixed priority scheduling, under Rate Monotonic, RM, [10] priority assignment (the greater period the task has the lower priority it is assigned). They gave a utilization bound, assuming the execution time sequence of each multiframe task has a particular restrictive property that they called *Accumulatively Monotonic*, AM, (see section 2). Subsequent papers (Section 3.1) have improved this utilization bound but their tests remain inexact (i.e. sufficient but not necessary).

In this paper we provide an exact and tractable analysis based upon the response time formulation for multiframe tasks when this AM restriction is applied. In general, to test

J.S. Fitzgerald, A.E. Haxthausen, and H. Yenigun (Eds.): ICTAC 2008, LNCS 5160, pp. 410–424, 2008.

the schedulability of a set of multiframe tasks, regardless to the AM restriction, requires examining all possible phasings of the tasks [17]; which leads to an intractability problem for the scheduling analysis. But, having the AM restriction applied to a multiframe task, we show that only *critical* frame can give rise to the worst-case response times for lower priority tasks. As a result the analysis is tractable.

This paper is organised as follows. In the next section our system model and notation are introduced whilst prior work is summarised in Section 3. Section 4 gives the exact response time analysis of AM multiframe tasks; then the analysis is developed to include blocking. In Section 5, we give a numeric example to illustrate our analysis. Section 6 provides an analysis of randomly generated task sets to show how our response time test is better than any one previously published. Conclusions are provided in Section 7 as a summary of the contribution.

2   System Model

Consider a system S consisting of N multiframe tasks. Each multiframe task τ_i consists, in its turn, of a repeating sequence of n_i frames. Frames are executing on a uniprocessor using the preemptive fixed priority scheduling policy. Priorities of multiframe tasks in the system are ordered consecutively with τ_1 having the highest priority in the system and τ_N the lowest priority (i.e 1 in τ_1 refers to the highest priority and N in τ_N refers to the lowest priority). All frames of the multiframe task have the same priority – the priority of the relative multiframe task.

Each frame in the multiframe task might have a worst case execution time that may be different from other frames in the same multiframe task with the assumption that the execution time sequences of all multiframe tasks in the system satisfy the AM restriction that is given below. In other words, a multiframe task, τ_i, has n_i worst case execution times $(C_i^k; k = 0..n_i - 1)$ that satisfy Equation (1). All frames in the same multiframe task are released with a fixed or minimum time interval T_i and have the same deadline represented by the single parameter D_i. In all situations we assume (in this paper) that $D_i \leq T_i$. The worst case response time R_i of the multiframe task τ_i is the maximum time of any of its frames from when the frame is released until it completes.

As an illustration of the multiframe scenario, Table 1 represents a simple example with just 2 tasks τ_1 and τ_2 where τ_1 is a multiframe task with 4 frames represented by the execution time values 8, 4, 3 and 1; and τ_2 has just one frame. To simplify the explanation of the multiframe concept, all tasks in the example are assumed to have zero blocking time and have $D_i = T_i; i = 1, 2$.

Table 1. Attributes of tasks in the example

task	C	$T = D$	priority
τ_1	8, 4, 3, 1	10	1
τ_2	x	20	2

Table 2. Possible interference from τ_1

release	exe seq.	1 inv	2 inv	3 inv	4 inv
8	8, 4, 3, 1	8	12	15	16
4	4, 3, 1, 8	4	7	8	16
3	3, 1, 8, 4	3	4	12	16
1	1, 8, 4, 3	1	9	13	16

Finding the worst case response time R_2 of τ_2, whatever its execution time, requires finding the maximum amount of possible interference from τ_1. Table 2 shows all values of interference that task τ_1 generates from different initial frames in the execution sequence and for numbers of invocations up to the number of frames (i.e. 4). It can be seen from Table 2 that the maximum amount of interference τ_1 generates, in the case of one, two, three or four invocations, is when it is released having an execution time of 8. None of the other releases of τ_1 generates a greater amount of interference than the release of 8. That is because the multiframe task τ_1 satisfies the Accummulatively Monotonic, AM, restriction.

In the AM multiframe task, one of the frames, whose execution time is maximum, always generates the maximum amount of interference within the execution of lower priority tasks; for any number of its invocations (i.e. interference). We call the frame whose execution time is maximum the *Peak Frame*.

Definition 1. A Peak Frame of a multiframe task *is one of the frames, in the multiframe task, whose execution time is the maximum of the execution times of this multiframe task.*

For example, the multiframe task τ, whose execution time sequence is $(8, 4, 8, 3)$, has two peak frames with locations 0 and 2; where their execution times are both 8.

Mok and Chen [12] mathematically formalize the AM restriction by an equation using the *mod* function to reach the execution time from its sequence whatever the number of invocations is. Equation (1) represents this AM restriction

$$\sum_{k=m}^{m+j} C^{(k \bmod n)} \geq \sum_{l=i}^{i+j} C^{(l \bmod n)}; \tag{1}$$

$$\forall i, j = 0, 1, 2, .., n - 1;$$

where C^m is one of the peak values in a list of execution times $(C^0, C^1, .., C^{n-1})$ that satisfies Equation (1). For example, for the multiframe task whose execution time sequence is $C = (8, 4, 8, 3)$, $m = 0$ and $C^0 = 8$. We call the peak frame whose execution time is C^m the *Critical Frame*.

Definition 2. A Critical Frame of an AM multiframe task *is one of the peak frames, in the multiframe task, whose execution time satisfies the AM restriction (i.e. Equation (1)).*

For example, the critical frame of the multiframe task whose execution time sequence is $C = (8, 4, 8, 3)$, is the first frame whose execution time is 8.

The first step in the schedulability analysis of a task is to identify the instant that leads to the maximum load for its execution. In terms of the response time analysis of a multiframe task τ_i, we now introduce the critical instant of τ_i as the instant that leads to the worst case response time of τ_i. Mok and Chen [12] show in their paper that the critical instant of an AM multiframe task is when its peak frame is released simultaneously with all critical frames of all higher priority AM multiframe tasks.

Definition 3. Critical instant of an AM multiframe task τ_i *is the simultaneous release, of the peak frame of* τ_i *with all critical frames of the higher priority multiframe tasks.*

We employ this critical instant of the AM multiframe task τ_i to analyse its worst case response time and therefore its schedulability status.

3 Related Work

Because we are concerned with the response time analysis of AM multiframe tasks, previous contributions must be covered within two fields. The first field is the schedulability analysis of the multiframe tasks; which is presented in the following subsection. The second field is response time analysis; which is presented in the later subsection.

3.1   Schedulability Analysis of the Multiframe Tasks

As the research into schedulability analysis starts from the *utilization* point of view, we introduce here the beginning of the utilization's research. Liu and Layland [10] and Serlin[15], with the RM priority assignment algorithm and assuming a constant execution time for each multiframe task in the system, introduced a sufficient but not necessary feasibility test. The test was based upon the least upper bound of the processor utilization factor; which is given by $\sum_{i=1}^{i=N} \frac{C_i}{T_i}$. The test is based on the criteria that a task set is schedulable if its processor utilization is less than a given upper bound; which is $N(2^{\frac{1}{N}} - 1)$ which simplifies to .693 for large N. Symbolically,

$$\sum_{i=1}^{i=N} \frac{C_i}{T_i} \leq N(2^{\frac{1}{N}} - 1).$$

This upper bound has been employed by different researchers to serve the multiframe model.

Although research on multiframe tasks began when Mok and Chen [12,13] introduced this multiframe concept and gave the utilization bound (as explained in the introduction), Han [6] gave another schedulability test, under RM priority assignment, that was better than Mok's test in the sense that multiframe task sets with peak utilization (i.e. the utilization of the peak frame) larger than Mok's bound are not feasible using Mok and Chen's utilization bound but can be found feasible by Han's test.

Baruah et al. [3] gave another tractable but sufficient response time analysis of a system of multiframe tasks. They applied a fixed point algorithm to determine the worst case response time of the peak frame of multiframe tasks taking into account the maximum amount of interference that higher priority multiframe tasks provide.

Traor et al. [18] mentioned in their paper that the multiframe model was a particular case of tasks with offset (transactions), so they assumed that their offset analysis can be applied to the multiframe model. However, we assume in our model that the priorities of the tasks are assigned according to the multiframe task so all frames in a multiframe task have the same priority which means the AM multiframe model is a restricted form of the transaction model.

Kuo et al. [8] gave another improved utilization bound for the schedulability test of systems with AM multiframe tasks. The main idea of the test was to merge tasks with harmonic periods to reduce the number of tasks that has to be considered in the schedulability test and then apply Mok's bound to the merged tasks. The combined task, under Kuo's test, will have a period of T^{merg} and a sequence of execution times (C^j) with the size n^{merg}; where T^{merg} is the maximum period of the merged tasks, n^{merg} is the least common multiple, LCM, of the number of frames of the merged tasks, for example, if N MF tasks in the system have harmonic periods then n^{merg} is LCM of $n_1, n_2, .., n_N$. The value of C^j is given by the following formula (assuming that we are merging N multiframe tasks)

$$C^j = \sum_{i=1}^{N} (\sum_{k=0}^{(\frac{T^{merg}}{T_i})-1} C_i^{(j(\frac{T^{merg}}{T_i})+k) \ mod \ n_i}); j = 0, .., n^{merg} - 1$$

More recently, Lu et al. [11] improved Kuo's utilization test and presented new scheduling conditions for AM multiframe tasks within the utilization domain and assuming the RM priority assignment. They considered the ratio of the periods in their test. The improvement was that they used Kuo's method to merge the tasks and then they applied their test to the merged tasks. The schedulability status, under their approach, depends on the total peak utilization, U, of the AM multiframe tasks being less than a defined upper bound. They call this upper bound the *Conditional Bound* function, CB. Symbolically, the AM task set is schedulable if the inequality (2) is satisfied.

$$U \leq CB; \tag{2}$$

where the total peak utilization, U, is the summation of all peak utilizations of the multiframe tasks in the system; and it is given by

$$U = \sum_{i=1}^{N} \max_{0 \leq j \leq n_i - 1} \{ \frac{C_i^j}{T_i} \}.$$

While the CB function is defined by Equation (3); for number of tasks, $N > 1$, and with regard to two parameters r and z.

$$CB(r, z) = z + r(z - 1) + r(N - 1)((\frac{1}{z})^{\frac{1}{N-1}} - 1) \tag{3}$$

where n_i and T_i are respectively the number of frames and period of the ith multiframe task. r is given as

$r = \min_{1 \leq i \leq N} \{r_i\}$, where r_i is defined depending on n_i as
$r_i = \frac{C_i 0}{C_i 1}$; $for\ n_i > 1$, and $r_i = 1$; $for\ n_i = 1$.
z is given as
$z = \max \{\min_{1 \leq i \leq N-1} \{\frac{V_i}{T_N}\}, \frac{r}{1+r}\}$, where V_i is a virtual period and given by
$V_i = \lfloor \frac{T_N}{T_i} \rfloor T_i$.

Although Lu's analysis improves previous results, it still remains inexact. In this paper we compare our schedulability analysis with Lu's analysis since Lu's analysis is the most recent improved scheduling analysis.

As can be seen from all of the above contributions, all published schedulability approaches are inexact since all of them are either in the utilization domain or are only sufficient. While in this paper, we provide exact scheduling analysis within the response time domain. In the following, we cover relevant contributions in the response time domain.

3.2   Standard Response Time Analysis

In terms of schedulability under response time analysis, we say that the task τ_i is schedulable if its worst case response time R_i is less than or equal to its deadline. Usually, the response time of a task represents two kinds of execution: execution of the task itself and execution of the other tasks in the system. The execution of the tasks other than the task itself is presented as the interference from higher priority tasks.

The research into response time analysis began with Joseph and Pandya [7] followed by Audsley et al. [1]. They introduced an iterative equation, Equation (4), for finding the worst case response time of a task τ_i within specific restrictions and assuming the execution times of the tasks in the system are constant for all phases of their execution. They consider in the formula Liu and Layland's critical instant [10]; where Liu and Layland's critical instant, and so the worst case response time, of a task is when this task is released simultaneously with all higher priority tasks.

$$R_i = C_i + \sum_{j=1}^{i-1} \lceil \frac{R_i}{T_j} \rceil C_j \qquad (4)$$

where $\sum_{j=1}^{i-1} \lceil \frac{R_i}{T_j} \rceil C_j$ is the amount of interference from tasks whose priorities are higher than the priority of τ_i.

From the blocking point of view, the blocking time of a task τ_i is the time for which τ_i is stopped in its execution because of the execution of some lower priority task. In other words, a task τ_i is subjected to blocking when this task is blocked awaiting a lower priority task to complete its execution. This scenario happens when a concurrency control protocol is used with the fixed priority scheduling scheme. Priority ceiling protocol [16] and stack resource protocol [2] are the most famous concurrency control protocols. Audsley et al. [1] enhanced the response time formula (i. e. Equation (4)) to include blocking time, B_i, as in Equation (5).

$$R_i = C_i + B_i + \sum_{j=1}^{i-1} \lceil \frac{R_i}{T_j} \rceil C_j \qquad (5)$$

To solve Equation (5), a recurrence relation is given as in Equation (6); where $w = 0, 1, 2, ...$ and $r_i^0 = C_i$. The smallest solution of Equation (6) represents the worst case response time of τ_i. In other words, the worst case response time is obtained when it is found that $r_i^{w+1} = r_i^w (= R_i$ for the smallest value of w). However, in the case that r_i^{w+1} becomes greater than the deadline of the task, τ_i is not guaranteed to meet its deadline, so we say that the task is unschedulable.

$$r_i^{w+1} = C_i + B_i + \sum_{j=1}^{i-1} \lceil \frac{r_i^w}{T_j} \rceil C_j \tag{6}$$

The critical instant of the task is not affected by changing the release frame of higher priority tasks; because all frames in a standard task generate the same amount of interference. In our contribution, the restriction of having constant execution times of the tasks is removed. So, the response time formula requires modification and specifically the side that calculates interference from the higher priority multiframe tasks.

4   Exact Response Time Analysis for AM Multiframe Tasks

In this section, we use the framework of response time analysis to provide the exact scheduling analysis of AM multiframe tasks. The analysis is done in two steps, in the first step we provide the basic response time formula when no blocking of the multiframe task is considered while in the second step we introduce the blocking term into the formula. Then, we show the applicability of this response time scheduling analysis by showing that its coverage is wider than the utilization based analysis.

4.1   Basic Response Time Analysis of the AM Multiframe Tasks

This section covers the response time analysis of a multiframe task assuming that all multiframe tasks in the system satisfy the AM restriction (i.e. Equation (1)). The main concern of the response time analysis of the multiframe task is to find a function that can account for the amount of interference an AM multiframe task, τ_j, generates for a specific number of its invocations, k. We call the function with this property the *cumulative function*, ξ_j, Definition 4 provides a full description of this function.

Definition 4. *Given an AM multiframe task τ_j with n_j execution times $(C_j^0, C_j^1, ..., C_j^{n_j-1})$. A cumulative function (ξ_j) of τ_j for a given number of its invocations is the amount of interference that τ_j generates starting from the critical frame and proceeding for that number of invocations. Equation (7) represents the cumulative function of the jth AM multiframe task, τ_j, for k number of its invocations assuming that its critical frame is indexed as m_j.*

$$\xi_j(k) = \sum_{l=m_j}^{m_j+k-1} C_j^{l \bmod n}; k = 1, 2, .. \tag{7}$$

For example, the value of $\xi_1(3)$ for the task τ_1 whose execution times are $(8, 4, 8, 3)$ is 20.

In fact, for an ordinary single frame task the cumulative function is well defined as $\xi_j(k) = kC_j$ because of the constancy of C_j for all frames of the multiframe task. So, using Equation (7) to present the amount of interference the higher priority multiframe tasks generate, the basic response time formula represented by Equation (4) is modified to be in the form used in the following theorem (i.e. Theorem 1).

Theorem 1. *Given a real time system consisting of N AM multiframe tasks, the worst case response time of the multiframe task τ_i is given by the smallest non-negative solution to Equation (8):*

$$R_i = C_i^{m_i} + \sum_{j=1}^{i-1} \xi_j(\lceil \frac{R_i}{T_j} \rceil) \tag{8}$$

where $\xi_j(\lceil \frac{R_i}{T_j} \rceil)$ is the cumulative function of the critical frame of τ_j as defined by Equation (7).

Proof. Assume R_i is the worst case response time of the task τ_i, then for each multiframe task whose priority is higher than the priority of τ_i (i.e. $\tau_j; j = 1..i - 1$); the number of invocations of τ_j within R_i is given by $\lceil \frac{R_i}{T_j} \rceil$ where the critical instant of an AM multiframe task is as in Definition 3 [12,13]. So, when τ_j is released at the critical frame, the amount of interference that τ_j generates within R_i is given by:

$$\xi_j(\lceil \frac{R_i}{T_j} \rceil). \tag{9}$$

In addition, the maximum amount of interference that any τ_j generates within a lower priority task is when it is released at its critical frame (i.e. Definition 3), so the amount of interference that all higher priority multiframe tasks generate within R_i is given by:

$$\sum_{j=1}^{i-1} \xi_j(\lceil \frac{R_i}{T_j} \rceil) \tag{10}$$

On the other hand, the maximum time τ_i takes for execution is represented by $C_i^{m_i}$. So the response time of τ_i is given by Equation (8); in which presents the execution of both the multiframe task τ_i as well as interference from all higher priority tasks.   □

Equation (8) that can be solved by a recurrence relation, provides an exact test of schedulability as the response time calculation is exact, assuming that there is no blocking time. So, the schedulability test, of a system with AM multiframe tasks, is presented as follows: a system with AM multiframe task set is schedulable if and only if all its multiframe tasks meet their relative deadlines. Where the AM multiframe task meets its deadline if its worst case response time, that is calculated by Equation (8), is less than or equals its deadline.

4.2   Adding Blocking Time to the Response Time Analysis

As mentioned earlier, blocking of a task is when this task stops its execution awaiting lower priority tasks to complete their execution. So, when we have a system of multiframe tasks, we expect more than one blocking values for the execution of τ_i since also all lower priority tasks are multiframes and therefore could have different execution times. However, using priority ceiling protocol [16,14] allows the task to be blocked at most once during its execution, so we only add, to the worst case response time formula, the maximum of the expected blocking values which we symbolize it as B_i. Thus, assuming that τ_i has a maximum blocking of B_i, we now say that the worst case response time formula (i.e. Equation (11)), is represented as a collection of three kind of execution: maximum execution of the task itself $C_i^{m_i}$, maximum blocking time B_i and maximum interference from the higher priority multiframe tasks, $\sum_{j=1}^{i-1} \xi_j(\lceil \frac{R_i}{T_j} \rceil)$.

$$R_i = C_i^{m_i} + B_i + \sum_{j=1}^{i-1} \xi_j(\lceil \frac{R_i}{T_j} \rceil) \tag{11}$$

Similar to the given solution of the standard response time, Equation (11) is solved using a recurrence relation as in Equation (12); where $w = 0, 1, 2, \ldots$ and $r_i^0 = C_i^{m_i}$. The worst case response time is obtained when it is found that $r_i^{w+1} = r_i^w (= R_i$ for the smallest value of w). While, in the case that r_i^{w+1} becomes greater than the deadline of the task, τ_i is not guaranteed to meet its deadline, so we say that the task is unschedulable.

$$r_i^{w+1} = C_i^{m_i} + B_i + \sum_{j=1}^{i-1} \xi_j(\lceil \frac{r_i^w}{T_j} \rceil) \tag{12}$$

4.3   Coverage of the Analysis

So far, research into schedulability tests has two formulations: the utilization domain and the response time domain. In our framework within this paper, we consider the response time scheduling test as better than the utilization based test because of the wider coverage the response time test gives for a less restricted system model.

From the utilization point of view, the scheduling test mostly depends on the chosen priority assignment, for example, Lu's approach considers RM priority assignment which is optimal when the deadlines of the tasks in the system are identical to their relative periods. However, when the deadlines of the tasks are permitted to be less than their relative periods; RM priority assignment is not optimal and Deadline Monotonic DM priority assignment takes its place (DM is a priority assignment where the lower deadline the relative task has, the higher priority it is assigned [9]). But, Lu's approach, for instance, is not applicable to the systems whose tasks' priority assignment is DM.

On the other hand, the response time scheduling analysis is a flexible test, better than the utilization test, from two points of view. Firstly, the response time test is applicable to the system model when the tasks have deadlines less than their relative periods. Secondly, the response time test does not depend on the priority assignment scheme of the tasks in the system. For example, response time test is still applicable to the system model where priorities are assigned according to RM, DM or even any other priority assignment scheme; while the utilization based test is not. For more illustration of the efficiency of the response time test, the following numeric example is given.

5   Numeric Example

In this section, we show the efficiency of the response time analysis by giving a numeric example and comparing the response time schedulability result with Lu's schedulability

Table 3. System Example

task	C	T = D	R
τ_1	1	3	1
τ_2	2	9	3
τ_3	3, 1	18	8
τ_4	2, 1	20	14
τ_5	6, 3	60	32

result. Table 3 represents an example task set of 5 AM multiframe tasks with their parameters and their worst case response times according to RM priority assignment (the smaller period the task has the higher priority it is assigned). To simplify the example, we assume that all deadlines are identical to their relative periods and all blocking terms are zero.

Lu et al. [11] note that the schedulability of this task set is unknown using Kuo's [8] method, while response time analysis shows that the task set is schedulable. Moreover, the analysis in this paper gives an exact value of the worst case response time of each task in the system. All worst case response times of all the tasks are given in Table 3 calculated by applying Equation (8). As all of the worst case response times are less than their deadlines, all multiframe tasks in the system are schedulable. So, the system is schedulable.

However, if we modify the execution times of task τ_4 to be $(3, 2)$ instead of $(2, 1)$ and keep all other parameters as in Table 3; we find that the system schedulability is unknown using Lu's method but it is schedulable using our response time analysis. That is because, in Lu's approach τ_1, τ_4, and τ_5 will be merged using Kuo's method to $\hat{\tau}_1$ with the execution times $(34, 30)$ and the period of 60 while τ_2 and τ_3 are merged to $\hat{\tau}_2$ with execution times $(7, 5)$ and a period of 18 (see Section 3.1 for all calculation details'). Therefore, the total peak utilization of the merged tasks is $U = 0.95556$ and Lu's conditional bound function (CB) of the merged tasks is 0.91259. So $U > CB$ which means using Lu's test that the system schedulability is unknown; whilst the exact response time analysis given in this paper shows that the system is schedulable because:

$R_1 = 1 \; < \; 3,$
$R_2 = 3 \; < \; 9,$
$R_3 = 8 \; < \; 18,$
$R_4 = 15 \; < \; 20,$
$R_5 = 35 \; < \; 60.$

6   Evaluating Exact Response Time Schedulability Analysis

We show in this section how the worst case response time test is a clear improvement, compared to the most recent schedulability test that is represented by Lu et. [11]. Comparison in this section requires the generation of the real time systems to check their schedulability under each approach (i.e. each of response time and Lu approaches) and then compare between these two to determine the best. This scenario is presented as simulations that are explained in three steps, the first step shows how each experiment is constructed, the second step illustrates how each experiment is run, and the third step shows the results of the experiments.

6.1 Experimental Setup

The generation of the real time system means the generation of the size of the system as well as the generation of the multiframe tasks that form the system. From the system size point of view, we assign the number of tasks in the system for each experiment to be one of the values $\{5, 20, 100\}$. While from the multiframe task's generation point of view, we require the generation of four parameters for each multiframe task, τ_i, (i.e. n_i, T_i, D_i, C_i; which are: number of frames, Period, Deadline, and the execution time sequence).

The four parameters of a multiframe task are generated, in summary, as follows. The first parameter that is the number of frames of the multiframe task is assumed as fixed for all multiframe tasks in the system and is chosen, for each experiment, as one of the values $\{3, 7, 13, 23\}$. The values are chosen to be prime numbers so that no task can have a repeating pattern of frames. The second and third parameters are the period and deadline of the multiframe task, they are assumed to be identical to each other for each multiframe task and are randomly generated in the range of $[1, 2500]$ using the uniform distribution. Once the deadlines are assigned to each task, the priorities of the tasks are also assigned according to DM (=RM) assignment.

The sequence of the execution times, which is the fourth parameter, is generated in two steps. In the first step we generate the utilization for each frame of the multiframe task, while in the second step we assign the execution time of this frame by multiplying its utilization by its period. The following is the full details the generation scheme for the execution times.

First of all, we give an overall utilization of the system and then we distribute this utilization to all multiframe tasks in the system using the UUnifast algorithm [4]. We consider each portion of the utilization for each multiframe task as the mean utilization of this multiframe task, and we multiply this mean by the number of frames, then we again apply the UUnifast algorithm to the results of the multiplication. In this case, we get the utilization of each frame in the multiframe task and therefore the execution time of this frame is the multiplication of its utilization by its period. Once we get the execution time sequence we re-arrange it to be AM using Mok's algorithm [13].

For each experiment, we modify one and fix two of the three attributes of the analysed system: utilization, number of frames and number of tasks. All experiments show, as expected, that the number of schedulable systems when the exact response time test is applied is always greater than when Lu's test is applied.

6.2 Scope of Running the Experiments

We run each experiment 1000 times, for each chosen number of frames, in four steps as following. Firstly, we generate the parameters of the experiment (i.e. number of frames, periods, deadlines, and execution time sequences) as previously explained. Secondly, we check the worst case response time of each task, using Equation (8), whether it is less than the relative deadline. In other words, we check the schedulability of the system by checking if the worst case response time of all multiframe tasks in this system are within their relative deadlines. Thirdly, for the same parameters of the system we check the schedulability of the same generated system using Lu's test. Lastly, for each of the two tests, we count the percentage of the number of schedulable systems out of the 1000 ones that are randomly generated.

6.3   Results of the Experiments

From the utilization point of view, we investigate the values of the utilizations that are in $(0.1, 0.2, 0.3, 0.4, 0.5, 0.6, 0.7, 0.8,)$. Figure 1 shows the percentage of the schedulable systems versus the overall utilization of the systems regarding two parameters: number of tasks, N, and number of frames, n. Each line in each graph in Figure 1 shows the results of the schedulability percentages for a value of n and a value of N. To simplify the presentation of the results, we present only two values of n in each graph. So, each graph has four lines, each two lines have the same values of parameters and present the results of both the response time test and Lu's test. For example, graph (a) in Figure 1 shows the results for 5 number of tasks and two values of n, that are 3 and 13; and likewise all graphs of Figure 1 show the results for different values of the number of tasks and number of frames.

Figure 1 shows that when the overall utilization of the system is very low, 0.1, both of the response time and Lu's tests give the same performance of 100% schedulable systems. While when the utilization is very high, greater than 0.6, although the exact test is better than Lu's one, the success of both tests is very low (as these systems are indeed unschedulable). So, we emphasize the range $[0.2, 0.6]$ of the overall utilization to show how much the exact response time test is better than Lu's test.

Graph (a) in Figure 1 shows that there is less than 10% better performance of the exact test than Lu's test; when the overall utilization of the system is 0.2, for 5 tasks in the system, and number of frames equal to 13. While this standard of performance rises to 20% in graph (a1) (i.e. percentage of the number of schedulable systems is 100%, according to the exact test, while this percentage is 80%, according to Lu's test), when the number of frames is 23 for the same other parameters. The performance decreases by increasing the number of tasks and increases by increasing the number of frames. For example, graph (b) and (b1) show that there is 55% better performance of the exact test than Lu's test; when the overall utilization of the system is 0.2, for 20 tasks in the system, and number of frames is 13 or 23. While this standard of performance rises to 95% in graph (c1) (i.e. percentage of the number of schedulable systems is 100%, according to the exact test, while this percentage is 5%, according to Lu's test); when the number of tasks is 100 and the number of frames becomes 23 for the utilization 0.2.

All graphs apart from (a1), in Figure 1, show that when the overall utilization of the system increases up to 0.4 (and sometimes 0.5 like in graphs (b) and (c)) and the number of frames is 3, *or* 7; the performance of the exact test stays higher than 90% for all studied number of tasks (i.e. 5, 20, *and* 100) while at the same time, graph (b1) shows that the performance of Lu's test decreases to about 22% when the utilization is 0.3, number of tasks is 20 and number of frames is 7. Also, from graph (c1), there is around 97% better performance of of the exact than Lu's test; when the overall utilization of the system is 0.3, for 100 tasks in the system, and number of frames is 23.

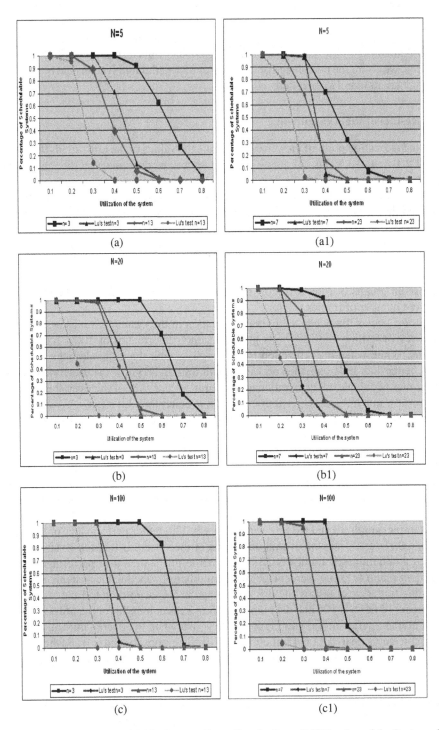

Fig. 1. Percentage of Schedulable Systems Regarding the Overall Utilization of the System after Applying Response Time and Lu's Tests

In addition, graph (b) shows that there is about 42% better performance of the exact test when the overall utilization of the system is 0.4, the number of frames is 13 and the number of tasks is 20. While graph (b1) shows that there is 80% better performance of the exact when the overall utilization of the system is 0.3, the number of frames is 23 and the number of tasks is 20; where 80% of the number of the random tasks are schedulable by the response time test but none of them were schedulable using Lu's test.

So, the percentage of the schedulability performance of the exact response time test is much more better than Lu's test and some times could reach to around 100% better performance. For example, graph (c) shows that 100% of the random systems are schedulable using exact test while non of the systems are schedulable using Lu's test; when the overall utilization is 0.3, the number of tasks is 100 and number of frames is 13. Similarly, graph (c1) shows that when the overall utilization is 0.3, the number of tasks is 100 and number of frames is 23; the percentage of the schedulable systems using exact test is about 97% while 0% of the systems are schedulable using Lu's test.

7   Conclusions

In this paper, we present an exact schedulability test for a system of AM multiframe tasks. The schedulability analysis is given in terms of the response time analysis of the AM multiframe tasks. The response time test, that is presented in this paper, shows a clear improvement in the schedulability tests from three points of view, firstly, the test is exact and tractable. Secondly, the test is applicable to the system model when deadlines of the tasks are less than their relative periods and regardless to the scheme for priority assignment. While thirdly, evaluations show that this exact response time test has better performance than the most improved utilisation bases schedulability test of the AM multiframe tasks. This improvement varies between 10% and 100% (for the relative three parameters: overall utilization of the system, number of tasks and number of frames).

References

1. Audsley, N.C., Burns, A., Richardson, M., Tindell, K., Wellings, A.J.: Applying New Scheduling Theory to Static Priority Preemptive Scheduling. Software Engineering Journal 8(5), 284–292 (1993)
2. Baker, T.P.: Stack-based scheduling of realtime processes. The Journal of Real Time Systems 3(1), 67–99 (1991)
3. Baruah, S.K., Chen, D., Mok, A.: Static-priority scheduling of multiframe tasks. In: Proceedings 11th Euromicro Conference on Real-Time Systems, pp. 38–45 (June 1999)
4. Bini, E., Buttazzo, G.C.: Biasing effects in schedulability measures. In: ECRTS 2004: Proceedings of the 16th Euromicro Conference on Real-Time Systems (ECRTS 2004), Washington, DC, USA, 2004, pp. 196–203. IEEE Computer Society Press, Los Alamitos (2004)
5. Burns, A., Wellings, A.J., Forsyth, C.H., Bailey, C.M.: A performance analysis of a hard real-time system. Control Engineering Practice 3(4), 447–464 (1995)
6. Han, C.J.: A better polynomial-time schedulability test for real-time multiframe tasks. In: Proceedings of 19th IEEE Real-Time Systems Symposium, December 1998, pp. 104–113 (1998)

7. Joseph, M., Pandya, P.: Finding Response Times in a Real-Time system. The Computer Journal 29(5), 390–395 (1986)

8. Kuo, T.W., Chang, L.P., Liu, Y.H., Lin, K.J.: Efficient on-line schedulability tests for real-time systems. IEEE Trans. on Software Engineering 29(8) (2003)

9. Leung, J.Y.T., Whitehead, J.: On the Complexity of Fixed Priority Scheduling of Periodic, Real Time Tasks. Performance Evaluation 2(4), 237–250 (1982)

10. Liu, C.L., Layland, J.W.: Scheduling Algorithm for Multiprogrammimg in a Hard Real-Time Environment. Journal of the Association for Computing Machinery 20(1), 46–61 (1973)

11. Lu, W.C., Lin, K.J., Wei, H.W., Shih, W.K.: New schedulability conditions for real-time multiframe tasks. In: 19th Euromicro Conference on Real Time Systems (ECRTS 2007), Pisa, Italy, July 4-6 (2007)

12. Mok, A.K., Chen, D.: A multiframe model for real time tasks. In: Proceedings of IEEE International Real Time System Symposium, December 1996, pp. 22–29 (1996)

13. Mok, A.K., Chen, D.: A multiframe model for real-time tasks. IEE Trans. on Software Engineering 23(10), 635–645 (1997)

14. Pilling, M., Burns, A., Raymond, K.: Formal specification and proofs of inheritance protocols for real-time scheduling. Software Engineering Journal 5(5), 263–279 (1990)

15. Serlin, O.: Scheduling of time critical processes. In: AFIPS Spring Computing Conference (1972)

16. Sha, L., Rajkumar, R., Lehoczky, J.P.: Priority Inheritance Protocol: An Approach to Real Time Synchronization. IEEE Transactions on Computers 39(9), 1175–1185 (1990)

17. Takada, H., Sakamura, K.: Schedulability of generalized multiframe task sets under static priority assignment. In: Real Time Computing Systems and Applications, pp. 80–86 (1997)

18. Traor, K., Grolleau, E., Rahni, A., Richard, M.: Response-time analysis of tasks with offsets. In: 11th IEEE International Conference on Emerging Technologies and Factory Automation (ETFA 2006), Prague, Czech Republic (September 2006)

Endomorphisms for Non-trivial Non-linear Loop Invariant Generation

Rachid Rebiha[1,3], Nadir Matringe[2], and Arnaldo Vieira Moura[3,*]

[1] Faculty of Informatics, University of Lugano, Switzerland
rachid.rebiha@lu.unisi.ch
[2] Institue de Mathematiques de Jussieu (UMR 7586) Université Paris 7-Denis
Diderot, France
matringe@math.jussieu.fr
[3] Institute of Computing, University of Campinas, SP.Brasil
arnaldo@ic.unicamp.br

Abstract. Present approaches for non-linear loop invariant generation
are limited to linear (affine) systems, or they relay on non scalable methods which have high complexity. Moreover, for programs with nested
loops and conditional statements that describe multivariate polynomials
or multivariate fractional systems, no applicable method is known to lend
itself to *non-trivial* non-linear invariants generation. We demonstrate
a powerful computational *complete* method to solve this problem. Our
approach avoids first-order quantifier elimination, cylindrical algebraic
decomposition and Grobner bases computation, hereby circumventing
difficulties met by recent methods.

1 Introduction

In this paper, we present a new method that addresses the various deficien-
cies of state-of-the-art non-linear invariant generation methods. An invariant at
a location in a program is an assertion true of any reachable program states
associated to this location. We provide mathematical techniques and design efficient algorithms to automate the discovery and strengthening of non-linear
interrelationships among the variables of a program containing non-linear loops
(multivariate polynomial and fractional manipulation).

It is well-know that the automation and effectiveness of formal verification of
programs depend on the ease with which strong invariants can be automatically
generated [1] (e.g. safety properties can be reduced to invariant properties). Furthermore, the standard techniques use invariant assertion [2] to prove program
properties or to provide lemmas that can establish other safety and liveness
program properties. We also know that the weakest precondition method [3, 4]
requires loop invariants to be completely automatic.

Non-linear loop invariant generation methods have seen tremendous progress
[5, 6, 7, 8, 9, 10, 11, 12] in recent years. But these approaches are limited to

---

* Supported by CNPq grant 472504/2007-0.

J.S. Fitzgerald, A.E. Haxthausen, and H. Yenigun (Eds.): ICTAC 2008, LNCS 5160, pp. 425–439, 2008.

linear (affine) system or relay on non scalable methods (with complexity at least doubly exponential). Moreover, they require Grobner Bases computations, first-order quantifier elimination [13, 14] or cylindrical algebraic decomposition. In [5], the non-linear invariant generation problem is reduced to a numerical constraint solving problem over indeterminate polynomial coefficients. In [7] similar forward propagation techniques use an abstract interpretation [15] framework and Grobner bases construction to compute invariants as fixed points of operations on ideals. In [16], techniques from abstract interpretation and Grobner bases computation are used to calculate a polynomial ideal that represents the weakest precondition for the validity of the polynomial relations at a given program point. The main challenge for these techniques is that abstract interpretation introduces imprecision (*widening*) to assure termination. This is the main reason why these approaches often produce null or trivial invariant due to a too coarse abstraction. In [17, 10], the methods use techniques from algebra and combinatorics (Grobner bases, variable elimination, algebraic dependencies and symbolic summation). They attempt to generate (not in an completely automatic way) all polynomial invariants from a restricted class of linear (P-solvable) loops. Also conditional statement are "omitted"[10]. On the other hand, [5, 18, 12] use the theory of polynomial algebra to generate multivariate polynomial invariants. However, the main weakness of these approaches is that they relay on methods with at least a doubly exponential complexity: Grobner Bases computation, first-order quantifier elimination. Also, these approaches omit conditional statements and deal with conjunctions of linear [5] and polynomial equations [18, 12]. Recently, [9] proposed the first methods to handle conditional statements by directly solving semi-algebraic systems, but the authors pointed out that this is not a practical method since the complexity remmains at least doubly exponential (single exponential w.r.t the number of program variables and parameters, and doubly exponential w.r.t the number of parameters).

For each type of semi-algebraic loop (affine, multivariate fractional and polynomial) we can summarize our contribution as follosw: (i) in contrast with the mentioned approaches, our methods do not required computation of Grobner bases, quantifier elimination, cylindrical algebraic decomposition or direct resolution of semi-algebraic system and do not depend on any abstraction methods; (ii) we succeeded in reducing the non-linear loop invariant generation problem to the intersection between eigenspaces of specific endomorphisms and initial linear or semi-affine/algebraic constraints; (iii) we present the first non-linear invariant generation methods that handle multivariate fractional instructions (as far as we know it is the first method that handles multivariate fractional systems), conditional statement, and nested inner-loops; (iv) we present necessary and sufficient conditions for the existence of *non-trivial* non-linear loop invariants; and (v) considering the problem of invariant generation, we identify large decidable and undecidable classes.

In Section 2 we present ideals of polynomials and their possible interactions with inductive assertions. In Section 3 we consider the case where loops describe an affine system. We also present a complete decision procedure for the automatic generation of *non-trivial* non-linear invariants. In Section 4 we present results for non-linear loops and the associated endomorphisms. Next, we present results for the existence of *non-trivial* invariants, decidable and undecidable classes and a generalization of the decision procedure to multivariate polynomial loops. In Section 5 we provide a complete generalization by considering loops describing multivariate fractional systems. We finally conclude our approach by showing how we handle nested loops and conditional statements in Section 6.

Details of all proofs and examples can be found in [19].

2   Ideals of Polynomials and Inductive Assertions

Let $A_n = K[X_1, .., X_n]$ be the ring of multivariate polynomials over the set of variables $\{X_1, .., X_n\} \subset K$. An ideal $I \in A_n$ is closed under addition, it includes 0 and it is closed by multiplication with each element in A_n (for all $P \in A_n$ and $Q \in I$, $PQ \in I$). Let $E \subseteq A_n$ be a set of polynomials, the *ideal generated* by E is given by the following set of *finite* sums: $(E) = \{\sum_{i=1}^{k} P_i Q_i \mid P_i \in K[X_1, \ldots, X_n], Q_i \in E, k \geq 1\}$. In other words, the set of *finite* sums $\sum_{Q \in E} A_n Q$. A set of polynomials E is said to be a *basis* of an ideal I if $I = (E)$. By Hilbert's Basis Theorem, we know that all ideals have a *finite* basis. An *algebraic* assertion is of the following form $\bigwedge_i p_i(x_1, ..., x_n) = 0$ where each $p_i \in A_n$. Let $\phi(x_1, ..., x_n) \equiv (\bigwedge_i p_i(x_1, ..., x_n) = 0)$ be an algebraic assertion and let $S_\phi \subseteq A_n$ be the associated set of polynomials p_i that appear in ϕ. For S_ϕ we define the *algebraic set* (or *variety*) as the set of common zeroes of all the polynomials in S_ϕ: $V(S_\phi) = \{(x_1, ..., x_n) \in \mathbb{C}^n \mid \forall p \in S_\phi, p(x_1, ..., x_n) = 0\}$. Consider a polynomial $Q \in A_n$, an algebraic assertion ϕ with its associated polynomial set S_ϕ and the ideal $I = (S_\phi)$. The *Ideal Membership* problem $(Q \in I)$ can be understood by the equivalent inclusion problem $V(I) \subseteq V(Q)$. The weak version of Hilbert's Nullstellensatz Theorem states that if $(Q \in I)$ then $\phi(x_1, \ldots, x_n) \models (Q(x_1, \ldots, x_n) = 0)$.

We use transition systems as representations of programs.

Definition 1. *A transition system is given by $\langle V, L, \mathcal{T}, l_0, \Theta \rangle$, where V is a set of variables, L is a set of locations and l_0 is the initial location. A state is given by an interpretation of the variables in V. A transition $\tau \in \mathcal{T}$ is given by a tuple $\langle l_{pre}, l_{post}, \rho_\tau \rangle$, where l_{pre} and l_{post} name the pre- and post- locations of τ. The transition relation ρ_τ is a first-order assertion over $V \cup V'$, where V correspond to current-state variables and V' to the next-state variables. Θ is the initial condition, given as a first-order assertion over V.*

Definition 2. *$W = \langle V, L, \mathcal{T}, l_0, \Theta \rangle$ is a transition system. An invariant at location $l \in L$ is defined by an assertion over V which holds on all reachable states at location l. An invariant of W is an assertion over V that holds at all locations.*

Definition 3. *Let $W = \langle V, L, \mathcal{T}, l_0, \Theta \rangle$ be a transition system and let D be the domain of assertions. An assertion map for W is a map $\eta : L \to D$. We say that η is inductive if and only if the Initiation and Consecution conditions hold:*

– $\Theta \models \eta(l_0)$ *(Initiation)*
– $\forall \tau \in T$ *s.t* $\tau = \langle l_i, l_j, \rho_\tau \rangle$ *we have* $\eta(l_i) \wedge \rho_\tau \models \eta(l_j)'$ *(Consecution).*

From [4], we know that if η is an inductive assertion map then $\eta(l)$ is an invariant at l. We will use the following notions of consecution.

Definition 4. *Let* $\tau = \langle l_i, l_j, \rho_\tau \rangle$ *be a transition for a given algebraic transition system and let* η *be an algebraic inductive map. We identify the following complete* notion of consecution:

1. η *satisfies the* Fractional-scale *consecution for* τ *if and only if there exists a multivariate fractional* $\frac{T}{Q}$ *such that:* $\rho_\tau \models (\eta(l_j)' - \frac{T}{Q}\eta(l_j) = 0)$
2. η *satisfies the* Polynomial-scale *consecution for* τ *if and only if there exist a multivariate polynomial* T *such that :* $\rho_\tau \models (\eta(l_j)' - T\eta(l_j) = 0)$
3. η *satisfies the* Constant-scale *consecution for* τ *if and only if there exists a constant* $\lambda \in K$ *such that :* $\rho_\tau \models (\eta(l_j)' - \lambda\eta(l_j) = 0)$

Constant-scale consecution encodes the fact that the numerical value of the assertion after the transition τ is given by λ times the numerical value prior the transition τ. *Polynomial-scale* consecution encodes the fact that the numerical value of the assertion after the transition τ has been multiplied after the transition by a multivariate polynomial T. *Fractional-scale* consecution encodes the fact that the numerical value of the assertion after the transition τ is a $\frac{T}{Q}$ multivariate fractional multiple of the numerical value prior to the transition.

3   When to Use Constant Scale Consecution

Definition 5. *Let a transition system corresponding to loop* $\tau = \langle l_i, l_i, \rho_\tau \rangle$ *be*

$$\rho_\tau \equiv [x_1' = L_1(x_1, \ldots, x_n) \wedge \ldots \wedge x_n' = L_n(x_1, \ldots, x_n).] \tag{1}$$

A polynomial $Q \in K[X_1, ..., X_n]$ *is said to be a* λ-*invariant for constant-scale consecution* with parameter λ *for the loop* τ *if and only if*

$$Q(X_1', .., X_n') - \lambda Q(X_1, .., X_n) = 0,$$

modulo the ideal of $K[X_1', .., X_n', X_1, .., X_n]$ *corresponding to the loop generated by the basis* $(X_1' - L_1(X_1, ..., X_n), ..., X_n' - L_n(X_1, ..., X_n)).$

Theorem 1. *(λ-invariant characterization) Consider a transition system corresponding to a loop* τ *as described in Definition 5. Let* $Q(X_1, ..., X_n)$ *be a multivariate polynomial with indeterminate coefficients.* Q *is a* λ-*invariant for constant-scale consecution with parameter* $\lambda \in K$ *for* τ *if and only if*

$$Q(L_1(X_1, \ldots, X_n), .., L_n(X_1, \ldots, X_n)) = \lambda Q(X_1, \ldots, X_n).$$

Consider the case of *affine* transition systems corresponding to a loop as described in Definition 5, where $L_i(x_1, ..., x_n) = \sum_{k=1}^{n} c_{i,k-1} x_k + c_{i,k}$ are affine forms. In this case, let $Q \in A_n$ be a multivariate polynomial of degree r, with indeterminate coefficients (a template), which is going to be a λ-invariant candidate for constant-scale consecution with parameter λ. We show that for good choices of λ there always exists such a λ-invariant that is not trivial. As Q is of degree r, it has coefficients $a_0, .., a_t$, each corresponding to a monomial in the expansion of Q with respect to the total-degree lexicographic ordering ($t + 1$ being the number of monomials of degree inferior to r, so that a_t is the coefficient of the constant term). Notice that $Q(L_1(X_1, .., X_n), .., L_n(X_1, .., X_n))$ is also of degree r because all L_i's are of degree one. Writing the problem using linear algebra, and using the canonical basis of $K[X_1, .., X_n]$, we immediately see that it is equivalent to solve the following: $(M - \lambda I) \vec{a} = \vec{0}$, where $\vec{a}$ is the column vector with coordinates a_i, and M is a $(t+1) \times (t+1)$ matrix whose coefficients depend on the $c_{i,k}$'s. To be more precise, let V_r be the subspace of $K[X_1, .., X_n]$ consisting of polynomials of degree less than r, then M is the matrix of the endomorphism of V_r given by

$$(P(X_1, .., X_n) \mapsto P(L_1(X_1, ..., X_n), .., L_n(X_1, ..., X_n))$$

in the canonical basis of V_r consisting of terms of degree less then r with total-degree lexicographic ordering (this is indeed an endomorphism because all L_i's are of degree one). That is, λ must be an eigenvalue of M if we want to find a non null λ-invariant whose coefficients will be those of an eigenvector.

Theorem 2. (*Existence of λ-invariants*) *Let V_r and M be as above. A polynomial Q of V_r is λ-invariant for scale consecution if and only if there exists an eigenvalue λ of M such that Q belongs to the eigenspace corresponding to λ.*

We also notice that the last column of M is always $(0, .., 0, 1)^t$ by definition of the matrix M. Thus 1 is always an eigenvalue of M, with a corresponding eigenvector being $\vec{a}$ with $a_i = 0$ except for a_t, which gives the trivial λ-invariant $Q(X_1, .., X_n) = a_t$, i.e. the constant polynomial. Eigenvalue 1 always gives the constant polynomial as a λ-invariant, but it might give better invariants for other eigenvectors if $dim(Ker(M - \lambda I)) \geq 2$, as we will see in the sequel.

Example 1. **General Case for 2 Variables.** We first treat the general case where the transition system has only two variables, we will look for a λ-invariant candidate of degree 2, where

$$\rho_\tau \equiv \begin{bmatrix} x_1' = c_{1,0}x_1 + c_{1,1}x_2 + c_{1,2} \\ x_2' = c_{2,0}x_1 + c_{2,1}x_2 + c_{2,2} \end{bmatrix}.$$

And we look for an invariant polynomial $Q(X_1, X_2) = a_0 X_1^2 + a_1 X_1 X_2 + a_2 X_2^2 + a_3 X_1 + a_4 X_2 + a_5$ for constant scaling with parameter λ. Recall that we must solve the equation $Q(c_{1,0}X_1 + c_{1,1}X_2 + c_{1,2}, c_{2,0}X_1 + c_{2,1}X_2 + c_{2,2}) = \lambda Q(X_1, X_2)$.

Thus for M we get the following matrix:

$$\begin{pmatrix} c_{1,0}{}^2 & c_{1,0}c_{2,0} & c_{2,0}{}^2 & 0 & 0 & 0 \\ 2c_{1,0}c_{1,1} & c_{1,0}c_{2,1}+c_{1,1}c_{2,0} & 2c_{2,0}c_{2,1} & 0 & 0 & 0 \\ c_{1,1}{}^2 & c_{1,1}c_{2,1} & c_{2,1}{}^2 & 0 & 0 & 0 \\ 2c_{1,0}c_{1,2} & c_{1,0}c_{2,2}+c_{1,2}c_{2,0} & 2c_{2,0}c_{2,2} & c_{1,0} & c_{2,0} & 0 \\ 2c_{1,1}c_{1,2} & c_{1,1}c_{2,2}+c_{1,2}c_{2,1} & 2c_{2,1}c_{2,2} & c_{1,1} & c_{2,1} & 0 \\ c_{1,2}{}^2 & c_{1,2}c_{2,2} & c_{2,2}{}^2 & c_{1,2} & c_{2,2} & 1 \end{pmatrix}.$$

We see that the last column is as predicted, plus the matrix is block diagonal. Thus its characteristic polynomial is $P(\lambda) = (1-\lambda)P_1(\lambda)P_2(\lambda)$, with P_1 being the characteristic polynomial of $\begin{pmatrix} c_{1,0} & c_{2,0} \\ c_{1,1} & c_{2,1} \end{pmatrix}$ and P_2 being the one of

$$\begin{pmatrix} c_{1,0}{}^2 & c_{1,0}c_{2,0} & c_{2,0}{}^2 \\ 2c_{1,0}c_{1,1} & c_{1,0}c_{2,1}+c_{1,1}c_{2,0} & 2c_{2,0}c_{2,1} \\ c_{1,1}{}^2 & c_{1,1}c_{2,1} & c_{2,1}{}^2 \end{pmatrix}.$$ Here P_2 is of degree 3 and has at least

one real root, which can be computed by Lagrange's resolvent method. Choosing λ to be this root, the corresponding eigenvectors will give non-trivial λ-invariants of degree two as at least a_0, a_1 or a_2 must be non null for such an eigenvector.

Example 2. Now, suppose the transition system is given by $\tau = \langle l_i, l_i, \rho_\tau \rangle$ with $\rho_\tau \equiv [x'_1 = 2x_1 + x_2 + 1 \wedge x'_2 = 3x_2 + 4]$. Then $P_2(\lambda) = (4-\lambda)(6-\lambda)(9-\lambda)$. So fix λ to be 4. We get that the corresponding eigenspace is generated by the following vector: $(1, -2, 1, -6, 6, 9)^t$. So that as a λ-invariant polynomial for scale consecution with parameter 4, we get $1X_1{}^2 - 1X_1X_2 + X_2{}^2 - 6X_1 + 6X_2 + 9$.

Example 3. (**With 4 Variables**). We study the following transition system [5] corresponding to the multiplication of 2 numbers and where the transition considered is $\tau = \langle l_i, l_i, \rho_\tau \rangle$ with $\rho_\tau \equiv [s' = s+i \wedge j' = j+1 \wedge i' = i \wedge j'_0 = j_0]$. We are looking for a degree two invariant of the form $Q(s, j, i, j_0) = a_0 s^2 + a_1 sj + a_2 si + a_3 sj_0 + a_4 j^2 + a_5 ji + a_6 jj_0 + a_7 i^2 + a_8 ij_0 + a_9 j_0{}^2 + a_{10} s + a_{11} j + a_{12} 2i + a_{13} j_0 + a_{14}$. We need to solve $Q(s+i, j+1, i, j_0) = \lambda Q(s, j, i, j_0)$. Here an evident eigenvalue is 1, as it is clear in view of the matrix M that $dim(Ker(M-I)) \geq 2$. For example the vector $(1, 0, 0, 0, 0, 1, 0, 0, -1, 0, 0, 0, 0, 0)^t$ is the eigenvector corresponding to the λ-invariant $s + ji - ij_0$. Note that without Grobner bases and quantifier elimination we find the invariant obtained in [5].

3.1   What Happens in Practice

We have seen that for an affine transition system of the type describe in Definition 5 where $L_i(x_1, ..., x_n) = \sum_{k=1}^{n} c_{i,k-1}x_k + c_{i,k}$ are affine forms, the scaling consecution technique with parameter λ works if and only if λ is an eigenvalue of M. Since eigenvalues are calculated as the roots of the characteristic polynomial of M, we can state three facts: 1 is always an eigenvalue as we have seen, but if the corresponding eigenspace is of dimension one exactly, the eigenvectors correspond to constant of λ-invariants, which are trivial. Apart from 1, other eigenvalues might not be real, but complex. If a polynomial is of degree equal to or greater than five, finding its roots becomes undecidable [20], so even if there are eigenvalues different than 1, one is not always certain to obtain them.

Theorem 3. *(Undecidability of constant scale consecution) Let M the matrix introduced in this section and let ϕ_λ be its characteristic polynomial. Finding a non trivial λ invariant is equivalent to finding a root of ϕ_λ different than 1, if 1 has multiplicity one. If the degree of ϕ_λ is equal to or greater than six, then $\phi_\lambda/(X-1)$ has degree equal to or greater than five.*

Theorem 4. *(Some decidable classes) Let M the matrix introduce in this section. The problem of finding a non-trivial λ-invariant is decidable if one of the following assertions are true:*

- *M is block triangular (with 4×4 blocks or less) ,*
- *Eigenspace associated with eigenvalue 1 is of dimension greater than 1.*

3.2 Initiation Step

Intersection with an Initial Hyperplane Consider the affine system associated with an affine loop (see Definition 5), and an invariant candidate Q of degree r. Q is a λ-invariant for constant scale consecution, meaning that $Q(L_1(X_1, .., X_n), .., L_n(X_1, .., X_n)) = \lambda Q(X_1, .., X_n)$. Now let $u_1, ..., u_n$ be the initial values of $X_1, ..., X_n$. For the initial step we need $Q(u_1, ..., u_n) = 0$.

In the space V_r of polynomials of degree less or equal to r, we have the following linear form on this space: $P \mapsto P(u_1, ..., u_n)$. Hence initial values correspond to a hyperplane in V_r, given by the kernel of $P \mapsto P(u_1, ..., u_n)$. Now, if we add the initiation step, $Q(X_1, ..., X_n) = 0$ will be an invariant (see Definition 2) if and only if there exists an eigenvalue λ of M such that Q belongs to the intersection of the eigenspace corresponding to λ and the hyperplane $Q(u_1, ..., u_n) = 0$ given by the initial values $(u_1, ..., u_n)$. Given our encodings, the algebraic assertion map $\eta : L \mapsto (Q(X_1, ..., X_n) = 0)$ is inductive (see Definition 3).

Theorem 5. *(Invariants and constant scale consecution) A polynomial Q in V_r is an invariant for the affine loop (see Definition 5) with initial values $(u_1, ..., u_n)$ if and only if there is an eigenvalue λ of M such that Q is in the intersection of the eigenspace of λ and the hyperplane $Q(u_1, ..., u_n) = 0$.*

The previous paragraph describes the case when variables are initial constraints with constant values. In the following theorem, we state the most important result: we consider the more general case where variables are assigned a set of parameter variables (that could be subject to any type of constraint).

Theorem 6. *(Non-null invariants and constant scale consecution) There will be a non-null invariant polynomial for any given initial values if and only if there exists an eigenspace of M with dimension greater than 2.*

Reconsider the example where $\rho_\tau \equiv [x_1' = 2x_1 + x_2 + 1 \wedge x_2' = 3x_2 + 4]$. Matrix M has six distinct eigenvalues, so that eigenspaces are of dimension 1. We denote by

E_λ the eigenspace corresponding to λ. E_4 has basis $(1, -2, 1, -6, 6, 9)^t$, E_6 has basis $(0, 1, -1, 2, -5, 6)^t$, E_9 has basis $(0, 0, 1, 0, 4, 4)^t$, E_2 has $(0, 0, 0, 1, -1, -3)^t$, E_3 has basis $(0, 0, 0, 0, 1, 2)^t$, and E_1 has basis $(0, 0, 0, 0, 0, 1)^t$. Suppose that the initiation step is given by $(x_1 = 0, x_2 = -2)$, i.e. $(u_1, u_2) = (0, 2)$, which corresponds to the hyperplane $Q(0, 2) = 0$ in V_2, or $4a_2 - 2a_4 + a_5 = 0$ in $\mathbb{R}^6$, using the canonical basis of V_2. It is clear that $(0, 0, 1, 0, 4, 4)$ belongs to this hyperplane, so that $X_2^2 + 4X_2 + 4$ is an invariant polynomial for the loop with initial step $(x_1 = 0, x_2 = -2)$. Now, reconsider Example 3 where $dim(Ker(M - I)) \geq 2$, so that according to the previous subsection, the consecution scale technique will give a non-null invariant whatever the initial values are (which explains why a non-trivial invariant was found in [5]).

3.3   When Constant Scale Consecution Never Works

Let's consider an algebraic transition system

$$
\rho_\tau \equiv \begin{bmatrix} x_1' = P_1(x_1, \ldots, x_n) \\ \vdots \\ x_m' = P_m(x_1, \ldots, x_n) \end{bmatrix}, \tag{2}
$$

where $P_1, \ldots, P_m \in A_n$. In the case where each polynomial P_i has a degree greater than 1, the constant-scale consecution encoding proposed by existing methods [5],[10] unfortunately generates trivial (constant or null) invariants. Moreover, if each P_i is of degree greater or equal than 2, the previous methods can only generate trivial invariants.

Example 4. Let's consider the following loop: $\rho_\tau \equiv \begin{bmatrix} x' = x(y+1) \\ y' = y^2 \end{bmatrix}$. At step k of the iteration, this loop computes the sum: $1 + y + \cdots + y^{2^k - 1}$. Let $P(x, y) = a_0 x^2 + a_1 xy + a_2 y^2 + a_3 x + a_4 y + a_5$ be a candidate λ-invariant. Modulo the loop ideal of $\mathbb{K}[x', y', x, y]$ (ordering by the precedence: $x' > y' > x > y$.), we have $P(x', y') = P(x(y+1), y^2)$ and we write $P'(x, y) = P(x(y+1), y^2)$. After expanding we get $P'(x, y) = a_0 x^2 y^2 + a_1 xy^3 + a_2 y^4 + 2a_0 x^2 y + a_1 xy^2 + a_0 x^2 + a_3 xy + a_4 y^2 + a_3 x + a_5$. If we try the constant-scale consecution with parameter λ we obtain, after simplification: $a_0 = a_1 = a_2 = a_3 = a_4 = 0$ and $a_5 = \lambda a_5$. If $\lambda \neq 1$ then $a_5 = 0$, which leads to a *null* invariant. Otherwise $\lambda = 1$ and we obtain a *constant* invariant (a_5). Also, by considering the initial condition, we note that it will imply that the constant invariant a_5 is null.

4   Non-linear Algebraic Transition Systems

4.1   T-Invariants Generation

Definition 6. *Consider an algebraic transition system corresponding to an algebraic loop $\tau = \langle l_i, l_j, \rho_\tau \rangle$ as in Equation 2 where $P_1, ..., P_n \in \mathbb{K}[x_1, ..., x_n]$. A polynomial $Q \in K[X_1, ..., X_n]$ is said to be a T-invariant for polynomial-scale* *consecution for τ if and only if there exists a polynomial $T \in K[X_1, ..., X_n]$, verifying $Q(X'_1, ..., X'_n) = T(X_1, ..., X_n)Q(X_1, ..., X_n)$ modulo the ideal of $K[X'_1, ..., X'_n, X_1, ..., X_n]$ corresponding to the loop, and generated by the base $(X'_1 - P_1(X_1, ..., X_n), ..., X'_n - P_n(X_1, ..., X_n))$.*

Theorem 7. *(T-invariant characterization) Consider an algebraic transition system corresponding to an algebraic loop τ as in Equation 2. Let $Q \in K[X_1, ..., X_n]$ be a multivariate polynomial with indeterminate coefficients (a template). Q is a T-invariant for polynomial scale consecution with parametric polynomial $T \in K[X_1, ..., X_n]$ for τ if and only if*

$$Q(P_1(X_1, ..., X_n), ..., P_n(X_1, ..., X_n)) = T(X_1, ..., X_n)Q(X_1, ..., X_n).$$

Reconsider Example 4. We take $(y = y_0, x = 1)$ as initial values. We propose to use *polynomial scale consecution* with a parametric polynomial $T(x, y) = b_0y^2 + b_1x + b_2y + b_3$. We obtain $P'(s, x) = (b_0y^2 + b_1x + b_2y + b_3) \cdot P(x, y)$. In other words, we obtain the following multi-parametric linear system (with parameters b_0, b_1, b_2, b_3):

$$\begin{cases} a_0 = b_0a_0 \quad 0 = b_2a_5 + b_3a_4 \quad a_3 = b_1a_4 + b_2a_3 + b_3a_1 \\ a_1 = b_0a_1 \quad 0 = b_0a_4 + b_2a_2 \quad a_4 = b_0a_5 + b_2a_4 + b_3a_2 \\ a_2 = b_0a_2 \quad a_3 = b_1a_5 + b_3a_3 \quad a_1 = a_3b_0 + b_1a_2 + b_2a_1 \\ a_5 = b_3a_5 \quad a_0 = b_1a_3 + b_3a_0 \\ 0 = b_1a_0 \quad 2a_0 = b_1a_1 + b_2a_0 \end{cases}$$

Now we describe a decision procedure for parameter valuations. Considering the first three equations, choose $b_0 = 1$ in order to keep a high degree invariant (otherwise the coefficients a_0, a_1, a_2 of the highest degree terms would be null). Then we obtain another system with $b_1a_0 = 0$. For the same degree, choose $b_1 = 0$. Then we have $b_2a_0 = 2a_0$. As a direct consequence, the parameter b_2 is set to 2. Since equation $b_3a_0 = a_0$ is in the resulting system, b_3 is set to 1. We obtain $a_3 + a_1 = 0$, $a_4 + 2a_2 = 0$ and $a_2 - a_5 = 0$. With less equations than variables, we will have a *non-trivial* solution for the generation of a T-invariant. Now we add the hyperplane corresponding to the initial values: $a_2y_0^2 + (a_1 + a_4)y_0 + a_0 + a_1 + a_5 = 0$. As there are six variables and four equations, we will have a *non-trivial* solution for the problem of invariant generation. A possible solution is the vector $(y_0(1 - y_0), 1, 1, -1, -2, 1)^t$, that is, $y_0(1 - y_0)x^2 + xy + y^2 - x - 2y + 1 = 0$ is an invariant. Note that $T(x, y) = y^2 + y + 1$.

That is a simple decision procedure, which can fail in more complex cases. Shortly, we will present a superior technique, with a more global point of view.

4.2 A General Theory for Polynomial Scale Consecutions

We need a T-invariant of degree r for an algebraic loop $\tau = \langle l_i, l_i, \rho_\tau \rangle$ (as in Equation 2), that is, a polynomial Q of degree r such that there exists a polynomial T, verifying $Q(P_1(X_1, .., X_n), .., P_n(X_1, .., X_n)) = T(X_1, .., X_n)Q(X_1, .., X_n)$.

We write again the T-invariant ordered candidate's coefficients $a_0, ..., a_t$ ($t + 1$ being the number of monomials of degree inferior to r). Let d be the maximal degree of the P_i's. We are going to look for T of degree $e = dr - r$. Let's write its ordered coefficients $\lambda_0, ..., \lambda_s$ ($s + 1$ being the number of monomials of degree inferior to e). Recall that V_m designates the subspace of $\mathbb{K}[x_1, \ldots, x_n]$ of degree inferior to or equal to m. Let M be the matrix, in the canonical basis of V_r and V_{dr}, of the morphism from V_r to V_{dr} given by $P(X_1, \ldots, X_n) \mapsto P(P_1(X_1, \ldots, X_n), \ldots, P_n(X_1, \ldots, X_n))$. The coefficients of M will be polynomials in the coefficients of the P_i's. Let L be the matrix, in the canonical basis of V_r and V_e, of the morphism from V_r to V_{dr} given by $P \mapsto TP$. Matrix L will be ssen to have a very simple form. Now we just claim that its non zero coefficients are the λ_i's, and that it has a natural block decomposition. Let u be the number of terms of degree less than dr (i.e. the dimension of V_{rd}). Our problem is equivalent to finding a matrix L, such that $M - L$ has a non trivial kernel. In other words, such that $M - L$ is of rank less than u. We know that a matrix is of rank less than $k \in \mathbb{N}$ if and only if it has an *invert* $k * k$ sub-matrix.

Theorem 8. *(Existence of T-invariant vectorspaces) Consider M as described above. There will be a T-invariant polynomial if and only if there exists a matrix L (corresponding to $P \mapsto TP$) such that $M - L$ has a nontrivial kernel. Further, any vector in the kernel of $M - L$ will give a T-invariant polynomial.*

Again the last column of M is $(0, ..., 0, 1)^t$, and the last column of L is $(0, .., 0, \lambda_0, .., \lambda_s)^t$. Hence, choosing every λ_i to be zero, except for $\lambda_s = 1$, the last column of M - L will be null. With this choice of L (or $T = 1$), we at least always get T-invariants corresponding to constant polynomials. Now, $M - L$ having a non trivial kernel is equivalent to its rank being less than the dimension $d(r)$ of V_r. This is equivalent to the fact that each $d(r) \times d(r)$ subdeterminant of $M - L$ is equal to zero [20]. Those determinants are polynomials with variables $(\lambda_0, \lambda_1, \cdots, \lambda_s)$, which we will denote by $D_1(\lambda_0, \lambda_1, .., \lambda_s), .., D_t(\lambda_0, \lambda_1, .., \lambda_s)$.

Theorem 9. *(Undecidability of finding T-invariants) There will be a non trivial T-invariant if and only if the polynomials $(D_1, .., D_r)$ described above admit a common root, other than the trivial one $(0, .., .., 0, 1)$. Those roots are, in general, not calculable.*

Example 5. **Loop with Two Variables, T-Invariant of Degree Two** We first study the general case of degree two algebraic transition systems with two variables in the loop. The transition system has the form:

$$\rho_\tau \equiv \begin{bmatrix} x' = c_0 x^2 + c_1 xy + c_2 y^2 + c_3 x + c_4 y + c_5 \\ y' = d_0 x^2 + d_1 xy + d_2 y^2 + d_3 x + d_4 y + d_5 \end{bmatrix},$$

$$M = \begin{pmatrix} c_0^2 & c_0 d_0 & d_0^2 & 0 & 0 & 0 \\ 2c_0 c_1 & c_0 d_1 + c_1 d_0 & 2d_0 d_1 & 0 & 0 & 0 \\ 2c_0 c_2 + c_1^2 & c_0 d_2 + c_1 d_1 + c_2 d_0 & 2d_0 d_2 + d_1^2 & 0 & 0 & 0 \\ 2c_1 d_1 & c_1 d_2 + c_2 d_1 & 2d_1 d_2 & 0 & 0 & 0 \\ c_2^2 & c_2 d_2 & d_2^2 & 0 & 0 & 0 \\ 2c_0 c_3 & c_0 d_3 + c_3 d_0 & 2d_0 d_3 & 0 & 0 & 0 \\ 2(c_0 c_4 + c_1 c_3) & c_0 d_4 + c_1 d_3 + c_3 d_1 + c_4 d_0 & 2(d_0 d_4 + d_1 d_3) & 0 & 0 & 0 \\ 2(c_1 c_4 + c_2 c_3) & c_1 d_4 + c_2 d_3 + c_3 d_2 + c_4 d_1 & 2(d_1 d_4 + d_2 d_3) & 0 & 0 & 0 \\ 2c_2 c_4 & c_2 d_4 + c_4 d_2 & 2d_2 d_4 & 0 & 0 & 0 \\ 2c_0 c_5 + c_3^2 & c_0 d_5 + c_3 d_3 + c_5 d_0 & 2d_0 d_5 + d_3^2 & c_0 & d_0 & 0 \\ 2(c_1 c_5 + c_3 c_4) & c_1 d_5 + c_3 d_4 + c_4 d_3 + c_5 d_1 & 2(d_1 d_5 + d_3 d_4) & c_1 & d_1 & 0 \\ 2c_2 c_5 + c_4^2 & c_2 d_5 + c_4 d_4 + c_5 d_2 & 2d_2 d_5 + d_4^2 & c_2 & d_2 & 0 \\ 2c_3 c_5 & c_3 d_5 + c_5 d_3 & 2d_3 d_5 & c_3 & d_3 & 0 \\ 2c_4 c_5 & c_4 d_5 + c_5 d_4 & 2d_4 d_5 & c_4 & d_4 & 0 \\ c_5^2 & c_5 d_5 & d_5^2 & c_5 & d_5 & 1 \end{pmatrix} \quad L = \begin{pmatrix} \lambda_0 & 0 & 0 & 0 & 0 & 0 \\ \lambda_1 & \lambda_0 & 0 & 0 & 0 & 0 \\ \lambda_2 & \lambda_1 & \lambda_0 & 0 & 0 & 0 \\ 0 & \lambda_2 & \lambda_1 & 0 & 0 & 0 \\ 0 & 0 & \lambda_2 & 0 & 0 & 0 \\ \lambda_3 & 0 & 0 & \lambda_0 & 0 & 0 \\ \lambda_4 & \lambda_3 & 0 & \lambda_1 & \lambda_0 & 0 \\ 0 & \lambda_4 & \lambda_3 & \lambda_2 & \lambda_1 & 0 \\ 0 & 0 & \lambda_4 & 0 & \lambda_2 & 0 \\ \lambda_5 & 0 & 0 & \lambda_3 & 0 & \lambda_0 \\ 0 & \lambda_5 & 0 & \lambda_4 & \lambda_3 & \lambda_1 \\ 0 & 0 & \lambda_5 & 0 & \lambda_4 & \lambda_2 \\ 0 & 0 & 0 & \lambda_5 & 0 & \lambda_3 \\ 0 & 0 & 0 & 0 & \lambda_5 & \lambda_4 \\ 0 & 0 & 0 & 0 & 0 & \lambda_5 \end{pmatrix}$$

For the rank of $M - L$ to be less than 6, one has to calculate each 6×6 subdeterminant obtained by canceling 9 lines of $M - L$. They will be polynomials of degree less than 6 in variables $(\lambda_0, ..., \lambda_5)$. Now, L is such that $M - L$ will be of degree less than 6 if and only if $(\lambda_0, ..., \lambda_5)$ are roots of each of those polynomials.

Remark 1. (**Decidable classes**) In many cases, it is easy to find a matrix L such that $M - L$ has a non trivial kernel. We describe two decidable classes: (i) suppose that in the previous case, c_2, c_4 and c_5 are null, then one can choose $(\lambda_0, \ldots, \lambda_s)$ in order to make the first column zero; and (ii) the third column can be canceled using good choices for the λ_i's, if d_0, d_3 and d_5 are zero.

For example, suppose that in the previous case c_2, c_4 and c_5 are null. Then one can choose $(\lambda_0, \ldots, \lambda_s)$ in order to make the first column zero. Now consider Example 4 in Section 3.3. Here we have $c_0 = 0, c_1 = 1, c_2 = 0, c_3 = 1, c_4 = 0, c_5 = 0$, and $d_0 = 0, d_1 = 0, d_2 = 1, d_3 = 0, d_4 = 0, d_5 = 0$. Then $M - L$ is:

$$
\begin{pmatrix}
-\lambda_0 & 0 & 0 & 0 & 0 & 0 \\
-\lambda_1 & -\lambda_0 & 0 & 0 & 0 & 0 \\
1-\lambda_2 & -\lambda_1 & -\lambda_0 & 0 & 0 & 0 \\
0 & 1-\lambda_2 & -\lambda_1 & 0 & 0 & 0 \\
0 & 0 & 1-\lambda_2 & 0 & 0 & 0 \\
-\lambda_3 & 0 & 0 & -\lambda_0 & 0 & 0 \\
2-\lambda_4 & -\lambda_3 & 0 & -\lambda_1 & -\lambda_0 & 0 \\
0 & 1-\lambda_4 & -\lambda_3 & -\lambda_2 & -\lambda_1 & 0 \\
0 & 0 & -\lambda_4 & 0 & -\lambda_2 & 0 \\
1-\lambda_5 & 0 & 0 & -\lambda_3 & 0 & -\lambda_0 \\
0 & -\lambda_5 & 0 & 1-\lambda_4 & -\lambda_3 & -\lambda_1 \\
0 & 0 & -\lambda_5 & 0 & 1-\lambda_4 & -\lambda_2 \\
0 & 0 & 0 & 1-\lambda_5 & 0 & -\lambda_3 \\
0 & 0 & 0 & 0 & -\lambda_5 & -\lambda_4 \\
0 & 0 & 0 & 0 & 0 & 1-\lambda_5
\end{pmatrix}
$$

Now, taking $\lambda_0 = \lambda_1 = \lambda_3 = 0, \lambda_2 = 1, \lambda_4 = 2, \lambda_5 = 1$, the first column of $M - L$ is zero, and the second column is equal to the fourth. hence, $M - L$ will be of rank equal to or less than four, i.e. with kernel of dimension equal to or more than two. Any vector in this kernel will be T-invariant.

4.3   Initiation Step

We are looking for an invariant $Q \in k[X_1, ..., X_n]$. Let $u_1, \ldots, u_n$ be the initial values of the variables $X_1, ..., X_n$. For the initial step we need $Q(u_1, \ldots, u_n) = 0$. Considering the space V_r of polynomials of degree less or equal to r, $P \mapsto P(u_1, \ldots, u_n)$ is a linear form in this space. Initial values then correspond to a hyperplane of V_r, given by the kernel of $P \mapsto P(u_1, \ldots, u_n)$.

Theorem 10. *(Non trivial invariants and polynomial consecution) There will be a non trivial invariant if and only if there exists a matrix L such that the intersection of the kernel of $M - L$ and the hyperplane given by the initial values is not zero. The invariants correspond to vectors in the intersection.*

We deal with practical cases using the following theorem. All variables are initially constrained to initial parameters (subject to other types of constraint).

Theorem 11. *(Non trivial invariant and polynomial scale consecution for any initial values) If one can find T (i.e. L) with $\dim(Ker(M - L)) \geq 2$ for any initiation step, then there will be non trivial invariants.*

Reconsider the preceding example, with $T(x, y) = y^2 + 2y + 1$, $M - L$ verifying the hypothesis of the theorem. Then there will always bee an invariant, whatever the initial values. Note that for the initial step ($y = y_0, x = 1$), a possible invariant is given by $y_0(1 - y_0)x^2 + xy + y^2 - x - 2y + 1$.

5   Fractional Scale Consecution

We now want to deal with transition systems like

$$
\rho_\tau \equiv
\begin{bmatrix}
x_1' = P_1(x_1, \ldots, x_n)/Q_1(x_1, \ldots, x_n) \\
\vdots \\
x_n' = P_n(x_1, \ldots, x_n)/Q_n(x_1, \ldots, x_n)
\end{bmatrix},
\tag{3}
$$

where P_i and Q_i belong to $K[X_1, ..., X_n]$, and P_i is relatively prime to Q_i.

Definition 7. *A polynomial $Q \in K[X_1, \ldots, X_n]$ is said to be a T-invariant for polynomial-scale consecution for the loop τ if and only if there exists a rational function $F \in K(X_1, ..., X_n)$, corresponding to the loop, with $Q(X_1', ..., X_n') = F(X_1, .., X_n)Q(X_1, .., X_n)$, modulo the fractional ideal of $K(X_1', .., X_n', X_1, .., X_n)$, and generated by $\left(X_1' - \frac{P_1(X_1, ..., X_n)}{Q_1(X_1, ..., X_n)}, \ldots, X_n' - \frac{P_n(X_1, ..., X_n)}{Q_n(X_1, ..., X_n)} \right)$.*

Theorem 12. *(F-invariant characterization) Consider an algebraic transition system corresponding to an algebraic loop τ as described in Definition 7. Let $Q \in K[X_1, \ldots, X_n]$ be a multivariate polynomial with indeterminate coefficients (a template). Q is a F-invariant for polynomial scale consecution with parametric polynomial $F \in K(X_1, \ldots, X_n)$ for τ if and only if*

$$
Q\left(\frac{P_1(X_1, ..., X_n)}{Q_1(X_1, ..., X_n)}, \ldots, \frac{P_n(X_1, ..., X_n)}{Q_n(x_1, ..., x_n)} \right) = F(X_1, ..., X_n)Q(X_1, ..., X_n).
$$

Let d be the maximal degree of the P_i's and Q_i's, and let Π be the lcm of the Q_i's. Now let $U = X_1^{i_1}..X_n^{i_n}$ be a monomial of degree less than r (i.e. $i_1 + .. + i_n \leq r$). Then, $\Pi^r U(P_1/Q_1, \ldots, P_n/Q_n) = \Pi^r(P_1/Q_1)^{i_1}...(P_n/Q_n)^{i_n}$. But as $Q_j^{i_j}$ divides Π^{i_j}, for all j, we see that $Q_1^{i_1}...Q_n^{i_n}$ divides $\Pi^{i_1 + \cdots + i_r}$ which divides Π^r. We deduce that $\Pi^r Q(P_1/Q_1, \ldots, P_n/Q_n)$ is a polynomial for every Q in V_r. Now suppose that $F = T/S$ (T relatively prime to S) satisfies the equality of the previous theorem and suppose that we are looking for an invariant Q of degree r. Then, multiplying by Π^r we get $\Pi^r Q(P_1/Q_1, \ldots, P_n/Q_n) = (\Pi^r TQ)/S$. As we have no "a priory" information on Q, in most of the cases Q will be relatively prime to S. In this case we see that S will divides Π^r, and we can suppose that it has denominator Π^r. So, let F be of the form T/Π^r (we just argued that this constraint is weak). Now let m be the morphism $Q \mapsto \Pi^r Q(P_1/Q_1, \ldots, P_n/Q_n)$ from V_r to V_{nrd}, and let M be its matrix in a canonical basis. Let T be a polynomial in V_{nrd-r}, let l denote the morphism $Q \mapsto TQ$ from V_r to V_{nrd}, with L as its matrix in a canonical basis. Combining theorem 11 and the preceding discussion, we have the following:

Theorem 13. *Let M be as described above. There will exist a F-invariant (with the restriction that F is of the form T/Π^r) polynomial if and only if there exists a matrix L (corresponding to $Q \mapsto TQ$) such that $M - L$ has a nontrivial kernel. Any vector in the kernel of $M - L$ will give a F-invariant polynomial.*

Similar to Theorems 9 and 10. For the initiation step we have a hyperplane in V_r. In order for the transition system to make sense, the n-tuple of initial values must not be a root of any of the Q_i's, and so must be their iterates, as long as the loop is applied. So, they will not cancel Π^r. We have the following:

Theorem 14. *(Non trivial invariants using Fractional scale consecution) There is a non trivial invariant if and only if there exists a matrix L (the one of $Q \mapsto TQ$ in the canonical basis, with the coefficients of T being $\lambda_0, ..., \lambda_s$), such that the intersection of the kernel of $M - L$ and the hyperplane given by the initial values (good initial values) is not zero, the invariants correspond to vectors in the intersection.*

We also have the important theorem:

Theorem 15. *(Non trivial invariants using Polynomial scale consecution for any initial value) We will have a non trivial invariant for any "good"(non-trivial) initial value if there exists a matrix L such that the kernel of $M - L$ is of dimension equal or greater than 2.*

Example 6. We consider the system $\rho_\tau \equiv \begin{bmatrix} x_1' = x_2/(x_1 + x_2) \\ x_2' = x_1/(x_1 + 2x_2) \end{bmatrix}$. We are looking for a F-invariant polynomial of degree two. The lcm of $(x_1 + x_2)$ and $(x_1 + 2x_2)$ is their product, so that m is given by: $[Q \in V_2 \mapsto [(x_1 + x_2)(x_1 + 2x_2)]^2 Q(x_1/(x_1 + x_2), x_2/(x_1 + 2x_2))]$. As both $x_2/(x_1 + x_2)$ and $x_1/(x_1 + 2x_2)$ have "degree" zero, $[(x_1 + x_2)(x_1 + 2x_2)]^2 Q(x_2/(x_1 + x_2), x_1/(x_1 + 2x_2))$ will be a linear combination of degree four terms, if it is non null. Hence, m has values in $Vect(X_1^4, X_1^3 X_2, X_1^2 X_2^2, X_1 X_2^3, X_2^4)$. For T and Q in V_2 to verify $[(x_1 + x_2)(x_1 + 2x_2)]^2 Q(x_2/(x_1 + x_2), x_1/(x_1 + 2x_2)) = TQ$, as the left member is in $Vect(X_1^4, X_1^3 X_2, X_1^2 X_2^2, X_1 X_2^3, X_2^4)$, T must be of the form $\lambda_0 X_1^2 + \lambda_1 X_1 X_2 + \lambda_3 X_2^2$ and Q of the form $a_0 X_1^2 + a_1 X_1 X_2 + a_3 X_2^2$. We see that we can take Q in $Vect(X_1^2, X_1 X_2, X_2^2)$, and similarly for T. Then both m and $l : (Q \mapsto TQ)$ will be morphisms from $Vect(X_1^2, X_1 X_2, X_2^2)$ in $Vect(X_1^4, X_1^3 X_2, X_1^2 X_2^2, X_1 X_2^3, X_2^4)$. In the corresponding canonical basis, the matrix $M - L$ is

$$\begin{pmatrix} -\lambda_0 & 0 & 1 \\ -\lambda_1 & 1 - \lambda_0 & 2 \\ 1 - \lambda_2 & 3 - \lambda_1 & 1 - \lambda_0 \\ 4 & 2 - \lambda_2 & -\lambda_1 \\ 4 & 0 & -\lambda_2 \end{pmatrix}.$$

Taking $\lambda_0 = 1, \lambda_1 = 3$ and $\lambda_2 = 2$ cancels the second column and L, $M - L$ will have kernel equal to $Vect(0, 1, 0)$. It was clear from the beginning that the corresponding polynomial $X_1 X_2$ is $(X_1^2 + 3X_1 X_2 + 2X_2^2)/[(X_1 + X_2)(X_1 + 2X_2)]^2$-invariant. It is an invariant (see Definition 2) for initial values $(0, 1)$ (whose iterates clearly never cancel $X_1 + X_2$ and $X_1 + 2X_2$, because they are of the form $(a, 0)$ or $(0, b)$ with a and b strictly positive).

6   Branching Conditions and Nested Loops

Here, we show how our method deals with the conditional statements.

Theorem 16. *Let* $I = \{I_1, ..., I_k\}$ *a set of ideals in* $K[X_1, ..., X_n]$ *such that* $I_j = (f^{(j)}_1, ..., f^{(j)}_{n_j})$ *where* $j \in [1, k]$. *Let's* $\nabla(I_1, ..., I_k) = \{\delta_1, ..., \delta_{n_1 n_2 ... n_k}\}$ *such that all elements* δ_i *in* $\nabla(I_1, ..., I_k)$ *are formed by the product of one element from each ideal in* I. *Assume that all* I_js *are ideals of invariants for a loop at location* l_j *described by a transition* τ_j. *Now, if all* l_j *describe the same location program point, then we have several transitions looping at the same point. So we obtain an encoding of possible execution paths of a loop containing conditional statements. Then* $\nabla(I_1, ..., I_k)$ *is an ideal of non-trivial non-linear invariants for the entire loop located at* l_j.

Example 7. Let's consider the following loop:

```
int u_0;//(M > 0)&&(Z = 1)&&(U = u_0) While ((X>=1) || (Z>=z_0)){
  if(Y > M){X = Y / (X + Y);
            Y = X / (X + 2 * Y);}
  else{Z = Z * (U + 1);
       U = U^2;}}
```

The resulting invariant given by our prototype is: [_WHILE_1][Invariant:=] [u_0*(1-u_0)*X*Y*Ẑ*+X*Y*Z*U +X*Y*Û2-X*Y*Z-2*X*Y*U+X*Y]

Once again, here there are no need for Grobner Basis computation and the complexity of the steps described remain linear. For nested loops, our prototype generates ideals of invariants for each inner-loop and then generates a global invariant considering the non-linear system composed of pre-computed invariants.

7   Conclusion

Our methods do not required computation of Grobner bases, quantifier elimination, cylindrical algebraic decomposition or direct resolution of semi-algebraic system, as well as they do not depend on any abstraction methods. We succeeded in reducing the non-linear loop invariant generation problem to the intersection between eigenspaces of specific endomorphisms and initial linear or semi-affine/algebraic constraints. Our non-trivial non-linear invariant generation method is *sound* and *complete* as we provide a complete encoding to handle multivariate fractional loops (algebraic system with multivariate rational functions) where variable are initially constrained by parameters. As far as we know, these are the first non-linear invariant generation methods that handle multivariate fractional instructions, conditional statement and nested inner-loops. Also, for each type of system, we presented necessary and sufficient conditions for the existence of *non-trivial* non-linear loop invariants. Considering the problem of invariant generation, we identified a large decidable class together with an undecidable class. Finally, our methods generates ideals of non-trivial non-linear loop invariants (in a polynomial number of steps) and we believe that our methods could complete the framework proposed in [9].

References

[1] Tiwari, A., Rueß, H., Saïdi, H., Shankar, N.: A technique for invariant generation. In: Margaria, T., Yi, W. (eds.) TACAS 2001. LNCS, vol. 2031, pp. 113–127. Springer, Heidelberg (2001)

[2] Manna, Z., Pnueli, A.: Temporal Verification of Reactive Systems: Safety. Springer, New York (1995)

[3] Dijkstra, E.W.: A Discipline of Programming. Prentice-Hall, Englewood Cliffs (1976)

[4] Floyd, R.W.: Assigning meanings to programs. In: Proceedings of the 19th Symphosia in Applied Mathematics, pp. 19–37 (1967)

[5] Sankaranarayanan, S., Sipma, H.B., Manna, Z.: Non-linear loop invariant generation using grobner bases. In: POPL 2004: Proc. of the 31st ACM SIGPLAN-SIGACT symposium on Principles of programming languages, pp. 318–329. ACM Press, New York (2004)

[6] Bensalem, S., Bozga, M., Ghirvu, J.C., Lakhnech, L.: A transformation approach for generating non-linear invariants. In: Static Analysis Symposium, pp. 101–114 (2000)

[7] Rodríguez-Carbonell, E., Kapur, D.: Automatic generation of polynomial invariants of bounded degree using abstract interpretation. Sci. Comput. Program. 64(1), 54–75 (2007)

[8] Bensalem, S., Lakhnech, Y., Saidi, H.: Powerful techniques for the automatic generation of invariants. In: Alur, R., Henzinger, T.A. (eds.) CAV 1996. LNCS, vol. 1102, pp. 323–335. Springer, Heidelberg (1996)

[9] Chen, Y., Xia, B., Yang, L., Zhan, N.: Generating polynomial invariants with discoverer and qepcad. In: Formal Methods and Hybrid Real-Time Systems, pp. 67–82 (2007)

[10] Kovacs, L.: Reasoning algebraically about p-solvable loops. In: Ramakrishnan, C.R., Rehof, J. (eds.) TACAS 2008. LNCS, vol. 4963, pp. 249–264. Springer, Heidelberg (2008)

[11] Cousot, P.: Proving program invariance and termination by parametric abstraction, lagrangian relaxation and semidefinite programming. In: Cousot, R. (ed.) VMCAI 2005. LNCS, vol. 3385, pp. 1–24. Springer, Heidelberg (2005)

[12] Rodríguez-Carbonell, E., Kapur, D.: Generating all polynomial invariants in simple loops. J. Symb. Comput. 42(4), 443–476 (2007)

[13] Weispfenning, V.: Quantifier elimination for real algebra - the quadratic case and beyond. Applicable Algebra in Engineering, Communication and Computing 8(2), 85–101 (1997)

[14] Collins, G.E.: Quantifier Elimination for the Elementary Theory of RealClosed Fields by Cylindrical Algebraic Decomposition. LNCS. Springer, Heidelberg (1975)

[15] Cousot, P., Cousot, R.: Abstract interpretation and application to logic programs. Journal of Logic Programming 13(2–3), 103–179 (1992)

[16] Müller-Olm, M., Seidl, H.: Polynomial constants are decidable. In: Hermenegildo, M.V., Puebla, G. (eds.) SAS 2002. LNCS, vol. 2477, pp. 4–19. Springer, Heidelberg (2002)

[17] Kovacs, L., Jebelean, T.: Finding polynomial invariants for imperative loops in the theorema system. In: Proc.of Verify 2006 Workshop, pp. 52–67 (2006)

[18] Kapur, D.: Automatically generating loop invariants using quantifier elimination. In: Proc. IMACS Intl. Conf. on Applications of Computer Algebra (2004)

[19] Rebiha, R., Matringe, N., Vieira-Moura, A.: Non-trivial non-linear loop invariant generation. Technical-Report-IC-07-045 (December 2007)

[20] Lang, S.: Algebra. Springer, Heidelberg (January 2002)

Instantiation for Parameterised Boolean Equation Systems

A. van Dam, B. Ploeger, and T.A.C. Willemse*

Department of Mathematics and Computer Science,
Eindhoven University of Technology
P.O. Box 513, 5600 MB Eindhoven, The Netherlands

Abstract. Verification problems for finite- and infinite-state processes, like model checking and equivalence checking, can effectively be encoded in Parameterised Boolean Equation Systems (PBESs). Solving the PBES solves the encoded problem. The decidability of solving a PBES depends on the data sorts that occur in the PBES. We describe a manipulation for transforming a given PBES to a simpler PBES that may admit solution methods that are not applicable to the original one. Depending on whether the data sorts occurring in the PBES are finite or countable, the resulting PBES can be a Boolean Equation System (BES) or an Infinite Boolean Equation System (IBES). Computing the solution to a BES is decidable. Computing the global solution to an IBES is still undecidable, but for partial solutions (which suffices for *e.g.* local model checking), effective tooling is possible. We give examples that illustrate the efficacy of our techniques.

1 Introduction

Parameterised Boolean Equation Systems (PBESs) [8,11], a specialisation of fixed-point equation systems [13] have emerged as a versatile vehicle for studying and solving verification problems for complex systems. Prime examples are the encoding of the first-order modal μ-calculus model-checking problem over (possibly infinite) labelled transition systems [6,7]; equivalence checking of various bisimulations on (possibly infinite) labelled transition systems [3]; and static analysis of code [5]. The solution to the encoded problem can be found by solving the resulting PBES. Solving PBESs is, much like the problems that can be encoded in them, generally undecidable. The outlook, however, is not that bleak: practical applications have demonstrated that a pragmatic approach can lead to promising results [7].

Among the techniques for solving PBESs are *symbolic approximation* [7] and *pattern matching* [8]. We here report on techniques for partially and fully *instantiating* a PBES. In general, this results in a new PBES. Ultimately, the transformation can yield a *Boolean Equation System* (BES) [9] when all involved data sorts are finite, or an *Infinite Boolean Equation System* (IBES) [10] when

---

* This research has been partially funded by the Netherlands Organisation for Scientific Research (NWO) under FOCUS/BRICKS grant number 642.000.602.

J.S. Fitzgerald, A.E. Haxthausen, and H. Yenigun (Eds.): ICTAC 2008, LNCS 5160, pp. 440–454, 2008.

some data sorts are countable. Hence, from a theoretical viewpoint, our transformations firmly relate the abovementioned different formalisms and help in understanding the quite complex theory underlying PBESs. In particular, they confirm the intuition that the inherent computational complexity in PBESs is due to the complexity of the data sorts that appear in the equations.

On a more practical level, we illustrate that our technique for *partially* instantiating a PBES leads to a wider applicability of existing solution techniques — such as the aforementioned use of *pattern matching* — even in the presence of countable and uncountable data sorts. A full instantiation of PBESs to BESs is important for automation purposes: BESs form a subset of PBESs for which computing the solution is effectively decidable. As such, both types of instantiation are welcome additions to the collection of PBES manipulation methods. As an aside, we show that the instantiation of PBESs involving countable data sorts can indeed lead to effective tooling for particular verification questions.

Independently of this work, the approach taken in [11] has recently been implemented in a tool called EVALUATOR 4.0 [12]. In essence, this tool employs alternation-free PBESs to solve the on-the-fly model-checking problem of MCL formulas on finite systems. Our approach is not restricted to alternation-free PBESs and can be used for model-checking both finite and infinite systems.

This paper is structured as follows. In Section 2, we introduce the relevant concepts and properties. Partial and full instantiation for finite data sorts in PBESs is detailed in Section 3, and full instantiation to IBESs for PBESs involving countably infinite data sorts is discussed in Section 4. In Section 5, we demonstrate the power of all involved instantiation schemes and our concluding remarks can be found in Section 6.

2 Preliminaries

2.1 Data

We assume that there are nonempty data sorts, generally written using letters D, E and F, and that every sort has a collection of *basic elements* to which every term can be rewritten. For a sort D, we write $v \in D$ to denote that v is a basic element of D and we use set notation to list the basic elements of D, e.g. $D = \{v_1, \ldots, v_n\}$. With every sort D we associate a semantic set $\mathbb{D}$ such that every syntactic term of type D can be mapped to the element of $\mathbb{D}$ it represents. The set of basic elements of a sort D is isomorphic to the semantic set $\mathbb{D}$.

We have a set $\mathcal{D}$ of *data variables*, with typical elements $d, d_1, \ldots$, and we assume that there is some data language that is sufficiently rich to denote all relevant *data terms*. We assume an interpretation function $[\![\_]\!]$ that maps every closed term t of type D (denoted $t{:}D$) to the data element $[\![t]\!]$ of $\mathbb{D}$ it represents. For open terms we use a *data environment* ε that maps each variable from $\mathcal{D}$ to a data element of the right sort. The interpretation $[\![t]\!]\varepsilon$ of an open term t is given by $\varepsilon(t)$, where ε is extended to terms in the standard way.

We assume the existence of a sort $B = \{\top, \bot\}$ representing the Booleans $\mathbb{B}$, and a sort $N = \{0, 1, \ldots\}$ representing the natural numbers $\mathbb{N}$. For these sorts, we assume the usual operators are available and we do not write constants or operators in the syntactic domain any different from their semantic counterparts. For example, we have $\mathbb{B} = \{\top, \bot\}$ and the syntactic operator $\_\wedge\_{:}B \times B \to B$ corresponds to the usual, semantic conjunction $\_\wedge\_{:}\mathbb{B} \times \mathbb{B} \to \mathbb{B}$.

2.2   Parameterised Boolean Equation Systems

We want to solve sequences of fixpoint equations, each of which is of the form:

$$\sigma X(d_1{:}D_1, \ldots, d_n{:}D_n) = \varphi.$$

The left-hand side of each equation consists of a *fixpoint symbol* $\sigma \in \{\mu, \nu\}$, where μ indicates a least and ν a greatest fixpoint, and a *predicate variable* $X{:}D_1 \times \ldots \times D_n \to B$ (from a set of variables $\mathcal{X}$) that depends on data variables $d_1, \ldots, d_n$ of possibly infinite sorts $D_1, \ldots, D_n$. We call n the *arity* of X and if $n = 0$ then we call X a *proposition variable*. In the sequel, we restrict ourselves to predicate variables of arity ≤ 2 which does not incur a loss of generality. The right-hand side of each equation is a *predicate formula* as defined below.

Definition 1. *Predicate formulae φ are defined by the following grammar:*

$$\varphi ::= b \mid X(e) \mid \varphi \oplus \varphi \mid Qd{:}D.\varphi$$

where $\oplus \in \{\wedge, \vee\}$, $Q \in \{\forall, \exists\}$, b is a data term of sort B, X is a predicate variable, d is a data variable of sort D and e is a data term.

Note that negation does not occur in predicate formulae, except as an operator in data terms. As a notational convenience, we use the operators $\oplus$ and Q throughout this paper when the exact operator is of lesser importance. Also, we call a predicate formula φ *closed* if no data variable in φ occurs freely. We now formalise the notion of a *Parameterised Boolean Equation System*.

Definition 2. *A parameterised Boolean equation system (PBES) is inductively defined as follows, for every PBES $\mathcal{E}$:*

- *ϵ is the empty PBES;*
- *$(\sigma X(d{:}D) = \varphi)\, \mathcal{E}$ is a PBES, where $\sigma \in \{\mu, \nu\}$ is a fixpoint symbol, $X{:}D \to B$ is a predicate variable and φ is a predicate formula.*

A special class of PBESs is the class of *Boolean Equation Systems* (BESs). BESs have been studied extensively in the literature [9]. Formally, we have:

Definition 3. *A Boolean equation system is a PBES in which every predicate variable has arity 0 and every formula φ adheres to the following grammar (hereafter referred to as* proposition formulae*):*

$$\varphi ::= \top \mid \bot \mid X \mid \varphi \oplus \varphi$$

where $\oplus \in \{\wedge, \vee\}$ and X is a proposition variable.

The set of predicate variables that occur in a predicate formula φ, denoted by $\mathrm{occ}(\varphi)$, is defined recursively as follows, for any formulae φ_1, φ_2:

$$\mathrm{occ}(b) \quad \stackrel{\Delta}{=} \emptyset \qquad\qquad \mathrm{occ}(X(e)) \quad \stackrel{\Delta}{=} \{X\}$$
$$\mathrm{occ}(\varphi_1 \oplus \varphi_2) \stackrel{\Delta}{=} \mathrm{occ}(\varphi_1) \cup \mathrm{occ}(\varphi_2) \qquad \mathrm{occ}(Qd{:}D.\varphi_1) \stackrel{\Delta}{=} \mathrm{occ}(\varphi_1).$$

For any PBES $\mathcal{E}$, the set of *binding predicate variables*, $\mathrm{bnd}(\mathcal{E})$, is the set of variables occurring at the left-hand side of some equation in $\mathcal{E}$. The set of *occurring predicate variables*, $\mathrm{occ}(\mathcal{E})$, is the set of variables occurring at the right-hand side of some equation in $\mathcal{E}$. Formally, we define:

$$\mathrm{bnd}(\epsilon) \stackrel{\Delta}{=} \emptyset \qquad \mathrm{bnd}((\sigma X(d{:}D) = \varphi)\,\mathcal{E}) \stackrel{\Delta}{=} \mathrm{bnd}(\mathcal{E}) \cup \{X\}$$
$$\mathrm{occ}(\epsilon) \stackrel{\Delta}{=} \emptyset \qquad \mathrm{occ}((\sigma X(d{:}D) = \varphi)\,\mathcal{E}) \stackrel{\Delta}{=} \mathrm{occ}(\mathcal{E}) \cup \mathrm{occ}(\varphi).$$

A PBES $\mathcal{E}$ is said to be *well-formed* iff every binding predicate variable occurs at the left-hand side of precisely one equation of $\mathcal{E}$. Thus, $(\nu X = \top)(\mu X = \bot)$ is not a well-formed PBES. We only consider well-formed PBESs in this paper.

A PBES $\mathcal{E}$ is called *closed* if $\mathrm{occ}(\mathcal{E}) \subseteq \mathrm{bnd}(\mathcal{E})$ and *open* otherwise. An equation $\sigma X(d{:}D) = \varphi$ is called *data-closed* if the set of data variables that occur freely in φ is either empty or $\{d\}$. A PBES is called *data-closed* iff each of its equations is data-closed. We say an equation $\sigma X(d{:}D) = \varphi$ is *solved* if $\mathrm{occ}(\varphi) = \emptyset$, and a PBES $\mathcal{E}$ is *solved* iff each of its equations is solved.

Finally, we give the denotational semantics of predicate formulae and PBESs. Predicate formulae are interpreted in a context of a data environment ε and a *predicate environment* $\eta{:}\mathcal{X} \rightarrow (\mathbb{D} \rightarrow \mathbb{B})$. For an arbitrary environment θ, we write $\theta[v/d]$ for the environment θ in which the variable d has been assigned the value v. For substitution on tuples we define $\theta[(v_1, \ldots, v_n)/(d_1, \ldots, d_n)]$ to be equivalent to the simultaneous substitution $\theta[v_1/d_1, \ldots, v_n/d_n]$.

Definition 4. *For any data environment ε and predicate environment η, the interpretation $[\![\varphi]\!]\eta\varepsilon$ is inductively defined as follows:*

$$[\![b]\!]\eta\varepsilon \quad \stackrel{\Delta}{=} [\![b]\!]\varepsilon \qquad\qquad [\![\varphi_1 \oplus \varphi_2]\!]\eta\varepsilon \stackrel{\Delta}{=} [\![\varphi_1]\!]\eta\varepsilon \oplus [\![\varphi_2]\!]\eta\varepsilon$$
$$[\![X(e)]\!]\eta\varepsilon \stackrel{\Delta}{=} \eta(X)([\![e]\!]\varepsilon) \qquad [\![Qd{:}D.\varphi]\!]\eta\varepsilon \stackrel{\Delta}{=} Qv{\in}D : [\![\varphi]\!]\eta(\varepsilon[v/d]).$$

The predicate formula φ in an equation $\sigma X(d{:}D) = \varphi$ must be interpreted as a fixpoint over the set of functions with domain D and co-domain $\mathbb{B}$. Note that the existence of such fixpoints follows from the following observations. The variable d, which may occur freely in φ, is effectively used as a formal, syntactic function parameter. Semantically, this is achieved by associating the interpretation of φ to the functional $(\lambda v{\in}D.\, [\![\varphi]\!]\eta\varepsilon[v/d])$, which relies on the data environment to assign specific values to variable d. The set of (total) functions $f{:}\mathbb{D} \rightarrow \mathbb{B}$, denoted by $\mathbb{B}^{\mathbb{D}}$ can be equipped with an ordering $\sqsubseteq$, defined as follows:

$$f \sqsubseteq g \stackrel{\Delta}{=} \forall d \in \mathbb{D} : f(d) \Rightarrow g(d).$$

The set $(\mathbb{B}^{\mathbb{D}}, \sqsubseteq)$ is a complete lattice. The functional $(\lambda v{\in}\mathbb{D}. \; [\![\varphi]\!]\eta\varepsilon[v/d])$ can be turned into a predicate formula transformer by employing the predicate environment η in a similar manner as the data environment is used to turn a predicate formula into a functional. Assuming that the domain of the predicate variable X is of sort D, the functional $(\lambda v{\in}\mathbb{D}. \; [\![\varphi]\!]\eta\varepsilon[v/d])$ yields the following predicate formula transformer:

$$\lambda g{\in}\mathbb{B}^{\mathbb{D}}. \; (\lambda v{\in}\mathbb{D}. \; [\![\varphi]\!]\eta[g/X]\varepsilon[v/d]).$$

The resulting predicate formula transformer is monotone over the complete lattice $(\mathbb{B}^{\mathbb{D}}, \sqsubseteq)$. As a corollary of Tarski's fixpoint Theorem [14], the existence of least and greatest fixpoints of the predicate formula transformers is guaranteed. This leads to the following interpretation for PBESs.

Definition 5. *The solution of a PBES in the context of a predicate environment η and a data environment ε is inductively defined as follows, for any PBES $\mathcal{E}$:*

$$[\![\epsilon]\!]\eta\varepsilon \quad \triangleq \quad \eta$$
$$[\![(\sigma X(d{:}D) = \varphi)\mathcal{E}]\!]\eta\varepsilon \quad \triangleq \quad [\![\mathcal{E}]\!](\eta[\sigma f \in \mathbb{B}^{\mathbb{D}}. \; \lambda v{\in}\mathbb{D}.[\![\varphi]\!]([\![\mathcal{E}]\!]\eta[f/X]\varepsilon)\varepsilon[v/d]/X])\varepsilon.$$

The solution of a PBES prioritises the fixpoint signs of equations that come first over the signs of equations that follow. In that sense, the solution is sensitive to the order of equations in a PBES. Moreover, the solution of a PBES only assigns functions to the *binding* variables of that PBES; other predicate variables are left unmodified. This follows from the following lemma:

Lemma 1 (see [4]). *Let $\mathcal{E}$ be an arbitrary PBES. Then for all $X \notin \mathsf{bnd}(\mathcal{E})$ and all environments η, ε: $[\![\mathcal{E}]\!]\eta\varepsilon(X) = \eta(X)$.*

2.3   Infinite Boolean Equation Systems

Mader [9] introduces *Infinite* Boolean Equation Systems *(IBESs)* as a vehicle for solving a model checking problem for infinite state systems. IBESs resemble BESs but differ in the following aspects: (1) finite *and* (countably) infinite conjunction and disjunction over proposition variables are allowed, and, (2) finite *and* (countably) infinite sequences of equations are allowed (but still only finitely many *blocks* of equations).

Definition 6. Infinite proposition formulae ω *are defined by the following grammar, for any countable sorts I and $J \subseteq I$:*

$$\omega ::= \top \mid \bot \mid X_i \mid \omega \oplus \omega \mid \bigoplus_{j \in J} \omega$$

where $\oplus{\in}\{\wedge, \vee\}$, $\bigoplus{\in}\{\bigwedge, \bigvee\}$ and $X_i{:}\mathbb{B}$ is a proposition variable for any $i \in I$.

Here, $\bigwedge_{j \in J}$ and $\bigvee_{j \in J}$ denote the infinite conjunction and disjunction over basic elements of a countable sort J, respectively.

Definition 7. *An* infinite Boolean equation system *(IBES) is inductively defined as follows, for every IBES $\mathcal{E}$:*

- ϵ *is the empty IBES;*
- $(\sigma\mathcal{B})\,\mathcal{E}$ *is an IBES, where $\sigma \in \{\mu, \nu\}$ is a fixpoint symbol and $\sigma\mathcal{B}$ is a block of equations $\{\sigma X_j = \omega_j \mid j \in J\}$ where J is a countable sort, and for each $j \in J$, $X_j{:}B$ is a proposition variable and ω_j is an infinite proposition formula.*

Notice that BESs are, syntactically, exactly in the intersection of PBESs and IBESs. The notions of binding and occurring variables, and the induced notions of *open*, *closed* and *well-formedness*, that are defined for PBESs transfer to IBESs without problems. We also restrict to IBESs that are well-formed.

The semantics of infinite proposition formulae is defined in the context of a proposition environment $\eta{:}\mathcal{X} \to \mathbb{B}$. For any countable sort I, environment η and function $f{:}I \to \mathbb{B}$ we denote by $\eta[f/X_I]$ the simultaneous substitution of $f(i)$ for X_i in η for all $i \in I$, i.e. $\eta[f/X_I](X_i) = f(i)$ if $i \in I$ and $\eta(X_i)$ otherwise.

Definition 8. *Let $\eta{:}\mathcal{X} \to \mathbb{B}$ be a proposition environment. The* interpretation $[\![\omega]\!]\eta$ *that maps an infinite proposition formula ω to $\top$ or $\bot$, is inductively defined as follows:*

$$
\begin{aligned}
[\![\top]\!]\eta &\overset{\Delta}{=} \top & [\![X_i]\!]\eta &\overset{\Delta}{=} \eta(X_i) \\
[\![\bot]\!]\eta &\overset{\Delta}{=} \bot & [\![\omega_1 \oplus \omega_2]\!]\eta &\overset{\Delta}{=} [\![\omega_1]\!]\eta \oplus [\![\omega_2]\!]\eta \\
[\![\bigoplus_{j \in J} \omega]\!]\eta &\overset{\Delta}{=} \mathsf{Q}v \in J : [\![\omega[v/j]]\!]\eta
\end{aligned}
$$

where $\mathsf{Q} = \forall$ if $\bigoplus = \bigwedge$, and $\mathsf{Q} = \exists$ otherwise.

The set of functions $f{:}I \to \mathbb{B}$, where I is some (countable) sort, is denoted by $\mathbb{B}^I$. Together with the ordering $\sqsubseteq$, the set $(\mathbb{B}^I, \sqsubseteq)$ is a complete lattice. Let $\Omega = \{\omega_i \mid i \in I\}$ be a countable set of infinite proposition formulae. The functional induced by the interpretation of Ω is written $(\lambda i \in I.\, [\![\omega_i]\!]\eta)$, with $\omega_i \in \Omega$. This leads to the following transformer on infinite proposition formulae:

$$\lambda g \in \mathbb{B}^I.\, (\lambda i \in I.\, [\![\omega_i]\!]\eta[g/X_I]).$$

The transformer is a monotone operator on the complete lattice $(\mathbb{B}^I, \sqsubseteq)$, guaranteeing the existence of its least and greatest fixpoints.

Definition 9. *Let η be a proposition environment, $\mathcal{E}$ be an IBES and $\sigma\mathcal{B} = \{\sigma X_i = \omega_i \mid i \in I\}$ be a block for some countable sort I. The* solution *of an IBES is inductively defined as follows:*

$$
\begin{aligned}
[\![\epsilon]\!]\eta &\overset{\Delta}{=} \eta \\
[\![\sigma\mathcal{B}\,\mathcal{E}]\!]\eta &\overset{\Delta}{=} [\![\mathcal{E}]\!]\eta[\sigma f \in \mathbb{B}^I.\, \lambda i \in I.[\![\omega_i]\!]([\![\mathcal{E}]\!]\eta[f/X_I])/X_I].
\end{aligned}
$$

The solution of an IBES assigns a value to *every* binding proposition variable of that IBES. Often, only the value for a specific proposition variable is sought, *e.g.* in local model checking. In such a case, equations that are unimportant to the solution of that variable can be pruned, yielding a smaller IBES, or even a BES. This follows from the following result.

Proposition 1 (see [4]). *For all IBESs $\mathcal{E}, \mathcal{F}, \mathcal{G}$ and all environments η:*

$$\mathsf{occ}(\mathcal{E}\ \mathcal{G}) \cap \mathsf{bnd}(\mathcal{F}) = \emptyset \implies \forall X \notin \mathsf{bnd}(\mathcal{F}) : [\![\mathcal{E}\ \mathcal{F}\ \mathcal{G}]\!]\eta(X) = [\![\mathcal{E}\ \mathcal{G}]\!]\eta(X).$$

The above result turns out to be useful in Section 4, and also provides the necessary foundation for the correctness of parts of the algorithm in [11].

3   Instantiation on Finite Domains

Without loss of generality, we assume that all predicate variables in this section are either of type $D \times E \to B$ or of type $E \to B$, for some finite sort D and some possibly infinite sort E. To each predicate variable $X{:}D \times E \to B$, we associate a finite set of predicate variables $\mathsf{all}(X) \stackrel{\Delta}{=} \{X_d{:}E \to B \mid d{\in}D\}$. For a set of predicate variables $\mathcal{P}$ we write $\mathsf{all}(\mathcal{P})$ for $\bigcup_{X\in\mathcal{P}} \mathsf{all}(X)$. For any PBES $\mathcal{E}$, we say X is *instantiation-fresh* for $\mathcal{E}$ iff $\mathsf{all}(X) \cap (\mathsf{bnd}(\mathcal{E}) \cup \mathsf{occ}(\mathcal{E})) = \emptyset$.

Instantiation replaces a single equation $(\sigma X(d{:}D, e{:}E) = \varphi)$ by an entire PBES $(\sigma X_{d_1}(e{:}E) = \varphi_{d_1}) \cdots (\sigma X_{d_n}(e{:}E) = \varphi_{d_n})$. The transformation can be lifted to general PBESs and to arbitrary subsets of binding variables (see Algorithm 1). Although the basic idea of the transformation is intuitive, the devil is in the technical details: careful bookkeeping and a naming scheme have to be applied to make the transformation work. This is taken care of by the function $\mathsf{Sub}_{\mathcal{P}}$ that is used in the main transformation $\mathsf{Inst}_{\mathcal{P}}$. It ensures that new predicate variables are introduced correctly in the right-hand sides of the equations of a PBES. In the definition of $\mathsf{Sub}_{\mathcal{P}}$, the operand $\bigvee_{v\in D}$ abbreviates a finite disjunction over all basic elements in D.

The soundness of the transformation is far from obvious due to newly introduced predicate variables. Proposition 2 phrases a precise correspondence between the solution of the original PBES and a partially transformed PBES. In

---

Algorithm 1. The instantiation algorithm $\mathsf{Inst}_{\mathcal{P}}$

For any $\mathcal{P} \subseteq \mathcal{X}$ with $\mathcal{P} \neq \emptyset$:

$$\mathsf{Inst}_{\emptyset}(\mathcal{E}) \stackrel{\Delta}{=} \mathcal{E}$$
$$\mathsf{Inst}_{\mathcal{P}}(\epsilon) \stackrel{\Delta}{=} \epsilon$$
$$\mathsf{Inst}_{\mathcal{P}}((\sigma X(d{:}D, e{:}E) = \varphi)\ \mathcal{E}) \stackrel{\Delta}{=}$$
$$\begin{cases} \{(\sigma X_v(e{:}E) = \mathsf{Sub}_{\mathcal{P}}(\varphi[v/d])) \mid v{\in}D\}\ \mathsf{Inst}_{\mathcal{P}}(\mathcal{E}) & \text{if } X{\in}\mathcal{P} \\ (\sigma X(d{:}D, e{:}E) = \mathsf{Sub}_{\mathcal{P}}(\varphi))\ \mathsf{Inst}_{\mathcal{P}}(\mathcal{E}) & \text{otherwise} \end{cases}$$

where

$$\mathsf{Sub}_{\emptyset}(\varphi) \stackrel{\Delta}{=} \varphi$$
$$\mathsf{Sub}_{\mathcal{P}}(b) \stackrel{\Delta}{=} b$$
$$\mathsf{Sub}_{\mathcal{P}}(X(d,e)) \stackrel{\Delta}{=} \begin{cases} \bigvee_{v\in D}(v = d \wedge X_v(e[v/d])) & \text{if } X{\in}\mathcal{P} \\ X(d,e) & \text{otherwise} \end{cases}$$
$$\mathsf{Sub}_{\mathcal{P}}(\varphi_1 \oplus \varphi_2) \stackrel{\Delta}{=} \mathsf{Sub}_{\mathcal{P}}(\varphi_1) \oplus \mathsf{Sub}_{\mathcal{P}}(\varphi_2)$$
$$\mathsf{Sub}_{\mathcal{P}}(Qd{:}D.\ \varphi) \stackrel{\Delta}{=} Qd{:}D.\ \mathsf{Sub}_{\mathcal{P}}(\varphi)$$

---

order to facilitate the proof of the main claims in this section, we first address several lemmata concerning the functions $\mathsf{Sub}_{\{X\}}$ and $\mathsf{Inst}_{\{X\}}$, which we abbreviate to Sub_X and Inst_X for conciseness.

Lemma 2. *Let φ be a predicate formula and $X{:}D \times E \to B$ be a predicate variable. Let η be an enviroment such that $\eta(X)(\llbracket v \rrbracket) = \eta(X_v)$ for all $v \in D$. Then for any enviroment ε: $\llbracket \varphi \rrbracket \eta \varepsilon = \llbracket \mathsf{Sub}_X(\varphi) \rrbracket \eta \varepsilon$.*

Proof. By means of an induction on the structure of formula φ. For full details, see [4]. □

Lemma 3. *Let $X{:}D \times E \to B$ be a predicate variable. Let $\mathcal{E}$ be a PBES for which X is instantiation-fresh and $X \notin \mathsf{bnd}(\mathcal{E})$. Let η be an environment such that $\eta(X)(\llbracket v \rrbracket) = \eta(X_v)$ for all $v \in D$. Then for arbitrary environment ε, we have:*

$$\llbracket \mathcal{E} \rrbracket \eta \varepsilon = \llbracket \mathsf{Inst}_X(\mathcal{E}) \rrbracket \eta \varepsilon.$$

Proof. Let ε be an arbitrary data environment, and let η be a predicate environment satisfying the conditions of the lemma. We prove the lemma by induction on the length of $\mathcal{E}$. If $\mathcal{E}$ is of length 0 then: $\llbracket \epsilon \rrbracket \eta \varepsilon = \eta = \llbracket \mathsf{Inst}_X(\epsilon) \rrbracket \eta \varepsilon$. Suppose $\mathcal{E}$ is of length $m + 1$, and for all $\mathcal{E}'$ of length m, we have, for all environments υ:

$$\llbracket \mathcal{E}' \rrbracket \eta \upsilon = \llbracket \mathsf{Inst}_X(\mathcal{E}') \rrbracket \eta \upsilon. \tag{IH}$$

Necessarily, $\mathcal{E}$ is of the form $(\sigma Z(f{:}F) = \varphi)\ \mathcal{F}$, where $\mathcal{F}$ is of length m. We derive:

$$\llbracket \mathcal{E} \rrbracket \eta \varepsilon$$
$$= \llbracket (\sigma Z(f{:}F) = \varphi)\ \mathcal{F} \rrbracket \eta \varepsilon$$
$$= \llbracket \mathcal{F} \rrbracket \eta [(\sigma g \in \mathbb{B}^F.\ \lambda v{\in}F.\ \llbracket \varphi \rrbracket (\llbracket \mathcal{F} \rrbracket \eta [g/Z] \varepsilon) \varepsilon [v/f]) / Z] \varepsilon$$
$$\overset{*}{=} \llbracket \mathcal{F} \rrbracket \eta [(\sigma g \in \mathbb{B}^F.\ \lambda v{\in}F.\ \llbracket \mathsf{Sub}_X(\varphi) \rrbracket (\llbracket \mathcal{F} \rrbracket \eta [g/Z] \varepsilon) \varepsilon [v/f]) / Z] \varepsilon$$
$$\overset{(\text{IH})}{=} \llbracket \mathsf{Inst}_X(\mathcal{F}) \rrbracket \eta [(\sigma g \in \mathbb{B}^F.\ \lambda v{\in}F.\ \llbracket \mathsf{Sub}_X(\varphi) \rrbracket (\llbracket \mathsf{Inst}_X(\mathcal{F}) \rrbracket \eta [g/Z] \varepsilon) \varepsilon [v/f]) / Z] \varepsilon$$
$$= \llbracket \mathsf{Inst}_X((\sigma Z(f{:}F) = \varphi)\ \mathcal{F}) \rrbracket \eta \varepsilon$$
$$= \llbracket \mathsf{Inst}_X(\mathcal{E}) \rrbracket \eta \varepsilon.$$

At * we used the following equivalence:

$$(\sigma g \in \mathbb{B}^F.\llbracket \varphi \rrbracket(\llbracket \mathcal{F} \rrbracket \eta [g/Z] \varepsilon) \varepsilon) = (\sigma g \in \mathbb{B}^F.\llbracket \mathsf{Sub}_X(\varphi) \rrbracket(\llbracket \mathcal{F} \rrbracket \eta [g/Z] \varepsilon) \varepsilon)$$

which follows readily from Lemma 2. Observe that this lemma applies because $(\llbracket \mathcal{F} \rrbracket \eta [g/Z] \varepsilon)(X)(\llbracket v \rrbracket) = (\llbracket \mathcal{F} \rrbracket \eta [g/Z] \varepsilon)(X_v)$ for all $v \in D$ by assumption on η, instantiation-freshness of X in $\mathcal{E}$, $X \notin \mathsf{bnd}(\mathcal{F})$ and Lemma 1. □

Suppose we have a PBES $\mathcal{E}$ in which the first equation is for variable $X{:}D \times E \to B$ and the domain D of X is instantiated in that PBES, *i.e.* we use the transformation $\mathsf{Inst}_X(\mathcal{E})$. The PBES resulting from the transformation will consist of $|D|$ equations replacing the single equation for X, plus the remaining $|\mathcal{E}| - 1$ equations from $\mathcal{E}$. The following lemma states that the solution to X in the original PBES and the solutions to its instantiated counterparts in the resulting PBES correspond. Note that it does not state that the transformation does not have undesirable side-effects. This property is addressed in Lemma 5.

Lemma 4. *Let $\mathcal{F}$ be a PBES of the form $(\sigma X(d{:}D, e{:}E) = \varphi)\, \mathcal{E}$ such that X is instantiation-fresh for $\mathcal{F}$. Then for any environment η, ε:*

$$\forall v \in D : (\llbracket \mathsf{Inst}_X(\mathcal{F}) \rrbracket \eta\varepsilon)(X_v) = ((\llbracket \mathcal{F} \rrbracket \eta\varepsilon)(X))(\llbracket v \rrbracket).$$

Proof. Assume that $D = \{v_1, \ldots, v_n\}$; then $|D| = |\mathbb{D}| = n$ and take $1 \le i \le n$. We abbreviate $\mathsf{Inst}_X(\mathcal{E})$ by $\mathcal{E}_\iota$. First, we rewrite the left-hand side of the equality as follows:

$$(\llbracket \mathsf{Inst}_X(\mathcal{F}) \rrbracket \eta\varepsilon)(X_{v_i})$$
$$=^\ddagger (\sigma g{\in}\mathbb{B}^{\mathbb{D} \to \mathbb{E}}.\ (\lambda u{\in}\mathbb{D}.\lambda w{\in}\mathbb{E}.$$
$$\llbracket \mathsf{Sub}_X(\varphi) \rrbracket (\llbracket \mathcal{E}_\iota \rrbracket \eta[g(\llbracket v_1 \rrbracket)/X_{v_1}, \ldots, g(\llbracket v_n \rrbracket)/X_{v_n}]\varepsilon)\varepsilon[u/d, w/e]))(\llbracket v_i \rrbracket).$$

At $\ddagger$ we used Bekič's theorem [1] to replace n nested σ-fixpoints by one simultaneous σ-fixpoint over an n-tuple, the fact that $X_{v_i} \in \mathsf{bnd}(\mathsf{Inst}_X(\mathcal{F}))$, the assumption that the data theory is fully abstract, and the isomorphism between $\mathbb{B}^{\mathbb{E}|\mathbb{D}|}$ and $\mathbb{B}^{\mathbb{D} \to \mathbb{E}}$ to replace a tuple of functions $(g_{v_1}, \ldots, g_{v_n})\text{:}(\mathbb{E} \to \mathbb{B})^n$ by a single function $g\text{:}\mathbb{D} \to \mathbb{E} \to \mathbb{B}$ such that for any $u \in D\text{:}\ g(\llbracket u \rrbracket) = g_u$.

For the right-hand side, we can derive:

$$(\llbracket \mathcal{F} \rrbracket \eta\varepsilon)(X(\llbracket v_i \rrbracket \varepsilon))$$
$$= (\sigma f \in \mathbb{B}^{\mathbb{D} \to \mathbb{E}}.\ \lambda u{\in}\mathbb{D}.\ \lambda w{\in}\mathbb{E}.\ \llbracket \varphi \rrbracket (\llbracket \mathcal{E} \rrbracket \eta[f/X]\varepsilon)\varepsilon[u/d, w/e])(\llbracket v_i \rrbracket).$$

So it suffices to show the following equivalence:

$$(\sigma f \in \mathbb{B}^{\mathbb{D} \to \mathbb{E}}.\ \lambda u{\in}\mathbb{D}.\ \lambda w{\in}\mathbb{E}.\ \llbracket \varphi \rrbracket (\llbracket \mathcal{E} \rrbracket \eta[f/X]\varepsilon)\varepsilon[u/d, w/e])$$
$$= (\sigma g \in \mathbb{B}^{\mathbb{D} \to \mathbb{E}}.\ (\lambda u{\in}\mathbb{D}.\ \lambda w{\in}\mathbb{E}.$$
$$\llbracket \mathsf{Sub}_X(\varphi) \rrbracket (\llbracket \mathcal{E}_\iota \rrbracket \eta[g(\llbracket v_1 \rrbracket)/X_{v_1}, \ldots, g(\llbracket v_n \rrbracket)/X_{v_n}]\varepsilon)\varepsilon[u/d, w/e]))$$

which follows readily from:

$$\llbracket \varphi \rrbracket (\llbracket \mathcal{E} \rrbracket \eta[h/X]\varepsilon)v \tag{$*$}$$
$$= \llbracket \mathsf{Sub}_X(\varphi) \rrbracket (\llbracket \mathcal{E}_\iota \rrbracket \eta[h(\llbracket v_1 \rrbracket)/X_{v_1}, \ldots, h(\llbracket v_n \rrbracket)/X_{v_n}]\varepsilon)v$$

for all environments v and $h \in \mathbb{B}^{\mathbb{D} \to \mathbb{E}}$. Lemmata 2 and 3 can be used to show ($*$). For full details, see [4]. $\qquad\square$

Lemma 5. *Let $\mathcal{F} \triangleq (\sigma X(d{:}D, e{:}E) = \varphi)\, \mathcal{E}$ be a PBES and let X be instantiation-fresh for $\mathcal{F}$. Then for all environments η, ε:*

$$\forall Y \in \mathcal{X} : Y \notin \mathsf{all}(X) \cup \{X\} \implies (\llbracket \mathsf{Inst}_X(\mathcal{F}) \rrbracket \eta\varepsilon)(Y) = (\llbracket \mathcal{F} \rrbracket \eta\varepsilon)(Y).$$

Proof. Let $Y \in \mathcal{X}$ such that $Y \notin \mathsf{all}(X) \cup \{X\}$. Let $g : \mathbb{D} \times \mathbb{E} \to \mathbb{B}$ be such that:

$$\forall v \in D : g(\llbracket v \rrbracket) = (\llbracket \mathsf{Inst}_X(\mathcal{F}) \rrbracket \eta\varepsilon)(X_v).$$

Then by Lemma 4, we have $g = (\llbracket \mathcal{F} \rrbracket \eta\varepsilon)(X)$ and:

$$(\llbracket \mathsf{Inst}_X(\mathcal{F}) \rrbracket \eta\varepsilon)(Y)$$
$$= (\llbracket \mathsf{Inst}_X(\mathcal{E}) \rrbracket \eta[g(\llbracket v_1 \rrbracket)/X_{v_1}, \ldots, g(\llbracket v_n \rrbracket)/X_{v_n}]\varepsilon)(Y)$$
$$= (\llbracket \mathsf{Inst}_X(\mathcal{E}) \rrbracket \eta[g/X][g(\llbracket v_1 \rrbracket)/X_{v_1}, \ldots, g(\llbracket v_n \rrbracket)/X_{v_n}]\varepsilon)(Y)$$
$$=^\dagger (\llbracket \mathcal{E} \rrbracket \eta[g/X][g(\llbracket v_1 \rrbracket)/X_{v_1}, \ldots, g(\llbracket v_n \rrbracket)/X_{v_n}]\varepsilon)(Y)$$
$$= (\llbracket \mathcal{F} \rrbracket \eta\varepsilon)(Y)$$

where at $\dagger$ we used Lemma 3. $\qquad\square$

Proposition 2. *Let $\mathcal{E}$ be a PBES and $X \in \text{bnd}(\mathcal{E})$ be instantiation-fresh. Then for all environments η, ε:*

$$\forall v \in D : (\llbracket \text{Inst}_{\{X\}}(\mathcal{E}) \rrbracket \eta \varepsilon)(X_v) = (\llbracket \mathcal{E} \rrbracket \eta \varepsilon)(X(\llbracket v \rrbracket)) \tag{2a}$$

$$\forall Y \in \mathcal{X} : Y \notin \text{all}(X) \cup \{X\} \implies (\llbracket \text{Inst}_{\{X\}}(\mathcal{E}) \rrbracket \eta \varepsilon)(Y) = (\llbracket \mathcal{E} \rrbracket \eta \varepsilon)(Y). \tag{2b}$$

Proof. Observe that $\mathcal{E}$ is of the form $\mathcal{E} \triangleq \mathcal{E}_1 \, \mathcal{F}$ where $\mathcal{F} \triangleq (\sigma X(d{:}D, e{:}E) = \varphi) \, \mathcal{E}_2$. The property can be shown by means of structural inductions on the sizes of $\mathcal{E}_1$ and $\mathcal{E}_2$, relying on Lemma 2 and Lemmata 4 and 5 for the base cases. and Lemma 2 for the inductive step. For full details, see [4]. □

Instantiation for a set of variables $\mathcal{P}$ in a PBES can be achieved by applying $\text{Inst}_{\{X\}}$ for all $X \in \mathcal{P}$ repeatedly. However, sound as this strategy may be, it is undesirable as it is highly inefficient. We therefore prove that the instantiation algorithm $\text{Inst}_{\mathcal{P}}$ is sound for a general set $\mathcal{P}$. To this end, we introduce the following shorthand notation for functional composition of Inst functions over a set of variables $\mathcal{P}$:

$$\bigcirc_{X \in \mathcal{P}} \text{Inst}_{\{X\}} = \begin{cases} \mathcal{I} & \text{if } \mathcal{P} = \emptyset \\ \text{Inst}_{\{Y\}} \circ \bigcirc_{X \in \mathcal{P} \setminus \{Y\}} \text{Inst}_{\{X\}} & \text{for some } Y \in \mathcal{P}, \text{ otherwise} \end{cases}$$

where $\mathcal{I}$ denotes the identity function for PBESs, *i.e.* $\mathcal{I}(\mathcal{E}) = \mathcal{E}$ for all $\mathcal{E}$. The following lemma formalises that instantiating a set of variables $\mathcal{P}$ yields the same equation system as successively instantiating for every variable in $\mathcal{P}$.

Lemma 6. *Let $\mathcal{E}$ be a PBES and $\mathcal{P}$ be a set of instantiation-fresh predicate variables such that $\mathcal{P} \subseteq \text{bnd}(\mathcal{E})$. Then:*

$$\text{Inst}_{\mathcal{P}}(\mathcal{E}) = (\bigcirc_{X \in \mathcal{P}} \text{Inst}_{\{X\}})(\mathcal{E}).$$

Proof. By means of an induction on the structure of the equation system $\mathcal{E}$, using an auxiliary lemma to prove $\text{Sub}_{\mathcal{P}}(\varphi) = \text{Sub}_X(\text{Sub}_{\mathcal{P} \setminus \{X\}}(\varphi))$ for all formulae appearing in the equation systems $\mathcal{E}$. For full details, see [4]. □

Theorem 1. *Let $\mathcal{E}$ be a PBES and $\mathcal{P} \subseteq \text{bnd}(\mathcal{E})$ be a set of instantiation-fresh predicate variables. Then for all environments η, ε:*

$$\forall X \in \mathcal{P} : \forall v \in D : (\llbracket \text{Inst}_{\mathcal{P}}(\mathcal{E}) \rrbracket \eta \varepsilon)(X_v) = (\llbracket \mathcal{E} \rrbracket \eta \varepsilon)(X(\llbracket v \rrbracket)) \tag{2a}$$

$$\forall Y \in \mathcal{X} : Y \notin \text{all}(\mathcal{P}) \cup \mathcal{P} \implies (\llbracket \text{Inst}_{\mathcal{P}}(\mathcal{E}) \rrbracket \eta \varepsilon)(Y) = (\llbracket \mathcal{E} \rrbracket \eta \varepsilon)(Y). \tag{2b}$$

Proof. By means of an induction on the size of $\mathcal{P}$, relying on Lemma 6 and Proposition 2. □

The above result allows for a full instantiation of a PBES to a BES. This is viable when (1) all data sorts that occur in the PBES are finite, (2) the PBES is closed and data-closed, and (3) it is possible to rewrite every data term that occurs in the right-hand side expressions of the PBES to either $\top$ or $\bot$. We assume that the latter is achieved by a data term evaluator eval; notice that eval can be lifted to PBESs in a straightforward manner.

Corollary 1. *Let $\mathcal{E}$ be a PBES. If $\mathcal{E}$ is closed and data-closed, all data sorts in $\mathcal{E}$ are finite and a term rewriter exists then $\text{eval}(\text{Inst}_{\text{bnd}(\mathcal{E})}(\mathcal{E}))$ is a BES.*

Algorithm 2. The instantiation algorithm Inst_∞ for countable domains D

$$\mathsf{Inst}_\infty(\epsilon) \qquad\qquad \overset{\Delta}{=} \epsilon$$
$$\mathsf{Inst}_\infty((\sigma X(d{:}D) = \varphi)\ \mathcal{E}) \overset{\Delta}{=} \{(\sigma X_v = \mathsf{Sub}_\infty(\varphi[v/d])) \mid v{\in}D\}\ \mathsf{Inst}_\infty(\mathcal{E})$$

where

$$\mathsf{Sub}_\infty(b) \qquad\quad \overset{\Delta}{=} \mathsf{eval}(b)$$
$$\mathsf{Sub}_\infty(X(d)) \qquad \overset{\Delta}{=} \bigvee_{v\in D}\ (\mathsf{eval}(v = d) \wedge X_v)$$
$$\mathsf{Sub}_\infty(\varphi_1 \oplus \varphi_2) \overset{\Delta}{=} \mathsf{Sub}_\infty(\varphi_1) \oplus \mathsf{Sub}_\infty(\varphi_2)$$
$$\mathsf{Sub}_\infty(\mathsf{Q}d{:}D.\ \varphi) \overset{\Delta}{=} \bigoplus_{v\in D} \mathsf{Sub}_\infty(\varphi[v/d]) \qquad \text{where } \bigoplus = \bigwedge \text{ if } \mathsf{Q} = \forall, \text{ else } \bigoplus = \bigvee.$$

4   Instantiation on Countable Domains

In the previous section, we assumed that the domain D of the instantiated parameter was finite. Instantiation then resulted in a PBES in which the predicate variables still carried parameters with a (possibly) infinite domain. In this section, we lift the restriction of finiteness and consider PBESs in which each variable is of type $D \to B$ or of type B, where D is a possibly infinite, yet countable domain. Note that neither the restriction to a single parameter nor the use of a single domain D incur a loss of generality. To each predicate variable $X{:}D \to B$, we associate a countable set of proposition variables $\mathsf{all}(X) \overset{\Delta}{=} \{X_d{:}B \mid d{\in}D\}$.

The instantiation algorithm is Algorithm 2; it generates an IBES from a PBES. For every equation $\sigma X(d{:}D) = \varphi$ in the PBES, a block of countably many equations is generated, each of which is of the form $\sigma X_v = \omega_v$ for some $v \in D$ and infinite proposition formula $\omega_v = \mathsf{Sub}_\infty(\varphi[v/d])$. To ensure that every ω_v is indeed a proper infinite proposition formula, we rely on the term evaluator eval to rewrite every data term in $\varphi[v/d]$ to either $\top$ or $\bot$. Hence, $\varphi[v/d]$ must be closed, *i.e.* φ may contain no free data variables other than d.

Theorem 2. *For all data-closed PBESs $\mathcal{E}$ for which every $X \in \mathsf{bnd}(\mathcal{E})\cup\mathsf{occ}(\mathcal{E})$ is instantiation-fresh, and all environments η satisfying:*

$$\forall Y \in \mathsf{occ}(\mathcal{E}) \setminus \mathsf{bnd}(\mathcal{E}) : \forall w \in D : \eta(Y_w) = \eta(Y)(\llbracket w \rrbracket) \tag{1}$$

it holds that, for any environment ε:

$$\forall X \in \mathsf{bnd}(\mathcal{E}) : \forall v \in D : (\llbracket \mathsf{Inst}_\infty(\mathcal{E}) \rrbracket \eta)(X_v) = (\llbracket \mathcal{E} \rrbracket \eta\varepsilon)(X)(\llbracket v \rrbracket).$$

Proof. Let $\mathcal{E}$ be a data-closed PBES and η, ε be environments such that $\mathcal{E}$ all variables $X \in \mathsf{var}(\mathcal{E})$ are instantiation-fresh, and η satisfies (1). The proof goes by induction on the length of $\mathcal{E}$. If $\mathcal{E} = \epsilon$ the statement holds vacuously. For the inductive case we assume, for all PBESs $\mathcal{E}'$ of length m for which all variables are instantiation-fresh and environments η', ε' satisfying (1):

$$\forall X \in \mathsf{bnd}(\mathcal{E}') : \forall v \in D : (\llbracket \mathsf{Inst}_\infty(\mathcal{E}') \rrbracket \eta')(X_v) = (\llbracket \mathcal{E}' \rrbracket \eta'\varepsilon')(X)(\llbracket v \rrbracket). \tag{IH}$$

Suppose $\mathcal{E}$ is of length $m + 1$, so $\mathcal{E} = (\sigma Y(d{:}D) = \varphi) \; \mathcal{E}'$ for some PBES $\mathcal{E}'$ of length m. We define the following shorthands:

$$\sigma\mathcal{B} \triangleq \{\sigma Y_w = \mathsf{Sub}_\infty(\varphi[w/d]) \mid w \in D\}$$
$$f \quad \triangleq \sigma g \in \mathbb{B}^D. \; \lambda w \in D. \; [\![\mathsf{Sub}_\infty(\varphi[w/d])]\!]([\![\mathsf{Inst}_\infty(\mathcal{E}')]\!]\eta[g/Y_D])$$
$$h \quad \triangleq \sigma k \in \mathbb{B}^\mathbb{D}. \; \lambda w \in \mathbb{D}. \; [\![\varphi]\!]([\![\mathcal{E}']\!]\eta[k/Y]\varepsilon)\varepsilon[w/d].$$

Let $X \in \mathsf{bnd}(\mathcal{E})$ and $v \in D$. Then:

$$\begin{aligned}
&[\![\mathsf{Inst}_\infty((\sigma Y(d{:}D) = \varphi) \; \mathcal{E}')]\!]\eta(X_v) \\
&= [\![\sigma\mathcal{B} \; \mathsf{Inst}_\infty(\mathcal{E}')]\!]\eta(X_v) \\
&= [\![\mathsf{Inst}_\infty(\mathcal{E}')]\!]\eta[f/Y_D][h/Y](X_v) \\
&\overset{*}{=} ([\![\mathcal{E}']\!]\eta[f/Y_D][h/Y]\varepsilon)(X)([\![v]\!]) \\
&= ([\![(\sigma Y(d{:}D) = \varphi) \; \mathcal{E}']\!]\eta\varepsilon)(X)([\![v]\!]).
\end{aligned}$$

At $*$ we used (IH), which applies since one can prove:

$$\forall X \in \mathsf{var}(\mathcal{E}') : \mathsf{all}(X) \cap \mathsf{var}(\mathcal{E}') = \emptyset \tag{2}$$
$$\forall Z \in \mathsf{occ}(\mathcal{E}') \setminus \mathsf{bnd}(\mathcal{E}') : \forall x \in D : \tag{3}$$
$$\eta[f/Y_D][h/Y](Z_x) = \eta[f/Y_D][h/Y](Z)([\![x]\!]).$$

For full details of the proofs of 2 and 3, we refer to [4]. $\qquad\square$

As a corollary of Theorem 2, we have the following result:

Corollary 2. *Let $\mathcal{E}$ be a PBES. If $\mathcal{E}$ is closed and data-closed, all data sorts in $\mathcal{E}$ are countable and a term rewriter* eval *exists then* $\mathsf{Inst}_\infty(\mathcal{E})$ *is an IBES.*

Note that a reverse transformation from an IBES to a PBES is elementary: the sort of an IBES block acts as the sort of a PBES equation and the infinite conjunctions/disjunctions occurring in the infinite proposition formulae can be mapped to equality tests and universal/existential quantifications, respectively.

For typical verification problems, such as (local) model checking and equivalence checking, a partial solution to the PBES is sufficient. In that case, Proposition 1 allows one to prune the infinite blocks from an IBES, often resulting in a BES. Pruning can be done on-the-fly by means of a depth-first or breadth-first exploration of all the equations for the required (instantiated) binding variables of the theoretical IBES. A similar technique is discussed in [11], and, thence, we do not further explore this issue here.

5   Examples

In this section, we illustrate the various uses of the basic instantiation techniques of the previous sections. First, we demonstrate that the partial instantiation of a PBES is a powerful manipulation in itself. Two prime –but lengthy– example applications of the manipulation are already contained in the full version of [3]. A smaller example is given below. This problem appeared in [2] and [9]. Another problem of this type, also appearing in both [2,9] can equally well be solved using partial instantiation, see [4].

Example 1. Consider the infinite transition system depicted below. The property that Bradfield [2] and Mader [9] verify is that every path that starts in s has only finite length, a property that is given by the following modal μ-calculus formula: $\mu X.[-]X$. Notice that the number of paths in the system is infinite.

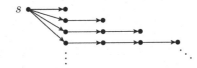

The following PBES, consisting of a single fixpoint equation, encodes the above model checking problem, where state s corresponds with $X(\top, 0)$:[1]

$$\mu X(b:B, n:N) = (\forall i:N. \neg b \vee X(\neg b, i)) \wedge (b \vee n = 0 \vee X(b, n-1)).$$

A solution technique based on a straightforward symbolic approximation as described in *e.g.* [8] does not terminate. Patterns [7] for solving PBESs, which allow one to "look up" a solution for equations of a particular shape, are also not applicable. Instantiation of Booleans leads to the following PBES:

$$(\mu X_\perp(n:N) = (n = 0) \vee X_\perp(n-1)) \quad (\mu X_\top(n:N) = \forall i:N. \ X_\perp(i)).$$

The equation for $X_\perp$ can easily be solved by means of a pattern, immediately leading to the following equivalent equation system:

$$(\mu X_\perp(n:N) = \exists i:N. \ n = i) \quad (\mu X_\top(n:N) = \forall i:N. \ X_\perp(i)).$$

The above equation system can immediately be rewritten to the following:

$$(\mu X_\perp(n:N) = \top) \quad (\mu X_\top(n:N) = \top).$$

Hence the property holds. The proof in [9] requires a manual construction of a set-based representation of an IBES, and requires showing the well-foundedness of mappings of this representation. The tableau-based methods of [2] require the investigation of *extended paths*. Our proof strategy requires less effort.   □

The next examples demonstrate the feasibility of instantiating to (I)BESs. All specifications contain infinite data sorts such as natural numbers.

Example 2. The algorithm has been implemented in a tool[2] that instantiates a given PBES, and, upon termination has computed a BES that holds the answer to whether a particular equation in the original PBES is true for some data value. The table below shows the time performance of this tool on several publicly available benchmarks, consisting of industrial protocols and systems (first four) and games (second three). The property encoded in the PBES was absence of deadlock, which would require all reachable states to be computed. This allows for a fair comparison with explicit state space generating tools. Of course, more involved properties can also be encoded, *e.g.* fairness and liveness properties.

---

[1] Notice that the PBES can be obtained fully automatically, for details, see [8]. For an implementation, see a.o. the tool *lps2pbes* of mCRL2 [http://mcrl2.org].

[2] The tool is part of the mCRL2 toolset (revision 4413) and is called *pbes2bool*.

	BRP	IEEE-1394	car-lift	chatbox	domineering	clobber	othello
States (#)	10,548	188,569	4,312	65,536	455,317	600,161	55,093
Transitions (#)	12,168	340,607	9,918	2,162,688	2,062,696	2,221,553	88,258
LTS (sec)	7	215	14	37	78	148	159
BES (sec)	6	232	10	15	82	182	186

We added the performance of the tool that would generate the state space. Our performance is in general comparable; differences are likely to be caused by minor differences in rewriting strategies. Our experience with memory usage is similar. Note that the BES generation time includes solving the BES using a BES-solver that is sufficiently efficient for alternation-free BESs. □

Example 3. The previous example illustrated the efficacy of full instantiation of PBESs to (I)BESs for alternation-free PBESs. We next consider the encoding of the branching bisimulation equivalence problem [3], which yields PBESs with alternation depth 2. The table below shows the time performance of our tool on instantiating three PBESs encoding the equivalence between the *Concurrent Alternating Bit Protocol* (CABP), the *Alternating Bit Protocol* (ABP) and the *One-Place Buffer* (OPB). Each protocol has ten different messages. The reported times do not include solving the BESs as our BES-solver currently cannot handle large, alternating BESs very well. □

	OPB	ABP	CABP	ABP $\approx$ OPB	CABP $\approx$ OPB	ABP $\approx$ CABP
States (#)	11	362	3,536			
Transitions (#)	20	460	13,791			
BES (# equations)				2,884	35,104	268,064
BES (sec)				< 1	2	13

6   Conclusions

Parameterised Boolean Equation Systems have demonstrated to be quite suited for studying various formal verification problems. Several unique solution techniques for solving PBESs have been studied and shown to be effective.

To this set of solution techniques, we have added a new set of manipulations, which admit a wider class of PBESs to be solved either automatically or by means of (syntactic) manipulations. From the point of view of the basic theory of PBESs, the manipulations firmly relate PBESs to two other prominent notions of equation systems, viz. BESs and IBESs. This provides a different angle on the somewhat complex basic theory of PBESs.

We have also reported on the efficacy of our manipulations (see Section 5). Among others, we report on the results of typical verification problems conducted using a tool that implements the transformation from PBESs to (I)BESs. In this respect, the approach taken in the tooling is reminiscent of the approach outlined in [12] but slightly more general.

Acknowledgements. We thank Wieger Wesselink and Jan Friso Groote for valuable feedback on the implementation.

References

1. Bekič, H.: Programming Languages and their Definition. LNCS, vol. 177. Springer, Heidelberg (1984)
2. Bradfield, J.C.: Verifying Temporal Proporties of Systems. Birkhäuser (1992)
3. Chen, T., Ploeger, B., van de Pol, J., Willemse, T.A.C.: Equivalence checking for infinite systems using parameterized boolean equation systems. In: Caires, L., Vasconcelos, V.T. (eds.) CONCUR 2007. LNCS, vol. 4703, pp. 120–135. Springer, Heidelberg (2007)
4. van Dam, A., Ploeger, B., Willemse, T.A.C.: Instantiation for parameterised boolean equation systems. CS-Report 08-11, TU Eindhoven (2008)
5. Gallardo, M.M., Joubert, C., Merino, P.: Implementing influence analysis using parameterised boolean equation systems. In: Proc. of ISOLA 2006. IEEE, Los Alamitos (2006)
6. Groote, J.F., Mateescu, R.: Verification of temporal properties of processes in a setting with data. In: Haeberer, A.M. (ed.) AMAST 1998. LNCS, vol. 1548, pp. 74–90. Springer, Heidelberg (1998)
7. Groote, J.F., Willemse, T.A.C.: Model-checking processes with data. Sci. Comput. Program 56(3), 251–273 (2005)
8. Groote, J.F., Willemse, T.A.C.: Parameterised boolean equation systems. Theor. Comput. Sci. 343(3), 332–369 (2005)
9. Mader, A.: Verification of Modal Properties Using Boolean Equation Systems. PhD thesis, Technische Universität München (1997)
10. Mader, A.: Verification of modal properties using infinite boolean equation systems. Technical Report CSI-R9727, University of Nijmegen, Nijmegen (1997)
11. Mateescu, R.: Local model-checking of an alternation-free value-based modal mu-calculus. In: Proc. 2nd Int'l Workshop on VMCAI (September 1998)
12. Mateescu, R., Thivolle, D.: A model checking language for concurrent value-passing systems. In: Cuellar, J., Maibaum, T.S.E. (eds.) FM 2008. LNCS, vol. 5014. Springer, Heidelberg (2008)
13. Tan, L., Cleaveland, R.: Evidence-based model checking. In: Brinksma, E., Larsen, K.G. (eds.) CAV 2002. LNCS, vol. 2404, pp. 455–470. Springer, Heidelberg (2002)
14. Tarski, A.: A lattice-theoretical fixpoint theorem and its applications. Pacific J. Mathematics 5(2), 285–309 (1955)

Author Index

Lecture Notes in Computer Science

Sublibrary 1: Theoretical Computer Science and General Issues

For information about Vols. 1– 4926
please contact your bookseller or Springer